# Beyond the Enclave

Towards a Pro-Poor and Inclusive
Development Strategy for Zimbabwe

*Edited by*

Godfrey Kanyenze, Timothy Kondo,
Prosper Chitambara and Jos Martens

Published in 2011 by
Weaver Press, Box A 1922, Avondale, Harare
in association with
ANSA (Alternatives to Neo-liberalism in Southern Africa)
LEDRIZ (Labour & Economic Development Research Institute, Zimbabwe)
and the
ZCTU (Zimbabwe Congress of Trade Unions)

© LEDRIZ, 2011

ISBN: 978-1-77922-151-3

Typeset by TextPertise, Harare
Cover design: Danes Design, Harare
Cover photographs: Mike Danes, Danes Design
Printed by Précigraph Ltd., Mauritius

# Contents

# Foreword

The Zimbabwe Congress of Trade Unions (ZCTU) published its groundbreaking analysis of the Economic Structural Adjustment Programme (ESAP), *Beyond ESAP: Framework for a Long-term Development Strategy for Zimbabwe*, in 1996. The book marked a new era for the labour movement, moving beyond simply criticizing government policies to offering detailed policy alternatives. It also marked an attempt by the labour movement to put its positions together into a cogent policy framework covering the macro and sectoral levels.

*Beyond ESAP* therefore provided a reference point for the policies of the ZCTU, and was used extensively by policy-makers, academics, students and other interested parties. The government team working on the Zimbabwe Programme for Economic and Social Transformation (ZIMPREST), 1996–2000, also made extensive use of it. Furthermore, the far-reaching recommendations of the *Beyond ESAP* study, the proposal to establish a national institutional framework for stakeholder participation in national decision-making processes, the Zimbabwe Economic Development Council, culminated in the formation of the National Economic Consultative Forum in July 1997 and the Tripartite Negotiating Forum in September 1998.

The Zimbabwean economy of 1996 is barely recognizable now, having gone through eleven years of crisis (1997–2008) and far-reaching changes. The economy analysed in *Beyond ESAP* and the one existing now are structurally different. For instance, a year before the onset of the crisis (1996), Zimbabwe's GDP of US$8.6 billion was the second largest of the fifteen-country SADC, behind that of South Africa at US$143.7 billion. At the height of the economic paralysis in 2008, Zimbabwe's GDP reached only US$4.8 billion, falling to the rank of eleventh in SADC, a position that was maintained in 2009. Instructively, while South Africa's GDP was almost 17 times that of Zimbabwe in 1996, it was almost 58 times larger by 2008.

Looking at the periods 1980–1989 and 1990–1999, Zimbabwe's real GDP growth at 5.2 per cent and 2.6 per cent in these periods was higher than the average for Sub-Saharan Africa at 2.2 per cent and 2 per cent. In the new millennium (2000–2006), the average GDP of Sub-Saharan Africa increased by 4.6 per cent while Zimbabwe's decreased by 5.8 per cent. Zimbabwe's persistent decline since the late 1990s does not, therefore, follow the general trend. Most African countries took advantage of the commodity price boom of 2002–2007 to improve their performances. Such has been Zimbabwe's fall in status that a country that used to be in the medium human-development category was at the bottom of the 169 countries reported on in the 2010 global *Human*

*Development Report*. As the economy collapsed, Zimbabwe's human resources went into the diaspora. Today almost a third of the population is estimated to be living abroad.

It is against this background of wrenching structural changes that the General Council of the ZCTU requested the Labour and Economic Development Research Institute of Zimbabwe (LEDRIZ), its research think-tank, to update the *Beyond ESAP* study. ZCTU leaders felt the need to ascertain the extent of economic regression and to establish baselines for launching the new, pro-poor, inclusive and humane recovery and development policies so urgently needed. This directive to update *Beyond ESAP* book took advantage of the fact that the Alternatives to Neo-liberalism in Southern Africa (ANSA) project, a regional initiative of the ZCTU and the Southern African Trade Union Co-ordination Council, is promoting country-level studies in the region.

In delivering this mandate, LEDRIZ and ANSA commissioned fourteen papers during the second half of 2008, which provided the basis for the chapters of this book. The research team was guided by two policy editors drawn from the Board of LEDRIZ, Dr Elizabeth Marunda and Cde Wellington Chibebe (also Secretary-General of the ZCTU), while the technical editorial team comprising Dr Godfrey Kanyenze (LEDRIZ Director), Timothy Kondo (ANSA Programme Co-ordinator), Prosper Chitambara (LEDRIZ Senior Economist) and Jos Martens (ANSA Associate) guided the research work. Following the production of the first drafts, the papers were presented to the General Council of the ZCTU at a workshop held in August 2009, where detailed comments were provided. The updated papers were further scrutinized at the annual retreat of the LEDRIZ board and staff in December 2009, attended also by the Executive Council of the ZCTU and its heads of departments as well as staff from ANSA.

The analysis in this book is informed by the understanding that most African economies are characterized by the existence of two radically different parts: a modern or formal segment employing a small proportion of the labour force, and a traditional or non-formal segment employing the bulk of the labour force. This feature is a product of colonial capitalism that captured a small segment of the economy, the formal sector, leaving the bulk of the economy, the non-formal segment, under pre-capitalist modes of production. It also reflects the failure of post-independence policies to deal with this structural deformity. As such, this disarticulate structure of the economy implies that the formal sector has a growth momentum of its own, and relates to the non-formal segment in a manner that marginalizes and impoverishes the latter, resulting in uneven development – indeed, an enclave economy. This structural distortion implies that even in the presence of growth, the economy is unable to absorb the vast numbers of the unemployed and underemployed into the mainstream economy.

This book argues that the post-independence policies have failed to address the inherited enclave structure of the economy, resulting in the continued marginalization of the majority of the population and the entrenchment of poverty. By 2004, instead of the economy being formalized, four out of every five jobs were informalized, with the decent-work deficits that this implies. This is the underlying factor behind the current crisis. The solution should therefore be steeped in the adoption of people-driven policies that redress this enclave and dual structure to achieve inclusive growth and human development.

While one can categorize the experiences of ESAP as largely manifesting market failure, the period since 1997 has clearly been dominated by state failure. The hand of the state has never been as visible in the affairs of the economy as it was during this period. It was an era characterized by policy inconsistencies and contradictions, even policy reversals, along with institutional overlap and decay. Never have so many policies been made in the name of the people without benefiting them, as was the case during this phase: inordinate price controls, multiple exchange rates, and land redistribution and indigenization initiatives. During this period, the state clearly showed signs of having been captured by a few individuals for their private benefit (a predatory state), eventually failing to provide basic services such as education, health and sanitation (a failed state). Furthermore, the state displayed lack of respect for the individual and collective rights of the people of Zimbabwe. Reconstituting the state, and transforming it into a democratic, accountable developmental state, is therefore a critical component of the recovery process.

As is now the emerging consensus, for development policies to be sustainable, they should be formulated with broad-based stakeholder participation to engender national ownership. It is for such reasons that the book recommends the rationalization of the various forums for social dialogue to create one legislated national stakeholder consultative body, as is the case with the National Economic Development and Labour Council of South Africa. This book therefore represents our desire for such an inclusive, participatory approach, and represents our input into the recovery and development of Zimbabwe 'Beyond the Enclave' to secure pro-poor, inclusive (shared) growth and development.

*Lovemore Matombo*
President, ZCTU

# Acknowledgements

During the course of the production of this book, several people and organizations played a part from its genesis to completion. Firstly, we would like to thank the General Council of the ZCTU, which made the decision to update the *Beyond ESAP* book and provided the impetus for the project. The General Council also engaged the writers of the individual chapters and gave detailed comments through a workshop held in August 2009. The Board of LEDRIZ played a central role in guiding the project, commenting on the various drafts of the chapters. We also want to put on record the immense role and contribution of the policy editors of the project, Dr Elizabeth Marunda and Cde Wellington Chibebe, both Board members of LEDRIZ, who gave direction and guidance from the time of the inception of the work to its completion. It is our hope that the work truly reflects the policy template that you so vigorously articulated at various stages of the work.

Special thanks go to the writers of the individual papers, which formed the basis for the chapters of the book, who were willing to work inordinate hours to get them to an acceptable level of quality. These writers and their contributions are as follows: Dr Godfrey Kanyenze [Chapters 1, 7, 8 and 13]; Prosper Chitambara [Chapter 2]; Dr Prosper Matondi [Chapter 3]; Best Doroh [Chapter 4]; David Matyanga [Chapter 5]; Tsitsi Mariwo-Mbanje and Naome Chakanya [Chapter 6]; Dr Henry Chikova [Chapter 9]; Benson Zwizwai [Chapter 10]; Dr Medicine Masiiwa and Rongai Chizema [Chapter 11]; Dr Joseph Muzulu and Simbarashe Mashonganyika [Chapter 12].

The conceptual framework that informs the book owes a lot to the work of the late Professor Guy C. Z. Mhone, who developed and applied the notion of enclave growth to the economies of Africa. May this book be a celebration of his life and enduring work.

We are especially indebted to Roger Stringer of TextPertise, who meticulously edited the book for publication. The book benefited from his extensive experience and expertise. Furthermore, the project owes a huge debt of gratitude to our co-operating partners, whose financial support made this book possible. ANSA supported the work from its inception, while the Royal Danish Embassy and AusAID generously funded the project. The other co-operating partners who provide institutional support to LEDRIZ (FNV-Mondiaal, SASK-Finland, FOS-Belgium, Steelworkers Humanity Fund of Canada, Solidarity Centre and Rosa Luxembourg Foundation) enabled LEDRIZ staff to work on the project, for which we are grateful. Finally, we would like to thank our publishers, Weaver Press for their unwavering support and commitment throughout the process of producing this book. We appreciate your commitment to excellence.

*The Editors*

# Acronyms

| | |
|---|---|
| ACP | African, Caribbean and Pacific group of countries |
| AFC | Agricultural Finance Corporation |
| AfDB | African Development Bank |
| AGRITEX | Agricultural Technical and Extension Services |
| ANSA | Alternatives to Neo-liberalism in Southern Africa |
| ARDA | Agricultural and Rural Development Authority |
| ATM | Automated Teller Machine |
| AU | African Union |
| BEAM | Basic Education Assistance Module |
| CEDAW | Convention on the Elimination of All Forms of Discrimination Against Women |
| COMESA | Common Market for Eastern and Southern Africa |
| CSO | Central Statistical Office |
| CZI | Confederation of Zimbabwe Industries |
| DDF | District Development Fund |
| DfID | Department for International Development (UK) |
| DRC | Democratic Republic of Congo |
| ECD | Early Childhood Development |
| EMA | Environmental Management Agency |
| EMCOZ | Employers' Confederation of Zimbabwe |
| EPA | Economic Partnership Agreement |
| EPO | Exclusive Prospecting Order |
| EPZ | Export Processing Zone |
| ESAP | Economic Structural Adjustment Programme |
| FCA | Foreign Currency Account |
| FDI | Foreign Direct Investment |
| FTA | Free Trade Area |
| GAPWUZ | General Agriculture and Plantation Workers' Union |
| GATT | General Agreement on Tariffs and Trade |
| GDP | Gross Domestic Product |
| GMB | Grain Marketing Board |
| GMO | Genetically Modified Organism |
| GPA | Global Political Agreement |
| GTZ | German Agency for Technical Co-operation |
| HIPC | Highly Indebted Poor Country |
| ICT | Information and Communication Technology |
| IFIs | International Financial Institutions |
| ILO | International Labour Organization |
| IMF | International Monetary Fund |

| | |
|---|---|
| IOM | International Organization for Migration |
| LBMA | London Bullion Market Association |
| LEDRIZ | Labour and Economic Development Research Institute of Zimbabwe |
| LSCF | Large-Scale Commercial Farm |
| MDC | Movement for Democratic Change |
| MDG | Millennium Development Goal |
| MDRI | Multilateral Debt Relief Initiative |
| MMCZ | Minerals Marketing Corporation of Zimbabwe |
| MTA | Money Transfer Agency |
| MVA | Manufacturing Value-Added |
| NEC | National Employment Council |
| NEDLAC | National Economic Development and Labour Council (South Africa) |
| NGO | Non-Governmental Organization |
| NIC | Newly Industrializing Country |
| NSSA | National Social Security Authority |
| NUST | National University of Science and Technology |
| OECD | Organization for Economic Corporation and Development |
| OGIL | Open General Import Licence |
| OVC | Orphans and Vulnerable Children |
| PASS | Poverty Assessment Study Survey |
| PGMs | platinum group metals |
| POSB | People's Own Savings Bank (formerly Post Office Savings Bank) |
| POTRAZ | Post and Telecommunications Regulatory Authority of Zimbabwe |
| PPP | Public–private partnership |
| PRSP | Poverty Reduction Strategy Paper |
| RBZ | Reserve Bank of Zimbabwe |
| R&D | Research and Development |
| RISDP | Regional Indicative Strategic Development Plan |
| RTGS | Real Time Gross Settlement |
| SADC | Southern African Development Community |
| SAP | Structural Adjustment Programme |
| SAPRIN | Structural Adjustment Participatory Review International Network |
| SARDC | Southern African Research and Documentation Centre |
| SARIPS | Southern African Regional Institute for Policy Studies |
| SAZ | Standards Association of Zimbabwe |
| S&T | Science and Technology |
| SEDCO | Small Enterprises Development Corporation |
| SHD | Sustainable Human Development |
| SIRDC | Scientific and Industrial Research and Development Centre |

| | |
|---|---|
| SMEs | Small and Medium-scale Enterprises |
| SSA | Sub-Saharan Africa |
| STERP | Short-Term Emergency Recovery Programme |
| STIs | Sexually Transmitted Infection |
| TNDP | Transitional National Development Plan |
| TNF | Tripartite Negotiating Forum |
| TVET | Technical and Vocational Education and Training |
| UNDP | United Nations Development Programme |
| UNICEF | United Nations Children's Fund |
| USGS | United States Geological Survey |
| VTC | vocational training centre |
| WAG | Women's Action Group |
| WEF | World Economic Forum |
| WFFC | A World Fit for Children |
| WTO | World Trade Organization |
| ZANU(PF) | Zimbabwe African National Union (Patriotic Front) |
| ZCTU | Zimbabwe Congress of Trade Unions |
| ZESA | Zimbabwe Electricity Supply Authority |
| ZJC | Zimbabwe Junior Certificate |
| ZMDC | Zimbabwe Mining Development Corporation |
| ZIMDEF | Zimbabwe Manpower Development Fund |
| ZIMPREST | Zimbabwe Programme for Economic and Social Transformation |
| ZISCO | Zimbabwe Iron and Steel Corporation |
| ZWRCN | Zimbabwe Women's Resource Centre and Network |

*Chapter 1*

# Conceptual Framework and Overview

## 1.1 Introduction

Zimbabwe attained independence in 1980, much later than most other African countries, and it was hoped that the country would learn from their experiences. It was reported that, on the eve of independence, the late President of Mozambique, Samora Machel, advised his ally and colleague Robert Mugabe to avoid being driven by revolutionary zeal and learn from Mozambique's experience when it chased the Portuguese from the country and nationalized the economy. A similar message came from another close ally, the late President Nyerere of Tanzania, who implored his friend to 'preserve the jewel in Africa' he had inherited. This was amplified in Zimbabwe's *Transitional National Development Plan*:

> In some of these countries growth and development have been impeded by a number of external and internal constraints. Some of them have adopted inappropriate policies and strategies and have misallocated much human and material resource in building costly, unproductive and often unnecessary capacity. Often the result has been uneven development, stagnation, even decline, leading to no significant and sustained improvement in living standards of people as a whole [Zimbabwe, 1982: 1].

The issue of learning from good and bad experiences is not a trite one. According to a World Bank study, behind the 'East Asian miracle' was the countries' willingness to experiment, and an ability to learn from, rather than persist in, their mistakes (World Bank, 2005: 15). In an attempt to understand the policies and strategies that underlie rapid and sustained economic growth and poverty reduction – and how other developing countries can emulate them following more than two decades of structural adjustment programmes (SAPs) with disappointing results – the World Bank launched the Commission on Growth and Development in April 2006.

The Commission brought together twenty-two leading practitioners from government and business and policy-makers, mostly from the developing world. After two years, it produced its report, *The Growth Report*, which noted that, since 1950, only thirteen economies had grown at an average annual rate of at least 7 per cent for 25 years or longer: Botswana, Brazil, China, Hong Kong, Indonesia, Japan, the Republic of Korea, Malaysia, Malta, Oman, Singapore, Taiwan and Thailand (World Bank, 2008: 1). India and Vietnam were identified as being on their way to joining them.

The Commission emphasized that fast, sustained growth does not occur spontaneously as it requires long-term commitment by a country's political leaders, a commitment pursued with patience, perseverance and pragmatism. Although these countries have often been referred to as 'economic miracles', the Commission argues that this is a misnomer because, unlike miracles, sustained, high growth can be explained and, hopefully, repeated elsewhere: 'Since learning something is easier than inventing it, fast learners can rapidly gain ground on the leading economies. Sustainable, high growth is catch-up growth. And the global economy is the essential resource' (World Bank, 2008: 2). The fact that thirteen countries achieved it suggests that fast, sustained growth, while not easy, is possible.

*The Growth Report* recalls that, when Japan grew at this pace, commentators remarked that this was a special case driven by post-war recovery. When Hong Kong, Taiwan, Singapore and South Korea (the four 'East Asian tigers') followed suit, it was deemed possible only because they were so small; when China surpassed them, it was argued that this was only because China was so big.[1] The truth of the matter is that all thirteen countries' experiences were remarkably diverse, even though some characteristics are similar, in which case some generalizations and lessons can be drawn from them. In fact, demonstration effects had a profound effect on these countries; Deng Xiaoping, the reform-minded leader of China, was reportedly positively influenced by his first encounters with Singapore and New York city when on a visit to the United Nations.[2]

These high-growth economies benefited in two ways: they imported ideas, technology and know-how from the rest of the world; and they exploited global demand, which provided them with a deep, elastic market for their goods. What is remarkably similar among all thirteen high-growth countries is that they did not have to originate much of this knowledge but had only to assimilate it quickly.[3] Significantly, the inflow of knowledge dramatically raised their economies' productive potential. What they did was simply to import what the rest of the world knew and export what they wanted. And the good news is that ideas are a public good characterized by non-rivalry in consumption: if one person uses them, it does not stop others from also using them.

Zimbabwe not only failed to learn from other countries' experiences but

---

[1] In his book with Janet Switzer, *The Success Principles: How to Get from Where You Are to Where You Want to Be* (HarperElement, 2005), Jack Canfield observes that 99 per cent of failures come from people in the habit of making excuses; he refers to this 'disease' as 'excusitis'.

[2] The *Growth Report* observes that the shift from closed and heavily regulated economies in China and India was partly motivated by 'the force of international example' (World Bank, 2008: 19).

[3] According to *The Growth Report*, knowledge refers to any trick, technique or insight that enables an economy to generate more out of its existing resources (land, labour and capital), including codified knowledge set out in books, blueprints and manuals, and the tacit know-how acquired through experience. 'The value of knowledge in the global economy is high and rising' (ibid., 41–2).

descended into crisis and paralysis and is now a classic example of how not to do it. Yet Zimbabwe's per capita GDP was more or less at the same level as those of South Korea and Thailand during the 1950s and 1960s. By 2003, however, South Korea's per capita GDP was almost sixteen times larger than Zimbabwe's, and Thailand's was seven times greater. Per capita GDP levels of the newly emerging economies, China and India, were below Zimbabwe's level until 1990. By 2003, Zimbabwe's per capita GDP amounted to almost a fifth of that of China and half of that of India (Table 1.1). This trend is aptly captured in Figure 1.1, Zimbabwe being left behind when these countries undertook reforms.

Lessons could have been drawn – and still could be – from these case studies, as well as from Zimbabwe's pre-independence experience when a seemingly invincible regime was overcome through sheer conviction, determination and

**Table 1.1: Per capita GDP, 1950–2003 (selected years)**

|             | 1950 | 1960  | 1970  | 1980  | 1990  | 2000   | 2003   |
|-------------|------|-------|-------|-------|-------|--------|--------|
| China       | 448  | 662   | 778   | 1,061 | 1,871 | 3,421  | 4,803  |
| India       | 619  | 753   | 868   | 938   | 1,309 | 1,885  | 2,160  |
| South Korea | 854  | 1,226 | 2,167 | 4,114 | 8,704 | 13,985 | 15,732 |
| Thailand    | 817  | 1,078 | 1,694 | 2,554 | 4,633 | 6,398  | 7,195  |
| Zimbabwe    | 701  | 938   | 1,282 | 1,295 | 1,356 | 1,328  | 1,070  |

*Source:* Angus Maddison <http://www.ggdc.net/MADDISON/oriindex.htm>.

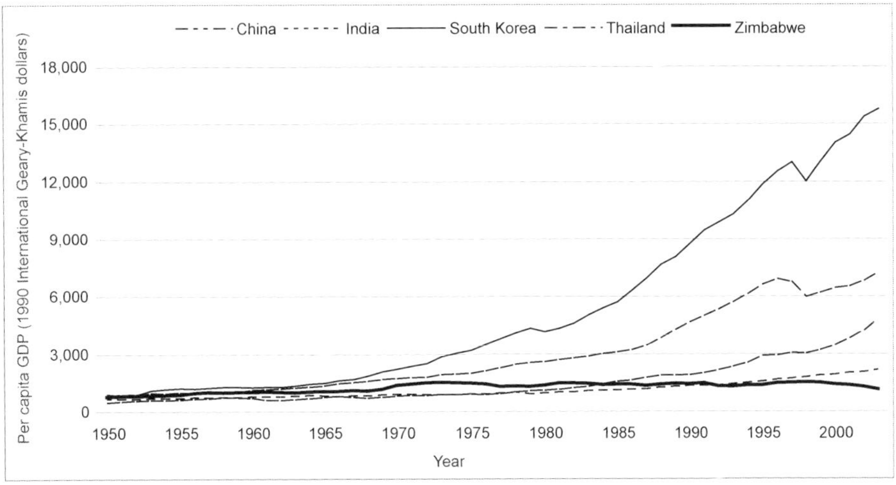

*Source:* Angus Maddison <http://www.ggdc.net/MADDISON/oriindex.htm>.

**Fig. 1.1: Per capita GDP cross-country comparison, 1950–2003**

resilience by a guerrilla movement with limited resources. Similarly, the success in the social sectors during the first decade of independence could provide useful lessons for the future.[4] Another example is the smallholder-led agricultural revolution of the 1980s that followed the provision of support services – credit, fertilizer, seed-distribution systems and marketing, extension services and financial resources. During this period, Zimbabwe earned a reputation as the regional 'bread basket' and did not import grain even during spells of drought. As Eicher *et al.* (2006) point out, these prime movers of agriculture were decimated after the ESAP period,[5] and Zimbabwe is now a net food importer. Ironically, the country imports maize from Malawi, a country which until recently was import-dependent, transforming itself into a net exporter only after adopting farmer-support measures borrowed from Zimbabwe's experience during the 1980s.

## 1.2 The Legacy of Enclavity and Dualism

Zimbabwe inherited at independence a relatively developed and diversified economy by African standards. An often-used measure of development is the share of agriculture and industry in an economy: with increasing development, the industrial sector's role rises relative to that of agriculture, and vice versa. At 12.2 per cent, the contribution of agriculture to GDP in Zimbabwe was much lower than the 31.6 per cent average for Sub-Saharan Africa (SSA) between 1980 and 1989. On the other hand, in 1980 the manufacturing sector was already the largest contributing sector to GDP at 25 per cent; the average for SSA between 1980 and 1989 was only 10.4 per cent, yet it was 23.3 per cent for Zimbabwe.[6]

Apart from its relative size, the manufacturing sector was so diversified that, at the advent of independence, industry already consisted of some 1,260 separate units producing 7,000 different products. This relatively high level of diversification was also reflected in the relatively broad export base, with agriculture accounting for 41 per cent of export earnings in 1984, followed by manufacturing at 32 per cent and mining at 27 per cent. Thus, the economy that the independent state inherited was far from the mono-cultural economy of typical SSA economies. Of the 37 African countries whose trade statistics are reported in the 1997 *World Development Indicators*, 31 derived more than 70 per cent of their export earnings from primary commodities (1993 statistics), and 15 of these derived at least 90 per cent.

However, if Zimbabwe was a 'jewel' at independence, it was certainly a flawed one. The inherited economy was based on a philosophy of white supremacy that resulted in the evolution of a relatively well-developed and modern formal

---

[4] See Chapters 8 and 9.

[5] See Chapter 2.

[6] World Bank, *World Development Report* (various years).

sector, employing about one million people (a fifth of the labour force), that existed alongside an underdeveloped and backward rural economy, the home of 70 per cent of the black population. The 'jewel' was the 'enclave' part of the economy, which had been developed on the ruthless dispossession of the source of livelihood of the majority of the people, in particular their access to land, which forced them into wage employment. Movement across these sectors was strictly controlled such that the prevailing relationship between them was an exploitative one.

Moreover, the relatively diversified manufacturing sector, which was part of this formal sector, had its own contradictions. Firstly, the import-substitution industrialization strategy that had performed well during the sanctions period (particularly during the fastest growth period, 1966–74) was showing signs of severe stress by 1980; all the easy and moderately hard industrialization had been achieved by 1975 (Green and Kadhani, 1986). Secondly, the deliberate policy of compressing imports to contain the balance-of-payments situation left capital stock in an obsolete and depleted state. The manufacturing sector itself became a net user of foreign exchange. For instance, although it contributed 32.1 per cent of export earnings in 1984, it accounted for 90.6 per cent of imports during the same year. Thirdly, the high level of protection created a monopoly structure such that 50.4 per cent of manufactured products were produced by single firms, 20.6 per cent in sub-sectors with two firms, and 9.7 per cent where there were three firms, implying that 80 per cent of goods produced in Zimbabwe were monopoly or oligopoly products (Ndlela, 1984; UNIDO, 1986). This market structure was exacerbated by the concentration of production in the two major towns, Harare and Bulawayo, accounting for 50 per cent and 25 per cent, respectively, of all manufactured products.

The dualism that characterized the economy then, and continues to do so, explains the perennial problem of the underutilization of resources, implying underdevelopment (Fig. 1.2).[7] Underdevelopment is therefore a reflection of the embedded economic dualism associated with the 'grafted' type of capitalism that developed after colonization. The low labour absorptive capacity of the economy is related to the enclave growth emanating from the structural legacy of economic dualism, which explains the vicious circle of perpetual under-employment that afflicts the majority of the labour force, especially women. The evolving social formations reflect the co-existence of the dominant capitalist and pre-capitalist modes of production that have been fused together in a rather uneasy and tenuous manner (grafted capitalism).

---

[7] While the notion of dualism is implied in the concept of enclavity, it requires its own identification in that the formal sector is predicated on the behavioural and organizational rules and imperatives of the market; the non-formal economy relies on a combination of market and traditional modes of economic behaviour and resource utilization (see Mhone, 2000).

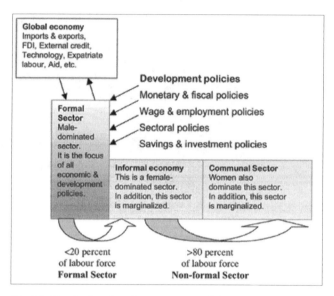

**Fig. 1.2: The dual and enclave structure of the economy**

The question to be asked now is whether or not the post-independence government transformed the inherited structural deformities that reflected and reinforced gender inequalities.

From the capitalist perspective, pre-capitalist forms of work constitute non-productive labour in that they are not profit-oriented, being of a survivalist nature. From a market, and therefore capitalist, point of view, underemployment manifests itself as non-productive labour in that it is not harnessed by capital for accumulation. The capitalist part of the economy is the formal sector, the pre-capitalist part being the non-formal sector (the informal and subsistence sectors). The non-formal sector therefore accommodates the remnant of pre-capitalist forms of production, the non-productive labour. An important requirement for development under capitalism is the need to capture non-productive labour into its realm of operation; in this way, a dynamic impulse is imparted to social relations based on the imperative to accumulate. Thus, the disruption of pre-capitalist relations provides a country with the potential for internally driven growth.

While both developed and developing countries have elements of productive and non-productive labour, it is the predominance of non-productive labour in developing countries that constitutes their major problem. The majority of the labour force, mainly women, are trapped in pre-capitalist forms of production, which are not driven by the need to employ labour to generate profit and the further expansion of capital.

Apart from the underutilization of resources, especially labour, another legacy of colonization is the absence of an internal (endogenous) dynamism for growth and transformation since the economies are dependent on, and constrained by, external factors. In the absence of an internally motivated and conscious process of transformation, the growth process would not only marginalize the majority of the labour force but also marginalize the developing country itself in the international arena.

An enclave economy will also be limited by the very nature of the system itself: the fact that a large segment of the labour force is engaged in low-productivity activities implies that effective demand is low, limiting the market for formal activities to expand. This deficiency in effective demand also makes the formal economy more reliant on external demand, thereby reinforcing dependency. Furthermore, the fact that a large segment of the labour force cannot engage in productive activities implies they are not available for accumulation by the capitalist sector. In addition, the fact that a majority of the labour force lives close to subsistence level implies that they cannot save and, if they do, their savings are not captured through financial intermediation because of missing linkages and gaps in the financial market.

Thus, an enclave economy tends to lack the capacity to generate internal savings and hence relies on foreign investment and aid, which pre-empts the need for self-generated savings. The implication of this structural deformity is that the trickle-down effects from the formal sector are too weak to transform and absorb these sectors into formal activities. Thus, market forces on their own would simply perpetuate this dualism, even in the presence of some growth.

The Zimbabwean experience amply demonstrates the inability of market forces to address this dualism. As will be illustrated in all the chapters in this book, not only has this dualism been preserved, it has also been exacerbated to the extent that the formal sector is much smaller than it was in 1980. A related issue has been the systematic decimation of the middle class, the 'missing middle'.[8] This is contrary to the expectation that, with sustained (inclusive) growth, the non-formal segment would be formalized; instead, it is the formal sector that has been informalized, with the resultant extension of decent-work deficits.

In this regard, the state needs to take a proactive role to integrate the non-formal economy and endogenize the growth process in a manner that allows the majority of the labour force to engage in productive activities. The strategy recommended involves targeted supply-side measures to resolve market failures through the redistribution of productive assets and building the capabilities of those in the non-formal sector.

---

[8] The issue of the informalization of the economy and the 'missing middle' are discussed extensively in Simpson and Ndlela (2010); and see also UNDP (2008).

## 1.3 Rethinking Development: The International Context

In the aftermath of the Second World War, the development discourse has gone through fads, starting with state intervention (dirigisme) during the 1950s and 1960s. Following the oil-price hikes of the mid- and late 1970s, state intervention-ism became increasingly discredited in the wake of stagflation (a combination of stagnation and inflation); in addition, a body of literature emerged in the early 1970s that questioned the efficacy of state interventions. The most critical analyses invoked rent-seeking behaviour to discredit the notion of the welfare state, arguing that politicians were inherently self-serving.

Accordingly, a market-oriented approach that emphasized the role of the price system and outward-orientation was the preferred option. This line of thinking found political expression with the emergence of Margaret Thatcher as the British Prime Minister in 1979 and Ronald Reagan as the President of the USA in 1981. This market-orientation permeated the work of the World Bank and IMF with the adoption of structural adjustment programmes as the premier lending programme.

The policy advice given to developing countries under SAPs can be reduced to the mantra 'stabilize, privatize and liberalize'. This became the central tenet of what economist John Williamson in 1990 called the 'Washington Consensus' (Rodrik, 2006; 2007).[9] After nearly two decades of implementing such reforms, the World Bank sought to understand the factors underlying their disappointing results. Its detailed assessment of the lessons were distilled into two seminal reports: *Economic Growth in the 1990s: Learning from a Decade of Reform* (World Bank, 2005); and *The Growth Report: Strategies for Sustained Growth and Inclusive Development* (World Bank, 2008).

*Economic Growth in the 1990s* observes that, more than a decade into tran-sition, many countries of Eastern Europe that embraced market-driven reforms had still not achieved their 1990 levels of output. Despite having implemented significant policy reforms, the economies of Sub-Saharan Africa failed to take off, with the success stories few, and even these were considered fragile more than a decade later.[10] Paradoxically, the region that tried the most to remodel itself on the advice of the Washington Consensus, Latin America – where countries such as Mexico, Argentina, Brazil, Colombia, Bolivia and Peru liberalized, deregulated and privatized more in a few years than the East Asian countries did in four decades – achieved little growth (Rodrik, 2007).

Contrasting the Washington Consensus growth model with that of South-East Asia suggests that countries such as South Korea and Taiwan adopted growth

---

[9] See Chapter 2.

[10] The often cited success stories include Ghana, Uganda, Tanzania and Mozambique.

policies that were at odds with those prescribed by the mainstream. None of these had significantly deregulated or liberalized their trade and financial systems well into the 1980s; in fact, they relied heavily on public enterprises and made use of industrial policies that included directed credit, trade protection, export subsidization and tax incentives, among others. The same applies to the recent experiences of China and India where, even with increased reliance on market forces, their policies were highly unconventional. They applied high levels of trade protection, did not privatize, resorted to extensive industrial policies, and followed lax fiscal and financial policies throughout the 1990s. In the case of India, the policy regime was deregulated only slowly, with very little privatization; well into the 1990s, India's trade regime remained restricted.

China did not change its private-property-rights regime, simply appending a market system on to its planned economy. Since the late 1980s, Vietnam has also experienced rapid growth owing in the main to heterodox (unconventional) policies, only gradually moving towards markets and greater reliance on private entrepreneurship. Thus, the extensive role of the state and the property-rights regime adopted are not in line with the tenets of the Washington Consensus. As Rodrik (2007) argues, if they had failed, they would have been presented as stronger evidence in support of mainstream policies.

A refreshing approach that characterizes the ground-breaking World Bank reports (2005 and 2008) is the absence of confident assertions on what works and what does not as they desist from recommending 'blueprints' for policy-makers.[11] They contend that what they have learned 'is the folly of assuming that we know too much', emphasizing the need to downplay grandiose claims, move cautiously, and concentrate efforts where the payoffs seem the greatest.[12] Humility is therefore an overriding attribute of these two documents, which argue for policy diversity, for selective and modest reforms, and for experimentation. They offer no unique universal set of rules and move away from formulas and the promotion of elusive 'best practices'.[13]

The key lessons from experience that are highlighted in the two reports are now discussed.

---

[11] As Rodrik (2007: 3) correctly points out: 'The economics that the graduate student picks up in the seminar room – abstract as it is and riddled with a wide variety of market failures – admits an almost unlimited range of policy recommendations, depending on the specific assumptions the analyst is prepared to make.' Hence the conventional advice 'is a derogation rather than a proper application of neoclassical economic principles' (ibid.). 'Neoclassical economics is a lot more flexible than its practitioners in the policy domain have generally given it credit for' (ibid.: 15).

[12] The Commission on Growth and Development (World Bank, 2008) admits that growing evidence suggests that the economic and social forces underlying rapid and sustained growth are not as well understood as had been thought, lamenting that economic advice to developing countries has been given with more confidence than justified by the state of knowledge.

[13] Rodrik's (2007) study is appropriately titled *One Economics, Many Recipes*.

*Promote [inclusive, shared] growth, not just efficiency*

*Economic Growth in the 1990s* criticizes the obsession of conventional packages with achieving efficiency gains, mistakenly equating policy reforms with growth strategies. It argues thus:

> In retrospect, it is clear that in the 1990s we often mistook efficiency gains for growth ... Expectations that gains in growth would be won entirely through policy improvements were unrealistic. Means were often mistaken for goals – that is, improvements in policies were mistaken for growth strategies, as if improvements in policies were an end in themselves. Going forward, the pursuit of policy reforms for reform's sake should be replaced by a more comprehensive understanding of the forces underlying growth. Removing obstacles that make growth impossible may not be enough: growth-oriented action, for example on technological catch-up, or encouragement of risk taking for faster accumulation, may be needed [World Bank, 2005: 11].

In its view, the policy focus of reforms in the 1990s enabled better use of existing capacity, but did not provide sufficient incentives for expanding that capacity. Thus, emphasis on efficiency explains the frequent instances of stabilization or liberalization without growth. While better policies can bring efficiency gains, and may increase incentives for investment, they do not amount to a growth strategy. What matters for growth is not the extent to which policies approximate the ideal, but 'the extent to which a given development strategy is able to mobilize the creative forces of society and achieve even-higher levels of productivity' (Alejandro Foxley, quoted in ibid.: 11).

The UNDP has over the years questioned the presumed automatic link between expanding income and expanding human choices and hence the tendency to see growth as an end in itself (see also World Bank, 2008); they have popularized the alternative concept of human development. Since the publication of the first global *Human Development Report* in 1990, the UNDP has refined the concept of human development to imply 'a process of enlarging people's choices' so that they live 'long, healthy and creative lives',[14] to which the aspect of 'sustainability' was added, borrowing from the Brundtland Commission report of 1987 (UN, 1987). Sustainable human development (SHD) meets the needs of the present generation without compromising the ability of future generations to meet their own needs.

The essence of SHD is that it places people at the centre of the development process, while its central tenet involves the creation of an enabling environment where people can enjoy long, healthy and creative lives. The global *Human Development Report, 1994* broadened the concept as follows:

---

[14] See *Zimbabwe Human Development Report 1999* (Harare: UNDP, Poverty Reduction Forum and Institute of Development Studies, 1999), 2.

Sustainable human development is pro-people, pro-jobs, and pro-nature. It gives the highest priority to poverty reduction, productive employment, social integration, and environmental regeneration. It brings human numbers into balance with the coping capacities of societies and the carrying capacities of nature ... It also recognizes that not much can be achieved without a dramatic improvement in the status of women and the opening of all opportunities to women [UNDP, 1994: 4].

The link between growth and SHD is strengthened by the following:

- Equity: the more equitable the distribution of resources, the greater the likelihood of growth benefiting the majority of the people.
- Job opportunities: Economic growth is easily transferred to people's lives when all people have access to productive and well-paid jobs.
- Access to productive assets: Access to productive resources by everyone – and especially to land, physical infrastructure and financial credit – empowers people to participate in and benefit from growth.
- Social spending: By channelling resources into social expenditure (health, education, shelter, water and sanitation, transportation, etc.), governments and communities can influence SHD.
- Gender equality: Better opportunities for women, and better access to education, child care, credit and employment, facilitate women's SHD. Other family members also benefit.
- Good governance: The link between growth and SHD is stronger and durable when governments prioritize the needs of the whole population and when people participate in decision-making.
- An active civil society: An active civil society supplements government services, and plays a vital advocacy role, mobilizing public opinion and community action.

In the context of SHD, economic growth is seen as a means rather than an end in itself. Such an approach acknowledges that a country may achieve high levels of growth, but that does not mean that it has a high level of human development. The UNDP (1996) articulated the conditions under which growth does not result in SHD:

- Jobless growth (growth that does not expand employment opportunities).
- Ruthless growth (growth associated with increasing inequality and poverty).
- Voiceless growth (growth in the absence of democracy or empowerment).
- Rootless growth (growth that withers cultural identity).
- Futureless growth (growth that squanders resources needed by future generations).

In this regard, economic growth is a necessary, but insufficient, condition for SHD. What is essential for human well-being, therefore, is the quality and distribution of growth, not just its quantity, hence the notion of pro-poor, shared, broad-based or inclusive growth;[15] these links may not exist in the marketplace, which can further marginalize the poor. The link between growth and human well-being has to be created consciously through deliberate public policies such as public spending on social services and infrastructure, enhancing individual (human) capabilities to redress capability deprivation and fiscal policy to redistribute income and assets.[16]

An economic strategy that empowers the poor through the redistribution of the means of production enhances the integrability of hitherto marginalized groups and sectors into the mainstream of the economy by redressing the capability-deprivation factor, thereby facilitating broad-based and inclusive growth. In this regard, human development is not only an input to growth but is also an output. Thus, SHD is the sustained elevation of an entire society towards a better and more humane life.

Looking at development from such a holistic framework has implications for the role of the state. Under SHD, the state plays a strategic and developmental role in expanding capabilities and opportunities and ensuring that growth is broad-based and inclusive. Thus, governments must go beyond merely creating an enabling environment to improve empowerment, co-operation, equity, sustainability and security of livelihoods through strategic interventions to correct market failures and to ignite economic growth by leading the market.

### Common principles and diverse ways to implement them
A related issue is that the broad objectives of economic reform (market-oriented incentives, macroeconomic stability, and outward orientation) do not translate into a unique set of policy actions. As stated in *Economic Growth in the 1990s*,

> The principles of ... 'macroeconomic stability, domestic liberalization, and openness' have been interpreted narrowly to mean 'minimize fiscal deficits, minimize inflation, minimize tariffs, maximize privatization, maximize liberalization of finance', with the assumption that the more of these changes the better, at all times and in all places – overlooking the fact that these expedients are just *some* of the ways in which these principles can be implemented [World Bank, 2005: 11].

There are many ways of achieving macroeconomic stability, openness, and domestic liberalization. For example, achieving macroeconomic stability does

---

[15] See Chapters 2 and 7.
[16] See Chapter 8.

not necessarily imply a need to minimize fiscal deficits at all times. A lower fiscal deficit achieved today through off-budget contingent liabilities or by cutting back public investments and thus reducing long-run growth and the future tax base may lead to a higher fiscal deficit in the future. Moreover, 'getting the policies right' mistakes means for ends. 'Clearly, not everything can be right at once, and not everything needs to be "right" for growth to take place – as witnessed in examples from Bangladesh, China, India, Indonesia, and many other countries' (ibid.: 12). This implies that solutions are to be found in specific country contexts rather than applied from blueprints, hence the need for more openness about the range of solutions possible.

## Common functions and diverse ways to achieve them

*Economic Growth in the 1990s* notes that, although key functions must be fulfilled to achieve growth, there is no unique combination of policies and institutions for doing so, as exemplified by the successful growth experiences in eight East Asian economies. Significantly, the fulfilment of four functions was common to all successes: rapid accumulation of capital, efficient resource allocation, technological progress, and sharing of the benefits of growth.

> Sharing the benefits of growth has been important in all sustained growth experiences, and particularly in countries with authoritarian forms of government, where it has helped to legitimize regimes that often were neither fully representative nor democratic. Various policies have been used to promote the sharing of the benefits of growth [including] land reform and redistribution of other assets; public expenditures on infrastructure ...; social spending ...; policies to increase the opportunities to economically underprivileged groups ...; and poverty-targeted programmes [ibid.: 14].

## Government discretion needs to be managed and checked, not replaced by rules

Policy reforms focusing on 'privatization, financial liberalization and the removal of quantitative restrictions' sought to limit the discretion of governments in growth strategies and minimize demands on institutions since developing countries 'resolve agency, predation and collective decision-making problems' less effectively than industrialized countries. But because government discretion cannot be dispensed with altogether, it becomes important to find ways in which it can be used effectively.

Above all, the experience showed that government discretion cannot be by-passed. It is needed for a wide range of activities that are essential for sustaining growth, ranging from regulating utilities and supervising banks to providing infrastructure and social services. Improving institutions that support the implementation of policies, and strengthening checks on the use of discretion, are more promising guiding principles than seeking to eliminate government discretion.

Much of the growth success of East Asian countries can be attributed to these countries' ability to allow discretion by different government agencies, alongside checks on this discretion that made them accountable [ibid.: 14].

*Move away from formulaic policy-making and focus on the binding constraint(s)*

Both *Economic Growth in the 1990s* and *The Growth Report* eschew the universal application of comprehensive, top-down blueprints, arguing that, to be successful, reforms should be selective and focus on the 'binding constraints' on economic growth rather than take a laundry-list approach. Experimentation and learning about the nature of these binding constraints is seen to be a critical starting point for reform efforts. Situations in which a country might face many constraints that have to be addressed simultaneously are considered rare: 'In most cases, countries can deal with constraints sequentially, a few at a time' (World Bank, 2005: 16).

Rodrik (2007) reinforces the need for a practical agenda for formulating growth strategies, involving a pragmatic, cautious, experimentalist approach with three sequential elements. The first involves undertaking a diagnostic analysis to flag the most significant constraints to economic growth in a given setting; the second concerns creative and imaginative policy design to target the constraints identified, which is followed by the institutionalization of the process to ensure that growth does not fizzle out and that the economy remains dynamic.

Growth diagnostics helps uncover the major constraints to growth, thereby addressing the ineffectiveness associated with post-Washington Consensus policy reforms which do not closely target the key factors hindering growth. The focus should be on those areas that will yield the greatest return rather than using the 'spray-gun' approach of conventional strategy. Institutional reforms in these areas are difficult to implement and take time, hence there is a need to begin with a less ambitious, more selective and more carefully targeted policy approach that can ignite growth in the short run.

Therefore, top-down, comprehensive, universal solutions should be replaced with a case-by-case approach. This calls for modesty and humility, and an emphasis on pragmatism, experimentation and local knowledge. China is cited as an example of a country that during the 1980s and 1990s adopted an approach defined by its leader Deng Xiaoping's often-quoted dictum as 'crossing the stream by groping for stones'.[17] A participatory political system is considered to be the most effective mechanism for processing local knowledge (Rodrik, 2006; 2007).

---

[17] In World Bank (2008: 4 and 23) it is stated as 'to cross the river by feeling for the stones'.

### 1.3.1 Key learning points from the success stories

The Commission on Growth and Development identified some of the characteristics of high-growth economies, which included (a) serving the global economy, (b) macroeconomic stability, (c) future-orientation (high levels of savings and investment), (d) market allocation, and (e) leadership and governance, including credible commitment to growth and inclusion, and capable administration.

All the sustained, high-growth economies prospered by serving global markets, which provided them with an elastic market for their goods and services; they were also a source of ideas, technology and know-how. Most adopted a variety of policies to encourage investment in the export sectors in the early stages of their development, which included tax breaks, direct subsidies, import tariff exemptions, cheap credit, dedicated infrastructure, or the bundling of all of these in export zones.

While macroeconomic stability had been pursued in all the success stories, moderately high inflation was tolerated from time to time. For instance, Korea had double-digit inflation during much of the 1970s and China's inflation reached about 24 per cent in 1994. Many of these countries had budget deficits over extended periods, while some had high ratios of debt to GDP; but these did not get out of hand as the countries' economies grew faster than the stock of public liabilities.

The critical issue is that these countries did not sacrifice long-term objectives for short-term ones, hence their tendency to run moderate deficits while securing long-term development goals (e.g. raising the levels of investment). Recurrent expenditure was not allowed to crowd out capital investment so critical for accumulation. Thailand, China and Vietnam are often cited as examples of countries that sustained spending on critical aspects such as infrastructure and social services without undermining prudential management requirements (Roy and Heuty, 2009).

Critically, therefore, none of the economies that sustained rapid growth achieved this without recording high rates of investment, both public and private, in infrastructure, education and health. This investment was drawn from available savings, and such economies accrued national saving rates of 20–25 per cent or higher. Although countries could finance investment needs from foreign capital, the record of inflows is not impressive. Their view is that foreign saving is an imperfect substitute for domestic saving (World Bank, 2008: 3).

The advantage of public investment is that it does not crowd out private investment but rather 'crowds it in'. Public spending on infrastructure expands investment opportunities and helps raise the net return to private investment by reducing the cost of production. It paves the way for new industries and facilitates structural transformation and export diversification. Yet investment in infrastructure is widely neglected (World Bank, 2008). As the deputy chairman of the Planning Commission of India, Montek Singh Ahluwalia, expressed it,

> International financial institutions, the IMF in particular, have tended to see public investment as a short-term stabilization issue, and failed to grasp its long-term growth consequences. If low-income countries are stuck in a low-level equilibrium, then putting constraints on their infrastructure spending may ensure they never take off [ibid.: 36].[18]

Equity and equality of opportunity are critical to sustainable growth. Equity refers to outcomes or results, while equality of opportunity refers to the starting points: access to nutrition, education and job opportunities. As Robert Solow, one of the two economists that participated in the Commission on Growth and Development, aptly stated (ibid.: 62):

> In many ways, the more equitable the growth, the more sustainable it's likely to be, because there will be less controversy, less disagreement, less resistance, and also there's an enormous amount of talent in populations that needs to be tapped. Excluding some parts of the population, whether by gender, age, or ethnicity, from the benefits of growth loses the talents that they have. So in my view, it is not only desirable that they go together, it's useful that they go together.

In this regard, promoting gender equality and equity in education and productive employment will positively impact long-term growth and poverty reduction.

Another characteristic shared by the successful cases is a capable, credible and committed government (strong political leadership) to ignite and sustain high growth over a long period. It is incumbent upon policy-makers to identify a growth strategy (through a consultative and participatory approach), communicate their vision, and convince the public that the future rewards are worth the sacrifice. The extent to which they succeed depends on the credibility and inclusiveness of the agenda, and requires patience, a long planning horizon, as well as conviction about the merits of inclusive (shared) growth.

While in some instances such success cases were driven by a single-party government that had a long planning horizon, in others it was done through multi-party democracies with or without a bipartisan growth strategy. Since fast, sustained growth is not spontaneous, it requires long-term commitment by the political leadership. Thus, the role of government was a strategic and co-ordinating one which went beyond enabling markets to function well (ensuring property rights, contract enforcement and macroeconomic stability) (Rodrik, 2007; World Bank, 2008).

The strategic role of the state is supported by the responses of developed countries to the global financial crisis that emerged after August 2007. Contrary to advice given to developing countries, these countries implemented large

---

[18] See also Roy and Heuty (2009) for a detailed discussion.

fiscal and monetary stimulus measures to kick-start recovery, a far cry from the austerity measures that developing countries would have been required to implement under similar circumstances.[19] Analysing the historical experiences of developed economies, Chang (2002) contends that the set of 'good policies' and 'good institutions' being foisted on to developing countries by the International Financial Institutions (IFIs) are not the policies that were used by the developed nations during the early phases of their development. They applied the so-called 'bad policies', such as protection of infant industries and export subsidies, which they now discourage. The chief proponents of open markets and free trade, the USA and the UK, employed such 'bad policies' in the earlier stages of their development (Stiglitz, 2002), a development that Chang argues is tantamount to 'kicking away the ladder' they used to develop.

In addition to strong political leadership, strong technocratic teams tasked with promoting long-term growth provided the necessary institutional memory and policy continuity. Good ethics and a culture of honest public service is the hallmark of credible policy formulation and implementation. To achieve this requires the attraction and retention of talented people. In the context of the East Asian success stories, the challenge of 'feeling for the stones' rested with the highly qualified technocrats who worked in small, dedicated 'reform teams' (World Bank, 2008: 28).

The issue of the environment is also critical. Unfortunately, most developing countries are too concerned with growth and consider the environment only as an afterthought, indeed a costly mistake. They should instead plan the evolution of the economy, bearing in mind environmental costs and implications (ibid.: 65).

### 1.3.2 Beyond the rhetoric

The stylized facts from lessons of experience with reforms are reduced to the following:

(a) In practice, growth spurts are associated with a narrow range of policy reforms.
(b) The policy reforms that are associated with these growth transitions typically combine elements of orthodoxy with unorthodox institutional policies.
(c) Institutional innovations do not travel well.
(d) Sustaining growth is more difficult than igniting it, and requires more extensive institutional reform (see Rodrik, 2007: 35–43).

Considered at face value, these nuggets distilled from lessons of experience entail a radical rethink of development policy. However, the reality remains different from what is espoused in these two influential documents, as the

---

[19] See the G20 communiqué of April 2009: <http://www.g20.org/Documents/final-communique.pdf>.

operational activities of the Bank are yet to reflect these lessons. The IMF has tended to remain behind in its thinking and policy action, as reflected in its 2005 report that sought to explain the disappointing growth experience, arguing that 'reforms were uneven and remained incomplete' (quoted in Rodrik, 2006: 977). Its former Deputy Managing Director, Anne O. Krueger, still maintained that failures were the result of advisees undertaking too little reform.[20] The point being made here is that the standard policy reforms did not produce the expected results because of weak institutions and poor implementation.

The addition of institutional reforms to the standard package of the Washington Consensus meant that the original list was augmented by a long list of 'second-generation' reforms of an institutional nature.[21] While the original list amounted to 'market fundamentalism', the augmented one is tantamount to 'institution fundamentalism' that can be reduced to the mantra of 'getting the institutions right'. The focus on institutions in the 'Augmented Washington Consensus' required institutional transformation in the areas of rule of law, property rights protection, and governance, among others.

As Rodrik (2006; 2007) points out, the problem with this approach is that cross-national literature has not found a strong link between any particular design feature of institutions and economic growth. For instance, a comparison of the experiences of Russia and China in the mid-1990s is instructive. While China attracted inordinate amounts of private investment within the framework of state ownership (township and village enterprises), Russia could not do so under Western-style private ownership. This suggests that common goals – in this case, protection of property rights – can be achieved under a different set of rules, as indicated in *Economic Growth in the 1990s* (World Bank, 2005). The rapid growth that China experienced in the late 1970s was achieved with marginal changes in its system of incentives and with no significant change in its ownership or trade regime. Likewise, no identifiable institutional changes preceded India's transition to high growth in the early 1980s (Rodrik, 2006; 2007).

> In the limit, the obsession with comprehensive institutional reform leads to a policy agenda that is hopelessly ambitious and virtually impossible to fulfil. Telling poor countries in Africa or Latin America that they have to set their sights on the best-practice institutions of the US or Sweden is like telling them that the only way to develop is to become developed – hardly useful policy advice! ... So open-ended is the agenda that even the most ambitious institutional reform efforts can be faulted ex post for having left something out [Rodrik, 2006: 980].[22]

---

[20] See her speech aptly entitled 'Meant well, tried little, failed much', <http://www.imf.org/external/np/speeches/2004/032304a.htm>.

[21] A comparison of this with the original list is outlined in Chapter 2 (see also Rodrik, 2006; 2007).

[22] Rodrik's article is sarcastically entitled 'Goodbye Washington Consensus, Hello Washington Confusion'.

Scarce political and administrative capacity could be better saved by targeting the most binding constraints on economic growth.

## 1.4 The International Aid Architecture[23]

When the current crisis in Zimbabwe began in 1997, international aid architecture was undergoing reform, which suggests that Zimbabwe will have to catch up on the latest developments as it seeks to re-engage the international community as partners. The international community has moved on without Zimbabwe's meaningful participation, so the country will have to invest in understanding these developments if it is to be a strategic player at the global level.

One of these developments is the shift in aid delivery from project-based approaches towards programme-based strategies in which support is provided to the various sectors through Sector-Wide Approaches and the national budget of partner countries. The Paris Declaration of 2005 provides an international framework guiding donor–partner relations. It sets out five principles to improve the efficiency of aid and its overall impact. The first relates to 'ownership', where it is the primary responsibility of the partner country to exercise leadership over its development policies and strategies and to co-ordinate development actions. Under the second principle of 'alignment', donors undertake to base their support on partner countries' national development strategies, to be guided by their priorities, and to use their systems and procedures.

The third principle of 'harmonization' requires donors to set up common arrangements within countries in the areas of planning, funding, disbursement, monitoring and reporting so that they are transparent and collectively effective. The fourth principle, 'managing for results', focuses on implementing aid in a way that improves decision-making to achieve development objectives. The fifth principle, 'mutual accountability', underscores the joint responsibility of donor and partner countries for development outcomes.

Partner countries should strengthen the role of their legislative bodies in the design of national strategies and budgetary processes and ensure the participation of the general public in the formulation, implementation, monitoring and evaluation of these strategies. Donors are required to provide timely information on their aid flows to allow partner countries to present comprehensive budget reports to their parliaments and citizens. Both donors and partner countries should undertake mutual assessment reviews (e.g. annual consultations) to monitor progress. Since 1999, countries requesting the assistance of the IFIs have had to craft a comprehensive and technically sound national development strategy, a Poverty Reduction Strategy Paper (PRSP).

---

[23] While the discussion here will outline the key aspects of the evolving aid architecture, a detailed presentation appears in Simpson and Doré (2009), as well as in other studies.

One of the criticisms that has been levelled against project-based lending, where discrete interventions are externally funded, is that there has been little co-ordination among the donors, and also between them and the partner country government, resulting in duplication and waste. It has also been argued that this form of aid delivery is often accompanied by a brain drain from the public sector to the donor sector. In addition, owing to the ad hoc manner in which projects are often implemented, this often results in the emergence of contingent liabilities that governments later find difficult to meet. For instance, after the handover of a project to the host government, 'recurrent expenditures, such as maintenance costs for infrastructure projects and personnel costs for social service delivery projects, are often extremely onerous for governments to sustain' (Simpson and Doré, 2009: 3).

As a result of these challenges, the past decade has witnessed a shift towards programme-based approaches. However, the situation on the ground shows that this shift is still low, suggesting that fiduciary risks still loom large in considerations by donors to transfer funds through the systems of partner countries.[24] In addition, the pull factors associated with project aid – such as the availability of parallel funding and the material and non-material incentives associated with projects (salary top-ups, vehicles, consumables, training and travel opportunities) – continue to exert pressure in favour of its sustenance. Furthermore, the high visibility of stand-alone projects holds sway, as well as the ease of attribution and evaluation of the impact of stand-alone projects compared to programmatic aid flows (ibid.: 4).

### 1.4.1 Poverty Reduction Strategy Papers and international debt relief

Developments in the late 1990s played a critical role in reshaping the aid architecture. The adoption of PRSPs by the boards of the IMF and World Bank in September 1999 had a major influence. All concessional lending by the IFIs and debt relief became conditional on the development of PRSPs. According to the IMF, these PRSPs had the characteristics that they

- were country-driven, developed by governments with the broad participation of civil society, elected institutions and relevant IFIs;
- were developed from an understanding of the nature and determinants of poverty and the links between public actions and poverty outcomes;
- recognized that sustained poverty reduction will not be possible without rapid growth; and
- were oriented toward achieving outcome-related goals for poverty reduction [IMF, 2000: 2].

---

[24] Fiduciary risk is the possibility that funds are not properly accounted for and that they are not used for their intended purpose.

The PRSP also acts as a framework for co-ordinating development assistance. It is prepared through a consultative process every three years, with annual updates. All countries seeking assistance (debt relief) under the Highly Indebted Poor Country initiative (HIPC) are required to have a PRSP, or an interim one (I-PRSP), in place by the decision point.[25] When a country is unable to prepare a PRSP by the HIPC decision point, an I-PRSP should be endorsed by the boards of the IMF and World Bank. To access debt relief, an eligible country must have adopted a PRSP and made some progress in implementing it (for at least one year) by the completion point. The I-PRSP covers the following:

- broad elements of the poverty reduction strategy and an outline of the timeframe and consultative process to develop a full PRSP;
- jointly agreed three-year macroeconomic framework;
- policy matrix on poverty reduction.

According to Simpson and Doré (2009), the fact that PRSPs now lie at the heart of the international development discourse is reflected in that, by March 2008, over seventy full PRSPs had been submitted to the Boards of the IMF and World Bank for 'sign off'.

While PRSPs have resulted in an increased focus on poverty by governments, civil society and international partners, as well as a noticeable improvement in national poverty analysis, enhanced databases and statistical skills, trade unions and other civil society groups have raised concerns about the macroeconomic framework, which reflects that of the discredited SAPs (ANSA, 2006).[26]

At the 2005 summit of the G8 countries, it was proposed that the IMF, World Bank and African Development Bank (AfDB) cancel 100 per cent of the debt of countries that had reached, or would reach, completion point under the HIPC initiative. Debt accumulated prior to end of 2004 was covered under this initiative. By the end of January 2009, 23 countries that had reached HIPC completion point had benefited from this Multilateral Debt Relief Initiative (MDRI). Ten HIPCs currently at decision point (the Interim Countries) were also eligible for MDRI once they reached HIPC completion point. By the end of 2006, 22 post-completion-point HIPCs (18 from SSA) had benefited from the HIPC initiative (and these also benefited from the MDRI), 10 post-decision-point HIPCs (8 from SSA), and 9 pre-decision-point countries (7 from SSA) (Simpson and Doré, 2009).

Evidence suggests that the reduction in debt-servicing requirements increased poverty-reducing spending through enhanced fiscal space arising from debt relief, reflecting the link between HIPC, MDRI debt relief and PRSPs. However,

---

[25] A detailed discussion of the processes involved can be found in Simpson and Doré (2009).

[26] The World Bank and IMF assumed that the SAPs and PRSP policies could be integrated into 'a consistent macroeconomic framework' with the two working in the same direction – reducing poverty. In this regard, PRSP policies have not integrated the need to move away from universal policy blueprints.

these countries have not made significant improvements in domestic resource mobilization, and export performance has remained stagnant. Worse still, given that international debt-relief efforts were meant to ensure a permanent exit from rescheduling, some slippage is evident. Of the 13 post-completion countries for which data were available in 2005, external-debt sustainability deteriorated in 11 cases, with 8 above HIPC thresholds.

As Simpson and Doré (2009: 13) note, 'One possible lesson to be drawn is that international debt relief efforts, in and of themselves, are not sufficient to improve export diversification, national debt management capacity or the ability of developing economies to cope with external shocks through either a deterioration of terms of trade or fluctuations in exchange rates'. Apart from the dangers of slippage, another worrying issue is the 'moral hazard' associated with continual extensions of international debt relief, which might constitute an incentive for debtor countries to increase their borrowings to unsustainable levels and avail themselves once again of debt relief.

These issues are of particular importance to Zimbabwe given its debt burden, which is unsustainable. If Zimbabwe were to follow the international debt-relief approach, it would first have to be reclassified as a Low-Income Country, an issue that has created heated exchanges within the Inclusive Government. One approach favoured by some civil-society groups involves developing a negotiating strategy based on the need for a resource audit in order to evaluate the extent of the 'odiousness' of the debt.[27]

### 1.4.2 The Millennium Development Goals

In September 2000, 189 heads of states and governments adopted an ambitious programme of poverty reduction at the UN. This programme set out eight goals to be achieved by 2015 – the Millennium Development Goals (MDGs). As a signatory to the Millennium Declaration, Zimbabwe sought to address all eight MDGs, prioritizing the following three: Goal 1: 'Eradicate Extreme Poverty and Hunger'; Goal 6: 'Combat HIV and AIDS, Malaria and Other Diseases'; Goal 3: 'Promote Gender Equality and Empower Women'.

The UN Millennium Project (2005) sees the current levels of foreign aid to be the major constraint on global poverty reduction, and calls for a significant increase in aid to finance public investments in infrastructure and human capital, and to enhance health-care delivery and the productivity of agriculture. The understanding of the UN Millennium Project is that Low-Income Countries are stuck in a low-level equilibrium, a 'poverty trap' which requires a 'big push' by way of external aid. Its premise is that we know enough to mount 'a bold, ambitious, and costly effort' to eradicate world poverty. It computes the required

---

[27] See Chapter 2.

growth rates (7 per cent for Africa) in order to meet the first MDG. However, this viewpoint has been criticized for failing to be modest about what is known about the determinants of growth, which are country-specific (Rodrik, 2006). The fact that no SSA country is in a position to meet the first goal is illustrative of the ambitiousness of the project, and calls for a more cautious, pragmatic, experimental case-by-case approach (Rodrik, 2006; 2007). Furthermore, the issue of increasing aid is coming at a time when strident calls are being made to improve its effectiveness (Simpson and Doré, 2009).

## 1.5 The Underlying Values and Principles of the Alternative Framework

As stated above, there is a rare historic opportunity for implementing alternative policy frameworks based on the distillation of lessons from experience. Convictions on either extreme of the policy divide (statism v. markets) are showing signs of softening, creating space for creativity and innovation. Significantly, the responses to the current global crisis in the developed world, evinced in fiscal and monetary stimulus packages, provide a critical departure point from the erstwhile faith in unbridled market forces.

Furthermore, the state of aid architecture, with its emphasis on country ownership of development strategies, provides a unique historical opportunity for country-based strategies that are collectively formulated, implemented, monitored and evaluated. In addition, the emergence of China, India and Vietnam, countries that were the epitome of statism on the basis of 'feeling for the stones' in order to cross the river, is instructive and demystifies the notion that those countries that have defied the odds and made it are 'economic miracles'. We agree with the Commission on Growth and Development (World Bank, 2008) that this term is a misnomer; sustained and inclusive growth can be explained and is achievable.

The alternative development framework espoused in this book draws from and builds upon the policy frameworks outlined in the *Beyond ESAP* (ZCTU, 1996) and *The Search for Sustainable Human Development in Southern Africa* (ANSA, 2006). It implies a human-rights approach as a critical aspect of it. Three variants of human rights can be identified: (a) political or civil rights ('blue rights'); (b) economic rights ('red rights'); and (c) social and cultural rights ('green rights'). These rights are universal and mutually inclusive, implying that one cannot be fully enjoyed without the other.

The right to an adequate standard of living encompasses several more specific rights: the right to food, the right to health, the right to water, the right to necessary social services, the right to clothing, and the right to housing. The right to an adequate standard of living requires governments to improve these rights consistently. Because of their public-good status (non-rivalry in consumption and non-excludability), human rights should not be put on the market, which discriminates, especially against the poor; they should be in the public domain. Their enjoyment is facilitated by the adoption and implementation of people-centred and -driven inclusive (humane) development strategies, implying that a human-rights approach to development is essential.

The ANSA (2006) study develops a comprehensive alternative strategy, with key building blocks based on humane principles and values. It hinges on a 'bottom-up' process that looks at the development process in a holistic manner, (Fig. 1.3). This means considering three basic factors:

1. The social factor – how people's basic human rights are safeguarded and how vulnerable people are protected against poverty and exploitation.

2. The democratic factor – how the political system functions, how decisions are made and implemented, how resources and opportunities are distributed, and how justice and fairness are achieved.

3. The global factor – how the system works at global level, how decisions are taken and implemented, how global resources are controlled and distributed, and how this global system affects Africa.

This entails a human-rights approach to development which encompasses human rights, community rights, and the right to national or regional self-determination. It also deals with issues of equity and fairness in the distribution of resources at local, national, regional and global levels. The provision of social services such as water, energy, health and education cannot be guaranteed for all if they are left to market forces. Social services and public utilities are not matters to be privatized as they are part of basic human rights, and states have the responsibility to secure them for all their people. The state must therefore be developmental as well as ethical, responsible and accountable to the people.

### Summary of the ANSA strategy

The main elements of the proposed ANSA strategy can be summarized into ten points:

1. It is a people-led (as opposed to an IMF–World Bank–WTO donor-led) strategy. It proposes:

2. An alternative production system based primarily on domestic demand and human needs and the use of local resources and domestic savings. It also proposes the 'horizontal' integration of agriculture and industry.

3. Grassroots-led regional integration rather than the current fragmentation by the powerful forces of globalization.

4. Strategic engagement with the international community in order to protect and advance national and regional interests.

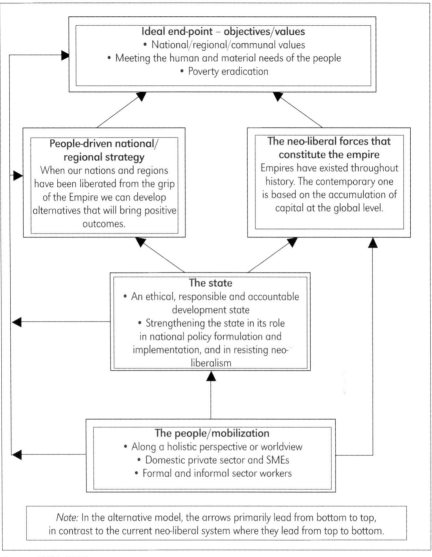

**Ideal end-point – objectives/values**
- National/regional/communal values
- Meeting the human and material needs of the people
- Poverty eradication

**People-driven national/regional strategy**
When our nations and regions have been liberated from the grip of the Empire we can develop alternatives that will bring positive outcomes.

**The neo-liberal forces that constitute the empire**
Empires have existed throughout history. The contemporary one is based on the accumulation of capital at the global level.

**The state**
- An ethical, responsible and accountable development state
- Strengthening the state in its role in national policy formulation and implementation, and in resisting neo-liberalism

**The people/mobilization**
- Along a holistic perspective or worldview
- Domestic private sector and SMEs
- Formal and informal sector workers

*Note:* In the alternative model, the arrows primarily lead from bottom to top, in contrast to the current neo-liberal system where they lead from top to bottom.

*Source:* ANSA (2006).

**Fig. 1.3: A holistic bottom-up approach**

5. An alternative policy on science and technology based on harnessing the collective knowledge and wisdom of the people.
6. The forging of strategic alliances and networks with progressive forces at national, regional and global levels.
7. A politically governed redistribution of wealth and opportunities from the formal to the non-formal sectors of the economy.
8. Women's rights as the basis for a healthy and productive society.

9. An education system that addresses the need for sustainable human development by improving technical, managerial, research and development skills.
10. The creation of a dynamic, participatory and radical democracy, which regards people's mobilization, demonstrations and open hearings to be part of the struggle for an ethical and developmental state.

## 1.6 Methodology of the Analysis and Overall Structure

Throughout this book, the chapters grapple with the issue of the inherited dual and enclave structure of the economy, under the sector being discussed. This dual and enclave framework, and the related concepts of capability deprivation, vulnerability and marginalization, is applied within the sectoral analyses that follow, and a pro-poor (i.e. broad-based and inclusive) approach is recommended. It is the view of the authors that the underlying cause of the current crisis lies in the failure by the state to initiate and sustain a growth process that is robust and inclusive, hence the loss of popular support for the ruling party which failed to develop a credible economic strategy, resulting in deteriorating governance and, ultimately, paralysis.

For the past three decades, government veered from one economic strategy to another in what became a game of hit and miss, played with more enthusiasm than success. It is probably instructive that at least ten economic blueprints were implemented during the period 1980–2008.[28] The first decade saw government adopt a cautious approach to policies, virtually retaining the system of controls and inward-oriented policies that were used during the pre-independence era. However, an emphasis on social welfare saw the health-care and education systems, in particular, receiving much attention. In the context of anaemic and lacklustre growth, this social thrust could not be sustained.

Under pressure from international and domestic capital, government went to the opposite extreme, implementing an Economic Structural Adjustment Programme (ESAP) on the recommendation of the IMF and World Bank in 1991. Although the ESAP period officially ended in 1995, the World Bank (2000: 2) argued that the 'unexpected and rapid deterioration of the economy since mid-1997 forced Bank assistance to Zimbabwe to be flexible and responsive, and has consequently differed from what was envisaged in the Country Assistance Strategy (CAS) dated May 1, 1997'. As a result, 1991–1996 has been taken as the reform (ESAP) period. Critically, ESAP took the economy on a path that entrenched dualism and enclavity.

---

[28] See Chapter 2.

As the World Bank's 'performance audit' of ESAP conceded,

> the concerns, however, go beyond the issues of pace and design: the comprehensiveness of the program seems a fundamental issue, especially given the objective of reducing poverty. Given the highly dualistic nature of Zimbabwe's economy (where the white minority dominates formal sector economic activity and owns two-thirds of high potential land, and the black majority is concentrated in rural, communal areas and the urban informal sector), it would appear that some basic questions were not explicitly addressed at the outset. First, would ESAP, predicated on the formal sector acting as an engine of growth, create sufficient jobs, quickly enough, to address the serious problems of employment? ... Even realization of the most optimistic scenarios for formal sector growth will not provide a quick solution to the unemployment problem [World Bank, 1995: 11].

The crisis started in earnest following the events of 14 November 1997, when the Zimbabwe dollar depreciated under pressure from the unbudgeted gratuity and pension pay-out to pacify war veterans, culminating in the paralysis of 2007/2008. This period saw the economy descend into hyperinflation, with inflation levels of 50 per cent per month. The year 2009 marked the emergence of the Inclusive (power-sharing) Government, following the signing of what came to be known as the Global Political Agreement (GPA) on 15 September 2008.

The analysis that follows in each chapter therefore follows these structural breaks in policies: 'The First Decade, 1980-90', the interventionist period of the first years of independence; 'The ESAP Period, 1991-96'; 'The Crisis Period, 1997-2008'; and finally the period following the formation of the Inclusive Government in February 2009, 'The Transitional Period'. This analysis, together with the assessment of the state of development thinking in the subject area covered by the chapter, is used to tease out a way forward. In other words, each chapter pays due regard to the principle of logical derivation.

A recurring challenge is the absence of good and credible up-to-date data. As highlighted in *Comprehensive Economic Recovery in Zimbabwe* (UNDP, 2008), Zimbabwean data deteriorated markedly during the new millennium. Under the circumstances, each writer sought to make the most of existing data and also made extensive use of available secondary sources.

In arranging the chapters, every effort was made to ensure the flow of the analysis. This chapter having provided the conceptual framework and overview, Chapter 2 focuses on the macroeconomic framework; Chapter 3 looks at agriculture, Chapter 4 at manufacturing, and Chapter 5 mining; Chapter 6 discusses gender issues; Chapter 7 is on the labour market, Chapter 8 on issues of education and training, and Chapter 9 on social services; Chapter 10 deals with science and technology, Chapter 11 trade, and Chapter 12 finance; finally, Chapter 13 provides a synthesis and concluding remarks.

# References

ANSA 2006. *The Search for Sustainable Human Development in Southern Africa* (Harare: Alternatives to Neo-liberalism in Southern Africa).

Chang, Ha-Joon 2002. *Kicking away the Ladder: Development Strategy in Historical Perspective* (London: Anthem Press).

Eicher, C. K., P. Tawonezvi and M. Rukuni 2006. 'Synthesis', in M. Rukuni *et al.* (eds.) *Zimbabwe's Agricultural Revolution Revisited* (Harare: University of Zimbabwe Publications).

Green, R. H. and X. Kadhani 1986. 'Zimbabwe: Transition to Economic Crisis, 1981–1983: Retrospect and Prospect', *World Development* 14(8).

IMF 2000. 'Poverty Reduction Strategy Paper and the New Poverty Reduction and Growth Facility'. Prepared by the Staff of the IMF in consultation with the Staffs of the World Bank and the African Development Bank, Libreville Conference, 18–19 January.

Mhone, G. C. Z. 2000. 'Enclavity and Constrained Labour Absorptive Capacity in Southern African Economies' (Harare: ILO/SAMAT, Discussion Paper No. 12).

Ndlela, Dan B. 1984. 'Sectoral analysis of Zimbabwe economic development with implications for foreign trade and foreign exchange', *Zimbabwe Journal of Economics*, 1(1).

Rodrik, D. 2006. 'Goodbye Washington Consensus, hello Washington confusion? A review of the World Bank's *Economic Growth in the 1990s: Learning from a Decade of Reform*', *Journal of Economic Literature*, XLIV (December), 973–87.

Rodrik, D. 2007. *One Economics, Many Recipes: Globalization, Institutions, and Economic Growth* (Princeton and Oxford: Princeton University Press).

Roy, R. and A. Heuty 2009. 'Investing in development: The Millennium Development Goals, aid and sustainable capital accumulation', in R. Roy and A. Heuty (eds.), *Fiscal Space: Policy Options for Financing Human Development* (London: Earthscan), 15–30.

Simpson, M. and D. Doré 2009. 'International Aid and its Management: Some Insights for Zimbabwe in the Context of Re-engagement', Comprehensive Economic Recovery in Zimbabwe, Working Paper No. 2 (Harare: UNDP).

Simpson, M. and D. Ndlela 2010. 'Informal economy, and the "Missing Middle" in Zimbabwe: Some Observations', Comprehensive Economic Recovery in Zimbabwe, Working Paper No. 9 (Harare: UNDP).

Stiglitz, J. 2002. *Globalisation and Its Discontents* (Harmondsworth: Penguin).

UN 1987. *Report of the World Commission on Environment and Development: Our Common Future*, <http://www.un-documents.net/wced-ocf.htm>.

UN Millennium Project 2005. *Investing in Development: A Practical Plan to Achieve the MDGs* (New York: Earthscan).

UNDP 1994. *Human Development Report 1994: New Dimensions of Human Security* (New York: UNDP).

UNDP 1996. *Human Development Report* (New York: Oxford University Press).

UNDP 2008. *Comprehensive Economic Recovery in Zimbabwe: A Discussion Document* (Harare: UNDP).

UNIDO 1986. *The Manufacturing Sector in Zimbabwe* (Vienna: UNIDO).

World Bank 1995. *Performance Audit Report: Zimbabwe Structural Adjustment Program* (Washington, DC: World Bank, Operations Evaluation Department).

World Bank 2000. 'Zimbabwe: Interim Strategy, 2000–1' (draft).

World Bank 2005. *Economic Growth in the 1990s: Learning from a Decade of Reform* (Washington, DC: World Bank).

World Bank 2008. *The Growth Report: Strategies for Sustained Growth and Inclusive Development* (Washington, DC: World Bank, Commission on Growth and Development).

ZCTU 1996. *Beyond ESAP: Framework for a Long-term Development Strategy for Zimbabwe* (Harare: Zimbabwe Congress of Trade Unions).

Zimbabwe 1982. *Transitional National Development Plan, 1982/83–1984/85: Volume 1* (Harare: Ministry of Economic Planning and Development, 2 vols.).

# Towards a Macroeconomic Framework for Pro-poor and Inclusive Growth

## 2.1 Introduction

Conventional macroeconomic policy frameworks have often confused means with ends, with macroeconomic stability (typified by single-digit inflation, low budget deficits, and a sustainable debt position) being seen as an end in itself rather than as an instrument for poverty reduction and the attainment of human development. Quite often, quantitative macroeconomic benchmarks have been set to guide policy-makers. While macroeconomic stability should provide a framework for the implementation of pro-poor and inclusive policies, focusing inordinately on it (i.e. stabilization) can throw an economy into a stabilization trap characterized by low inflation, low investment, low growth rates and high unemployment (Heintz, 2008).

With the re-emergence of social objectives such as employment creation and poverty reduction and eradication, especially at the start of the new millennium, the traditional macroeconomic framework has been considered inadequate and restrictive, even though the goal of achieving macroeconomic stability is accepted as a useful building plank (Heintz, 2008). A focus on quantitative macroeconomic targets increasingly came to be seen to be misplaced, since governments could achieve these simply by cutting back on social and infrastructural spending, areas with a high payback in the longer term, while maintaining recurrent expenditure (Roy et al., 2007).

In reality, no country has sustained rapid growth without achieving high rates of public investment, especially in infrastructure, education and health (World Bank, 2008a). Empirical evidence shows that cuts in public investment are not compensated for by private investment, as expected in the conventional framework, owing to the complementary relationship between public and private investment. Rather, public investment 'crowds in' private investment. Therefore, the short term becomes a binding constraint on the long term, as the positive endogenous effects on solvency and stability of spending in developmental activities, such as public investment, are ignored. A transformative, and hence developmental, approach to macroeconomics requires a better understanding of the long-term effects of fiscal expansion on economic growth and human development (Roy et al., 2007).

• The focus on fiscal deficits introduces a strong bias against expenditures with high short-term costs and long-term returns, such as infrastructure projects. Experience has shown that countries whose macroeconomic frameworks included strong public-investment strategies achieved sustained high levels of economic growth with high capacity to reduce poverty, while those that sought to achieve deficit targets without reference to growth and poverty objectives experienced economic stagnation. In this regard, fiscal strategies that complement social and economic policies to secure a development thrust that is transformational require a departure from conventional fiscal planning. The issue is not only about the levels of spending, but rather where the spending is going: the sustainability of macroeconomic policies depends on what the expenditures are used for.

Moreover, an economy's future stream of revenues will depend on whether it remains trapped in poverty or unlocks a new equilibrium. This implies that fiscal plans that may appear to be unsustainable become sustainable once the links between fiscal policy and development are explicitly included in the analysis. Restrictive macroeconomic approaches often miss the fact that social goals are not only ends in themselves but are also capital inputs, the very means to productive life, economic growth and further development. Where the development payback is sufficiently high, then deficit-financed public investments are compatible with fiscal sustainability.

## 2.2 Evolution in Macroeconomic Thinking:
### From the Washington Consensus to Pro-poor and Inclusive Growth

The macroeconomic framework that has been followed in most developing countries since the 1980s was based on the philosophy of 'getting the prices right'. This was codified and distilled by Williamson (1990) into the Washington Consensus, which has been at the heart of conventional economic policy formulation for some time. The Washington Consensus has been simplified into the mantra 'stabilize, privatize and liberalize' (Rodrik, 2006).

The Washington Consensus provided the framework for many of the reforms that were implemented during the 1990s by a variety of countries around the world. According to the Washington Consensus, stabilization, privatization and liberalization were regarded as the central objectives of growth-oriented policy in the belief that, once growth is achieved, society benefits through 'trickle-down'. Consequently, most governments were seized with the objective of 'getting the prices right' to the detriment of other, equally important, social imperatives and objectives such as employment creation and poverty reduction. Key aspects of the Washington Consensus were reflected in the World Bank's *World Development Report, 1991* (World Bank, 1991).

It has now been demonstrated both theoretically and empirically that economic growth on its own does not necessarily ensure human development and poverty reduction.[1] It leads to human development and poverty reduction only when it is accompanied by the rapid growth of productive and remunerative employment; it is not just the quantum and pace of economic growth that matters but also the quality and pattern of that growth (Ehrenpreis, 2007). The much touted 'trickle-down', whereby economic gains slowly filter to the bottom strata of society, either has not occurred or, at best, has been slow to materialize. Macroeconomic policies therefore need to promote both the pace of economic growth and its pattern, i.e. the extent to which the poor actively participate in growth both as agents and as beneficiaries (Klasen, 2003).

Stiglitz (1994) argues that, while the Washington Consensus rightly emphasized the need for macroeconomic stability and liberalization, its policies were sometimes misguided in those areas and it failed to recognize the need for complementary measures to ensure sound financial regulation and an effective role for the state in areas such as human capital formation and technology transfer, all of which are essential for 'making markets work'. Furthermore, the Washington Consensus approach to economic reforms overlooked the fact that in many cases countries lack the capacity and resources to attack all distortions in an economy simultaneously (Rodrik, 2006 and 2007).

The original Washington Consensus was expanded in the late 1990s to reflect the new thinking of the International Financial Institutions (IFIs) towards 'getting the institutions right', the second-generation reforms (Table 2.1). This Augmented Washington Consensus, which was more institutional in nature and targeted problems of 'good governance', came about after the realization that 'getting the prices right' was not sufficient to address structural and institutional bottlenecks and distortions. Moreover, the 'big bang' liberalization of markets made economies more prone to financial crisis and contagion: the 1997 East Asian financial crisis and the global financial crisis which began in August 2007 are cases in point.

Although vast parts of the world's economy have been doing quite well in the last quarter century,[2] this success has not come from following a particular sequence of policy reforms and prescriptions (World Bank, 2005 and 2008a; Rodrik, 2007). For instance, even though China and India increased their economies' reliance on free-market forces to some extent, their general economic policies remained the exact opposite of the main tenets of the Washington Consensus and Augmented Washington Consensus, as they both had high levels of protectionism, no privatization, extensive industrial-policy planning, and lax fiscal and financial policies throughout the 1990s. Surprisingly, Williamson himself

---

[1] Since the launch of the first global *Human Development Report* of 1990, the UNDP has defined human development as 'a process of expanding people's choices by enabling them to enjoy long, healthy and creative lives'.

[2] Studies on poverty reveal that 400 million fewer people are living in extreme poverty than in the early 1980s.

**Table 2.1: The Washington Consensus and Augmented Washington Consensus**

| Washington Consensus | Augmented Washington Consensus |
| --- | --- |
| Secure property rights | Anti-corruption |
| Deregulation | Corporate governance |
| Fiscal discipline | Independent central bank and IT |
| Tax reform | Financial codes and standards |
| Privatization | Flexible labour markets |
| Reorientation of public expenditures | WTO agreements |
| Financial liberalization | 'Prudent' capital-account opening |
| Trade liberalization | Non-intermediate exchange-rate regimes |
| Openness to FDI | Social safety nets |
| Unified and competitive exchange rates | Targeted poverty reduction |

*Source:* Rodrik (2006: 978).

summarized the overall effects on growth, employment and poverty reduction in many countries as 'disappointing'.[3] He attributed this limited impact to the following factors: firstly, the Washington Consensus per se placed no special emphasis on mechanisms for avoiding economic crises, which have proved very damaging; secondly, the reforms were incomplete; thirdly, the reforms cited were overly ambitious with respect to targeting improvements in income distribution.

The World Bank's report *Economic Growth in the 1990s* showed that there was an unexpectedly deep and prolonged collapse in output in countries making the transition from communism to market economies (World Bank, 2005 and 2008a). More than a decade into the transition, many former communist countries had still not achieved their 1990 levels of output. Sub-Saharan African (SSA) economies completely failed to take off, in spite of significant policy reform, changes in the political and external environments, and the continued heavy influx of foreign aid. There were several successive and painful financial crises in Latin America, East Asia, Russia and Turkey. The Latin American recovery in the first half of the 1990s was very short-lived: there was less growth in per capita GDP in Latin America than in the period 1950–80 (Rodrik, 2006).

In view of the above, it is now generally agreed that economic development is about structural transformation and that, as markets generally under-provide incentives for such a transformation to occur, governments have to play a strategic and proactive role in initiating and spurring development. This explains why countries that have developed successfully have used government-driven industrial policy as the norm rather than as the exception. For growth strategies to be effective, they should focus on attacking the binding constraints on

---

[3] J. Williamson, 'Did the Washington Consensus Fail?' Remarks at the Center for Strategic and International Studies, 6 November 2002, <http://www.iie.com/publications/papers/paper.cfm?researchid=488>.

growth rather than addressing many weaknesses simultaneously. Development success requires not a 'big bang' approach but, rather, a selective, sequential and often unorthodox approach that accounts for country-specific circumstances (ibid; World Bank, 2008a).

Another key lesson from the past few decades is the need to move away from economic formulas and to understand that economic policies and institutional reforms must address whatever is the binding constraint on growth at the right time, in the right manner, and in the right sequence, instead of addressing any constraint at any time. This much more targeted, sequential and incremental approach requires recognizing country specificities, and calls for greater economic, institutional and social analysis and rigor than a simple formula-based approach to policy-making (ibid.).

A development strategy that identifies and deals with country-specific barriers to growth is the key to sustained growth. Different countries have different binding constraints and hence a 'one size fits all' strategy does not necessarily work (Rodrik, 2006 and 2007; World Bank, 2005 and 2008a). In Zimbabwe, a major binding constraint to pro-poor, inclusive and broad-based economic growth is the dual and enclave economic structure. Past macroeconomic policies have failed to address this structural distortion.[4]

The first decade after independence (1980–90) was characterized by state welfarism and limited redistribution of resources as the government sought to address some of the challenges inherited from the previous regime. A number of economic blueprints were adopted, including *Growth with Equity* in 1981, the *Transitional National Development Plan* (1982–85) and the *First Five-Year National Development Plan* (1986–90). The resultant unsustainable budget deficit that emerged at the end of the first decade depressed investment (and savings), and rising unemployment and shortages of foreign currency resulted in the introduction of market-led economic reforms (ESAP) in 1991, on the recommendation of the IMF and World Bank, and entailed the liberalization of markets, the deregulation of the economy, and the partial privatization of parastatals, among other measures.

The economic and social hardships that resulted from ESAP led to the abandoning of market reforms. The period that followed saw the economy descend into crisis, culminating in the economic paralysis of 2007/08. Most economic policies crafted during the period were not implemented, as government resorted to knee-jerk measures. The rapidly deteriorating social, economic and political situation eventually gave rise to the formation of an Inclusive Government in February 2009 following the signing of the interparty political agreement in September 2008. This chapter explores each of these phases in greater detail.

---

[4] A more detailed discussion on enclavity and dualism can be found in Chapter 1.

## 2.3 Post-Independence Performance of the Economy

### 2.3.1 The first decade after independence, 1980–1990

Following the attainment of independence in 1980, the economic policy framework was shaped by the need to achieve both economic growth and equity. The new nationalist government, intent on establishing an egalitarian society, embarked on a largely interventionist development strategy, which led to increased expenditure on health, education and other social welfare programmes. These socio-economic objectives were well articulated in the *Growth with Equity* policy document (Zimbabwe, 1981).

On the back of the end of the liberation war, the country's re-integration into the international community following the removal of international sanctions in 1980, access to international aid and lines of credit, favourable weather conditions and terms of trade, the first two years of independence witnessed an economic boom. Data from the Central Statistical Office suggests that GDP grew at phenomenal rates of 11 per cent and 10 per cent in 1980 and 1981, respectively. Gross investment in capital stock as a percentage of GDP rose steadily, from 13.7 per cent in 1979 to 14.8 per cent in 1980 and 15.5 per cent in 1981. Capacity utilization followed the same trend, rising from 76 per cent in 1979 to 83 per cent in 1980 and 95 per cent in 1981. However, the economy began to show symptoms of over-heating in 1981, with the rate of inflation rising from 7 per cent in 1980 to 14 per cent in 1981. The current account deteriorated from a surplus of US$2.5 million in 1978 to deficits of US$74 million in 1979, US$157 million in 1980, US$439 million in 1981, and US$533 million by 1982.

Government had banked on the US$2.2 billion that had been promised at the Zimbabwe Conference on Reconstruction and Development (ZIMCORD) donors' conference in March 1981. However, by the end of 1984, only a fifth of the amount had been disbursed (World Bank, 1985). To meet its obligations, government borrowed indiscriminately, especially from non-concessionary commercial sources, with short maturity periods and high interest rates. As a result, total debt rose markedly from US$786 million in 1980 to US$2,304 million by 1983 (World Bank, 1993). The debt-service ratio, which represented 1.3 per cent of export earnings in 1979, had risen to 25 per cent by 1983, generating additional pressure on the balance of payments.

The budget deficit, which averaged 8.5 per cent of GDP in 1980/81, improved to 6.6 per cent of GDP in 1981/82 before deteriorating to an average of 8.7 per cent for the period 1982/83–84/85. It remained high owing to security commitments in Mozambique and at home, expenditure on drought relief, and because social services were sustained. By the end of 1982, it was clear that the incipient crisis was not transitory and that the situation required intervention.

In response to the balance-of-payments crisis, the government adopted a 'home-grown' stabilization programme which started with a 20 per cent devaluation of the local currency in December 1982.

The *Transitional National Development Plan* (*TNDP*) of 1982–85 sought to accelerate the process of post-war reconstruction, achieve sustained economic growth, and redress the social imbalances that had prevailed in the pre-independence political dispensation (Zimbabwe, 1982). On the macroeconomic front, the *TNDP* envisaged: GDP growth of 8 per cent per annum; an increase in investments from 19 per cent of GDP achieved in 1981/82 to 23 per cent in 1984/85; an increase in domestic savings from 11 per cent of GDP in 1981/82 to 17 per cent by 1984/85; an increase in the GDP shares of imports and exports to 26 per cent and 23 per cent, respectively, over the same period; and a 3 per cent annual growth in wage employment.

Overall, real GDP registered negative growth in 1982 (–2 per cent) and 1983 (–3 per cent), with a slight (1.3 per cent) recovery in 1984; and its distribution showed a pattern quite the opposite of the intended growth structure, with production in the non-material sectors (mostly government-related) growing at 4.2 per cent per year, and material production registering only 1.4 per cent – in both cases, still falling far short of the 8 per cent overall target. Employment generation was still poor, with significant job losses being experienced (except in the social sectors) in spite of administrative interventions aimed at protecting jobs. Investment declined significantly over the three-year plan period. By 1985, the volume of investment in fixed assets was one fifth below its 1982 level, and the share of productive sectors in total investment fell below 40 per cent.

In 1986, the government adopted the *First Five-Year Development Plan* as the official framework for managing socio-economic development over the period 1986–1990 (Zimbabwe, 1986). The Plan noted that socio-economic performance over the first five years of independence was below that envisaged under *Growth with Equity* and the *TNDP*. The major economic objectives included an average annual GDP rate of growth of 5.1 per cent and the creation of 28,000 jobs per annum.

In terms of real GDP growth, the economy grew at close to the target rate of 5.1 per cent, averaging 4.6 per cent per annum for the period 1986–90. Employment grew at an average annual rate of 2.7 per cent during the same period. This average annual rate of growth was inadequate to deal with new entrants into the labour market, as indicated by the growth rate of the labour force of around 3 per cent per annum. The budget deficit for the period 1986–90 averaged 9.8 per cent of GDP.

Meanwhile, the World Bank and IMF continued to put pressure on the government to adopt market liberalization and deregulation. For instance, in 1987, the World Bank refused to sign an agreement for an extension of the export revolving fund until measures were taken to liberalize trade. The adoption of investment guidelines in April 1989 marked a major shift in government policy. This was followed by the establishment of the Zimbabwe Investment Centre in mid-1989, a move designed to create a 'one stop' investment window. In a bid to reassure investors, government signed the World Bank's Multilateral Investment Guarantee Agency Convention in September 1989, and, in June 1990, signed the USA's Overseas Private Investment Corporation Agreement.

There was a general consensus among stakeholders during this period on the need for some reforms in order to boost depressed investment, streamline inefficient labour regulations, and to restructure the economy to achieve growth with equity, promote exports and create employment. There was, however, no consensus on the nature of the reforms to be adopted.

However, a key highlight of economic policy during the first decade of independence is that, while the government publicly espoused socialism, in practice it implemented a conservative macroeconomic agenda designed to retain the relatively developed formal economy with a strong dose of social development, especially in the areas of education and health. The fear was that irresponsible radicalism would destroy what was a relatively developed and diversified formal economy (Nyawata, 1988). Furthermore, the negotiated settlement that brought about independence (the Lancaster House Conference) emphasized continuity rather that change in economic policy. Furthermore, the internal disturbances in Matabeleland and the military expedition in Mozambique, worsened by destabilization from a hostile South Africa under apartheid, necessitated the adoption of a cautious approach to economic management. In addition, the unsatisfactory experiences of Tanzania and Mozambique with nationalization were still fresh in the minds of the liberation war protagonists who were now in government.[5]

### 2.3.2 The ESAP period, 1991–1996

When it became clear that the economy was not generating sufficient jobs, especially in the context of depressed investment, government adopted a market-led reform programme, the Economic Structural Adjustment Programme (ESAP), in 1991 on the recommendation of the World Bank and the IMF. ESAP marked a paradigm shift from the state-led economic development of the 1980s to a more market-driven development strategy. The key targets of ESAP were to:

- achieve annual GDP growth of 5 per cent over the period 1991-95;
- raise savings to 25 per cent of GDP;
- raise investment to 25 per cent of GDP;
- achieve export growth of 9 per cent per annum;

[5] See Chapter 1.

• reduce the budget deficit from over 10 per cent of GDP to 5 per cent by 1995;

• reduce inflation from 17.7 per cent to 10 per cent by 1995.

To achieve these objectives, the government set out to liberalize markets, in line with prescriptions of the World Bank and IMF. The trade regime was liberalized, and so were the financial and labour markets. Price controls, subsidies and other regulations were dismantled as the economy changed to rely increasingly on markets.

ESAP, however, had a stagflationary effect on the economy, which was exacerbated by the drought of 1991/2 (Table 2.2). Economic growth declined, average annual inflation rose markedly, and employment growth slowed. To deal with such inflationary pressures, monetary policy was tightened by keeping the benchmark rediscount rate high. Other interest rates also remained high, with harmful consequences on the private sector's demand for credit. With the depreciation of the Zimbabwe dollar as a result of the high inflation rate, the servicing of the external debt also rose, and this, together with the high domestic interest rates, resulted in high interest expenses. The share of manufacturing in GDP declined, and a similar downward trend prevailed in the agriculture and mining sectors. The budget deficit deteriorated and export growth declined. However, both the savings and investment ratios registered some improvements.

The number of employees in the non-agricultural sector declined from about 929,800 in 1991 to about 844,000 in 1992 as retrenchments accelerated and many private employers of low-skilled workers shed permanent employees in favour of casual workers (World Bank, 1995; ILO, 1993); by August 1995, 20,000 workers had been retrenched in the public sector. Real wages were generally declining

**Table 2.2: Zimbabwe's economic performance, 1980–1996**

| Economic indicators | 1980–1990 | 1991–1996 |
|---|---|---|
| | % | % |
| Real GDP growth | 4.2 | 2.8 |
| Average annual inflation | 12 | 26.6 |
| Employment growth | 1.9 | 0.12 |
| Manufacturing/GDP | 20.35 | 16 |
| Agriculture/GDP | 16.2 | 14 |
| Mining/GDP | 4.3 | 4 |
| Savings/GDP | 18 | 23 |
| Investment/GDP | 17 | 21.7 |
| Budget deficit/GDP | –3 | –5.8 |
| Export growth | 0.2 | 0.1 |
| Exports/GDP | 23 | 41 |

Source: Central Statistical Office; Reserve Bank of Zimbabwe (various publications).

for most workers, and especially for low-skilled workers. A study by the Central Statistical Office (Zimbabwe, 1998) suggested that the incidence of poverty in Zimbabwe increased from 40.4 per cent in 1990/91 to 63.3 per cent in 1995/96, while extreme poverty (households that cannot meet basic food requirements) increased from 16.7 per cent to 35.7 per cent over the same period.

After some years in denial, the World Bank eventually admitted that ESAP had failed. Addressing the First Forum of the Structural Adjustment Participatory Review Initiative (SAPRI) in Zimbabwe on 2 September 1999, Tom Allen, then Resident Representative of the World Bank, attributed its failure to the following factors:

- Growth needs to be inclusive.
- Social sector expenditures need to be protected, and targeted measures to deal with poverty should not be seen as 'add ons' but as an integral part of the programme.
- State intervention is necessary – 'getting the prices right' and making markets work better are important, but these need to be complemented with measures to ensure that the 'unequal' balance of power of those who can readily engage in the market and those who cannot does not lead to dangerous levels of social tension.
- National ownership is critical.

More importantly, the failure to consult other social partners hindered progress. In the words of the World Bank, 'the Zimbabwe case demonstrates the importance of popular ownership and participation throughout the process of adjustment. An open, transparent dialogue can help generate realistic expectations, reduce uncertainty, and contribute to a unified sense of national ownership for reforms' (World Bank, 1995).

Although the IMF moved much more slowly than the World Bank, it had been steadily reforming its operations. In the light of the Asian financial crisis of 1997, the IMF had to change its position, arguing vigorously for the regulation of financial markets and calling for a new International Financial Architecture (Swoboda, 1999). At the 1999 annual meetings held in October, the World Bank and the IMF adopted a new Poverty Reduction and Growth Facility that was to

- be country-driven, with the broad participation of civil society, elected institutions, key donors and relevant IFIs;
- be developed from an understanding of the nature and determinants of poverty and the links between public actions and poverty outcomes;
- recognize that sustained poverty reduction will not be possible without rapid economic growth;
- be oriented towards achieving outcome-related goals for poverty reduction.

### 2.3.3 The crisis period, 1997–2008

Following the failure of ESAP, and the hardships that resulted in growing discontent and the rise of civil society from its slumber, subsequent economic policies were generally characterized by irrational controls, policy inconsistencies and reversals. The Zimbabwe Programme for Economic and Social Transformation (ZIMPREST) was presented to the nation as the successor to ESAP in March 1998, almost two years late, as it was meant to cover the period 1996–2000. ZIMPREST targeted budget-deficit cuts to 6.5 per cent of GDP by 2001, inflation reduced to 5 per cent by the end of 2000, GDP growth of 6 per cent per annum, and the creation of 42,000 jobs in the next three years. In spite of these impressive targets, ZIMPREST was never implemented and remained largely a paper tiger.

It is generally agreed that the massive crash of the Zimbabwe dollar on 14 November 1997, commonly referred to as 'Black Friday', marks the onset of the crisis. The crash was precipitated by the government's unbudgeted payment of gratuities to war veterans of the liberation struggle. Each of the estimated 50,000 ex-combatants received a once-off gratuity of Z$50,000 (US$4,167) by 31 December 1997, and a monthly pension of Z$2,000 (US$140) from January 1998. Government sought to fund this through the introduction of a war veteran's levy, which was rejected by workers through ZCTU-organized demonstrations, and had to seek recourse to borrowing and printing money.

As a result of the massive depreciation of the Zimbabwe dollar, input costs soared, thereby undermining the viability of producers; farmers, in turn, demanded that the producer price of maize be raised. Millers hiked prices by 24 per cent in January 1998 following increased input costs, and the increase in the price of maize-meal triggered nationwide riots during the last week of January 1998. Government immediately intervened by introducing price controls on all basic commodities. The exchange rate was then fixed at Z$38 to the US dollar.

In August 1998, government unilaterally sent troops to the Democratic Republic of Congo (DRC) to help the government of that country repel rebels who were on the brink of taking over the capital city, Kinshasa. Zimbabwe's involvement in the DRC war was estimated to cost US$33 million a month. This was followed by a decision to increase civil servants' salaries by between 69 per cent and 90 per cent at the beginning of 2000, just before a referendum in February 2000 on a government-proposed new constitution. Since these salary increases had not been budgeted for, government had to borrow again to meet the expenditure. In the February referendum, Zimbabweans rejected the proposed constitution. A process of occupation of white-owned commercial farms then ensued, and in June 2001 the fast-track land-reform programme was officially launched. This followed accusations by government that white farmers had provided transport for their workers to vote against the proposed constitution.

In July 2001 the government decided to resume control over food supplies. Maize and wheat were declared controlled products, which made it illegal to buy, sell or move them within Zimbabwe other than to the Grain Marketing Board (GMB); the Zimbabwe Agricultural Commodity Exchange (ZIMACE) was officially suspended. In December 2001, further restrictions compelled farmers to deliver their maize and grain stocks to the GMB within fourteen days of harvesting. By 2002, all holding of grain stocks by farmers was banned and grain supplies were seized, leaving the livestock industry and farm-workers facing a crisis.

Against this background, the relationship between Zimbabwe and its development partners deteriorated to a degree that Zimbabwe earned itself a high-risk profile (pariah status). Donors and investors deserted the country, resulting in an acute shortage of foreign currency. As a result, a thriving parallel market emerged, which became virtually the only port of call for foreign-currency seekers. The impact of all these irrational decisions was particularly acute with respect to the budget deficit (Fig. 2.1).

The deficit deteriorated progressively from about 6 per cent of GDP in 1998 to about 18 per cent by the end of 2000; it had been targeted to decline to 3.8 per cent of GDP by then, so this largely reflected the impact of the unbudgeted expenditures. It declined noticeably to about 1 per cent in 2009, though it was projected to deteriorate to about 8 per cent in 2010 on the back of rising recurrent government expenditure. Because these deficits, as well as

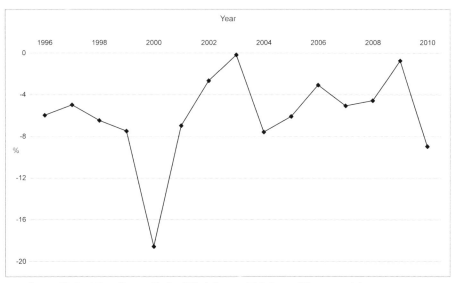

*Source:* Derived from Reserve Bank of Zimbabwe and Ministry of Finance statistics. The figure for 2010 is projected.

**Fig. 2.1: The budget deficit as a percentage of GDP, 1996–2010**

new borrowing, were being incurred primarily to support recurrent expenditure rather than investments in infrastructure or productive capital, the domestic and external debt burden increased significantly. The country accumulated arrears on its foreign-debt repayments in 1999, which had risen to US$1.3 billion by December 2002 and about US$6 billion by 2009. By 2009, external debt as a proportion of GDP stood at about 120 per cent, down from about 190 per cent in 2008 (Fig. 2.2). On the other hand, the external debt as a percentage of exports and imports stood at about 400 per cent and 200 per cent, respectively. External debt continued to grow as a consequence of new payment arrears and interest and penalty charges on existing payment arrears, and according to the Ministry of Finance was projected to reach US$7.6 billion by the end of 2010.

The balance-of-payments position also deteriorated, with annual fluctuations (Fig. 2.3). The overall balance deteriorated progressively from about US$200 million in 2000 to reach an all-time low of about US$1.9 billion in 2009. This came against a backdrop of slow export growth, increasing imports, and lack of external financing and investment. The deterioration of the current and capital account reflects the persistent loss of competitiveness of the economy. The financing of the current and capital accounts remains contingent on foreign direct investment (FDI), short-term capital inflows and short-term borrowing.

That the crisis emanated from a descent into lawlessness and bad governance was reinforced by the Tripartite Negotiating Forum where, in its Kadoma Declaration of August 2001, government, business and labour agreed that the way forward involved the ascent to good governance. The Kadoma Declaration emphasized internal factors as the cause of the crisis, not external intervention.

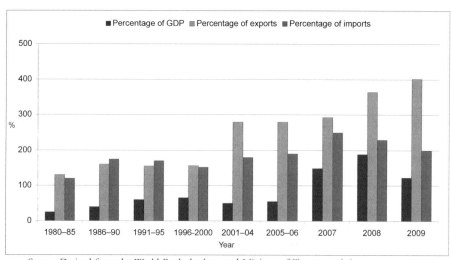

*Source:* Derived from the World Bank database and Ministry of Finance statistics.

**Fig. 2.2: Total external debt as a percentage of GDP, exports and imports, 1980–2009**

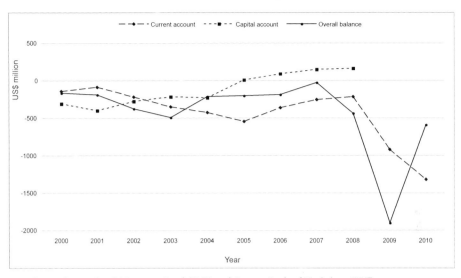

Source: International Monetary Fund (IMF) and Reserve Bank of Zimbabwe (RBZ).
The figure for 2010 is projected.

**Fig. 2.3: Balance-of-payments position, 2000–2010**

The argument that external forces, disgruntled by the seizure of white farms, were the reason for the crisis is highly contested, especially when the descent into crisis is explored in historical, chronological order. The land grab started in earnest after the February 2000 referendum, when, in fact, the crisis had already started, as evidenced by the economic decline from 1997. In fact, the US Zimbabwe Democracy and Economic Recovery Act (ZDERA) came into force only in 2001 when the crisis had already set in. Furthermore, Zimbabwe had stopped accessing balance-of-payments support from the IMF in 1998, owing chiefly to its failure to service its outstanding debt.

Measures taken to address the crisis were knee-jerk, targeting the symptoms and not the underlying factors. After the emergence of the crisis in 1997, a number of economic strategies were adopted: ZIMPREST, which was supposed to run from 1996 to 2000; the Millennium Economic Recovery Programme (MERP), launched early in 2000, an 18-month programme that was supposed to run concurrently with the Millennium Budget announced on 21 October 1999; the Ten-Point Plan, with an emphasis on agriculture, launched in 2002; the National Economic Revival Programme (NERP) in 2003; the Macroeconomic Policy Framework (2005–2006): 'Towards Sustained Economic Growth'; expansive 'monetary policies' between 2003 and 2008; and the National Economic Development Priority Programme (NEDPP) in 2007. However, a common feature of all these programmes and efforts is that they were not implemented; the documents were used more for propaganda purposes than as instruments to turn around the economy.

A new Governor of the Reserve Bank of Zimbabwe (RBZ), Gideon Gono, was appointed at the end of 2003 to spearhead the country's economic turnaround efforts. With time, the RBZ started to depart from conventional central-bank functions and its legal mandate over monetary policy. Its interventions took the form of quasi-fiscal activities,[6] funded through the printing of money, which increased sharply after 2004 and included monetary operations to mop up liquidity, subsidized credit, subsidized exchange rates for selected government purchases, and multiple currency practices. The RBZ created subsidized lending programmes to support priority sectors like agriculture such as the Productive Sector Facility (PSF) and the Agricultural Sector Productivity Enhancement Facility (ASPEF) introduced in 2007. It also provided support to insolvent banks in the form of access to a Troubled Banks Fund (TBF). Since lending under these schemes was larger than the statutory reserves, the RBZ printed money to cover the difference, thereby increasing the monetary base.

While central-bank losses in most countries have not exceeded ten per cent of GDP, Zimbabwe's flow of realized central-bank quasi-fiscal losses are estimated to have amounted to 75 per cent of GDP in 2006. The escalation of inflation was fuelled by rapid money growth arising from these quasi-fiscal activities. There is a close relationship between inflation, growth in broad money supply (M3) and quasi-fiscal disbursements.[7] The hyperinflation, which was primarily driven by high money-supply growth on the back of increasing quasi-fiscal activities by the central bank, was compounded by speculative activities in financial markets and the underlying severe supply constraints in the economy. At the last count before the inception of the Inclusive Government in February 2009, the official rate of inflation had reached a staggering 231 million per cent, which independent analysts considered conservative.[8]

From a high rate of 9.7 per cent in 1996, economic growth suffered a sharp decline reaching a nadir of –14.8 per cent in 2008 (Fig. 2.4). The unprecedented economic downturn brought about increased poverty, which in turn increased the social and economic marginalization of already disadvantaged groups. By 2003, 72 per cent of the population was below the poverty line, up from 55 per cent in 1995. Female-headed households had a higher incidence of poverty

[6] Mackenzie and Stella (1996, quoted in Munoz, 2007: 3) define a quasi-fiscal activity as 'an operation or measure carried out by a central bank or other public financial institution with an effect that can, in principle, be duplicated by budgetary measures in the form of an explicit tax, subsidy, or direct expenditure and that has or may have an impact on the financial operations of the central bank, other public financial institutions, or government'.

[7] See Zimbabwe. Ministry of Finance. *The 2009 Mid-Year Fiscal Policy Review Statement: STERP in Motion*, p. 39, <http://www.zimtreasury.org/downloads/293.pdf>.

[8] The New Hyperinflation Index for Zimbabwe estimated in mid-November 2008 that Zimbabwe's monthly inflation rate was 79,600,000,000 per cent, which gives an equivalent daily inflation rate of 98.0 per cent and an annualized inflation rate of 89.7 sextillion per cent: <http://www.cato.org/Zimbabwe>.

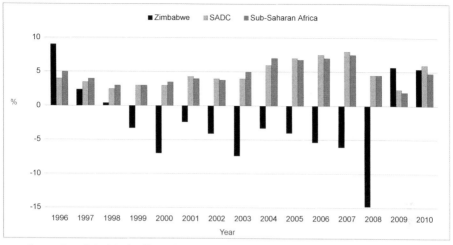

Source: Central Statistical Office and Ministry of Finance. The figure for 2010 is projected.

**Fig. 2.4: Trends in real GDP growth, 1996–2010**

at 68 per cent compared to male-headed households at 60 per cent – poverty had 'a rural face and a woman's face' (Zimbabwe, 2006). The percentage of the population employed in the formal sector had declined from 14 per cent in 1980 to 10 per cent by 2004 and about 6 per cent by 2007.

More importantly, economic policies failed dismally to address the structural distortions prevailing in the economy. In fact, the dual and enclave structure was further entrenched, as the informal economy became the largest segment of the economy, and the middle-class disappeared (the 'missing middle'); inequality worsened, the Gini coefficient rising from 0.53 in 1995 to 0.61 by 2003 (Zimbabwe, 2006).[9] As the economic crisis deepened, the government became reactionary, adopting conflicting policies, reversing some, and, as the popularity of the ruling party waned, irrational price controls, in which prices were set below their viable levels, became a central aspect of macroeconomic policy.

Owing to the unviable pricing regime and the debilitating macroeconomic environment, capacity utilization declined to below 10 per cent, with commodities virtually disappearing from the market in 2007 and 2008 – the period of economic paralysis. The Mid-Term Monetary Policy Review Statement of 1 October 2007 introduced the Basic Commodities Supply-Side Intervention Facility (BACOSSI) with the objective of boosting production through targeted financial support to producers of basic commodities. As the Monetary Policy

---

[9] The Gini coefficient is a measure of inequality, ranging from 0 (complete equality) to 1 (complete inequality).

Statement of January 2008 conceded, BACOSSI was 'a crisis management intervention in the aftermath of the mid-2007 price blitz' to foreclose the possible collapse of companies. This in itself highlights the policy conflict or contradictions alluded to above, where in one swoop government introduced a price blitz and the next moment introduced a quasi-fiscal intervention to subsidize producers, yet what was required was the relaxing of the pricing regime.[10]

On 10 September 2008, the RBZ introduced Foreign Exchange Licensed Warehouses and Retail Shops (FOLIWARS), Foreign Exchange Licensed Oil Companies (FELOCs) and Foreign Exchange Licensed Outlets for Petrol and Diesel (FELOPADs). Under these schemes, licensed businesses would be allowed to sell commodities in foreign currency. Their objectives included harnessing the foreign currency floating around in the country, increasing local industry capacity utilization and, most importantly, improving the availability of basic goods and commodities. While this initiative improved the availability of commodities on the local market, it represented only a partial approach to resolving the problems affecting the economy, which required a more holistic approach.

The rapidly deteriorating socio-economic and political situation resulted in the three political parties signing an Interparty Political Agreement – which has now become known as the Global Political Agreement (GPA) – in September 2008. Article 3.1(a) of the GPA states:

> The Parties agree to give priority to the restoration of economic stability and growth in Zimbabwe. The Government will lead the process of developing and implementing an economic recovery strategy and plan. To that end, the Parties are committed to working together on a full and comprehensive economic programme to resuscitate Zimbabwe's economy, which will urgently address the issue of production, food security, poverty and unemployment and the challenges of high inflation, interest rates and the exchange rate.

The GPA also envisages the creation of a National Economic Council comprising the political parties that signed the GPA, sectoral representatives of employer organizations, the Zimbabwe Congress of Trade Unions (ZCTU) and academia. However, its relationship to already existing consultative forums – such as the National Economic Consultative Forum established in July 1997, in which invited individuals participate, and the Tripartite Negotiating Forum created in September 1998 by the Employers' Confederation of Zimbabwe, the ZCTU and government to negotiate policy – is not clarified.

---

[10] In the 2003 national budget statement, the Minister of Finance and Economic Development, Herbert Murerwa, observed with respect to price controls: 'Efforts to protect the consumer from spiralling prices are being undermined by price controls that focus mostly on the final product, ignoring developments affecting inputs into the production process. This has affected production viability and the sustainability of the controlled price levels.'

## 2.3.4 The Transitional Period, 2009–2010

### 2.3.4.1 The 2009 national budget

The budget presented to Parliament on 29 January 2009, just before the formation of the Inclusive Government in February, saw the estimates being presented for the first time in Zimbabwe dollars, United States dollars and South African rand.[11] The budget statement acknowledged that the economy was in deep crisis, which it blamed largely on internal policies. Even though it still apportioned some blame to external factors, such as drought and sanctions, the emphasis was clearly on internal factors.

The budget statement also acknowledged the importance of a stable macroeconomic environment that allows forward planning and transacting in stable currencies while implementing reforms aimed at restoring the value of the local currency. The statement highlighted the importance of holistic policies, unity of purpose among stakeholders, and the re-engagement of international partners to ensure regular and sustainable inflows of, and access to, foreign currency to achieve the anticipated economic turnaround. The need to remove existing distortions arising from multiple exchange rates and the licensing of businesses to transact in foreign currency alongside the local currency was also highlighted.

Clearly, therefore, the budget statement broke ranks with the 'populist' approach that had resulted in the implementation of half-hearted and wrong-headed interventions, including price controls that undermined viability and resulted in widespread shortages of basic commodities and the collapse of industry and the economy:

> Excessive money supply growth rates, emanating from unbudgeted expenditures made through the Reserve Bank, as well as low supply of goods and services remain the major sources of inflation [para. 80].

> The 2009 Budget thrust should, therefore, shift from policies that promote and fuel consumption to those which create wealth, through supporting our productive sectors, particularly agriculture, mining, tourism and manufacturing, whose capacity utilization is now below 30 per cent [para. 83].

> Essential for shoring up the value of the Zimbabwe dollar will be implementation of a combination of strict and painful fiscal and monetary measures that relate the Zimbabwe dollar monetary base to developments in the real sector, and avoidance of recourse to money printing beyond the economy's production of goods and services [para. 145].

[11] <http://www.zimtreasury.org/downloads/196.pdf>.

Realising this requires discipline and commitment to our expenditure and revenue targets and, therefore, expenditures outside the Budget will not be entertained [para. 146].

One of the key policy proposals in the budget was the liberalization of the foreign-exchange market, implying that all transactions could be legally undertaken in foreign currency alongside the local currency. The budget merely recognized and legitimized the status quo: 'In line with the prevailing practices by the general public, Government is, therefore, allowing the use of multiple foreign currencies for business transactions, alongside the Zimbabwe dollar' (para. 139). The role of the National Incomes and Pricing Commission was reviewed 'to focus on monitoring price trends obtaining in the sub-region and beyond, guiding producers and retailers as well as advising Government on import parity based pricing' rather than impose price controls (para. 232).

Following the formation of the Inclusive Government, the new Minister of Finance, Tendai Biti, presented a National Budget Review Statement to Parliament on 18 March 2009.[12] This was followed by the Short-Term Emergency Recovery Programme (STERP), launched by President Robert Mugabe on 19 March 2009.[13] The Budget Review Statement was necessitated by the need to achieve the alignment of tax and other economic measures to STERP, downward revision of the overall 2009 budget framework in line with actual developments, and reconfiguration of the estimates of expenditure to incorporate additional ministries in line with the formation of the Inclusive Government (para. 1.1.8).

The focus of the budget review was on the following:
• Adoption of a cash budgeting system.
• Use of multiple currencies as legal tender and adoption of the rand as a reference currency.
• Revised estimated revenue and expenditure of US$1 billion.
• Dismantling of foreign-currency controls.
• Upward review of the tax-free threshold from US$125 to US$150.
• Payment of US$100 allowance to civil servants.
• Rehabilitation and development of irrigation systems.
• Resuscitation of the social contract.

### 2.3.4.2 Short-Term Emergency Recovery Programme (STERP)

In an effort to address the economic crisis and paralysis, the Inclusive Government came up with STERP, a short-term emergency programme aimed at stabilizing the macro- and microeconomy, recovering levels of savings, investment and growth, and laying the basis for a more transformative mid-term to long-term

---

[12] <http://www.zimtreasury.org/downloads/198.pdf>.

[13] <http://www.zimtreasury.org/downloads/31.pdf>.

economic programme that will turn Zimbabwe into a progressive developmental State (para. 6).

STERP was to focus on the following short-term emergency policy areas (para. 46):

- Social protection measures meant to mitigate poverty and suffering by resuscitating public services' delivery, and strengthening humanitarian assistance, particularly focusing on Specially Targeted Vulnerable Groups including women, children, the disabled, the elderly and child-headed families;
- Support for the revival of productive sectors;
- Creation of a conducive investment climate in the country;
- Establishing a sound macroeconomic environment conducive for stabilization through demand side management measures, in particular capacity expansion in all sectors;
- Strengthening the regulatory environment of the financial sector; and
- Finalizing the national employment policy.

On account of its bloated structure, the Inclusive Government is overly consumption-oriented, comprising 71 ministers, deputy ministers and governors. This figure is far too high, and is unsustainable for an economy and population the size of Zimbabwe. Moreover, Zimbabwe cannot afford such a bloated government at a time when the economy is still in distress and the treasury is bankrupt. Quite clearly, therefore, the little revenue that will trickle into state coffers will go largely towards meeting the day-to-day recurrent expenditures of the government, leaving very little for social protection and the rehabilitation of infrastructure.

The absence of an overarching developmental vision that will underpin and anchor the short-term macroeconomic policy framework, as well as provide a guiding framework of where the country is going, remains a limiting factor. STERP is only a short-term economic revival document and therefore contains no specific measures to deal with the structural distortions and rigidities arising out of the dual and enclave economic structure. The absence of supply-side incentives to resuscitate and engender inclusive, pro-poor growth, coupled with the likely adverse impacts of the global financial crisis and anti-inflation measures, implies that the decent-work deficits that characterize the economy and entrench poverty and its feminization will abound. More importantly, STERP fails to provide stimuli for a new paradigm that is pro-poor and inclusive, fails to promote the integrability[14] of marginalized groups (women, youths, people with disabilities and people living with HIV and AIDS) and sectors, especially the

---

[14] 'Integrability' refers to the extent to which the poor are able to integrate into economic processes such that, as growth and employment expand, they can take advantage of the opportunities that arise to improve the quality and quantity of their employment (Osmani, 2004).

informal and rural economy, and unleash a more employment-intensive pathway out of poverty. The dilapidated state of infrastructure provides an opportunity to leverage pro-poor, employment-intensive infrastructure programmes.

### 2.3.4.3 A critical look at dollarization

Dollarization refers to the adoption by a sovereign country of the national currency of another country to fulfil part or all of the basic functions of money.[15] Dollarization does not imply that only one foreign currency is adopted. Many countries have adopted dual and/or multiple exchange-rate regimes, whereby more than one currency is officially adopted. There are two forms of dollarization: official/de jure and unofficial/de facto. Official dollarization entails a foreign currency (or foreign currencies) becoming the exclusive legal tender; unofficial dollarization entails the de facto adoption of foreign currency, either exclusively or in parallel with the domestic currency.

Zimbabwe adopted a de facto dollarization regime in February 2009 following the introduction of the multiple currency regime, with the South African rand acting as the reference currency for accounting purposes, under which all transactions are now conducted in hard currencies. Generally, dollarization is seen as a response to a loss of confidence in the local currency owing to sustained bouts of hyperinflation and currency crisis. Countries experiencing severe episodes of lack of policy credibility and uncertainty may also adopt dollarization. The main economic rationale for dollarization is to bring about monetary stability in the dollarizing country, but it may also help to broaden and deepen financial integration with the anchor country.

*Benefits of dollarization*

Dollarization has been applied in Argentina, Mexico, Bolivia, Peru, Georgia, Russia, Ukraine, Turkey, Romania, Mozambique, Zambia and Zimbabwe. In most of these, it stemmed from a loss of confidence by economic agents in the domestic currency owing to chronic high inflation, currency crises and the absence of policy credibility. Most chronic high-inflation countries have successfully eliminated inflation after the adoption of dollarization. There is a reduction in exchange-rate risk and volatility, and a reduction in the possibility of currency crises and capital flight. Dollarization eliminates the need to print money to finance fiscal deficits, which helps to foster sound fiscal policy. It also reduces currency speculation and other rent-seeking economic behaviour that may be detrimental to the overall welfare of the economy.

The adoption of dollarization in Zimbabwe had the immediate impact of

---

[15] These basic functions include money as a medium of exchange, store of value, unit of account, and standard for deferred payment.

eliminating hyperinflation, resulting in an improvement in the business climate and economic stability. Annual inflation declined from the official 231 million per cent in July 2008 to 7.7 per cent in 2009 and 3.6 per cent in August 2010; it is expected to end the year 2010 at 4.5 per cent. There has also been a significant improvement in product availability in retail and wholesale outlets, with capacity utilization having improved markedly from below 10 per cent to around 30–50 per cent.[16]

*Cost of dollarization*

There is a loss of seigniorage in the dollarized nation. Seigniorage is the profit that accrues to the central bank from printing money and minting coins. By creating fiat money,[17] the central bank can purchase real resources almost without cost, except for those of printing the notes and the interest on bank reserves. This profit normally amounts to about 1–1.5 per cent of GDP.

Dollarization results in a loss of the 'lender of last resort' function of the central bank, as it leaves it with only limited resources. Hence, the impact of a financial (or banking) crisis may be more accentuated and pronounced, as the ability of the central bank to mitigate it will be severely constrained. There is a loss of an independent monetary and exchange-rate policy, as the central bank's ability to control its money supply, interest rates and exchange rate to influence the domestic economy is undermined. This leaves the dollarized economy vulnerable to external shocks.

There is also compelling evidence that dollarization has pernicious effects on marginalized and vulnerable groups, such as the poor and SMEs; this is already becoming evident in Zimbabwe. The elite, on the other hand, favour dollarization as a way to protect their asset portfolios. Once an economy has dollarized it is usually difficult to de-dollarize – the 'dollarization trap'. This trap may be caused by a number of factors, such as the fact that economic agents may be heavily indebted in US dollars, by the increasingly constrained policy regime, as well as by general economic uncertainties.

### 2.3.4.4 Is dollarization the panacea?

Dollarization should not be viewed as the panacea to Zimbabwe's economic problems. It cannot be a substitute for the adoption and implementation of structural, institutional and political reforms necessary to create a stable political and macroeconomic environment. Most importantly, the pace and sustainability of economic progress in Zimbabwe will depend on developments on the political front. At the moment, a number of would-be investors and co-operating partners

---

[16] *Mid-Term Fiscal Policy Review Statement*, 14 July 2010, p. 16.

[17] Fiat money is money that is not backed up by any physical commodity such as gold or silver.

are still sceptical and risk-averse; they are in a wait-and-see mode. However, as more robust political and institutional reforms are implemented, it is most likely that this scepticism and risk-aversion will subside.

Dollarization has indeed eliminated Zimbabwe-dollar hyperinflation and helped to restore price stability, thereby bringing convenience to consumers. However, there is a potential downside risk of greater economic contraction if foreign money supply does not improve. The current-account deficit is likely to worsen, as imports from neighbouring countries continue to flood the domestic market. This is not favourable to Zimbabwe's local industries, as they face stiff competition from those foreign products at a time when they are still struggling to stand on their feet.

### 2.3.4.5 Evaluation of STERP

There has been a notable improvement in the performance of the key sectors of the economy, and a number of firms have registered significant improvements in their levels of capacity utilization. Having cumulatively declined by more than 50 per cent over the period 1999–2008, the economy grew by an estimated 5.7 per cent in 2009 (the average for SADC was 2.4 per cent and for Sub-Saharan Africa 2 per cent) and is forecast to expand by 5.4 per cent in 2010.

Even though the economy has been on a relative stabilization trajectory since the formation of the Inclusive Government in February 2009, that recovery remains delicate. The major constraint to full economic recovery is the highly volatile and unstable political milieu (which increases the country/political-risk premium). There are also economic uncertainties, especially with regard to the implementation of the indigenization and empowerment regulations which were gazetted with minimal stakeholder involvement and participation. Consequently, there has been very little inflow of investment and capital into the country as most potential investors and co-operating partners adopt a wait-and-see attitude: FDI rose marginally to US$60 million in 2009 from US$52 million in 2008.[18]

These political and economic uncertainties have contributed to a general dearth of competitiveness in the economy. The *2010–2011 Global Competitiveness Report* compiled by the World Economic Forum ranked Zimbabwe 136 out of 139 countries (WEF, 2010); in the previous year's rankings, Zimbabwe came 132 out of 134 countries (WEF, 2009). According to the *Report*, a combination of dilapidated infrastructure, limited health-care and education services and poor institutional frameworks have conspired to render Zimbabwe less competitive in the global marketplace. Zimbabwe also fares badly in the World Bank's *Doing Business* report, being ranked 159 out of 183 countries (World Bank, 2009). This

---

[18] 'Modest rise in FDI for Zimbabwe', *ZimOnline*, 23 July 2010, <http://www.zimonline.co.za/Article.aspx?ArticleId=6230>.

therefore means that the country is rated very unfavourably as a business and investment destination.

To deal with the political risk, there is an urgent need for the implementation of the Kadoma Declaration on Country Risk, in which the Tripartite Negotiating Forum observed that technical solutions will not work on a sustainable basis without the 'political-risk factor' being addressed. The Declaration identifies what each social partner – government, labour and business – should do to create a new order based on a 'win–win' consensus approach. It is therefore necessary to build the necessary political will and commitment to implement this Kadoma Declaration.

It is also imperative to ensure policy coherence and consistency. For instance, on 29 January 2010, Indigenization and Economic Empowerment Regulations were gazetted, stipulating that any business with an asset value of US$500,000 should 'cede' 51 per cent of ownership to indigenous Zimbabweans.[19] It later emerged that there had not been any consultations, even within the Inclusive Government itself. The lack of broad consultations on the issue, and the fact that it remains unresolved, implies that uncertainties regarding future policies will persist.

The economic prospects and outlook for the country will depend on the expeditious resolution of the outstanding political issues,[20] as well as the attendant implementation of robust institutional and economic reforms. This will infuse confidence and certainty into the economy and minimize the high levels of uncertainty and risk that are prevalent. Furthermore, the issue of the limited fiscal space available needs to be addressed, especially in the context of the unsustainable debt situation and limited external assistance. For instance, in the first half of 2010, as much as 82 per cent of expenditure went to recurrent expenditure; employment costs took up 53 per cent of total revenue, leaving very little for capital expenditure.

### 2.3.4.6 Impact of the global financial crisis

The global financial crisis that was triggered by the sub-prime mortgage crisis in the USA in August 2007 saw the world economy slide into its worst recession since the Great Depression of the 1930s. In June 2009, the World Bank predicted that the world economy would shrink by 2.9 per cent in 2009, more than double the 1.3 per cent it forecast just two months earlier. Most African countries have suffered significantly from a decline in investment and tourism

---

[19] The regulations were promulgated to implement the Indigenization and Economic Empowerment Act (No. 14 of 2007). Following their gazetting, stock market capitalization had fallen from US$3.97 billion in January 2010 to US$3.19 billion by June 2010.

[20] Key outstanding issues, among many, include governance reforms, bringing closure to the land issue, which includes implementing an agreed land audit, and the appointment of senior government officials.

receipts as well as falling export earnings. The value of Zimbabwe's exports declined from US$1,819 million in 2007 to US$1,657 million in 2008 and an estimated US$1,591 million in 2009. Meanwhile, the balance-of-payments deficit deteriorated from US$323 million in 2007 to US$725 million in 2008 and an estimated US$1,908 million in 2009. As a result of firming commodity prices, the balance-of-payments deficit is projected to improve to US$597 million in 2010.[21]

### 2.3.4.7 Evaluation of the national budget framework as pro-poor and inclusive

The national budget should be an instrument of resource allocation in order to ensure not just a rapid pace of GDP growth but also the achievement of important social objectives such as employment creation, poverty elimination and overall development. The ability of ordinary citizens to achieve their basic social and economic rights is a useful measure of the adequacy or otherwise of the budget. Previous budgets have tended to allocate more funds towards recurrent expenditure than to capital expenditure and social investment. A pro-poor and inclusive budget framework should be employment-intensive while also promoting macroeconomic stability. Fiscal policy should influence the processes of income generation and distribution in such a way that it benefits the poor by directing resources disproportionately to:
- sectors in which the poor work (such as agriculture, construction and manufacturing);
- areas in which they live (such as underdeveloped regions);
- factors of production which they possess (such as unskilled labour);
- outputs which they consume (such as food).

Sustained economic growth, in which poor women and men participate directly as both agents and beneficiaries, is essential for reducing poverty.

Furthermore, a transformative budget is judged by how it treats short-term exigencies (recurrent expenditure) and longer-term developmental capital expenditure on infrastructure, education and health, for example. As indicated above, the budget focuses predominantly on recurrent expenditure, with sub-optimal allocations for capital investment.

Of a total budget of US$2,250 million, capital expenditure is US$571.8 million and recurrent expenditure is US$1,678.2 million, of which the wage bill accounts for US$600 million. Recurrent expenditure therefore constitutes about 75 per cent of total expenditure (Table 2.3). With an estimated GDP of around US$5,561 million in 2010,[22] recurrent expenditure represents 30.42 per cent of GDP while capital expenditure represents only 10.36 per cent. Ideally, in

---

[21] *Mid-Term Fiscal Policy Review Statement*, 14 July 2010.

[22] Ibid., p. 103.

**Table 2.3: Government expenditure as a percentage of GDP and the budget, 2010**

|  | Percentage of budget | Percentage of GDP |
|---|---|---|
| Recurrent expenditure | 75 | 30.42 |
| Capital expenditure | 25 | 10.36 |
| TOTAL | 100 | 40.78 |

*Source:* Calculated from national budget statements.

a developing country like Zimbabwe, capital expenditure should constitute at least 50 per cent of the total budget and at least 25 per cent of GDP.

Allocations to the agriculture sector deteriorated from 2.55 per cent to 2.48 per cent of the budget between 2009 and 2010 (Table 2.4); however, as a percentage of GDP, they rose from 0.66 per cent to 1.01 per cent. Since the agriculture sector is the mainstay of the economy and the majority of the poor live in rural areas and depend directly or indirectly on it for their livelihood, budgetary allocations to the sector should be prioritized. A budget strategy favouring pro-poor growth must of necessity place greater emphasis on improving agricultural productivity and incomes. Pro-poor growth must be strategically focused on rural areas and the informal economy by enhancing incomes in agriculture and making intensive use of labour (leveraging employment-intensive growth).

**Table 2.4: Government expenditure by sector as a percentage of GDP and the budget**

| Sector | 2009 | | 2010 | |
|---|---|---|---|---|
|  | Percentage of budget | Percentage of GDP | Percentage of budget | Percentage of GDP |
| Agriculture | 2.55 | 0.66 | 2.48 | 1.01 |
| Education | 11.68 | 3.11 | 12.3 | 5.02 |
| Health | 8.7 | 2.32 | 6.98 | 2.84 |
| Energy | 0.09 | 0.02 | 0.07 | 0.03 |
| Transport and infrastructure | 0.88 | 0.23 | 0.92 | 0.38 |
| Public works | 0.58 | 0.16 | 0.26 | 0.10 |
| Housing | 0.24 | 0.06 | 0.16 | 0.06 |
| Water | 0.29 | 0.08 | 0.12 | 0.05 |
| Science and technology | 0.10 | 0.03 | 0.14 | 0.06 |
| Mining | 0.28 | 0.07 | 0.17 | 0.07 |
| Industry | 0.67 | 0.18 | 0.12 | 0.04 |
| SMEs | 0.08 | 0.02 | 0.06 | 0.02 |
| Gender | 0.18 | 0.05 | 0.17 | 0.07 |
| Youths | 1.25 | 0.33 | 0.66 | 0.27 |
| Defence | 4.11 | 1.09 | 4.37 | 1.78 |

*Source:* Calculated from national budget statements.

Budget allocations to the education and health sectors also need to be prioritized and ring-fenced. The Abuja Declaration stipulates a minimum allocation of 15 per cent to health, while the Dakar Declaration says that at least 20 per cent should be channelled towards education.[23] The defence allocation remains relatively high for a developing country that is not at war. In Uganda, for example, the most recent National Budget Framework Paper envisaged a real reduction in expenditure of 3 per cent on security, justice and governance between 2008 and 2011 to allow increased pro-poor expenditure on rural development, energy, road infrastructure and human development over the next three years.[24]

The 1991 *Human Development Report* (UNDP, 1991) came up with four Human Development Expenditure Ratios:

- Public Expenditure Ratio (PER), a ratio of public expenditure to national income (this helps to distinguish between current and capital expenditure).
- Social Allocation Ratio (SAR), the percentage of public expenditure earmarked for social services.
- Social Priority Ratio (SPR), the percentage of social expenditure devoted to human priority concerns.
- Human Expenditure Ratio (HER), the percentage of national income devoted to human priority concerns.

The *Report* stated that a PER at 25 per cent, an SAR at 40 per cent, an SPR at 50 per cent, and an HER at at least 5 per cent are necessary to ensure adequate resources for human development priority sectors in an average developing country.

The current national budget framework does not have a clear focus on employment or on employment-intensive growth. Given that the National Employment Policy Framework should inform the overall development strategy by prioritizing the goal of creating decent work for all,[25] this objective should be reflected – and, indeed, integrated – in all macroeconomic and sectoral policies if full employment is to be attained. It has been demonstrated empirically that it is not only the quantity of growth that matters for employment: it is both sustained high levels of growth and employment intensity that make the difference.[26] This has been a missing link, as past policies tended to be crafted in isolation from each other and, in recent years, as the objectives of employment creation and poverty reduction have been treated as residual, stabilization has taken centre stage.

[23] A summit of African Health Ministers (2001) and an Education for All meeting (2000), respectively.

[24] See <http://www.finance.go.ug>.

[25] The National Employment Policy Framework outlines an employment-intensive growth path and how employment and the Decent Work Agenda should be mainstreamed in all sectors (see Chapter 7).

[26] See Chapter 1.

The budget framework also contains few specific measures to deal with the dual and enclave economic structure outlined in Chapter 7. The demise of the formal sector, and the absence of supply-side incentives to resuscitate and engender inclusive, pro-poor growth, implies that the decent-work deficits that characterize the economy and entrench poverty and its feminization will abound. By focusing largely on the formal sector, which is male-dominated, the budget neglects the non-formal sectors that accommodate the majority of the population, and especially women. It therefore reinforces the inherited dual and enclave structure of the economy, especially in the context of a highly informalized economy.

Zimbabwe, like most developing countries, has a very low tax/GDP ratio (Table 2.5). The ratio averages 31.3 per cent for developed countries, 25.4 per cent for transitional countries, and 17.4 per cent for developing countries (Jha, 2007: 4). Challenges in raising tax revenue in Zimbabwe arise from the large informal sector, the narrow tax base, volatile tax revenues, relatively low tax/ GDP ratios, and over-reliance on indirect taxes. It is imperative that the tax/ GDP ratio is increased to ensure a stable tax base.

**Table 2.5: Structure of taxes (as a percentage of GDP)**

|              | 2009  | 2010  |
|--------------|-------|-------|
| VAT          | 5.15  | 6.34  |
| Customs duty | 3.43  | 2.41  |
| PAYE         | 2.00  | 3.06  |
| Corporate tax| 0.49  | 1.82  |
| Excise duty  | 0.85  | 1.38  |
| Other        | 1.19  | 1.86  |
| TOTAL        | 13.12 | 16.87 |

*Source:* Derived from national budget statements.

### 2.3.4.8 Reorientation of the national budget

Since 1991, Zimbabwe has followed a largely market-based approach to development, with basic social and economic rights in terms of food security, access to health care, education, shelter, transport and basic utilities (mainly electricity and water) becoming market-driven. Because even basic rights have been put on to the market, the majority of Zimbabweans, who are living in poverty, cannot access them. It is therefore important to return to a basic-needs approach (or a rights-based strategy), which begins and ends with people, the real object of development. It is imperative to ensure that there is a human-centred approach to development, and that a people-oriented budget is adopted. Such a shift entails upholding the following principles:

- gender-sensitivity;
- stakeholder participation in the formulation, implementation, monitoring and evaluation of development programmes and budgets at all levels;
- sensitivity to the needs of special groups, such as children, youths, those with disabilities, and those living with HIV/AIDS;
- prioritizing people's needs and ring-fencing expenditures thereto;
- shifting from supply-based to more demand-driven systems of delivery;
- adopting a holistic approach to issues of development (realizing that everything depends on everything else and taking advantage of synergies).

In short, a pro-people budget is pro-poor, pro-women, pro-disadvantaged groups, pro-basic needs, and therefore inclusive. It allocates resources to communities, and not just for recurrent purposes, and is concerned with broad-based ownership. Such a strategy requires the prioritization of basic needs such as food security, health care, education, housing, transport, and basic utilities (water and electricity). This approach is also often referred to as a human-rights approach to development. The South African government has consciously adopted a human-centred approach by adopting a 'people's contract' to deliver basic social services.

In Zimbabwe, the focus is on the supply-driven provision of social and other services. Thus, service delivery is concentrated on ministries, resulting in a national budget that is recurrent and hence consumptive. Other countries have since moved to the more efficient and effective demand-driven systems. In other countries, for instance, vocational education and training are run by a more demand-focused stakeholder board and not by a ministry. Stakeholders, not only the fiscus, contribute resources, thereby reducing the pressure on government.

Zimbabwe can learn from its past, where, at varying times, the governments manipulated policy instruments strategically to achieve desired goals. The economic management of the period 1966–75 is particularly outstanding in that, through strategic import-substitution industrialization, much of the manufacturing sector was built against a background of international sanctions and war. During the 1980s, following a modest land-redistribution exercise, government provided strategic support to the new farmers in the form of subsidized inputs, finance and extension services, and the result was what became known as an 'agricultural revolution' and earned the country the title of 'regional bread basket'. The President won international accolades for this successful 'revolution'.

The strategic role of the state in development needs to be strengthened in order to transform it into a developmental state and to promote good governance, as well as to expand and strengthen the national institutional framework for broad-based stakeholder participation in decision-making, implementation, monitoring and evaluation.

## 2.4 Recommendations and the Way Forward

### 2.4.1 Engendering a pro-poor and inclusive macroeconomic framework

In the context of a dual and enclave economic structure it is imperative that any future growth be pro-poor and inclusive. This can be achieved and enhanced by ensuring the 'integrability' of the poor in the growth dynamic. Economic growth must be translated into productive-employment growth, which is a key nexus between growth and poverty reduction. It has been demonstrated that economic growth does not necessarily ensure poverty reduction and development but does so only when it is accompanied by a rapid expansion of productive employment. A number of nations that have successful poverty-reduction credentials – such as the East Asian 'tigers' (South Korea, Hong Kong, Taiwan and Singapore) – have also followed robust employment-creation strategies. The emergence of sustained high levels of growth in these countries was preceded by the equitable redistribution of resources, especially land. Furthermore, economic growth is pro-poor and inclusive if it utilizes the factors of production that the poor possess. The poverty-reduction records of countries such as the High-Performing Asian Economies (HPAEs) demonstrate that poverty reduction was greatest when economic growth made use of those assets.

The extent to which economic growth is pro-poor and inclusive will also depend greatly on the amount of human capital that the poor possess, which has been amply demonstrated in the HPAEs (World Bank, 2008a). Thus, economic growth is higher in countries with sufficient human capital (Barro, 1991; Mankiw *et al.*, 1992). Consequently, many of the returns to growth accrue primarily to those with high human capital, although there may be some 'trickle-down' effects to the less skilled over time. Heavy investment in the human capital of the poor will yield two poverty-reduction benefits: it will increase economic growth, and it will make growth more pro-poor and inclusive. In the HPAEs, high human capital accumulation spurred economic growth and poverty reduction.

As the majority of the poor live in rural areas and depend directly or indirectly on agriculture for their livelihood, the factor of production that they possess and use most is labour. The informal economy also accounts for a large proportion of the poor in Zimbabwe. Thus, pro-poor growth must be strategically focused on rural areas and the informal economy. It must also enhance incomes in agriculture and make intensive use of labour.

To make a significant impact on poverty, much greater emphasis must be placed upon improving agricultural productivity (Eastwood and Lipton, 2001). To achieve high agricultural productivity, increased investment in agriculture (including basic and applied research, extension, irrigation, rural credit and expanding technological access to small-holder farmers) is urgently needed. In addition, there is an urgent need to strengthen land-tenure and security rights.

The rehabilitation of existing irrigation infrastructure is imperative to mitigate the effects of adverse weather conditions, as well as to increase agricultural output. There is scope for public–private partnerships (PPPs), especially in the area of infrastructure rehabilitation and development. The government should collaborate with the private sector to facilitate the mobilization of resources to invest in the expansion and building of dams, in tapping underground water resources for sustained irrigation development, and to support the establishment of more dam sites and facilitate river irrigation mechanisms.[27]

'Public–private partnership arrangements may provide a better means of sharing the investment costs, benefits, and risks associated with infrastructure projects between the public and private sector' (Ter-Minassian *et al*, 2008: 14). PPPs usually take the form of joint ventures, concessions, or design–build–finance–operate arrangements between the government and private firms.

> South Africa has the longest and broadest experience with PPPs in the region, with more than 50 projects in development or implementation at the national level and over 300 at the municipal level since 1994. South African experience with PPPs over the past decade has underscored the benefits of
> * putting in place a clear legal and regulatory framework for PPPs from the start ...
> * starting small and expanding gradually ...
> * building central capacity to evaluate the affordability, value for money, and risk transfer of proposed PPP contracts [ibid.].

A pro-poor approach to development can also benefit from the promotion of industrial clusters and the enhancement of backward and forward linkages (e.g. value chains) within and across sectors.[28] In addition to using the cluster and value-chain approach to support the informal economy and its integration into the formal economy, investment in basic infrastructure such as roads and energy must be prioritized. Merely relying on the private sector is not enough: it is imperative that government be actively involved in these areas. Integrating the informal economy into the mainstream of the economy can also be achieved by consciously directing resources to uplift marginalized groups (women and youths) and underdeveloped sectors. Therefore, macroeconomic policy needs to be employment-oriented and gender-focused. In this regard, an employment-oriented national budget has to be crafted on the basis of stakeholder-agreed priority areas.

Ensuring pro-poor and inclusive economic growth requires that the people and their needs come first, implying a human-rights strategy to development. Thus, the prioritization of people and their basic needs (food security, health

---

[27] See Chapter 3.
[28] See Chapter 4.

care, education, housing, transport, access to public utilities, decent jobs and infrastructure) should occupy pride of place in macroeconomic policy and pro-poor national budgeting.

### 2.4.2 Increasing expenditure on infrastructure

In Zimbabwe, there is a huge infrastructure gap, caused by years of neglect and decay owing to lack of investment and maintenance; infrastructure also suffered from severe cuts in public spending after the 1990s. It has now been shown that, in the absence of accessible transport, power and water, the poor pay heavily in time, money and health. When roads are impassable, power cuts frequent, water services dysfunctional and telecommunications absent, countries and regions have great difficulty in achieving pro-poor economic growth. There is strong evidence that good and equitable access to infrastructure is beneficial to the poor (Kanyenze, 2009).

Reliable and affordable infrastructure reduces the production and transaction costs of doing business: it helps to connect poor people to the growth process by improving their access and mobility. Access to infrastructure services contributes to the achievement of several MDGs.

In China, for instance, the rapid expansion of infrastructure has been an important factor in sustaining that country's growth. Most of this infrastructure has been developed through a policy of 'cost recovery' that prices infrastructure services at levels sufficient to finance their capital cost as well as operations and maintenance. China has been able to expand its infrastructure network rapidly by borrowing at commercial interest rates and servicing the resulting debt through appropriate prices for power, roads, rail and telecommunications. Central government played an initial catalytic role by providing some budget capital. However, there has recently been little budgetary support for infrastructure, which is now priced to cover the full cost of the initial capital outlay as well as the subsequent costs of maintenance.

Dollar (2008) notes that in the power sector, for example, China set its reform course with the 1985 State Council Decree, 'Diversify the Sources of Financing for the Power Sector and Implement Debt-Repayment Electricity Price for New Power Plants'. This decree put an end to central government being the sole source of financing for power-sector investment and allowed local government, as well as public and private, and foreign and domestic investors, to participate. The decree allowed the electricity price to be set high enough to recoup initial capital outlay, service all the debts, and make a reasonable profit. Consequently, capacity increased from 67 gigawatts in 1981 to 622 in 2006. The first 'Build–Operate–Transfer' power plant put together by foreign investors, in any developing country, was completed in China in 1987. The result of this cost-recovery policy is that China has relatively expensive power for industrial use but a power network that is extensive and reliable. If infrastructure services are priced too low, then it will be impossible to expand the system in a sustainable manner.

China's experience shows that, even in a low-income country, firms can be highly competitive while still paying the full cost for infrastructure services. Another lesson from China is that the government has been pragmatic about ownership. State firms play an important role in power generation, rail and water. But the government has also permitted foreign investment in all these sectors, and at times has privatized infrastructure assets in order to obtain revenue to expand the system.

### 2.4.3 Increasing expenditure on health and education

Zimbabwe should also prioritize investment in health and education, particularly basic education and primary health care, which contribute towards ensuring that the poor benefit from economic growth. Key strategic interventions should revolve around the following:

- equipping and capitalizing educational and health institutions;
- reviewing remuneration and conditions of service;
- implementing a comprehensive primary health care and universal education plan;
- promoting a national health insurance scheme;
- support the strengthening of the District Health Management Systems initiative of the Ministry of Health and Child Welfare.

It is also important to focus on vocational training and overcome gender-based discrimination in the education sector.[29]

### 2.4.4 Fiscal space

Fiscal space can be defined as 'the financing that is available to government as a result of concrete policy actions for enhancing resource mobilization, and the reforms necessary to secure the enabling governance, institutional and economic environment for these policy actions to be effective, for a specified set of development objectives' (Roy *et al.*, 2007: 6). The motive for creating fiscal space is to enable additional financial resources to be freed and mobilized towards high-priority government spending such as investment in infrastructure and social services. The 'fiscal space diamond' can help and guide policy-makers in ways and means of creating fiscal space (Fig. 2.5).

There is great scope for the creation and expansion of fiscal space in Zimbabwe in a variety of ways, which include:

- tax policy – by improving administration, collection, performance, compliance and broadening the tax base;

---

[29] For more detail on this, see Chapters 8 and 9.

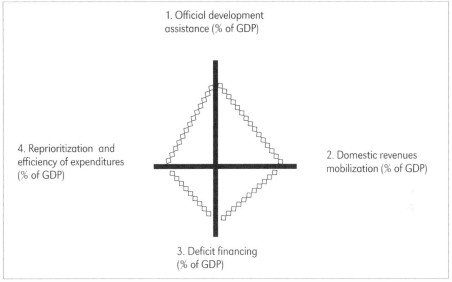

Source: Roy, Heuty and Letouze (2007).

**Fig. 2.5: The Fiscal Space Diamond**

- reallocation and rationalization of expenditures – by shifting resources from less efficient to more efficient uses and eliminating relatively inefficient programmes;
- expansion of government spending financed from restructuring/ privatization proceeds and internal non-tax revenues such as minerals.

Reprioritization should be predicated on the extent that expenditures contribute to MDGs. There is also scope for public–private partnerships for the rehabilitation of infrastructure and the provision of social protection.

Reducing unproductive expenditures, particularly those of a recurrent nature, should be the first priority. One way in which fiscal space can be created in Zimbabwe is by rationalizing the size of government, which is bloated relative to the size of the economy. This would imply reducing the number of ministries to a sustainable level – say, to less than twenty. The government should learn to cut its coat according to its cloth, which implies restructuring government to reflect its resource base and agreed national priorities. Merely encouraging line ministries to live within their budgets in the midst of a bloated government structure will not work, as has been the case in the past. The efficiency of expenditure could also be enhanced through the rationalization of the civil service to remove 'ghost workers'.[30]

---

[30] 'Ghost workers' are former workers or employees who, though no longer on the payroll, continue to use and access organizational resources.

There is also scope for more fiscal space from revenue mobilization. According to the World Bank's *Doing Business* report (World Bank, 2008b), between 1991 and 2008, taxation as a percentage of GDP (the tax ratio) averaged about only 7 per cent. In comparison, the average for low-income countries is 14.5 per cent, for low-middle-income countries it is 16.3 per cent, and it is 21.9 per cent for upper-middle-income countries. A tax ratio of 15 per cent of GDP should be a minimum objective for low-income countries. The same *Doing Business* report ranked Zimbabwe 157th out of 181 countries in the ease of paying taxes. Companies must make 52 payments a year, involving 256 hours of work and an overall tax rate as a percentage of profits of 63.7 per cent. The next year's edition, however, ranked Zimbabwe 130th, with an overall tax rate of 39.4 per cent from 51 payments involving 270 hours of work (World Bank, 2009).

Empirical evidence strongly supports the simplification of tax systems. Countries with more tax payments per year have fewer formal businesses per capita and lower rates of business entry. Similarly, countries that make it easier to pay taxes also have higher rates of workforce participation in the formal economy as well as lower unemployment rates among women. It has been shown that burdensome tax systems hurt smaller businesses disproportionately, especially in the services sector, which is where most women work (World Bank, 2008b).

There is therefore a need to simplify personal and corporate tax systems by reducing the number of tax rates and tax-relief measures, thus producing a system with low rates and a broad base. This can be achieved by combining taxes. Where the tax base is the same (wages, salaries, profits or property) it makes sense to levy a single tax. Reducing the number of taxes simplifies both the payments system for businesses and the collection system for revenue agencies. Minor excise taxes and stamp duties that are costly to collect do not raise much revenue and distort costs and prices and should be abolished. In terms of individual income tax, the tax-free threshold needs to be continuously adjusted in line with the prevailing Poverty Datum Line. It is also important to reduce the high marginal tax rates by introducing a low and flat tax regime.

### 2.4.5 Debt strategy[31]

The total external-debt stock amounted to US$6,532 million as at 31 August 2010, which constituted about 118.4 per cent of GDP. About 37.2 per cent of the country's external debt was owed to multilateral creditors, while 33.9 per cent was owed to bilateral creditors and 28.9 per cent to commercial creditors.[32] To deal with the high debt levels, three debt-clearance strategies have been proffered:

---

[31] Much of the information used in this section has been drawn from the Summary of Proceedings of the International Conference on Sustainable Debt Strategy, 17–18 May 2001, NICON Hilton Hotel, Abuja, Nigeria: <http://www.odiousdebts.org/odiousdebts/index.cfm?DSP=content&ContentID=2752>.

[32] Reserve Bank of Zimbabwe, unpublished data.

applying for Highly Indebted Poor Country (HIPC) status, debt restructuring/ rescheduling, and using revenue from local resources such as minerals.

The HIPC initiative was adopted in 1996 (by the World Bank and the IMF) as a way of providing sustainable external-debt relief to the world's most highly indebted poor countries. The HIPC initiative was designed along the conventional lines of conditionality. Debtor countries would become eligible for the HIPC initiative (reach the 'decision point') only when they had maintained stable macroeconomic conditions under IMF programmes for at least six years, and would then receive a permanent reduction in their official debt stock (reach the 'completion point') after another three years of satisfactory progress. By 1999, only six countries (Bolivia, Burkina Faso, Ivory Coast, Guyana, Mozambique and Uganda) had reached the decision point, and only Uganda had reached the completion point.

In September 1999 an enhanced form, HIPC II, was launched in order to simplify the qualifying conditions and processes; its main aim was to improve the link between debt relief and poverty reduction. HIPC II required countries to formulate national strategies called Poverty Reduction Strategy Papers (PRSPs) for reducing poverty which detailed how the money saved will be spent on the social sector. To qualify for HIPC II, the ratio between a country's debt and its exports should be no higher than 150 per cent; where a debt-to-revenue ratio is used instead, this should not exceed 250 per cent. According to the World Bank, a country with a ratio lower than 150 per cent should be earning enough export revenue to service its debt, and hence the debt would be sustainable. In spite of the improvements to the original initiative, the enhanced HIPC has had its fair share of problems and progress has been much slower than anticipated. Indicators show that an increasing number of beneficiary countries are not likely to attain sustainable debt levels even after graduating from the initiative (Simpson and Doré, 2009).

There now seems to be an emerging consensus, however, that many African countries continue to suffer from a 'debt overhang', despite the HIPC initiative and various actions in the context of the Paris Club.[33] The fact that even those countries that have reached the completion point will soon find themselves in an unsustainable-debt situation points to the inappropriateness of the criteria applied in the debt-sustainability analysis. And the fact that several more debt-distressed African countries are not eligible for HIPC debt relief reflects the lack of objectivity in the eligibility criteria.

At the 2005 Gleneagles G8 summit, it was proposed that the International Financial Institutions write off 100 per cent of the outstanding debt claims

---

[33] The Paris Club is an informal group of official creditors whose role is to find co-ordinated and sustainable solutions to the payment difficulties experienced by the debtor countries: <http://www.clubdeparis.org/en/>.

on developing countries that reached completion point by end of 2004. This initiative became known as the Multilateral Debt Relief Initiative (MDRI). By July 2008 the total amount of debt relief granted under this initiative was US$49 billion. However, in spite of the introduction of MDRI, the debt situation in most developing countries has not changed significantly:

> Data on the face value of debt can give a misleading impression on the actual change in the value of external debt of developing countries. Part of the reduction in external debt was due to debt relief under the HIPC initiative. However, some of the cancelled debt had a present value which was well below its face value. Focusing on the net present value of debt shows a smaller decline in public external debt (5 versus 10 percentage points). In fact, debt relief under the HIPC Initiative has not been fully successful in achieving long-term debt sustainability. According to the 2007 HIPC and MDRI Status of Implementation Report, more than half of the post-completion point countries are still considered as having either a moderate or a high risk of debt distress and only 10 out 22 post-completion point countries have graduated to the low risk category ...
>
> The evidence summarized above points to the fact that it would be wrong to claim, as it is often done, that developing countries no longer have an external debt problem [Panizza, 2008: 3].

The second option of debt restructuring/rescheduling would entail Zimbabwe negotiating with its bilateral and multilateral creditors to have its debt rescheduled from short-term obligations into long-term debt. This option, however, has the problem that most of the country's debt has been owing for a long period of time; in addition, Zimbabwe has a bad credit record – it has long had a record of defaulting on its debt – so many creditors may not favour this approach. Also, debt restructuring does not lessen the debt burden but only pushes it forward. Hence, debt restructuring may not be a feasible or a good option.

The third option entails using revenue derived from resources such as minerals to retire the debt. However, in spite of boasting of abundant mineral wealth such as gold, diamonds and platinum, Zimbabwe has not been able to derive any significant economic and financial benefit from these resources; the nation continues to be prejudiced of significant mineral resources through smuggling. There is a need for strong political will and commitment to deal with these and other forms of leakages so as to harness the revenues towards economic development.

Arrears clearance is a prerequisite for full engagement and the ability to borrow from the IFIs. Zimbabwe is currently not HIPC-eligible and, as the list was closed in 2005, the process would have to be reopened for Zimbabwe to be included. Zimbabwe should, however, vigorously pursue all the options for debt relief, including outright cancellation. From the outset, it will be important that a clear legal framework and national debt strategy be developed. The legal framework should clearly state who is able to contract new debt on behalf of the state, the purpose of the debt and the limit of the debt, as well as spell out clearly the role of parliament in oversight functions, among other issues. This will help to ensure the effective and efficient use of present and future national resources so as to prevent waste.

For effective debt management, it is crucial to have firm political will and a commitment to adhering to sound legal frameworks. In designing a debt strategy, there is need for close co-ordination and co-operation among different government agencies to ensure synergy with overall macroeconomic and developmental policies. Social partners and civil society should also participate in the development of a debt-management system. The debt strategy should include an audit (review) of each of the projects for which past loans were incurred. This would enable the government to verify the genuineness (or otherwise) of the debts and to see what percentage of the debt might be odious.

The national debt should also be viewed and treated as a symptom of the wider structural and political challenges inherent in the economy. Dealing with these challenges should therefore form an integral part of a sustainable debt strategy. The high country risk represents a major constraint to both sustainable poverty reduction and debt strategy. Without addressing this risk and the resultant uncertainty inherent in the economy, it will be difficult to prevent future indebtedness. The government should therefore simultaneously implement structural, political and sound economic policies as part of a sustainable debt strategy. Such a cocktail of reforms should address the poor state of infrastructure, enforce the rule of law, and minimize the risks and uncertainties associated with the political and economic environment.

### 2.4.6 Currency reforms
Zimbabwe can opt to continue with its de facto dollarization regime, reintroduce the Zimbabwe dollar underpinned by mineral resources, or join the Rand Monetary Area by adopting the South African rand.

The costs and benefits of dollarization have been outlined above. Although experience from other countries has shown that dollarization in itself is not a panacea to all the economic challenges facing the nation, it does, however, help to lay a firm foundation for sustainable economic development. To date, a number of notable achievements have been made thanks to the introduction of dollarization: an end to hyperinflation, an increase in capacity utilization by industry, and growing confidence in the economy, among others. In spite of these gains, however, the economic environment still remains very delicate and the recovery is fragile.

In terms of the reintroduction of the Zimbabwe dollar, which is not likely to be soon, certain benchmarks will need to be met, which will include:

- attaining a sustainable GDP growth rate of at least 7 per cent;
- low and stable inflation and interest rates;
- reducing the high debt ratios to very low and sustainable levels;
- increasing the level of savings and investments to at least 25 per cent of GDP;
- reducing the balance-of-payments deficit to less than 5 per cent of GDP;
- increasing the export level to at least 25 per cent of GDP;
- high levels of productive capacity;
- financial and political stability.

Foreign-currency reserves will also need to be built up to sustainable levels to anchor the Zimbabwe dollar and to defend it in the event of a currency or speculative attack. With the painful experience of the demise of the Zimbabwe dollar still fresh in people's minds, it may take even longer to restore public confidence in the national currency. Its reintroduction might result in further erosion of public confidence in the financial sector, precipitating disintermediation and a run on the banks as people take rational steps to protect their wealth, including shunning the banking system altogether.

The RBZ has been proposing the reintroduction of a Zimbabwe dollar that will be anchored on gold valued by an independent body comprising all stakeholders, akin to the gold standard.[34] However, this system has a number of problems. Firstly, the monetary base (money supply) is determined by the supply or production of gold. Hence, there is a loss of control over economic policy and, in particular, over monetary policy, which will be determined by the rate of gold production. If the rate of gold production slumps, it will mean that money supply will go down, and this may induce deflation; if the rate of production of gold goes up, it implies that money supply will go up, which may induce inflationary pressures in the economy. This therefore leaves the economy susceptible to speculative attacks and recessions.

Moreover, it is now believed that the use of the gold standard played a significant role in preventing governments from countervailing the Great Depression and played a catalytic role in transforming the recession of 1929–31 into the Great Depression of 1931–41. It has been found that countries that were not part of the gold standard escaped the Great Depression largely unscathed, and countries that left the gold standard in 1930 and 1931 suffered much less.[35]

---

[34] Under the gold standard the value of the currency is anchored or tied to a specific weight of gold. A pure gold standard system was used by a number of trading nations between 1879 and 1914 and their currencies were convertible based on the gold value.

[35] See B. Bernanke, 'Money, Gold and the Great Depression', Remarks by Governor Ben S. Bernanke at the H. Parker Willis Lecture in Economic Policy, Washington and Lee University, Lexington, VA, 2 March 2004, <http://www.federalreserve.gov/boarddocs/speeches/2004/200403022/default.htm>; J. Bradford DeLong, *Slouching Towards Utopia?: The Economic History of the Twentieth Century XIV: The Great Crash and the Great Slump*, 1997, <http://www.j-bradford-delong.net/tceh/slouch_crash14.html>.

Another problem is that the value of the currency will be determined by the price of gold, and hence swings in the price of gold will leave the currency volatile, thereby increasing exchange-rate risks and volatility. This system also works better when other countries form part of it, as this makes it easier for the process of self-correction to take place in the event of a balance-of-payments surplus or deficit.

Another currency option for Zimbabwe would be to join the Rand Monetary Area (RMA) by adopting the South African currency. The RMA currently comprises Lesotho, Swaziland, Namibia and the Republic of South Africa. Under the terms of the RMA agreement, the rand is the legal tender throughout this region, although other countries have the right to issue their own national currencies, which should be fully backed by foreign-exchange reserves. They therefore have limited control over their own monetary policy and financial system.

Anticipated benefits from membership of the RMA include:

- saving in currency conversion costs in all trade with South Africa and other countries in the RMA;
- reduction in transaction costs involved in cross-border trade;
- reduced foreign-exchange-rate uncertainty and risk;
- gains from trade creation between Zimbabwe and other members of the RMA;
- opportunity for improvements in monetary policy;
- the possibility of seigniorage.

Anticipated costs include:

- a loss of policy space with respect to the exchange rate, interest rates and money supply;
- the possibility of asymmetric shocks;[36]
- changeover costs;
- possible dispute over seigniorage apportionment;
- reduced opportunities for currency substitution could make policy less time-consistent;[37]
- the possibility of intra-union factor immobility.[38]

Being a member of the RMA will not guarantee higher economic growth unless the country deals with the structural and institutional bottlenecks inherent in the economy. Growth and development is essentially a function of economic, political, structural and institutional reforms. An additional challenge will be the

---

[36] Asymmetric shocks occur when an external change in economic conditions affects differently the different parts of a region.

[37] A policy is time-consistent if an action planned at time $t$ for time $t+i$ remains optimal to implement when time $t+i$ actually arrives (Walsh, 2003: 363).

[38] This occurs when a factor of production (such as labour or capital) cannot easily move from one country to another.

need to maintain adequate foreign-currency reserves, which may prove difficult for Zimbabwe.

Given the extensive trade and financial ties between Zimbabwe and South Africa, the rand represents a credible monetary anchor. It has been demonstrated empirically that countries that trade more with each other benefit more from adopting the same currency (Alesina and Barro, 2002). Also, smaller countries should, other things being equal, be more inclined to give up their currencies. Empirical evidence on the relationship between currency integration and intra-regional trade has concluded that using a common currency increases trade by up to three times (Engel and Rose, 2002).

Therefore, the greater the level of existing trade, or the potential for increased trade, between prospective members of a currency union, the greater the expected benefits will be. SADC's *Regional Indicative Strategic Development Plan* (RISDP) has set the goals of establishing a SADC monetary union by 2016 and a common currency by 2018.[39] However, certain macroeconomic convergence criteria with respect to inflation, interest rates, budget deficits, national debt and exchange rates should not exceed predetermined thresholds. When countries are targeting macroeconomic convergence, they are likely to have different costs of adjustment. Therefore, it will be important to determine how these adjustment costs will be financed and who will finance them.

### 2.4.7 Macroeconomic stability

Even though macroeconomic stability is important in underpinning pro-poor and inclusive growth, if it is attained through cutbacks in public expenditure (on infrastructure and social services), growth may be retarded. This is especially true for developing countries such as Zimbabwe that have serious infrastructure deficits and endemic poverty. Overly focusing on stabilization may undercut the basis for pro-poor and inclusive growth in the long term and consign an economy into a stabilization trap typified by low deficit, low inflation, low investment, and low economic growth with high unemployment. Macroeconomic stability should not be an objective in itself but rather should provide a framework for the attainment of pro-poor and inclusive growth.

Pasha argues that

> contrary to the view that higher fiscal deficits 'crowd-out' private investment by raising interest rates, there is persuasive empirical evidence that if higher fiscal deficits are caused by larger public investment outlays then this may actually 'crowd-in' private investment on a net basis by removing physical bottlenecks of infrastructure and thereby raising the factor productivity of private investment.

---

[39] See Chapter 10, and <http://www.sadc.int/attachment/download/file/74>.

In addition, larger public outlays on education and health raise the productivity of the poor and equip them better to get out of the poverty trap.[40]

Employment creation and poverty reduction should be viewed as central objectives and outcomes of macroeconomic policy and not as an afterthought. These outcomes should be pursued through the selective adoption of macro-economic policies that pursue low external indebtedness (public and private); competitive exchange-rate regimes; countercyclical fiscal policies; rising tax/GDP ratios, and sustained investment in public goods.

## 2.5 Conclusion

It has been demonstrated that past macroeconomic policies have failed to deal with the structural distortions and bottlenecks inherent in the Zimbabwean economy. Moreover, even when the country has recorded a positive economic growth rate, that growth rate has been neither pro-poor nor inclusive. 'Trickle-down', whereby economic pay-offs drip down to the poor and marginalized in society, is yet to materialize, as the majority of people continue to wallow in poverty and deprivation. Future macroeconomic policies therefore need to promote both the pace of economic growth and its pattern, i.e. the extent to which the poor actively participate in growth, both as agents and beneficiaries.

Macroeconomic reforms should be context-specific and implemented in an incremental and non-formulaic way. They should be targeted at the binding constraints to economic growth and development at a given point in time. It is also important to involve key stakeholders in the formulation, implementation, monitoring and evaluation processes so as to ensure buy-in and ownership. This can be achieved by coming up with an institutional framework for social dialogue along the lines of the National Economic Development and Labour Council (NEDLAC) of South Africa.[41]

It is imperative that the government deal with the inherited dual and enclave structure of the economy so as to unlock its potential to generate pro-poor and inclusive growth. Focus should be on increasing expenditures on infrastructure and basic social services (health and education), improving agricultural productivity, and promoting pro-poor private-sector development initiatives such as industrial clusters and value chains. It is important to strengthen the strategic role of the government as the driver and facilitator of sustainable (human) development.

In light of the tenuous economic gains that have been achieved to date, it is imperative to consolidate macroeconomic stability by introducing institutional and political reforms so as to enhance confidence, credibility and certainty in

---

[40] H. A. Pasha, 'Pro-poor Policies', paper presented at the Fourth Global Forum on Citizens, Businesses, and Governments: Dialogue and Partnerships for the Promotion of Democracy and Development, Marrakech, Morocco, 12–13 December 2002.

[41] See Chapter 7.

the economy. There is also scope for the creation of fiscal space through the reprioritization (and efficiency) of expenditures, domestic revenue mobilization and official development assistance, and to inculcate a developmental budget framework that prioritizes capital over recurrent expenditure. The government should adopt a sustainable-debt and optimal-currency strategy to buttress economic stability and lay a solid foundation for pro-poor and inclusive growth and sustainable (human) development.

## References

Alesina, A. & R. Barro 2002. 'Currency unions', *Quarterly Journal of Economics*, 117(2), 409–36.

Barro, R. J. 1991. 'Economic growth in a cross-section of countries', *Quarterly Journal of Economics*, 106(2), 407–43.

Dollar, D. 2008. *Lessons from China for Africa* (Washington, DC: World Bank, World Bank Policy Research Working Paper 4531).

Eastwood R. and M. Lipton 2001. 'Pro-poor growth and pro-growth poverty reduction: Meaning, evidence, and policy implications', *Asian Development Review*, 19, 1–37.

Ehrenpreis, Dag 2007. *Poverty in Focus*, 10: 'Analysing and Achieving Pro-Poor Growth'.

Engel, C. and A. Rose 2002. 'Currency unions and international integration', *Journal of Money, Credit and Banking*, 34(4), 1067–89.

Heintz, J. 2008. 'Reintroducing employment into macroeconomic policy', in Dag Ehrenpreis, *Poverty in Focus*, 16: 'Jobs, Jobs, Jobs: The Policy Challenge', 18–19.

ILO 1993. *Structural Change and Adjustment in Zimbabwe* (Geneva: International Labour Office, Occasional Paper No. 16).

Jha, R. 2007. *Fiscal Policy in Developing Countries: A Synoptic View*, ASARC Working Paper 2007/01

Kanyenze, G. 2009. 'Restructuring Public Enterprises and the Rehabilitation of Infrastructure in Zimbabwe' (Harare: UNDP-Zimbabwe, Comprehensive Economic Recovery in Zimbabwe, Working Paper Series No. 3).

Klasen, S. 2003. 'In Search of the Holy Grail: How to Achieve Pro-Poor Growth?' (Göttingen: University of Göttingen, Discussion Paper No. 96), <http://129.3.20.41/eps/mac/papers/0401/0401005.pdf>.

Mankiw, N. G., D. Romer, and D. N. Weil 1992. 'A contribution to the empirics of economic growth', *Quarterly Journal of Economics*, 107(2): 407–37.

Munoz, S. 2007. 'Central Bank Quasi-fiscal Losses and High Inflation in Zimbabwe: A Note' (Washington, DC: International Monetary Fund, Working Paper WP/07/98).

Nyawata, O. I. 1988. 'Macroeconomic management, adjustment and stabilisation', in Colin Stoneman (ed.), *Zimbabwe's Prospects* (London: Macmillan).

Rodrik, D. 2006. 'Goodbye Washington Consensus, hello Washington confusion? A review of the World Bank's *Economic Growth in the 1990s: Learning from a Decade of Reform*', *Journal of Economic Literature*, XLIV (December), 973–87.

Rodrik, D. 2007. *One Economics, Many Recipes: Globalization, Institutions, and Economic Growth* (Princeton and Oxford: Princeton University Press).

Roy, Rathin, Antoine Heuty and Emmanuel Letouze 2007. 'Fiscal Space for What? Analytical Issues from a Human Development Perspective', Paper for the G20 Workshop on Fiscal Policy, Istanbul, July 2007.

Swoboda, A. 1999. 'Reforming the international financial architecture', *Finance & Development*, 36(3), <http://www.imf.org/external/pubs/ft/fandd/1999/09/swoboda.htm>.

Stiglitz, J. 1994. 'The role of the state in financial markets', in M. Bruno and B. Pleskovic (eds.), *Proceedings of the World Bank Conference on Development Economics, 1993* (Washington, DC: World Bank), 41–6.

Ter-Minassian, T. *et al.* 2008. 'Creating Sustainable Fiscal Space for Infrastructure: The Case of Tanzania' (Washington, DC: IMF, Working Paper WP/08/256).

UNDP 1991. *Human Development Report, 1991* (New York: Oxford University Press for the United Nations Development Programme).

Walsh, C. 2003. *Monetary Theory and Policy* (Cambridge, MA: MIT Press, 2nd edn.).

Williamson, J. 1990. 'What Washington means by policy reform', in J. Williamson (ed.), *Latin American Adjustment: How Much Has Happened?* (Washington, DC: Institute for International Economics).

World Bank 1985. *Zimbabwe: Country Economic Memorandum, Performance, Policies and Prospects* (Washington, DC: World Bank, 3 vols.).

World Bank 1991. *World Development Report 1991: The Challenge of Development, Volume 1* (Washington, DC: World Bank).

World Bank 1993. *World Debt Tables: External Finance for Developing Countries* (Washington, DC: World Bank).

World Bank 1995. *World Development Report, 1995* (Washington, DC: World Bank).

World Bank 2005. *Economic Growth in the 1990s: Learning from a Decade of Reform* (Washington, DC: World Bank).

World Bank 2008. *The Growth Report: Strategies for Sustained Growth and Inclusive Development* (Washington, DC: World Bank, Commission on Growth and Development).

World Bank 2008b. *Doing Business, 2009* (Washington, DC: World Bank).

World Bank 2009. *Doing Business, 2010* (Washington, DC: World Bank).

WEF 2009. *2009–2010 Global Competitiveness Report* (Geneva: World Economic Forum).

WEF 2010. *2010–2011 Global Competitiveness Report* (Geneva: World Economic Forum).

Zimbabwe 1981. *Growth with Equity: An Economic Policy Statement* (Harare: Ministry of Economic Planning and Development).

Zimbabwe 1982. *Transitional National Development Plan, 1982/83 – 1984/85: Volume 1* (Harare: Ministry of Economic Planning and Development, 2 vols.).

Zimbabwe 1986. *First Five-Year National Development Plan, 1986–1990: Volume 1* (Ministry of Finance, Economic Planning and Development, 2 vols.)

Zimbabwe 1998. *Poverty in Zimbabwe* (Harare: Central Statistical Office).

## Chapter 3

# Land, Agriculture and Rural Development

## 3.1 Introduction

In recognition of its potential role in unlocking sustainable human development, the World Bank's 2008 *World Development Report* focused on 'Agriculture for Development'. The *Report* notes that agriculture can be a vital development instrument for achieving the first Millennium Development Goal of halving poverty by 2015. This is particularly so because three out of every four people in developing countries live in rural areas and the majority depend on agriculture for their livelihoods: 'Agriculture contributes to development as an economic activity, as a livelihood, and as a provider of environmental services, making the sector a unique instrument for development' (World Bank, 2008: 2–3).

The option of using agriculture to drive growth, overcome poverty and enhance food security is particularly strong in Sub-Saharan Africa. According to the *Report*, scope for this lies in enhancing productivity growth in smallholder farming, as well as in effective support to those coping as subsistence farmers. Furthermore, in such agriculture-based economies, food is imperfectly tradable owing to high transaction costs and the prevalence of staple foods that are lightly tradable. In such countries, people have to feed themselves. In the context of globalization, rising land and water scarcity, the *Report* believes that the future of agriculture is closely tied to better stewardship of natural resources, and says that the promise of agriculture can be realized only with 'the visible hand of the state' providing core public goods, improving the investment climate, regulating natural resource management, and securing desirable social outcomes (ibid.: 2).

The *Report* cites a number of countries where agricultural growth was the precursor to industrial growth: England in the mid-18th century, Japan in the late 19th century, and, more recently, China, India and Vietnam. With the new focus on pro-poor growth at the turn of the millennium, agriculture is seen as one of the sectors with huge potential to trigger such growth.[1]

Agriculture is the mainstay of the economy in Zimbabwe, with 65 per cent of the population's livelihood directly dependent on the sector.[2] At the advent of independence in 1980, the agricultural sector accounted for 17 per cent of GDP and 32.4 per cent of formal employment. Its importance in the economy

---

[1] See, for instance, Ehrenpreis (2008).
[2] See Zimbabwe (2002) and Zimbabwe (2006).

is also evidenced by studies that found a strongly positive correlation between agriculture and the country's overall economic performance (World Bank, 2008; FAO, 2003). This is also borne out by the fact that, in the mid-1990s, over half of the inputs into agriculture were sourced from the manufacturing sector, while 44 per cent of agricultural output went to the manufacturing sector (UNDP, 2008), implying strong backward and forward linkages between the sectors. Those sectors that do not depend directly on agriculture benefit indirectly, especially in relation to food security: improved agricultural production obviates the need for food imports, quite often resulting in much lower food prices and an improved balance-of-payments position (World Bank, 2008).

Critically, as Zimbabwe is still a predominantly agricultural country, any forward-looking, pro-poor policy framework has to be based on the development of its agriculture sector. However, development of the agricultural sector cannot be considered without addressing rural development in its broader sense. The development of the rural areas helps to minimize labour migration to the already populated urban areas, and helps transform rural areas from being reservoirs of cheap labour and a dumping ground for the unemployed, the retrenched, and the old and sick. A prerequisite for secure livelihoods in rural areas is security in land access and ownership.

In addition, a massive support programme, geared particularly towards small-holder agriculture, led and supported by the state, has to be embarked upon. The focus should be on restoring Zimbabwe's agricultural production, with an emphasis on attaining food security, and the creation of jobs and income-generation through, among other means, the development of agro-industries in the rural areas. Simultaneously, a deliberate rural-development strategy will have to be implemented, based in the first instance on the development of backward and forward linkages between agricultural production and the manufacturing sector. If done properly, with the needs and skills of the local people in mind, this will enable rural people to find employment not only in agriculture but also in local, rural-based, labour-intensive industries and services (Jonasson, 2008).

## 3.2 The Inherited Dual and Enclave Structure of Agriculture

After failing to locate mineral deposits in the country on the scale of those discovered in South Africa, and following the crash of the Johannesburg stock market in 1901, the white settlers moved quickly into agriculture. Over time, a dual structure emerged, with a large-scale commercial agricultural sector existing alongside small-scale communal agriculture which was largely subsistence based. By 1980, some 6,600 white farmers occupied 15.5 million hectares of the best land while some 7 million people were crowded into some of the most infertile, dry areas. By 1997, commercial farming land had decreased marginally by 3.6 million hectares, most of it having gone to the government resettlement programme (Table 3.1). The historical fact of extreme concentration of land ownership remained the same throughout that period as, by 1997, although the number of white commercial farmers had decreased to about 4,500, they still held over 30 per cent of the most productive land under freehold.

**Table 3.1: Land-ownership patterns, 1980 and 1997**

| Sector | Area in hectares (1980) | | Area in hectares (1997) | |
|---|---|---|---|---|
| | millions | % | millions | % |
| Large-scale commercial sector | 15.5 | 39.10 | 12.1 | 30.60 |
| Small-scale commercial sector | 1.4 | 3.5 | 1.4 | 3.5 |
| Resettlement areas | – | – | 3.6 | 9.1 |
| Communal areas | 16.4 | 41.4 | 16.4 | 41.4 |
| State farms | 0.3 | 0.8 | 0.1 | 0.3 |
| National parks and urban settlements | 6.0 | 15.20 | 6.0 | 15.20 |
| TOTAL | 39.6 | 100 | 39.6 | 100 |

*Source:* Matondi (2001).

The racially skewed agrarian structure that favoured mostly the large white-owned commercial farms formed the basis of historical grievances resulting in the First *Chimurenga* of 1896, the Second *Chimurenga* ending in 1980, and the fast-track land-reform programme (the 'Third *Chimurenga*') of 2000, which was an expression of growing demand for the redistribution of land by a variety of existing and potential small- and large-scale indigenous land-users.

Zimbabwe has a total land area of 39.6 million hectares, of which 33 million are reserved for agriculture while the rest is reserved for national parks, forests and urban settlements. The country has a variable rainfall pattern, occurring mainly between October and March, and total rainfall and its distribution are the over-riding factors limiting agricultural production. Average annual rainfall varies from below 300 mm in the low-lying areas of the country to over 1,000 mm on the central watershed; a small area in the eastern border mountains receives over 1,500 mm annually. The reliability of rainfall increases with altitude, and only 37 per cent of the country receives more than the 700 mm annual average considered necessary for semi-intensive farming, with less than a third of this area being arable (Muir-Leresche, 2006) (Fig. 3.1).

Furthermore, in the last decade there has been a remarkable shift in seasons in Zimbabwe due to climatic changes. Chasi (2008) notes that annual rainfall across Zimbabwe decreased by between 5 and 20 per cent of the 1961–80 average, and this is likely to decrease further owing to the warming of the atmosphere. Mano and Nhemachena (2007) examined how Zimbabwe's agricultural production would respond to climate change. Their scenarios showed that a 2.5°C increase in temperature would decrease net farm revenues by US$0.4 billion for all

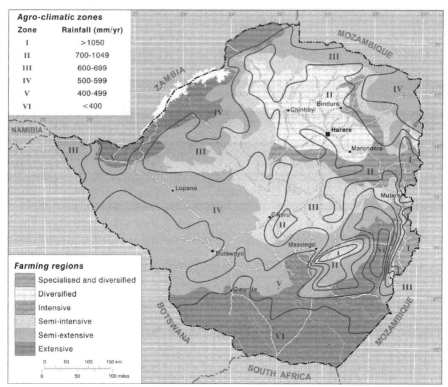

Source: *Moving Forward in Zimbabwe: Reducing Poverty and Promoting Growth* (Brooks World Poverty Institute, University of Manchester, 2009; reproduced with permisison).

**Fig. 3.1: The Natural Regions of Zimbabwe**

farms and increase it for farms with irrigation by US$0.3 billion. The study also examined the impact of a 5°C increase in temperature and the results showed that net revenues would decrease across all farms, rain-fed farms and farms with irrigation by US$0.4 billion, US$0.5 billion and US$0.003 billion, respectively. A 7 per cent and a 14 per cent decrease in precipitation would result in a decrease in net farm revenue by US$0.3 billion for all farms. Assuming a total contribution from agriculture to GDP of around US$3.3 billion per year (at factor cost between 1990 and 1998), the various scenarios predict a decrease in agricultural revenue, other things remaining equal, of around 10 per cent to 30 per cent, which is dramatic.

Any agricultural policy will therefore have to anticipate the adverse effects of climate change. According to the Central Statistical Office, in 2000 only 0.2 per cent of the communal areas was under irrigation, less than 1 per cent of the 75,000 hectares cropped in the small-scale commercial sector, approximately 5 per cent of the 165,000 hectares in the resettlement areas, and 35 per cent of the 500,000 hectares under crops in the large-scale sector (Muir-Leresche, 2006). Next to this total of slightly less than 200,000 hectares of irrigated land, another

250,000 hectares can be irrigated (Makhado, 2006). This means that around 90 per cent of the arable land is not irrigable, which stresses the need for ecological, drought-adapted agricultural policies and strategies if Zimbabwe is to safeguard its agricultural base.

## 3.3 Land, Agriculture and Rural Development in the 1980s

### 3.3.1 The agrarian base at independence
Agriculture stands out as having been the most developed sector at independence in 1980, to the extent that it can be said that it underpinned Nyerere's literal description of Zimbabwe as the jewel of Africa (Kanyenze, 2006). The infrastructure in both rural and urban areas was impressive, with a sophisticated and largely commercially driven agricultural sector. However, Zimbabwe's large-scale agriculture was an enclave which was developed on the basis of ruthless land dispossession for a period of over ninety years after 1890. On the other hand, many of the black African population were condemned to below subsistence farming in neglected, marginal and overcrowded 'Tribal Trust Lands' which could not provide a decent livelihood, forcing many into (low) wage employment.

Nevertheless, agricultural activities such as crop production, food processing and animal husbandry had been the core means of subsistence for the people of Zimbabwe before colonization, to the extent that commercial farming by the white settlers benefited immensely from the basic farming skills and a culture of hard work that the black population possessed prior to being forced into wage employment on white-owned farms. The dispossessed black majority's need for land, coupled with their undoubted capability to use the land to produce surplus for the market, compelled the Rhodesian government to introduce small-scale farms for black farmers, particularly for those to whom they awarded Master Farmer certificates. The small-scale farms for blacks established before independence included farming areas such as Chitomborwizi, Zowa, Mushagashi, Gandami, to mention but a few.

### 3.3.2 Resettlement and the nagging land question
In the early 1980s, the government embarked on an ambitious programme to resettle 162,000 families on three million hectares of land by 1985.[3] By the target date, only 35,000 households had been resettled on areas that accounted for 11 per cent of commercial land (Moyo, 1995; Alexander, 1994; Kinsey, 1998). Land acquisition reached a high point in the first few years of independence in 1981 to 1982, when over 2.1 million hectares were transferred. Much of the resettlement

---

[3] The 162,000 families target was derived from the 18,000 families suggested by the Zimbabwe-Rhodesia government of 1978–79, which was simply multiplied by three at independence to 54,000 families and then by three again to 162,000 families, which stood as the target until 1997.

in the 1980s was facilitated by low-cost acquisition of abandoned land and the selection of some people who were already squatting on commercial land (Table 3.2). In fact, by the end of the 1980s, it became increasingly difficult to find land suitable for resettlement. Land-owners were resisting sales, and the cost of land was rising in a context in which agricultural growth was increasing, with large farmers diversifying from extensive field crops to intensive, high-yielding crops, especially in the horticulture sector.

**Table 3.2: The land acquisition process in Zimbabwe, 1980–1990**

| Period | Laws and instruments | Total number of hectares acquired | Average hectares per year | Number of households resettled |
|---|---|---|---|---|
| 1980–1985 (5 years) | Constitutional constraints (willing-seller, willing-buyer) | 2,147,855 | 429,571 | 30,000 |
| 1985–1990 (6 years) | Land Acquisition Act 1985 (willing-seller, willing-buyer, and government issues certificate of no present interest) | 447,791 | 74,632 | 20,000 |

*Source:* Moyo (2001).

However, a coincidence of economic and political considerations led to a de-emphasis on resettlement and a shift towards other policies, such as commercialization, to meet national agricultural objectives. The government began to experience problems with funding for resettlement. Firstly, it failed to match the United Kingdom's co-funding; resettlement on a massive scale had proved too costly (Moyo, 1993). Secondly, the pace of land acquisition slowed, targets were not met, and issues of equity and racial bias in capital and resource-ownership markets once again became starkly obvious. The sellers of land (white farmers) were the determinants of the land-acquisition policy based on the land they put on the market. The state, especially after 1985, became the buyer of first resort, even though there were budget limitations. These factors led to a marked slowdown in the pace of the land transfers, as government changed its priority after 1990 to the development of the resettled farmers.

Early evaluations of the resettlement exercise revealed that the agricultural activities of resettled farmers produced yields that were below expected targets, and the resettlement exercise was widely criticized (Masters, 1994; Von Blackenburg, 1994). However, some observers pointed out that judgements were premature given that the criteria originally employed to choose participants emphasized the selection of the poor and landless people (who were usually without draught animals) and that the planners themselves anticipated a 15–20-year maturation period which would be completed for the earliest schemes only in the late 1990s (Kinsey, 1998). Studies started to indicate that farmers in resettlement areas were beginning to lift themselves out of poverty as they learned better farming techniques and accumulated sufficient farming and other livelihood resources to better utilize available land (Matondi, 2001).

### 3.3.3 Continuity without change in large-scale commercial agriculture

In the 1980s, there was little change in the direction of government policy with respect to land reform, only in emphasis. The government ring-fenced the large-scale commercial farming sector (LSCF) as the anchor for the economy. This was not only prudence from the side of government; it was also constrained by the Lancaster House Agreement, which stipulated that during the first ten years land redistribution could take place only on a willing-seller basis.

The large-scale commercial farms were basically left intact, and the expectation of a mass exodus of whites in all sectors of the economy in fear of a vindictive state was quashed by the reconciliation policies espoused by the new Prime Minister of Zimbabwe. Thus, for most of the white farmers, it became 'business as usual', leaving politics to blacks while they themselves concentrated on economic accumulation. The large-scale farming sector was complex and highly developed, with some of the best infrastructure and capabilities for farming in comparison with most of Africa. The further development of large-scale farms drew on cheap, long-term finance that was secured on the domestic market and offshore. Investors had confidence in large-scale commercial farming and the fact that government policy-making was done in a very sensitive manner that did not affect the operations of markets.

At the same time, a heavy bias remained towards the LSCF sector. For instance, infrastructural services such as dams, irrigation and water rights remained concentrated in the LSCF areas. They also received the bulk of agricultural credit from the parastatal Agricultural Finance Corporation (AFC) because of pressure from its lender, the World Bank; between 1981 and 1991, the LSCF sector received 3.5 times more credit from the AFC than Communal Land farmers. Later on, the transformation of the LSCF sector to focus on high-value, capital-intensive export products (mostly horticulture and wildlife) resulted in a division of labour as smallholders focused on labour-intensive maize and cotton production.

### 3.3.4 Unbalanced growth in communal area agriculture

The 1980s were characterized by the growth of smallholder agriculture, resembling, in the words of Rukuni, a second agricultural revolution (Rukuni and Eicher, 1994; Rukuni *et al.*, 2006). Agricultural growth after 1980 increased substantially, as reflected in the output from smallholder farmers. Communal Land maize output rose from 35 per cent to 63 per cent of total national output, while their share of cotton increased from 26 per cent to 50 per cent between 1980 and 1990. With respect to cotton, the area planted almost quadrupled, while crop yields remained almost static at around 0.7t/ha. There was a dramatic increase in smallholder output of cotton, burley tobacco and groundnuts in the 1980s and 1990s, which was due to increases in the cropped areas and improved yields in some cases, particularly in tobacco. The rapid growth in the area planted for cotton was due largely to the increase in growers in the communal areas from less than 90,000 in 1980 to 215,000 in 1987 (Takavarasha, 1994).

In the case of burley tobacco, there was a 500 per cent increase in the area planted to the crop between 1980–85 and 1996–2000 (Shumba and Hwingwiri, 2006), due largely to the entry of new tobacco farmers. Smallholder farmers also gained a foothold in the commercial production of sunflower, sorghum and millets. In the livestock sector, the number of animals increased substantially. However, animal husbandry remained relatively unsophisticated and the farmers were unwilling to sell. This remained a key challenge, given that livestock mortality during drought years, particularly in 1991, was very high. The ZCTU *Beyond ESAP* study questioned the quality of the growth of communal agriculture (ZCTU, 1996) when considering issues of food security and poverty eradication. World Bank figures showed that, overall, maize, groundnut and cotton yields declined during the 1980s, while the acreage under maize and groundnuts decreased as well. Tobacco increased both in acreage and yield (Table 3.3).

**Table 3.3: Average annual rate of growth in national crop yields and planted area, 1980–1991**

|         | Tobacco | Maize | Soya beans | Wheat | Sugar | Groundnuts | Sunflower | Cotton |
|---------|---------|-------|------------|-------|-------|------------|-----------|--------|
| Yields  | 2.3     | -3.2  | 1.1        | 1.0   | -0.6  | -2.2       | -0.7      | -6.9   |
| Acreage | 3.4     | -3.1  | 3.5        | 5.2   | 1.1   | -1.4       | 20.6      | 7.4    |

*Source:* World Bank (1995).

In the communal and resettlement areas, the total area under maize increased in the first half of the 1980s but decreased thereafter, while the area under small grains decreased by almost 40 per cent during the 1980s. This was mainly due to unattractive government-set prices: between 1970 and 1989 the growth rates of producer prices for farmers were negative for maize, small grains, groundnuts and soya beans (Food Studies Group, 1990). The cash crops cotton and sunflower gained more and more ground within the communal areas, despite the fact that the producer price for cotton also decreased in the 1980s (Table 3.4).

Marketing trends show a similar path. The marketed value of major crop and livestock products from communal and resettlement areas rose sharply until 1985 and gradually declined thereafter. The value of major crops and livestock for the large-scale commercial sector also declined after 1985, but this was more than offset by a sharp increase in the marketed volume and value of tobacco and horticulture. Growth rates among crops varied, revealing a shift from food crops to cash crops (Table 3.5).

**Table 3.4: Trends in crop acreage in communal and resettlement areas (1,000 ha)**

| Crop | 1980/81 | 1984/85 | 1989/90 | Change (ha) 1989/89 v. 1980/81 | Acreage in 1989/90 as a percentage of 1980/81 |
|---|---|---|---|---|---|
| Maize | 1,086 | 1,160 | 1,030 | -56 | 98.84% |
| Pearl millet | 401 | 303 | 167 | -234 | 41.65% |
| Finger millet | 118 | 154 | 124 | 6 | 105.08% |
| Sorghum | 214 | 247 | 158 | -56 | 73.83% |
| All small grains | 733 | 704 | 449 | -284 | 61.26% |
| Groundnuts | 243 | 149 | 173 | -70 | 71.19% |
| Sunflower | 24 | 31 | 111 | +87 | 462.50% |
| Cotton | 62 | 146 | 180 | 118 | 290.33% |
| TOTAL | 2,148 | 2,190 | 1,943 | 205 | 90.46% |

*Source:* World Bank (1995).

**Table 3.5: Average annual growth rates (%) in marketed output, 1980–1990**

| High growth | | Moderate growth | | Slow growth or decline | |
|---|---|---|---|---|---|
| Sunflower[a] | 28.4 | Cotton | 2.5 | Sugar | 0.4 |
| Horticulture[b] | 26.2 | Groundnuts | 2.1 | Maize | -4.2 |
| Wheat | 6.2 | Cattle | 1.8 | Sorghum | -25.2 |
| Tobacco | 4.9 | Pigs | 1.6 | | |
| Milk | 4.7 | | | | |
| Soya bean | 4.0 | | | | |

*Notes:* [a] 1983–1992; [b] High-value horticultural crops. *Source:* World Bank (1995).

Even the spectacular increase in maize output from communal areas in the 1980s benefited only a small proportion of the communal population. According to the ILO, only 11 per cent of the communal farmers (i.e. 114,000) produced a surplus for the market in the late 1980s, with the top 8,000 contributing 45 per cent. This was because Natural Regions II and III contain only 38 per cent of the smallholder population, grow 60 per cent of the total maize and market 80 per cent (ILO, 1993). At least half of the smallholders remained in maize deficit.

### 3.3.5 Exports

During the 1980s, Zimbabwe gradually increased the value of its agricultural exports from Z$409.2 million in 1981 to Z$1.1 billion in 1988. In real terms, exports increased by less than 10 per cent over this period, or at an average of close to 1 per cent per year. As a matter of fact, about 75 per cent of the income from exports was accounted for by three crops: tobacco (50 per cent), cotton (15 per cent) and sugar (10 per cent). However, while overall exports increased during the first decade of independence, the proportion of exports to the regional markets decreased dramatically over the same period (ZCTU, 1996).

### 3.3.6 Employment

Total formal employment in agriculture (including forestry and fishing) decreased from 327,000 in 1980 to 284,600 in 1989. The use of casual labour increased in the LSCF sector: permanent employment decreased from 215,000 in 1980 to 150,000 in 1989, while casual employment increased from around 55,000 to 110,000 in the same period (ZCTU, 1996). The communal lands had to absorb an increasing proportion of the population: workers who had lost their jobs in agriculture plus the growing number of school-leavers who could not find employment in industry. In addition, environmental degradation further increased in the rural areas.

### 3.3.7 Lessons from the first decade, 1980–1990

Growth in smallholder agricultural production was due to the subsidy programme in which communal area farmers had access to free seed and fertilizer packs, improved availability of high-yielding seed varieties, and access to credit, while large numbers of extension workers were trained and deployed at the ward level. The next level of support was the systematic establishment of marketing depots in rural areas, mainly by state parastatals such as the Grain Marketing Board, Cold Storage Company, and Cotton Marketing Board. In order to spearhead infrastructural development in rural areas, government established the District Development Fund (DDF), which was responsible for rural development, re-settlement, road maintenance and water management, with a focus on the establishment of medium-sized dams in each district.

The government's recognition of the critical role of the agricultural sector in national development was first emphasized in the *First Five-Year Development Plan*, 1986–1990, which stated that 'the agricultural sector must be in the centre of the development strategy' (Zimbabwe, 1986). It is worth noting that there is a difference between an 'agricultural revolution' riding on the waves of the commercialization of smallholder farming, and equitable agricultural and rural development. Proponents of the former seem to assume implicitly that, when the prime movers (skills, supporting institutions for marketing, credit, research and extension, access to land, a favourable economic policy, etc.) are in place, sustainable agricultural development will occur. However, this rather technocratic approach was insufficient to uplift the lives of the masses in the rural areas as the 'success story' of Zimbabwe in the 1980s shows. Maize sales by communal farmers increased from a yearly average of 54,000 tonnes in the five years before independence to an average of 550,000 tonnes between 1988/89 and 1991/92. This was all due to conscious government efforts to get the prime movers working countrywide: making inputs and technology available, disbursement of credit, opening up depots even in the most remote rural areas, etc.

Underlying this problem is, amongst others, the unequal access to financial resources under the Agricultural Finance Corporation, most of whose loans went to the better-endowed provinces; Mashonaland West and Central accounted for 57 per cent of all the AFC's loans. Loans reached only a small percentage of the rural population: only 5 per cent out of an estimated 1,000,000 communal area households between 1981 and 1991. Even for those who received loans, the road to success was far from guaranteed: by January 1998, 80 per cent of communal area farmers, 68 per cent of small-scale commercial farmers and 77 per cent of resettlement farmers were in arrears (Chimedza, 1994). As Bond and Manyanya (2003: 54) wondered, 'is agricultural credit – sourced from hard-currency World Bank loans, lent under neo-liberal conditionality, and recycled through bureaucratic state agencies in local currency – the most useful input for rural peasants, especially women?' Certainly, a lot more has to happen to augment policy towards 'getting the prime movers right' to increase food security, uplift the rural masses, in particular the women, and induce equitable agricultural and rural development.

## 3.4 Land, Agriculture and Rural Development, 1991–1996

### 3.4.1 Agricultural policies during ESAP

With the publication of the *Economic Policy Statement* in 1990 and the *Framework for Economic Reform* in 1991, the government formally embarked on its stabilization and structural adjustment programme, ESAP. In its *Second Five-Year Development Plan*, 1991–1995, government stated its development objectives for the agricultural sector as 'the production of enough food for the population as well as an increase in exports, expansion of employment and production of sufficient raw material for the manufacturing industry' (Zimbabwe, 1991).

In its critique of ESAP, the ZCTU (1996) argued that the government implicitly made the incorrect assumptions that:

- the agricultural sector was homogenous, with everybody having equal chances to enter and gain within a capitalist, liberal market-place (no market distortions);
- liberalization would improve efficiency of production through the adoption of improved technology and would stimulate diversification;
- a free market improves net returns to farmers;
- ESAP would increase employment and food production.

Government's specific policy thrust was to concentrate agricultural production on non-traditional exports, on activities related to tourism, and liberalizing domestic markets which were considered to be the main constraints to agricultural growth. The expectation of greater agricultural diversification (Matondi, 1997; Moyo, 2000) was premised on the need to raise new sources of foreign-currency earnings, employment and income growth.

The implementation of ESAP resulted in cuts in government budgets, and spending on agricultural services such as extension, research, finance and market outlets deteriorated in real terms throughout the 1990s. The Grain Marketing Board (GMB) sharply reduced its number of temporary collection points within communal areas; loans to the communal sector declined further, both in value and number; the quality of research and extension deteriorated further. Markets were also steadily liberalized, and government's involvement in the determination of agricultural prices was actively reduced, the GMB setting a bottom price for maize only. Only the producer price of wheat remained controlled by government as it aimed at self-sufficiency in this respect.

Thus, small-scale farmers were increasingly left to fend for themselves in a liberalized market environment where the odds were heavily stacked against them. Even in cases where government intervened through legislation, it did not actively support small-scale farming: the 1995 Water Act committed only ten per cent of Zimbabwe's water to the communal areas, thereby completely ignoring the importance of water distribution for increasing and improving agricultural production in the smallholder sector.

### 3.4.2 Resettlement and its challenges

The ESAP period coincided with the new land policy in 1990 that was adopted as a basis for resolving the land issue. This policy was backed by legal changes in the form of the Land Acquisition Act of 1992 [*Chapter 20:10*], which aimed at the compulsory acquisition of land through a process of designation. However, following a serious drought in 1991/92, and in the light of the economic liberalization programme, the government took a cautious approach to land reform. According to Moyo (2000), the government's land policy seemed to have been redefined through a gradual revision of what was a radical strategy of compulsorily expropriating underutilized land towards an even more liberal market land policy. This policy was based on the use of donor funds to buy land on a willing-buyer–willing-seller basis.

Resettlement did not receive adequate attention from the government during the ESAP period. For instance, the revised policy proposals of 1996 emphasized the transfer of land to the 'better-off black farmers' and not the needy. In addition, government's budgetary allocations for land acquisition remained at around Z$10 million per annum; the actual area of LSCF land that the government could therefore purchase – with its available financial allocations at the prevailing cost per hectare after 1990 – was reduced to about 35 per cent. Furthermore, throughout the late 1980s and 1990s, the government had not responded to rising land prices in the LSCF sector (Rugube *et al.*, 2004). For example, land prices based upon sales to the government had already increased by 50 per cent between 1989 and 1991 at the time ESAP was being initiated.

This price trend was then met by the Land Acquisition Act of 1992, which reflected political concern over the increases. Surprisingly, however, LSCF land prices continued to rise steadily, only to decline by 1996 to pre-1990 levels owing to the effects of droughts, high interest rates and the gradual downward trend of real farm commodity prices (ibid.).

### 3.4.3 Commercial agriculture during the ESAP period, 1991–1996

The 1990s were a growth period for the large-scale commercial farming sector as the deregulation of agricultural markets led to an increase in access to foreign currency. The devaluation of the Zimbabwe dollar presented major changes and opportunities for the sector.[4] The large-scale agricultural sector became increasingly intensified: there was a strong movement towards the intensification of commercial crops (maize, cotton, tobacco, wheat), and diversification into horticulture and new income streams such as ostrich-farming and game-ranching. In areas close to urban and tourist centres, and in areas with significant wildlife, some farmers reported higher returns from tourism than from tobacco.

There was an increase in conventional plant and animal breeding in conjunction with advances in agronomy, farm mechanization and crop protection, which helped agriculture reach its peak level in Zimbabwe in the 1990s. While biotechnology promised to provide additional opportunities in agriculture (Sithole-Niang, 2006; Muchena, 2006), there was a robust debate on the possibilities of genetically modified organisms (GMOs) in agriculture, which government cautiously put on trial but did not approve for large-scale production. Other notable scientific advances, in remote sensing and geographical information systems, backed by the introduction of the Internet and rural cellphone coverage, underpinned Zimbabwe's agricultural diversification process during the ESAP period.

It should be realized, however, that profits attained by large-scale commercial farms were at the expense of the farm-workers. While formal employment in the LSCF sector remained at around 300,000 in the first years of ESAP, the real value of agricultural wages in 1992 was half its 1990 level because of ESAP-induced inflation. The share of wages in the value of LSCF-marketed output fell from an average of 26 per cent in the 1980–83 period, and 35 per cent during the 1988–91 period, to less than 15 per cent by 1993. Moreover, employment figures show that casual labour increased at a rate almost twice that of the increase in permanent employment (ZCTU, 1996).

---

[4] Real exchange-rate depreciation changes relative prices in favour of the tradable-goods sector. It shifts the terms of trade in favour of the tradable-goods sector, where profitability is expected to improve relative to the non-tradable-goods sector.

### 3.4.4 Communal area agriculture loses out

As discussed above, the 1990s were characterized by a number of economic changes. Macroeconomic reforms had major effects on formal-sector employment and agricultural prices. Marketing reforms led to greater participation in and reliance on private-sector marketing initiatives. However, the international marketing channels could not easily be accessed by smallholders because of stringent phyto-sanitary (health and hygiene) requirements, complex international markets, poor market information, and so on. The occurrence of drought exacerbated the negative aspects of these changes. The area under maize production in the communal areas rose from around 1 million hectares in the 1980s to around 1.2 million in the 1990s (Rukuni, 2006), while average yields per hectare declined somewhat in the 1990s (with large variations between seasons). The acreage under small grains decreased further, and groundnuts continued to lose ground. The total acreage under crops in the communal and resettlement areas declined (ZCTU, 1996).

The acreage under seed cotton in the communal sector increased further under the liberalized regime, while the commercial sector's acreage gradually decreased. Cotton production increased, despite the fact that world market prices had dropped sharply in the 1980s, remained somewhat constant between 1990 and 1997, and then dropped by 45 per cent in the period between 1997 and 2000 (Bond and Manyanya, 2003). Cotton yields per hectare remained almost constant in both communal and commercial sectors, with the latter's yields about double those in the communal sector (Table 3.6).

Real producer prices went up slightly in the early 1990s for maize, wheat and soya beans, remained constant for sunflower, but declined for sorghum, ground-

**Table 3.6: Acreage and yields of seed cotton in the 1990s**

| Growing season | Communal sector | | | Commercial sector | | |
| --- | --- | --- | --- | --- | --- | --- |
| | Area (ha) | Yield (kg/ha) | Production (mt) | Area (ha) | Yield (kg/ha) | Production (mt) |
| 1990/91 | 197,000 | 700 | 137,900 | 77,222 | 1,595 | 123,151 |
| 1991/92 | 183,000 | 195 | 35,700 | 52,777 | 768 | 40,532 |
| 1992/93 | 199,000 | 676 | 134,500 | 47,300 | 1,687 | 79,800 |
| 1993/94 | 181,150 | 612 | 110,805 | 40,150 | 1,760 | 70,675 |
| 1994/95 | 179,760 | 312 | 56,100 | 33,800 | 1,078 | 36,440 |
| 1995/96 | 217,620 | 724 | 157,584 | 40,000 | 1,827 | 73,070 |
| 1996/97 | 267,500 | 740 | 197,825 | 45,755 | 1,756 | 80,359 |
| 1997/98 | 239,000 | 764 | 182,550 | 47,000 | 1,921 | 90,300 |
| 1998/99 | 274,500 | 686 | 188,350 | 188,350 | 1,407 | 76,630 |
| 1999/2000 | 326,000 | 808 | 263,400 | 63,668 | 1,742 | 110,935 |

*Source:* Mariga (2006).

nuts, beef and tobacco (Zimbabwe, 1994). As was the case in the 1980s, only a small fraction of the communal farming sector gained: ten districts accounted for approximately two-thirds of the smallholder-marketed output of maize, cotton and other crops.[5]

The ESAP framework did not directly address the key constraints confronting small-scale or communal area farmers, including the discriminatory land and financial markets, distorted water rights, and the lack of access to essential infra-structure for more effective land use such as dams, irrigation and transport. Given that the central focus of ESAP was on efficiency, the large-scale com-mercial sector became a priority at the expense of the smallholder sector. Communal areas were thus constrained by generally poor infrastructure (roads, communication), which hindered access to markets and services.

The vicious cycle of poverty for many households, particularly those in communal areas, and displaced farm-workers increased; the 1990s witnessed a growth in both poverty and vulnerability in rural areas, rather than the expected economic growth.[6] Between 1990 and 2001, up to 57 per cent of the population in Communal Lands was classified as having, on average, insufficient food entitlements to ensure basic food security at some point in time (Stack and Sukume, 2006).

### 3.4.5 Lessons from the ESAP period

With its emphasis on real exchange-rate depreciation, ESAP contributed to the growth of export-oriented commercial farming through the development of new land use in the area of wildlife and tourism and horticulture, especially the floriculture sector. Unfortunately, during this period land reform was not a priority, suggesting that there was less money for land purchases, resettlement planning and rural-development support. The large-scale sector continued to blossom amid the growing poverty that afflicted the smallholder sector. Irrigation development, infrastructure renewal, and new market streams all contributed to make the large-scale commercial farms grow. The more land, capital and technical resources that commercial farmers had, together with their superior links with national and international markets, the greater their influence on agri-cultural policy, which ensured that they were more able than the peasants to exploit the new market opportunities.

Peasants were ill-equipped to meet the challenges and opportunities presented by the market reforms under ESAP. In addition, many people retreated to subsistence agriculture as an adaptation and coping mechanism when they

---

[5] They comprised Hurungwe, Gokwe, Murehwa, Mount Darwin, Makoni, Guruve, Shamva, Uzumba-Maramba-Pfungwe (UMP), Buhera and Gutu (ZCTU, 1996).

[6] See Chapter 7.

were made redundant from industry and the civil service. However, given the unequal land-ownership patterns, they found themselves in communal areas that were already overpopulated and faced a range of constraints in terms of poor soils, shortage of land, market constraints, a reduction in public extension services, tillage problems and land insecurity. A minority of peasant groups with better resources, entrepreneurial skills, locational advantages or access to the development programmes of NGOs tried in vain to adapt (Moyo, 2000). In fact, there was a renewed growth in inequality, reversing the small gains that had been made in the 1980s (Rukuni *et al.*, 2006).

Hence, ESAP further entrenched and deepened the inherited dual and enclave nature of the agricultural sector in Zimbabwe, since its policy thrust deliberately left out the rural population, despite government's original goal to uplift the standard of living of rural people through various support mechanisms aimed at boosting rural agricultural production, which was abandoned or scaled down during ESAP. In the words of Moyo (1999: 2), 'In spite of the liberation war, a narrow racial and class monopoly over land has been consolidated through the extra market processes for decades'.

## 3.5 The Land Issue during the Crisis Period, 1997–2000

### 3.5.1 The trigger of the land crisis
While the pressure to redistribute land had emanated largely from the nationalist liberation movement, the impetus for land reform in the latter part of the 1990s came from civil society. In October 1996, in defiance of government policy, two hundred land-hungry peasants invaded an idle state farm adjacent to the Matobo Research Station in Matabeleland, illustrating growing impatience with the slow pace of resettlement and anger at the allocation to senior government officials and politicians of land meant for resettlement. Land occupations assumed greater prominence, with fifteen major land invasions taking place in 1997 and 1998 in prime farmlands in the three Mashonaland Provinces (Moyo, 1999). In June 1998, the Svosve people from Marondera and Wedza districts invaded large commercial farms in Mashonaland East and refused to move until land was made available to them. They even occupied land belonging, or leased by the state, to prominent political leaders, suggesting that the peasants' impatience was now directed at government and not just at the colonial legacy of inequality. Such invasions spread to other parts of the country, but had been contained by November 1998.

Meanwhile, government gazetted 1,471 commercial farms for resettlement in November 1997. However, 625 were then de-listed for a variety of reasons – that they were not multiple-owned, they were owned by indigenous (black) people, they were productive, established or new estates, and for the likely developmental and social impact (Moyo, 1999). Thus, following legal challenges, this initiative was halted. During this time, government noted the loopholes in the legal framework and started to work on amendments to change the process from designation to compulsory acquisition. They also expected that the action of listing the commercial farms would have the effect of forcing negotiation, particularly with the British government.

### 3.5.2 The land issue takes a political dimension

The British government, which had largely supported land reform, raised some concerns. The labour government that came into office in May 1997 had this to say in a letter from Clare Short to Minister Kumbirai Kangai: 'I should make it clear that we do not accept that Britain has a special responsibility to meet the costs of land purchase in Zimbabwe. We are a new government from diverse backgrounds without links to former colonial interests. My own origins are Irish and, as you know, we were colonized not colonizers' (Matondi, 2008b).[7] This seems to have seriously angered the Zimbabwe government.

This statement gave the government of Zimbabwe the ammunition it needed to blame the labour government for reneging on the promises made during the political settlement at Lancaster House in 1979. All attempts by the British government to exonerate itself – by observing that the £44 million they had provided during the first phase from 1980 to 1997 was not all spent (Matondi and Moyo, 2002), and further promises of £26 million at the height of the land occupations and negotiation through the UNDP and the Commonwealth in Abuja – did not yield any political settlement on the land question. Faced with increasing opposition, especially following the launch of the Movement for Democratic Change (MDC) in September 1999, the government was forced to act. In January 2000, it proposed an amendment to clause 57 of the draft new constitution, allowing compulsory acquisition of land without compensation. The government broadened the discussion on land in the constitution-making exercise to legitimize the actions that it had taken. The debate during the drafting of the constitution for the first time clearly stated that the formerly disadvantaged Zimbabwean people were not responsible for payment for the soil, and dispossessed farmers would be paid only for improvements, and that responsibility for compensation lay with the British because they had a colonial responsibility. The British government, through its foreign office, rejected such demands, which made the negotiations over land untenable. Although the draft constitution was rejected in a referendum in February 2000, the government introduced compulsory land acquisition through parliament.

[7] In fact, in November 1997, Clare Short, then Secretary of State for International Development, reaffirmed the British government's position that they would only support a programme of land reform that was part of a plan to help reduce poverty in Zimbabwe, stressing the importance of transparency and cost-effectiveness.

### 3.5.3 Land negotiations

To break the stalemate with its development partners, the government hosted a land conference in Harare in September 1998, involving key domestic stakeholders, international donors and multilateral institutions. The conference agreed on fundamental principles to govern land redistribution: transparency, respect for the rule of law, poverty reduction, affordability, and consistency with Zimbabwe's wider economic interests. It was also agreed that there should be a first phase, during which government resettlement schemes would be tried alongside schemes from the private sector and civil society. On this basis, the government published an 'inception phase' document in March 1999 for a two-year period, but progress in its implementation was slow.[8]

The Commercial Farmers' Union sought to negotiate by offering land for resettlement, and in 2000 tried to make about 1.5 million hectares available along with a Z$15 billion aid package through the Zimbabwe Joint Resettlement Initiative; it never got off the ground because the government had by then taken the position that the British government and commercial farmers were not serious about the land-reform programme. The international community did not rise to underpin this initiative with any support, which would probably have positively changed the course of the land negotiations.

At the same time, the government began negotiating directly with the British government by sending missions to find common ground. During the negotiations, the British government raised various issues with respect to corruption in the land allocations, lack of a poverty-reduction focus, an inclination towards cronyism by party functionaries, and the government's inability to make use of all the British aid for resettlement, as well as broader political issues of democracy, transparency, accountability, etc. Such a political perspective angered the Zimbabwe government, who felt that it required a countervailing political response: they targeted white commercial farmers in land takeovers, and sought to make a loud political statement in the international and local media on the necessity of taking over the farms for historical reasons.

Thus, the two-year inception phase that had been agreed at the land conference in 1998 was interrupted by farm occupations and violence (*jambanja*) in the aftermath of the referendum and during the run-up to the June 2000 parliamentary elections. However, the government was aware that something needed to be done on the land issue, particularly since the ZCTU had succeeded in organizing nationwide riots over food in 1998, so government was pushed

---

[8] In its background briefing document of March 2000, the British Department for International Development (DfID) stated that the UK was not convinced that the Zimbabwe government had a serious poverty-eradication strategy, and questioned whether it was giving priority to land reform to help the poor. It also raised concern about transparency in the selection of settlers and the arrangements in place to help resettlement. It noted that against this background the best way to help the poor was to support land resettlement through non-government channels (the private sector and NGOs).

to work on a socially and politically appealing way of addressing the land question.

## 3.6 Land, Agriculture and Rural Development, 2000–2008

### 3.6.1 Land reform prioritized and executed

ZANU(PF)'s political message at the height of the land reforms and elections became 'Land is the Economy and the Economy is Land'. Government had to deal with land occupations while also taking the legal route of constitutional changes (Madhuku, 2004). Constitution of Zimbabwe Amendment (No. 16) Act (No. 5 of 2000), backed by amendments to the Land Acquisition Act (No. 15 of 2000), allowed the state to acquire land compulsorily, without compensation for the land but only for improvements. The responsibility for compensation was then, as in the rejected draft constitution, transferred to the former colonial power, the British government. While acknowledging its debt on financing land reform, the British government was vehemently opposed to the fast-track land-reform programme. The violence associated with the programme, the poor planning, and the unfair redistribution to politicians and elites within the ruling ZANU(PF) party deepened the sharp differences.

The fast-track land-reform programme was indeed fast, and clearly it was about taking the land and giving it to black farmers as the custodians of the land. Most rules, processes, administrative mechanisms, and issues of resource mobilization were put aside because they were seen as a hindrance to achieving the objectives of the programme. Some constitutional and legal imperatives were also suspended and, if challenged by white farmers, were amended to meet this one objective. In a short space of time, white farmers had lost hope, confidence and a sense of place in the Zimbabwean body politic and started trooping out of the farms. While there was a good deal of uncertainty by the peasantry on the sustainability of government's action to acquire almost all commercial farms, they still applied to be resettled on the land.

Land reform therefore assumed a political dimension, with politicians taking advantage of the reality that the majority blacks favoured land repossession based upon grievances over historical injustices. It also turned out to be a major political issue as it entailed a deep-seated challenge to the property rights of a powerful propertied class. Thus, the fast-track land-reform programme became an instrument to redress political injustices of the past, while the political elites took advantage of the situation for their own political ends, as well as benefiting from the reforms, as has been illustrated in the outstanding issue of multiple farm ownership.

The key milestones around the land issue during the period 1997–2009 are summarized in Box 3.1.

---

**Box 3.1: Milestones of the fast-track land-reform programme**

**1997: Economic spin as war vets went on the offensive**

- UK–Zimbabwe bilateral negotiations on land reform reach a deadlock.
- Government lists 1,471 farms for compulsory acquisition.

**1998: Government and donors negotiate**

- Land donors' conference between government and donors. There is an agreement to try out a combined market and state acquisition through an Inception Phase Framework Plan. The plan was delayed and there was very slow progress from both government and donors.
- Svosve land occupations spread throughout the country, but were effectively contained by November of 1998.

**1999–2000: The constitutional year and land occupations**

- Referendum on constitution has a strong provision for the land question and makes it a responsibility for the British to pay for land compensation, with government paying for improvements.
- Abuja Commonwealth Agreement accepts that the land question is at the root of the political crisis in Zimbabwe.
- Zimbabwe Joint Resettlement Initiative, where white commercial farmers are offered land and mobilization of finance to support the resettlement programme on the basis of negotiations on land reforms.
- Electoral campaigns ('land is the economy and the economy is land'). Government takes land acquisition to a higher political profile, and acts to transfer and place beneficiaries on the land with minimum support.

**2000–2003: Implementation: Acquisition and allocation, and evaluation**

- The Buka audit unearths the extent of multiple farm ownership, land underutilization, especially on the A2 farms [see 3.6.3], as well as inequitable allocation by gender, etc.
- The Utete committee acknowledges positive developments of the transfers, but identifies teething problems with implementation of the programme from district to national level. Significantly recommends the separation of the Ministry of Lands from that of Agriculture.

**2003–2007: Self-assessment and reflection on land reform, with political hesitancy**

- Government continues with its programme of mass land transfer, but there are problems that result in numerous audits whose recommendations are rarely implemented.
- Empowered Reserve Bank of Zimbabwe takes its quasi-fiscal activities to a higher level in support of agriculture through crop inputs, farm mechanization, support to horticulture producers, etc. But all actions are in vain, with temporary relief to a few only.

**2008–2009: Collapse of the economy and rethinking governance**

- Severe food shortages permeated by inadequate food in all the land sectors seem to imply that the land reform has been a huge flop in terms of agricultural production.
- Economic collapse forces the political players into a state of negotiation that results in the GPA with Section V of the agreement devoted to land issues.
- Formation of an inclusive government halts the fast-track land-reform programme, though pressure remains from sceptics who are suspicious that the Inclusive Government wants to reverse land reforms.

---

*Source*: Rukuni *et al.* (2010).

### 3.6.2 The fast-track land-reform programme

The fast-track land-resettlement programme was defined by government as an elaborate plan of the 'Land Reform and Resettlement Programme – Phase II' that had been presented at the donors' conference held towards the end of 1998, in which it outlined a programme aimed at acquiring five million hectares and settling 91,000 families (Zimbabwe, 1998).[9] The beneficiaries were to include the landless poor and overcrowded families and youths as well as graduates from agricultural colleges and others with experience in agriculture, who were to be selected in a gender-sensitive manner. Phase II was expected to bring the total redistributed area to about 8.3 million hectares, and its basic objectives included reducing poverty, increasing agriculture's share of GDP by increasing the number of commercial small-scale farmers, promoting environmentally sustainable land use, and enhancing conditions for sustainable peace and social stability.

Over time this target was changed to 12 million hectares in response to political pressure from war veterans, ZANU(PF), and popular demands for land, but also in response to court cases launched by the Commercial Farmers' Union, who represented mostly white farmers. At a practical level, meeting the objectives of the programme was a challenge, because most of the institutions involved had been allocated shoestring budgets yet were expected to implement it without fail. Thus, resources meant for other agricultural programmes, as well as those meant for other ministries, were usurped for the land-reform programme, but the implementing agencies did not have the equipment or personnel to engage in such a massive programme. The army, students in colleges, and the unemployed were mobilized in the process of surveying and demarcating farms. At the same time, a fast-track process of training agricultural extension personnel was extended to the youth training centres throughout the country. The fast-track programme was further premised on minimum support being available to new settlers in the form of inputs. The longer-term social and agricultural services were expected to be invested later over time.

Furthermore, land allocation under the fast-track programme was complex, given the varied pressures of many people wanting land. This gave rise to a wide range of problems that included double allocations, occupations without an offer letter, forged offer letters, boundary conflicts, settlers being denied access to their plots, sharing of infrastructure, as well as vandalism and theft of equipment.[10] Multiple land-allocation authorities created conditions that supported the development of these problems. The co-ordination of land-allocation

---

[9] The additional area of resettlement was, on the basis of independent research, regarded as one that would not prejudice the strategic role of large-scale commercial farming in national agricultural production.

[10] See Zimbabwe (2003) and Parliament of Zimbabwe, Second report of the Portfolio Committee on Lands Agriculture Water Development Rural Resources and Resettlement, Third Session, Fifth Parliament, 11 June 2003 [S.C. 11, 2003].

activities met several challenges, and accordingly figures for the total number of people allocated land showed wide variations: several institutions at district and national level had different figures for people to be allocated land. According to the Utete Report (Zimbabwe, 2003), traditional leaders, war veterans, the security forces, women's organizations, provincial task forces, the ministries of agriculture and land resettlement, and others, all had their own lists of potential beneficiaries. This meant that there were parallel land-allocation processes taking place, creating confusion. This was exacerbated by the fact that some of the A2 settlers had offer letters that came direct from the parent ministry's headquarters in Harare, whereas the procedure was that they should go through the province and the district. Table 3.7 shows the results of land distribution by 2008.

### 3.6.3 The agrarian sector under fast-track land reform

*The A1 resettlement model*
During the fast-track phase, some 145,775 farmers were settled in a social scheme named A1,[11] in which they got smaller-sized land-holdings (usually twelve acres, in the most productive natural regions) and were to receive minimum support from government. The government planned the farms through demarcation by AGRITEX. In general, a villagized scheme, with residential areas, separate fields, and grazing areas was designed. However, given that government had very few resources, the beneficiaries were supposed to oversee the construction of their own residencies. Often, settlers pushed farm-workers out of their compounds, others constructed temporary shelter, while some turned sheds and other buildings into residential accommodation (Matondi, 2009). It was difficult to establish the criteria used by the land committee to decide who was allocated land under the A1 model. The modus operandi seems to have been no different from beneficiaries choosing which plot to occupy by pulling numbers out of a hat.

*The A2 resettlement model*
The A2 resettlement model is largely contested in political terms, as it is seen by donors and other critics as a sanctuary for the political elites. In contrast, government sees it as offering options for the development of black commercial farmers. Some 16,386 farmers have benefited in the commercial A2 scheme, in which they are provided with medium- to large-sized land-holdings and are expected to provide their own resources. The Ministry of Lands, Agriculture and Rural Resettlement placed advertisements in the five main national newspapers inviting people to apply for the model A2 scheme. Application forms were

---

[11] A study for the UNDP, however, puts the total number of resettled communal households much lower, at about 75,000 (Doré, 2009).

**Table 3.7: Land distributed to A1 and A2 farmers by 2008, by province**

| Province | A1 resettlement[a] | | | A2 resettlement[b] | | |
|---|---|---|---|---|---|---|
| | No. of farms | Area (ha) | Beneficiaries | No. of farms | Area (ha) | Beneficiaries |
| Manicaland | 223 | 215,427 | 12,309 | 258 | 102,215 | 1,232 |
| Mashonaland Central | 243 | 568,197 | 16,853 | 342 | 259,489 | 2,434 |
| Mashonaland East | 384 | 437,269 | 17,731 | 349 | 314,233 | 4,703 |
| Mashonaland West | 476 | 811,033 | 28,435 | 592 | 873,111 | 4,460 |
| Masvingo | 248 | 750,563 | 33,197 | 155 | 341,000 | 1,351 |
| Matabeleland North | 281 | 520,214 | 9,394 | 88 | 259,659 | 421 |
| Matabeleland South | 151 | 383,140 | 10,812 | 194 | 288,324 | 765 |
| Midlands | 282 | 451,242 | 17,044 | 317 | 243,611 | 1,019 |
| TOTAL | 2,288 | 4,137,085 | 145,775 | 2,295 | 2,681,642 | 16,386 |

[a] Peasant farmers. [b] Commercial farmers. *Source:* Ministry of Lands and Rural Resettlement.

available for collection at the offices of the Department of Land Acquisition and Rural Resettlement, the Provincial Administrator and the District Administrator. Officials explained, on television and radio, the details needed on the application forms and the attachments required. Land allocation was then done through the office of the Provincial Governor and Resident Minister. An offer letter was provided by the Minister of Lands and Land Reform to the successful applicant.

The scoring system for A2 applicants was developed by the former Ministry of Lands and Agriculture. The government mooted the idea of aspiring A2 farmers undergoing a means test for them to qualify: they needed to have any (or a combination) of the following: agricultural training, financial resources (proven through bank records), a viable farm production proposal, experience in farming, and the ability to employ a farm manager. However, the temptation to please followers and close associates felt by politicians meant that the well-developed and rigorous system was put aside.

### The large-scale commercial sector under the fast-track programme

Until the fast-track programme, large-scale (white) commercial farmers had bene-fited from government support more than smallholder farmers. Although they had huge tracts of underutilized land – in the range of 40 per cent of total productive land (Moyo, 1995) – the area on which they practised their farm-ing sufficed for commercial production. By 2009, less than 200 white farmers remained on the land; a few black-owned commercial farms had also been compulsorily acquired. Table 3.8 shows the patterns of landholdings by 2009. Production on the remaining farms had gone down, reflecting the general econ-omic meltdown of the country.

**Table 3.8: Landholding patterns in Zimbabwe in 2006/07 and 2008/09**

| | No. of farmers ('000) | | Arable landholding (ha) | | Total arable land ('000 ha) | | Cultivated land ('000 ha) | | Land utilization (%) | |
|---|---|---|---|---|---|---|---|---|---|---|
| | 06/07 | 08/09 | 06/07 | 08/09 | 06/07 | 08/09 | 06/07 | 08/09 | 06/07 | 08/09 |
| Communal Land | 1,132 | 1,200 | 2.2 | 2.1 | 2,491 | 2,500 | 1,924 | 2,332 | 77 | 93 |
| Old resettlement | 160 | 160 | 5 | 5 | 800 | 800 | 241 | 217 | 30 | 27 |
| A1 | 145 | 146 | 5 | 5 | 725 | 725 | 357 | 385 | 49 | 53 |
| A2 | 15.5 | 16.5 | Variable | Variable | 710 | 710 | 161 | 162 | 55 | 49 |
| Small-scale commercial | 30 | 8.5 | | | | | 116 | 107 | | |
| Large-scale commercial | 0.9 | 0.8 | | | | | 113 | 77 | | |
| TOTAL | 1,484 | 1,531 | – | – | 4,726 | 4,735 | 2,911 | 3,279 | 62 | 69 |

*Source:* FAO and WFP (2009).

## The plight of the farm-workers

The issue of farm-workers in Zimbabwe draws emotional debates and is very complex. The large-scale commercial farming areas were dominated by a large labour population, especially in the Mashonaland and Manicaland provinces. In the 1980s and 1990s, the number of farm-workers servicing the agricultural sector ranged from 250,000 to 350,000. Given that large-scale farms numbered only about 4,500, it can be directly argued that the success of the sector was due to this labour.

However, it is also clear that much of the success of the LSCF sector was based on the exploitation of farm-workers through bad labour relations practices (Amanor-Wilks, 1995; Loewenson, 1992; Rutherford, 2001). Rutherford (1996) has documented these as having included poor contractual terms, poor wages (lowest of any worker in any sector), poor living conditions on the farms (poor housing, poor sanitation, lack of services), minimal education and health delivery (the responsibility of the farm-owners), etc. The neglect of farm-workers cannot be blamed only on white farmers, but it epitomizes how farm-workers had become second-class citizens in a country that viewed them as being foreigners. Government did not regard them as an important constituency that needed attention: for instance, it was not until 1998 that farm-workers could exercise their right to vote.

According to Sachikonye (2003) and Doré (2009), more than half of the farm-workers (around 200,000) lost their jobs in the first wave of the fast-track programme, while over the last nine years hundreds of thousands lost their liveli-hoods, though a few were incorporated into the current agrarian arrangements as employees of A1 or A2 farmers, as well as being beneficiaries (Chambati,

2007). Evictions and 'voluntary' departures continued over the years. According to the General Agriculture and Plantation Workers' Union (GAPWUZ), by 2009 some 71 per cent of farm-workers had been evicted (GAPWUZ, 2009).

The fate of the few farm-workers who found employment with new black employers did not improve much: the minimum wage in agriculture was artificially suppressed under the pretext that the new farmers needed breathing space to develop before they could pay higher wages. For example, in the inflation-ravaged economy of 2008, average wages hovered around US$0.50 cents per month, improving marginally to US$12 per month in 2009 following the dollarization of the economy. Nine years after the reforms commenced, farmers in both A1 and A2 schemes continue to call themselves 'new', and give this as an excuse for not paying their workers adequately. It also explains the paradox of labour shortages being experienced in the agricultural and agro-industrial sectors amid high levels of unemployment. Given a choice, farm-workers opted to become gold-panners, cross-border traders, etc., or migrated to urban areas. At the same time, less than one per cent of seized farm lands was distributed to farm-labourers (GAPWUZ, 2009).

### The communal and old resettlement farmers

As land-reform gathered momentum, the state seemed to have forgotten that it also had responsibility for the communal and old resettlement areas. Since the 1980s, the farmers in these two sectors had produced the bulk of the commercially marketed maize and cotton (over 60 per cent). In the 1980s, input packs (seed and fertilizer) had been directed to these farmers, but under the fast-track programme they were directed towards the new farmers in the resettled areas, who ironically lacked commercial farming skills. The communal and old resettlement farmers faced a drought not only in terms of rainfall but also in terms of inputs, which adversely affected their productivity.

As the economy continued on its free fall, government 'for security and strategic reasons' started to commandeer inputs away from open markets to its own subsidy programmes. The agencies appointed by government to redistribute the inputs – such as the GMB, the Cold Storage Company, ARDA and AGRITEX – diversified their operations to add this new 'lucrative' responsibility. In a high-inflation economy, civil servants and politicians found a new avenue for pilfering state resources through self-allocations. A few unfortunate ones were arrested and prosecuted, but by and large the majority got away with it. The parastatals proved to be inefficient and self-serving because they were held captive by the politicians. By 2008 the communal and old resettlement farmers received very few of these subsidies, so production under the fast-track programme declined markedly. Some areas in Mashonaland, for instance, that were usually known to be food-reliant needed food relief even in the best farming seasons.

### 3.6.4 Agriculture under the fast-track programme

*Factoring economic decline into agricultural performance*

The fast-track programme marked a structural break in the performance of the Zimbabwean economy, and notably its agricultural sector; virtually all commodities were adversely affected. Table 3.9 compares the rates of growth of agriculture and the economy as a whole over the period 2000–2009. Poor agricultural performance literally dragged the rest of the economy into a depression, and the sector led the recovery in 2009.

**Table 3.9: Agricultural and GDP growth rates (%), 2001–2009**

|  | 2000 | 2001 | 2002 | 2003 | 2004 | 2005 | 2006 | 2007 | 2008 (est.) | 2009 (est.) |
|---|---|---|---|---|---|---|---|---|---|---|
| Real GDP | –7.0 | –2.4 | –4.1 | –7.4 | –3.3 | –4.0 | –5.4 | –6.1 | –14.1 | 5.7 |
| Agriculture | 2.0 | 14.0 | –24.0 | –15.0 | –9.0 | –5.0 | –4.0 | –7.0 | –39.3 | 14.9 |
| Agriculture/GDP | 23 | 21 | 18 | 10 | 7 | 11 | 15 | 21 | 24 | |

*Source:* Unpublished data from the Ministry of Finance, and the 2010 Mid-Term Fiscal Policy Review Statement, July 2010.

Land-use intensity had been low due to low plot up-take levels and slow A2 allocations. In addition, the country had suffered from a low level of financial resources and other inputs, which affected cropping and grazing intensities. Potentially arable land was largely underutilized owing to resource limitations among the beneficiaries and the high cost of inputs; an unknown amount of acquired land remained unallocated, leading to its non-utilization. To fully appreciate the extent of the agrarian crisis one needs to examine the productivity patterns of key commodities, especially during the fast-track years (see below).

*Food security under the fast-track programme*

For a variety of reasons, food security has been a perennial problem since the year 2000. As wages failed to keep pace with inflation, access to food was reduced for the ordinary person. This was worsened by unviable pricing policies (and price controls) that created shortages of basic commodities, as well as policies that restricted the movement of grain. Because of price controls on basic commodities, most commodities could not be obtained on the formal markets and were available only on the black market at much higher prices. Restrictions placed on the movement of maize grain in 2003 also resulted in shortages.

While the area under maize increased between 2001 and 2005, and from 2007 to 2008, the total yield decreased during the period, signifying a further decrease in yield per hectare compared to the 1980s and 1990s. The acreage under sorghum was comparable to that in the 1980s, but the area under millets decreased considerably (Table 3.10). Zimbabwe has gone through consistent food deficits in the nine years of the fast-track programme; the humanitarian crisis is reflected by the fact that over two million Zimbabweans were food insecure in 2008, and this rose to 3.8 million people during October–December, reaching 5.1 million in January 2009 (FAO and WFP, 2009).

**Table 3.10: National crop productivity trends**

| Crop | Area ('000 hectares) | | | Yield (t/ha) | | | Production ('000 tonnes) | | |
|---|---|---|---|---|---|---|---|---|---|
| | 2006/07 | 2007/08 | 2008/09 | 2006/07 | 2007/08 | 2008/09 | 2006/07 | 2007/08 | 2008/09 |
| Maize | 1,446 | 1,730 | 1,426 | 0.66 | 0.28 | 0.80 | 953 | 496 | 1,140 |
| Sorghum | 255 | 291 | 362 | 0.30 | 0.26 | 0.43 | 75 | 75 | 156 |
| Millets | 194 | 193 | 238 | 0.26 | 0.20 | 0.31 | 50 | 37 | 74 |
| Wheat | | 10.3 | 4 | | 3.00 | 2.88 | | 31 | 12 |
| All cereals | | 2,224.3 | 2,030 | | 0.29 | 0.68 | | 639 | 1,382 |

*Source:* FAO and WFP (2008 and 2009).

## Cotton and tobacco production

Production suffered across the range of commodities, where land utilization in any farming season is generally around 40 per cent in the new resettlement areas. The most conspicuous production losses have been in tobacco, which was a major foreign-currency earner. By the end of 2000, Zimbabwe had become the world's third-largest producer of flue-cured tobacco. If these levels of production had been maintained and the current world tobacco price applied, the country would have earned at least US$1 billion per season, especially with new markets in the Far East, particularly China. The highest tobacco yields were achieved in 2000 when 236,946 tonnes of flue-cured tobacco were sold. The area put to tobacco and the output in 2001/02 had declined by 56 per cent compared to the 1990s average, and continued to decline during the fast-track period (Table 3.11). Total tobacco production fell dramatically after 2001 and showed no sign of recovery after then (FAO and WFP, 2009). Tobacco output in the resettlement sector grew from 5,000 tonnes in 1999/2000 to 16,628 tonnes in the 2003 season. Increased tobacco production in resettlement areas suggests some potential for new farmers in the agricultural export sector.

## Livestock production patterns

There has been a shift in cattle ownership in the country linked to the fast-track land-reform programme (Table 3.12). Since 2000, there has been a decrease in the number of cattle in the A2 and large commercial farms, with increases in the communal areas. Communal areas now hold the bulk of cattle in the country as there has been a significant drop in numbers within the large-scale commercial farming areas. This is a problem, given the fragile nature of the ecology of most

**Table 3.11: Cotton and tobacco production trends, 2000–2009**

| | | Cotton | | | Tobacco | |
|---|---|---|---|---|---|---|
| Growing season | Area | Yield (kg/ha) | Production (mt) | Area (ha) | Yield (kg/ha) | Production (mt) |
| 1999/2000 | 415,000 | 850 | 353,000 | 85,000 | 2770 | 236,000 |
| 2000/01 | 397,000 | 840 | 337,000 | 76,000 | 2650 | 202,000 |
| 2001/02 | 229,000 | 850 | 195,000 | 71,000 | 2330 | 166,000 |
| 2002/03 | 282,000 | 850 | 240,000 | 54,000 | 1510 | 82,000 |
| 2003/04 | 389,000 | 850 | 331,000 | 41,000 | 1580 | 65,000 |
| 2004/05 | 350,000 | 560 | 198,000 | 56,000 | 1330 | 75,000 |
| 2005/06 | 300,000 | 860 | 258,000 | 27,000 | 2030 | 55,000 |
| 2006/07 | 354,000 | 840 | 300,000 | 53,000 | 2160 | 79,000 |
| 2007/08 | 431,000 | 520 | 226,000 | 62,000 | 1100 | 70,000 |
| 2008/09 | 338,000 | 730 | 247,000 | 48,000 | 1330 | 64,000 |

*Source:* FAO and WFP (2009).

**Table 3.12: Livestock numbers by sector, 2006**

| Sector | Cattle | Sheep | Goats | Pigs | Donkeys | Horses |
|---|---|---|---|---|---|---|
| A1 | 311,556 | 20,745 | 100,790 | 7,636 | 20,573 | 202 |
| A2 | 651,436 | 79,282 | 377,524 | 44,240 | 107,846 | 934 |
| Communal | 3,311,913 | 202,406 | 2,407,764 | 148,268 | 240,907 | 27 |
| Resettlement | 500,494 | 16,652 | 148,476 | 7,133 | 21,490 | 59 |
| Small-scale | 210,918 | 13,637 | 103,414 | 10,830 | 6,738 | 14 |
| Grand total | 4,986,318 | 333,721 | 3,137,969 | 218,108 | 397,553 | 1,236 |

*Source:* FAO and WFP (2009)

communal areas owing to a lack of grazing land and water, and, following the almost complete decimation of the LSCF sector, the livestock in this sector have now been categorized under the A1 and A2 resettlement schemes.

### 3.6.5 Lessons from the fast-track land-reform programme

*Misunderstanding of farming systems complementarities*
The impact of the fast-track programme has been much wider than the architects of the programme had in mind. Their thinking was that reorganization would affect only commercial farmers. Government ministers, politicians and government-aligned academics argued that, in any case, smallholders produced the bulk of the maize, cotton, and so on, and therefore deserve the land. It is true that the smallholder farmers produced the bulk of the maize and cotton, but the sector also needed a functional commercial sector to balance food production and produce in other sectors. It was stated that white farmers had in fact abandoned maize production in the 1980s and were producing only for

livestock (Moyo, 2001). On the basis of these arguments, they reasoned that land reform would not affect the economy and would actually enhance it with more producers. As shown above, this did not turn out as expected.

In general, there was a progressive deterioration in the commercial farming sector at a time when smallholders in communal areas were struggling equally. Farmers who moved into the resettlement areas, together with communal, old resettlement and small-scale commercial farmers, failed to fill the production gap created through the forced departure of white commercial farmers. The prime movers of agriculture (Rukuni *et al.*, 2006) have been decimated, including the research and development services, with equipment going to waste, and dams and irrigation infrastructure being either underutilized or rarely serviced.

## Misconstruing land ownership with agricultural success

When we examine food insecurity in Zimbabwe from 2000, it points to the multi-dimensional impact of the fast-track land-reform programme and the politics surrounding it. Although new settlers felt empowered in the early period, up to 2002, the positive expectations associated with the initial land takeover have waned. The hardships associated with minimum support to agriculture in a context of the country's inability to raise private-sector resources for farming has affected the confidence of the producers. It has emerged that access to land is not the same as making it productive: it takes much more than redistributing land to ensure that it is used productively.

While there are pockets of managing and success, the new farmers have generally struggled for a variety of reasons to do with continued conflicts over land ownership, hurried survey and demarcation (which led to mistakes), inadequate state support at individual farmer level, lack of farming resources (especially tillage and harvesters), shortage of labour, inadequate extension when new farmers needed to manage large landholdings, pilferage of products because of insecurity, inadequate irrigation support, poor pricing of products controlled by government (especially maize and wheat), transport bottlenecks, as well as the effects of global warming – for instance, lack of planning to mitigate droughts or manage too much rain, as in the 2007/8 season, one with great potential (the government had called it the 'Mother of All Farming Seasons' in the national press), which ended up being a disappointment in terms of production.

## Inequitable distribution of land

*The Economist* quotes land and agrarian expert Sam Moyo as conceding that at least 15,500 beneficiaries were part of the security apparatus of government (police, army, CIO) as well as officials from the then ruling party, ZANU(PF).[12]

---

[12] 'Whose land?', *The Economist*, 5 March 2009, <http://www.economist.com/node/13240812>.

Civil servants, judges, ministers and members of parliament were also given priority in the allocations. Although applications for land were open to any Zimbabwean who wanted to farm, allocations were made by a committee heavily patronized by ruling-party functionaries represented by war veterans and district co-ordinating committees of the party. It is on this basis that the 'open application' process can be qualified in political terms, as potential beneficiaries outside the party could have been left out of the programme. For instance, farm-workers, women, youths and people from districts without commercial farms received least consideration during the allocations. Moreover, there were localized incidences when people who were perceived to belong to another political party or were affiliated to organizations perceived to have been opposed to land reform were not considered, even when they had expressed a desire to be settled.

### Key challenges on the farms

It must be stated that the necessity for land reform in Zimbabwe cannot be questioned, given the manifestly inequitable land-distribution patterns before independence. However, this should have been the rallying call for mastering the energies of all Zimbabweans to implement a well-conceived land-reform programme. The Utete Report (Zimbabwe, 2003) noted that the fast-track land-reform was dominated by corrupt tendencies, opportunism, discrimination based on political party affiliation, and self-enrichment tendencies by senior officials. This abuse of political office for unfair gain in the land-reform programme has made critics within and outside Zimbabwe roundly condemn the programme.

Most of the critics were opposed to the speed of the programme and the violent manner of the exercise. Some of those who had forcibly occupied farms took over not only the land but also the farmhouses, confiscated equipment and livestock, as well as seizing produce in contravention of the state's own laws targeting only land (Zimbabwe, 2003; Marongwe, 2008; Sadomba, 2008; Matondi, 2008). Furthermore, there was no intent to harness 'the skills and farm-management capacity of the former land owners', but if this had been done, it could perhaps have made land reform different. The result was that skilled and experienced farm-owners and farm-workers were immediately lost to the sector. A new breed of farmers, some experienced in communal farming, others without any idea of what farming entailed, took charge of productive land. The euphoria of owning a piece of land, of grabbing a farmhouse, of seizing a farmer's produce and household property engulfed the farming areas.

A new breed of people termed the 'pirates of the land' emerged who were on a perpetual search for new farms as their own booty. This group was usually 'supported' at the highest level or simply exploited the policy gap; they were people with the machinery and connections to convince the administrators to give them land. In general, they could not have been more than ten per cent of the total beneficiaries (Moyo and Yeros, 2005). They could even go to the courts to contest land takeovers and were ready to use force by mobilizing their own eviction teams. They engaged in the political mischief of wanting to harvest other people's crops. This form of pirating in the new farms made the newly resettled areas places for the fittest survivors, leaving women vulnerable. Their targets were not just white-owned farms but also A1 farms that they thought were 'nicer' than the ones they already had.

The result was that the fast-tracked commercial areas became places for competition for access to resources rather than competition for production and use of the land. If the energy displayed in fighting for access to implements, farmhouses, the best farm location, etc., had been translated into intense production, Zimbabwe's agriculture would have been transformed. Yet, when questioned about poor production, the new farmers gave numerous excuses and, almost every year, a self-serving defence line as to why they were not performing: 'We are new, there are no implements, there are no inputs.'

## Fear of self-correction by government

Government did not pay attention to serious self-assessment and evaluation of the impact of the programme on production. The land audits commissioned were not accompanied by serious attention to the many anomalies identified at the policy level and in the field. As a result, problems identified went uncorrected, production continued to go down, farmers continued to suffer from disjointed support, etc. In addition, while government defined the tenure system in the form of leases for A2 farmers and permits for A1 farmers, these remain just paper policies. Many financial institutions still have no confidence in the land-ownership arrangements, so there has not been any substantial investment in the resettlement areas. As the government audits have illustrated, there is scope for restructuring, refinement and improvement. A huge constraint to agricultural recovery was the inadequate budget allocations to the administration of the reform programme, caused, among other reasons, by poor planning and untimely requests for money. A number of those that received inputs and subsidized fuel 'round-tripped' them, selling them at inflated parallel-market prices.

A major problem has been weak policy communication on land-reform matters, especially on the process and outcomes. Those responsible for the land-reform policy were very strong at defending it, but developed cold feet when it came to policy correction or rationalization processes. For instance, many of the land audits (full and partial) were not published in full, and recommendations have been only partially adopted.[13] Not surprisingly, therefore, the Global Political

---

[13] Those by Flora Buka in 2002, by the Utete Commission in 2003, and by the Ministry of Lands and Rural Resettlement and SIRDC in 2006.

Agreement (GPA) identified the need to bring the land-reform programme to closure as an urgent issue. A Land Commission is proposed in the GPA whose mandate is to correct the anomalies identified, such as multiple ownership of farms and dealing with the issue of security of tenure.

### The land-reform programme and the decongestion of communal areas

Another major justification for the redistribution of land was to reduce land pressure in the crowded Communal Lands, and their decongestion was a central objective of the reforms. With chiefs and local communities complaining that the programme had been hijacked by undeserving urban elements, civil servants and elites (Zimbabwe, 2003; Sadomba, 2008), it is questionable whether the exercise has decongested the communal areas as expected. Government assumed that simply targeting people for land allocation would lead to automatic de-congestion. In reality, decongestion has not occurred, as civil servants and urban people with greater negotiating capacity had greater access to the land.

Decongestion of the communal areas, though desirable and rational, is a very static concept. It assumes that uplifting people from one locality to another would on its own alleviate the challenges presented by overcrowding. However, in the absence of a deliberate economic-development policy for the Communal Lands, decongestion will not achieve the poverty-reduction objectives of the fast-track land-reform programme. In fact, during the programme, resources were targeted at the newly resettled areas, implying a progressive decline in the capacity and quality of agriculture in the communal areas.

Sukume et al. (2004) concluded that there is an inherent limitation in reducing overcrowding in communal areas, given the finite nature of the land resource. There is, in fact, a limit to the extent to which a programme such as the fast-track land-reform programme can achieve low densities in communal areas via land redistribution. Households in newly resettled areas still maintain homes in communal areas, which effectively undermines productivity, as little investment is made in the new resettlement areas in the absence of security of tenure.

### The fast-track programme and political, economic and social stability

The socio-economic objectives of the fast-track land-reform programme have been the most difficult to achieve. In fact, it was not until 2009 that space for political activity was opened. The fast-track programme actually brought political instability, given the differences amongst Zimbabweans on its methodology, as well as the personal interests that crept into the programme; the former ruling party ring-fenced commercial farms as their own territories. Furthermore, the litigation brought by the former land-owners, who naturally took government to local, regional and international justice forums, had the effect of perpetuating political hostility. The government reacted by closing political space and creating further alienation amongst Zimbabweans and from the international development community. Hence, the political environment of the fast-track programme was not conducive for investment in agriculture.

The fast-track land-reform programme contributed to the disruption of society, and brought fear, anxiety and uncertainty to community life in Zimbabwe. Apart from the social disruptions associated with the programme, the process of removing land-occupiers without offer letters created further social instability. Families were separated, as men and boys occupied farms, leaving women behind in the communal areas. Farm-worker communities have perhaps been the greatest casualties of the fast-track programme, as many had to endure accusations of being aliens, of being saboteurs supporting the white farmers, and of being members of opposition political parties. Though some were members of GAPWUZ, they were unintended victims as government pushed for reforms.

The stabilization of land resettlement in Zimbabwe has taken longer than with similar programmes in other countries. Though the fast-paced programme was declared to have officially ended in 2002, it has remained open-ended. It must be noted that difficulties in the first years of any resettlement exercise are to be expected, and match historical patterns in other countries. Studies of a longitudinal database in Shamva showed that welfare levels are almost universally lower following resettlement than they were before (Kinsey, 1998). The period following resettlement is one of stress and adjustment from which most households, but not all, will recover. There is then an upturn as farmers complete the post-relocation adjustment process and begin to reap benefits from their enhanced resource base. As experience accumulates and collaborative efforts begin, benefits continue to grow, often quite rapidly. However, a crucial factor is the degree of growth in the national economy. Unless growth is dynamic enough to absorb a growing rural population, the increase in the size of resettled households will tend to bring down the standard of living.

*Women lose out*

While the government stated in October 2000 that it would ensure a 20 per cent quota for women under the fast-track land-reform programme, by the official end of the programme in 2002, the number of women allocated land was low countrywide. As shown in Table 3.13, female-headed households who benefited under the model A1 scheme constituted 18 per cent of the total number of households, while female beneficiaries under the model A2 scheme amounted to only 12 per cent of the total. Within the A1 model, Mashonaland East allocated the highest percentage, 24 per cent, to women, while in the A2 model, only Matabeleland South, where many men are working in neighbouring countries, achieved the 20 per cent quota target.

While women were free to apply for land under both models, those interested

**Table 3.13: Land allocation patterns by gender, by province, 2003**

| Province | Model A1[a] Males No. | % | Females No. | % | Model A2[b] Males No. | % | Females No. | % |
|---|---|---|---|---|---|---|---|---|
| Midlands | 14,800 | 82 | 3,198 | 18 | 338 | 95 | 17 | 5 |
| Masvingo | 19,026 | 84 | 3,644 | 16 | 709 | 92 | 64 | 8 |
| Mashonaland Central | 12,986 | 88 | 1,770 | 12 | 1,469 | 87 | 215 | 13 |
| Mashonaland West | 21,782 | 81 | 5,270 | 19 | 1,777 | 89 | 226 | 11 |
| Mashonaland East | 12,967 | 76 | 3,992 | 24 | * | * | * | * |
| Matabeleland South | 7,754 | 87 | 1,169 | 13 | 215 | 79 | 56 | 21 |
| Matabeleland North | 7,919 | 84 | 1,490 | 16 | 574 | 83 | 121 | 17 |
| Manicaland | 9,572 | 82 | 2,190 | 18 | 961 | 91 | 97 | 9 |
| TOTAL | 106,986 | 82 | 22,723 | 18 | 6,043 | 88 | 796 | 12 |

[a]Peasant farmers. [b]Commercial farmers. *Figures not available.
*Source:* Zimbabwe (2003: 40).

in the A1 model had to apply through their traditional leadership if they lived in Communal Lands, or through councillors if they lived elsewhere. In these structures, patriarchal and customary practices discriminated against women. Furthermore, under the A2 model, applicants were required to have resources (human and material) to develop and utilize the land effectively, a condition that disqualified most women from applying and getting the land.

Significantly, the Presidential Land Review Committee, appointed in 2003, recommended a different gender share in the allocation of land, with a quota of at least 40 per cent of the land allocations to women, especially in A1 areas. In addition, it proposed a quota of 40 per cent of funding to be reserved for women and other new farmers, for credit and other purposes.

## 3.7 Land, Agriculture and Rural Development, 2009–2010

The GPA signed between the three main political parties in September 2008 that led to the Inclusive Government formed on 13 February 2009 provided an opportunity to resolve the contentious aspects of land reform. The Inclusive Government immediately formulated a Short-Term Emergency Recovery Programme, known as STERP;[14] it was operationalized by a 100-day programme for ministries to meet specific targets. For the Ministry of Lands, the targets were to secure the farming environment, carry out a land audit, and secure tenure and the provision of support services for new farmers. The targets for the agriculture ministry revolved around mobilization and the provision of inputs for key agricultural enterprises (Zimbabwe, 2009b).

The implementation of the targeted issues under the Inclusive Government

[14] <http://www.zimtreasury.org/downloads/31.pdf>.

has been very slow. The modalities of the land audit have still not been agreed upon. In the absence of title to land, no sustainable financing can be invested in agriculture, as has been the case over the last eleven years since the start of the land-redistribution exercise. The political struggle around land is far from over.

## 3.8 Strategies for Agricultural Recovery and Rural Development

### 3.8.1 Prerequisites

As long as Zimbabwe does not resolve its political problems, the land-reform question cannot be addressed properly, and agricultural and rural development will be virtually impossible. Therefore, a new people-driven and people-oriented constitution, followed by democratic and transparent elections, is a pre-requisite. The new government that comes into place after elections carried out under a new constitution has to choose clearly a development path based on solidarity, equity, sustainability and co-operation from the bottom up.

The common people in the towns and the rural areas have to claim back primacy over their development. True development based on the sharing of resources, equality and solidarity can only occur if people join hands and take the lead in this process, which is too important, and potentially detrimental, to leave to politicians and professionals. It needs a dynamic, participatory and radical democracy built from below and not imposed from above.[15] This notion has to be the basis of all policy formulation, implementation, monitoring and evaluation processes, and will have to pervade any action. Making Zimbabwe's agriculture work must start with a favourable socio-political climate, adequate governance and macroeconomic fundamentals, underpinned by robust and responsive institutions (Fig. 3.2).

The four main policy objectives in rebuilding agriculture after the land-reform struggles must include the following:

- *Agriculture must improve food security and the livelihoods of the poor:* To sustain the popular legitimacy of the land-reform programme, and to improve the quality of human development, the agrarian-reform strategy must be supported by a social-protection programme. The objective of the strategy is to improve the productive capacities and self-sustenance of the poor as they settle on the land.
- *Agriculture for community and self-employment:* In order to address problems of unemployment, agriculture has a role to play in terms of self-employment. In Zimbabwe, with two million communal farmers – 71,000 in old resettlement schemes, 145,775 in the A1 resettlement areas, 16,386 in the A2 resettlement areas, and around 80,000 in the

---

[15] ANSA Principle No. 10: see Chapter 1.

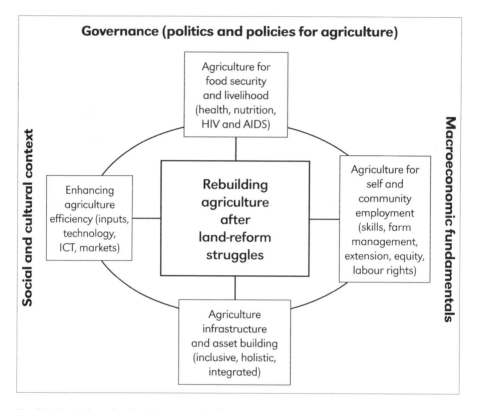

**Fig. 3.2: Agriculture for development after land-reform struggles**

farm-worker community – agriculture can directly absorb 2.5 million
people. If those who work in the agricultural services sectors (finance,
tertiary institutions, extension, manufacturing, retail, etc.) are added
to the numbers directly working in agriculture, then a significant
population of Zimbabweans is dependent on agriculture. Therefore,
issues such as skills, farm management, and the labour rights of workers
in agriculture need to be addressed.

• *Enhancing agricultural efficiency to better the yields and increase
  output*: Opening the inputs markets and removing the monopoly of
  the state, which has used inputs for its political objectives within the
  context of land reform, must be a priority. The government must also
  not look for quick-fix solutions, such as the use of GMOs in seed
  multiplication, but must opt for conventional breeding as well as using
  indigenous hybrids that local farmers are better able to control. The
  farmers must also have access to technology, water resources, labour
  that is fairly remunerated, credit facilities, and subsidies targeting the
  poor where necessary to boost yields and outputs.

• *Rebuilding agricultural assets and infrastructure*: Zimbabwe's world-class agriculture infrastructure has deteriorated in the last nine years and will require focused attention. However, farmers now possess inadequate assets for them to be able to translate their labour into increased production. For this reason, government will have to build the assets of the poor. At the same time, smallholder agricultural support programmes (inputs support, marketing, pricing, etc.) should play a critical social as well as economic policy function.

Agriculture will most likely benefit from other policy reforms in the area of decentralization to address the heterogeneity of rain-fed agricultural systems (World Bank, 2008). When generating employment and raising income streams through agriculture must be a priority, additional employment has to be generated through the development of labour-intensive, small- and medium-scale rural industries, trade and services. Broad-based farm mechanization, in which allocations are based on the competencies of the farmers, is a must if commercial production is to be revived. Appropriate technologies that are available for smallholders to produce and market must be part of any deal for agricultural growth, because these are the farmers likely to reduce food insecurity and hunger in the short to medium term.

### 3.8.2 Need for a comprehensive land policy

Zimbabwe will need to look again at its land policy, given the drastic changes that have occurred to the agrarian base. The racial structure of land ownership has changed, and so have the land sizes per beneficiary – generally decreasing from an average of 2,000 hectares to less than 600 hectares in the A2 scheme, with increases in land-holding sizes for the majority poor from less than one hectare to an average of twelve hectares (Matondi, 2001; Moyo, 1995; Zimbabwe, 2003; Rukuni *et al.*, 2006). These fundamental demographic, land-area and institutional changes require new benchmarks for land policy. It also has to be recognized that the land changes have been accompanied by conflicts and problems of governance on the farms and outside. Given that the land issue became the primary focus of political contests nationally and internationally, there is a need for a clear policy position on land. Box 3.2 explores some of the key building blocks of such a land policy.

During the fast-track period it seemed that the main vision for land reform was defined in implicitly political terms, relying on the strong moral grounds for returning land to the historically disadvantaged black people who had endured years of neglect. What Zimbabwe needs is a vision for a land policy that outlives generations. Such a vision should provide the basis for developing an overall framework that defines the key measures required to address the critical issues of land-tenure security, land administration, access to land, land-

---

**Box 3.2: Strategic goals of Zimbabwe's future national land policy and plan**

**Equity and justice issues**

- Address historical and potential conflicts, inequities and injustices based on race, social status, gender, political affiliation, and other such differences. Ensuring access to land for all Zimbabweans that will make it possible and affordable to access farm land and residential land.

**Tenure insecurity**

- Policy must ensure security of tenure for all Zimbabweans, regardless of their system of land-holding, the aim being to bring confidence to the land-reform process and to resolve questions of tenure insecurity.

**Enhance optimal land use**

- Ensure that land transferred will be used productively for the production of food, secure employment, and to produce agricultural commodities needed for backstopping the economy.

**Reduce poverty and misery**

- Reduce poverty in rural areas and contribute to economic growth through capital formation, addressing income inequalities, provision of basic needs and more secure livelihoods.

**Strengthen land management**

- Streamline land administration and information as part of enhancing land reforms. This includes upgrading the cadastral and land-registry systems, and carrying out a land audit as part of a broader land-management information system. The expectation is that these elements will be integrated with the financial services grid for all categories of land, including land held under traditional tenure.

**National healing and stability**

- Without peace in rural areas there can be no political stability or economic prosperity. The land-reform programme must be a basis for national healing and stability as it was central to the social and political problems that Zimbabwe faced. Dialogue should inform the way forward.

---

use planning, restitution of historical injustices, environmental degradation, conflicts, an outdated legal framework, institutional framework and information management.

Through the land policy, the main goal should be to build justice, to enhance national healing, to provide stability, and to contribute to economic growth in the country. The land policy emerges within the context of a highly polarized environment, where Zimbabweans have been divided. The current land patterns demonstrate a changed agrarian base, where issues of racial land ownership have been addressed. Race should no longer be a cause of insecurity and should not feature as central to Zimbabwe's political and economic progress. The land policy should rather deal with how to get the best out of the land-reform programme, focusing on land tenure, sustainable use and administration.

### 3.8.3 Addressing land tenure and land rights

The Inclusive Government's constitution-making process should aim to provide a lasting solution to the land issue in Zimbabwe. The process of addressing the land issue in the new constitution should entail the following:

• Look critically at the Lancaster House Constitution as regards the land issue, including all the laws or Acts of Parliament passed after independence to address the land question, identifying what is still relevant to put in the new constitution from all these enactments.

• Consider the land audits commissioned after independence (Rukuni, Buka, Utete, among others), taking into account the recommendations made by each.

It will also be useful to consider the recommendations made by other land conferences held in Zimbabwe involving communal/commercial farmers and non-state actors at large, with particular reference to recommendations made by the National Working People's Convention of 26–28 February 1999, a year before the fast-track programme. Among the recommendations on the land issue made by that convention were that:

Land redistribution and resettlement should be taken out of the hands of politicians and be made a social and economic issue in the hands of the people themselves. To this end, without further delay, democratic structures, transparent procedures and clear criteria should be adopted to guide the process of land redistribution and resettlement. ... Democratic committees should be set up involving Chiefs/headmen, District Administrators, Provincial Administrators, Local Authorities, grassroots organizations, Farmers' organizations, Civic organizations, trade unions, NGOs, etc. With the help of technocrats [AGRITEX], critical gender sensitization is essential [Recommendation 5].

The key political parties agreed in the GPA that land reform after 2000 was irreversible.[16] In the same document they also agreed to work towards producing a national land policy, taking into consideration land tenure, land administration, and compensation for acquired land, as well as looking at investment and productivity on commercial and other categories of land in Zimbabwe. The land audit proposed by the GPA is a first step towards designing an effective land policy and should help in the consideration of issues that underpin injustices. The land policy should then create the conditions for government and stakeholders to design strategies to help to revive agriculture as well as to grow the economy.

Lastly, the consolidated land audit report should be subjected to intense scrutiny and critical discussion at land conferences at local, district, regional

---

[16] 'Agreement between the Zimbabwe African National Union-Patriotic Front (ZANU(PF)) and the two Movement for Democratic Change (MDC) Formations, on Resolving the Challenges Facing Zimbabwe' ['Global Political Agreement', GPA], 15 September 2008, Clause 5.5.

and national levels involving all stakeholders and interested parties. The recommendations from these conferences should feed into a new land policy as a basis for reviving agriculture.

A priority area for Zimbabwe is the completion of the judicial framework governing property rights, especially land. The country will need to come up with clear, unambiguous tenurial regimes. While the leasehold tenure arrangement was a first stage in clarifying the relationship between the state and its citizens, a second is to give real land rights to the producers as attempted through leasehold policy. However, the country needs to move to more secure forms of tenure to give confidence to the producers. This means that the government must not play a prominent interfering role in the lives of producers, who must be provided with secure ownership and the necessary public support to produce for the nation. In other words, all farmers in Zimbabwe should enjoy security of tenure defined in the form of a basket of rights that Rukuni (pers. comm.) outlines as:

a)  user rights – defining what use the land can be put to;
b)  transfer rights – so as to be clear on the rights to sub-divide, sell, bequeath, and so on;
c)  exclusion and inclusion rights – to clarify who else may have access to that land and for what;
d)  enforcement rights or the rights to protection by the state – to clarify the administrative and judicial provisions that will intervene, and that are available for the land user to appeal to if they feel any of their rights are being violated.

While diversity and differentiation will have to be celebrated in agriculture, government and the people will have to be aware that new forms of dualism and enclavity will (re)emerge. Firstly, there is the danger that a new upper class of A2 and large-scale commercial farmers will fill the vacuum left by the formerly white enclave. Government, in particular a neo-liberal or an 'old-boys' one, might be tempted to ring-fence and unduly support such a group, and hence perpetuate dualism instead of focusing on creating forward and backward linkages between agricultural production by the masses and other economic sectors (industry and commerce).

Secondly, there is a danger that in a society where water and irrigation will become increasingly important, a new elite with access to and control over irrigation water will emerge, supported by government for the same reasons as above. While it will be government's responsibility and duty to develop and make use to the maximum of the country's irrigation potential, a dichotomy in its policies, where it gives priority to irrigated agriculture to the detriment of developing the agricultural potential of the other 90 per cent of the arable land and grazing lands, has to be prevented.

### 3.8.4 The need for technical land administration

In order to be able to formulate a meaningful agricultural policy, insight into the underlying situation is needed. Moreover, it is necessary to look into the whole land-redistribution process of the past years to prevent multiple ownership, etc., and hence prevent the birth of a new crony-capitalist elite.

The land audit should consider the idea that tenure be granted on a 99-year-lease basis, and only to the people who actually work the land (no absentee landlords); that land should not be turned into a commodity which is freely available on the market, but that transfers should be carefully monitored by independent, decentralized land committees to prevent speculation and accumulation in the hands of a few. Land should not be sold to foreign nationals, companies or governments, particularly if they want to acquire it for the production of biofuel, export crops, or even for food for the North. Such is the importance of national land sovereignty that it should be grounded in the new constitution.

To this end, Zimbabweans must review existing land administration structures. Land resources must be regarded as a key security and strategic asset for the nation and must be used as such. A new integrated system of land administration in the form of a Land Commission should be set up as an independent agency regulated by the government. It should co-ordinate all activities to do with land issues, and should rationalize access to land and its utilization while promoting and facilitating land-tenure lease variations that enhance tenure security and land-use optimization. An important concern of this system should be to guarantee the physical security of leases and their infrastructure and equipment as well as their products (livestock and crops) in collaboration with relevant institutions. This should be adequately funded and well staffed, and there should be public access to its information and reports on land control, use and transfers. A well-enforced government regulatory framework is required to encourage production, hence the need for integrated land management to ensure adequate provision of land for both human settlement and wildlife conservation. In the broader public domain, and within the political parties forming the Inclusive Government, land provisions in the GPA and the proposed Land Commission have not been interrogated. It is hoped that in future Zimbabweans will debate the merits and demerits of the Commission against the backdrop of a need to design an institutional framework that works best for agriculture and the economy.

### 3.8.5 A land law for Zimbabwe

The government has had to rely mainly on the Land Acquisition Act to guide almost all aspects of land reform. This is not enough, because the land-acquisition instrument serves mainly acquisition matters and does not address other elements that constitute the land policy. It is for this reason that it would be desirable to have a Land Act that addresses all land issues. Most of the benchmarks alluded to in the land policy will need legal back-up so that litigants and legal authorities will have the necessary tools for adjudication. The process of making laws is basically a trade-off between different interest groups; resolving land disputes should therefore be a collective process to deal with all disputes ranging from land administration (duplication of roles) and on-farm disputes for all categories of land. However, to deal with such conflicts requires clear and robust legislation, which needs to be defined within the constitution together with aspects that deal with the Bill of Rights and property rights.

### 3.8.6 Agricultural support to small farmers

In order to build a new agrarian structure, there is a need to strengthen the prime movers of agricultural development, on which the ability to bring about an agricultural revolution is critically dependent (Box 3.3). The bottom line is that the ultimate success of agriculture hinges crucially on the ability of the government to launch a 'fast-track smallholder improvement programme' that can turn the formerly landless people into farmers who produce an economic surplus for the market. The centrepiece of the revolution is the mobilization of farmers, in particular new settlers, who must be equipped with the tools and knowledge to increase food, livestock and cash-crop production, and rural employment, which, in turn, will generate effective demand for food and products from the industrial sector.

Without question, subdividing large farms into small-scale family farms can help put more people to work in rural areas. However, households without adequate land or sufficient resources to meet their family's food-security needs from farming will need to find off-farm jobs in the private sector or in government-financed rural employment programmes with support from food safety nets. Nevertheless, it should be remembered that the agricultural-technology-driven model of development is applicable only to rural households who have access to adequate land and the resources (credit, draught animals, markets) to adopt new technology and employ the available family labour in farming.

A comprehensive development plan, from village to ward to district and province, has to be developed and decided upon with the maximum involvement and decisive power of the people at the lowest level, based on and with input from professionals. Consultations to define what this 'agriculture for development' entails will need to include farming unions, development agencies, rural development activists, farmers, and aspiring businesspeople (for services, trades and industries). At the same time, government – with the private sector, where appropriate – has to be in the forefront of defining the agricultural agenda for Zimbabwe.

Ideally, every district and ward should have a multidisciplinary team of professionals and professional institutions overseeing rural development, anchored

---

**Box 3.3: The prime movers in transforming land reform to agrarian reform**

**Land-tenure development**

- Land acquisition and redistribution has been done and needs to be concluded. Within this framework, the issues of agrarian reform and questions of tenure security remain outstanding but are key drivers of change.

**Human-capital development**

- Identifying and attracting capable farmers and policies that discourage incapable farmers. Identifying resettled farmers willing to undergo on-farm training. There is also a need for professional, managerial and technical skills produced by investments in schools, agricultural colleges, faculties of agriculture and on-the-job training and experience. Human development should develop self-standing business people in the commercial farms.

**Sustained growth of biological capital**

- Development of genetic and husbandry improvements of crops, livestock, and forests. The natural heritage must be protected in the farms, which requires development of appropriate policies to encourage environmental stewardship.

**Infrastructure development**

- Physical capital investments in dams, irrigation and roads. Synchronize the physical infrastructure of power, feeder roads, public transportation, communication, restocking the livestock herd, revamping veterinary institutions and the revival of on-farm agricultural research centres.

**Institutional performance**

- Enhancing the performance of institutions such as marketing, credit, research and extension, and settlement.

**Policy environment**

- Recent political development and economic policies such as STERP, the 100-day plan, and programmes of the Inclusive Government require support. Farmers now have incentives to produce in a liberalized environment. However, there is a need for political support for agriculture over the long haul.

**Technology revolution**

- Invest in new technology produced by public and private investments in agricultural research or imported from the global research system and adapted to local conditions. Restore seeds, fertilizer, machinery and irrigation, developing research and development so that industry is capable of restoring local technology.

*Source:* Adapted from Rukuni *et al.* (2010).

on the key agricultural enterprise of that area. The core should be agricultural competencies in the area of research, extension services, and enterprise development. Next to that, competencies are needed in backward and forward linkages in order to identify and stimulate small- and medium-scale industrialization, trades and services. Government's service institutions – such as the GMB, Agribank, DDF, etc. – that were already decentralized should be revamped in the light of a new agricultural policy responding to the changed agrarian base. Agricultural extension services and local research and training institutions should also be subject to the scrutiny and control of their stakeholders, i.e. the farmers.

Agricultural development will have to be, at minimum, inclusive, holistic, decentralized and sustainable, while a precondition will be completing land redistribution. Appropriate land sizes will have to be variable, depending on different local conditions, while aimed at achieving broad, sustainable land use and land development. The selection of resettled farmers and their allocation will have to be done by bottom-up, democratic, representative, stakeholder organs. Women farmers' and women farm-workers' interests should receive extra attention and priority. Farm-workers could be provided with residential land, some land to produce their own food, and/or a choice of alternative employment possibilities as a farm-worker, or as a resettled farmer, or in local employment (local industry, trade or services), or as an independent entrepreneur. In an alternative, new rural-development policy, these conditions will have to be created: a place outside the commercial farms where they can live, grow their own food if necessary, and look for/create employment; and preference to become resettled farmers.

Stimulating agricultural development cannot be seen as a technical process of simply 'getting the prime movers going'. Agricultural development is much more than increasing the yields of separate pieces of plots. Sustainable agriculture has to look at a much wider physical area as an interlocked ecosystem which will have to be very carefully handled to get extra yield for human use without disturbing its balance. Hence, it will be necessary for each district, ward or catchment area to study and analyse its specific potential as a sustainable agricultural-production base. Based on the established potential, and taking into consideration the human resources, the area could then be divided into viable small to medium farming enterprises for redistribution. The process will be less complicated in still-to-be-settled areas. In communal areas and those already resettled, such a pattern could be pursued only with a medium-term perspective, which will require a locally driven, bottom-up approach, with the democratic involvement of all stakeholders, supported by a multidisciplinary, holistically oriented team of professionals.

### 3.8.7 Climate and ecology

The climate and surrounding ecological system influence and limit agricultural options and potential as agriculture is an inextricable part of the local ecology. If Zimbabwe's climate, and therefore its ecology, changes in the future, adverse effects of up to 30 per cent loss in agricultural revenue can be expected in the region. This would, however, not be a blanket reduction; the hotter and drier regions, and those with little or no possibility of mitigation through irrigation, will be those most affected. However, as the ecological system will also change, adaptations will have to go far beyond putting in a few extra dams or introducing more drought-resistant crops. Government policies will have to anticipate these major climatological, ecological and agricultural changes, which means that agricultural research, extension, training and education institutions must not only receive adequate funding but will also have to take these changing conditions as a starting point. An ecological and agricultural audit will have to be carried out nationwide per ecological unit – a catchment area or other coherent ecological entity – to understand how it works, in all its complexity, what changes can be expected due to temperature and rainfall changes, and what forms of sustainable agriculture will be possible at present and in the future.

Contract farming, which took on a more prominent role under ESAP and in subsequent years, will still have a role to play in the whole complexity of ecologically sound agricultural development, but it will have to be well defined within strict boundaries and have to be closely monitored and guided by government policies. In this context, GMOs should be considered for what they are: dangerous and irresponsible tinkering with ecological systems, in most cases with only the aim of generating profits for large companies and making farmers more dependent on them instead of promoting food security, food sovereignty and food safety.

The new ecological approach will be based on at least three organizational principles:
- research, extension, training and education institutes and the private sector will have to (be made to) co-operate intensively;
- it will have to be decentralized owing to the site-specific nature of ecological systems;
- local stakeholders will have to be the drivers of the process as they possess the greatest knowledge about their locality and as they will have to be the implementers and beneficiaries of any agricultural and rural strategy for their locality.

Many recommendations of the commission of inquiry (Zimbabwe, 1994) can be applied to this huge undertaking, but more will be required. Government will have to play a facilitating, monitoring and managing role, while local people must spearhead the process at the local level and hold government and its institutions accountable. Once more, stakeholder participation and leadership should not only be through government structures like village and ward development committees but should be facilitated through an array of means, ways and organizations that will spring up from within the communities.

### 3.8.8 Rural development
The government should not fall into the trap of starting large-scale, capital-intensive manufacturing operations in major towns but instead should stimulate and spearhead the growth of small- and medium-scale, labour-intensive

manufacturing industries throughout the rural areas, as close as possible to the places where raw materials are being produced. At the same time it should also design and implement a variety of incentives to stimulate local, small-scale growth of services geared towards the agricultural sector. This will absorb surplus labour from the agricultural sector, generate income through increased employment, thus creating new demand and thereby engineering a process of rural development. Deliberate attention should be paid to the plight of women and former farm-workers, not only when creating opportunities within agriculture but also when promoting small- and medium-scale industries. Special attention should be given to those former farm-workers who were born on large-scale farms and have no link with any rural area within Zimbabwe but who would still like to reside and work there. Zimbabwe needs to develop a long-term vision about land, agriculture and rural development which is based on local needs and capabilities, inclusiveness and solidarity. This can only happen when the people themselves take the lead in such a process.

## References

Alexander, J. 1994. 'State, peasantry and resettlement in Zimbabwe', *Review of African Political Economy*, 61, 325–45.

Amanor-Wilks, D. 1995. *In Search of Hope for Zimbabwe's Farm Workers* (Harare: Dateline Southern Africa).

Bond, P. and M. Manyanya 2003. *Zimbabwe's Plunge: Exhausted Nationalism, Neoliberalism and the Search for Social Justice* (Harare: Weaver Press, 2nd edn.).

Chambati, W. 2007. *Emergent Agrarian Labour Relations in New Resettlement Areas* (Harare: African Institute for Agrarian Studies, Mimeograph Series).

Chasi, M. 2008. 'Climate change and coping strategies for the rural poor', *Building Bridges for Poverty Reduction and Sustainable Development*, 3(1).

Chimedza, R. 1994. 'Rural financial markets', in M. Rukuni and C. K. Eicher (eds.), *Zimbabwe's Agricultural Revolution* (Harare: University of Zimbabwe Publications).

Doré 2009. 'The Recovery and Transformation of Zimbabwe's Communal Areas' (Harare: UNDP, Comprehensive Economic Recovery in Zimbabwe, Working Paper 4), <http://www.undp.org.zw/images/stories/Docs/working%20papers/UNDP%20Working%20Paper%204%20-%20The%20Recovery%20and%20Transformation%20of%20Zimbabwe%27s%20Communal%20Areas.pdf>.

Ehrenpreis, D. 2008. *Poverty in Focus*, 16: 'Jobs, Jobs, Jobs: The Policy Challenge'.

FAO 2003. 'WTO Agreement on Agriculture: The Implementation Experience – Developing Country Case Studies (Zimbabwe)', Study Prepared for the FAO by Dr Moses Tekere (with assistance of James Hurungo and Masiiwa Rusare) Trade and Development Studies Centre, Harare.

FAO and WFP 2008. *Special report: FAO/WFP Crop and Food Security Assessment Mission to Zimbabwe, 18 June 2008,* <http://www.fao.org/docrep/010/ai469e/ai469e00.htm>.

FAO and WFP 2009. *Special report: FAO/WFP Crop and Food Security Assessment Mission to Zimbabwe, 22 June 2009,* <http://www.fao.org/docrep/011/ai483e/ai483e00.htm>.

Food Studies Group 1990. 'Agricultural Marketing and Pricing in Zimbabwe', background paper prepared for the World Bank, Zimbabwe Agriculture Sector Memorandum, Harare.

GAPWUZ 2009. 'If Something Is Wrong ...', report produced for GAPWUZ by the Research and Advocacy Unit and the Justice for Agriculture Trust, <http://www.kubatana.net/html/archive/agric/091111gapwuz.asp?sector=AGRIC>

ILO 1993. 'Structural change and adjustment in Zimbabwe' (Geneva: International Labour Office, Occasional paper 16).

Jonasson, E. 2008. 'Rural non-farm jobs: A pathway out of poverty?' in D. Ehrenpreis, *Poverty in Focus,* 16: 'Jobs, Jobs, Jobs: The Policy Challenge', 24–5.

Loewenson, R. 1992. *Modern Plantation Agriculture: Corporate Wealth and Labour Squalor* (London: Zed Books).

Kanyenze, G. 2006. 'Economic Policy Making Processes, Implementation and Impact in Zimbabwe', paper prepared for the Centre for Rural Development, Mount Pleasant, Harare.

Kinsey, B. H. 1998. 'Determinants of Rural Household Incomes and their Impact on Poverty and Food Security in Zimbabwe', resource paper for a discussion on Rural Household Dynamics, Bronte Hotel, Harare, 15–16 June 1998.

Madhuku, L. 2004. 'Law, politics and the land reform process in Zimbabwe', in M. Masiiwa (ed.), *Post Independence Land Reform in Zimbabwe: Controversies and Impact on the Economy* (Harare: Friedrich Ebert Stiftung).

Makhado, J, P. B. Matondi, and M. N. Munyuki-Hungwe 2006. 'Irrigation development and water resource management', in M. Rukuni *et al.* (eds.), *Zimbabwe's Agricultural Revolution Revisited* (Harare: University of Zimbabwe Publications).

Mano, R. and C. Nhemachena 2007. *Assessment of the Economic Impacts of Climate Change on Agriculture in Zimbabwe* (Washington, DC: World Bank, Policy Research Working Paper 4292).

Mariga, I. K. 2006. 'Cotton research and development 1920–2004', in M. Rukuni *et al.* (eds.), *Zimbabwe's Agricultural Revolution Revisited* (Harare: University of Zimbabwe Publications).

Marongwe, N. 2008. *Interrogating Zimbabwe's Fast Track Land Reform and Resettlement Programme: A Focus on Beneficiary Selection* (Cape Town: University of the Western Cape, Institute for Poverty, Land and Agrarian Studies, Ph.D. thesis).

Masters, W. A. 1994. *Government and Agriculture in Zimbabwe* (London: Praeger).

Matondi, P. B. 2001. *The Struggle for Access to Land and Water Resources in Zimbabwe: The Case of Shamva District* (Uppsala: Swedish University of Agricultural Sciences, Department of Rural Development Studies, doctoral thesis).

Matondi, P. B. 2008. 'Institutional and policy issues in the context of the land reform and resettlement programme in Zimbabwe', in C. T. Khombe and L. R. Ndlovu, *The Livestock Sector After the Fast Track Land Reforms in Zimbabwe* ([Zimbabwe]: Institute of Rural Technologies).

Matondi, P. B. and Moyo, S. 2002. 'Experiences with market based land reforms in Zimbabwe', in F. Barros *et al.* (eds.), *The Negative Impacts of World Bank Market-based Land Reform* (Brazil: CPT, MST and FIAN).

Moyo, S. 1993. 'The Land Question – Which Way Forward?', *Southern Africa Political Economy Monthly*, 7 (October), 37–41.

Moyo, S. 1995. *The Land Question in Zimbabwe* (Harare: SAPES Trust).

Moyo, S. 1999. *The Political Economy of Land Acquisition and Redistribution in Zimbabwe, 1990–1999* (Harare: Southern African Regional Institute for Policy Studies).

Moyo, S. 2000. *Land Reform Under Structural Adjustment in Zimbabwe; Land Use Change in Mashonaland Provinces* (Uppsala: Nordiska Afrika Institutet).

Moyo, S. 2001. 'The Interaction of Market and Compulsory Land Acquisition Processes with Social Action in Zimbabwe's Land Reform', paper presented at the SARIPS of the Sapes Trust Annual colloquium on Regional Integration: Past, Present and Future, Harare Sheraton Hotel and Towers, 24–27 September, <http://www.jointcenter.org/index.php/content/download/520/3031/file/The%20Interaction%20of%20Market%20and%20Compulsory%20Land%20Acquisition%20Processes%20with%20Social%20Action%20in%20Zimbabwe%27s%20Land%20Reform.doc>.

Moyo, S. and P. Yeros 2005. 'Land occupations and land reform in Zimbabwe: Towards the national democratic revolution', in S. Moyo and P. Yeros (eds.) *Reclaiming the Land: The Resurgence of Rural Movements in Africa, Asia and Latin America* (London: Zed Books).

Muchena, S. C. 2006. 'Agricultural diversification', in M. Rukuni *et al.* (eds.), *Zimbabwe's Agricultural Revolution Revisited* (Harare: University of Zimbabwe Publications).

Muir-Leresche, K. 2006. 'Agriculture in Zimbabwe', in M. Rukuni *et al.* (eds.), *Zimbabwe's Agricultural Revolution Revisited* (Harare: University of Zimbabwe Publications).

Rugube, L. *et al.* 2004. 'Government-assisted and market-driven land reform: Evaluating public and private land markets in redistributing land in Zimbabwe', in M. Roth and F. Gonese (eds.), *Delivering Land and Securing Rural*

*Livelihoods: Post-Independence Land Reform and Resettlement in Zimbabwe* (Harare: CASS, University of Zimbabwe, and Land Tenure Center, University of Wisconsin-Madison).

Rukuni, M. 2006. 'The Evolution of Agricultural Policy: 1890–1990', in M. Rukuni *et al.* (eds.), *Zimbabwe's Agricultural Revolution Revisited* (Harare: University of Zimbabwe Publications).

Rukuni M. and C. K. Eicher (eds.) 1994. *Zimbabwe's Agricultural Revolution* (Harare: University of Zimbabwe Publications).

Rukuni, M. *et al.* (eds.) 2006 *Zimbabwe's Agricultural Revolution Revisited* (Harare: University of Zimbabwe Publications).

Rutherford, B. 1996. 'Another side to rural Zimbabwe: Social constructs and administration of farm workers in Urungwe District, 1940s', *Journal of Southern African Studies*, 23(1).

Rutherford, B. 2001. *Working on the Margins: Black Workers, White Farmers in Post-Colonial Zimbabwe* (Harare: Weaver Press).

Sachikonye, L. 2003. 'The Situation of Commercial Farmers after Land Reform in Zimbabwe', report prepared for the Farm Community Trust of Zimbabwe.

Sadomba, W. Z. 2008. 'War Veterans in Zimbabwe's Land Occupations: Complexities of a Liberation Movement in an African Post-Colonial Settler Society' (Wageningen University, Ph.D. thesis).

Sithole-Niang, I. 2006. 'Biotechnology and the future of agriculture in Zimbabwe: Strategic issues', in M. Rukuni *et al.* (eds.), *Zimbabwe's Agricultural Revolution Revisited* (Harare: University of Zimbabwe Publications).

Shumba, E. M. and E. E. Hwingiri 2006. 'Commercialisation of smallholder agriculture', in M. Rukuni *et al.* (eds.), *Zimbabwe's Agricultural Revolution Revisited* (Harare: University of Zimbabwe Publications).

Stack, J. and C. Sukume 2006. 'Rural poverty: Challenges and opportunities', in M. Rukuni *et al.* (eds.), *Zimbabwe's Agricultural Revolution Revisited* (Harare: University of Zimbabwe Publications).

Sukume, C., S. Moyo and P. B. Matondi 2004. 'Farm Sizes, Decongestion and Land Use: Implications of the Fast-Track Land Redistribution Programme in Zimbabwe', paper for the Presidential Land Review Committee, Harare.

Takavarasha, T. 1994. 'Agricultural price policy', in M. Rukuni and C. K. Eicher (eds.), *Zimbabwe's Agricultural Revolution* (Harare: University of Zimbabwe Publications).

UNDP 2008. *Comprehensive Economic Recovery in Zimbabwe: A Discussion Document* (Harare: United Nations Development Programme).

Von Blackenburg, P. 1994. *Large Commercial Farmers and Land Reform in Africa* (London: Ashgate).

World Bank 1995. 'Zimbabwe: Achieving Shared Growth' (Washington, DC: World Bank, Country Economic Memorandum Volume 1).

World Bank 2008. *World Development Report: Agriculture for Development* (Washington, DC: World Bank).

ZCTU 1996. *Beyond ESAP: Framework for Long-term Development Strategy in Zimbabwe* (Harare: Zimbabwe Congress of Trade Unions).

Zimbabwe 1986. *First Five-Year National Development Plan, 1986–1990* (Ministry of Finance, Economic Planning and Development, 2 vols.)

Zimbabwe 1991. *Second Five-Year National Development Plan, 1991–1995* (Ministry of Finance, Economic Planning and Development)

Zimbabwe 1994. *Report of the Commission of Inquiry into Appropriate Agricultural Land Tenure Systems* [Chairman: M. Rukuni] (Harare, Government Printer, 3 vols.).

Zimbabwe 1998. *Land Reform and Resettlement Programme, Phase II: A Policy Framework* Harare: Government Printer).

Zimbabwe 2002. *Census 2002 National Report* (Harare: Central Statistical Office).

Zimbabwe 2003. *Report of the Presidential Land Review Committee on the Implementation of the Fast-track Land Reform Programme 2000-2002*, [Chairman: C. Utete] <http://www.sarpn.org.za/documents/d0000622/P600-Utete_PLRC_00-02.pdf>.

Zimbabwe 2006. *2004 Labour Force Survey* (Harare: Central Statistical Office).

Zimbabwe and SIRDC 2007. *National Land A2 Audit Report* (Harare: Ministry of Lands and Rural Resettlement and SIRDC).

Appendix to Chapter 3

**Table 3.A1: Development of agriculture in Zimbabwe since 1890**

| Period | Sector progress | Outcomes | Problems |
|---|---|---|---|
| 1890–1940 | • Large-scale farm sector grows<br>• Smallholder sector is weak | • Forty years of investment in the prime movers produces a robust commercial sector | • Inequitable land distribution, biased development of the large-scale sector |
| 1940–1980 | • Continued growth of the large-scale sector | • Large-scale sector manages to develop agriculture backed by import-substitution policies that create strong links with the commerce and manufacturing sector to withstand economic sanctions | • Large-scale sector remains biased towards white farmers and policies have racial connotation |
| 1980–1990 | • Large-scale sector remains undisturbed by the political changes<br>• Smallholder growth due to political prioritization | • Very little infrastructural and family development, though output increased in marketed commodities<br>• Greater food security, but land ownership becomes even more skewed, being conspicuous owing to demographic change | • Weak investment in the smallholder sector by the private sector and international finance |
| 2000–2009 | • Large-scale sector is almost obliterated with the fast-track land-reform programme<br>• Growth in the small and medium-scale farming sector | • Land inequalities being resolved under a contested circumstances, but the agrarian question remains hanging | • Food insecurity, land-tenure and rights problems<br>• Outstanding issues of land administration and compensation |

*Source*: Derived from Rukuni *et al.* (2010).

**Table 3.A2: Land, the constitution and the legal framework of Zimbabwe, 1979–2009**

| Year | Constitutional changes | Relevant legislation | Key Provisions |
|---|---|---|---|
| 1979–1984 | • Constitution of Zimbabwe (Section 16:1) | • Land Acquisition Act (Act 15 of 1979) | • Limits rights of compulsory acquisition<br>• Introduces 'willing seller, willing buyer criteria' for compensation<br>• Allows acquisition for resettlement with 'prompt and adequate' compensation |
| 1985–1990 | | • Land Acquisition Act (Act 21 of 1985). | • Repeals 1979 Act<br>• No reference to 'willing seller, willing buyer' criteria<br>• All commercial agricultural land sold on the open market had to first be offered to government. If government was not ready or interested in the property (Right of First Refusal), it would be issued with a Certificate of No Present Interest |
| 1990 | • Constitution of Zimbabwe Amendment Act (Act 30 of 1990, the 11th Amendment to the Constitution) | • Land Acquisition Act (Act 3 of 1992 and now Chapter 20:10) | • Repeals 1985 Act<br>• Introduces designation for up to 10 years as a prelude to compulsory acquisition<br>• Confirmation of compulsory acquisition through designation |
| 1992–1993 | • Constitution of Zimbabwe Amendment Act (Acts No. 4 and 9 of 1993, the 12th and 13th Amendments to the Constitution) | | • Right of First Refusal abolished<br>• Compulsory acquisition through designation |

**Table 3.A2** *cont.*

| Year | Constitutional changes | Relevant legislation | Key Provisions |
|------|------------------------|----------------------|----------------|
| 2000 | • Constitution of Zimbabwe Amendment Act (Act 5 of 2000, the 16th Amendment to the Constitution)<br><br>• Constitutional Amendment No 16A | • Land Acquisition Amendment Act (No. 15 of 2000)<br><br>• Land Acquisition Amendment Act (No. 14 of 2001)<br><br>• Land Acquisition Amendment Act (No. 6 of 2002)<br><br>• Land Acquisition Amendment Act (No. 10 of 2002) | • Absolves government from paying compensation for land, obliges paying for improvements (section 16A)<br><br>• Incorporates new position of 'no obligation to pay compensation for land<br><br>• Eliminates designation route, allows payment through instalments, bonds, and other long-term securities<br><br>• Maximum one-year preliminary notice of acquisition made valid indefinitely<br><br>• Condones Government's failure to comply with time limits imposed by the Land Acquisition Act<br><br>• Reduces indefinite validity of preliminary notice of acquisition to two years (increased to 10 years through section 14 of Act 7 of 2004)<br><br>• Required 'owners' of acquired land to cease operations within 45 days of service of the order and to vacate the living quarters within 90 days despite the fact that they are challenging the acquisition<br><br>• Introduces presumption that land to be acquired for resettlement is suitable for agricultural purposes<br><br>• Allows acquisition to proceed despite failure to serve notice on bondholders as required by law |

**Table 3.A2** *cont.*

| Year | Constitutional changes | Relevant legislation | Key Provisions |
|---|---|---|---|
| 2001 | | Rural Land (Farm Sizes) Regulations | Prescribed the maximum farm sizes per natural region |
| | | Rural Land Occupiers (Prevention from Eviction) Act (Act 13 of 2001, Chapter 20:26) | Allowed for occupier who had occupied land by March 2001 to stay on the land (Act repealed without substitution by the Gazetted Land (Consequential Provisions) Act (Act 8 of 2006, Chapter 20:28)) |
| 2004-2006 | | Acquisition of Farm Equipment or Material Act (Act 7 of 2004, Chapter 18:23) | Provides for compulsory acquisition of farm equipment and material on agricultural land which is not being used for agricultural purposes |
| | | Gazetted Land (Consequential Provisions) Act (Act 8 of 2006, Chapter 20:28) | Also amended the Land Acquisition Act by extending the validity of the preliminary notice of acquisition from two years to ten years, |
| | | | Requires former owners of land which has been compulsorily acquired and owners whose land is identified and gazetted for resettlement and other purposes to cease operations within 45 days and vacate the living quarters within 90 days of the gazetting unless authorised to remain on the land |
| 2005-2009 | Constitution of Zimbabwe Amendment Act (Act 5 0f 2005, the 17th Amendment to the Constitution) | | Takes away the right of former land owners to contest agricultural land acquisition in the Administrative Court or any other court in Zimbabwe although they can still challenge the fairness of the compensation offered |

*Source:* Derived from government sources (Madhuku, 2004; Statute Law of Zimbabwe; Constitution of Zimbabwe Section 16B

## Chapter 4

# Manufacturing

## 4.1 Introduction

The manufacturing sector is the central driver of growth in many countries. It assumes a key role in the growth process because of its ability to generate spill-overs, technical progress, economies of scale, induced productivity growth in the sector, and to raise the overall productivity of the economy (Felipe *et al.*, 2010). Kaldor (1967) postulated that manufacturing is the engine of growth in the sense that the faster the rate of growth of manufacturing output, the faster the rate of growth of overall output. This is because the manufacturing sector has strong linkages with the rest of the economy, has potential for capital accumulation, and its potential for technical progress is greatest.

The manufacturing sector in Zimbabwe has traditionally been a key driver of economic growth, contributing significantly to GDP, export receipts and employment: it was the biggest contributor to GDP between 1980 and 1990 at 22 per cent, followed by agriculture at 14 per cent (CZI, 2009). Moreover, it has significant backward and forward linkages with other key sectors of the economy, such as agriculture. The evolution of the manufacturing sector in Zimbabwe can be traced back to the beginning of the twentieth century. As early as the 1940s, the country had a relatively sophisticated industrial base, ranging from the only integrated iron-and-steel plant in Sub-Saharan Africa to basic consumer-goods industries; at that time around ten per cent of GDP and eight per cent of exports were derived from the manufacturing sector. In addition, about seven per cent of the labour force was also derived from the manufacturing sector (Riddell, 1990). Import-substitution industrialization was first pursued during the 1940s and continued during the Federation of Rhodesia and Nyasaland (1953–63) and the period of the Unilateral Declaration of Independence (UDI) (1965-79).[1]

The Federation resulted in the creation of an enlarged common market. Furthermore, UDI resulted in the imposition of an embargo on the country, causing the government to adopt an import-substitution industrialization strategy, further deepening and diversifying the manufacturing sector. The state played an active and central role by introducing a centralized foreign-exchange

---

[1] Import substitution involves the development of local industry through various forms of protection, its aim being to produce products that were previously not produced locally.

allocation system, an advanced system of parastatals and state-owned enterprises, and subsidies. Furthermore, a bilateral agreement with South Africa in 1964 provided the basis for sanctions-busting as well as the generation of much-needed foreign currency. By 1980, the manufacturing sector's share of GDP had grown to 25 per cent from 17 per cent in 1965.

This chapter deals with the state of the manufacturing sector from 1980: the first part during the first decade of independence, 1980–1990, the second during the ESAP period, 1991–1996, the third during the crisis period, 1997–2008, and the fourth in the transitional period from February 2009.

## 4.2 The First Decade of Independence, 1980–1990

At independence, Zimbabwe inherited a relatively developed and diversified manufacturing sector by Sub-Saharan African standards, producing many different products. The manufacturing industry consisted of some 1,260 separate units producing 7,000 different products, and played a key role in the economy through backward and forward linkages with other critical sectors such as agriculture and mining. It was a significant foreign-currency earner as well as a major employer. According to the Confederation of Zimbabwe Industries, manufacturing value-added (MVA) was estimated to be US$1.2 billion (CZI, 1986),[2] which was three times the African average and double that of Kenya, a country with a similar GDP and twice the population of Zimbabwe. The government maintained most of the controls that had been introduced during the UDI period.

A major downside, however, was that the structural distortions inherent in the economy (see Chapter 1) also extended to the manufacturing sector, where the informal and rural areas were home to micro- and small manufacturing enterprises, mostly labour-intensive in nature, and formed out of the need for subsistence. In contrast, most of the large manufacturing concerns were located in the urban areas, where they had access to skilled labour, an advanced business infrastructure, easy access to finance and markets, and could procure raw materials easily and cheaply. As a result of the unfavourable operating environment and a lack of support for manufacturers in informal and rural areas, most did not thrive, and rural–urban linkages were dominated by the urban manufacturing sector, which was the driver of economic growth because of its high gross value-added and its integration into the global economy. Moreover, government policy continued to favour big business, thwarting the growth of small and medium-sized enterprises.

---

[2] Manufacturing value-added is defined as the approximate value created in the process of manufacture, i.e. the contribution of manufacturing establishments to the value of finished manufactured products. Value-added is computed by subtracting the sum of the cost of materials, supplies, containers, fuels, purchased electricity, and contract work from the total value of products.

After the attainment of independence in 1980, industry remained protected through the foreign-exchange allocation system, which was inherited *in toto* from the previous regime (Herbst, 1990; Skalness, 1993). According to Skalness (1993: 412–13), the changes analysed by Herbst 'represented modifications of an inherited system of bureaucratic controls of a basically privately-owned, but protected market economy'. In fact, the sector became even more inward-looking. The ratio of exports to output in the manufacturing sector fell from 5 per cent in 1980 to 4.1 per cent in 1981, and although it started to rise thereafter, it remained below 10 per cent until 1985 when it rose to 12.1 per cent (Muzulu, 1993).

As already indicated above, much of Zimbabwe's industrial growth took place within a protective import-control regime via the foreign-exchange allocation system, which conferred an umbrella of protection as imports that competed with domestic production were effectively barred. Consequently, a heavy concentration developed in many sectors of the economy. However, the import-substitution industrialization strategy which had done well during the Federation and UDI years began to show signs of distress in the mid- and late 1980s. The deliberate policy of compressing imports to manage the balance-of-payments situation left capital stock in an obsolete and depleted state.

The manufacturing sector itself became a net user of foreign exchange. Although it contributed 32.1 per cent of export earnings in 1984, it accounted for 90.6 per cent of imports during the same year. Furthermore, the high level of protection created a monopoly structure whereby 50.4 per cent of manufacturing products were produced by single firms, 20.6 per cent in sub-sectors with two firms, and 9.7 per cent in sub-sectors with three firms. This meant that 80 per cent of goods produced in Zimbabwe were monopoly or oligopoly products (Ndlela, 1984; UNIDO, 1986). This market structure was further exacerbated by the concentration of production in the two major cities – Harare and Bulawayo accounting, respectively, for 50 per cent and 25 per cent of all manufactured products.

### 4.2.1 Structure of the manufacturing sector

The manufacturing sector comprises eleven major industrial groupings. Throughout the 1980s, the largest grouping in terms of gross output was the metals and metal products sub-sector, which accounted for an average of 24.7 per cent of total manufacturing output, followed by the foodstuffs (including stockfeeds) sub-sector at 14.3 per cent and textiles (including ginning) at 14.2 per cent (Table 4.1).

Although much of Zimbabwe's industrial growth took place within a protective import-control regime, the sector achieved a surprisingly high degree of efficiency. Studies suggest that, in the early 1980s, as much as half the country's

**Table 4.1: Average sub-sectoral contribution to manufacturing output, 1980–1990**

| Sub-sector | Percentage |
|---|---|
| Metals and metal products | 24.7 |
| Foodstuffs (including stockfeeds) | 14.3 |
| Textiles (including ginning) | 14.2 |
| Chemicals and petroleum | 13.6 |
| Drink and tobacco | 9.2 |
| Clothing and footwear | 7.4 |
| Paper, printing and publishing | 6.1 |
| Non-metallic mineral products | 4.0 |
| Wood and furniture | 3.4 |
| Transport equipment | 2.3 |
| Other | 0.8 |
| TOTAL | 100.0 |

*Source:* CSO, *Quarterly Digest of Statistics* (various issues).

industrial output was competitive in international markets, while only 12 per cent was assessed to be very inefficient (Jansen, 1983; World Bank, 1987).

In view of the above, one would have expected the manufacturing sector to oppose moves towards liberalization as it had invested heavily in production for the domestic market. However, by 1987, balance-of-payments problems became more binding as export receipts dwindled. At the same time, controls were intensified, culminating in the 1987 exchange-control measures that suspended dividend and profit remittances. Remittances of blocked funds were also stopped, except where this was done via government's four per cent bonds.[3]

The manufacturing sector became increasingly aware of the need to increase exports in order to generate more foreign exchange, and lobbied for export incentives in addition to the Export Revolving Fund (ERF), which had been introduced in 1983 with the help of the World Bank. The sector was wary of the liberalization of imports of goods produced at home, but was even more worried about the stricter price controls, as well as its inability to retrench workers (Skalness, 1993). When the foreign-exchange constraint became even more binding, especially following the 1987 economic slowdown, calls for a gradual liberalization of the economy grew louder.

The World Bank capitalized on this changed view by the manufacturing sector to press for market-led reforms. The publication of a document on the manufacturing sector and another on the economy as a whole, both of which put forward the case for liberalization, bear testimony to such external pressure (World Bank, 1987). In addition, the World Bank refused to renew the ERF

---

[3] For more details, see Muzulu (1993).

unless market reforms were carried out. Studies undertaken by a number of committees set up in 1989 showed that industries were generally supportive of the reform programme.[4] Thus, by 1990, there was overwhelming pressure on government in business circles to undertake market reforms.

## 4.3 The ESAP Period, 1991–1996[5]

The Economic Structural Adjustment Programme (ESAP), which encompassed domestic deregulation, trade liberalization and public-sector reform, began in earnest in October 1990 when some items were put on to the Open General Import Licence (OGIL) system. Trade liberalization was to be sequenced in such a way that 'raw materials, irrespective of whether or not they are domestically produced' were put on OGIL first in order to increase capacity utilization (Zimbabwe, 1991: 10). Once this stage had been achieved, it was to be followed with intermediate inputs being placed on to OGIL. As more and more products went on to OGIL and the foreign-exchange allocation system phased out, tariffs were to become the only means of providing protection to local industry.

Recognizing that import liberalization had to be accompanied by an appropriate exchange-rate policy, government decided to maintain the existing policy of allowing the Zimbabwe dollar to depreciate in real terms, believing that this would 'continue the existing resource shift in favour of export sectors and sustain export competitiveness' (ibid.: 12). In addition, and to encourage exports, a number of new incentives were introduced, over and above the ERF (Muzulu, 1993). Firstly, an export retention scheme was introduced whereby productive sectors were to retain a certain percentage of their export earnings in order to purchase machinery and raw materials needed to boost output. Although initially mining and agriculture were to retain 5 per cent of the value of exports, with manufacturing, tourism, construction and road hauliers retaining 7.5 per cent, the scheme was rationalized and increased in stages until it was abolished in 1994 with all exporters retaining 100 per cent of their export earnings.

Secondly, a wide range of incentives to attract foreign capital in mining and manufacturing were introduced, including easier access by export-oriented ventures to foreign exchange for essential imports. Furthermore, local borrowing rules were relaxed to allow foreign-owned firms to borrow an amount equal to 25 per cent of total shareholders' funds. Exchange-control measures pertaining to the remitability of dividends were also relaxed and, by 1995, companies could remit 100 per cent of their net after-tax profits. In addition, the Labour Relations Act was amended, introducing flexibility in issues of wage-bargaining and the

---

[4] Of note were the Industrial Review Committee and the Tariff Review Committee.

[5] For a detailed analysis of issues around the response of investment, exports, employment and manufacturing output to measures taken during ESAP, see *Beyond ESAP* (ZCTU, 1996).

hiring and firing of employees. Similarly, price controls were lifted on all but a few basic commodities.[6]

In anticipation of renewed growth and a concomitant increase in the demand for credit, the monetary authorities also adopted a restrictive monetary-policy stance designed to curtail inflationary pressures. Interest rates were liberalized. In view of the previous controls, nominal interest rates rose substantially in the first instance (Muzulu, 1995), but it was hoped that the policy would result in higher national savings as well as more efficient allocation of financial resources.

An evaluation of the effects of ESAP on industry in general and on the manufacturing sector in particular from 1991 to 1996 shows that, despite prices of tradable goods rising faster than those of non-tradable goods,[7] there was no shift towards production in the tradable-goods sectors as theory postulates. In fact, employment in the non-tradable-goods sectors grew faster than that in the tradable-goods sectors. In addition, output growth in the non-tradable-goods sectors was higher than that in the manufacturing sector. The implication of these findings is that, contrary to theoretical expectations, performance in non-tradable-goods sectors need not necessarily decline or lag behind that in tradable-goods sectors following the liberalization of the economy. In fact, some non-tradable-goods activities need to be expanded in order to improve productivity in the tradable-goods sectors. This point is important because it is often ignored in policy prescriptions involving economic liberalization (Muzulu, 1993).

During the ESAP period, the liberalization of competing imports resulted in some de-industrialization as domestic firms failed to compete with imported products. This process was exacerbated by high interest rates stemming from financial-sector reforms that raised the cost of capital. Using changes in manufacturing value-added as an indicator of the extent of de-industrialization, MVA growth per annum slowed from 3.4 per cent between 1980 and 1990 to 2.1 per cent during the ESAP period; it had been anticipated to grow by 5.4 per cent per annum.

On the question of whether firms became more labour-intensive following the higher increase in the price of capital relative to labour, the evidence appears to show the opposite. The capital–labour ratio actually rose in spite of the fact that real product earnings collapsed during the ESAP period.[8] In fact, the choice of techniques is influenced by a number of factors in addition to those such as the need to replace obsolete machinery following years of foreign-exchange

---

[6] For a detailed review of these issues, see Muzulu (1993).

[7] The non-tradable-goods sector includes: Electricity and Water, Construction, Finance and Insurance, Real Estate, Distribution, Hotels and Restaurants, Transport and Communication, Public Administration, Education, Health, Domestic and Other Services. Although electricity has been traded in Zimbabwe, it is difficult to disaggregate it from water services.

[8] For a detailed review of this issue, see Muzulu (1994).

constraints and to improve product quality, particularly for the export market. As Muzulu (1994) shows, because of foreign-exchange shortages for much of the 1970s and 1980s, Zimbabwean firms had adjusted to using the least capital possible. Thus, employment did not increase even though the cost of capital had risen substantially. But even if employment had grown, the question is whether it would have resulted in the rapid capital-intensive development seen in countries such as South Korea, whose experience shows that aspects other than factor prices need to be attended to if development is to be achieved.

The evaluation of the ESAP period also shows that the liberalization of the economy did not lead to significant increases in export volumes. While exports rose in the 1980s because of incentives to exporters, their removal following the adoption of ESAP resulted in non-traditional exports failing to respond strongly to price incentives generated by exchange-rate depreciation. In fact, according to Tekere (2001), traditional and high-technology industries performed poorly in the export market. Between 1991 and 1996, exports of high-technology products such as machinery, electrical machinery and transport equipment slowed down significantly, and Tekere attributes this development to Zimbabwe's 'technological weakness' in the manufacturing and export of these products. As shown in Table 4.2, while manufactured exports increased in nominal terms during ESAP, their share in total exports declined from 31 per cent to 22 per cent over the same period.

**Table 4.2: Zimbabwe's manufactured exports, 1991–1996**

|                            | 1991 | 1992 | 1993 | 1994 | 1995 | 1996 |
|----------------------------|------|------|------|------|------|------|
| Value (US$ millions)       | 533  | 546  | 634  | 751  | 898  | 684  |
| Percentage of total exports| 31   | 30   | 28   | 24   | 30   | 22   |

*Source:* CSO, *Quarterly Digest of Statistics* (various issues); Reserve Bank of Zimbabwe.

The poor export performance of the manufacturing sector during ESAP was due to the fact that Zimbabwe's industry was uncompetitive thanks to the protection it had received before the reforms started in 1991. As noted by Tekere (2001: 12), 'firms had a guaranteed domestic market and also concentrated on foreign markets, which came mainly as a result of past colonial arrangements such as the Rhodesia–South Africa trade agreement and Lomé Convention'. In addition, the removal of export incentives, the withdrawal of the cotton-lint subsidy for the textile sector, and increased competition from cheap foreign products following the removal of import-license restrictions all contributed to the sluggish performance of manufactured exports during ESAP.

The manufacturing volume index declined from about 3 per cent in 1991 to about –9 per cent in 1992, improving markedly in 1994 before declining again in 1995 to a record low of –13 per cent (Figure 4.1).

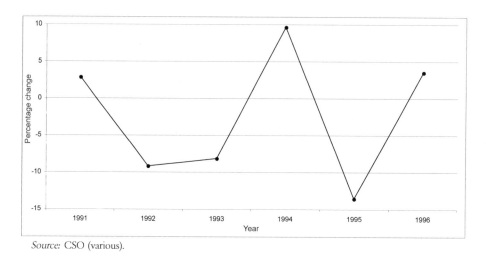

Source: CSO (various).

**Fig. 4.1: Changes in all manufacturing volume index, 1991–1996 (1980 = 100)**

## 4.4 The Crisis Period, 1997–2008

The ESAP period officially ended in 1996, after which the government experimented with a number of economic programmes. The post-ESAP period also coincided with the start of the fast-track land-reform programme, which led to a significant drop in agricultural production, as well as a fall in manufacturing output given that

> the sector was so closely integrated with commercial agriculture, the most devastating shock was the knock-on effect of the [fast-track programme]. In the mid-1990s over half the inputs into agriculture – fertilizer, stockfeeds and insecticides – were supplied by the manufacturing sector, while in the reverse direction 44 per cent of agricultural output was sold to the manufacturing sector [UNDP, 2008: 126].

Thus, the period after 1996 forms the genesis of a crisis for the manufacturing sector as a number of factors combined to weigh down its performance.

### 4.4.1 The behaviour of the relative prices of tradable and non-tradable goods

The analysis of the tradable-goods sectors below concentrates on the manufacturing sector. This is purely for convenience, and should not be taken to imply that other tradable-goods sectors, especially mining, are unimportant. The manufacturing sector has historically been the largest single tradable-goods sector, accounting for about 19 per cent of GDP between 1990 and 2008, contributing a third of the country's foreign-exchange earnings and accounting for about 15 per cent of formal employment (CZI, 2007).

Theoretically, the depreciation of the exchange rate should, all things being equal, result in a higher increase in prices of tradable goods (both exportables and import substitutes) than of non-tradables. Assuming that the economy is operating at full employment, and assuming that other things remain constant, these price incentives should encourage a shift in resources from the production of non-tradable goods to the production of tradable goods, of which manufacturing forms a big part, particularly in Zimbabwe where it accounts for 15 per cent of GDP. Consequently, the production of manufactured goods should expand, while that of non-tradable goods should fall. However, if the assumption of full employment is relaxed, there is no reason why both employment and output in the tradable-goods sector should expand at the expense of the non-tradable-goods sector. Under such circumstances, theory predicts that the performance of tradable-goods sectors (output and employment) should, all things being equal, outstrip that of the non-tradable-goods sector.

The devaluation of the Zimbabwe dollar, especially in 1997, and its subsequent continual depreciation, should have led, all things again being equal, to a greater increase in the prices of tradable goods (both exportables and import substitutes) than of non-tradable goods.[9] To trace the behaviour of the relative prices of tradable to non-tradable goods, Zimbabwe's GDP as reported in the national accounts was disaggregated into its tradable-goods and non-tradable-goods components in line with Muzulu (1993). This disaggregation was done in both nominal and real terms. From such data, prices were computed, being the implicit sectoral deflators. From the data, the relative price ratio of non-tradable-goods prices to tradable-goods prices was calculated.

Between 1997 and 2001 the ratio increased considerably, implying that during this period the prices of non-tradable goods rose faster than those of manufactured goods. This upward trend reflected the fact that the Zimbabwe dollar was appreciating in real terms even though it depreciated noticeably in nominal terms. Between 2002 and 2006, there was a sharp increase in the prices of tradable goods relative to non-tradable goods, resulting in a major decline in the relative price ratio. This came on the back of the large devaluation of the Zimbabwe dollar by the RBZ and the introduction of a foreign-currency auction system designed to boost the competitiveness of Zimbabwe's exports. However, this trend was reversed between 2007 and 2008 as the relative price ratio increased significantly in favour of non-tradable goods, once again reflecting the appreciation, in real terms, of the Zimbabwe dollar as hyperinflation set in.

### 4.4.2 Manufacturing output

Table 4.3 shows that, as the economic crisis intensified, manufacturing output declined significantly when compared to the non-tradable-goods sector in the

---

[9] Theoretically, this is true by definition, particularly if the real exchange rate is defined as the ratio of prices of non-tradable to tradable goods (Edwards and Ng, 1985).

period 1997 to 2008. In 1997, output in the manufacturing sector declined while output in the non-tradable goods sectors, inclusive of government, rose. This was at a time when the Zimbabwe dollar depreciated by 28 per cent in real terms in 1997 compared to 1996. In fact, much of the loss in the value of the currency occurred in a single day when, on 14 November 1997, the Zimbabwe dollar depreciated sharply by 46 per cent, in nominal terms.

From 1998 to 2008, output in the manufacturing sector continued to decline at a faster rate than that of the non-tradable goods sector (Table 4.3). The only exception was in 2005, when manufacturing output grew by 3.8 per cent, while that for the non-tradable-goods sector declined by 15 per cent. In 2002 and 2004, output from the non-tradable-goods sector increased, while that for the manufacturing sector contracted, reflecting the fact that, over the same period, the price ratio of non-tradable to tradable goods was increasing.

**Table 4.3: Growth in output, manufacturing sector and non-tradable sectors, 1997–2008 (%)**

|  | 1997 | 1998 | 1999 | 2000 | 2001 | 2002 | 2003 | 2004 | 2005 | 2006 | 2007 | 2008 |
|---|---|---|---|---|---|---|---|---|---|---|---|---|
| Manufacturing | −0.8 | −3.4 | −4.5 | −11.5 | −5.4 | −13.2 | −13.5 | −10.2 | 3.8 | −2.8 | −5.0 | −12.3 |
| Non-tradable | 1.7 | −0.1 | −1.4 | −4.2 | −1.5 | 1.0 | −8.8 | 2.4 | −15.0 | −3.5 | −2.5 | −4.1 |

Source: CSO, *Quarterly Digest of Statistics* (various issues); CZI.

While the near-drought situation in 2002 exacerbated the decline in manufacturing output in 2002, a number of other factors – such as limited export markets, increased foreign competition on the domestic market, and continued macroeconomic instability – were also responsible for the decline recorded in manufacturing output. Therefore, in all the years under review, growth in the manufacturing sector continued to lag behind that of the non-tradables sector. In the period 1997–2003, manufacturing output declined by an average of 7.5 per cent, compared to an average decline of 2.5 per cent for the non-tradables sector. According to the CZI (2008), by 2007, the manufacturing sector was producing only about 30 per cent of what it used to produce in 2003. The manufacturing sector recovered somewhat in 2005, with output increasing by 3.3 per cent, driven in the main by strong performances of the metals and metal products, textiles and ginning, clothing and footwear, drinks, tobacco and beverages, and paper, printing and publishing sub-sectors.

From the end of 2003, when a new Governor assumed office at the Reserve Bank of Zimbabwe, an expansionary monetary-policy stance was implemented, with a significant adverse impact on the performance of the manufacturing sector. In December 2003, the RBZ introduced the Productive Sector Facility (PSF), which offered concessional interest rates of 30 per cent to the manufacturing sector at a time when commercial lending rates were at about 600 per cent. When PSF was launched, it was designed 'to avoid company closures due to the high cost of borrowing; to stimulate employment creation through support of new and expansion of projects and providing funds for capital expenditure; to stimulate additional export earnings; and to increase capacity utilization' (RBZ, 2006: 6). Cumulative PSF support, including special facilities to the private sector over the period January 2004 to 26 May 2006, amounted to Z$6.3 trillion (US$315 million). However, the impact of the RBZ's intervention was limited, as manufacturing output declined by an average of 21.1 per cent between 2004 and 2007. Inflationary pressures arising from the resultant high money-supply growth worsened, with the year-on-year rate of inflation rising from 20.1 per cent in December 1997 to 231.1 million per cent by July 2008 (the last period for which official inflation data were released during the Zimbabwe dollar era). During this period, the rate of growth in broad money supply (M3) also rose, from 34.9 per cent in December 1997 to 344 quintillion per cent by December 2008.

The response of manufacturing output to the various concessional facilities introduced by the central bank during the period under review was not positive owing to other constraints bedevilling the sector.[10] According to a survey by the CZI, 80 per cent and 69.4 per cent of companies interviewed in 2005 and 2006, respectively, cited the lack of foreign currency as their major constraint to operating at full capacity. Other factors that adversely affected growth in manufacturing output were the unavailability of raw materials, weak domestic demand, fuel shortages and power cuts (CZ1, 2007). The performance of the manufacturing sector deteriorated significantly in the period 2000 to 2007, with output declining by an average of 12.2 per cent, compared to an increase in output of 0.45 per cent in the period 1990 to 2000.

Fiscal policy was also not helpful, with continued sustenance of high government budget deficits, which were financed largely from the domestic banking sector. The government's budget deficit as a percentage of GDP averaged 8.6 per cent in the period 1997–2007. However, if the quasi-fiscal activities of the RBZ are included, then the ratio is even higher – at close to 80 per cent for 2006 (Munoz, 2007). Indeed, the government crowded out the private sector from accessing funding from the banking sector, particularly in the period 2003–2008. In fact, according to the CZI's *Manufacturing Sector Survey* of 2008, companies lamented the failure to raise working capital, given that there was limited credit in the system (both domestic credit and international credit lines), as one of the major constraints to production.

From 2003, the government consistently reverted to the use of price controls as a means of controlling inflation, culminating in July 2007 when the National Incomes and Pricing Commission issued a directive ordering that the prices

---

[10] Various other concessional facilities included the Parastatals and Local Authorities Reorientation Programme (PLARP), Agricultural Special Productivity Enhancement Facility (ASPEF), and the Basic Commodities Supply Side Intervention (BACOSSI).

of all goods produced be taken back to their levels at 18 June 2007. Prices were, therefore, kept at artificially low levels, with no regard to the ever-rising cost of production for manufacturing firms in a hyperinflationary environment. The manufacturing sector responded by reducing production, which lowered capacity utilization and reduced the ability of shops to replace stock. In fact, there was a serious run-down on capital, which has since become a major constraint to improved production by industry (CZI, 2008).

### 4.4.3 Employment

While there was a decline in employment in the two sectors from 1999 to 2002 (Table 4.4), the decline was greater in the manufacturing sector than in the non-tradable-goods sector. For reasons discussed above, a significant decline had been recorded in manufacturing output over the same period. Employment levels declined particularly sharply in 2000 at the height of the often-violent invasions of commercial farms, which left many manufacturers with little or no raw materials and business from the agriculture sector.

**Table 4.4: Employment growth by sector, 1997–2004 (%)**

|  | 1997 | 1998 | 1999 | 2000 | 2001 | 2002 | 2003 | 2004 |
|---|---|---|---|---|---|---|---|---|
| Manufacturing | 7.1 | 5.6 | –4.0 | –10.0 | –0.6 | –6.7 | –4.2 | –3.1 |
| Non-tradable goods | 4.1 | 3.3 | –2.2 | –4.5 | –2.0 | –1.1 | 0.1 | – |

*Source:* CSO, *Quarterly Digest of Statistics* (various issues).

Employment decline in the non-tradable-goods sectors averaged about 0.3 per cent per annum between 1997 and 2003, while that in the manufacturing sector averaged 1.7 per cent. A further analysis of employment statistics for the manufacturing sector indicates that employment rose from an average of 197,800 in 1997 to as high as 207,600 in 1998. However, after 1999, employment in the manufacturing sector continued to fall on a year-on-year basis and, in fact, the figure of 160,900 in 2003 was the lowest recorded since 1985.[11]

The trend confirms a persistent reduction in employment numbers across the manufacturing sector owing to depressed business operating conditions. A number of manufacturing companies adopted coping strategies that included retrenchments and restructuring,[12] a shorter working week and reduced shifts (some companies no longer operated on a 24-hour day), and overtime was done away with.

[11] CSO, *Quarterly Digest of Statistics* (various issues).

[12] According to figures obtained from six National Employment Councils, which account for about 55 per cent of all of them, a total of 1,187, 3,858 and 2,575 employees were retrenched, respectively, in 2002, 2003 and 2004. The sub-sectors that had the highest number of retrenchees were those of leather, shoe and allied products, and furniture and textiles (CZI, 2003).

Although official data on the growth in employment levels in both the manufacturing and non-tradable-goods sectors are not available for after 2003, anecdotal evidence points to further deterioration in the employment situation in the manufacturing sector. In fact, based on a sample of firms, the CZI found that employment numbers in the manufacturing sector declined by 12.2 per cent from 2006 to 2007 (CZI, 2008). Furthermore, 'almost all [industrialists] interviewed identified the loss of skills and the deterioration in the country's training and education infrastructure as the most important single problem that industry will face in a post-crisis environment' (UNDP, 2008: 127). An executive with Zimbabwe's largest trainer of artisans was reported as having said that his company was losing about half of its qualified artisans each year (ibid.). As a result of the significant loss of qualified and experienced workers, there was a collapse in the labour market in 2008 as out-migration of labour intensified. In addition, the quality of the remaining labour force was also compromised: 'Personnel previously categorized as technicians are now graded engineers, reflecting a downgrade of industrial capability across the board' (ibid.: 128).

### 4.4.4 De-industrialization

There is no agreed statistic on de-industrialization. Although the CSO publishes some statistics on company insolvencies, the data are meaningless if the reasons for them are not given. Consequently, this study relied heavily on data obtained from manufacturing-sector surveys by the CZI. According to their evidence, company closures increased significantly owing to the harsh economic environment faced after 1997, since when the manufacturing sector recorded significant downsizing, and, in extreme situations, closures were effected to avoid additional losses. Robinson (2006) also attributed the 42 per cent fall in the volume index of manufacturing recorded between 1996 and 2006 to de-industrialization.

Incomplete data show that a total of 838 companies closed between 2000 and 2004 (Table 4.5). During the period under review, the furniture, leather, textiles, and food and allied products sub-sectors recorded the largest number of company closures. The footwear, electronics goods, and clothing and textiles sub-sectors did not recover from the liberalization of imports in the 1990s, which saw the importation of second-hand clothes and shoes, as well as cheap electrical goods, mostly from Asia and the Middle East.

Using the share of the manufacturing sector to total GDP as a measure of industrialization, statistics show that it declined progressively, from about 22 per

**Table 4.5: Company closures, 2000–2004**

|                  | 2000 | 2001 | 2002 | 2003 | 2004 |
|------------------|------|------|------|------|------|
| Company closures | 400  | 150  | 200  | 40   | 48   |

Source: CZI, *Manufacturing Sector Surveys* (various issues).

**Table 4.6: Growth of GDP and manufacturing value-added, 1980–2008**

|            | GDP growth (%) | MVA growth (%) |
|------------|----------------|----------------|
| 1980–1990  | 4.2            | 3.6            |
| 1991–1996  | 2.8            | 2              |
| 1997–2008  | -5.2           | -7.2           |

*Source:* CSO (various publications).

**Table 4.7: Manufacturing value-added per head, 1980–2006**

|                                      | 1980  | 1985  | 1990  | 1995 | 2000 | 2001 | 2002 | 2003 | 2004 | 2005 | 2006 |
|--------------------------------------|-------|-------|-------|------|------|------|------|------|------|------|------|
| Manufacturing value-added per head (US$) | 583.0 | 631.5 | 183.8 | 42.0 | 7.9  | 5.9  | 5.1  | 4.4  | 4.0  | 4.1  | 1.5  |

*Source:* Adapted from UNDP (2008: 125–6).

cent in 1991 to an estimated 8 per cent in 2008 (World Bank, 2009). Further evidence of the extent of de-industrialization can be gathered from an analysis of the share of manufacturing value-added (MVA) growth and MVA per head, which is 'the most widely-used measure of industrial progress' (UNDP, 2008: 125). MVA grew in the 1980s and early 1990s, though the rate of growth slowed during the ESAP period, until there was a marked decline during the period of the economic crisis (1997–2006) and its share in GDP almost halved from 20.5 per cent in the 1980s to as low as 13 per cent.[13]

MVA per head (Tables 4.6 and 4.7) rose gradually between 1980 and 1990, underpinned by strong domestic demand and import substitution. However, after 1990, de-industrialization set in, and MVA per head declined sharply from US$183.80 in 1990 to US$1.50 in 2006 as constraints such as foreign-currency and raw-materials shortages, occasioned in part by the decline in agricultural production following the fast-track land reform, worsened the situation.

In addition, as capacity utilization and output fell, domestic demand for products remained unsatisfied, which, in turn, necessitated re-opening the domestic market to cheap competing imports.

Apart from problems caused by the liberalization of competing imports, the evolving tariff structure also contributed to the de-industrialization of the Zimbabwean economy. Generally, duties on imported inputs were higher than those on finished products, which tended increasingly to turn manufacturers into traders. In the capital-goods sector, which uses imported steel plate, for example, import duties ranged from 30 per cent to 40 per cent, yet finished products that used steel plate as inputs were imported into the country duty-free.[14] Clearly, any

---

[13] It is important to note that a decline in MVA can be the result of (exogenous) factors other than de-industrialization. Thus, the use of MVA or MVA per head as the ultimate indicator of de-industrialization needs to be treated with caution.

[14] Statutory Instrument 23 of 1994.

domestically manufactured capital goods that used imported steel plate could not compete on the local market with imported goods, let alone on the export market. Consequently, firms tended to stop manufacturing products locally, preferring to import them directly and sell them to local consumers.

### 4.4.5 Exports

In a developing economy such as Zimbabwe, exports play a key role in terms of assisting in the achievement of economic growth and macroeconomic stability. The expansion of non-traditional exports, of which manufactured goods play a very significant part, is therefore critical in any economic-recovery process. For the generation of foreign currency and growth in exports to be sustained, the exchange rate plays a central role in making exports competitive in international markets. This section determines whether or not manufactured exports expanded during the post-1997 period, when economic reforms officially ended.

Manufactured exports declined progressively from a peak of US$853.3 million in 2001 to US$210.3 million by 2008 (Table 4.8), a quarter of their 2000 level. Over the same period, manufactured exports as a percentage of total exports also declined.

**Table 4.8: Zimbabwe's manufactured exports, 2000–2008**

|  | 2000 | 2001 | 2002 | 2003 | 2004 | 2005 | 2006 | 2007 | 2008 |
|---|---|---|---|---|---|---|---|---|---|
| Value (US$ millions) | 815.0 | 853.3 | 706.1 | 691.2 | 620.9 | 555.1 | 290.9 | 266.7 | 210.3 |
| Percentage of total exports | 37.0 | 40.4 | 39.2 | 41.4 | 36.9 | 34.6 | 16.8 | 17.7 | 15.3 |

Source: CSO, *Quarterly Digest of Statistics* (various issues); RBZ.

The sluggish performance of manufactured exports was also highlighted by the UNDP: 'exports of "pure" manufactures [i.e. excluding ferro-alloys, cotton and steel] halved between 1997 and 2004 while the number of products exported declined and export concentration increased in terms of both markets and products' (UNDP, 2008: 126–7). The adverse impact of export concentration is also supported by the World Bank, which argues that manufacturing firms 'export small quantities of products designed for the domestic market to nearby markets with similar tastes and requirements, but this type of exporting rarely represents a promising basis for significant export expansion' (World Bank, 1995b: 133).

It would appear, therefore, that manufactured exports did not grow as fast as was expected. In fact, evidence from the CZI (2008) indicated that, on average, the manufacturing sector exported only 20 per cent of its total output in 2007 compared with about 50 per cent in 2006. The main reasons cited by companies for not exporting included the uncompetitive export markets, high cost of production, low capacity utilization, lack of foreign currency, and working capital constraints (CZI, 2009). In its 2007 study, 17 per cent of the manufacturing firms sampled also cited non-tariff barriers as another major constraint to expanding exports, which included the fact that both established and potential clients in certain markets refused Zimbabwean products simply because of the source country (CZI, 2007). The study also highlights the fact that the destination of Zimbabwe's exports is primarily a function of real bilateral exchange-rate movements since 'companies will increase exports into a country against whose currency the Zimbabwe dollar has depreciated most and reduce exports to countries against which the Zimbabwe dollar has appreciated' (ibid.: 26). However, a more thorough study of the manufacturing sector in Zimbabwe shows how the provision of export incentives in the 1980s led to a significant growth in exports (Muzulu, 1993).

Not many export incentives were in place for manufacturing companies between 2000 and 2009. Apart from the various exchange-rate linked incentives – such as the introduction of the foreign-currency auction system in January 2005, which was later replaced by the Tradable Foreign Currency Balances System in October 2005 – and the 'carrot and stick' export retention scheme, in which numerous changes to exporters' surrender requirements were made, no specific incentives were put in place for manufacturers. Yet, according to evidence from firms, the non-existence of favourable incentives at a time when other countries in the region provided them not only led to low exports but to a decline in domestic demand caused by more competitive imports. In fact, as long as the macroeconomic fundamentals remain weak and volatile, business confidence will continue to wane. In this state, no amount of lower level incentives will impact positively on exports. The biggest incentive for reviving the supply side remains the creation of a stable macroeconomic environment accompanied by a competitive exchange rate (CZI, 2007).

Muzulu (1993) also identified a number of additional factors that militate against an expansion in exports, one of which was the lack of experience by local firms in marketing goods in foreign markets. A study by the World Bank (1995a) also found that marketing was one of the weakest points in Zimbabwe with regard to textiles and clothing.

Poor support services in terms of electricity and water supply, telecommunications services, and road and rail infrastructure also impact adversely on exports. Ten years of continuous economic decline have had a serious impact on Zimbabwe's infrastructure. No new investments have taken place other than a few re-investments accomplished through barter trade with friendly countries. Maintenance has been limited to what has been necessary to try to keep essential parts of the old systems working. The total generation of electricity of about 1,000 megawatts is well below the estimated peak domestic consumption of 2,400 megawatts.

In terms of water and sanitation, there has been an irregular supply of water to industry and homes all over the country, resulting in blockages and the outbreak of diseases. Burst pipes are left unrepaired and industrial production is disrupted: treated-water losses are estimated at between 35 per cent and 50 per cent. The national road network is in bad shape, with most of the trunk and urban tarred roads littered with potholes and in need of resurfacing and resealing. The rail track, signalling and telecommunications infrastructure has also collapsed, forcing most manufacturers to use more expensive road and air transport to move bulk raw materials and products to the market.

**Table 4.9: Projects approved by the Zimbabwe Investment Authority**

|                          | 2000  | 2001 | 2002 | 2003 | 2004  | 2005  | 2006  | 2007    |
|--------------------------|-------|------|------|------|-------|-------|-------|---------|
| Approved projects (US$ m) | 359.5 | 97.8 | 56.5 | 57.4 | 115.1 | 705.5 | 964.6 | 7,655.4 |

*Source:* Zimbabwe Investment Authority.

### 4.4.6 Investment

While information on the extent of foreign direct investment inflows destined for the manufacturing sector is not readily available, data on project approvals by the Zimbabwe Investment Authority (ZIA), formerly the Zimbabwe Investment Centre, indicate that investment in the manufacturing sector was also sluggish during the period under review (Table 4.9).[15] In addition to the noticeable decline in investment in the manufacturing sector, there was a major shift in the geographical origin of investment, with Europe and the United States contributing less to investment inflows into the country. The bulk of the investment projects approved by the ZIA, especially after 2003, came from the East, particularly from China and South Korea, who submitted 98.3 per cent of the manufacturing-sector projects approved in 2007. The proportion of manufacturing-sector projects approved by the ZIA to the total cumulative investment projects approved in 2007 was 44.2 per cent.

The adverse impact of the land-reform programme and the lack of respect for property rights, especially after 1999, affected both local and foreign investment, not only in the manufacturing sector but in all the other sectors of the economy. While most studies show that the foreign-exchange allocation system and the investment licensing that it gave rise to, as well as labour regulations, were largely responsible for the low investment levels during the 1980s, the unstable macroeconomic environment had greater impact on investment levels between 1997 and 2008.

Anecdotal evidence from a sample of firms interviewed by the CZI after

---

[15] Project approvals by the ZIA may be misleading as some of them are never implemented for a variety of reasons.

2004 shows that the rate of investment in the manufacturing sector was well below that required to keep pace with wear and tear and the obsolescence of existing capital stock. In fact, investment in the manufacturing sector continued to plummet in real terms. Firms were 'doing the barest minimum required to keep their plants running with little or no meaningful effort towards upgrading existing machines and technology. This is because in real terms, the companies are not making enough returns to afford this necessary retooling and upgrading' (CZI, 2007: 18).

A major reason for the low investment levels was the low savings rate, which was estimated to have been around 10 per cent of GDP in the period 1997–2007 (UNDP, 2008).[16] Since it is generally believed that the quantity of financial resources influences investment, inconsistent monetary policies during the period under review, when there were long periods of negative real interest rates, compromised growth in investment. In addition to the low responsiveness of savings, and hence investment, to negative real interest rates, the savings made by the private sector were used up by government, which has consistently been dis-saving. In fact, domestic financing of the government's budget deficit (excluding the RBZ's quasi-fiscal activities) as a percentage of GDP averaged 7 per cent in the period 1997 to 2007. This meant that the private sector was not able to access much-needed credit. Yet the experience of countries such as Uganda has shown that the availability of credit is crucial to private-sector investment.[17] Lack of access to credit is a major constraint to investment, particularly for small-scale producers, and perpetuates dualism in economic development.

Added to the low levels of savings, high lending rates have had a crowding-out impact on investment, with most firms financing fixed investment from retained earnings. Although this was at a cost in terms of the interest income forgone were the money invested in other interest-bearing assets, deposit rates were lower than lending rates between 1997 and 2008. In addition, debt financing has been found to contain other costs (such as transaction costs, costs of financial distress and asymmetric information), making it cheaper to finance investment through retained earnings (Fazzari et al., 1988).

Owing to the high nominal interest rates, not many firms were able to generate projects with concomitant high rates of return to make it profitable to borrow from formal financial institutions. According to the CZI's manufacturing sector surveys, most firms cited high interest rates as one of the major constraints to investment (CZI, 2007, 2008 and 2009). This situation arises from the fact that high nominal lending rates accompanied by high rates of inflation increase the risk of borrowing (Harvey & Jenkins, 1994): the higher the rate of inflation,

---

[16] See also Chapter 12.

[17] International Monetary Fund Survey, 11 December 1995.

the greater its variability, which sharply increases the cost of borrowing at high nominal rates. This factor highlights the need to reduce inflation to enable the monetary authorities to lower nominal interest rates, which should encourage more firms to borrow from the formal financial institutions. Indeed, financial deregulation succeeded in boosting investment in countries that maintained moderate inflation rates (Cho and Khatkhate, 1989).

The hyperinflationary environment during the post-March 2007 period also impacted adversely on the Public Sector Investment Programme, with most projects remaining as work-in-progress for a long time owing to ever-escalating costs. This resulted in the deterioration of infrastructure that is critical for both local and foreign private-sector investment. Research in countries such as Kenya has shown how public-sector investment 'crowds in' private-sector capital projects (Kariuki, 1993).

An additional factor that has continued to cloud Zimbabwe's investment climate has been the Indigenization and Economic Empowerment Act, which was introduced as a bill in 2007 and subsequently gazetted in 2008.[18] The act 'sets out mandatory indigenous shareholding thresholds of 51 per cent in every business that is being transferred, merged, restructured, unbundled or de-merged and in any new investments of a prescribed value'. In its current state it has had an adverse impact on investment decisions by foreign shareholders in large manufacturing entities, and may lead to little or no further investment in these companies. Indeed,

> successful companies have a strategic fit and alignment of the mission, vision, goals, strategy, programmes, policies and objectives. The founders of the company project their vision so that it consequently underpins the strategic fit. The unconditional takeover of the 51 per cent equity will derail the strategic fit and give birth to confusion as founders are controlled by people with other interests [Kundishora, 2009].

This highlights the deficiencies in the long-term sustainability of the indigenization and empowerment laws as viable and non-conflicting state intervention.

## 4.5 The Transitional Period, 2009–2010

The formation of the Inclusive Government in February 2009 paved the way for a number of structural changes in economic policy, both fiscal and monetary. The national budget for 2009 and monetary policy statements announced in January and February 2009, respectively, by the Ministry of Finance and the RBZ, brought about the dollarization of the economy and allowed the use of multiple foreign currencies as legal tender. Despite price controls on goods and services being removed, hyperinflation was ended overnight.

[18] Act No. 14 of 2007.

Further refinement and revision of the 2009 budget was done in March 2009 when the Minister announced further liberalization of the foreign-exchange market. The exporters' foreign-currency surrender requirements to the RBZ were removed, and the suspension of customs duty on the importation of basic commodities was extended to December 2009 when the Mid-Term Fiscal Policy Statement was made on 16 July 2009.[19] This measure has the potential to increase competition for domestic manufacturers, who are still trying to recapitalize and regain the market following years of under-capitalization and low capacity utilization. Ultimately, it may lead to further erosion of the manufacturing sector.

The two policy statements also emphasized the need to improve public service delivery through the payment of salaries to civil servants in foreign currency and the general improvement in their welfare. Reform of public enterprises was also highlighted in the 2009 national budget, and water and sewage management was transferred to local authorities from the Zimbabwe National Water Authority with effect from 1 February 2009, while the Grain Marketing Board's monopoly as the sole purchaser of grain was also removed.[20] Recapitalization of the real sectors of the economy (including the manufacturing sector) was also given high priority in the subsequent Short-Term Emergency Recovery Programme (STERP), which was launched in March 2009.

One of the key objectives of STERP was the resuscitation of the manufacturing sector, thereby increasing levels of capacity utilization from below 10 per cent to over 60 per cent by the end of 2009. Capacity utilization had been hampered over the years by chronic hyperinflation, foreign-exchange controls and shortages of foreign currency, disruption of electricity and water supplies, working-capital constraints and price controls, among others.

The 2009 Mid-Term Fiscal Policy Statement also reduced customs duty on finished goods used as raw materials from an average of 40 per cent to zero to 10 per cent with effect from 1 August 2009;[21] customs duty rates on raw materials, intermediate goods and capital goods were also reduced. These measures were expected to assist in the recovery of the manufacturing sector through cheaper access to imported raw materials, machinery and equipment, thus supporting the re-tooling and equipping of the local industry. However, it is pertinent to note that the major constraint to the full recovery of the manufacturing sector still remains the unavailability of credit lines. In fact, according to the Minister

---

[19] Commodities on which duty was suspended include cooking oil, margarine, rice, flour, salt, mealie-meal, bath and laundry soap, washing powder, toothpaste, and petroleum jelly.

[20] ZINWA reverted to its responsibility prior to the directive of 9 May 2005 of managing water systems in rural areas.

[21] These include: powdered milk; butter oil; leather in slabs, sheets or strip; palm stearine; waste leather; wadding textile fibres; binding and baler twine of sisal; twine of synthetic fibres, sisal, baler twine and manila hemp.

of Finance, 'immediate requirements for the manufacturing sector amount to US$1 billion. To date, only US$562 million has been identified as potential lines of credit' (Zimbabwe, 2009: 33).

Excise duty on the products of domestic manufacturers of cigarettes and tobacco and of wines and spirits was increased: such measures have the effect of forcing producers to pass on the increases to consumers via an upward adjustment in prices of the affected products and may lead to consumer resistance and a subsequent decline in output and exports.

Services provided by public enterprises and local authorities are essential inputs and enablers for the manufacturing sector, yet their collapse has been a major constraint to the sector. Since the advent of dollarization, the situation has not improved but worsened as the levels of tariffs being charged in foreign currency by utility companies, local authorities and some government departments, taking advantage of their monopolistic advantage, have remained too high. As a result, the domestic manufacturing industry has not been able to withstand them. An improvement in the efficiency of public enterprises and local authorities is, therefore, a critical element which must be addressed if the recovery of industry is to be sustainable.

The COMESA customs union was launched in June 2009 and, while it presents a wider potential market for local industry, the fact that local industry has been operating for many years at low capacity utilization with obsolete equipment means that it may not be able to cope with the competitive forces arising out of this new union. According to the 2009 CZI *Manufacturing Sector Survey*, there had been an improvement in capacity utilization, to levels of about 32.3 per cent for the first half of 2009 from an estimated level of below 10 per cent at the beginning of 2009 (18.9 per cent in 2007). The industry at large saw a staggering 72 per cent increase in working hours in the second quarter of 2009, largely on the back of increased demand for products, as companies built up volumes to meet demand. In line with the increase in the working hours, the total wage bill also increased by 72.9 per cent.

At its peak, the sector contributed up to 41.4 per cent of total exports. According to the 2009 CZI *Manufacturing Sector Survey*, total shipments by the manufacturing sector from 1 January to 30 June 2009 amounted to U$67.1 million, compared to US$123.5 million for the same period in 2008, reflecting a 46 per cent decrease. During the first six months of 2009, the sector accounted for only 14 per cent of export shipments (mining 44 per cent, tobacco 26 per cent, agriculture 13 per cent, horticulture 2 per cent and hunting 1 per cent). According to the survey, key constraints to business performance were lack of working capital, exorbitant utility tariffs, a tax structure higher than elsewhere in the region, high wage demands and expectations, and a credit and liquidity crunch.

According to the 2010 Mid-term Fiscal Policy Review Statement, the manufacturing sector was estimated to have grown by 10.2 per cent in 2009 from −33.4 per cent in 2008, largely underpinned by the liberalization and deregulation measures ushered in by STERP. In 2010 it is projected that the sector will grow by 4.5 per cent. However, as the Minister of Finance observed, the momentum that had been generated in the manufacturing sector was not sustained during the first half of 2010, as reflected by the sluggish gains in average capacity-utilization levels that are still hovering around 35–40 per cent. Notable exceptions have been in the food and beverages sub-sector, where major gains in capacity utilization have left some firms operating at about 70 per cent.[22]

The full recovery of the manufacturing sector is inextricably linked to the recovery of the agricultural sector. The government has identified strategic sub-sectors that will assist the manufacturing sector to improve capacity utilization, which include companies in food processing, beverages, textiles and ginning, clothing and footwear, fertilizers, pharmaceuticals, motor industries, packaging, paper, printing and publishing, chemical and petroleum products, non-metallic mineral products.[23]

## 4.6 Recommendations and the Way Forward

### 4.6.1 Strategic industrial and export policy
Zimbabwe has experimented with various policies and strategies from market-based policies to controls, but neither approach has proved to be sufficient to add value to raw materials and enhance international competitiveness as part of an industrial strategy. Given the pervasiveness of distortions in Zimbabwe, especially since 1997, the adoption of market-based policies alone may not produce the desired effects.

Zimbabwe can learn from the newly industrializing countries of East Asia that intervened strategically in various ways to nurture and promote specific manufactured exports of high technological sophistication. This was achieved by deliberately altering price incentives in order to promote manufacturing firms that required increasingly advanced skills and technology. Some of the interventions used included subsidizing the acquisition of certain technologies and providing tax breaks to industries judged most likely to foster further economic progress. These interventions were highly selective, specifically targeted, and conditioned on the eventual attainment of economic efficiency and international competitiveness (Smith, 1991).

---

[22] Mid-term Fiscal Policy Review Statement, 14 July 2010, 43.

[23] Section 184 of the STERP document.

Zimbabwe needs to come up with an industrial policy based on the following generic principles developed by Rodrik (2007: 114–16):

1.  Incentives should be provided only to 'new' activities. 'New' refers both to products that are new to the local economy and to new technologies for producing an existing product.
2.  There should be clear benchmarks or criteria for success and failure.
3.  There must be a built-in 'sunset' clause. This ensures that resources do not remain tied up for an inordinately long time in activities that are not paying off.
4.  Public support must target activities, not sectors.
5.  Activities that are subsidized must have the clear potential of providing spill-overs and demonstration effects.
6.  The authority to carry out industrial policies must be vested in agencies with demonstrated competence.
7.  The implementing agencies must be monitored closely by a principal with a clear stake in the outcomes who has political authority at the highest level.
8.  The agencies carrying out promotion must maintain channels of communication with the private sector.
9.  Mistakes that result in 'picking the losers' will occur.
10. Activities need to have the capacity to renew themselves, so that the cycle of discovery becomes an ongoing one.

Incentives can encourage firms to undertake technological capability building. The provision of protection to the industry affected needs to be consistent with a country trying to develop a dynamic comparative advantage in manufacturing. In this regard, it needs to be underpinned by a strategy designed to raise industrial competitiveness. This can be achieved by basing protection for certain industries and/or firms on the achievements of set export targets;[24] the failure to achieve such targets would see the removal of such protection. Thus, the strategy would entail selectivity in terms of which sectors or firms to support depending on perceived future comparative advantages.[25] However, such a strategy needs to be time-bound in order to remove the risk of its being abused. The adoption of such a strategy would provide the engine of growth in technological capability development, in spite of the protected domestic market.

### 4.6.2 Adequate infrastructure provision
Given that poor infrastructure for business (water, electricity, telecommunications, roads, railways and ports) impacts adversely on export growth, it is necessary for

---

[24] Zimbabwe Financial Holdings, *Zimbabwe Economic Review*, December, 1995.

[25] There is need to base this on the computation of effective rates of protection.

the state to play an active role in the provision of adequate infrastructure. This can also be achieved though public–private partnerships.[26]

### 4.6.3 Technology transfer

In addition to institutional support, industrial competitiveness can be improved by building industrial capabilities in the form of the provision of technical effort and skills (Lall, 1993b). No firm can achieve – and sustain – international competitiveness unless there is a conscious effort to acquire and assimilate technology. Product quality, which is extremely important in expanding exports in Zimbabwe (Muzulu, 1993), is a function of technical progress. In fact, for any post-crisis industrial strategy to be effective, there is an urgent need to develop skills and acquire state-of-the-art technology given that 'at a time when manufacturing industry worldwide is becoming more skills- and knowledge-intensive, Zimbabwe has fallen behind technologically' (UNDP, 2008: 130).

Although recent trade theories have tried to incorporate technological change into the analysis, the simplicity of the way this has been done (reducing it to 'learning curves') is 'reflected in the simplicity of the policy recommendations of how to slide along such learning curves' (Van Hulst *et al.*, 1992: 248). Technology is neither freely available to all countries and firms nor is its absorption costless and instantaneous. Firm-level research in South-East Asia has shown that investment in the necessary assimilation and adaptation of industrial technology is vitally important in the development process (Pack and Westphal, 1986).

The World Bank also admits that manufacturers' ability to compete depends on, among other things, the extent to which technological improvements are transferred 'to facilities manufacturing for the local market' (1995b: 32). However, it is not clear how this can occur if everything is simply left to market forces, as the Bank appears to imply. Given that technology is essential for improving product quality, and given also that it cannot be reduced to being perfectly tradable (Westphal, 1990), it follows that policies aimed at improving the competitiveness of the manufacturing sector need to address the technological factor seriously. African industry 'suffers from ... small ... technological capabilities for the efficient exploitation of existing physical capacity and the dynamic build-up of new areas of competitiveness ... [and unless] the base of capabilities is improved, no amount of tinkering with incentive structures will produce sustained export growth' (Lall, 1993a: 58). Indeed, research in both industrial and developing countries has shown that industrial competitive advantages arise from 'deliberate efforts to build industrial capabilities rather than "given" factor endowments' (Lall, 1993b: 4) since prices do not always carry sufficient information for economic decisions (Datta-Chaudhuri, 1990).

---

[26] See also Chapter 2.

Attracting foreign direct investment (FDI) may be one of the main vehicles for acquiring new technology and marketing strategies (Lall, 1993a), but, in more recent years, FDI was increasingly attracted to the developed world (Kaplinsky, 1991). Evidence from South Korea shows that multinational corporations played a crucial supporting role in the evolution of its comparative advantage (Westphal, 1990). Unfortunately, technological changes have encouraged FDI in locations that provide highly skilled labour, advanced infrastructure and stability (Lall, 1993a). While price signals may encourage domestic firms to develop technological capabilities, this may not be enough because of externalities, high risks, lack of technical knowledge, and so on (World Bank, 1992: 27). Consequently, firms may under-invest in such crucial areas. Thus, policy-makers have to encourage technological effort, for example, 'to subsidize R&D, provide technical extension services and information, and create a technology infrastructure to help firms do quality control, testing, design development, production "trouble-shooting", process adaptation, and so on' (Lall, 1993a: 60).

### 4.6.4 Promotion of small- and medium-scale manufacturing enterprises

The above strategy needs to be pursued concurrently with one that encourages the development of small- and medium-scale enterprises (SMEs) because they have proved to be the main hope of increasing employment owing to their low capital–labour ratios. The setting up of the Ministry of Small and Medium Enterprises Development in 2000, as well as institutions such as the Small Enterprise Development Corporation (SEDCO) to lend exclusively to small firms, has helped to promote the growth of this sector. However, both the Ministry and SEDCO have largely failed to deliver because of the under-funding of their activities; apart from its administrative problems, SEDCO remains under-capitalized. While the RBZ came in to support this sector – through such schemes as the Farm Mechanization Programme, the Distressed Companies Fund, the Productive Sector Facility, and the Basic Commodities Supply-Side Intervention Programme (BACOSSI) – its support was not sustainable. The bulk of its funding was diverted from production into speculative activities that offered better and quicker returns because the monitoring of beneficiaries was weak. For example, in June 2004 the RBZ allocated $50 billion (US$8.5 million) to SEDCO which was disbursed to 106 beneficiaries. While production improved temporarily in some of the companies, in most instances the amounts disbursed were too insignificant to have had any impact on capacity utilization, and macroeconomic conditions prevented any expansion of production.

Small businesses in Zimbabwe suffered from the following constraints: access to land; access to credit; inadequate management and technical skills; lack of means of transport for products; inadequate infrastructure; and a history of government policies that tend to favour large and existing industry, such as the foreign-exchange allocation system (World Bank, 1993). Such issues, if addressed by government, can lead to significant growth in output in this sector and, with it, employment. Indeed, land security is of crucial importance in the promotion of growth in the economy, which includes SMEs. As the World Bank (ibid.: 25) argued, it was almost impossible for SMEs to access credit unless they could offer title deeds as collateral.

According to Chambati (1995), industrialization will not take root in Africa as long as concentration is placed on supporting and assisting existing industries. He goes on to argue that industrialization can be aided by encouraging SMEs, especially in rural areas, with the help of the state. It is noteworthy that both the CZI and the Zimbabwe National Chamber of Commerce are supportive of the need to promote SMEs via subcontracting as well as setting up committees to look into the problems of this sub-sector. However, their efforts need to be part of a wider developmental initiative that addresses the problem as part of an industrial strategy.

### 4.6.5 Development of clusters

Cluster development in the manufacturing sector, targeting especially the SMEs, is a viable industrialization option for Zimbabwe, and is ideal in that it focuses development on groups of firms rather than on individual firms.[27] SMEs in the manufacturing sector stand to benefit from clustering as it provides and encourages collective efficiency and competitiveness, and fosters productivity and innovation. The development of clusters can also assist SMEs in rural and communal areas to obtain easier access to markets and technology. It is, therefore, important that there be a conscious and explicit cluster-development programme targeting the manufacturing sector.

Industrial clusters operating in the same sector can provide advantages to small firms, ranging from agglomeration economies and joint-action benefits. Emphasis in a cluster model is on internal linkages, within which cluster gains are enhanced by local firm co-operation, local institutions and local social capital. External linkages also come into play, with global buyers helping local clusters access global markets, acquire new knowledge and upgrade. However, the governance relationship between external buyers and local clustered firms is critical, as it determines the autonomy and power of the local firms. The value-chain approach helps understand how local clusters are inserted into global value-chains and provide a basis for exploring the link with poverty by identifying the poverty 'nodes'.[28]

---

[27] A cluster is defined by Porter (2001) as 'a geographic concentration of competing and co-operating companies, suppliers, service providers and associated institutions'.

[28] See UNIDO (2004) for an excellent discussion.

Importantly, industrial clusters can have direct links with poverty through employment, incomes, and the well-being generated for the working poor, and also indirect links through their wider impact on the local economy. From a conceptual perspective, clusters and poverty are related in three distinct ways: through cluster features, cluster processes and cluster dynamics. Certain types of clusters – such as those in rural areas and the urban informal economy, those with a predominance of SMEs, micro-enterprises and homemakers, those in labour-intensive sectors, and those that employ women, migrants and unskilled labour – have a direct impact on poverty. Agglomeration economies help reduce costs and improve the capabilities of workers and producers. These capabilities are further strengthened by cluster joint action, which also reduces vulnerability to external shocks. Because cluster growth produces winners and losers among workers and producers, it is important to understand which workers and producers win and which ones lose in order to enhance poverty outcomes (UNIDO, 2004).

By identifying business-environment constraints – inefficiencies and cost disadvantages – policy-makers have the opportunity to initiate reform processes that target priority areas along the product/service life-cycle – the value chain.[29] The policy and reform agenda that emerges from the value-chain approach relates to three core areas (FIAS, 2007):

- Product market issues – e.g. trade policy, competition policy, price distortions, subsidies, licensing, product standards, customs, logistics, property rights, enforcement of regulations.
- Factor market issues – e.g. wages, capital charges, utility-market issues, labour-market rigidities, land price, zoning.
- Market-related issues – e.g. market diversification, research and development, product diversification, supplier linkages.

### 4.6.6 Phased import liberalization

In order to minimize the adverse impact on the domestic industry of the removal of customs duty on imports, import liberalization should have been phased in gradually via a more selective, incremental and targeted intervention. Furthermore, it is crucial that stability be achieved in order to maintain low and predictable interest rates that are not inimical to increased investment needed to achieve sustainable growth.

### 4.6.7 Strengthening the human-capital base

In addition, the competitiveness of Zimbabwe's manufacturing sector can be

---

[29] Value-chain analysis is a method of accounting and presenting the value that is created in a product or service as it is transformed from raw inputs to a final product consumed by end-users.

further enhanced if firms have access to the requisite skills. It is generally agreed that there is need to strengthen the human-capital base of developing countries in a bid to enhance technological capabilities. According to Lall, 'even the simplest of technologies, if they are to be operated at world levels of efficiency, need a range of workers' supervisory, maintenance, quality control and adaptive skills. Advanced activities need more, not just in a static sense, but continuously as technical change for new capabilities' (1993b: 14–15). The market failures associated with the education system are well known and have been reviewed extensively (Kanyenze, 2009). The education system currently produces labour that has the wrong skills, basically because educational establishments are far removed from the needs of industry. It is not just volume of investment in education that is important: the relevance of the education provided is a vital determinant of its contribution to industrial development (Lall, 1990; Muzulu, 1993).

Since 1997, when macroeconomic conditions worsened in the country, the public education system has been under a lot of strain owing to inadequate funding, which resulted in qualified educators in technical colleges and universities emigrating into the region, particularly to South Africa, in search of better working conditions. The development of new forms of work organization, arising from the need to be competitive internationally, has made skills acquisition essential. Additionally, the general transition to 'quality at source' and cellular production (Kaplinsky and Posthuma, 1993) implies a shift away from unskilled towards more skilled labour. By its very nature, multi-skilling entails risks and externalities, which may lead firms to under-invest in human-resource development. Thus, the state needs to intervene to enhance special training.

## References

Chambati, A. 1995. 'Industrialisation of Africa', *Southern African Encounter*, 2(1).

Cho, Y. and D. R. Khatkhate 1989. 'Lessons of Financial Liberalization in Asia: A Comparative Study' (Washington, DC: World Bank, Discussion Paper 50).

CZI 2003. *Manufacturing Sector Survey, 2003* (Harare: Confederation of Zimbabwe Industries).

CZI 2007. *Manufacturing Sector Survey, 2007* (Harare: Confederation of Zimbabwe Industries).

CZI 2008. *Manufacturing Sector Survey, 2008* (Harare: Confederation of Zimbabwe Industries).

CZI 2009. *Manufacturing Sector Survey, 2009* (Harare: Confederation of Zimbabwe Industries).

Datta-Chaudhuri, M. 1990. 'Market failure and government Failure', *Journal of Economic Perspectives*, 4(3).

Edwards, S. and F. Ng 1985. 'Trends in Real Exchange Rate Behaviour in Selected Developing Countries' (Washington, DC: World Bank Country

Programs Department, Discussion Paper 16).

Fazzari, S. M., R. G. Hubbard and B. C. Petersen 1988. 'Financing Constraints and Corporate Investment', *Brookings Papers on Economic Activity* 1988(1).

Felipe, J., U. Kumar and A. Abdan 2010. *Exports, Capabilities and Industrial Policy in India* (Annandale-on-Hudson, NY: Levy Economics Institute, Working Paper No. 638).

FIAS 2007. *Moving Toward Competitiveness: A Value Chain Approach* (Washington DC: World Bank, Foreign Investment Advisory Service).

Harvey, C. and C. Jenkins 1994. 'Interest rate policy, taxation and risk', *World Development*, 22(12), 1869–79.

Herbst, J. 1990. *State Politics in Zimbabwe* (Harare: University of Zimbabwe Publications).

Jansen, D. 1983. 'Zimbabwe: Government Policy and the Manufacturing Sector', mimeo.

Kaldor, N. 1967. *Strategic Factors in Economic Development* (Ithaca, NY: Cornell University).

Kanyenze, G. 2009. 'Labour Markets and the Rebuilding of Human Capital' (Harare: UNDP, Comprehensive Economic Recovery in Zimbabwe, Working Paper 3).

Kaplinsky, R. 1991. 'TNCs in the Third World: Stability or discontinuity', *Journal of International Studies*, 20(3).

Kaplinsky, R. and A. Posthuma 1993. 'Organisational Change in Zimbabwean Manufacturing' (mimeo).

Kariuki, P. 1993. *Interest Rate Liberalisation and the Allocative Efficiency of Credit: Some Evidence from the Small and Medium Scale Industry in Kenya* (Brighton: University of Sussex, IDS, D.Phil. thesis).

Kundishora, H. 2009. 'Zimbabwe Economy – Indigenisation Not the Key', *The African Executive*.

Lall, S. 1990. *Building Industrial Competitiveness in Developing Countries* (Paris: OECD).

Lall, S. 1993a, 'Trade policies for development: A policy prescription for Africa', *Development Policy Review*, 11.

Lall, S. 1993b. 'What Will Make South Africa Internationally Competitive' (mimeo).

Munoz, S. 2007. 'Central Bank Quasi-Fiscal Losses and High Inflation in Zimbabwe: A Note' (Washington, DC: International Monetary Fund, Working Paper Number 07/98).

Muzulu, J. 1993. *Real Exchange Rate Depreciation and Structural Adjustment: The Case of the Manufacturing Sector in Zimbabwe* (Brighton: University of Sussex, D.Phil. thesis).

Muzulu, J. 1994. 'The Impact of Currency Depreciation on Zimbabwe's Manufacturing Sector', *Development Policy Review*, 12.

Muzulu, J. 1995. 'Beyond ESAP – Financial Policies for Sustainable Development', background paper for the ZCTU 'Beyond ESAP' Project, Harare.

Ndlela, Dan B. 1984. 'Sectoral analysis of Zimbabwe economic development with implications for foreign trade and foreign exchange', *Zimbabwe Journal of Economics*, 1(1).

Pack, H. and L. E. Westphal 1986. 'Industrial strategy and technological change: Theory versus reality', *Journal of Development Economics*, 22(1).

Porter, M. 2001. 'Clusters of Innovation Initiative: Regional Foundations of U.S. Competitiveness'.

RBZ 2006. *A synopsis of the impact of the Central Bank's interventions to the economy from Jan 2004 – June 2006* (Harare: Reserve Bank of Zimbabwe).

Riddell, R. 1990. 'Zimbabwe', in his (ed.), *Manufacturing Africa; Prospects and Performance in Seven Countries of Sub-Saharan Africa* (London, Overseas Development Institute).

Robinson, P. 2006. Zimbabwe's Hyperinflation: The House is on Fire – But Does the Government Know it is Dousing the Flames with Petrol (Bonn: Friedrich-Ebert-Stiftung, Referat Afrika).

Rodrik, D. 2007. *One Economics, Many Recipes: Globalization, Institutions, and Economic Growth* (Princeton and Oxford: Princeton University Press).

Skalness, T. 1993. 'The state, interest groups and structural adjustment in Zimbabwe', *Journal of Development Studies*, 29(3).

Smith, S. 1991. *Industrial Policy in Developing Countries: Reconsidering the Real Sources of Export-led Growth* (Washington, DC: Economic Policy Institute).

Tekere, M. 2001. 'Trade Liberalisation under Structural Economic Adjustment – Impact on Social Welfare in Zimbabwe' (Harare: University of Zimbabwe, Poverty Reduction Forum, SAPRI).

UNDP 2008. *Comprehensive Economic Recovery in Zimbabwe: A Discussion Document* (Harare: United Nations Development Programme).

UNIDO 1986. *The Manufacturing Sector in Zimbabwe* (Vienna: UNIDO).

UNIDO 2004. 'Industrial Clusters and Poverty Reduction: Towards a Methodology for Poverty and Social Impact Assessment of Cluster Development Initiatives' (Vienna: UNIDO).

Van Hulst, N., R. Mulder and, L. G. Soete 1991. 'Exports and technology in manufacturing industry', *Weltwirtschaftliches Archiv*, 27(2).

Westphal, L. E. 1990. 'Industrial policy in an export-propelled economy: Lessons from South Korea's experience', *Journal of Economic Perspectives*, 4(3).

World Bank 1987. *Zimbabwe: An Industrial Sector Memorandum* (Washington DC: World Bank).

World Bank 1992. *World Bank Support for Industrialisation in Korea, India and Indonesia* (Washington DC: World Bank).

World Bank 1993. *Zimbabwe: A Policy Agenda for Private Sector Development* (Washington DC: World Bank).

World Bank 1995a. 'Africa's Experience with Structural Adjustment – Proceedings of the Harare Seminar, May 23-24, 1994' (Washington, DC: World Bank Discussion Paper).

World Bank 1995b. 'Zimbabwe: Achieving Shared Growth' (Washington, DC: World Bank, Country Economic Memorandum Volume 2).

World Bank 2009. *World Development Indicators, 2009* (Washington, DC: World Bank).

Zimbabwe 2009. 'The 2009 Mid-Term Fiscal Policy Statement, 16 July 2009' (Harare: Ministry of Finance).

## Chapter 5

# Mining

## 5.1 The First Decade of Independence, 1980–1990

The years 1980 to 1990 could be viewed as a two-phase period, the first from 1980 to 1985, when the policies in place were a carry-over from those implemented by the pre-independence government. This period was characterized by declining volumes of most of the minerals produced. This was followed by the years from 1985 to 1990, when policy amendments to reverse declining production volumes were undertaken, with some positive outcomes.

Investor interest in mineral exploration, which had been affected by the war, started fairly early in 1980 with companies such as BP Coal Zimbabwe, *inter alia*, taking up ground for mineral exploration. The Zimbabwe Geological Survey played a critical role in providing technical papers, bulletins, maps and data on the country's geology which interested investors in mineral exploration. Between 1980 and 1990 the country attracted interest from many countries, resulting in government-to-government co-operation projects aimed at revealing the country's mineral potential. These include regional mapping and the generation of bulletins with such organizations as BGRM of France, the British Geological Survey, BGR of Germany, JICA (the Japanese International Co-operation Agency) and others. With aid from Germany, the Geological Survey established the National Remote Sensing Facility that provided additional tools for mineral exploration and land-use planning. In addition, the Canadian International Development Agency funded a number of projects, including the airborne aeromagnetic survey.

As a result of these and other initiatives, private-sector investment increased as the number of active Exclusive Prospecting Orders (EPOs) increased from 53 in 1980 to 59 in 1990, with 54 new applications having been received in 1990. These exploration activities resulted in some significant discoveries of mineral deposits and useful findings that included the Royal Family resource (gold) discovered in 1983 and becoming operational in 1984, and the Freda Rebecca resource (gold) discovered in 1985 with the mine opening in 1988. The feasibility study on the Hartley Platinum Mine by Delta Gold was conducted in 1988, the Sengwa tarred road as part of efforts to develop the Sengwa coal deposit was built, and test work on the Cam and Motor dump, which was geared to produce 650 kg of gold per year, were conducted among other investments. Government entered negotiations with Mobil Oil Corporation for hydrocarbon exploration in the Zambezi Valley in 1988 with the signing of an agreement in 1989; exploration work for hydrocarbon deposits started in 1990. Although the exercise did not find any oil, results pointed to the possibilities of a gas resource. There was need to sink a pilot well to confirm the existence of the gas, but Mobil Oil was not in a position to finance this exercise and the project was abandoned.

### 5.1.1 Foreign-currency shortages

The years 1980 to 1990 were characterized by severe shortages of foreign currency. Mining imports were acquired through permits obtained on application to the Ministry of Industry and Commerce. For the mining sector, government established the Mining Continuation Reserve (MCR) and the Mining Projects Fund (MPF). The MCR was used to import inputs meant to keep operations going, while the MPF was meant for capital projects to grow the production base. By 1983, allocations for the industry under these schemes were very low, impacting adversely on the availability of mining inputs. Shortages of mining inputs, combined with low revenues generated from exports, created production challenges. By 1984 a huge backlog of mining inputs had accumulated. With limited investment having been made before independence, the shortage of foreign currency to import spares badly affected the utilization levels of the aged equipment and machinery.

In 1985, allocations of Z$34.776 million (US$21.189 million) were made against bids of Z$74.934 million (US$45.658 million). Government negotiated a loan of £70 million from two British banks to augment the allocations made under the MCR and MPF.[1] This facility was available to exporters only under the Export Promotion Programme. Mining was allocated £35 million; the first tranche of Z$23.67 million (US$14.422 million) was made in September as an addition to the MCR and MPF. In 1987, government made allocations of Z$32.707 million (US$19.666 million) to the MCR and Z$15.724million (US$9.455 million) to the MPF. Demand for foreign currency for both recurrent and capital items was Z$90 million (US$54.116 million) annually during the period 1984 to 1990. The actual allocations were nowhere near these levels. By 1990, allocation of foreign currency was Z$112.414 million (US$45.550 million), inclusive of allocations made under the Export Promotion Programme. This compares unfavourably to Z$92.5 million (US$43.604 million) in 1989, Z$80.4 million (US$44.132 million) in 1988 and Z$48.43 million (US$29.120 million) in 1987.

To cater for non-exporters' requirements, a percentage of the exporters' foreign-currency entitlement under the MCR was set aside. Companies such as BIMCO, Hwange Colliery, Dorowa Minerals and others were able to maintain operations as a result of this arrangement.

---

[1] Information on the MCR and MPF is contained in the Chamber of Mines *Annual Reports*, 1980 to 1988. Additional information was sourced from the Secretary for Mines *Annual Reports*, 1988, 1989 and 1990.

### 5.1.2 Production

The decline in most mineral commodity prices during 1980 to 1985 combined with foreign-currency shortages and increases in the cost of production to create a harsh operating environment for mineral producers. The fuel shortages experienced during 1982 and 1983 also made operating mines much more difficult, and the 1984/85 drought brought water challenges for some mineral producers. Challenges were also faced in terms of providing sufficient food for the workers, but these were effectively resolved with the assistance of government, which allowed mines to access strategic grain reserves.

Gold prices peaked in 1980 as demand increased arising from investors taking gold positions. The war in Afghanistan and political instability in Iran created conditions of uncertainty leading to the hoarding of gold. Prices declined to a low of US$376.35/oz in 1982 owing to the recessions experienced in 1981 and 1982. The weak US dollar created demand for gold among jewellers and investors, which led to an increase in gold prices from 1985 to 1987. Asbestos prices declined from US$382/t in 1980 to US$262/t in 1990. Nickel prices declined from US$6,230/t in 1980 to US$4,670/t in 1983 owing to the world recession that reduced demand. Prices then increased from US$3,880/t in 1986 to US$13,800/t in 1987 because of a shortage of primary nickel on the market. Copper prices followed the nickel trend.

Production of most minerals declined from 1980 to 1984 as a result of inadequate mining inputs because of shortages of foreign currency. A combination

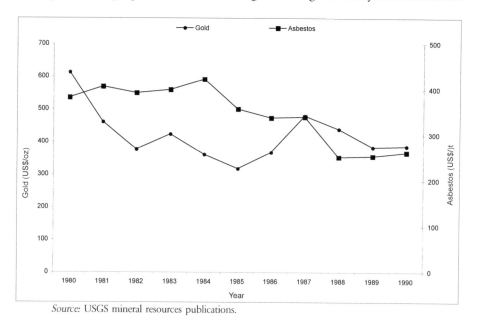

Source: USGS mineral resources publications.

**Fig. 5.1: Gold and asbestos prices**

of declining mineral revenues and limited availability of plant and equipment affected the production of most minerals. The MCR and MPF reduced the extent of the decline in mineral production.

The copper operations at Mhangura and Alaska mines were experiencing declining head grades,[2] leading to lower production levels during the period 1980 to 1984 at a time when copper prices were not favourable. The shortages of foreign currency and declining revenues combined to create difficult conditions for copper production. The major producer of copper, Messina (Transvaal) Development Company (MTD), indicated its intention to disinvest as early as 1988, citing the challenging operating environment. When MTD was allowed to disinvest, government handed their assets over to the Zimbabwe Mining Development Corporation (ZMDC).

Gold production increased from 11,444 kg in 1980 to 14,877 kg in 1984. This increase was attributed mainly to the growth in the number of producers during this period, from 389 in 1980 to 525 in 1985.[3] Although there was a decline in prices during this period, the contributions from the new producers compensated for the loss in production arising from declining revenues.

In 1984, the government, through the RBZ and in partnership with the mining industry, agreed to assist the gold industry maintain viability through the establishment of a gold-stabilization scheme. Under this scheme, the RBZ would buy gold from producers at a floor price of Z$500/oz. In the event that the market price was more than that, the RBZ would pay producers the Z$500/oz plus 75 per cent of the market differential. The remaining 25 per cent was to be retained by the RBZ to liquidate the account they used to pay producers when the price was less than Z$500/oz. The gold floor price was increased to US$950/oz in 1990. It was this policy position that was responsible for maintaining production at around 14,800 kg between 1984 and 1988.

The Roasting Plant Corporation, a government parastatal, was also facing challenges in toll processing refractory gold ores.[4] By 1984 the capacity at the plant was grossly insufficient to meet mine production, and a commitment was made to purchase an additional roaster. Construction of the roaster started in 1985 but its commissioning was delayed until 1987. The roasting process caused arsenic fumes to be released into the atmosphere, and environmental concerns raised by the government's environmental authority led to the suspension of the use of the third roaster. These developments affected producers of refractory ore, as limited revenue was generated as a result of constraints suffered by their only

---

[2] Head grade is the average grade of ore fed into a mill.

[3] Secretary for Mines *Annual Reports*, 1980 to 1985.

[4] Toll processing is an arrangement whereby a firm that has specialized processing facilities processes raw materials (in this case, refractory gold concentrates) on behalf of others.

processing facility. Although the Roasting Plant made efforts to find alternative technology for the treatment of refractory gold ores, by 1990 no satisfactory solution had been found. This led to the closure of a number of small gold mines in the Midlands area that relied on the Roasting Plant for the treatment of their ore. It is estimated that a refractory gold resource of 8.7 million tonnes grading 5.6g/t is available for exploitation within the Midlands area.[5]

As early as 1984, government considered the possibility of establishing a re-finery to process the ever-increasing gold that the country was producing; at this time all the gold was being refined in South Africa at the Rand Refinery. By the end of 1990 the refinery had been built and was operational as part of Fidelity Printers, a subsidiary of the Reserve Bank of Zimbabwe. This development was part of government's efforts to increase the level of beneficiation of minerals. The refining of gold locally saved the country foreign currency in processing fees.

### 5.1.3 Small-scale mining

In 1980 small-scale mining was only a small component of the mining industry, confined mainly to ex-servicemen from the Second World War. The Mining Industry Loan Fund was created specifically to assist those interested in mining to establish their operations. With the opening of the mining space to every Zimbabwean, interest in mining grew rapidly. The Small-Scale Miners Associ-ation was formed in the mid-1980s for the purpose of representing the interest of black small-scale miners. It received support from the Intermediate Technology Development Group to build a secretariat and structures that could best serve the interests of its members. One of the projects that was developed was the Shamva Mining Centre, which was a central processing facility for gold ore from mining communities around Shamva. Besides processing gold, the Centre provided technical assistance to miners in the catchment area to enable it to make full use of its installed milling and processing capacity. This ran successfully for some time until it ran into management difficulties.

Small-scale mining was confined to gold, emeralds, semi-precious stones (aquamarine and amethyst), chrome, talc, mica and tantalite. Most of these are high-value, low-volume products that are easy to transport. There has been limited involvement of the small-scale sector in base minerals such as limestone, nickel or copper because of the capital required for large volumes to generate sufficient returns, as well as the absence of a ready market.

Government promoted the establishment of mining co-operatives in the early 1980s. The ZMDC was mandated with overseeing their development, and a division was formed within the company that encouraged and registered co-operatives. The area in which the co-operatives thrived was chrome. The need

---

[5] *Zimbabwe Refractory Gold Ores: Reserves and Resources, 1993* - T. Nutt and Associates.

for a group to pull their resources together to generate sufficient volumes for sale can be cited as a reason for their success. The availability of a ready market in the form of ZIMASCO and Zimbabwe Alloys also helped in the development of these co-operatives.

## 5.2 The ESAP Period, 1991–1996

With the declining performance of the economy in the late 1980s, it became apparent that intervention was needed to reverse the fortunes of the economy. The government entered into negotiations with the World Bank that resulted in the introduction of the Economic Structural Adjustment Programme (ESAP) in 1991. When ESAP was announced, many commentators pointed to the failure of similar programmes elsewhere in Africa. The pillars of this programme were:
- Budget deficit reduction
- Fiscal and monetary reforms
- Trade liberalization
- Public enterprise reforms – privatization and commercialization
- Deregulation of investment, labour and price-control legislation

The mining industry benefited mainly from the deregulation of fiscal and monetary reforms, investment controls and trade liberalization. In this regard the removal of import-permit requirements in favour of the free importation of goods and services ensured that inputs such as chemicals, spares for equipment and machinery, explosives and replacement capital were acquired much more easily. The export retention scheme allowed exporters, of which mining is an important component, to retain and manage some of their foreign-currency earnings. The relaxation of exchange-control measures meant that the conduct of business was more in line with international norms.

### 5.2.1 Developments during ESAP

At this time the ability of the export sector to provide sufficient foreign currency for the country's requirements was very limited. Government's financial requirements were increasing against declining revenues; and inflation was rising.

Under ESAP, government introduced the Open General Import Licence (OGIL) scheme as part of the trade-liberalization measures. All goods could be imported without a permit, with the exception of materials of war and goods of overwhelming public interest. As for business, the move towards a free-market economy was a welcome departure from the bureaucracy of the permit system. The advantage to mineral producers was in the ability to plan and execute programmes and projects within budget times. Government also introduced the export retention scheme, removing the foreign-currency allocation system. Under the retention scheme exporters were allowed to retain 5 per cent of their total foreign-currency earnings with effect from 1 January 1991, which was increased to 30 per cent in December 1992. Foreign-currency-account resources could initially be held for only ninety days, but this retention period was removed in July 1994. The Minerals Marketing Corporation of Zimbabwe (MMCZ) used its position to secure foreign-currency-denominated loans, which were made available to mineral exporters for the importation of mining inputs and machinery. Three facilities were organized between 1991 and 1993, valued at over US$80 million.

To cater for the foreign-currency needs of non-exporting mines, 2.5 per cent of 15 per cent of the total retained export proceeds for the period July to December 1991 was reserved for non-exporting mines. This policy was made as an afterthought following the realization that non-exporting mines made a significant contribution to the economy. In the formulation of policy to make foreign currency available to exporters, very little consideration had been given to gold producers, who were considered non-exporters. The RBZ finally agreed to pay gold producers in foreign currency in 1996, which provided producers with some foreign currency with which to develop the industry. With foreign currency now available, mineral producers were able to acquire imported inputs more easily: as over 60 per cent of the inputs were imported, the importance of foreign currency cannot be overstated. Besides inputs such as spares, explosives, drilling accessories, grease and chemicals, replacement capital items such as fans, jack-hammers and compressors were needed following a ten-year period when such purchases were not possible. Production of non-export minerals such as coal, iron ore, phosphate and pyrites had declined as a result of the constant breakdown of machinery and equipment arising from shortages of spares and service kits.

These measures were meant to deal decisively with the perennial problem of shortages of imported inputs. The local manufacturing sector was able to provide some significant inputs into mining processes during this period.[6] Supplies such as drill bits, drill rods, pumps, underground wagons, underground locomotives, crushers, ball mills and grinding media were largely manufactured locally for the mining industry. However, the capacity of the local manufacturing sector to continue producing was hindered by the revaluation of the exchange rate that made the acquisition of foreign currency expensive. In addition shortages of foreign currency reduced the ability of manufacturers to maintain stocks of raw materials. With the reduction in duties of finished products, some local manufacturers could not compete on pricing with imported products, forcing some of them to become traders rather than manufacturers.

---

[6] Mining processes are a sequence of interdependent and linked procedures. For example, development drilling, rock support, rock and waste hauling, hoisting, ore crushing, milling, filtration, among others.

However, it appears government may have rushed into implementing a programme without having properly analysed the implication of some of the policy moves. With the experience gained with the Export Promotion Programme, the MCR and MPF, one would have expected government to have a thorough understanding of which sectors were in need of foreign currency and the levels required to achieve growth. Past experience with the import-licence system provided sufficient learning points on the importance of foreign currency to the minerals sector.

As part of ESAP, customs duty on capital goods was exempted. The mining sector benefited from the duty draw-back scheme. Government phased out the OGIL scheme at end of 1993: a 10 per cent temporary duty on OGIL was removed, while a 20 per cent surtax was reduced to 15 per cent with effect from 1 January 1994. However, there was an increase in general sales tax on vehicles and an increase in the cost of fuels, among other increases, which added to the tax burden. The overall impact of the measures was to increase the cost of doing business.

### 5.2.2 Small-scale mining
By 1990 government estimated that over 600,000 people were involved in gold-panning and almost all rivers were affected. In response to the growing number of illegal panners, and to provide the legal space for this activity, government promulgated the Mining (Alluvial Gold) (Public Stream) Regulations of 1991. The policy position was to allow panning in the middle of a river bed.

The ministry of mines granted licences to Rural District Councils in the form of special grants over large tracts of the river course within their jurisdiction. These councils were, in turn, required to issue licences to panners over 100 m stretches along the river. No panning was to take place on the river banks; supervision was to be provided by the councils. The Mining Engineering Department of the University of Zimbabwe under Prof. Voss designed a demonstration project at Makaha in Mutoko and at Filabusi in Matabeleland. Even though the financial viability of these projects was limited, they were a technical success in that areas that had been worked by the project were well rehabilitated and were not invaded again by panners. The projects managed to provide social benefits such as a vegetable garden, a sand-extraction project, a water reservoir for brick moulding, and other activities that were income-generating. In addition, the income from gold sales had a visible impact on the lives of the communities affected.

When this policy position was taken and the regulations developed, no capacity-building programmes were conducted for the councils to handle the technical side of mining; no resources were placed at their disposal to handle the extra responsibilities on mining matters. Although it was a practical activity, no know-how was imparted to council officials to provide regulatory oversight over these activities. As a result, there was huge resistance by councils to apply for special grants and implement provisions of the statutory instrument.

With the 1991/92 drought came a wave of more illegal gold-panners, and now their activities spread beyond river courses to disused mines and any property where gold might be found. Again, no policy intervention was taken to provide an alternative source of income to panning, such as 'food for work' programmes or other public-works initiatives. Sporadic raids were made by the police in areas of high panning activity, but they failed to deter the panners. Those found guilty were given light sentences by the courts. There were many fatal accidents involving illegal panners, most going unreported and unrecorded. Exposure to mercury was high, but the full impact of the panning on health is unknown.

In 1996, Fidelity Printers and Refiners made a decision to accept gold above 50 grams for refining. Those who produced less were forced to sell their production on the parallel (black) market, fuelling parallel-market activities, which further entrenched illegal gold dealings. The chrome co-operative continued to provide important quantities of chrome to the major smelters. The tribute agreements entered into between small-workers and ferrochrome producers involved the provision of technical support by the ferrochrome producers. Outside gold and chrome, small-scale mining activities were quite limited. The volumes of aquamarine, amethyst and talc produced declined during the ESAP period, which can be attributed to the tough social environment that prevailed.

### 5.2.3 Mineral production

Measures undertaken to attract foreign direct investment resulted in some increased investment in the mining sector. In April 1993 government announced a series of measures on investment, export promotion and trade liberalization that impacted positively on the mining industry. These measures included: an increase in the export retention level from 35 per cent to 50 per cent; the introduction of foreign-currency denominated accounts; unrestricted remittance of after-tax dividends accruing to foreign shareholders for new investments, these dividends being paid from funds made available through the export retention scheme market; companies exporting at least 75 per cent of turnover could use blocked funds for investments. In addition, restrictions on access to domestic borrowing by foreign investors were removed in December 1994. Foreign investors were allowed to invest on the Zimbabwe Stock Exchange, while export credit terms were doubled to 180 days.

One of the major investments in mining was the Hartley platinum mine development by BHP Inc. in 1995. In addition, Reunion Mining started copper production at the Munyati Copper Mine, while Ashanti Goldfields took over the Freda Rebecca mine and other properties owned by Cluff Resources. Rio

Tinto Zimbabwe undertook technical evaluation of the Gokwe power station project. These developments were mainly in response to the liberalization of the investment environment.

On the energy front, electricity supplies were disrupted by the 1991/92 drought, which was the worst in the country's history. The low water levels at Kariba affected electricity generation, requiring imports from South Africa, the DRC and Botswana to augment domestic generation. Zambia discontinued its export of power from Kafue owing to drought in April 1992, which caused some supply interruptions at operating mines. The supply position improved significantly in 1996 with the completion of the Matiba–Insukameni inter-connector and the Bindura link to the Cabora Bassa power station. With improved electricity supply came consistent mineral production.

## Coal

The decrease in coal production between 1991 and 1993 is associated with short-ages of foreign currency. Coal was one of the minerals that benefited little from the export retention scheme because most of its production was for domestic consumption. Thus the acquisition of imported spares critical for mining and mineral processing was problematic, and servicing foreign creditors became a challenge. This affected the availability of machinery and ultimately production levels. Production fell from 5,505,000 tonnes in 1991 to 5,174,000 tonnes in 1996, a decline of 6 per cent over the ESAP period (Fig. 5.2), though the number of people employed increased from 12,875 to 19,588 over the same years.

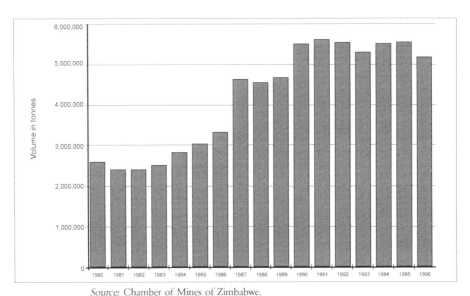

*Source:* Chamber of Mines of Zimbabwe.

**Fig. 5.2: Coal production, 1980–1996**

## Asbestos

The increase in asbestos production from 1991 to 1996 is directly attributable to the foreign currency retention scheme and duty reductions during this period. Production increased from 141,697 tonnes to 165,487 tonnes (Fig. 5.3). The foreign currency retained was used to service mining and mineral-processing equipment that had been run down during the first decade of independence. Of critical importance to underground production operations was drilling and hauling equipment, so the availability of plant and equipment resulted in an increase in production. Although the anti-asbestos lobby had started, its impact had not extended to the greater part of Europe by the end of the ESAP era. Constraints to operations included interruptions in electricity supply and delays in transporting export products to the various ports.

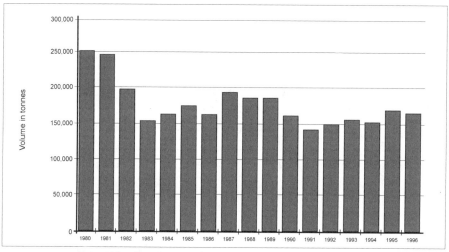

*Source:* Chamber of Mines of Zimbabwe.

**Fig. 5.3: Asbestos production, 1980–1996**

## Iron ore

BIMCO, the mining wing of ZISCO, depends on ZISCO for working capital to undertake the mining of iron ore and limestone that feed the furnaces. Production of iron ore declined from 1,260,000 tonnes in 1990 to 324,000 tonnes in 1996, a fall of 74 per cent (Fig. 5.4). Constant breakdowns of furnaces at ZISCO resulted in decreased demand from them for iron ore. In addition, the shortage of foreign currency affected iron-ore production in the same way that it affected coal operations.

## Copper

The decline in copper production was a function of the inadequate capitalization of copper-mining operations and the antiquated state of plant and machinery. The

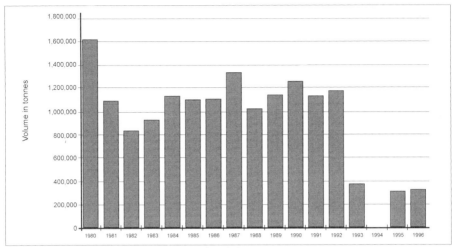

*Source*: Chamber of Mines of Zimbabwe.

**Fig. 5.4: Iron ore production, 1980–1996**

ZMDC operated the only copper mines in the country, and mineral exploration over time around existing mines had failed to yield additional resources. The mines at Alaska and Mhangura were low-grade operations of below 0.5 per cent copper. The ZMDC was struggling to maintain viable operations under difficult conditions. Copper prices declined from US$2,662.88/t in 1990 to US$2,028.60/t in 1993, and rose to US$3,043.90/t in 1995. This trend is reflected in the production volumes realized during this period (Fig. 5.5).

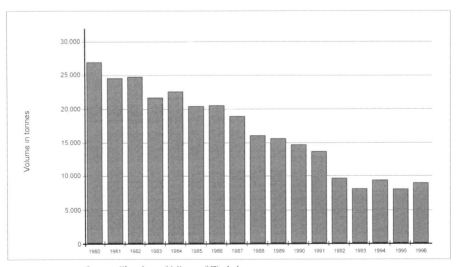

*Source*: Chamber of Mines of Zimbabwe.

**Fig. 5.5: Copper production, 1980–1996**

## Nickel

Nickel prices declined from US$8,864.10/t in 1990 to US$5,292.00 in 1993 and then rose to US$7,497.00/t in 1996. The availability of foreign currency and the increase in nickel prices resulted in increases in volumes produced from 1992 to 1994 (Fig. 5.6). The ability of nickel producers to take advantage of price signals was enhanced as a result of their access to inputs and their ability to service plant and machinery, the result of being able to access and manage foreign currency.

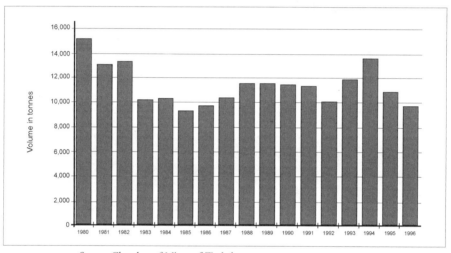

*Source:* Chamber of Mines of Zimbabwe.

**Fig. 5.6: Nickel production, 1980–1996**

## Chrome

Chrome production declined from 573,103 tonnes in 1990 to 516,801 tonnes in 1994, quickly rising to 707,433 tonnes in 1995 (Fig. 5.7). All the chrome produced in Zimbabwe is used in the production of ferroalloys, the primary input in the production of stainless steel. The production performance of chrome ore is a reflection of the demand for and price of ferroalloys, mainly high-carbon ferrochrome.

## Gold

Gold production increased from 16,920 kg in 1990 to 24,722 kg in 1996, a 46 per cent increase over a six-year period, having largely stagnated between 1984 and 1988 (Fig. 5.8). The growth of 6.67 per cent per year was achieved in spite of price stability between 1989 and 1996: the gold price increased by only 1.7 per cent during this period, rising from US$382.58/oz in 1989 to US$389.08/oz in 1996. The reasons for the production increase are therefore domestic. The availability of mining and mineral-processing inputs, such as spares, drilling rods

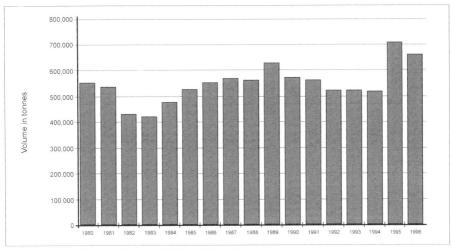

*Source:* Chamber of Mines of Zimbabwe.

**Fig. 5.7: Chrome ore production, 1980–1996**

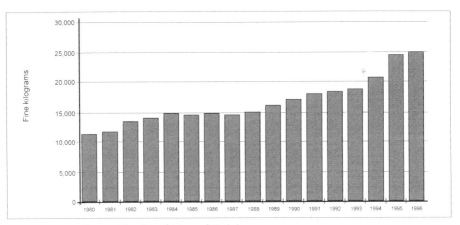

*Source:* Chamber of Mines of Zimbabwe.

**Fig. 5.8: Gold production, 1980–1996**

and accessories, explosives, cyanide and other chemicals, allowed gold producers to produce at higher levels. The liberalization of the import system and the reduction in duties also enabled gold producers to service production units efficiently and thus produce at higher levels. Formal employment increased from 12,300 people in 1990 to 19,588 in 1996. Many more were involved in the illegal panning of gold.

*Platinum*

In 1994, government amended the Mines and Minerals Act to include a section on Special Mining Leases, which provided for government to enter into an agreement with an investor and fix the operating conditions for that investment. Investments that qualified for the Special Mining Lease had a capital threshold of US$100 million. This clause was used to accommodate the requirements of BHP Inc. for the development of the Hartley platinum mine, which was the single largest investment since independence and opened up the Great Dyke to platinum production.

### 5.2.4 Mineral commodity prices

Gold prices moved between US$344.97/oz and US$389.08/oz during the ESAP period. The development of hostilities in the Persian Gulf, coupled with the dissolution of the Soviet Union and the weakening of the world economy, created conditions that weakened investors' appetite for gold as a safe haven for their investment; instead, investors preferred to hold bonds and other securities. Gold prices were relatively stable between 1993 and 1996 (Fig. 5.9).

The decision in 1989 by US automobile manufacturers to use palladium-only auto-catalysts drove down the demand and price of platinum, the latter declining from US$467/oz in 1990 to US$361/oz in 1992.

Palladium prices increased between 1991 and 1995. There was, however, some market resistance that resulted in a switch back to the use of platinum around 1995/96, which followed the application of stringent emission laws in the European Union. Since platinum-based auto-catalysts are said to be more efficient, the US market reverted to the application of platinum for diesel vehicles, resulting in palladium prices falling in 1996.

By 1989 stainless steel production in the West passed 10 million tonnes per year. The massive selling of nickel by Russia to raise foreign currency depressed the market, resulting in the price declining from US$8,864/t in 1990 to US$5,292/t in 1993.[7] Production cut-backs led to shortages of primary nickel resulting in a price recovery in 1994 and 1995.

Nickel prices were depressed in the early 1980s, owing primarily to the world recession that dampened demand for stainless steel, and were at their lowest in 1986. However, they increased between 1986 and 1987, driven by decreased availability of stainless-steel scape material, increased demand for nickel from stainless-steel producers, and reduced production capacity from primary nickel producers. The sustained low-price regime of early 1980 resulted in many nickel producers closing down throughout the world. Prices reached US$8.17/lb (US$17,974/t) in April 1988, only to decline annually until 1994 as a result of the increased production of primary nickel as mines sought to benefit from the high prices, the availability of scape stainless steel that provided alternative feed for stainless-steel plants, and increased exports from the Soviet Union (Fig. 5.10).

---

[7] Nickel is the main raw material, besides iron and ferrochrome, used in the production of stainless steel.

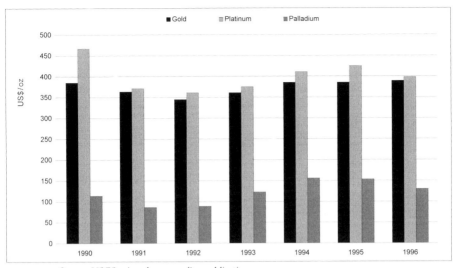

*Source:* USGS mineral commodity publications

**Fig. 5.9: Gold, platinum and palladium prices, 1990–1996**

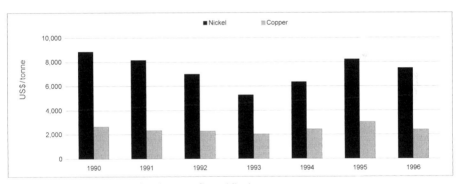

*Source:* USGS mineral commodity publications

**Fig. 5.10: Nickel and copper prices**

The factors that affected nickel prices also had an impact on copper prices – the recession in 1981/82 and the low demand for mineral commodities that ensued. Asbestos prices were fairly stable between 1980 and 1983. Prices then rose with the end of the recession as industrial applications of asbestos increased. However, the 1990s brought the anti-asbestos lobby to asbestos producers which resulted in many nations banning the use of all forms of asbestos, despite scientific evidence that not all types of asbestos were harmful.

In addition, the reduction in the customs duties resulted in a reduction in the cost of inputs, which impacted positively on business viability. Employment in the mining industry increased from 53,200 in 1991 to 59,800 in 1996.[8]

---

[8] Secretary for Mines *Annual Reports*, 1991 and 1997.

## 5.3 The Crisis Period, 1997–2008

Government's commitment to the ESAP programme appeared to wane around 1997. Pronouncements appeared in government circles that the programme was not in the best interests of the country. Although ESAP was considered to have been a failure for a number of reasons,[9] the mining industry performed well, as can be seen from the levels of production.

Government published the Zimbabwe Programme for Economic and Social Transformation (ZIMPREST) in April 1998, even though it was supposed to run from 1996 to 2000. It was meant to be a successor to ESAP with the intention of providing the economy with a firm basis for sustainable economic growth, greater employment and equitable distribution of income. Under the programme, mining was targeted for the facilitation of economic empowerment and private-sector development, the objectives being to:

- Actively encourage large-scale investment in new minerals. particularly platinum and diamonds.
- Provide assistance to small-scale miners in
  - extension services;
  - marketing of minerals;
  - provision of finance through the Mining Industry Loan Fund.
- Open greater opportunities to SMEs through administrative and legal changes.
- Provide adequate skills to the sector.
- Undertake a thorough review of the tax system and regulatory environment so that the public revenue system captures an appropriate share of returns from mineral exploitation.
- Provide incentives to encourage local beneficiation of minerals.

These objectives were similar to those announced under ESAP. The capacity did not exist within government to act on the programme as it was designed. Issues that did not require funding, such as administrative and legal reforms to provide opportunities for SMEs, were not attended to. The co-ordination of government departments to deliver on these objectives was weak, resulting in delays in the implementation of government programmes.

In 2000 government announced the Zimbabwe Millennium Economic Recovery Programme (MERP), an 18-month programme. Its objectives were targeted at arresting economic decline and stimulating the performance of the productive sectors. The minerals sector was expected to play a significant role through the generation of employment, foreign-currency generation, and the recapitalization of the Mining Industry Loan Fund to support small- and medium-scale mineral producers.

---

[9] See Chapter 2.

Measures targeted at the mining sector included the reduction of customs duties, speeding up the privatization of mining parastatals, attracting investment and stopping mineral leakages. The year 2003 saw the introduction of the National Economic Recovery Programme (NERP), which was followed by the National Economic Development Priority Programme (NEDPP) in 2007. All these economic blueprints had little positive impact on the declining performance of the mining industry. Little effort was placed on the core problems of shortages of foreign currency, the misaligned exchange rate, rising costs of production, erratic power supply and declining investor confidence.

### 5.3.1 Mine closures

In March 1998, after a year with no clearly articulated payment procedure for gold producers, the RBZ made a decision to pay gold producers in local currency with effect from that month. This move was to prove fatal to the gold-mining sector. With inflation and interest rates rising significantly, the sector found cost management a difficult exercise; the viability of the sector was under threat. Athens, Yellow Aster and other mines collapsed under the weight of costs. All sectors of the mineral industry were affected by these developments (Table 5.1). The social impact of these closures was felt mainly by the employees, who lost the incomes necessary to sustain their lives. No schemes were put in place by either the Associated Mine Workers' Union or the government to take care of the retrenched workers. Since the closure affected mainly medium-scale to small-scale miners, whose financial reserves were low to non-existent, no safety nets were available for former employees. Because lack of viability was the reason for the closures it was not possible for employers to fund social safety nets.

On the international scene, commodity prices were softening: gold prices averaged US$334/oz in 1997, US$292/oz in 1998 and US$286/oz in 1999. The trend of declining prices was felt in all the precious metals, with palladium being the only exception. Palladium prices increased from US$171/oz in 1997 to US$358/oz in 1999, associated with an increase in the demand for palladium by the automotive catalyst industry. In the base metals industry, the prices of nickel and copper declined significantly.

External and internal constraints combined to create an environment challenging for mining operations. Companies complained about the unsustainable increases in input costs and, as a result, a number sought exemption from the payment of the Mining Sector National Employment Council agreed wage rates, while other mines contemplated closure.

Problems identified in 1997 and 1998 received little attention during 1999, particularly the increase in inflation, increases in interest rates and high rates of duty. The shortage of foreign currency affected producers towards the end of 1999, and most affected were the gold producers, who were directed to source

**Table 5.1: Mines that closed between 1996 and 2001**

| Name of mine | Holding company | Annual production (kg) | Reason for closure | Year of closure |
|---|---|---|---|---|
| Boka 1 | Boka Investments | 47.4 | Viability problems | 1996 |
| Lonely | Mat Minerals | 7.5 | Viability problems | 1996 |
| Baffalo & Tigre | A.C. Lube T/A Milverton Eastates | 3.7283 | Not known | 1997 |
| Bonsor | R.B. Dollar | 13.4748 | Not known | 1997 |
| Eva | African Gold Mining | 4.3803 | Not known | 1997 |
| Mt Morgan | R.B. Dollar | 6.2821 | Not known | 1997 |
| Peccary 3 | Norman Levin Gold Mines Pvt Ltd | 29.2182 | Viability problems | 1997 |
| Prestwood | | 3.2636 | Not known | 1997 |
| Riverlea | | 21.0979 | Viability problems | 1997 |
| Athens | Lonhro | 348.1556 | Ore exhausted | 1998 |
| Bee Hive | African Gold Mining | 7.2372 | Viability problems | 1998 |
| Bonsor | Ngezi Mining Co. (Pvt) Ltd. | 6.0907 | Viability problems | 1998 |
| Coquette | W.J. Smit T/A Horseshoe Mine | 7.0559 | Not known | 1998 |
| Cut | Ngezi Mining Co. (Pvt) Ltd. | 3.4664 | Viability problems | 1998 |
| Damba North | Romjack Mining (Pvt) Ltd. | 2.7633 | Not known | 1998 |
| Gwizo | Ngezi Mining Co. (Pvt) Ltd. | 11.9706 | Viability problems | 1998 |
| Iron Mask | G.L. Niehaus | 3.2552 | Not known | 1998 |
| Mount Morgan | Ngezi Mining Co. (Pvt) Ltd. | 70.998 | Viability problems | 1998 |
| Red Rose | G & S Mining Syndicate | 27.7732 | Not known | 1998 |
| Whistlecock 7 | Falcon Gold Zimbabwe | 59.9733 | Viability problems | 1998 |
| Windmill II | W.J. Smit T/A Horseshoe Mine | 5.2265 | Not known | 1998 |
| Yellow Aster | Forbes and Thompson (Pvt) Ltd. | 91.7121 | Viability problems | 1998 |
| Budy | Dopey Mining Investments | 14.025 | Not known | 1999 |
| Claydon | Auld Mac Mining (Pvt) Ltd. | 160.9747 | Viability problems | 1999 |
| Lone Hand | Forbes and Thompson (Pvt) Ltd. | 11.9607 | Viability problems | 1999 |
| C Mine | Maple Leaf Mining | 103.6932 | Viability problems | 2000 |
| Connemara | Chase Minerals | ? | Viability problems | 2000 |
| Eureka II | Delta Gold | 78.9973 | Viability problems | 2000 |
| Gatling Hill 5 | Ngezi Mining Co. (Pvt) Ltd. | 70.5857 | Viability problems | 2000 |
| Kimberly Reef | R.A.N. Mines Limited | 38.9557 | Viability problems | 2000 |
| Peccary | Norman Levin Gold Mines (Pvt) Ltd. | 53.4577 | Viability problems | 2000 |
| Tebekwe | Ngezi Mining Co. (Pvt) Ltd. | 28.13 | Viability problems | 2000 |
| Camperdown | Reedbuck Gold | 75.9487 | Viability problems | 2001 |
| Gaika | Reedbuck Gold | 124.0635 | Viability problems | 2001 |
| Lenox | Reedbuck Gold | 259.2651 | Viability problems | 2001 |
| Motapa | Reedbuck Gold | 5.3169 | Viability problems | 2001 |
| Venice | Falcon Gold | ? | Viability problems | 2002 |

**Base-metal mine closures**

| | | | | |
|---|---|---|---|---|
| Molly | Mhangura Copper Mines | 2500 | Ore depletion | 2000 |
| Madziwa | Bindura Nickel Corporation | ? | Ore depletion | 2001 |

their requirements on the market, despite the fact that gold was then the second highest foreign-currency earner after tobacco. As a result, the number of gold mines that indicated their intention to close increased.

While increased costs of production, coupled with depressed commodity prices, exerted pressure on the viability of mining companies, the industry was able to remain in business by deferring such activities as exploration and development, by deferring the acquisition of new equipment, and by maintaining stores stocks at the minimum possible level. To remain viable, some companies extracted the very rich pockets of the ore deposit – a process called 'high grading' – to the detriment of the sector's future production performance.

The 1999/2000 rainy season saw 'war veterans' spearheading a farm-invasion campaign that also had an impact on the mining sector. The exploration activities that had been reduced as a result of viability problems were reduced further as hostile farm-invaders hindered fieldwork. Cases were reported of geologists and their crews being forced to leave rock and soil samples behind. Some areas became too dangerous to work, resulting in exploration campaigns being suspended. The country's risk-rating was dented by these developments.

A parallel market for foreign currency developed following the fixing of the exchange rate on 18 January 1999 at US$1:Z$38 and the unavailability of foreign currency within the banking system. The monetary authorities were not able to contain inflation until 2009, when the use of multiple currencies for the conduct of business was sanctioned at the end of January. The economy lost confidence in national data provided by the Central Statistical Office, resulting in rampant speculation driving parallel-market rates, which led to huge costs to business. Fuel shortages were experienced during this period, arising from an inappropriate pricing policy and the resultant withdrawal of investment in fuel procurement.

Monetary policy instability, particularly from 2004 onwards, when changes to the operating environment were made almost every month, made the planning and execution of mining activities very difficult. Changes made to the foreign-exchange management system were particularly damaging. Exchange-control measures were used in an attempt to manage foreign-currency outflows. Mining companies encountered delays in the approval of applications for foreign exchange; the prior exchange-control approval required for invoices above a certain threshold took too long to obtain. The overall impact was delays experienced by importers in receiving deliveries of imported goods, which were compounded by bureaucratic delays at ports of entry. Mines thus experienced production stoppages arising from these process inefficiencies in the import cycle.

The over-valued exchange rate resulted in low revenues in Zimbabwe dollar terms that did not cover the costs of production. The misaligned exchange rate that had been in place since 2000 was not dealt with effectively. It was considered a political issue in which the local currency was to be protected at all costs. Mining businesses, whose costs and revenues are largely US-dollar-based, experienced operational challenges arising from the misaligned exchange rate. Owing to the shortage of foreign currency on the formal market, parallel-market rates were used by suppliers to determine the Zimbabwe-dollar cost of inputs, while Zimbabwe-dollar revenues were determined using the official rate of exchange that was over-valued. This situation was compounded by the forced surrender of a portion of export revenue to the Reserve Bank; the surrender portion was reduced from 50 per cent of gross exports in 2002 to 15 per cent in 2008. This surrender requirement was effectively a tax on exports, as the exchange rate applied to convert to Zimbabwe dollars was greatly over-valued. Accompanying the surrender requirement was the retention period, the period of time that funds were allowed to reside in foreign-currency denominated accounts. The retention period, which was changed regularly, made it difficult for exporters to build up the cash reserves that are critical for mining business to weather periods of low prices. Mining companies were therefore not in any position to pay for capital equipment.

### 5.3.2 Mineral production

Production of most minerals declined in 2000 compared to their 1999 levels; this declining trend continued through 2008. The main reasons for the decline include the shortage of foreign currency, an increase in input costs, a fixed exchange rate, and the erratic supply of electricity and liquid fuels. Electricity supply constraints became worse after 2006. Inflation expectations were high, adding to the inflation problem that had taken root. The sense of insecurity brought about by pre-election violence before the parliamentary elections in June 2000 and the presidential elections in March 2002 further eroded investor and business confidence. This environment recurred around the 2005 and 2008 elections. Lack of decisive measures to deal with these constraints dented business confidence in the future of the sector.

### Gold

Gold production volumes increased from 24,669 kg in 1996 to reach a peak of 27,000 kg in 1999, with over 2,000 known producers; the number of individual producers also reached a peak in 1999. This increase in production was a result of full utilization of installed capacity. It was necessary then to produce more units of metal to cover the rising costs. Gold producers that performed well during the year included Reedbuck Mining, Trillion Mining, Independence Gold Mining and Ashanti Goldfields Zimbabwe.

In an effort to respond to the foreign-currency needs of the gold industry, in March 2000 the RBZ established a foreign-currency pool at Stanbic Bank. Stanbic retained a percentage of the foreign currency that flowed through the bank during its normal business operations. These resources were then made available to suppliers of goods to the mining sector on a first come, first served basis. The list of items to be imported through this facility included spares, explosives and chemicals, but excluded capital items. Foreign-currency inflows into the pool were erratic and the volumes too small to satisfy the sector's requirements. The Reserve Bank often requested Stanbic to surrender all the funds that they had accrued. These issues made the facility less effective than was intended, and in November 2000 it was suspended.

The RBZ introduced 20 per cent foreign-currency retention for gold producers at the beginning of 2001; the rest of the export sector retained 100 per cent of their foreign-currency earnings. This move was too little too late for some producers, who were forced to close their operations. In April 2001 government introduced a gold price support scheme at Z$18,868/oz. The impact of low gold prices and increasing operating costs had finally made the sector unviable. The introduction of a gold-support-price scheme was meant to provide sufficient Zimbabwe-dollar revenue to gold producers to stave off further mine closures and to encourage exploration and development. Government undertook to review the support prices in line with movements in the sector's cost structure. The support price was adjusted ten times before the Minister of Finance and Economic Development suspended the scheme at the beginning of March 2003 at a price of Z$97,712/oz. However, a small-scale producer price for gold of Z$7,000/g (equivalent to Z$217,721/oz), introduced in November 2002, was maintained. So the formal producers, who produced ninety per cent of the gold, were paid less than small-scale miners. This was meant to entice small-scale producers, who were more likely to sell to illegal buyers, to deposit their output through the formal channels.

In an effort to kill off parallel-market activities in gold, in 2004 the Governor of the Reserve Bank substantially increased the support price beyond what was paid by illegal gold buyers (Table 5.2). As a result, production for 2004 shot up to 21,330 kg, compared to the 12,564 kg recorded in 2003, as small-scale producers responded to higher prices. The formal producer benefited significantly from this move and responded by increasing production. However, gold producers who preferred to be paid in US dollars suffered in that the Zimbabwe-dollar portion (50 per cent in 2004) was paid at the market rate and not at the more attractive support-price-implied rate. Producers were forced to alternate between the two schemes in order to generate sufficient Zimbabwe dollars to pay local creditors and to generate US dollars for imports. This untidy arrangement created accounting challenges.

The process of reviewing the support price was onerous. The RBZ was largely unresponsive to requests for its review. All support-price reviews were effected late, resulting in revenues always lagging behind costs, given the environment in which the prices of inputs in Zimbabwe dollars were changing rapidly. The support price and the gold pool were able to stave off further mine closures but were not sufficient to encourage exploration and development.

**Table 5.2: Gold support prices**

| Date | Gold support price Z$\kg | Exchange rate US$1:Z$ | Equivalent US$/oz | LBMA price US$/oz |
|---|---|---|---|---|
| 23 Apr. 2001 | 606,522.96 | 54.964347 | 343.22 | 263.10 |
| 22 Aug. 2001 | 760,364.06 | 54.873647 | 430.98 | 276.30 |
| 21 Dec. 2001 | 767,983.77 | 54.903845 | 435.06 | 276.10 |
| 1 Mar. 2002 | 940,279.37 | 54.903845 | 532.67 | 296.85 |
| 1 July 2002 | 1,496,679.39 | 54.903845 | 847.87 | 318.50 |
| 2 Sept. 2002 | 1,526,097.28 | 54.903845 | 864.53 | 312.80 |
| 10 Dec. 2002 | 1,610,244.98 | 54.903845 | 912.20 | 325.10 |
| **Support price suspended on 3 March 2003** | | | | |
| 22 Apr. 2004 | 71,000,000.00 | 4619.24 | 478.07 | 392.75 |
| 27 July 2004 | 85,000,000.00 | 5357.93 | 493.43 | 390.75 |
| 29 Oct. 2004 | 92,000,000.00 | 5620.78 | 509.09 | 424.20 |
| 1 Feb. 2005 | 130,000,000.00 | 5957.09 | 678.75 | 422.15 |
| 20 May 2005 | 175,000,000.00 | 6125.20 | 888.63 | 420.80 |
| 7 June 2005 | 194,444,444.44 | 9499.07 | 636.67 | 425.85 |
| 21 July 2005 | 255,555,555.55 | 10801.10 | 735.90 | 422.15 |
| 17 Aug. 2005 | 263,496,901.38 | 18500.41 | 442.99 | 443.00 |
| 30 Nov. 2005 | 1,200,000,000.00 | 70477.00 | 529.59 | 496.00 |
| 12 Dec. 2005 | 1,300,000,000.00 | 76464.02 | 528.80 | 525.50 |
| **Support price suspended on 19 December 2005** | | | | |
| 27 Apr. 2007 | 350,000,000.00 | 250.00 | 43,544.20 | 673.00 |
| 1 Jun 2007 | 1,000,000,000.00 | 250.00 | 124,412.00 | 659.10 |
| 2 July 2007 | 3,000,000,000.00 | 250.00 | 373,236.00 | 650.50 |
| 1 Aug. 2007 | 3,500,000,000.00 | 250.00 | 435,442.00 | 665.50 |
| 3 Sept. 2007 | 4,000,000,000.00 | 250.00 | 497,648.00 | 672.00 |
| 1 Oct. 2007 | 5,000,000,000.00 | 30000.00 | 5,183.83 | 743.00 |
| 1 Nov. 2007 | 7,500,000,000.00 | 30000.00 | 7,775.75 | 789.50 |
| 3 Dec. 2007 | 10,000,000,000.00 | 30000.00 | 10,367.67 | 783.50 |
| 2 Jan. 2008 | 100,000,000,000.00 | 30000.00 | 103,676.67 | 836.50 |
| 3 Mar. 2008 | 700,000,000,000.00 | 30000.00 | 725,736.67 | 971.50 |

By 2005, the RBZ was experiencing difficulty in paying the US-dollar component for gold delivered to Fidelity Printers and Refiners. Despite repeated appeals for quick payment of this component, they fell on deaf ears. At year-end 2008, gold producers were owed in excess of US$35 million. Analysis of outstanding payments shows that some producers had not been paid by July 2008 for deliveries made in October 2007. There was no system used to pay for the arrears; in most cases lodgements made later were paid before lodgements made earlier were paid. Follow-up requests to senior RBZ officials for payment were not responded to. Gold producers continued to lodge declining volumes in an effort to maintain some semblance of production lest they were accused of sabotaging the economy.

As a result of these developments, gold production declined considerably (Fig. 5.11). From October 2008, many gold mines were unable to continue production owing to working-capital challenges and shortages of inputs; by the end of the year, most gold mines had suspended operations. Only 49 kg was produced in December 2008, most of which came from platinum operations.

Significant production resumed in April 2009 following the announcement of the liberalization of the marketing of gold, and the publishing of export modalities. Production for the first ten months of 2009 was 3,140 kg, with a projected 4,350 kg for the year.

The gold industry has been, and still is, experiencing challenges in securing funding to increase production, both working capital and long-term finance for capital projects. Given the requirement to build production capacities back to

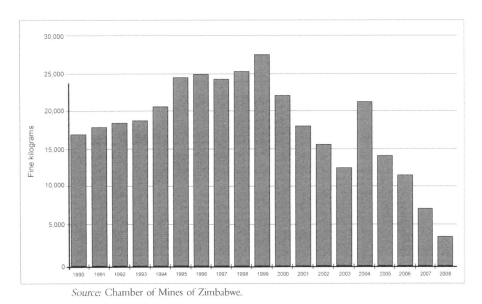

*Source:* Chamber of Mines of Zimbabwe.

**Fig. 5.11: Gold production 1990–2008**

levels that existed in 1999, there is need for significant capital expenditure in equipment, machinery, mineral exploration and development. The credit crunch and the high country-risk rating still placed on Zimbabwe has not helped the cause of gold producers.

## Platinum

The Special Mining Lease conditions negotiated by BHP Inc. for the development of the Hartley platinum mine were favourable to a foreign investor, which encouraged other investors to take an interest in the Great Dyke. The closure of BHP's Hartley mine in June 1999 resulted in a significant reduction in the production of platinum group metals (PGMs). The mine closed owing to difficult ground conditions that led to the production of ore at levels that could not support the investment. Zimplats took over these assets in 2000 and has, to its credit, developed world-class operations at Ngezi. Zimplats made its first shipment of saleable product in 2002, when production rose from 390 kg in 1999 to 2,306 kg. During this period, platinum prices were relatively stable at around US$539/oz. The palladium price that was US$899/oz in December 2000 declined to US$242/oz in December 2002. Platinum prices peaked in May 2008 at a monthly average of US$2,048/oz (Table 5.3). From the beginning of 2009, platinum prices were bullish, rising from US$949.76/oz in January to US$1,217/oz in June. Prospects for growth in output are bright, given the planned expansion programmes and new projects being assessed.

The other platinum operation, Mimosa, producing platinum at almost the same level as Zimplats, has also continued to expand its operations. Mimosa mine increased its platinum production from 500 kg per year to over 1,797 kg per year by 2003, and to 2,352 kg in 2008. Expansion programmes undertaken at both Zimplats and Mimosa have led to the growth of the platinum sector. International prices have also firmed beyond levels wished for in 2002. By 2007, platinum production had reached 5,085 kg, a growth of 880 per cent over a six-year period (Fig. 5.12).

Unki mine has been slow to take off as the project promoters have sought favourable operating conditions from government and cite delays in reaching agreements on the operation of the mine.

The PGM sector has the potential to exceed gold as the main foreign-currency earner in the mining industry. Potential exists for the development of additional mines along the Great Dyke. The difference between the PGM sector and that of all

**Table 5.3: Platinum prices, 2002–2008**

| Year | Annual average platinum price US$/oz |
|------|--------------------------------------|
| 2002 | 537.93 |
| 2003 | 691.91 |
| 2004 | 778.24 |
| 2005 | 876.39 |
| 2006 | 1,141.57 |
| 2007 | 1,304.87 |
| 2008 | 1,575.91 |

*Source:* <http://www.kitco.com>.

other minerals is its unhindered access to foreign currency in the form of off-shore accounts. A comparison needs to be made between PGMs and gold. While gold production declined considerably owing to the RBZ's policy on prices and the unavailability of foreign

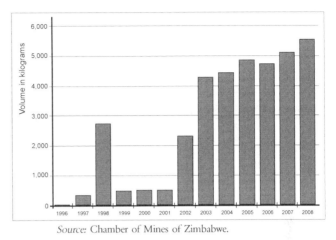

*Source:* Chamber of Mines of Zimbabwe.

**Fig. 5.12: Platinum production, 1996–2008**

currency, PGMs have blossomed as these factors were not interfered with.

## Coal

The increase in coal production from 2000 to 2001 can be attributed to improved operational efficiency at Hwange Colliery, although the production level of 4.064 million tonnes recorded in 2001 is below the 4.575 million tonnes recorded in 1999. Shortages of foreign currency led to frequent production stoppages: spares for the coal-haulage fleet were difficult to acquire during 2002, and foreign-currency problems also affected the blasting operation. As inflation continued to rise, production costs also increased, leading to increases in the price of coal, a development that impacted on the cost of electricity generation. The inability of the National Railways of Zimbabwe to supply the colliery with sufficient wagons affected production during 2002, and the persistent shortage of wagons led to reduced coal production and its availability on the market (Fig. 5.13).

The shortage of coal affected the agriculture and manufacturing sectors, where linkages are very strong, as well as the production of cement, which affected the construction industry. From the third quarter of 2002, ZESA was unable to operate all the electricity-generating units at Hwange power station because of the coal-supply situation. These problems persisted through to 2008, with little intervention being made to assist the sector. In 2007, a plan to tribute part of the Hwange coal fields to a private contractor was developed as a way to boost production, but these efforts had not materially changed coal-production levels by the end of 2008. Because of the linkages that exist between coal and other sectors of the economy, a responsible government would have provided the coal sub-sector with an operating framework conducive to its growth and development. Production capacity has been allowed to degenerate owing to inadequate foreign-currency provisions. Hwange Colliery had invested in equipment that allows for

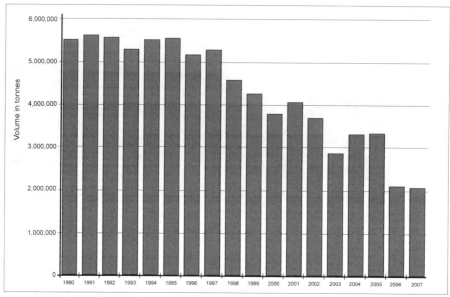

*Source:* Chamber of Mines of Zimbabwe.

**Fig. 5.13: Coal production, 1990–2007**

direct loading of coal into train wagons, but since the Railways can provide only 35 per cent of the daily wagon requirements, this has contributed greatly to the reduction in coal production and shortages on the market. As coal constitutes 11 per cent of mining GDP, these factors had an important bearing on the overall reduction in the mining sector's contribution to GDP.

### Nickel

Nickel and high-carbon ferrochrome have been affected principally by increases in input costs locally and by low prices on the external market. The Asian financial crisis of 1997, coupled with low economic growth rates in the industrialized economies, led to a reduction in demand for raw nickel and ferroalloys globally. These developments impacted on local production performance during the period under review. Nickel prices that increased during 1999 to US$8,000/t to peak at US$10,500/t in early 2000 decreased during the second half of 2000 to a minimum of US$4,500/t towards the end of 2001. These developments, together with the worsening domestic environment, impacted adversely on production levels during 2000 to 2002.

Despite these constraints, the sector performed reasonably well compared to other sectors between 2000 and 2008 (Fig. 5.14). Nickel production benefited significantly from the developments in the platinum sector, and the contribution of nickel from platinum operations increased from 7 per cent in 2004 to 41 per cent in 2007. However, this contribution, although significant, was not able to

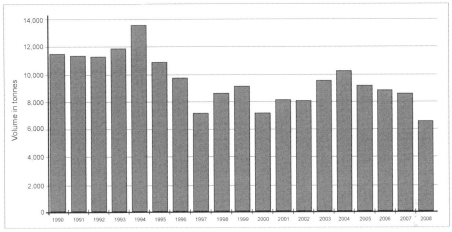

*Source:* Chamber of Mines of Zimbabwe.

**Fig. 5.14: Nickel production, 1990–2008**

reverse the declining production trend, though with the expansions envisaged in the platinum sector its contribution to nickel production is expected to increase.

### Asbestos

Shortages of foreign currency and lack of capitalization adversely affected production levels at African Associated Mines, where asbestos production decreased from 123,000 tonnes in 1998 to 115,000 tonnes in 1999. The only asbestos producer in the country, AA Mines has seen major reduction in its output from 2002 to 2008. Although production had increased to 168,000 tonnes in 2002, this was very low compared with the peak production of 250,000 tonnes recorded in 1980. This increase in output was the result of investments made to improve production capacity and efficiencies generated for system optimization. The shortages of power and foreign currency, as well as shareholder challenges affected production from 2004 (Fig. 5.15).[10]

---

[10] AA Mines operates as a division of SMM Holdings. Since its localization from Turner & Newall, this division was used by the new owners as a vehicle to diversify the portfolio of businesses. Thus, resources meant to fully recapitalize AA Mines' operations were partially diverted to acquire assets in banking, insurance and other businesses. It is alleged that the localization of AA Mines' operations was made through the aid of government guarantees. There appears to have been a fall-out of the AA Mines shareholders with government that saw the latter invoking the Reconstruction of State-Indebted Insolvent Companies Act [*Chapter 24:27*], which led to the appointment of an Administrator to run the affairs of the mines.

It can safely be said that the appointment of an Administrator who did not understand the business of mining was the main cause of the decline in performance of the mines. Poor management, non-replacement of capital, poor relations with creditors and other stakeholders – all combined to render the operations technically unviable. With declining production came a reduction in working capital, which in turn reduced the Mines' ability to continue to produce. There are allegations that the Administrator was paid huge sums of money at the expense of mines. At the time of writing, the matter is still in dispute.

Since the organization was placed under judicial management its performance has been dismal. Shortage of working capital resulted in high equipment and machinery downtime which, in turn, affected output. Production was also impacted by the anti-asbestos lobby, mainly in Europe and North America, which gained momentum and resulted in the shrinkage of the world market for asbestos.

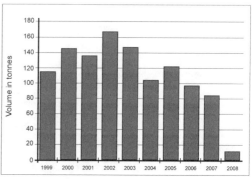

*Source:* Chamber of Mines of Zimbabwe.

**Fig. 5.15: Asbestos production, 1999–2008**

### 5.3.3 Mineral leakages/smuggling

Government has raised the issue of mineral leakages within the mining industry, particularly when foreign-currency inflows fell during 2001 and 2002. Leakages can occur in high-value, low-volume commodities such as gold and diamonds. The gold-buying permits introduced in 1996 in an effort to provide an avenue for small gold producers to sell their gold near their operations was suspended in 2001. A new system, in which one gold-buying permit was registered in the designated fourteen gold-buying districts, was introduced in December 2002.[11] This system required that all custom milling facilities become agents for the buyer in that area, and was meant to provide a better regulatory framework in the disposal of gold. This was a miscalculation on the part of the policy-makers.

Firstly, to avoid false declarations, there was a need for the verification of production data between the producer of ore, the miller and the buyer; the ministry of mines did not have the resources to undertake such verification. Secondly, the records of the buyers were difficult to verify as the buyer could connive with the producer. Thirdly, the price offered by Fidelity Printers and Refiners was considered to be too low, leaving room for arbitrage. As a result, the policy move did not achieve the desired results, and the system was abandoned in November 2003 after poor deliveries by gold buyers.

When the regulations were suspended, all producers were supposed to deliver their gold to Fidelity Printers and Refiners in Harare. Small-scale producers found this option unworkable. Fidelity Printers and Refiners did not have the geographical presence to compete with other buyers, who were now operating illegally, so this development reinforced illegal trading in gold.

In 2006/07, government undertook Operation Chikorokoza Chapera, a con-

[11] The registration of gold buyers and their obligations are contained in Statutory Instrument 328 of 2002.

certed effort to rid the country of illegal gold dealings. It was headed by the Police Minerals Unit, with back-up from the RBZ and the ministry of mines. As part of this exercise, small-scale miners were required to ensure that they complied with environmental requirements; those without valid Environmental Impact Assessments (EIAs) had their operations suspended. Many small-scale miners hired experts to write EIAs for their operations, but those hired charged huge sums of money that were beyond the reach of those involved. Furthermore, the charges made by the Environmental Management Agency for the review of these EIAs were also too high. As a result, a number of genuine operators went out of business. The illegal operators were affected temporarily, but were back at work barely four months after the start of the operation. Illegal gold mining continues – and will continue as long as the country offers no meaningful alternative option for those involved.

The institutional set-up in the regulation of the sector has the Ministry of Mines and Mining Development as the principal agency. The mining engineering department, with engineers and technicians, is mandated to ensure that production processes are not wasteful and are able to detect leakages. In addition, the MMCZ is mandated with the responsibility of monitoring the production and export of minerals. Over and above this, the police have a Gold Unit that was transformed into a Minerals Unit in 2006/07. The ministry of mines advised the mining industry in 2006 that government had also hired the services of Alex Stewart International to audit mining operations in an effort to stem leakages.[12] Since its appointment, there has been no review or report of the findings of the inspector contracted. Experience from other countries in Africa is that such organizations are paid huge sums of foreign currency and do not add any value. It would appear that, in bringing other institutions to reinforce the structures of the Ministry of Mines and Mining Development, government ended up undermining the authority and smooth administration of mining titles.

### 5.3.4 Diamonds

Since 2006, the country has been faced with illegal diamond mining in the Marange area. The area was initially under a diamond EPO issued to De Beers, and was handed over to Africa Resources Limited soon after the EPO for De Beers expired in 2005. People in the community used as labourers got to know that there were diamonds during their contract work with De Beers and, armed with this knowledge, took to the area in search of diamonds. The ministry of mines reacted slowly to protect the area against exploitation. Analysis of the reports by De Beers should have warned the ministry of the existence of alluvial diamonds

---

[12] This was done through Statutory Instrument 249 of 2006: Mines and Minerals (Contracted Inspectors) Regulations, 2006.

within this EPO, though it could be that De Beers did not report truthfully on the work that was done and the results obtained, or that the geological survey was inefficient. Either way, it is unforgivable that the information on diamonds in Marange was provided by the community of Marange. This exposes weakness in the EPO management system.

The ministry of mines directed the MMCZ to mop up all the diamonds produced in Marange, so the latter established buying points in Marange and Harare to purchase all diamonds. Information on how many were bought, and their value, is not readily available on the market. The ministry then proceeded to direct the ZMDC to conduct the proper mining of diamonds in the area. By July 2008 information indicated that no diamonds had been sold by ZMDC while a number of people had been arrested for being in possession of diamonds from Marange. Although the police have been in the area in an effort to enforce the reservation and to control the illegal mining of diamonds, it would appear that illegal activities are still rife.

Zimbabwe is a founding member of the Kimberley Process Certification Scheme (KPCS), whose mandate is to ensure that the sale of rough diamonds is not used to fuel conflict. Thus, governments and diamond producers work on transparent systems of regulating the rough-diamond trade. Since the discovery of diamonds at Marange, there have been reports of illegal trade in diamonds as people sought a quick solution to Zimbabwe's challenging socio-economic environment. At one time, it was estimated that over 400,000 people were involved in diamond panning in Marange. In an effort to allow the organized exploitation of this resource, government had to drive off the illegal workers that had invaded the area. There are allegations that this process resulted in human-rights abuses by the police and the army. The use of the army for the purpose of maintaining order is highly controversial; the question to be asked is, whose interests are being served by the presence of the army in the area? This research can point only to the irregular nature of this situation. The KP intersessional and plenary meeting held in India in November 2008 noted with concern challenges being experienced in the implementation of the KPCS and recommended further monitoring of developments. Its involvement will hopefully provide sufficient international scrutiny to induce government to ensure that the Marange resource is managed in accordance with best practices.

### 5.3.5 Employment

Average annual employment in the mining industry decreased from 43,713 in 1997 to 40,208 in 2008,[13] a result of the sustained challenging environment that

---

[13] These are employees who have direct contractual obligations with mining companies; those at smelters and refineries are not included.

has prevailed since 1999. The increase in employment that did occur between 2002 and 2008 is attributed to expansion in platinum.

During the period under review, those that left employment were hardly ever replaced unless their work could not be shared by those already employed. The loss of skills to the region and beyond had a telling effect on production and safety performance. Many supervisory positions in the industry are currently filled by young people who would ordinarily have been under supervision themselves. This has tended to mean that those in supervisory positions are less competent, thus leading to inappropriate and costly decisions that have impacted on equipment down-times and serious accidents.

A report commissioned by the Chamber of Mines in 2007 indicated that, in the 19 mining companies that provided data, 233 vacancies for graduate-level employees existed, including 28 geologists, 47 mining engineers, 30 metallurgical engineers, 34 mechanical engineers and 12 electrical engineers, among others. There were up to 445 vacancies for technicians, of which 78 were for mining technicians and 33 for geological technicians.[14] The capacity of the tertiary educational facilities and training institutions to produce quality graduates has deteriorated significantly, and there has been a major loss in the number of lecturers. In order to achieve high economic growth rates, the country must train large numbers of its population in order to generate sufficient human capital, particularly at graduate level, to support development efforts.

### 5.3.6 Export performance

The contribution of the mining sector to export earnings, inclusive of gold, ferroalloys and steel, peaked at 50.95 per cent in 1990. At the same time, non-metals comprised about 16 per cent of non-gold exports, the major ones being black granite (7.5 per cent), graphite (1.5 per cent), coke (3.3 per cent) and petalite (1.4 per cent). Metals comprise 83 per cent of mineral exports, excluding gold, the major metal exports being high-carbon ferrochrome, nickel, PGMs, steel products, copper, and cobalt in various forms. The contribution of gold to total mineral exports decreased from 42.86 per cent in 1999 to 41.39 per cent in 2001 but increased to 42.81 per cent in 2002. The increase in the price of gold during 2002, coupled with the reduced export performance of other commodities, more than offset the decrease in volume of gold production. Steel products have the potential to surpass all non-gold mining exports. However, management and cash-flow problems at ZISCO limited the contribution of steel products to only 3.2 per cent of mining exports, exclusive of gold, in 1990. Mining exports excluding gold grew from US$733 million in 2005 to US$849

---

[14] A survey of professional and technical vacancies in the mining industry was commissioned by the Chamber of Mines of Zimbabwe in 2007, and was conducted by Prof. Keith Viewing.

million in 2007,[15] principally a result of the surge in mineral commodity prices that was witnessed after 2003, the commodity super-cycle. Despite declining volumes of minerals produced, the industry managed to realize increased export revenues.

The mining sector is exposed to price shocks, as evidenced by the suspension of base-mineral operations during the last quarter of 2008, though the price fluctuations have not been the same for all commodities. Given the diversified mineral endowment, it is critical that the country encourages the exploitation of other minerals to avoid dependence on a few commodities. Platinum and diamonds have performed better than nickel and chrome, and while gold was least affected by the recession, local conditions were primarily responsible for the demise of the gold sector.

In March 2009, the Inclusive Government developed the Short-Term Emergency Recovery Programme (STERP) as its anchor policy for the year. Its principal objectives were the stabilization of the economy, dealing with the humanitarian crisis arising out of a failed 2008/09 agricultural season, and re-engaging the international community. On the economic front STERP sought to:
- Restore public institutions of governance.
- Halt economic decline.
- Lay the foundation for economic development.

With respect to mining in particular, STERP deals with the following:
1. Recovery of the mining sector through the promotion of joint ventures.
2. The development of exploration, registration and extraction mining policy.
    a. Amending mining legislation to discourage hoarding and speculation in EPOs.
    b. Improve the administration of mining title.
    c. Establish an institution responsible for exploration issues.
3. Ensuring that no pricing gaps for minerals exist.
4. The centrality of the MMCZ in the marketing of minerals.
5. The need to review mining taxation.
6. Earning greater levels of revenue through beneficiation and local toll processing of minerals.
    a. Resuscitation of Lomagundi Copper Refinery.
    b. Beneficiation of industrial minerals.
    c. Coal processing.
7. Mechanization of small-scale mining.

These policy intentions require concrete action if they are not to be permanent

---

[15] Monetary Policy Statements by the Governor of the Reserve Bank of Zimbabwe.

features in economic policy documents. Some issues in STERP were simply imported from previous documents, for example:

- Use of the Mining Industry Loan Fund as a vehicle for the mechanization of small-scale mining.
- Calls for the mining industry to increase mineral beneficiation.
- Establishment of an exploration company.

These issues are likely to remain rhetoric, as the real issues affecting mining lie elsewhere. The Mining Industry Loan Fund has played an important role as a vehicle for the development of small-scale mining in the past, and over the years the government has proposed recapitalizing the fund to ensure that sufficient resources are available to assist small-scale miners. However, owing to a combination of the erosion of capital by inflation and limited resources available for government to disburse, it has not been appropriately funded.

Recognition of the need for a mining policy to underpin legislative, institutional and fiscal developments targeting mining is a positive development. Currently there is no comprehensive policy document on mining, and there has been over-reliance on provisions of the Mines and Minerals Act in the past.

A growing shortage of personnel at all levels is impacting on production. Because remuneration packages in Zimbabwe fall far short of those prevailing in the region, the local labour market has been unattractive. Young professionals are not able to acquire assets such as cars and houses, and concerns about the deteriorating education system have forced professionals to seek employment outside the country's borders.

### 5.3.7 Marketing

The marketing of minerals has been a thorny issue since the establishment of the MMCZ. BHP Inc. negotiated and was granted the right to market its own output under the supervision of the MMCZ; AA Mines also negotiated and was granted the right to market its own produce. The marketing of gold was liberalized with effect from end of January 2009, and gold producers producing 20 kg per month have been allowed to apply for gold-dealing licences in order to export gold in their name in accordance with the Gold Trade Act [*Chapter 21:03*]. All other minerals produced in Zimbabwe are exported through the MMCZ.

In formulating this policy, government intended to ensure that the country derives maximum benefit from its mineral endowment. However, some past experiences have indicated that marketing through state institutions can be a barrier to the efficient sale of minerals and therefore to production. In the times when gold was sold through Fidelity Printers and Refiners, there were alarming increases in smelting and refining, but declining deliveries. MMCZ has been accused by some of rejecting marketing agreements on the pretext that the prices offered are too low while they could not offer better prices. Such accusations can be avoided through a transparent system of marketing that involves the producers at all levels.

Although government liberalized the marketing of gold under STERP, the move was not extended to other minerals. It would appear that the decision to liberalize the marketing of gold was forced on the government, otherwise they could have liberalized the marketing of all minerals. The Rand Refinery in South Africa had advised the Reserve Bank of Zimbabwe that it was not going to continue refining gold from Zimbabwe because the RBZ had not paid the gold producers. It would appear that the Rand Refinery was afraid of the reputational risks of continued relations with the RBZ, which was responsible for the demise of many gold operations, some of which were subsidiaries of South African companies.

### 5.3.8 Ownership and empowerment

Mining law in Zimbabwe allows for private-sector ownership of mining concerns. The ownership structure of businesses involved in mining range from those listed on the Zimbabwe Stock Exchange, government-owned and limited-liability companies, foreign-owned and indigenous companies, and co-operatives and syndicates, among others. The landscape of ownership has changed after Lonhro, Anglo American Corporation, Reedbuck Mining, Cluff Resources, BHP Inc. and Ashanti Goldfields pulled out of Zimbabwe. The number of multinational companies involved in the mining industry was considerably reduced between 1980 and 2009. Table 5.4 shows the ownership structure of the top twenty-two mining companies in Zimbabwe. There is need for the country to increase the number of mining investors in all categories.

The first time that the issue of broadening the ownership of mining companies was raised was when ZIMPREST was announced in 1998, one of whose objectives was economic empowerment in mining. In 2002 the minister of mines advised the mining industry to make proposals to government on how

**Table 5.4: Ownership structure of mining companies, 2009**

| Ownership | Number | Percentage |
|---|---|---|
| Government | 3 | 14 |
| Indigenous | 3 | 14 |
| Listed on ZSE | 4 | 18 |
| Local non-indigenous | 2 | 9 |
| Foreign | 10 | 45 |
| TOTAL | 22 | 100 |

*Source:* Chamber of Mines membership list.

indigenous Zimbabweans could be accommodated, saying that if nothing was done government would be forced to legislate for indigenization. Since then, the debate on indigenization has tended to be clouded by emotions and there has been little open and frank discussion based on the realities of the business. The mining industry has put it on record that it is not against indigenization and would like to see policies that do not hinder the growth of the sector.

Government's position, as stated in the Mines and Minerals Amendment Bill (H.B. 14 of 2007), was a mixture of nationalization and forced relinquishment of shares, requiring up to 51 per cent equity. The bill provided for the state to acquire 25 per cent non-contributory shares, not to be paid for, plus an additional 26 per cent shares paid for from dividends arising from shareholdings surrendered free of charge. For precious metals and stones, the 26 per cent would be achieved in stages as follows: 10 per cent in two years, 20 per cent in five years, and 26 per cent in seven years.

Those companies that did not surrender the initial 25 per cent to government for free would be levied a tax of 25 per cent of the value of their production. In the event that no production were realized, the 25 per cent tax would be levied on the estimated value of reserves they would be likely to produce in a year. If after two years 25 per cent of the shares in the company had not been surrendered, the tax applicable would increase by one per cent for every year the obligation remained outstanding.

From the viewpoint of foreign investors, this policy position is draconian, to the extent that foreign investors would not be likely to invest in such an arrangement. Despite it being the product of over six years of consultation between government and the mining industry, the bill was withdrawn in August 2009 to permit further consideration and consultation with all stakeholders. The mining industry, through the Chamber of Mines, has since presented a detailed proposal which government is considering. Areas of disagreement include the 51 per cent equity threshold: the mining industry believes that the equity component should be low (10 per cent to 15 per cent) to ensure that growth to the sector is not inhibited. This is premised on the long gestation period, long payback periods, technical and other risks associated with mining projects. The investment community in Zimbabwe does not have the risk capital that normally funds mining projects, particularly during the initial phases of such projects. The Chamber's proposal also targets broad-based empowerment through commitments from mines to invest continually in community and infrastructure projects, including assistance to small-scale miners and purchasing mining inputs from local suppliers.

The trading of indigenous shares was not dealt with in the bill. The interpretation of the provisions of the bill seem to suggest that, once an investment company complies with the requirements of the act in terms of an agreement with a indigenous partner, the investor's responsibility is over. As the environment in the life of a business is dynamic, some investors may wish to sell their shareholdings, but such a sale of indigenous shares could be made only to an indigenous Zimbabwean. This creates a captive market for the indigenous shares in that they could be sold only to the indigenous community. Such shares might always be discounted. In addition, if a call were to be made for capital injection from shareholders, those that are not in a position to contribute would have to accept the dilution of their stake in the project. If this were not acceptable, then any investor would find the indigenization framework difficult to comply with.

Zimbabwean investors who require higher equity positions in a mining company are encouraged to do so. It is estimated that over 600,000 Zimbabweans hold mining titles in one form or another. These people have to be capacitated to develop their claims through the provision of technical know-how, appropriate technology and access to capital. In addition, those willing to partner big mining organizations in the development of their properties would benefit their organizations and the country through foreign direct investment, export earnings, rural development and employment creation. This creates opportunities for those with entrepreneurial skills to explore possibilities of manufacturing mining inputs for the domestic and regional market.

Already a number of equipment producers have made their mark on the continent: ABJ Engineering and the Institute of Mining Research are two examples. Mines can play an important role in aiding indigenization by sourcing their inputs from local companies, as this is where most of the money is made. Partnerships on a commercial basis between formal and small-scale mines is an area that has not been exploited fully and that can be mutually beneficial for the parties involved. Forced partnerships that do not generate wealth and growth are bound to fail.

There are better options for empowering Zimbabweans in the mining industry than the government's model of sharing existing assets. In any event, the majority of Zimbabweans will not benefit from the sharing of existing assets. There is need to have Zimbabweans as owners of the wealth involved in many economic activities, including mining.

### 5.3.9 Beneficiation

The country beneficiates minerals extracted to varying degrees of purity. The primary extract in mining is the ore; any process that increases the quality and value of the sellable product is beneficiation. Thus, when ore is processed through the mill and concentrators to produce a concentrate, this is beneficiation. The production of metal ingots, as in the case of nickel, ferroalloys and iron bars in various forms, is a process of beneficiation. Asbestos is processed into fibre for export; the fibre is used in the manufacturing of various products locally, which include pipes, tiles, brake pads and other products. Black granite is processed into tiles and kitchen table-tops; the bulk is exported as blocks.

The platinum sector exports products in polymetallic concentrate and smelter matte form. The volume of PGM concentrates being produced are not large enough to justify the investment in smelting and refining operations. With the development of Unki mine, the viability of a smelter may become possible.

The skill sets required to process an iron bar into a plate, spoon or knife lie with industrialists. The call for mineral producers to beneficiate minerals is equivalent to a call for cotton farmers to make shirts, or a tobacco farmer to make cigarettes. With the competitive advantage of mineral-based raw materials, government has a duty to attract investment into areas that use these minerals as inputs in the manufacture of finished products, i.e. creating forward and backward linkages between the primary sector and the manufacturing sector. Hence, the proposed 'solution' of penalizing mining companies through taxes on exports for not investing in mineral beneficiation will only increase the cost of mining, thereby making local mining operations less competitive than those in the region.

### 5.3.10 Environmental protection, occupational health and safety

The Environmental Management Act [*Chapter 20:27*] provides the legal frame-work for the management of the environment. One of the tenets of this law is the 'polluter pays' principle. In the event that business and the public are forced to pollute through discharge of effluent, solid waste or gaseous emissions, a permit is issued for a fee by the regulator, the Environmental Management Agency (EMA). The fee is supposed to be used to clean up the environment.

In the mining industry, large-scale operators have traditionally tried to manage environmental issues, as required by the law. These organizations have partnered the ministry of mines to develop policies for the effective manage-ment of the environment around mining locations. Almost all the large-scale mining operations have environmental management plans that are certified by international standards' organizations such as ISO or NOSA. The exception is government-owned operations. It is a requirement of the Environmental Management Act to register an environmental management plan with the EMA. The challenge rests largely with small- to medium-scale operations, particularly those at the smaller end of the spectrum. These operations have neither the structures nor the resources to dedicate to environmental issues; compliance with environmental legislation is a cost to their operations. Those at the smaller end of the market require not only technical and material (financial) support but also strong supervision to ensure compliance with the minimum health and safety standards set by the law. The ministry of mines and the EMA are also constrained from providing the requisite oversight in terms of personnel and resources. This is an area that requires government investment in resources and guidelines for the protection of the environment.

In relation to global warming, many processing facilities in the mining industry do not produce greenhouse gasses. The few smelting facilities and coal fields that produce greenhouse gasses require new investment in the form of cleaner technologies. Such investments are generally expensive and, given the state of the economy, many businesses may not be able to afford the required investments at this point in time. However, a programme for compliance over an agreed period of time should see the industry commit to cleaner technologies.

The mining industry has one of the worst fatal-accident records of all the productive sectors of the economy, an average of twelve per year being reported between 2001 and 2007. In 2008, 24 accidents were reported involving 28 fatalities, and between January and September 2009 there were 18 accidents with 29 fatalities. In the years 2008 and 2009 there was an increase in the number of fatal accidents caused by gas; in most cases, these accidents involved multiple fatalities. The major cause of these accidents was the use of petrol engines to de-water mines, even though the Mining (Management and Safety) Regulations clearly prohibit the use of petrol engines in underground operations. The violation of safe work procedures, a lack of supervision and inexperience are some of the reasons for such a high incidence of fatalities within the sector, as well as collapses.

Zimbabwe lags behind countries in the region in managing occupational health within the mining sector, though occupational-safety programmes are well entrenched and systems well developed and observed within the formal mining sector. The poor resourcing of the ministry's department responsible for inspecting mines tends to affect compliance. Through the National Social Security Authority (NSSA) there is an elaborate scheme to monitor pneumo-coniosis, but there is a need to develop programmes to record and track occurrences of occupational health incidents and to provide interventions to prevent recurrences. Through the Zimbabwe Occupational Health and Safety Council, government is in the process of reviewing the various legal instruments governing occupational safety and health with a view to developing a comprehensive legal framework. The mining industry through the ministry of mines and the Chamber of Mines is fully represented in this exercise.

## 5.4 The Way Forward

### 5.4.1 Policy framework
The mining industry has the potential to be the impetus for the growth of Zimbabwe's economy, and areas with greatest potential include PGMs, asbestos, chrome, coal, iron and steel, gold and industrial minerals. In addition, the

recent discovery of diamonds is creating a new, infant industry in Zimbabwe. Significant work still needs to be done to explore for diamond resources, but given Zimbabwe's geographic location in the SADC region, the location of major diamond producers, there are great prospects for diamonds. Furthermore, mining should be viewed not only in terms of the employment that it generates but in terms of the secondary employment that is generated by the support infrastructure needed to keep the mining sector in production. Employment is also generated by those engaged in the beneficiation of the minerals that are produced locally, and there are many social and infrastructure projects that spin off from mining projects.

This potential can be realized, provided that consistent application of the right mix of policies is applied over a long period of time. These policies include the following:

- Sufficient foreign currency being available to the minerals sector for the importation of mining inputs and replacement of capital equipment.
- An exchange-rate management system that offers fair and competitive revenues for exports.
- Active exploration for minerals based on an effective 'use it or lose it' principle.
- The efficient and effective allocation and management of mining titles.
- Fair taxes that encourage efficient business practices, and incentives that encourage corporate social responsibility.
- Industrialization policies that encourage the creation of new businesses that utilize mineral-based raw materials.
- Adequate electricity supply at tariffs that encourage efficient energy utilization, and fiscal measures that reward efficient business practices.
- An efficient rail and road transport system linking the mines to other business and service centres in the country, regionally, on the continent and internationally.

The primary weakness in Zimbabwe is the fact that the country has operated for decades without a properly documented mining policy that would guide the development of legislation, regulations, programmes and projects in this sector. The mining policy should spell out the co-ordination of government efforts and initiatives in the development of the industry, and at the same time serve to inform investors of the government's medium- and long-term plans regarding the various issues pertinent to the development of this critical sector of Zimbabwe's economy.

The number one priority for Zimbabwe, therefore, is to develop a comprehensive policy framework for the mining sector. This should be formulated with the involvement and participation of all the stakeholders in the sector, which includes small-, medium- and large-scale mining companies (owners) and their associations; the trade union representing workers in the sector as well as the national trade union (ZCTU); other relevant ministries such as those responsible for energy, infrastructure, transport, trade and finance, among others; traditional leaders representing local communities from the mining areas; local and external experts in such areas as environment, geology and international trade.

In developing the national mining policy, past government interventions (discussed in this chapter) over the thirty years of political independence, as well as pre-independence policies, current mining laws/regulations, new bills proposed for the mining sector, STERP, and other national, regional and international studies carried out on the mining sector or the environment – all should be given thorough scrutiny to assess what is still relevant to a new comprehensive mining policy for Zimbabwe.

### 5.4.2 Institutional arrangements

The government's roles, responsibilities and functions over the past thirty years in the mining sector have been discharged through a ministry of mines, which collaborates with all the key players in the sector, such as the Chamber of Mines, the ZMDC, MMCZ, RBZ, CSO, mining-sector employers and worker representatives, and the National Employment Council, as well as at the inter-ministerial level and through structures cascading down to district and plant levels.

The supervisory work of the ministry is field-based work, reaching out to large and small mines, developed and underdeveloped rural areas, for the purposes of gathering data about minerals and the mining activities under way or in plan, distributing information about local and external market and price trends of minerals, and informing them about government programmes and constraints.

To accomplish its mission, vision, goals and objectives effectively, the ministry of mines urgently needs to be capacitated in the following areas:

*Human capital*
The first priority should be given to filling all the vacant posts in the ministry of mines, from the head office down to the local offices, including specialized personnel such as mining inspectors, environmental experts, geologists, and health and safety personnel.

The human capital and systems needed for effective communication internally and with stakeholders are critical. The high vacancy rate must be reduced through the recruitment of qualified and competent staff. The restructuring of the ministry at district level is critical to ensuring a more co-ordinated and targeted vehicle for mineral development. Finally, resources for mobility, data acquisition and analysis will be necessary in compiling the required information that feeds into policy formulation and monitoring the implementation of policy.

*Work ethic*

The historic decline of the economy of Zimbabwe, particularly during the crisis period, worsened the erosion of professional work ethics among workers in the ministry of mines and the public sector at large.

Priority should therefore be given to the present workforce who need to undergo re-training, re-skilling, reorientation and motivation in order to achieve full commitment to duty. In addition, there must be effective and efficient delivery of the diverse government services and support mechanisms towards the mining sector, which is critical to the development of the Zimbabwean economy as a whole.

Coupled with the re-training of staff, the workers in the public sector should be assured of decent working conditions and remuneration, and their rights and freedoms, employment security, social security and social advancement guaranteed.

Therefore, efforts to re-establish work ethics among the civil service should be given high priority through staff-development projects with clear short-, medium- and long-term indicators for attaining professionalism.

*Social dialogue*

The ministry of mines is a very important service provider to the mining sector, but it is not the only player or the only interested party: there are a variety of other important players, including quasi-government institutions, investors, labour, experts, and beneficiary or affected communities with whom the ministry needs to collaborate and network in supporting this critical sector.

If executed effectively, this will result in the active involvement and participation of all the stakeholders, and accountability and transparency being achieved in the sector.

Therefore, the ministry of mines should spearhead and establish social-dialogue platforms and processes between all players and interested parties in the sector and ensure that such dialogue is institutionalized, with clearly laid-out procedures, aims, goals and objectives that are strictly adhered to by all parties, with a clear mandate to implement recommendations from such dialogue, and with stipulated time-frames for review, progress monitoring and evaluation.

### 5.4.3 Legal framework

The country has been working on amendments to the Mines and Minerals Act since 2004, but to date the exercise has not been completed. However, this delay can be turned into an advantage if social dialogue takes effect immediately, with all large and small stakeholders contributing ideas effectively towards both a new act and the comprehensive national mining policy proposed earlier.

The process to produce a new Mines and Minerals Act and the national mining policy should be participatory, and stakeholders should take stock of existing laws and establish what is relevant and what is irrelevant in the present circumstances.

The new legal framework for the mining sector should ensure that the diverse rights and interests of the different players and interest groups are sufficiently harmonized, protected and promoted.

However, it has to be understood that the ministry of mines is not only a regulator but also a service provider, facilitator and co-ordinator of all players in the sector. In addition, governments elsewhere in the world are major stakeholders, beneficiaries, shareholders or custodians of the mineral wealth of their country. Minerals are very important natural resources to countries such as Zimbabwe, where there are precious minerals like gold, diamonds and platinum among others of good quality and quantity that make them the second highest foreign-currency earner for the country. Governments always play a very important role in this sector and Zimbabwe should not be an exception.

The process of amending the law requires finality in order to give confidence to investors regarding the nature of the country's legal framework as regards mining.

### 5.4.4 Monetary issues
Monetary issues have adversely affected the production capacity of mining organizations. The monetary environment has been very unstable, preventing the sector from adopting long-term strategies needed to grow the industry. The current use of multiple currencies has stabilized prices and is making cost management easy, but more long-term and stable monetary policies are very urgently required. Even if the dollarization is deemed suitable at this time, in the longer term it will be necessary to revert to a local currency, so macroeconomic fundamentals must be properly addressed.[16]

### 5.4.5 Foreign-currency management
Shortages of foreign currency over the years have seen the industry fail to acquire the inputs to remain in production. A regime put in place for the platinum sector, whereby producers were allowed to maintain offshore foreign-currency accounts, was instrumental in the growth of that sector. In contrast, the gold industry's access to foreign currency was restricted and led to a serious decline in production. Although the use of multiple currencies has now rendered this factor unimportant, future governments need to understand the impact that foreign-currency shortages have on mining. In the development of policy, mineral producers need to be assured of foreign currency at levels that sustain

---

[16] See Chapters 2 and 12.

their operations; they should be able to accumulate sufficient balances to pay for capital equipment.

However, the sad story about platinum in Zimbabwe is the fact that the life-span of the first mining venture by BHP at Hartley mine became very short: the mine was opened in 1995, in June 1999 its operations were suspended, and in 2001 the company was sold to Zimplats. Therefore, concessions and privileges offered by the government to foreign investors, such as tax holidays, duty-free imported equipment, offshore accounts, etc., may result in the state losing both the precious minerals and the revenue that could have been generated from the taxes and customs duties, as well as experiencing the loss of jobs that would have been created, foreign currency remitted, and damage to the environment.

Therefore, issues relating to customs duties, or to taxation, or to special concessionary arrangements for certain minerals must be thoroughly examined and properly documented in the proposed comprehensive national mining and minerals policy, and developed through collaborative strategies that involve all stakeholders and interested parties in the mining sector of Zimbabwe.

### 5.4.6 Fiscal issues

Taxation on mining has been fairly steady and progressive. The challenge for the fiscal framework has been to maintain the value of the various allowances provided for in the face of high inflation, as the industry did not benefit from those allowances as was intended in the design of policy. It is important to ensure, firstly, that capital allowances are set at realistic levels that encourage the building of clinics, the establishment of schools, the development of piped water systems and the purchase of equipment. In addition, adjustments for inflation will have to be made in order to preserve the value of these allowances.

Customs duties are a critical component of the input cost of mining goods and services, and currently some of the tariffs are extremely high. As the exchange rate is adjusted to reflect market fundamentals, assuming it is correct, customs duties can rise to unsustainable levels. In light of this, government is encouraged to review levels of duty to those of COMESA or the SADC common market.

Although the level of Zimbabwe's corporate tax is highly competitive, indirect taxes place a very high burden on mining companies. The effective corporate tax for mining ranges from 40 per cent for gold to 48 per cent for diamonds, which is high, and there is room for government to look realistically at indirect taxes. The World Bank ranked Zimbabwe 144th out of 178 countries on Ease of Paying Taxes, and 136th on Total Tax Rate at 53 per cent, while Botswana was ranked 8th with a Total Tax Rate of 17.2 per cent.[17] Current efforts by the Ministry of Finance to review taxation for mining should simplify the tax system

---

[17] *Paying Taxes 2008: The Global Picture*, <http://www.doingbusiness.org/documents/Paying_Taxes_2008.pdf>.

for ease of compliance and administration, as the mining industry currently pays a multitude of taxes and compliance costs are high. The intent of the tax system should not only be to raise revenue for the government but also to attract investment and encourage social spending, thereby assisting governments in rural development and wealth creation in more sustainable activities. This can only be achieved if mining companies are allowed to operate profitably.

The responsible use of revenues derived from mining is also of critical importance. Other countries have established sovereign funds and made appropriate use of these resources in the structural transformation of the economy. Revenues from mining should be used wisely, otherwise future generations will have nothing to show for the country's current minerals endowment. Government is encouraged to direct part of the royalties paid by mining companies to district councils that host mining projects, where they should be used for capital projects that impact on the standard of living of the people. Special committees comprising the mines (employers and employees), Rural District Councils and affected communities could be a vehicle to identify and prioritize projects, account for the resources and monitor implementation. This structure would allow all interested parties to have their voices heard in shaping the development of communities in which mines operate, and should also be covered in the proposed comprehensive national mining and minerals policy for Zimbabwe.

### 5.4.7 Small-scale mining

The small-scale mining sector requires nurturing if it is to grow; support for the institutions will go a long way towards providing the vehicles for technical support. In this regard the infrastructure that allows for assistance in terms of mineral identification, resource estimation, rock support, ventilation, drilling and blasting, safety, equipment maintenance, project management, etc., needs to be improved. These services can be made available through consultancy and government institutions. In addition, the financial-services sector needs to adopt the same strategy that it developed for the agriculture sector, where every bank had an 'agro' division. If each bank had a division that supported small-scale mining, the resources necessary to finance mining projects could be harnessed. Small-scale mining has to be treated as a business by the players themselves and by government. In this regard, small-scale miners require training in all aspects of business as well as in the technical aspects.

Furthermore, forward and backward linkages between the large-scale and small-scale mining companies should be nurtured consistently, and properly catered for in the comprehensive mining and minerals policy that is aimed at enhancing the indigenization agenda. Enhancing these linkages can take various forms that might include large mining companies subcontracting smaller companies and panners, or small-scale companies and/or co-operatives selling their ores through the large companies, or the large companies sharing their technical knowledge, experience, expertise and equipment with small-scale miners.

### 5.4.8 Mineral exports
The mining sector will continue to be a major export earner for the country; however, to enhance its contribution, a stable operating environment is required. Specific incentives are needed to encourage the sector to increase exports and to reward investment in exploration and development, a unique feature of the industry. In addition, because mining is capital intensive, any capital project will need incentives. Increases in export volumes should also be encouraged by fiscal and monetary incentives in the form of tax breaks, export bonuses, duty-free certificates, and reduced VAT levels for export performance, among others.

### 5.4.9 Mineral marketing
The MMCZ can play an important role in marketing minerals for those producers that are not big enough to justify a marketing department of their own. It is agreed that, because of the nature of minerals, the state has an interest in ensuring that the minerals the country is endowed with yield good returns. The state's function in the marketing of minerals is therefore in the areas of technical support, supervision and auditing. Where government does not have the capacity to do these on its own, it should hire reputable experts to do so on its behalf, as is the case in Namibia and Botswana in the form of a government valuator.

### 5.4.10 Beneficiation of minerals
Mineral producers beneficiate ore into a saleable form as a matter of course. The extent to which mineral producers climb the value-addition ladder depends on the economies of scale, market dictates and the returns earned. Market conditions should therefore be made to favour the beneficiation of minerals. The processing of minerals to finished products is not an extractive industry, and therefore industrial policies must be made that link with the mining policy.

### 5.4.11 Infrastructure
Reliable electricity supply is essential in mineral production, so the country must adopt policies that ensure an uninterrupted supply to the mining industry. Electricity self-sufficiency should be made a priority. This starts with allowing ZESA to charge tariffs that can sustain the sector, i.e. tariffs that take into full account the cost of supply and of future projects. Apart from increasing the national budget allocation towards electricity supply, government is urged to encourage investors to participate in the generation, transmission and dis-tribution of electricity. Utilities such as electricity supply play an important role

in facilitating low-cost production of goods and services not only in the mining sector but other in economic sectors as well.

The rehabilitation of rail, road and telecommunications networks should also be one of government's urgent priorities because they are essential for the development of all the economic sectors and in particular the minerals sector. Because mines are producers of bulk commodities usually located in remote areas, these services are critical to mining investment. In relation to this, government is encouraged as a matter of urgency to provide a working framework for the development of public–private partnerships, learning from the experiences of such countries as the United Kingdom, India and France in this regard.

### 5.4.12 Empowerment

The empowerment issue requires considerable debate to find a model most suited to Zimbabwe's development needs and should be well catered for in the national mining and minerals policy proposed above. The country needs to create an environment that offers opportunities for all, with a particular focus on the less privileged nationals, to participate in economic activities. Zimbabwe can benefit from policies that allow broad-based economic empowerment and the distribution of wealth to empower the indigenous people. The country therefore requires an environment that grows and equitably distributes its wealth for the benefit of the nation at large and not only to foreign investors or elites.

The empowerment issue should not be limited to the acquisition of shares in existing organizations or employee share-ownership programmes but should involve mentoring of young businesses, growth in local suppliers, technology transfer, development of land under mining title, and appropriate use of technology, among the many possible initiatives. In fact, the indigenization agenda is in essence part of an empowerment process for the less privileged indigenous people.

### 5.4.13 Environment

Mining causes permanent and massive damage to nature and the environment, apart from displacing people and animals. Environmental protection and rehabilitation measures should therefore always form part of any mining contracts and conditions for licensing. Strict adherence to the best practices, laws and regulations relating to environmental protection should be effectively enforced, and non-compliance and violations of the set standards or laws should be severely punishable offences, and even risk mining licences being withdrawn.

### 5.4.14 Foreign direct investment

Mining is a business that requires huge capital investment, and most often it is foreign investors and transnational corporations that are in a position to raise the huge financial capital required to establish and operate a mining venture. These investors also normally have the capacities to survive the long gestation period before mining activities start to generate profits.

The introduction of ESAP in Zimbabwe in 1991 was partly premised on attracting foreign direct investment, but the outcome was very disappointing, despite the measures taken by the government to deregulate labour laws, reduce tariff rates, and offer bonuses and tax holidays to new investors. Therefore, while the campaign for FDI should continue, greatest priority, encouragement and support should be given to local companies and the indigenous people to invest in this key economic sector for Zimbabwe.

Before accepting investment offers by foreign companies in the mining sector, it is important that thorough investigations are carried out on the track record of interested companies so as to be assured of their genuine interest in contributing to the overall development of Zimbabwe's economy. They should not be concerned only with making a quick profit before abruptly closing down, as was the case with the BHP Hartley mine referred to above.

### 5.4.15 Local communities
More often than not, local communities tend to lose more than they gain when a mine is opened in their area. Their losses come in such forms as environmental degradation, water and air pollution, displacement, cultural disruptions, loss of land for crop cultivation, and loss of pastures for their domestic and wild animals.

Communities should therefore be compensated against any such loses caused by the mine, and be able to benefit from the investment in ways that include employment opportunities for locals, community-development projects, environmental protection and rehabilitation projects such as reafforestation, infrastructure development such as roads, the construction of social facilities such as hospitals and schools, share-buying schemes, sport and recreation activities, and other projects funded by the mines.

### 5.4.16 Mineral reserves
Minerals, once extracted from the ground, cannot be replenished, therefore the government needs to ensure that the exploitation of minerals resources brings tangible benefits to current and future generations. Government has the responsibility to ensure that the exploitation of minerals is always conducted in a manner that derives tangible benefits to both the economy and the investor. The use of revenues generated from mineral resources must be invested in areas that lead to the development of more sustainable businesses.

Mines have a beginning and an end. This characteristic must guide policy to preserve and use effectively the investments that mines make during their lifespan.

To allow such investments to rot – as has been the case at Kamativi, Empress, Pangani, Mhangura and Inyati, to name just a few former mining centres – should be avoided at all costs. Inter-ministerial co-ordination is necessary for the provision of support services and policies that are needed to attract businesses that take over from mines as sources of economic activity.

*Chapter 6*

# Gender

## 6.1 Introduction

Over the years, policies implemented by the government have to a large extent failed to respond sufficiently to the needs and responsibilities of women, hence the persistence of gender inequality and inequity. Many of the policy responses have been poorly implemented for various reasons, which include capacity deficits, inadequate budget allocations and poor infrastructure. Furthermore, economic policy strategies adopted since 1980 have failed to address the inherited enclave and dual structure of the economy, which has strong gender dimensions with women being particularly disadvantaged.[1] As a result, several key indicators show that women have been, and continue to be, disproportionately affected by the thrust of policy strategies adopted by government that have not taken into account their needs, roles and responsibilities. Empirical evidence compiled by the Southern African Regional Institute for Policy Studies (SARIPS, 2000) suggests that Zimbabwe was ranked sixth in the Southern Africa Development Council (SADC) region for high gender inequalities. The Gender-related Development Index (GDI) for Zimbabwe of 0.47 implies that men receive higher income, have better access to education, and have a longer life expectancy than women.

The Poverty Assessment Study Survey (PASS) of 2003 found that the incidence of poverty was higher in female-headed households than in male-headed households, with levels of poverty of 72 per cent and 58 per cent, respectively (Zimbabwe, 2006a). Since 1998, the Human Development Index (HDI) for females has always been lower than males; for example, in 2003, the HDI for males was 0.429 and 0.373 for females.[2] One of the reasons given for the persistent low HDI for females is that gender equality goes beyond simply empowerment and encompasses issues of social justice, culture and discrimination (ZWRCN and SARDC-WIDSAA, 2005). Furthermore, the crisis that started in earnest in 1997 further entrenched women's poverty as women resorted to survival strategies that involved multiple jobbing and their participation in risky and illegal activities on

---

[1] Women are disadvantaged in the sense that issues of direct concern such as land, education, income, food security, health care, and participation in decision-making and the economy have not been addressed; as a result they find it difficult to sustain their livelihoods. Women have been marginalized as critical agents in these processes.

[2] HDI is a measure of well-being incorporating poverty, literacy, education, life expectancy and other factors. It is considered to be a good tool for measuring development as it takes into account both economic and social indicators.

the parallel market. In fact, there has not only been a feminization of poverty but also of responsibilities and obligations.

This neglect of women's needs and roles in the formulation of economic policy strategies persists, despite the fact that women make up about 52 per cent of Zimbabwe's population. Nevertheless, it should be noted that Zimbabwean women have always known what they wanted, which is what motivated them to join the liberation struggle in the first place (Chirimuuta, 2006). Over the years, they have not remained passive: several women's groups, organizations and initiatives have been set up by women themselves, especially during the economic crisis: the Indigenous Business Women's Organization; Women in Business and Skills Development in Zimbabwe; the Zimbabwe Women's Resource Centre and Network (ZWRCN); Women in Law and Development in Africa; Women's Action Group; the Zimbabwe Women Lawyers Association; the Women's Coalition of Zimbabwe; and others. They have played an active role in advocating and lobbying for women's empowerment in Zimbabwe. Hence, the rise of the women's movement was critical as a vehicle that would drive the women's agenda and organize the women's voice in the political, social and economic processes that continue to unfold in today's Zimbabwe (ibid.).

The primary objective of this chapter is to inform and influence the formulation of alternative policies that address the gender trauma characterizing Zimbabwean society. It begins by highlighting the impact of the different policies on gender equity since 1980. This analysis will be conducted in a holistic manner that ultimately seeks to draw conclusions about why Zimbabwean women have remained significantly marginalized in policy formulation, implementation and management, despite socio-economic policy and legal reforms formulated since the country's independence. Given that addressing gender issues holistically can be very broad, this chapter pays critical attention to the strategic areas most

---

**Box 6.1: The rise of women's groups in Zimbabwe**

The first women's group, the Women's Action Group (WAG), arose in 1983, initially as a pressure group resulting from government's actions that violated the rights of Zimbabwean women.

In October 1983, the government embarked on 'operation clean-up', carried out by police, to arrest women who were unaccompanied by males after sunset and were accused of being prostitutes. More than 6,000 women – old women, schoolgirls as young as 11, young mothers with babies on their backs, nurses coming off duty, as well as other thousands of other innocent women of all races were arrested.

As a result, a group of women, using their own resources, took up the fight against this injustice towards women, and this became the first step towards the struggle for women's rights and human rights by Zimbabwean women. Today, WAG is a formal organization and produces a quarterly magazine called *Speak Out*, which is also translated into the Shona and Ndebele languages.

*Source:* Watson (1998).

pertinent in unlocking the gender paralysis in Zimbabwe. In addition, it uses gender-based indicators that highlight the impact of selected economic policy strategies on women's employment and incomes, access to education, access to healthcare, access to socio-economic resources such as land, participation in the economy, and representation in politics and decision-making.[3] Furthermore, the chapter discusses the initiatives taken by women to address the challenges facing them.

## 6.2 Background to Gender Inequality in Zimbabwe

The roots of gender inequality in Zimbabwe lie in the structural inequalities that exist in the social, political and economic spheres. Certain groups in society, particularly women, are excluded from accessing the key resources necessary for the expansion of their capabilities.

### 6.2.1 Patriarchy and structures of society

Historically, the patriarchal system in Zimbabwe that has resulted in the persistence of gender inequalities is prescribed by tradition, culture and religion. Culturally, a woman is expected to be dependent, submissive, well mannered, enduring, emotional, fearful, soft-hearted, hard-working and conservative (inward-looking), while men are expected to be the opposite – independent, ambitious, brave, aggressive, without emotions, and economically empowered. In addition, a woman's place is in the kitchen and men are the bread-winners. Furthermore, the prevailing social norms subject women to societal discrimination. Customary practices – which include pledging a young woman to marriage with a partner not of her choice, forcing a widow to marry her late husband's brother, and offering a young girl as compensatory payment in inter-family disputes – are still rooted in the country.[4] Unequal power relations result in women not being able to exercise and enjoy their sexual and reproductive health rights, leaving them more vulnerable to STIs, HIV and AIDS (WAG, 2009).

Similarly, in the religious realm, men tend to dominate even in church leadership while women remain on the margins, passive and obedient; women's visibility in the religious environment is restricted. However, colonialism reinforced patriarchy in that discriminatory rules of customary law were codified by the colonial governments and did not evolve to keep pace with the international, regional and national values introduced by the concept of equality. These customary laws, particularly in the area of access to land in communal areas, have resulted in women having unequal access to land.

---

[3] Because a plethora of economic policy strategies have been adopted since 1980, it is not possible to discuss them all. For more detail on these economic policies, see Chapter 2.

[4] See <http://www.afrol.com/Categories/Women/profiles/zimbabwe_women.htm>.

In addition to this, colonialism strengthened patriarchy in that it created a division of labour at the household level. Initially, the settlers required men to work in the newly created mines, farms and emerging towns while women remained in the poor rural areas. Therefore, men were able to enter the labour market (paid employment) while women were relegated to subsistence farming in arid rural areas, then called 'Reserves', implying that they were reservoirs of cheap labour for the settler regime.

### 6.2.2 The structure of the economy and the marginalization of women

At independence, the new government inherited a dual and enclave economy, which still largely exists today and remains not only the cause of chronic poverty and vulnerability among the poor but also exacerbates gender inequality. Over the years, the formal, male-dominated economy has shrunk and those most affected are women, given that they are in the lower echelons of the economy. This has pushed more women into the informal economy as a survival strategy. Regrettably, despite the collapse of the formal economy, government policies have continued to target the formal economy, neglecting the informal and communal economies where the majority of people, particularly women, are located. Hence, the informal and communal economies remain marginalized from developmental socio-economic, fiscal and monetary policies.

Since the economic crisis in 1997, the informal economy has grown to unprecedented levels. The 2004 *Labour Force Survey* revealed that 53 per cent of those employed in the informal economy were females, an indication that women act as shock-absorbers of crises (Zimbabwe, 2006b). This has further entrenched the feminization of poverty, and required women to seek livelihoods outside the formal economy where they are not consistently and adequately absorbed. Women's business activities within the informal economy are generally small-scale or micro-enterprises and are concentrated in the services sector (e.g. hair-dressing salons, hotels and restaurants, health and distribution services), the retail sector (including street-vending), manufacturing (usually backyard production units), agriculture, cross-border trading, and 'other' services. Unfortunately, gender-based barriers inhibit women from accessing the socio-economic resources (credit, skills training, markets, information and policy environment, etc.) that are essential for supporting micro- and very small businesses.

The majority of women are found in the communal sector, where they remain disempowered as they have no access to land in their own right. Even after the fast-track land-reform programme of 2000, the inherited inequalities in the allocation of land by gender remain evident. Furthermore, rural women's informal activities in the communal areas generate very little income: they are not viable because of the lack of markets as rural folk seldom have any money to spend.

## 6.3 The Impact of Policies on Gender

### 6.3.1 The first decade of independence, 1980–1990

At independence, the government adopted various strategies aimed at addressing the historical imbalances of the colonial period. The priority in the first ten years was ensuring that the needs of the indigenous people were addressed. However, this majority-needs approach diluted the specific needs of women, which resulted in the continued development of strategies that were viewed largely as gender-neutral but had an adverse impact on women.

From a gender perspective, the policies during this period were focused on the black majority in general and were silent about gender. However, very few women benefited from the policies that were implemented, such as decentralization of primary health care, education, development of rural infrastructure, access to markets, and access to water through boreholes and tap water. The gender-central approach in all the policy strategies meant that women's practical needs in accessing crucial resources – land, credit and extension services – were not addressed.[5]

On the other hand, a major weakness at independence was that the women's organizations that existed before independence – such as the Young Women's Christian Association and the Association of Women's Clubs (formed in 1937), among others – were focused on moral and survival issues of women without seeking to address issues of gender rights, inequity, discrimination, harassment, abuse and empowerment. Hence, there was a yawning gap immediately after independence as regards women's lobby and advocacy networks or organizations that sought to advance women's rights and the gender-equity agenda.

*Access to land*

Statistics show that although a considerable number of households had been allocated land by 1990 the gender implications were not assessed. In the early and mid-1980s, the resettlement policy generally gave preference to landless married men with dependants, and permits were issued in their names (Ncube *et al.*, 1997). Women could be allocated land only if they were widowed, divorced or unmarried with dependants. The resettlement policy therefore excluded women as it was based not only on state law but on customary practices, and as a result 87 per cent of permit holders were men (ibid.).

---

[5] Practical gender needs are defined as those basic survival needs that are not unique to women, such as food, shelter, clothing and water. These can be met through the provision of direct material inputs and do not challenge the gender divisions of labour and women's subordinate position in society. Strategic gender needs refers to the socio-economic and political positions of women in relation to men. They are concerned with structures and systems that challenge the gender division of labour, power and control, such as domestic violence, equal wages, legal rights, etc.

## Education and training

The government also inherited an educational system that was not only characterized by racial inequalities but by gender disparities as well (ZWRCN, 2004). Hence, at independence, the government embarked on an aggressive and positive education policy that made education and training a basic human right and barred the provision of education on racial grounds. The strategy of free primary education for all, which was accompanied by the expansion of the school system throughout the country, ensured that all boys and girls had access to education; thus, there were fairly few gender disparities in the education of boys and girls during the first decade of independence.

While gender disparities were eliminated at the primary-school level, they persisted at secondary-school level, with the widest gap occurring during the period 1986 to 1990. More boys than girls enrolled at secondary schools, indicating lower completion and transition rates for girls. In fact, gender divergences were even higher at tertiary and university levels.[6]

## Health

The primary health care policy of the 1980s ensured the decentralization of health facilities and accessibility of health care to the majority of Zimbabweans, including women. This policy encompassed free ante-natal and post-natal care for pregnant women. Medication was largely available in hospitals and clinics, and the availability of trained and qualified medical staff ensured accessibility to a quality public health care delivery system, which to a large extent relieved women of the burden of looking after the sick, and providing health care services and needs to their families as mothers.

## Employment

The pattern of women's participation in the labour force in Zimbabwe has been shaped by particular historical circumstances in addition to the general issue of discrimination against women.[7] At independence, women were concentrated in the non-formal labour force, which was largely non-monetized, while men formed the majority of the formal labour force, which was monetized. This trend was also attributable to the fact that women had less access to education, and 80 per cent of them resided in rural areas and were involved in subsistence farming. After independence, more women joined the formal sector but mostly in semi- and low-skilled jobs with low pay, such as secretarial and clerical work.

---

[6] More detail on gender aspects of education and training during this period can be found in Chapter 8.

[7] A National Manpower Survey that was conducted soon after independence showed that African women, who comprised 95.5 per cent of the national female population, constituted only 39 per cent of the trained female workforce. On the other hand, European women, who comprised 2.9 per cent of the female population, constituted 54 per cent of the trained work force.

Significant increases in female employment were recorded in some sectors – agriculture, mining, electricity and water, construction, distribution, restaurants and hotels, public administration, education and private domestic (Table 6.1). However, in the finance, insurance and real-estate sector there was a continual decline in the percentage of females employed in the formal sector.

**Table 6.1: Percentage share of female employment in the formal economy, 1980–2002**

| Sector | 1980–1985 | 1986–1990 | 1991–1996 | 1997–2002 |
|---|---|---|---|---|
| Agriculture | 23.3 | 25.5 | 29.0 | 31.9 |
| Mining | 2.0 | 2.6 | 3.7 | 4.2 |
| Manufacturing | 7.8 | 7.0 | 7.6 | 8.7 |
| Electricity and water | 3.2 | 3.5 | 5.6 | 5.6 |
| Construction | 1.4 | 2.2 | 4.5 | 5.2 |
| Finance, insurance and real estate | 36.9 | 31.8 | 30.2 | 27.1 |
| Distribution, restaurants and hotels | 16.1 | 15.4 | 15.7 | 18.9 |
| Transport and communication | 6.2 | 6.6 | 7.5 | 9.5 |
| Public administration | 8.5 | 10.1 | 11.6 | 17.2 |
| Education | 35.5 | 34.3 | 32.4 | 43.0 |
| Health | 56.5 | 56.0 | 56.6 | 57.7 |
| Private domestic | 19.0 | 25.4 | 26.4 | 26.4 |
| Other services | 42.1 | 15.3 | 13.7 | 14.2 |
| All sectors | 16.6 | 17.9 | 19.7 | 22.8 |

*Source:* Calculated from unpublished CSO data.

### Decision-making positions

Despite women's considerable participation in liberating the country from colonialism, during the 1980s the patriarchal power system was hostile to the entry of women into politics. The first act of establishing 'women's minimal participation in decision-making' was at independence when only eight women were elected to Parliament, which had 100 seats (Ncube, 2005). While the creation of a Ministry of Women's Affairs in 1981 was first heralded as progressive, it turned out to be an appeasement strategy to the rising agitation from women while also successfully detaching women from the core of government's agenda (ibid.).

Another cause of the minimal participation of women was their lack of education, which limited their capacity to take opportunities. Thus, politics remained a male domain: women who could enter politics did so within parameters set by men and patriarchal bargaining and co-optation (Ncube, 2005). The codifying of women as peripheral participators came through the women's wings by political parties; these were the places to which women's issues were relegated, outside the main agenda of political decision-making (ibid.).

Although women's participation in political decision-making started to gain

---

**Box 6.2: Legislation affecting women passed between 1980 and 1990**

1 Sex Disqualification Act (1980), which allowed women to hold public office.

2 Equal pay legislation (1981).

3 Legal Age of Majority Act (1982), which conferred majority status on women. Before this law women were regarded as perpetual minors.

4 Labour Relations Act (1985), which prohibited employers from discriminating against any prospective employee in relation to their employment. The Act included maternity leave and breast-feeding time. Previously, women had to resign from work when they became pregnant.

5 Public Service Pensions (Amendment) Regulations (1985), which made provision for female workers in the public service to contribute to their pension at the same rate as males.

6 Matrimonial Causes Act (1987), which provided for the equitable distribution of matrimonial assets on divorce.

7 Maintenance Amendment Act (1989), which requires a negligent non-custodian parent to contribute regularly to the maintenance of minor children in the custody of the other parent.

8 Electoral Act (1990), which allowed women to participate in general and by-elections for the presidency or in parliamentary and local elections as voters or candidates without discrimination.

*Note:* Points 2, 3, 4 and 5 catered only for the minority of women who were in paid formal employment.

*Source:* Watson (1998) and Zimbabwe (2009b).

---

momentum after 1988, the levels still remained very low. For example, women's representation in political decision-making positions between 1980 and 1984 was only 9 per cent, and dropped to 8 per cent during the period 1985–1990. By 1990, women's participation in parliament was only 11 per cent, and there were only 9.4 per cent female ministers and 8.2 per cent deputy ministers in a country where 52 per cent of the population were women (ANSA, 2006). In realizing the need to increase the level of participation of women in politics, the government put in place the Electoral Act of 1990, which allowed women to participate in general and by-elections for the presidency, parliamentary or local elections as voters or candidates without any discrimination.

### 6.3.2 The ESAP period, 1991–1996

During ESAP, the government introduced several policies that sought to empower women as well as give them space to participate in the economy. In 1991, Zimbabwe signed the Convention on the Elimination of All Forms of Discrimination Against Women (CEDAW), under which all member states were obliged to take measures to eliminate all discrimination against women in order to ensure equal rights with men in education, by providing conditions that allowed equal access to vocational training, the same curricula, adult literacy programmes, a reduction in female drop-out rates, and equal access to sports and physical education.

However, the market-led economic prescriptions which informed ESAP centred on fiscal austerity, domestic deregulation, profit-driven markets and the 'roll back' of the state under the general belief that these prescriptions would have a 'trickle-down' effect leading to a decline in poverty and inequality, including gender inequality. A supposition was that women would be equal beneficiaries, leading to gender equality. Unfortunately, the benefits predicted were not realized, nor was there a fairer share between men and women of the unpaid work and costs in caring for the family and raising children. In fact, the rolling back of the state meant a reduction in government spending on social services such as education, health, transportation, utilities and food subsidies (welfare programmes).

## Education

In education, cost-recovery was introduced in urban areas, while development levies were raised in rural areas (ZWRCN, 2004), which had an impact on enrolments at both primary and secondary schools, with girls being affected more than boys. Although primary-education enrolments fluctuated, rising slightly overall, this was not the case with secondary schools. During ESAP, there was a huge drop in enrolments at secondary level, the worst affected being females, effectively reversing some of the gains that had been achieved during the first decade of independence. The 1992 census report showed that 34 per cent of school-going age children were still in school; 49 per cent had left and, of these, 51 per cent were females. The same report indicated that 17 per cent had never been to school and, of these, 60 per cent were female (ibid.). Even after the establishment of the second university in Zimbabwe, the National University of Science and Technology (NUST) in 1991, the enrolment of females remained low at 19 per cent (ZWRCN and SARDC-WIDSAA, 2005).

## Health

ESAP also placed the achievements made during the first decade of independence in the health sector under threat and reversed most of the gains that had been realized, also having a different impact on men and women. During ESAP, most hospitals were run on a cost-recovery basis with a business focus, where a patient was viewed as a client and services were 'commoditized'. Furthermore, the removal of health-care subsidies resulted in the imposition of user fees.

This had a great impact on poor households, especially female-headed households. Households adjusted by shifting more of the care on to the shoulders of women. The result was an increase in unpaid work for women on top of their usual responsibilities of caring for the family and raising children. It has to be noted that it was during ESAP that the HIV and AIDS pandemic began to manifest itself. The number of victims grew very quickly, and a new 'care economy' emerged in which women were the care-givers in the families and in society in general under home-based care schemes which were introduced by hospitals and clinics that were unable to take care of the ever-increasing number of HIV and AIDS patients.

## Employment

The opening of the Zimbabwean market through the liberalization agenda of ESAP made it difficult for local producers to compete with cheap imports. Thus, local companies either downsized or closed down, which led to massive job losses and redundancy in the manufacturing and industrial sectors. The sectors most affected were clothing and textiles, where the majority of female workers were found. From Table 6.2 it can be seen that the overall percentage share of employment of females dropped during the ESAP period to 55 per cent from 61.5 per cent during the period 1985–1990, eroding the gains that had been attained between 1980 and 1990. While job losses affect both women and men, women find it more difficult to regain employment or self-employment owing to a lack of education and skills (ANSA, 2006).

ESAP also brought with it Export Processing Zones (EPZs) in an Act that was passed in 1994 [*Chapter 14:07*]. More women than men were employed in EPZs, the reason for which has been linked to particular feminine characteristics which include their greater submission and docility and hence willingness to follow orders while being less likely to organize, their greater dexterity in the production of small objects or those processes that require care and patience, and their flexibility with respect to conditions of work (Deere, 2005).

While women gained more access to paid work in selected sectors, the nature of these jobs was, however, not decent. Deregulation of the labour market led to a shift from permanent jobs to 'flexible jobs' (part-time and casual) which are insecure in nature (ANSA, 2006), but the proportion of females to males remained low, indicating inequality between the sexes (Table 6.2). On the other hand, the rate of growth of female casual workers increased more than that of males, indicating that women are more vulnerable than their male counterparts. Clearly, therefore, even though the proportion of total female employment in the formal economy increased over time, precarious forms of employment (casual) grew at a faster rate.

**Table 6.2: Percentage share of female employment by tenure, 1990–2002**

| Year | Full-time | Part-time | Casual |
|------|-----------|-----------|--------|
| 1990 | 15.9 | 29.9 | 6.3 |
| 1991 | 16.0 | 26.3 | 7.7 |
| 1992 | 16.4 | 28.7 | 7.9 |
| 1993 | 16.6 | 21.0 | 8.7 |
| 1994 | 17.5 | 32.4 | 8.2 |
| 1995 | 18.0 | 21.9 | 8.3 |
| 1996 | 19.1 | 17.9 | 8.8 |
| 1997 | 18.9 | 17.6 | 9.6 |
| 1998 | 20.1 | 16.9 | 10.1 |
| 1999 | 20.2 | 15.9 | 10.6 |
| 2000 | 21.9 | 15.6 | 12.0 |
| 2001 | 22.1 | 27.1 | 12.1 |
| 2002 | 22.5 | 21.2 | 14.9 |

*Source:* Calculated from unpublished CSO data.

### 6.3.3 The crisis period, 1997–2008

Government policies during this period were largely reactionary.[8] Regrettably, all the policies were gender-blind. While the blueprints stated the need to reduce poverty levels, the measures for such action did not specifically target women who were, and continue to be, disproportionately affected by poverty, nor did they focus on addressing gender inequalities and the rising dominance of the non-formal sectors where women were concentrated.

They also failed to take cognizance of the roles, work and responsibilities of women that had been exacerbated during the ESAP period. For example, the Millennium Economic Recovery Programme was focused essentially on the manufacturing industry, a male-dominated sector, and thereby undermined sectors occupied by women and women's work (e.g. reproductive and care work). In addition, the reduction of tariffs on major inputs in the mining sector and recapitalization of the mining industry, in which very few women are involved, also shows the gendered nature of economic fundamentals in terms of what is considered productive or otherwise.

Like its predecessor, the National Economic Revival Programme focused on capacity utilization and the revival of industry, not at utilizing the capacity of women in the non-formal sectors and care work; the manufacturing industry was assumed to be the only sector that had been seriously affected by economic challenges such as input costs, high interest rates and price controls. On the other hand, although the Zimbabwe Economic Development Strategy formulation

[8] See Chapter 2 for details of the policies discussed here.

process was based on a broad and extensive nationwide consultation process by stakeholders, including women's groups, it failed to take off owing to financial difficulties.

### Access to land

In 2000, the government embarked on the accelerated land-reform programme which, however, did not correct past gender imbalances in land ownership; it focused on ability and not need, thereby disadvantaging women. Since 86 per cent of women in Zimbabwe live in the rural areas, where they depend on land for their livelihoods and families, women play a key role in agriculture (ZWRCN and SARDC–WIDSAA, 2005). The programme therefore provided an opportunity for the government to address the gender gaps in land ownership. However, the lack of gender-sensitivity in the implementation of the programme resulted in no significant change in women's access to land. In addition, because the policy had shifted from a social-justice approach to a political-reward system, very few women benefited.[9]

The Presidential Land Review Committee set up in 2003 to examine the impact and implementation of the 2000 land-reform programme clearly noted that women did not benefit equally with men (Zimbabwe, 2003).[10] This was despite the efforts of the Women Land and Lobby Group that had lobbied for 30 per cent of the land to be distributed to women and registered in their names (ZWRCN and SARDC–WIDSAA, 2005). The Committee also noted that women farmers did not have great opportunities in terms of access to inputs and labour-saving technology. As reported in Chapter 3, women constituted only 18 per cent of those allocated land under the A1 model and 12 per cent of those in the A2 model, despite the fact that the 2003 Committee had recommended a quota of 40 per cent of the land allocations, especially A1 farms, to women, and that 40 per cent of the funding be reserved for women. Thus, the majority of the women continued to have secondary-use rights, especially under the communal land-tenure system.

Furthermore, the marginalization of women's access to land was perpetuated by gender imbalances in terms of traditional leaders in rural areas. Zimbabwe has 266 chiefs, of whom only 5 are women, and 474 headmen, of whom 5 per cent are women, meaning that when unmarried women take their concerns to these leaders, only a few leaders may sympathize with them because they are also women (Women and Land in Zimbabwe, 2009).

The land-allocation structures in urban areas also marginalize women's access

---

[9] Women constitute less than 30 per cent of the politicians in Zimbabwe, mainly because the political terrain is set according to male standards which make it difficult for women to participate.

[10] In fact, the process of land redistribution did not even achieve the 20 per cent target for women set by the government.

to land. In the urban areas, land is allocated by local authorities for residential, commercial and peri-urban-agriculture purposes, and is sold to those who can afford to buy it and those who have collateral security. Women, however, disadvantaged by their lack of access to financial resources and collateral security, are unable to buy land and as a result the bulk of it is purchased by men who have collateral (ibid).

These gender imbalances have persisted despite the fact that Zimbabwe signed CEDAW, Article 14(g) of which stresses that 'State parties shall take all appropriate measures to ensure that women have access to agricultural credit and loans, marketing facilities, appropriate technology and equal treatment in agrarian reform as well as in land resettlement schemes' (ZWRCN and SARDC–WIDSAA, 2005). Furthermore, women's lack of access and control over land principally excludes them from accessing other resources such as credit, marketing facilities, decision-making powers over agricultural production activities and benefits, which impact adversely on their productive capacity (ibid). Given that 80 per cent of household food security is generated by women, their access to land and accompanying resources has a greater impact on household food security (Mushunje, 2001).

Another dimension in agriculture during this period was that there was a shift in incentives to promote cash crops such as tobacco and cotton, yet women focused on food crops. Thus, women were again in a disadvantaged state.

## Access to loans

Data available from the Small Enterprises Development Corporation (SEDCO) indicate that women tend to apply for loans in areas such as cross-border trading, general trading, vending, poultry-rearing and market gardening (Women and Land in Zimbabwe, 2009). Unfortunately, most of the data on access to credit are not disaggregated by gender.

The number of women who were given support by SEDCO increased significantly in 2001, but levels thereafter show a declining trend (Table 6.3). Even the Small to Medium Enterprise Revolving Fund that was introduced in September 2006 by the Reserve Bank of Zimbabwe indicated that, of the Z$16 billion (US$64 million) set aside, only 27 per cent had gone to women by March 2007.[11] By August 2007,

**Table 6.3: Women entrepreneurs supported by SEDCO, 2000–2005**

| Year | Women beneficiaries | |
|------|--------|------------|
|      | Number | Percentage |
| 2000 | 45     | 16         |
| 2001 | 483    | 45         |
| 2002 | 398    | 44         |
| 2005 | 112    | 38         |

*Source:* Women and Land in Zimbabwe (2009)

[11] The RBZ's official exchange rate of UD$1:Z$250 has been used here. On the parallel market, US$1 could be changed for around Z$3,000 in January 2007 and for between $100,000 and $150,000 by July.

women's projects had received nearly Z$14 billion (US$56 million) out of the Z$32 billion dollar facility (US$128 million), which was almost 44 per cent of the total fund (Women and Land in Zimbabwe, 2009). Although the levels look high, it is still necessary to channel more resources towards women.

*Education crisis*

Most of the gains that had been made during the 1980s and 1990s in the education sector were eroded during the crisis period. There were more cases of children dropping out of school, particularly those in difficult circumstances. Parents could not afford the high costs of fees, books, school uniforms and transport. Many bread-winners lost their jobs when companies restructured or closed down, while others lost their jobs owing to HIV and AIDS-related illnesses. This had an impact on the girl-child's education, as parents were forced to make choices that were guided by social beliefs about investing in the boy-child, who was the assumed bread-winner and the extender of the family, which involved fewer risks than the girl-child. Cultural beliefs and practices continued to be cited as the major promoter of gender inequality in education.

There has been a steady decline in the rate of children completing primary and secondary school, with males having higher completion rates than females, especially in secondary education.[12] The main reason for this can be attributed to economic hardships, which tend to sacrifice the girl-child and place more value on educating males. Other reasons include teenage pregnancies and early marriages, proximity of schools (especially in resettlement areas), and cultural beliefs, values and practices (Jirira and Masuko, 2009).

In the light of these challenges, in 2001 the government introduced a pro-gramme under the Enhanced Social Protection Project called BEAM (Basic Education Assistance Module) for primary and secondary schools, a community-driven programme in terms of beneficiary selection and programme monitoring. It meets the cost of tuition fees, levies and exam fees. However, its intended objective of reducing the number of vulnerable children dropping out of school, and/or of children who had never been to school as a result of the economic hardships, especially girls between the ages of 6 and 19, failed. The target set for BEAM was to reach 25 per cent of total enrolment each year and, for secondary schools, that 50 per cent of the beneficiaries be females (SARDC–WIDSAA, 2008). The number of children assisted under BEAM constituted an estimated 19.6 per cent of the enrolment in 2006 and 23.8 per cent in 2007, which are less than the target and clearly indicate that the programme is failing to achieve its objectives. This calls for more resources to be applied towards the girl-child.[13]

---

[12] This was noted in the Nziramasanga commission's report of 1999; see Chapter 8.

[13] See also Chapter 9.

BEAM has, however, faced a number of challenges, particularly the hyper-inflationary environment which saw the erosion of funds and the continual review of school fees, as well as human and technological constraints in the Ministry of Labour and Social Services which led to the late disbursement of funds and poor targeting. Other difficulties included a loss of continuity of support before students sat for examinations, poor fiscal resource allocations, numerous competing demands as poverty accelerated, and the daunting challenge of the increased number of HIV and AIDS orphans who are most in need of BEAM.

There are also gender disparities in terms of the subjects taken by females and males at high schools, and, in order to encourage females to take up technical subjects, maths and science camps have been introduced at selected schools (Zimbabwe, 2009b). However, limited success has been achieved because there are few career-guidance programmes at secondary and high schools. At higher institutes of learning, the government introduced an affirmative-action policy in 1995 which was meant to increase female enrolment: females were allowed to enrol in degree programmes at universities with one or two points fewer than males for the same degree. In line with the motive of increasing women's education at higher institutes of learning, the Women's University in Africa was established in 2002 (Box 6.3). Although this has created space for females to attain degrees, they remain concentrated in non-technical programmes such as

---

**Box 6.3: The Women's University in Africa**

Established in 2002, the University offers degree programmes and other courses for females ready to take up tertiary education at all levels up to 60 years. In most cases, these students are those who missed out on furthering their education owing to lack of finance, married women with family responsibilities, and working women. Learning schedules are very flexible as there are also evening and weekend lectures, which is not the case in most universities in the country. The degree programmes are as follows:

1 Agriculture: Women are the tillers of the land, yet because of lack of education in that field, they remain poor.

2 Reproductive health: Women are not in control of their reproductive health so there needs to be some formal training so that they can fill the gap between the nurse and the doctor.

3 Gender: Women should be taught at an early stage the technicalities of gender issues and the sociological connotations.

4 Management: This aims at empowering women who have become stuck in middle management by virtue of being female. This is a popular course. The aim is for women to rise above diploma level and get to the highest level – degree level.

*Note:* The University also enrols male students. However, the percentage of females is higher.

*Source:* Adapted from ZWRCN and SARDC–WIDSAA (2005).

arts and commerce; few are venturing into science subjects. This is, however, a reflection of the choice of the subjects they had taken at high schools.

Also of importance is access to education for those who are physically challenged, and although both males and females may face difficulties in accessing education, the girl-child is in a worse position.

Box 6.4: Advocacy initiatives by UNICEF in the education sector

1 *Campaign for Female Education (CAMFED)* was launched in 1993. It offers assistance for girls of school-going age in both primary and secondary schools in the rural areas.

2 *Go Back to School Campaign* which encourages young girls to go back to school.

*Source:* <http://www.uneca.org>.

She requires more attention as she suffers two kinds of discrimination – because of her sex and because of physical challenges (ZWRCN and SARDC–WIDSAA, 2005). This is coupled with the fact that many girls with disabilities are vulnerable to sexual abuse and therefore to STIs and HIV and AIDS.

In addressing the issue of pregnant girls and education, the Ministry of Education, Sports and Culture put in place Policy Circular No. 35 of 2001, which provided pregnant pupils with the opportunity to go back to school after delivery. Although this intervention was received with a lot of criticism by some parents, its aim is a step towards addressing the gender gaps in education in line with the Beijing Platform of Action, which stresses the need to address inequalities and inadequacies in, and unequal access to, education and training, and persistent discrimination against and violation of the rights of the girl-child.

*Health crisis*

The economic crisis exacerbated the health crisis which had already begun to emerge during the ESAP period. The deteriorating economy created severe health risks for women, even where they were not living in extreme poverty. The brain drain resulted in a shortage of medical staff (nurses, doctors, technicians, etc.) in government hospitals, and it became very difficult to obtain drugs and equipment because of cutbacks in government expenditure. All this meant that the burden on women increased as they had to spend more time dealing with health issues at the household level as the public system had failed. Many households were forced to resort to alternative (traditional) health-delivery systems or other coping strategies. The high cost of drugs and medical services, coupled with a lack of foreign currency, resulted in more families being unable to access such services.

The health crisis also dealt a huge blow to pregnant women, as the deterioration in public-health institutions greatly hindered women's access to care during pregnancy, delivery and after delivery, as well as to pap smears and family planning services (WAG, 2009). As a result, most pregnant women had to deliver at home (which is very risky for both the mother and the baby) and therefore missed out on prevention of mother-to-child transmission of HIV support. Cases of maternal and newborn morbidity were higher than in previous periods (ibid.).

The outbreak of cholera in 2008 had a woman's face because women had to bear the brunt of caring for the sick, and some were blamed for spreading cholera as their roles involved maintaining household hygiene (WAG, 2009). The health crisis also manifested itself in a decline in life expectancy. Female life expectancy dropped from about 62 years in 1992 to 57 years in 1997, while that of males declined from 58 years to 53 years over the same period. The figures fell further to reach 43.6 years for females and 42.6 years for males, clearly indicating gender disparity in life expectancy.[14]

The scourge of HIV and AIDS also has a woman's face. The HIV/AIDS pandemic has led to child-headed families – or, rather, 'girl-child-headed and granny-headed families' – which has an impact on the education of the girl-child who has to forgo education so as to look after the other family members. Overall, the HIV and AIDS pandemic has increased the burden for women. Poor households adjust by shifting more of the care into the household and on to the shoulders of women and girls:

> We have a cultural tradition of extended families. If somebody gets sick with HIV or AIDS, they are returned to their homes and to the care-giver, who is usually the mother or the grandmother. If the sick person dies, the orphans are then left in the hands of the grandmothers or the aunts or sisters; so there is such a huge responsibility around issues of poverty that women face on a day-to-day basis.[15]

---

**Box 6.5: Response by women's organizations to the HIV and AIDS pandemic**

Advocacy work by various women's organizations led to the enactment of the Sexual Offences Act of 2001, which is now part of the Criminal Law (Codification and Reform) Act [*Chapter 9:23*]. The act recognizes the important role of women's sexual and reproductive health.

*Source:* WAG (2009).

---

In response to the HIV and AIDS crisis, the government, instead of expanding the hospital infrastructure, chose to capacitate existing clinics with HIV and AIDS-related facilities for treatment, such as prevention of mother-to-child transmission facilities in 2001 and sourcing of anti-retroviral drugs. Various awareness-raising activities, such as voluntary counselling and testing, and New Start centres were set up in almost all the cities and towns in the country. Victim-friendly units were also established at various police stations, and survivors of rape have

---

[14] UNDP, *Human Development Report, 2009.*

[15] Lucia Matibenga, 'Fighting for Zimbabwean women', *The Guardian*, 1 August 2007, <http://www.guardian.co.uk/world/2007/aug/01/zimbabwe-women>.

access to post-exposure prophylaxis, medicine given within 72 hours to reduce the chances of HIV infection.

## Employment crisis

At the onset of the economic crisis in 1997, it was found that more women than men worked in the informal economy,[16] the percentage increasing from 51 in 1991 to 52 in 1997. The figures continued to rise, the ILO reporting in June 2005 that between 3 million and 4 million Zimbabweans earned a living in the informal sector, the majority of these being women. The data showed that the low number of women employed in the formal sector was accounted for by the high number in the informal sector.

However, labour-market segregation is also permeating the informal economy. Within the informal economy, women continue to face challenges as there is a growing trend in the feminization of certain jobs that do not pay as much as those undertaken by men. For instance, most women in the informal economy concentrate on buying and selling vegetables, sweets and clothing, and on cross-border trading. Men are involved in what has been termed 'small to medium-sized enterprises' such as carpentry, welding, tailoring, construction and sculpture, among others, which receive some support from the Ministry of Small and Medium Enterprises as they are viewed as sustainable and profitable. Furthermore, after 2000, many female agricultural workers lost their jobs when they were displaced after the land-reform programme, and there were also widespread retrenchments across all sectors of the economy in the same period.

As if this was not enough, the government-led Operation Murambatsvina in 2005 stripped women of their livelihoods. The majority of women in the informal sector lost their sources of income, some were displaced and were left to look for alternative livelihoods. Some ended up staying wherever there were services such as water, electricity and schools. It was the women and girl-children who had to walk long distances in search of water and firewood, and some girls had to forgo their education.

## Participation in politics and decision-making

Although the participation of women began to gain momentum during the late 1980s, and the rate increased in the late 1990s and after, it still remains minimal and falls short of the SADC target of 50 per cent and the 52 per cent of the National Gender Policy (Table 6.4). The percentage share of female ministers declined disappointingly between 1990 and 1995 before rising to 16.7 per cent in 2009, and the percentage share of female deputy ministers had declined sharply to 5 per cent in 2005 before rising to about 16 per cent in 2009 (Table 6.5).

---

[16] The 1997 intercensal demographic survey.

**Table 6.4: Women's representation in political decision-making positions, 1980–2009**

| Period | Percentage representation |
|---|---|
| 1980–1984 | 9 |
| 1985–1990 | 8 |
| 1991–1995 | 11 |
| 1996–2000 | 10 |
| 2000–2005 | 16 |
| 2005–2008 | 25 |
| 2009 (Inclusive Government) | 20 |

*Source:* UNDP reports, ZWRCN and SARDC-WIDSAA (2005),
Parliament of Zimbabwe.

**Table 6.5: Political decision-making positions by gender and portfolio in Zimbabwe (%)**

| Portfolio | 1988 Female | 1988 Male | 1990 Female | 1990 Male | 1995 Female | 1995 Male | 2005 Female | 2005 Male | 2009 Female | 2009 Male |
|---|---|---|---|---|---|---|---|---|---|---|
| Ministers | 12.5 | 87.5 | 9.4 | 90.6 | 8.7 | 91.3 | 12.9 | 87.1 | 16.7 | 83.3 |
| Deputy ministers | 16.7 | 83.3 | 8.2 | 91.8 | 26.7 | 73.3 | 5 | 95 | 15.8 | 84.2 |
| MPs | 13 | 87 | n.a. | n.a. | n.a. | n.a. | 16.7 | 83.3 | 33.3 | 66.7 |
| Senators | 7.5 | 92.5 | n.a. | n.a. | n.a. | n.a. | 34.8 | 65.2 | 34.8 | 65.2 |

*Source:* Various Sources; Jirira and Masuko (2009).   n.a. = not available.

However, there was an improvement in the percentage share of female Members of the House of Assembly (MPs) and Senators, though both the Speaker and Deputy Speaker were men, and of the thirteen Parliamentary Portfolio Committees, only one was chaired by a woman. Remarkably, the President of the Senate was a woman, and in 2001, a Women's Parliamentary Caucus was established following the realization of the need for women parliamentarians to work together on gender issues across the political divide (ZWRCN and SARDC-WIDSAA, 2005). The increase in female Senators can be attributed to increased awareness among the top leadership of the need to augment the number of women in decision-making bodies, and to lobbying by civil-society organizations (ibid.).

Although 58 female candidates (21.3 per cent) contested the 2005 parliamentary elections, less than half managed to win a seat, mainly because of sexist and gender-stereotyping attitudes. Even after the 2008 harmonized elections, the main parties came forward with policies that at least 30 per cent of the contested seats should be reserved for female candidates, but this has not materialized; a woman could still lose the seat to a contesting male. There is no legislated quota system that would ensure that a fair number of women found their way into parliament and are guaranteed political positions.

The percentage share of women in decision-making positions in the public

---

**Box 6.6: Women's participation in the constitutional reform process, 1999–2000**

During the 1999 and 2000 period, the Women's Coalition mobilized women to take up leadership positions in the constitutional reform process and to participate in information-gathering and the writing of the constitution. The Coalition managed to engender the National Constitutional Assembly (NCA) and constitutional processes.

The NCA was made up of a task force of which 30 per cent were women from women's groups. From August 1999 to November 2001, it was led by an outspoken woman, Thoko Matshe. Hence, women were active in the leadership, implementation, and participation in the growing political debate on the constitutional reform process, and this created space strategically for women to discuss their political issues. However, in March 1999 a Constitutional Commission (CC) was set up whose mandate was to consult Zimbabweans widely and draw up a constitution reflecting the views of the people. Unfortunately, only 13 per cent of that body were women.

It was at this point that the women decided to form a separate process parallel to the NCA and CC processes as a way of adequately giving voice to women or to address their needs. Thus, the Women's Coalition was formed. It comprised women's groups, NGOs and academics across the political-party divide whose aim was to ensure the full participation of women in the ongoing constitutional reform process and the creation of a gender-sensitive national constitution.

Women did not pull out of the NCA or the CC processes, but used the input from the Women's Coalition to strengthen their participation in these other processes.

*Source:* Adapted from Ncube (2005).

---

sphere remained low, especially in local government (Table 6.6). This falls short of the policy requirement which states that 50 per cent of the posts in the public service be occupied by women; two-thirds of the Public Service Commissioners are women. On the other hand, there is only a 32 per cent representation of women on the Select Committee on constitution-making, which is still low.

The *Progress of the World's Women, 2008/2009* (UNIFEM, 2009) demonstrated that, for women's rights to be translated into substantive improvements in their lives, and for gender equality to be realized in practice, women must be able to participate fully in public decision-making at all levels and hold those responsible to account when their rights are infringed or their needs ignored. What remains is to translate their visibility into leadership positions and influence over the decision-making process.

**Table 6.6: Decision-making positions in the public sphere by gender (%)**

|  | Female | Male |
| --- | --- | --- |
| Urban councils | 13 | 87 |
| Rural district douncils | 3 | 97 |
| Judiciary | 41 | 59 |
| Public service | 30 | 70 |
| Zimbabwe Republic Police | 11 | 89 |

*Note:* Positions include councillors, commissioners, chairpersons, managers, judges, magistrates, etc. *Source:* Jirira and Masuko (2009).

## Gender-based violence

The growth of the economic crisis saw an increase in gender-based violence against women. It has been suggested that a contributing factor was that the economic crisis stripped men of their traditional role as breadwinners, and women took over this role in many families. Consequently, there were tensions at home, which resulted in domestic violence. For example, domestic violence accounted for six out of ten murder cases in the courts (SARDC–WIDSAA, 2008). As a result, the Musasa Project launched the White Ribbon Campaign in 2003 as a national year-long campaign to protest against family violence (ZWRCN and SARDC–WIDSAA, 2005).

With the growing rate of domestic violence, several women's rights groups emerged, including the Zimbabwe Women Lawyers Association, WAG, the ZWRCN, and the Women and AIDS Support Network. These organizations provide services such as legal representation, training and counselling for victims of gender-based violence, and impart information to women about their legal rights.

> **Box 6.7: Some of the initiatives to address domestic violence at national level**
>
> A national gender-based violence-prevention strategy was developed by the Ministry of Women's Affairs, Gender and Community Development, in collaboration with the United Nations Population Fund, in 2005. The strategy focuses on prevention, service provision, research, documentation and advocacy in the area of gender-based violence.
>
> 1 Enactment of the Domestic Violence Act [*Chapter 5: 16*] in 2006, which criminalizes domestic violence as well as providing relief and protection to victims.
>
> 2 An Anti-Domestic Violence Council has been established to constantly monitor the problem of domestic violence in the country.
>
> *Source:* Ministry of Women's Affairs, Gender and Community Development.

## Participation in the media

The participation of women in the media is very important as it gives an indication of the extent to which women's issues are covered by media. Although the National Gender Policy highlights the need to transform the media to make it gender-sensitive through training, make media personnel gender-sensitive and thus facilitate a positive portrayal of women in the media, for example, this has not been supported by any legislation.

There is an overall under-representation of women in the media (Table 6.7). Only in institutions of higher learning do we find females constituting more than 50 per cent of the students in media studies. Unfortunately, this positive trend is not reflected in the labour market. For example, only 10 per cent of those in senior management in the media industry are women, while only 13 per cent are in the top management. Such under-representation of women in decision-making positions in all the media houses results in an unbalanced and stereotyped portrayal of women in society.

**Table 6.7: Percentage of women's participation in the media**

| Indicator | Percentage of women |
|---|---|
| Overall | 13 |
| Board of directors | 38 |
| Senior management | 10 |
| Top management | 13 |
| Female staff in institutions of higher learning | 25 |
| Proportion of students in institutions of higher learning | 57 |
| New sources | 16 |

*Source:* 2010 SADC Gender Barometer.

## 6.4 Initiatives to Address Gender Inequality and Inequity

While there have been various initiatives at country level over the years, the government adopted various initiatives at national, regional and international levels in an effort to address existing gender imbalances. These initiatives included the establishment of national gender institutional frameworks, legal and policy reforms.[17]

### 6.4.1 International frameworks

The government of Zimbabwe has signed and ratified the majority of relevant international documents, indicating government's commitment to address gender imbalances. These instruments contain provisions that proscribe discrimination on the basis of sex and guarantee the equality of men and women before the law. They include:

- The United Nations Declaration of Human Rights (1948)
- The International Covenant on Economic, Social and Cultural Rights (1966)
- The Convention on the Elimination of Discrimination Against Women (CEDAW) (1979)

The Zimbabwe government participated in the Nairobi Conference in 1985 which deliberated on the UN Decade for Women, and in 1995 it was part of the Beijing Conference and ascribed to principles aimed at addressing the twelve critical areas of concern under the Beijing Platform of Action (BPFA).[18]

---

[17] This section discusses only the key initiatives that are related to the key strategic areas on gender. It is not possible to cover all the legal, policy and pragmatic measures.

[18] The critical areas of concern include: the persistence and increasing burden of poverty on women; inequalities and inadequacies in and unequal access to education; violence against women; effects of armed conflict on women; inequalities in accessing resources; insufficient mechanisms for the advancement of women; lack of respect for women's human rights; stereotyping of women; violations of the rights of the girl-child; and gender inequalities in the management of natural resources.

---

**Box 6.8: The Convention on the Elimination of Discrimination Against Women (CEDAW)**

This convention is the cornerstone of measures that have to be taken to address gender inequality, and is the only human-rights treaty that affirms the reproductive rights of women and targets culture and tradition as influential forces shaping gender roles and family relations.

It further provides directives to governments on the most critical dimensions of gender inequality, including cultural stereotypes, political and public participation, educational opportunities, employment opportunities, economic resources, legal rights, health care and gender-based violence. CEDAW also calls upon governments to put in place institutional mechanisms to address gender inequality.

*Source:* <http://www.un.org/womenwatch/daw/cedaw>.

---

Furthermore, Zimbabwe was one of the 189 member states that reached a global consensus that culminated in the Millennium Declaration in the year 2000 that seeks to ensure the improvement of the condition of humanity throughout the world in the areas of development, poverty eradication, peace, security, protection of the environment, human rights and democracy. The Declaration outlined eight Millennium Development Goals, one of which is to achieve gender equality and empower women by 2015. Interestingly, the other seven goals are linked to the goal of achieving gender equality and empowering women and are useful in terms of implementing CEDAW and the BPFA.[19]

The government also ratified international conventions in the field of employment that seek to advance gender equality at the workplace. These include the ILO's Convention (No. 111) concerning Discrimination in Respect of Employment and Occupation of 1958 and Convention (No. 100) concerning Equal Remuneration for Men and Women Workers for Work of Equal Value. Although the government is yet to ratify other gender-sensitive employment-related conventions,[20] measures have been put in place at national level to advance gender equality in the field of work. However, a weakness of Zimbabwe's legal system is that a ratified convention does not have any automatic legal effect, and must be domesticated in legislation passed by parliament; this has not been done with regard to the above-mentioned conventions.

### 6.4.2 Regional frameworks

At the regional level, government has ratified the African Charter on Human and Peoples' Rights of 1981, and is also committed to implementing sub-regional initiatives such as the SADC Gender and Development Declaration of 1997 and

---

[19] See <http://www.un.org/millenniumgoals> for details of the Millennium Development Goals.

[20] Such as Convention 103 on Maternity Protection, Convention 175 on Part-time Work, and Convention 156 on Workers with Family Responsibilities. See <http://www.ilo.org/ilolex/english/convdisp1.htm> for details of all these ILO conventions.

its Addendum on Domestic Violence of 1998. Furthermore, in 2003, it also adopted the SADC Charter of Fundamental Social Rights, which focuses on employment and social-security concerns and recognizes the need to ensure gender equity, equal treatment and opportunities for men and women in all aspects of life.

Later in 2006, Zimbabwe signed the Protocol to the African Charter on Human and Peoples' Rights on the Rights of Women in Africa (Women's Protocol) of 2003, which came about after the realization that gender issues were not being considered seriously at the African Union (Banda, 2005). In order to take the issue of women's empowerment further, Zimbabwe signed the SADC Protocol on Gender and Development in 2008. However, these protocols still remain to be domesticated in Zimbabwean law so that they become legally binding and usable in the courts.

### 6.4.3 National frameworks

*National gender machinery*
The Ministry of Women's Affairs, Gender and Community Development was so named in 2005. Its mandate is to advance women, and to promote gender equality and community development, and it seeks to address gender inequalities in a multi-sectoral and integrated manner. The ministry receives funding from the national budget and international development partners. However, its greatest challenges remain financial constraints and high staff turn-over due to low remuneration. High staff turnover has resulted in the loss of institutional memory. Supporting the ministry's work are Gender Focal Persons, Gender Committees, the Women's Parliamentary Caucus, and the Parliamentary Portfolio Committee on Gender.

a) *Gender Focal Persons and Gender Committees* are responsible for monitoring and evaluation. However, there are no feedback mechanisms for quarterly reports submitted to the ministry, inadequate training on gender mainstreaming, and the Gender Focal Persons are excluded from senior management and policy-planning meetings (Zimbabwe, 2009b).

b) *The Women's Parliamentary Caucus* is responsible for promoting the gender agenda in parliament, and is very active in the constitution-making process.

c) *The Parliamentary Portfolio Committee on Gender* assesses progress and monitors the activities and implementation of gender equality and women's empowerment policies in the country.

Responsible for co-ordination are the UN Gender Thematic Group and the Inter-ministerial Committee on Gender, both of which are chaired by the Ministry of Women's Affairs, Gender and Community Development; unfortunately, by 2009, the Inter-ministerial Committee had not been put in place (ibid.). For this committee to be effective, it should ensure that it provides adequate space for the participation of non-state actors such as civil-society organizations, non-governmental organizations, trade unions and development partners to exercise their role as strategic partners in policy formulation, implementation, monitoring and evaluation. This creates joint ownership and allows the pooling of internal and external capacities and capabilities (Chakanya and Makanza, 2009). Apart from this, the capacity of the ministry's officers to implement gender mainstreaming effectively at both provincial and district level largely remains limited.

## Gender focal points

The government has established gender focal points in all line ministries, supported by the Ministry of Women Affairs, Gender and Community Development through capacity-building programmes. Their mandate is to mainstream gender in all ministries. However, 'no accountability mechanism has been established by the ministry to determine [their] effectiveness' (Zimbabwe, 2009b: 12).

## The national constitution

The Zimbabwe constitution, particularly section 23(1), which was amended in 1996 in order to ensure the elimination of discrimination on the basis of gender,[21] is another overarching document for the advancement of gender inequality. The development of a constitutional framework meant that all laws had to be in line with the supreme law in terms of eliminating discrimination against women. However, there is still a claw-back clause that allows for discrimination on the basis of customary law, which is a challenge to women who, more often than not, are adversely affected by customary practices and norms.[22]

However, although policies and legislation have been put in place (Table 6.8), this is not an end in itself. Achieving gender equality encompasses not only the adoption of specific laws and policies but their implementation. Laws and policies provide just the essential foundation for the realization of rights. In reality, women's legal rights go beyond these and depend more on women's socio-economic empowerment.

## The Global Political Agreement

From a gender perspective, the Global Political Agreement (GPA) – the political settlement entered into by the three main political parties after the disputed

---

[21] Constitution of Zimbabwe Amendment (No. 14) Act (No. 14 of 1996).

[22] Section 23(3)(f).

**Table 6.8: Policy and legal measures at sectoral level**

| Legal/Policy instrument | Objectives/Purpose | Effectiveness / Achievements | Challenges |
|---|---|---|---|
| **Education** | | | |
| Universal free primary education policy (1980) | Primary education for all (boys and girls) | • Expansion of school infrastructure and training of teachers<br>• High enrolment and literacy rates characterizing the period between 1980 and late 1990s | • Substituted by the introduction of school fees after the adoption of ESAP |
| Affirmative Action Policy (1990s) | To ensure the participation of women in higher institutions of learning | • Increased enrolment of females in universities in the late 1990s and early 2000<br>• Not effective as gender imbalances continue despite gender parity being reached in 2000 | • Introduction of fees in tertiary institutions has hampered the participation of female candidates<br>• Lack of implementation owing to inadequate resources |
| National Strategic Plan for the Education of Girls (2006) | To address the gender imbalance in education | • No longer effective. Education is now a right for children whose parents can afford the direct and indirect costs of education | • Lack of implementation due to inadequate resources. |
| Education Act (2004) | To provide for the legal framework that ensures every child has the right to education | • Worked only during the 1980s and early 1990s | • Not coupled with public financing that ensures the accessibility of education to children from poor households, particularly the girl-child |
| **Employment** | | | |
| Labour Act as amended | Non-discrimination clauses in employment, based on sex, gender and marital status | • Women continue to be discriminated against in the absence of a changed mindset | • Lack of employment gender policies and their implementation |
| | Equal pay for work of equal value | • Largely effective | • Societal attitudes based on women's inferiority to men |
| | Prohibition of sexual harassment at the workplace | • Sexual harassment continues, though largely unreported | • Prevalence of women in the informal sector where the principle does not apply. |
| | Recognition of women's reproductive roles through the provision of full-paid maternity leave, 100 per cent job security during maternity leave, and an hour breastfeeding break per day for six months | • Effective | • Lack of a clear legislative framework for lodging complaints on sexual harassment<br>• Absence of criminal and civil remedies for victims of sexual harassment |

| Legal/Policy instrument | Objectives/Purpose | Effectiveness / Achievements | Challenges |
|---|---|---|---|
| National Social Security Act (1989) | Provides the legal framework for equal social security services for men and women | • Poor returns from invested funds owing to inflation and poor management | • Limited to women in the formal sector, who form less than 20 per cent of the formal sector |

**Access to resources/Economic participation**

| Legal/Policy instrument | Objectives/Purpose | Effectiveness / Achievements | Challenges |
|---|---|---|---|
| General Laws Amendment Act (2005) | Recognizes the equal status of men and women to transact on an equal basis | • Not effective | • Cultural norms, values and attitudes mean women are still looked down upon. |
| Communal Lands Act (1992) | Allows for the acquisition of rural land for redistribution to men and women | • Not effective. Few women own land in their own right | • Lack of a proper institutional mechanism on land to address gender disparities in land ownership |
| Agricultural Lands Resettlement Act | Allows for the acquisition of land by the state for agricultural settlement | • Not effective. Few women own land in their own right | • Cultural attitudes do not recognize women as individuals who can own land in their own right |
| Land Acquisition Amendment Act (2000) | Provides for the acquisition of privately owned land for distribution to the landless | • Not effective. Few women own land in their own right | • Lack of political will to address gender disparities in land ownership |
| Amendment of the Deeds Registry Act | Allows married women to register property in their own name | • Not effective. Few women have the necessary financial resources to acquire property | • Structural inequalities in resources ownership |
| Small and Medium Enterprises Policy (2002) | Provides an extensive framework for the support of SMMEs | • Not very effective. The policy targets the manufacturing industry in terms of value-addition where men are concentrated | • Absence of a gender lens on the focus of the policy results in the marginalization of the sectors in which women are concentrated – farming, cross-border trading, vending |
| POSB Act (1965) Building Societies Act (1965) | Allow women to have bank accounts in their own names and confidentiality in their financial details | • Fairly effective as many women now own bank accounts | • New requirement of utility bills to open bank accounts impacts on women as the majority do not own property in their own names |

**Table 6.8** *cont.*

| Legal/Policy instrument | Objectives/Purpose | Effectiveness / Achievements | Challenges |
|---|---|---|---|
| **Participation in politics and decision-making** | | | |
| Electoral Act (1980) and consolidated to 17 March 2008 | Facilitates the participation of men and women in the electorate process | • Not very effective. Very few women hold political and decision-making positions | • Absence of a legislated quota system for women's participation in politics<br>• Raw deal from male counterparts within the same political party<br>• Societal attitudes based on the patriarchal ideology that a woman's place is in the home<br>• Violent political environment<br>• Limited resources for campaigning processes |
| Sex Discrimination Removal Act (2001) | Entitles women to hold public office and exercise public functions on an equal basis with men | • Not effective, as men and women face different barriers to participating in public office | • Absence of a quota system to ensure that a certain percentage of women hold public office |
| **Access to health care** | | | |
| Primary Health Care Policy (1980) | Ensures the accessibility of basic health care to men, women and children | • Effective, as measured by the expansion of clinics and hospitals throughout the country<br>• Expansion of ante-natal clinics | • Introduction of user fees<br>• Brain drain<br>• Cutbacks on government expenditure impacting on the availability of drugs and further expansion of clinics and hospitals |
| Sexual Offences Act (2001) | To combat deliberate transmission of HIV/AIDS and marital rape. | • Not utilized fully by women | • Hampered by cultural norms and beliefs and also the cumbersome judicial framework |
| Termination of Pregnancy Act (1977) | Permits abortion in limited cases where the health of the mother is threatened or where the foetus was conceived as a result of unlawful intercourse | • Not very effective | • Cumbersome procedural framework<br>• Negative societal attitudes towards abortion<br>• Limited grounds for abortion |
| National AIDS Policy (1999) | Provides for the provision of AIDS-related medication, prevention of mother-to-child transmission (PMCT), and provision of home-based care facilities | • Not effective. Few women are accessing PMCT and AIDS-related drugs. | • Brain drain<br>• Poor management of the AIDS Fund, and inflation. |

presidential election run-off in 2008 – recognizes, acknowledges and accepts non-discrimination and respect of all persons without regard to gender as the bedrock of democracy and governance. Furthermore, Article XX of the GPA seeks to create gender parity in the appointment of women to strategic decision-making positions. Better representation of women in high-level and decision-making positions assists in getting women into the economic mainstream. In addition, Article 5.8 recognizes the need for women's access to and control over land in their own right, which is also an important element in ensuring the growth and development of women, and has implications for the success of initiatives intended to support women's participation.

In order to engender the constitutional process, a number of initiatives were put in place to mobilize women through the ministry and NGOs that focus on the education and mobilization of women both in and outside decision-making positions (Jirira and Masuko, 2009). However, the negotiating process leading to the GPA excluded non-state actors, who were denied participation by the SADC-appointed facilitator (Thabo Mbeki) despite their concerted efforts. Except for Article XX, which was temporarily incorporated into the constitution as Schedule 8, the GPA is not a legally binding document, hence its implementation depends entirely on the good faith and sincerity of the parties to it.

### 6.4.4 Policies to address gender equality and women's empowerment

*The National Gender Policy*

The National Gender Policy, launched in 2004, is the overarching instrument designed to guide the implementation of gender-sensitive legislation and socio-economic policies, programmes and projects. Its overall objective is to mainstream gender in all sectors in order to eliminate all political, economic, social and cultural practices that impede equality of the sexes. The policy calls for the redress of numerical imbalances in decision-making and political positions by increasing women's representation to 52 per cent.

The National Gender Policy is to be implemented through the National Gender Policy Implementation Strategy and Work-plan (2008–2012). The Work-plan is premised on the recognition that gender inequalities continue to permeate all aspects of human interaction and development in Zimbabwe. The vision of the Work-plan is of a society where there is economic, political, religious and social equality and equity among women and men in all spheres of life and at all levels. The Implementation Strategy and Work-plan is also intended to be fully integrated into national sectoral plans as a reference point for mainstreaming gender and women's empowerment issues at all development levels by line ministries and government institutions. Its main strategic approach is to ensure that these objectives are realized by strengthening the capacities of these institutions and improving the co-ordination and harmonization of gender-equity initiatives.

Although the National Gender Policy has been translated into indigenous languages, its crippling challenge is that it is under-resourced (with inadequate fiscal support) resulting in limited awareness of it. It therefore remains largely unimplemented and its objectives unrealized.

### The Inclusive Government's 100-day plan

The 100-day plan period ran from 29 April to 6 August 2009, and mapped key result areas for the Ministry of Women's Affairs, Gender and Community Development as follows:

- Ensure women's household to food security.
- Increase women's participation in the economy (mines, agriculture, cottage and home industry).
- Compile statistical data on the status of women in the economy.
- Engender constitutional structures, processes and products.
- Promote national healing through community development projects.

However, there is still no clear action plan for addressing the unequal gender–power relations that perpetuate gender inequality.

### The Short-Term Emergency Recovery Programme (STERP)

STERP was a short-term programme running from February to December 2009.[23] It acknowledged the marginalization of women, especially in key decision-making positions, highlighting that there were only seven women cabinet ministers out of a total of thirty-five and proposing the adoption of various measures to ensure the de-marginalization of women (paras. 35–45). In support of this, STERP proposed a constitutional review process that addressed critical aspects of women's rights, particularly in the areas of control and ownership of resources, decision-making and personal law, as well as the amendment of laws that continue to discriminate against women. However, there were still inadequate resources to implement the policy to achieve the full realization of gender equality.

## 6.5 Alternative Pro-Gender Development/Equity Policies

Following this analysis of the position of women and the persistence of gender inequality in Zimbabwe, the recommendations below are proposed in order to ensure that policy strategies developed take into account the practical and strategic needs of women and their current position, geographically, politically, socially, economically and culturally.

---

[23] <http://www.zimtreasury.org/downloads/31.pdf>.

### 6.5.1 Addressing the dual and enclave economy and marginalization of women

As indicated above, the inherited dual and enclave economy is the foundation of the economic structure that continues to marginalize women. It is therefore important to bring the hitherto excluded sectors and groups, which include women, into the mainstream of the economy and that economic and developmental policies – fiscal, monetary, financial and trade – be focused on the marginalized sectors: the informal economy and the communal sector. Such policies also need to be reviewed so that they take into account the increasing unpaid care and household work, and appreciate the value of those sectors with a high concentration of females, such as agriculture. It has been shown that 'one size fits all' strategies are inefficient as they fail to take into account their impact from a gender perspective.

### 6.5.2 Mainstreaming women into the economy and employment creation

One specific strategy to mainstream women in the economy has been proposed by the African Development Bank and the ILO (Fig. 6.1). This useful framework illustrates how women can be supported, and also provides a possible way in which women-owned enterprises can become mainstreamed in the Zimbabwe economy.

The government could offer a variety of SME support programmes that can be roughly divided into five main types: financial assistance, enterprise culture, advice and assistance, technology, and management training. When it comes to promotion of women entrepreneurs, there is need to match these with the implementation strategies and budget allocations necessary to translate them into a transformation of women's lives, including removing administrative barriers to investment and to the legalization of enterprises.

A pro-poor approach that ensures that women are included in cluster development and participate in value-chains grows the economy for women. In addition, the active labour-market policy interventions outlined in Chapter 7 can help address the enclave nature of the economy and promote equitable growth.

### 6.5.3 Domestication of international and regional instruments

As reported above, Zimbabwe has signed and ratified a number of international and regional conventions and instruments on gender that have not been domesticated into Zimbabwean law so as to create an environment where gender equality can be monitored. Line ministries in charge of the enhancement of the status of women, ministries responsible for SME development, NGOs, women's organizations, and technical co-operation projects and programmes can play an active role in seeking the domestication of these conventions and instruments, thereby ensuring that an enabling business environment, especially for women-owned enterprises, is created.

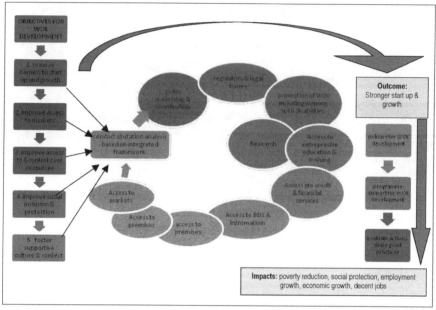

Source: ILO (2007).

**Fig. 6.1: The AfDB/ILO integrated framework: Growing women's enterprises**

These instruments should also be translated into indigenous languages, as has been done with the National Gender Policy. In addition, complementary literacy programmes and public campaigns to promote and respect the rights enshrined in them should be carried out to ensure that they become values at the household, local and national levels. The capacity of civil-society organizations to provide subsidized or free legal-support services also needs to be strengthened.

### 6.5.4 Implementation of engendered national policies

While it is commendable that Zimbabwe has drafted a progressive National Gender Policy, has put in place policies and laws that promote social justice for women, and has ratified a number of regional and international gender protocols and instruments, these efforts unfortunately fall short when it comes to implementation. Zimbabwe has been hailed for coming up with very good policy documents, but fails on implementation.

In fact, during the crisis period, government embarked upon a strategy of responding with violence to human, civil, political and economic rights pressure groups or activists or critics. During this period, the feminization of violence was prevalent. Female lawyers (e.g. Beatrice Mtetwa), journalists (e.g. Grace Kwinjeh), trade union leaders (e.g. Lucia Matibenga and Thabitha Khumalo), leaders of civil-society organizations (e.g. Jestina Mukoko) and politicians (e.g. Sekai Holland) were victims of state-orchestrated violence despite such 'progressive gender policies, protocols and acts' being either already in place or in the making.

Implementation is critical, otherwise these policies, protocols and acts will exist only on paper and not in reality. Therefore, the strengthening of existing machinery or institutional structures through capacity-building, complemented by adequate budget allocations and political will, is needed to bring identified targets and strategies into concrete results. Such structures should have full authority to influence motions for promoting gender equality, and should implement, monitor and evaluate the successes and failures of various national policies on women.

### 6.5.5 Greater coherence and co-ordination of national policies

Addressing gender inequality and equity goes beyond the jurisdiction of the Ministry of Women's Affairs, and a positive development is that there are already a number of initiatives arising in other ministries to address gender inequality and equity. Regrettably, however, they lack coherence in terms of design and implementation. Good examples are laws on land, which are fragmented across different ministries and different legal documents; there is no solid coherent law on land access, distribution and control, which leaves women with no legal protection whatsoever (Women and Land in Zimbabwe, 2009).

As a result, these initiatives have remained weak and ineffective and have been infested with duplication or oversights. Hence, it is vital that all initiatives are co-ordinated and that internal and external capacities and capabilities are drawn together. This will reduce duplication and strengthen the impact of gender programmes. At the civil-society level, there is great potential for coherence as there are already vibrant women's organizations and co-ordination networks in Zimbabwe, as mentioned above. There exists a unique opportunity, therefore, for effective, co-ordinated strategies among these organizations to approach various ministries on matters that relate to policy implementation, monitoring and evaluation, and to demand accountability, transparency and pragmatism.

### 6.5.6 Greater ownership of and participation in national policies by women

The emerging discourse on pro-poor, human-centred development promotes a culture of continuous stakeholder involvement and participation through effective consultation in the formulation, implementation, monitoring and evaluation of policy programmes and initiatives. This culture reinforces the national ownership of programmes, which is essential for their success. This therefore implies that the Inter-Ministerial Committee on gender should ensure adequate space for the participation of non-state actors such as women-based civil-society organizations, trade unions and the donor community to exercise their role as strategic partners. Already, as shown in this chapter, women's organizations have vast potential which can be tapped into and is valuable in building national strategic interventions. A good example is the Women's Economic Development Plan, developed in 2009 in the Deputy Prime Minister's office through a national stakeholder consultative process that brought together women from various sectors of the economy across the country (Zimbabwe, 2009a). As a test case, the stakeholder representatives that participated in the development of this plan could be constituted into a 'reference group' that meets regularly to review progress, undertaking continuous reflection and analysis of issues and prevailing situations, and making concrete recommendations on appropriate short-, medium- and long-term interventions to ensure the successful and coherent implementation of gender-policy programmes and plans. However, they should also ensure effective communication within their organizations so that they represent the interests of their constituencies.

### 6.5.7 An enabling legal and economic environment to improve security of tenure, access, control and ownership of resources

There is need to harmonize the customary norms and values with received norms and values that promote gender equality to remove conflicts and ingrained hindrance to gender equality. For example, Section 23(3)(f) of the constitution states that there shall be no discrimination on the basis of race, tribe, gender, sex or political affiliation, yet the customary law has differential treatment in the allocation of land in communal lands. In terms of the Communal Land Act [*Chapter 20:04*] the rural authority should have regard to customary law relating to the allocation, occupation and use of the land in the area concerned.[24] In light of the fact that customary law, as alluded to earlier, gives married men primary-use rights, these guidelines are discriminatory in effect as they exclude women. Thus, women are reduced to agricultural workers with no rights, despite their being the primary producers of agricultural output and guardians of household food security.

In addition, rural freehold tenure also operates in a manner that excludes women. This is land acquired upon an individual's capacity to command the financial resources necessary to purchase it. It is common cause that, relative to men, women have limited access to money and credit (Ncube and Nkiwane, 1994), and few women therefore have the capacity to purchase land. Consequently, there is need for a review of existing laws and policies on women's right to land, e.g. Section 23 of the constitution that limits that right.

To improve women's access to credit and loans, initiatives such as women's banks, including mobile banks, that focus on women's specific needs in all

---

[24] Sections 8(2) (a) and (b).

economic sectors, and linking women with networks that facilitate access to resources, markets, supportive marketing arrangements and information, are critical. These call for co-ordinated efforts by all stakeholders, who include government, the private sector, civil-society organizations and development partners (Zimbabwe, 2009a).

In this regard, an enabling legal and economic environment is a prerequisite. Therefore, the opportunity should be seized by all gender-rights and gender-development advocacy networks, organizations, programmes and projects to formulate recommendations collectively and present them as part of the process under way to make a new national constitution. These stakeholders should also carefully study all the drafts produced in the process, and be in a position to comment, propose amendments, corrections or additions before encouraging their constituencies to vote either Yes or No in the referendum on the final draft document.

## 6.5.8 Adequate public spending on social services (education, health care, public utilities) and enabling infrastructure

A reduction in budget allocations for education, health and public utilities (water, electricity) has greater impact on women than on men. There is therefore a need to refocus on building the state's capacity to provide these services by rehabilitating existing infrastructure and extending service provision, as was done during the first decade of independence, and subsidies are needed in order to promote equitable access to utility services. More research is needed to identify the impact of the various forms of subsidy targeting the poor in national poverty-reduction strategies, and the link between them and the provision of social services must be re-emphasized.

As for education, the case goes beyond just the provision of financial resources to the creation of conditions that allow the girl-child to remain at school despite the increasing burden of the care economy. The education curriculum requires the introduction of entrepreneurship skills for both boys and girls, as well as offerng them equal opportunities to learn and cultivate their skills from an early age. To this end, teachers should be trained in teaching entrepreneurial skills and sensitized to the gender issues involved in education (Chakanya and Makanza, 2009).

In terms of health, greater involvement by civil society will help to ensure that these services are delivered effectively, and that women and adolescent girls are fully educated and empowered to make sound reproductive and health choices.[25]

---

[25] See Women's Economic Development Outreach (2002), MDG discussion paper for UNDP, draft document, <http://www.undp.org/women/docs/mdgs-genderlens.pdf>.

### 6.5.9 Promotion of gender budgeting

Gender budgeting is a tool that is being used to ensure that national budgets are pro-poor and gender-equitable in the sense that they take into account the different needs of women, men, boys and girls (ZWRCN, 2004). Hence, in 2007, the Ministry of Women's Affairs, Gender and Community Development, in partnership with the ZWRCN, launched the Gender Budgeting and Women's Empowerment Programme, which led to a memorandum of understanding between the ZWRCN and the ministry. According to the ZWRCN, the initiative also seeks to track the impact of national expenditure on women and men with a view to highlighting the gaps in the manner in which resources are allocated.

While this is a commendable effort, more such arrangements need to be promoted. It is still essential that the government fully institutionalizes and sustains gender-responsive budgeting initiatives: all stakeholders, including national machineries, line ministries, parliament and civil-society organizations, especially women's organizations, must have the capacity to engage fully in the budget process. The engagement process – or, rather, the social dialogue process – in national budget formulation needs a constituted platform that functions effectively and meets regularly and whose submissions are taken seriously by the responsible ministry.

Ministries of finance and other ministries need to build capacity to develop, implement and monitor gender-sensitive policies, programmes and budgets, and national machineries need capacity to promote, support and monitor such efforts. The development and use of tools such as guidelines, budget instructions, directives and gender-sensitive indicators, could support such capacity-building efforts. South Africa, Tanzania (through Feminist Activism, FemAct) and Uganda (through the East African Gender Budget Network) have good experience in the promotion of gender budgeting.

### 6.5.10 Participation of women in politics and decision-making positions

Sustainable development cannot take place unless women also have the political space to contribute to the process of national development. It is generally agreed that if more women are involved in policy- or decision-making, either in government or private sector, then the decisions made are likely to take the concerns of women on board.

There is therefore a need to review the Electoral Act to ensure that it contains provisions that give effect to the SADC Gender Protocol that requires the 50 per cent female representation that Zimbabwe agreed to. Without the legislated and effective implementation of a gender-equity system, women will continue to be marginalized from the political process, even at party level (Ncube, 2005). A legislated gender-equity system should be accompanied by a peaceful political environment that guarantees equal rights and freedoms to all players without bias, fear or favour, and the necessary financial support should be rendered to women candidates in order to enable them to participate on an equal basis with men. In this regard, political will at the highest level is necessary if any intervention to support gender equality and equity is to succeed.

In addition, civil-society organizations should play a proactive role by providing training for women in political leadership and empowerment to enable both women and men to demystify the stereotypes around women's participation in decision-making (Zimbabwe, 2009b). Furthermore, training media personnel to be gender-sensitive can facilitate a positive portrayal of women in the media and in society at large. Already commendable work is being done by civil-society organizations and trade unions in this direction. Examples include the UNFPA training of media personnel in gender-sensitive reporting on HIV and AIDS and the Domestic Violence Act, and a platform to promote gender equality and the empowerment of women on programmes like *Gender Diaries* put out by civil society (Zimbabwe, 2009b: 16). However, several challenges need to be addressed regarding guaranteeing the enjoyment of all the human rights and freedoms provided in the country's current constitution.

### 6.5.11 Gender-disaggregated data
The lack of data disaggregated by gender and gender-sensitive indicators in the country poses a problem, as it limits effective policy-making and budgetary processes as well as the monitoring and evaluation of policies, plans and programmes at national, provincial and community levels. Although there is a gender department at the Central Statistical Office, it needs to be supported to strengthen its initiative to collect, analyse and publish timeously core indicators for gender-related parameters in all relevant socio-economic and political spheres. For example, a gender-sensitive manpower survey to establish Zimbabwe's human-resource base (including those in the diaspora) should be introduced by government as a matter of extreme urgency with the meaningful involvement and active participation of all non-state actors.

### 6.5.12 Systematic research on the practical and strategic needs of women
It is of paramount importance that systematic research on the practical and strategic needs of women be carried out. In order to maximize women's efforts in the productive economy, it is necessary to intensify efforts that facilitate the improvement of their practical needs such as access to credit, land, inputs, markets for their produce, transport for their goods, and skills development. The output of the research will be useful in terms of informing any strategy-formulation process that is all-inclusive.

In addition, research on best practices of gender equality and equity elsewhere is critical, so an inventory of regional and international initiatives targeting women should be compiled and used to promote best-practice approaches at the household, local and national level.

### 6.5.13 Elimination of stereotypes based on patriarchy and subordination of women

It is important to emphasize communication for social change, which is aimed at eliminating attitudes, stereotypes and practices based on patriarchy that reinforce women's assumed roles and inferiority. For example, despite their education, most women find themselves trapped in oppressive traditional notions of 'respectable' women, and most female students and academics who strive for such a label risk being called unrespectable and unmarriageable (Chirimuuta, 2006). Thus, training for the patriarchal gate-keepers – who include traditional leaders, village and ward heads and peer educators – is important (ibid).

The religious, cultural and traditional norms, values, practices and orientation that seek to promote the suppression, oppression, exploitation and subjugation of women to men should be categorically denounced, discouraged and, where necessary, outlawed. There is a definite need for reorientation, gender sensitization, awareness-creation and transformation in most church-, culture- and tradition-related organizations to understand and appreciate present-day requirements of gender equity and equality, and they should team up with others in advocating the same, even within their own organizations.

A good example of such an initiative is the Padare/Ekhudhleni Men's Gender Forum, a social-dialogue forum that brings together men and boys to discuss gender equality. Padare challenges patriarchal attitudes, beliefs and practices and gender-based violence through the mobilization of males in schools, rural communities and urban areas (Zimbabwe, 2009b). This forum does not work in isolation, but partners with women's organizations.

## 6.6 Conclusion

Empirical evidence points to the fact that most of the gains in the economy made during the first decade of independence were eroded first by ESAP and then by the economic crisis. ESAP failed to generate human-centred development wherein gender equality and equity co-exist. Instead, the deflationary bias created under ESAP led to slow growth and recession, which resulted in high unemployment levels for women, increased responsibilities of unpaid care work, and increased poverty among women. In fact, the benefits of the Social Dimensions Fund safety net were short-lived as it was poorly managed, lacked adequate resources, and was centralized, so the majority of women were plunged into the informal economy.

Furthermore, the collapse of service-delivery systems during the crisis period also worsened the burden on women. The water and sanitation crisis, food crisis, health crisis, education crisis and energy crisis have had the greatest impact on women, especially on female-headed households. Women have had to spend more time searching for food, water, alternative traditional medicines and herbs, and firewood, on top of the already over-burdening care economy. As a result, women's practical needs were neglected and most of the gains of early independence were eroded.

Although the government of Zimbabwe has ratified several international and regional conventions, and taken measures at national level towards the elimination of discrimination against women, these formal measures did not address the structural gender inequality that is rooted in socio-economic, political and cultural dynamics and institutions. Thus, they are blind to structural and material inequalities and to the empirical content and context of inequality experienced by women. Furthermore, these measures are more often than not de-linked from the processes that formulate, implement and manage policy strategies, particularly those related to the budget, as demonstrated by the limited resource allocations. Even judicial pronouncements during this period indicated the pervasiveness and unrepentant nature of the patriarchal ideology, despite government's commitment on paper to address gender imbalances.[26]

As a result, these formal policy frameworks have to a large extent not been translated into practical actions, either because of inadequate budget allocations or human capacity, and the absence of implementation of gender-sensitive policy measures partly explains the persistence of gender inequality.

Therefore, the formulation of pro-gender development policies, which can be assured only by the allocation of adequate resources and changes in attitudes towards women, is critical for the eradication of gender-based inequalities in all sectors of Zimbabwean society. All stakeholders – government, development partners, civil-society organizations, labour and the private sector – have a part to play in achieving women's politico-socio-economic empowerment and thereby reducing gender disparities. It is now widely acknowledged in the development discourse that a greater sense of investment in development often occurs when direct and indirect stakeholders are responsible for, and in charge of, development processes and outcomes. In this way, they are engaged not only in immediate, ongoing development interventions, but also in establishing mechanisms for sustained impact (Kapur and Duvvury, 2006).

Thus, principle number 8 of the ANSA initiative, which states that 'gender rights are the basis for development', can be achieved where a dynamic,

---

[26] For example, the Supreme Court in *Magaya* v. *Magaya* 1999 (1) ZLR 100 held that '[G]reat care must be taken when African customary law is under consideration. In the first instance, it must be recognized that customary law has long directed the way African people conducted their lives ... In the circumstances, it will not be readily be abandoned, especially by those such as senior males who stand to lose their positions of privilege.'

participatory and radical democracy is functioning properly, i.e. where people-driven initiatives and people-centred development, aimed at narrowing and eventually eradicating current gender disparities and gaps, are given space and recognition, and their recommendations are taken into account. This requires vibrant women's organizations and effective gender programmes and projects that aggressively and proactively advance the gender equity and equality agenda at all platforms and at all levels from the household to the national. And this equally requires a government that upholds principles of political tolerance, plurality, accountability and transparency.

## References

Banda, F. 2005. *Women, Law and Human Rights: An African Perspective* (Oxford: Hart).

Chakanya, N. and T. Makanza 2009. 'Women and the Economy: An Evidence Based Approach', paper presented at the Women's Economic Summit and Conference, Harare.

Chirimuuta, C. 2006. 'Gender and the Zimbabwe Education Policy: Empowerment or Perpetuation of Gender Imbalances?', <http://www.quietmountainessays.org/Chirimuuta>.

Deere, C. D. 2005. *The Feminization of Agriculture?: Economic Restructuring in Rural Latin America* (Geneva: United Nations Research Institute for Social Development).

ILO 2007. *Assessing the Enabling Environment for Women in Growth Enterprises: An AfDB/ILO Integrated Framework Assessment Guide* (Geneva: International Labour Office), <http://www.ilo.org/empent/Whatwedo/Publications/lang–en/docName–WCMS_116163/index.htm >.

Jirira, K. and T. Masuko 2009. 'A Gender Analysis of the Zimbabwe Education Sector Policies Programmes and Budget', paper prepared for the Zimbabwe Women's Resource Centre and Network, Harare.

Kapur, A. and N. Duvvury 2006. *A Rights-Based Approach to Realizing the Economic and Social Rights of Poor and Marginalized Women* (Washington, DC: International Center for Research on Women), <http://www.icrw.org/files/publications/A-Rights-Based-Approach-to-Realizaing-the-Economic-and-Social-Rights-of-Poor-and-Marginalized-Women.pdf>.

Mushunje, M. T. 2001. *Women's Land Rights* (Madison, WI: Broadening Access and Strengthening Input Systems, BASIS Management Entity).

Ncube, J. 2005. 'The Women's Movement in the Zimbabwe Constitutional Debate: The Continuous Journey to a Gender fair Constitution', <http://www.siyanda.org/docs/gender_and_costitution_building_zimbabwes_story_050907060455.doc>

Ncube, W. and V. Nkiwane 1994. 'Review of current legislation governing land

and natural resources in Zimbabwe', in Zimbabwe, *Report of the Commission of Inquiry into Appropriate Agricultural Land Tenure Systems* [Chairman: M. Rukuni] (Harare: Government Printer, 3 vols.).

Ncube, W. *et al.* 1997. *Paradigms of Exclusion: Women's Access to Resources in Zimbabwe* (Harare: Women and Law in Southern Africa).

SARDC-WIDSAA 2008. *Beyond Inequalities 2008: Women in Southern Africa* (Harare: Southern African Research and Documentation Centre – Women in Development in Southern Africa Awareness Programme).

SARIPS 2000. *SADC Regional Human Development Report 2000* (Harare: Southern African Regional Institute for Policy Studies of the SAPES Trust).

Watson, P. 1998. *Determined to Act: The First 15 Years of the Women's Action Group (WAG), 1983-1998* Harare: Women's Action Group).

Women and Land in Zimbabwe 2009. *Report* (Harare: Women and Land in Zimbabwe).

WAG 2009 *Quarterly Reports* (Harare: Women's Action Group).

Zimbabwe 2003. *Report of the Presidential Land Review Committee on the Implementation of the Fast-track Land Reform Programme 2000-2002*, [Chairman: C. Utete] <http://www.sarpn.org.za/documents/d0000622/P600-Utete_PLRC_00-02.pdf>.

Zimbabwe 2006a. *Poverty Assessment Study Survey Report* (Harare: Ministry of Public Service, Labour and Social Welfare).

Zimbabwe 2006b. *2004 Labour Force Survey* (Harare: Central Statistical Office).

Zimbabwe 2009a. *The National Women Economic Development (WED) Plan: January 2010 – December 2015* (Harare: Office of the Deputy Prime Minister).

Zimbabwe 2009b. *Progress Report of the Republic of Zimbabwe on the Implementation of the Beijing Declaration and Platform for Action (1995) and the Outcome of the Twenty-third Special Session of the General Assembly (2000)* (Harare: Ministry of Women's Affairs, Gender and Community Development), <http://www.uneca.org/eca_programmes/acgd/beijingplus15/Questionnaire/DAW/English/Zimbabwe.pdf>.

ZWRCN 2004. *Gender Budget Watch: Hands up for Girls Education* (Harare: Zimbabwe Women Resource Centre and Network).

ZWRCN and SARDC-WIDSAA 2005. *Beyond Inequalities 2005: Women in Zimbabwe* (Harare: Zimbabwe Women Resource Centre and Network and Southern African Research and Documentation Centre – Women in Development in Southern Africa Awareness Programme).

## Chapter 7

# The Labour Market

## 7.1 Introduction

In economic terms, labour is a measure of the work done by human beings, and labour markets occur wherever workers supply labour services (the supply side) in return for conditions of service provided by those who demand such services (employers).[1] Labour markets function through the interaction of workers and employers, resulting in a pattern of wages, employment and income (Ashenfelter and Card, 1999). The administration of the labour market – labour administration – refers to public administration activities in the area of national labour policy. The 'system of labour administration'

> covers all public administration bodies responsible for and/or engaged in labour administration – whether they are ministerial departments or public agencies, including parastatal and regional or local agencies or any other form of decentralized administration – and any institutional framework for the co-ordination of the activities of such bodies and for consultation with and participation by employers and workers and their organizations.[2]

The multiplicity of stakeholders requires that the functions and responsibilities of labour administration should be properly co-ordinated, which implies that consultation, co-operation and negotiation between the public authorities and the most representative organizations of employers and workers is essential at the national, regional and local levels and within the various sectors. To implement these effectively, qualified staff with the material means and finances are needed.

The key aspects of the labour administration system include:
- Labour standards – to regulate terms and conditions of employment.
- Labour relations – where the system ensures the free exercise of employers' and workers' rights of association.
- Employment – the preparation, administration, co-ordination and review of national employment policy; co-ordination of employment services, employment promotion and creation programmes; vocational guidance and training programmes and unemployment benefit schemes; and

---

[1] As the renowned economist, Alfred Marshall put it, 'The worker sells his work, but he himself remains his own property'.

[2] ILO Labour Administration Convention No.150, 1978, <http://www.ilo.org/ilolex/cgi-lex/convde.pl?C150>.

sharing responsibility for the management of funds created to counter underemployment and unemployment or assisting the employment of certain categories of workers.
- Labour research – the system of labour administration must carry out research and encourage others to do so.

Labour administration plays a critical role in socio-economic development by
- ensuring social stability for wealth creation;
- enhancing productivity and economic growth through skill formation;
- assisting in the eradication of poverty through empowerment initiatives for (self-)employment;
- promotion of decent work and incomes policy;
- promoting social justice and shared growth.

Thus, labour administration plays its full role in development if it contributes to the maintenance of a healthy social climate, if the services that it offers are effective and correspond to the needs of users, if the services and products contribute to the design of development strategies, and if the social partners participate.

This chapter explores the role of the labour market in Zimbabwe since the attainment of independence in 1980 up to 2009.[3] The first section focuses on the role of labour administration and, by inference, the labour market in poverty reduction. Labour-market policy interventions covering the period 1980–2008 are discussed in the second section, which analyses the developments in policy during the three phases: the first decade of independence, 1980–1990, the period of the Economic Structural Adjustment Programme (ESAP), 1991–1996, and the crisis period (1997–2008). The processes that saw the emergence of a dual labour market during the colonial era are traced to provide a historical understanding of the forces that resulted in labour-market segmentation. Discussion of the performance and outcomes of the labour market then follows, while the next section examines developments during the transitional period following the inception of the Inclusive Government in February 2009. Conclusions and recommendations are the subject of the last part of the chapter.

## 7.2 The Role of the Labour Market in Poverty Reduction

The resurgence of neo-liberal policies in the 1980s and 1990s resulted in social objectives – and in particular poverty reduction and its eventual eradication – being treated as residuals in the development process. Such approaches, and especially the structural adjustment programmes (SAPs) implemented in most developing countries on the recommendation of the IMF and World Bank, focused exclusively on achieving macroeconomic stability, believing that this

---

[3] Aspects of the analysis in this chapter draw from and expand the discussion in Kanyenze (2009).

would result in sustained growth, which in turn would 'trickle down' to benefit the poor through employment effects. As things turned out, macroeconomic stabilization was often achieved, but at the expense of sustained levels of economic growth, employment and poverty reduction – the stabilization trap (Islam, 2003).

By focusing on macroeconomic stability, deregulation and privatization, such policies confused means for ends. The exclusive emphasis on macroeconomic stability was based on the questionable assumption that 'macroeconomic stability is a public good and might be expected to affect all equally. There is a well-established association between macroeconomic stability and long-term growth, and growth typically brings expansion opportunities to everyone' (World Bank, 2005a: 198). However, stability is a means to an end, the ultimate goal being poverty eradication. With hindsight, it is now widely accepted that the link between growth and poverty reduction is not automatic (World Bank, 2005b; Ehrenpreis, 2007 and 2008; ILO, 1999 and 2005). In fact, growth on its own is considered a necessary but inadequate condition for sustained poverty reduction. This is the case because the quality of growth matters as much as its quantum. In this regard, economic growth does not ensure poverty reduction; it leads to poverty reduction only when it is accompanied by the rapid growth of productive and remunerative employment. Hence, countries that have succeeded in reducing poverty have followed strong employment-creation policies. With this recognition of the limits to growth re-emerged a central and critical role for labour markets, and decent work in particular, as the nexus between growth and poverty reduction (Ehrenpreis, 2008).[4]

As a result, poverty reduction and its eventual eradication has assumed prominence in the new millennium; in fact, the first Millennium Development Goal targets halving poverty by 2015. In this framework, the labour market, and decent employment in particular, are expected to play an intermediating role (the nexus) between growth and poverty reduction, in which case a development strategy that fully employs a country's human resources and raises the returns to labour is considered a powerful tool for poverty reduction and eradication (Islam, 2003). Critical to income growth is the expansion of decent jobs, and this is where the labour market comes in as the framework for connecting growth to poverty reduction.

For the poor to participate in, and benefit from, economic growth, they need skills and assets. Land is one such asset, so critical for agricultural development. In addition, access to education and capital – and infrastructure such as rural feeder roads, electricity and irrigation – are as important to make land assets productive. Such broader assets allow the rural poor to connect to markets for

---

[4] Recent work from the International Finance Institutions acknowledges this fact (Fox and Sekkel, 2008).

their goods and to access inputs for their production. It was found that, for example, agricultural productivity increased by four per cent for every additional year of formal schooling following the Green Revolution in Asia (Lucas and Timmer, 2005). Where there are relatively high levels of inequality in land-holdings, agricultural growth does less than non-agricultural growth to raise the incomes of the very poor. In most cases, the inequality of land distribution hinders the growth of agricultural outputs. Such inequality can be addressed through land reform.

Apart from the ownership of assets, personal and household capabilities and the potential to improve them are often defined by less tangible assets involving levels of education and health. Arguably, education plays a key role in enabling farmers to increase their productivity and workers to move from agriculture to other rural economic activities, or from the informal to formal sector. It has been found that in many poor countries people with just one additional year of schooling earn ten per cent higher wages. In addition, no country has sustained rapid growth without reaching an adult literacy rate of at least 40 per cent. Better educated people are able to prevent disease and use health services effectively, with young people between the ages of 15 and 24 years who have completed primary education less than half as likely to contract HIV than those who have little or no schooling. Furthermore, greater female education has been associated with more-productive farming and high returns in other areas, leading to lower fertility rates, lower infant-mortality levels, and higher education rates for the next generation (Lucas and Timmer, 2005).

Investments in health have also been found to have had significant impact on economic growth and poverty reduction. Healthy workers are generally more productive over longer lives. In states where female literacy and female labour participation were highest in the 1960s in India, growth over the subsequent three decades was higher and more effective in reducing poverty. Gender inequality therefore makes it difficult for women to participate in, and benefit from, the growth process, particularly in higher-skill areas of employment.

In addition, as labour is the main resource that most poor people have, labour-intensive growth is the most effective way to reduce poverty. Thus, sustained poverty reduction requires improving the labour productivity of poor women and men, whether as paid or self-employed workers. Reducing the costs for the poor to access sectors where growth is occurring, and to promote growth in the sectors where the poor are located, is a critical mechanism for translating growth into sustainable poverty reduction. Consequently, public investment in the capacity of the poor to participate in, and benefit from, economic growth becomes imperative (Lucas and Timmer, 2005).

The relationship between growth and employment therefore depends on the initial structure of the economy and the sectors in which growth is concentrated. If the growth sectors are employment-intensive and their growth is rapid, increases in economy-wide productive employment could follow, though this would also depend on whether the growth sectors are large and closely linked to the rest of the economy. In this regard, it is important to know where poor people are concentrated. Generally, rural poverty accounts for at least 70 per cent of total poverty.

The share of agriculture in the national economy and the share of the national labour force employed in agriculture determine the potential of agricultural development as an engine of growth and poverty reduction. It has been found that the concentration of agricultural growth is important in poverty reduction, especially in countries that have very unequal land distribution and bi-modal agricultural sectors, a dynamic large-scale commercial sector sitting alongside an underdeveloped and isolated small-scale rural sector. In such instances, agricultural growth has been concentrated in the commercial, export-oriented sectors, and has not translated into broad-based poverty reduction.

Inevitably, therefore, the level of, and change in, income inequality determines the extent to which growth is pro-poor (Kakwani et al., 2004; Ehrenpreis, 2007). Hence, the initial levels of inequality and changes in inequality cause rates of poverty reduction to differ across similar growth experiences, with higher rates of initial inequality leading to fewer gains for the poor from growth. In countries with very high rates of inequality, growth may be ineffective in reducing poverty. Apart from limiting the earning potential of women, gender inequality in both education and employment also slows economic growth by reducing the pool of people contributing to it. Gender inequalities can also hinder the potential for growth to reduce poverty.

However, employment is not the only means of translating growth into poverty reduction. Social provisioning, especially with respect to basic services encompassing education, health and income grants, among others, is critical. Hence a viable employment-centred strategy for development should also integrate social policies (see, for instance, Heintz, 2006).

Osmani (2004) developed a conceptual framework for analysing the link between growth and poverty reduction, identifying three underlying factors: the growth factor, the elasticity factor, and the 'integrability' factor. The growth factor refers to the rate at which an economy grows, while the elasticity factor relates to the extent to which growth is associated with employment (in both quantity and quality). The integrability factor refers to the extent to which the poor are able to integrate into economic processes such that, as growth and employment expand, they can take advantage of the arising opportunities. This framework will be used to assess the extent to which there has been sustained employment-intensive growth and poverty reduction in Zimbabwe.

## 7.3 Labour–Market Policy in Zimbabwe, 1980–2008

### 7.3.1 Shaping the labour market in Zimbabwe: The colonial experience

The idea that the structural features of developing economies are different from those of developed economies is long established.[5] Three important features distinguish developing countries from developed ones. The first is dualism: the existence of two radically distinct parts, a modern or formal segment employing a small proportion of the labour force, and a traditional or non-formal segment (the rest of the economy) employing the bulk of the labour force. Whereas production in the formal segment involves the use of reproducible capital (including advanced technology) as well as labour (skilled and unskilled), that in the non-formal segment involves the use of predominantly unskilled labour, using natural resources and simple tools and implements. In the formal segment, production is for profit, which is saved and used to reproduce capital; in the non-formal segment it is for subsistence. Workers in the formal segment are engaged as regular, full-time, waged employees, while in the non-formal segment they are either self-employed or engaged as casual, irregularly waged workers. Huge gaps in labour incomes and productivity characterize the two segments, with poverty (and the use of child labour) prevalent in the non-formal segment. Government regulations and institutions of collective bargaining generally exist in the formal segment but are absent in the non-formal segment.

The second distinguishing feature is the availability of surplus labour in the non-formal segment, implying that a substantial portion of workers in the non-formal sector are under-employed (engaged in work- and income-sharing). Therefore, a substantial proportion of workers in this segment could be withdrawn into the formal segment without affecting the labour input used in production (Lewis, 1954).

The third feature is the absence of institutionalized social security: only a few people from well-off households can survive without working – most people must work to survive. In such a situation, unemployment – conventionally measured as the population aged fifteen years and above who, during a seven-day reference period, did not work and had no job or business to go back to, but who were available for work – is a poor indicator of the state of the labour market. In this case, growth in 'employment' does not reflect the growth of productive jobs in the economy as it may imply increased underemployment in the non-formal segment. It is only in the formal segment where growth in employment may be interpreted as growth in productive jobs.

Thus, it is only in the movement of workers from the non-formal into the formal segment, or from casual to regular, full-time, waged employment, or

---

[5] See Ghose *et al.* (2008) for a recent discussion.

from low-productivity employment to high-productivity employment, or from unregulated into regulated employment, that one can speak of an improving employment situation. More generally, a worker's move from the non-formal to the formal sector is considered positive; hence a rising share of the formal sector in total employment indicates an improvement in the overall employment situation. A decline in underemployment or low-productivity survival activities results in increased labour productivity in the non-formal sector, and such an improvement in labour productivity implies an improvement in the employment situation.

The labour market in Zimbabwe was shaped during the colonial period, where the ideology of white supremacy resulted in a distorted dual and enclave structure.[6] The capitalist mode of accumulation was partially grafted on to the pre-colonial economy such that the imperative of surplus accumulation applied only in the formal sector, while a subsistence mode of production drove the processes in the communal sector (formerly known as Tribal Trust Lands). The dual and enclave nature of the inherited economy in Zimbabwe was such that the formal sector accounted for about a fifth (one million) of the potential labour force, while the remainder were either underemployed in the informal and communal sectors, or openly unemployed.

The dual and enclave structure of the economy and, by implication, the labour market was shaped largely by the ideology of white supremacy upon which colonial policies were predicated. Apart from its marginalized role as a source of raw materials, the local economy retained a disarticulate structure where capitalist relations of production, and especially the profit motive, drove the activities of the formal sector, while the pre-capitalist relations of production, based on subsistence, characterized the peasant rural economy, the domain of the majority of the black population. By virtue of the racial prejudice, super-imposed on patriarchy, the emerging gender relations perceived women as third-level citizens.

No sooner had the colonial powers conquered and subjugated the indigenous population in 1890 than they began a systematic process of undermining the capacity of the indigenous population to sustain themselves independently, effectively forcing them into wage employment and dependency. As well as confiscating the cattle, grain and other possessions of the indigenous people, the colonizers devised additional coercive means of generating a constant flow of cheap labour for the emerging farms and mines. This included the use of taxes to be paid for in cash and, more fundamentally, the expropriation of land, the very source of livelihood of the indigenous population. It was this

---

[6] The evolution of the colonial economy has been articulated in a variety of studies: Palmer (1977), Phimister (1976), Arrighi and Saul (1973), Gann (1965), among many. A good summary appears in Sibanda (1992) and Amanor-Wilks (2001).

expropriation of their means of livelihood that caused the 1896/97 uprisings by the indigenous population.

To create a stable workforce, the Master and Servants Ordinance was passed in 1901, which made it a criminal offence to break a labour contract. Pass laws were introduced in 1904, limiting the movement of workers and effectively putting them under the control of their employers. When these measures proved inadequate, land expropriation was effected. The Land Apportionment Act of 1930 and the Land Tenure Act of 1969 facilitated the expropriation of land, the latter parcelling out 50 per cent of the land to the 5 per cent white population. Consequently, able-bodied black men had to look for wage employment to fend for their families and pay taxes. Wage employment therefore became the new source of livelihood, with accommodation of the dormitory-type meant exclusively for the employed men; their families remained in the rural areas. This marked the birth of the migratory labour system characterized by split families, an aspect of the social and gender relations that apply to this day. The migratory labour system, and its attendant cheap-labour policy, was designed to ensure the cheap reproduction of the labour force and maximization of surplus value. Employees that fell ill or died had to be catered for by their families, implying that the rural economy should become the source of social security for the employed.

This policy of separate development and the migratory labour policy was aptly described by Phimister:

> Because the [Rhodesia Native Labour Bureau] recruits and other migrant workers still retained rights to land in rural areas, the wages paid by the mining industry were generally fixed at, or slightly above, the level of subsistence of the individual worker. The needs of his family were to be met by agricultural production in African rural areas. By obliging the rural economy to undertake social security functions for migrant labour, capitalist enterprises thus relieved themselves of important expenditure in this sphere. This was of immense value for profit maximization by the mines as it allowed capital to pay the worker below the cost of his reproduction [1976: 476].

This system was particularly pronounced in large-scale commercial agriculture, where workers were treated as part of the employer's 'domestic governance'. As Rutherford (1997) explained, farm-workers were viewed as less a government responsibility and more a domestic responsibility of white farmers, thereby placing them in the private rather than the public domain. While industrial relations in other sectors were governed under the Industrial Conciliation Act of 1934, agricultural workers came under the Master and Servants Ordinance of 1901.[7] The Ordinance did not provide for terms and conditions of employment,

---

[7] The Masters and Servants Act ceased to apply only in 1979.

and trade unions were specifically prohibited. To the extent that farmers exercised quasi-political and judicial authority on the farms, the employer had the upper hand as he/she was free to run the farm as he/she saw fit (domestic governance). It is in this context that Loewenson (1992) saw the contradictory situation in agriculture as representing 'corporate wealth and labour squalor'.

Mining, which had suffered earlier set-backs because of the absence of deposits of the same magnitude as those discovered in South Africa, recovered owing to cheap labour such that the colony's Auditor-General proclaimed that 'in Western Australia, where there is no native labour, mines which are of higher grade than ours cannot be worked at a profit though ours, the lower grades, produce profits. The inference is clear. Our mines are profitable only because of native labour available' (quoted in Phimister, 1976: 481).

As more white settlers came into the country, bringing with them trade-union traditions that were quite developed in their home countries, they found the situation in Rhodesia, and in particular the Master and Servants Ordinance, reprehensible. They particularly disliked the lack of trade-union protection against competition from the cheap and unskilled African labour. As a result, the Industrial Conciliation Act was passed in 1934, providing for the regulation of trade unions, employers' organizations and the settlement of disputes, and setting up industrial councils and boards for white workers. The Act applied only to white employees.

Following labour unrest, the colonial authorities passed the Native Labour Boards Act of 1947, whose functions were to advise the minister in regard to legislation for the improvement of employment of Africans, and to prevent and settle disputes. These boards were made up of government appointees, representatives of employers, and persons skilled in African affairs who were not themselves African workers. The Act did not apply to workers in agriculture, domestic service, mining and the civil service. Realizing the futility of suppressing the growth of trade unionism, government amended the Industrial Conciliation Act in 1959, legalizing the formation of trade unions, albeit under strict conditions. Trade unions could be registered only if they were representative, non-political, financially healthy, and had the consent of the employer. The amendment was geared towards the maintenance of industrial peace through: joint representation of employers and employees where no industrial council existed; collective bargaining; and the prevention and settlement of disputes through negotiation, conciliation boards, and voluntary and compulsory reference of disputes to the industrial tribunal. However, as the struggle for independence intensified, the government escalated its anti-union repression in view of the close links between the nationalist movement and the trade unions.

Thus, to sustain the process of capitalist accumulation in the formal economy, an underdeveloped and marginalized peasant (rural) sector, dominated largely by women, had to exist alongside a more dynamic and better-developed formal sector. As Harris (1977: 28) observed, 'White capitalists and landowners receive satisfactory profits, and white workers satisfactory wages. The returns are secured out of the relative deprivation of black industrial workers and peasants.' While black men had to eke out a living in the development enclaves controlled by white employers, women were pushed to the extreme margins of this development – indeed, resigned to a triple jeopardy.

Women, who constituted over half the population, accounted for only about 17 per cent of the total employment of slightly over one million workers in the formal sector in 1980. Of the thirteen sectors that constitute the formal sector, female employment was dominant only in the health sector, at 57 per cent of the workforce. In the two traditional sectors of agriculture and mining, female employment constituted, respectively, 26 per cent and a mere 2 per cent of the employees. In the manufacturing sector, women constituted only 7 per cent of the employees at independence, and only 3 per cent in the highest-paying sector of electricity and water. In the public-administration sector, women accounted for only 7 per cent of the workforce in 1980. Tellingly, by the late 1970s, the communal areas, the location of most women, with a carrying capacity of 275,000 farming units, were already overcrowded with 700,000 units (Riddell, 1979). Given the prevalence of women in the non-formal sectors and the dominance of men in the formal sector, the marginalization and vulnerability of women therefore remains a feature of the economy.

Because of the inequitable distribution of resources, income distribution followed a similar pattern. Blacks' and whites' share of wages and salaries was disproportionate to their share of the population (Table 7.1). On the whole, an estimated three per cent of the population controlled two-thirds of gross national income (Stoneman and Cliffe, 1989). The World Bank (1987) found that, at independence, black incomes were one-tenth of those of whites, with the wage differentials as high as 24 times for whites over blacks in agriculture. The differential stood at 7.3 times for manufacturing, with the lowest at 3.5 for the financial services sector. The trend appears to be that the lower the average skill level in a sector, the higher the average wage differentials between black and white, and vice versa.

**Table 7.1: The distribution of income by race**

| Group | Proportion of population | Share of wages and salaries |
|---|---|---|
| African | 97.6 | 60.0 |
| European | 2.0 | 37.0 |
| Coloured | 0.3 | 2.0 |
| Asian | 0.2 | 1.0 |

*Source:* Zimbabwe (1981a).

As stated above, growth under such conditions of gross inequality would not lift the majority of the population out of poverty in a situation where the 'integrability' of the disadvantaged groups and sectors was weak. Such a racially segmented labour market was a basis for conflict and instability. Pro-poor and inclusive growth would entail the implementation of redistributive policies to address inherited inequalities in the allocation of resources while raising agricultural productivity in the peasant sector and bringing the majority of the people into productive and remunerative formal-sector employment. That, in essence, is the development challenge that Zimbabwe faces.

### 7.3.2 The first decade of independence, 1980–1990

Before and after the inauguration of the new government in April 1980, the country was engulfed in strikes emanating from a 'crisis of expectations' on the part of workers. The new government responded by intervening extensively in the labour market. These interventions were meant to promote security of employment, to raise the standard of living of the people – in particular, of the lowly paid, to narrow income differentials, and to reduce inflationary pressures, especially after 1982 (Zimbabwe, 1986: 90). Government responded to the strikes by promulgating a Minimum Wages Act in 1980, but employers responded with retrenchments. In order to forestall further retrenchments, government then responded with an Employment Act, which stipulated that no retrenchments could take place without ministerial approval. Further protection from employers resorting to casuals was instituted by making their remuneration double that of permanent employees.

To deal with wider issues of incomes policy, in September 1980 the government constituted a Commission of Inquiry under the chairmanship of Roger Riddell to look at incomes, prices and conditions of service, with a view to correcting inherited anomalies. The Riddell Commission's report observed that, 'the necessity for action and for the introduction of policies directed specifically at alleviating poverty and narrowing differentials is apparent when one considers the implications of a "no" or status quo type of policy scenario' (Zimbabwe, 1981b: 84). According to the report, there was a need for a policy shift towards 'growth with equity through planned change' from the prevailing situation of 'growth with widening inequalities' (ibid.: 85).

Buoyed by the economic boom of the first two years of independence – in which GDP grew at 11 per cent and 10 per cent, respectively – government pursued an expansionary incomes policy influenced by the Poverty Datum Line. On the recommendations of the Riddell Commission, a sliding-scale mechanism was adopted whereby those at the bottom of the earnings structure received higher percentage increases, and vice versa. Government also fixed ceilings beyond which no increase could be granted. However, following three years of consecutive droughts and world recession beginning in 1982, a 'home-grown' stabilization programme was introduced with a wage-restraint component. Until 1988, minimum wages were set unilaterally by government on a two-tier system (domestic and agriculture, and industry and commerce) and were announced annually at the Workers' Day rally on 1 May. In 1989, government allowed National Employment Boards and National Employment Councils to negotiate within a 5–16 per cent range. In 1990 the negotiations started at 10 per cent with 'the sky' as the limit; this was part of the measures undertaken to deregulate the economy.

In the absence of a strong trade-union movement and its fragmented nature, with six federations, each aligned to a political party, the government felt duty-bound to intervene in the labour market, as was the case with the rest of the economy. Realizing its weak hold on trade unions since it did not have its own federation, the ZANU(PF) government organized the merger of the six federations to establish a pro-government umbrella body, the Zimbabwe Congress of Trade Unions (ZCTU), in February 1981. Thereafter, it took a paternalistic and corporatist approach to trade unionism, taking over the role of wage-setting ostensibly to improve the working conditions of workers and to redress the gross income inequalities.

The initial pieces of legislation were incorporated into a comprehensive Labour Relations Act (No. 16 of 1985), which for the first time provided for fundamental rights of employees (including the establishment of workers' committees at the shop floor), defined unfair labour practices, regulated conditions of employment, and introduced a highly centralized and elaborate dispute-resolution mechanism.[8] The route followed in dispute resolution was such that, from a labour relations officer, a case would follow the line of appeal to a hearing officer, to a regional hearing officer, to the Labour Relations Board, to the Labour Relations Tribunal (which was at par with the High Court), and then to the Supreme Court. Clearly, the dispute procedure was long-winded and the security-of-employment regulations were indeed onerous – in fact, those of India and Zimbabwe were considered to be among the most onerous in developing countries (Fallon and Lucas, 1993). Termination of employment was governed by Statutory Instrument 371 of 1985, which prohibited any employer from terminating employment without ministerial approval.

While these measures advanced the overall position of the workers, they undermined trade unions in several ways. Their role in wage-setting and the resolution of disputes had largely been vested in the Minister of Labour. While the justification for state intervention was understandable at independence,

---

[8] The Labour Relations Act repealed the Industrial Conciliation Act, the Minimum Wages Act and the Employment Act of 1980. It was known as the Labour Relations Act until 7 March 2003, when the short title was changed to the present Labour Act by Act No. 17 of 2002.

especially given the weak and divided situation among unions, continued state intervention effectively made it difficult for unions to justify their existence. The cumbersome dispute procedures made it difficult for workers to obtain quick justice. Moreover, the Labour Relations Board's and Tribunal's lack of adequate resources created a huge backlog of cases, and justice delayed was effectively justice denied. The overriding powers given to the minister undermined good governance in industrial relations. In addition, an aggrieved party could circumvent the labour courts and seek redress through the civil courts, creating parallelism in dispute resolution.

The workers' committees that were adopted as shop-floor-level structures at independence were not trade-union committees in practice: members could be drawn from non-trade-union members. Thus, the shop-floor-level structures were not linked to trade-union structures, resulting in competition between the two. More fundamentally, the Labour Relations Act made it difficult for workers to undertake strike action – in fact, it was impossible to go on a legal strike under the Labour Act. The implication of this is that striking workers are exposed to their employer, who can easily use the illegality of strike action to dismiss employees.

By the late 1980s, it became increasingly clear that the labour legislation was too restrictive and suffered from inordinate delays in resolving disputes, and the unions and employers were agitating for a more proactive role in industrial relations. In 1987, a tripartite technical committee was constituted to identify and recommend areas of the Act that required adjusting. By the end of the decade, consensus had been reached regarding the areas that had to be changed; however, the changes that were adopted by government did not reflect this consensus, as highlighted below.[9]

### 7.3.3 The ESAP period, 1991–96

While the social partners had sought to enhance the efficiency of the industrial-relations management framework without changing its underlying philosophy of creating a more humane system, the advent of ESAP changed that. Under the market reforms, government blamed past interventions in the labour market as having 'contributed to the present high levels of unemployment' (Zimbabwe, 1989: 10). This assessment was in line with that of the International Finance Institutions which insist on countries creating flexible labour-market regimes to facilitate the downward movement of real wages (real-wage flexibility) in order

---

[9] A fundamental structural change implemented by the government in 1988 was the transfer of skills-training from the Ministry of Labour and Social Welfare to the newly created Ministry of Higher and Tertiary Education. This effectively diluted the influence of tripartism in skills-formation, giving it an academic focus. With this restructuring, the department for manpower planning and research was split between the two ministries, with adverse implications for labour-market research and information.

to 'price workers into jobs' (employment flexibility).[10] In addition, the internal labour market at the level of the firm is expected to be flexible (functional flexibility), enabling workers to do multiple tasks (multi-tasking) and move easily between job categories (multi-skilling). Thus, according to government, this new approach entailed 'a more rationale and market-oriented method of determining prices and incomes' (ibid.).

The regulations dealing with retrenchment were restructured through Statutory Instrument 404 of 1990, which provided that any employer wishing to retrench should give written notice of his/her intention to the works council established for his/her undertaking, or, if there is no works council or if the majority of the workers concerned agree to such a course, to the employment council or employment board.[11] In his/her letter of notice, the employer was expected to give details of every employee affected and the reasons for the proposed retrenchment. A copy of the notice had to be sent to the retrenchment committee, to which the matter was to be referred if it was not resolved within a month.

Far-reaching changes were also made to the law dealing with dismissals and disputes. Statutory Instrument 379 of 1990 required workplaces and employment councils/employment boards to establish employment codes (codes of conduct). Once an employment code was registered with the Ministry of Labour, Statutory Instrument 371 of 1985 would cease to apply. However, Statutory Instrument 379 was silent in terms of what would happen should both a workplace and employment council register an employment code. Through Statutory Instrument 356 of 1993, this issue was clarified: a works council was allowed to register a code notwithstanding that an employment council had applied for, or proposed to apply for, the registration of a code. In the event that both the workplace and employment council had registered codes, the statutory instrument made the code registered by the works council binding, implying that shop-floor-level arrangements superseded any arrangement at the industrial level.[12]

While the decentralization of industrial-relations management was welcome, it was the nature and extent of that decentralization that presented problems; both the Employers' Confederation of Zimbabwe (EMCOZ) and the ZCTU had preferred that authority be derogated from the minister to national employment councils (NECs), where structures were established. Giving powers to the shop-floor level, where workers' committees were not trade-union committees, effectively undermined the role of unions. In addition, requiring codes at shop-floor level is an administrative nightmare, considering the multiplicity of organizations and

---

[10] Real-wage and employment flexibility are referred to as numerical flexibility.

[11] A works council is a decision-making body at the shop-floor level comprising equal representation of workers and management. All employment boards have now been abolished, so all sectors that had boards had to form employment councils.

[12] These changes were formally incorporated in the amendments to the Labour Relations Act of 1992.

firms. The courts also experienced serious problems with codes, as reflected in the case of *ZFC Limited* v. *Malayani*,[13] where the Supreme Court remarked:

> We have often remarked that Codes of Conduct are badly drafted ... This one is particularly so ... It would seem imperative to us that a great deal more care should be taken by the Registrar of Labour Relations before he agrees, in terms of section 101(2) of the Act, to register a Code of Conduct. This Code in particular needs redrafting.

Other important changes arising from the 1992 amendments to the Labour Relations Act included streamlining of the dispute procedure, allowing for the formation of committees for managerial employees, the abolition of the principle of 'one industry, one union or employers' association', and minor amendments to the provisions on maternity leave. The cumbersome dispute procedures were amended to allow quick decision-making: the number of stages to be followed in resolving a dispute was substantially reduced. The new structure was such that an appeal could be made from the workplace to the employment council, from where the dispute could be taken to the Labour Relations Tribunal, which was made full-time, and finally to the Supreme Court. Time limits were also set for handling cases at all stages, which was expected to quicken their resolution.

However, in spite of this streamlining, the backlogs remained. The Tribunal, for instance, had only two full-time judges, who were easily overwhelmed by the number of cases awaiting resolution. It was also highly centralized, based only in Harare. The involvement of the civil courts in labour matters exacerbated the situation, as they interpreted the spirit of deregulation liberally. For example, in the case of *Lancashire Steel* v. *Zvidzai and Others*,[14] the definition of a collective job action was extended to include gatherings that are disrespectful and disobedient to management. The judge argued that 'We cannot subscribe to the view that when mature men jeer, boo and offer insulting behaviour to management they are unaware that such conduct is unlawful'. The judgment determined that participation in collective job action is sufficient grounds for the termination of employment in terms of Statutory Instrument 371 of 1985,[15] and that it is legally permissible to punish only the ringleaders (selective dismissal).

In the case of *Continental Fashions (Private) Limited* v. *Elliot Mupfuriri and Others*,[16] the judge noted that the legislation with respect to retrenchment was not helpful to practitioners. In his judgment, Justice McNally made it clear that

> where, as here, the purpose of retrenchment is to avoid the collapse and liquid-ation of the company, the well-being of the retrenchees cannot be the only

[13] SC 34/99

[14] SC 29/95.

[15] As for the codes, whether dismissal is permissible depends on its provisions.

[16] SC 161/97.

consideration. The survival of the company is the motivating consideration. The purpose of the exercise is to save the company. In so doing, care must be taken to cushion the blow to the workers. But to say, as the Labour Relations Tribunal has done in this case, that it is almost irrelevant whether or not the company can afford the package, is a fundamental misdirection. The immediate objective of retrenchment remains the saving of the company and of the jobs of the remaining employees.

Clearly therefore, although it is not stated in the Regulations, the ability of the company to pay the retrenchment package is the ultimate criterion – the bottom line. If the company cannot pay what it is ordered to pay, it must go into liquidation, which is what the retrenchment exercise was designed to avoid.

This judgment undermined the ability of unions to negotiate good retrenchment packages. It undermined the principle of mitigation of loss of employment.

Yet, in another case, *Charles Ambali* v. *Bata Shoe Company Limited*,[17] the judgment took away the right to reinstatement of a wrongfully dismissed worker. Justice McNally opined:

I think it is important that this court should make it clear, once and for all, that an employee who considers, whether rightly or wrongly, that he has been unjustly dismissed, is not entitled to sit around and do nothing. He must look for alternative employment. If he does not, his damages will be reduced. He will be compensated only for the period between his wrongful dismissal and the date when he could reasonably have expected to find alternative employment ... There are also those, and Ambali is one of them, who seem to believe that they must on no account look for alternative employment; that so long as their case is pending they must preserve their unemployed status; that if they look for and find a job in the meanwhile they will destroy their claim. It cannot be emphasized too strongly that this is wrong.

This judgment undermined the right to reinstatement, and hence significantly reduced the level of damages an unfairly dismissed worker can have. It had the effect of rubbing salt into the injury, blaming the victim for his or her plight. This judgment came at a time when the economic crisis was biting deeper and many workers were losing their jobs. In other words, the judgment took away a right when it was needed most. The worker was being asked to mitigate his or her loss by seeking alternative employment at a time the unemployment rate was high. This is illustrated in *Olivine Industries (Pvt) Ltd* v. *Caution Nharara*,[18] where the Supreme Court ordered the High Court to deduct an amount earned by the employee through repairing cell phones and selling tomatoes.

The Act retained the proscription of the right to strike. Worse still, what was

---

[17] 1999 (1) ZLR 374.
[18] SC 88/05.

intriguing was the use of the Law and Order Maintenance Act (No. 53 of 1960), which was later superseded by the Public Order and Security Act [*Chapter 11:17*] of 2002, to deal with strikes. This law criminalized collective job action, with imprisonment of up to seven years for using inflammatory language and up to five years for inciting strike action in essential services. Ironically, this law had been put in place during the colonial era to deal with the rise of nationalism.

Furthermore, the industrial-relations scene during this phase was characterized by the existence of a multiplicity of labour laws: the Labour Relations Act and its amendments, the Public Service Act [*Chapter 16:04*], the Urban Councils Act [*Chapter 29:15*], special regulations for Export Processing Zones, and various other regulations. These created numerous problems for workers. The Public Service Act does not recognize the collective-bargaining rights of public employees, and its structures for dealing with grievances and disputes is heavy-handed and unilateral. In fact, the Public Service Act does not have provisions for unions, and the various associations in existence do not have trade-union rights. Although a Joint Negotiating Forum was established in 1998, its role is merely advisory. The Urban Councils Act offered procedures and conditions at variance with those in the Labour Relations Act, resulting in a conflict of laws.

While the establishment of Export Processing Zones was effected in 1995, the enabling act [*Chapter 14:07*] excluded the Labour Relations Act from applying in them. It was not until 1998 that employment regulations were put in place to cover these zones and only in January 2000 that a Labour Board for them was established. The segmentation of workers by sector effectively undermined the establishment of a strong, united labour movement.

### 7.3.4 The crisis period, 1997–2008

More fundamentally, with the adoption of ESAP in 1991, the relationship between the ZCTU and the state deteriorated progressively. The ESAP-induced hardships alienated the government and civil society and, in particular, the trade-union movement. In the late 1990s, strikes became a regular feature of the industrial-relations scene. In 1997, for instance, 231 strikes were recorded.[19] Worker resistance became increasingly more militant and varied, and included demonstrations and stay-aways.

In response to the growing militancy of the working people, and the growing influence of the ZCTU, government abolished the ZCTU's monopoly by registering the Zimbabwe Federation of Trade Unions (ZFTU) in July 1998. What is interesting is that almost all of the latter's thirteen affiliates were registered after its registration, suggesting a top-down approach. The actual members of its

---

[19] It is necessary to recall that there has never been a legal strike in Zimbabwe.

affiliates are not known, but indications suggest that some had only a handful of members at registration.

To deal with increasing worker militancy, especially at the national level, government used the Presidential Powers (Temporary Measures) Act [*Chapter 10:20*] to issue labour regulations.[20] These measures, which came into effect in November 1998 following threats by the ZCTU to go on further weekly stay-aways, imposed heavy penalties on employers, employees, trade unions and employers' organizations that incited or facilitated strikes, stay-aways or other forms of unlawful collective action. Unlawful collective action refers to any strike, boycott, lock-out, sit-in, stay-away or other such action on the part of employers or employees which is:

- prohibited under section 104(3) of the Labour Relations Act; or
- engaged in wholly or mainly for the purpose of
  - resisting any law or lawful measure of the government; or
  - inducing or compelling the government to alter any law or lawful measure.

Section 4 of the regulations empowered the minister to issue a 'show cause' order in terms of section 106 of the Labour Relations Act in respect of any unlawful collective action that was threatened, anticipated, in force or had taken place. The minister could vary, suspend or rescind the registration or certification of a trade union, employers' organization, or federation of trade unions, or employers' organization if the minister was satisfied that any of these bodies had:

- recommended, encouraged or incited persons to engage in unlawful collective action;
- associated itself with any such recommendation, encouragement or incitement, or
- organized any unlawful collective action.

In such cases the minister would have to be satisfied that the unlawful action had caused or would cause substantial prejudice to the economy. Additional penalties included a fine of Z$100,000, or up to three years' imprisonment, or both. Liability for any loss or damage to property and any injury or death of a person caused by or arising out of any collective action was provided for. Furthermore, any employer could dismiss an employee on the ground of involvement in unlawful collective action. The employer would not have to seek ministerial approval, as with Statutory Instrument 371 of 1985.[21]

An operator of a passenger transport service who

- encouraged or incited people to engage in unlawful collective action;

---

[20] Presidential Powers (Temporary Measures) (Labour Relations) Regulations: Statutory Instrument 368A of 1998.

[21] See *At the Ready Wholesalers (Pvt) Ltd trading as Power Sales* v. *Innocent Katsande and 5 others*, SC 7/03.

- organized or assisted in the organization of any unlawful collective action; or
- knowingly facilitated any unlawful collective action through the withdrawal of services

would have its operator's licence suspended or cancelled. Clearly, these measures were draconian in nature and violated the liberties guaranteed in the constitution (sections 20 and 21) on freedom of expression and association.

These measures were incorporated into the Labour Amendment Act (No. 17 of 2005), one of whose major objectives was to harmonize all labour laws in Zimbabwe. However, the amended act only partially did so. It excluded civil servants from the labour legislation in two areas:

- in matters relating to misconduct, where they will remain under the authority of the Public Service Commission;
- where the President is given prerogative to determine whether or not other government employees can be covered by the Labour Relations Act.

Clearly, therefore, this undermined the concept of harmonization. However, by making the Labour Act superior to any other law in dealing with labour matters, Section 3 of the amended act removed the previous conflict of laws, where the Urban Councils Act, for instance, undermined the operation of the Labour Relations Act with respect to local authority employees (section 141), as did the Export Processing Zones Act with respect to EPZ employees (section 56).

Probably the most draconian part of the amended act is with respect to strikes/stay-aways. Here, the act incorporated the presidential ban on stay-aways originally contained in Statutory Instrument 368A of 1998. This was done by:

- inserting a new definition of unlawful collective job action (section 3);
- giving the minister the power to de-register trade unions organizing stay-aways (section 11);
- prohibiting an employer from collecting union dues on behalf of a suspended or de-registered trade union (section 14);
- providing for new offences by trade-union leaders who organize stay-aways (clause 30);
- providing for the easy dismissal of employees involved in stay-aways (clause 29);
- maintaining excessive powers of the Minister of Labour.

Furthermore, the amended act requires that a strike should be endorsed by a majority of workers through a secret ballot, a measure taken from the British experience in the 1980s under Margaret Thatcher as she sought to weaken unions in that country. These draconian measures clearly violate the fundamental human and trade-union rights enshrined in the various instruments that Zimbabwe has ratified. The amendments also increased the number of days of maternity leave from 90 to 98, and increased pay for those on maternity leave from 75 per cent to 100 per cent, though these benefits were restricted to those employees who had served one year. The amendments made sexual harassment an 'unfair labour practice', which is commendable. The amendments also formalized the provisions of Statutory Instrument 202 of 1998, Labour Relations (HIV and AIDS) Regulations, which make it an offence for an employer to compel an employee to undergo testing for HIV and forbid any form of discrimination and the termination of employment on the basis of a person's HIV status.

The amendments now allow for the formation of trade-union committees at the shop-floor level where a trade union commands more than 50 per cent of the employees. Persons employed without termination dates are now considered to be permanent employees, and so are casuals whose work exceeds six weeks in four consecutive months, and someone on a fixed-term contract that is not renewed but where the employer engages another person instead. To deal with cases of dismissal where an employment code is non-existent, the employer is now required to do so in terms of the Labour (National Employment Code of Conduct) Regulations, 2006.[22] Prior to these amendments, employees were entitled to only 22–26 days' sick leave on full pay; the Labour Act now provides for up to six months' sick leave, with three months on full pay and the rest on half pay. Vacation leave was extended to one month, and an employee is now entitled to special leave of twelve days per calendar year.

The Labour Tribunal was transformed into a Labour Court, empowered to exercise the same powers as the High Court with respect to labour issues and to hear and determine applications and appeals from authorities under it. The Labour Court does not follow strict rules of evidence like the civil courts, and allows trade unionists to represent members, effectively reducing the legal charges of legal practitioners. The dispute-resolution procedure was streamlined such that conciliation and arbitration are provided for, with labour officers given thirty days to conciliate a matter instead of the twelve months that applied previously. In addition, parties can go for voluntary arbitration in order to speed up the process of dispute resolution. An appeal on a question of law from an arbitrator's or employment code now lies in the Labour Court. Once an appeal is noted to the Labour Court, it does not suspend the determination or decision appealed against, effectively undermining frivolous appeals.

While both the employer representatives (EMCOZ) and worker representatives (the ZCTU) were generally part of the consultations and endorsed the 2002 amendments, the workers have reservations on the provisions criminalizing strike action and undermining the right to conduct their business without interference;

---

[22] Statutory Instrument 15 of 2006.

the act did not fully address this issue. Even though the amendments had partially included the public sector under the Labour Act [*Chapter 28:01*], the Labour Amendment Act took them back to the Public Service Act.

From the foregoing analysis, it is clear that Zimbabwe's labour laws remain fragmented and contain elements that undermine human and trade-union rights, which makes trade-union work extremely difficult and hazardous. It is also clear that amendments to the laws have been governed more by political expediency than by consensus, resulting in the insertion of unpopular and draconian provisions. Section 104 of the Labour Act, as read with the Labour (Settlement of Disputes) Regulations,[23] effectively makes it impossible to go on a legal strike. The regulations prescribe ambiguous and strict procedures that must be complied with before employees embark on strike action, including giving fourteen days' written notice to the employer, voting by secret ballot supervised by the few labour officers or National Employment Council agents, or be referred to compulsory arbitration, thereby terminating the right to strike.

Strikes are banned in the widely defined 'essential' services, which are the prerogative of the Minister of Labour to demarcate. The Labour (Declaration of Essential Service) Regulations provide sectors unilaterally classified as essential by the Minister of Labour,[24] which include the entire civil service and parastatals. Employees absent from work for more than five days without reasonable cause can be fired through recourse to the code. Apart from criminalizing participation in an unlawful collective job action, Section 109 of the act empowers an affected party to claim damages from an employee or trade union for losses incurred as a result of the strike. The union risks its registration being suspended for a period of twelve months and cannot collect subscriptions during this period.

As the economic and social crisis gripping the economy deepened, the relationship between the ZCTU and the government deteriorated. This was worsened when the ZCTU, together with other civil-society groups, facilitated the formation of a formidable opposition party, the Movement for Democratic Change (MDC) in 1999. Since then, labour legislation proposed has included draconian measures. Splinter unions have been facilitated by government and, at one point in 2001, war veterans became involved in settling labour disputes. At this stage in the country's development, the management of industrial relations is inextricably linked to issues of national governance.[25]

Although Zimbabwe has ratified the core ILO conventions that place emphasis

---

[23] Statutory Instrument 217 of 2003.

[24] Statutory Instrument 137 of 2003.

[25] For instance, in 2005, the Police Fraud Squad raided the ZCTU offices alleging misappropriation of funds and illegal dealing in foreign currency on the parallel market. Through Section 120 of the Labour Act, the state appointed an investigator who produced a pro-government report, on the basis of which the matter was put before the courts.

on freedom of association,[26] its conduct has been in violation of these funda-mental standards. Freedom of association is a fundamental human right enshrined in most national constitutions and in major international instruments like the Universal Declaration of Human Rights 1948,[27] the International Covenant on Economic, Social and Cultural Rights, the International Covenant on Civil and Political Rights, and the African Charter on Human and Peoples' Rights – all ratified by Zimbabwe. These international instruments are specific on the right of workers, employers and the population at large to form and join their own associations, assemble and carry out their activities unhindered by the state.

However, these international conventions and recommendations are under-utilized by the courts in interpreting legislation on the strength that the con-stitution requires that international law be first approved by parliament and incorporated into Zimbabwean law before it can be used locally. In the case of *Communications and Allied Services Workers Union of Zimbabwe v. Zimpost,*[28] the trade union tried unsuccessfully to justify the right to strike by making reference to ILO Conventions 87 and 98.

Sections of the Labour Act outlined above – and other non-labour laws such as the Public Order and Security Act, the Access to Information and Protection of Privacy Act [*Chapter 10:27*] and the Criminal Law (Codification and Reform) Act [*Chapter 9:23*][29] – which are interfering in the regulation of industrial relations violate the principles enshrined in the ILO and other international conventions. Even though the High Court ordered the state not to interfere with trade-union meetings in 2002,[30] this is ignored, implying that the rule of law is not adhered to. As the violations of workers' and trade-union rights intensified, the ILO conference of June 2008 decided to send a Commission of Inquiry to investigate violations of Conventions 87 and 98; it came to Zimbabwe from 12 to 25 August 2009.

In summarizing the developments during this crisis phase, it is important to note that the focus of government was on reigning in growing worker militancy rather than on dealing with underemployment, unemployment and poverty. Government policies during this phase were of an ad hoc, fire-fighting nature, dealing with short-term crises rather than focusing on medium- to long-term development issues such as employment creation and poverty reduction,[31] with

---

[26] Conventions 87, the Freedom of Association and Protection of the Right to Organize convention, 1948, and 98, the Right to Organize and Collective Bargaining convention, 1949.

[27] Articles 20.1 and 23.4.

[28] Case No. LC/H/180/2004.

[29] Under the Criminal Law (Codification and Reform) Act, protest actions are regarded as an obstruction to traffic, and hence are deemed illegal.

[30] *Zimbabwe Congress of Trade Unions v. The Officer Commanding Police Harare District and the Commissioner of Police,* H-H 56/2002.

[31] See Chapter 2.

catastrophic consequences, as the analysis above shows. An attempt to craft an employment policy framework that was revived in 1999 was effectively shelved and only achieved in 2009.

## 7.4 Labour-Market Performance and Outcomes, 1980–2008

### 7.4.1 Real-wage trends

The evolution of wage policy was discussed above. What was noteworthy was the change in policy during the ESAP period to achieve real-wage and employment (numerical) flexibility. Real average earnings peaked in 1982, before collapsing by 2004 (Fig. 7.1). Within the accumulation strategy of SAPs, a fall in real wages is

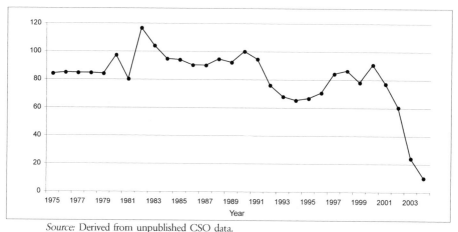

*Source:* Derived from unpublished CSO data.

**Fig. 7.1: Real average earnings index (1990 = 100)**

considered positive. According to the World Bank (1989: 29), the collapse in real wages in Sub-Saharan Africa, represented 'a brutal but necessary adjustment to reflect a labour force that has outstripped job creation and the need to become internationally competitive'. As for Zimbabwe, Collier (1995: 5) observed:

> Certainly, inflation has been faster during the liberalization than prior to it, and so it is reasonable to conclude that the liberalization has contributed to the decline in real unskilled wages. Note that this is not a decline in the equilibrium real wage, but rather acceleration in what was already a gradual adjustment to the equilibrium. Such an adjustment raises employment. The transfer from wages to profits may also raise savings.[32]

---

[32] The World Bank's *Country Assistance Study* noted that Zimbabwe's labour costs 'are now very competitive in international terms' (World Bank, 1997: 3).

However, studies on low-wage policies have linked them to poor morale, shirking, moonlighting, multiple-jobbing, low productivity, high turn-over and corruption, which undermine human development (Schiller, 1990). The 2008 CZI *Manufacturing Sector Survey* found such survivalist strategies to be applicable to industry in Zimbabwe. It argues that, while workers may turn up for work, the greater part of the day is devoted to private business using the company's infrastructure such as telephone services. A detailed World Bank study of labour markets and adjustment highlighted the downside of such a development, contending that 'beyond a certain point the macroeconomic consequences of real wage declines may lead to an additional cost of adjustment that relies too heavily on labour markets' (Horton *et. al.*, 1991: 5). Indeed, that is what happened in Zimbabwe with the collapse of real earnings in the new millennium, especially during the hyperinflationary period after June 2007.

The 2007 *Manufacturing Sector Survey* observed that the collapse in real wages was having adverse effects on the economy, arguing that 'In addition to a shrinking economy, this has had a multiplier effect of seriously depleting the country's disposable incomes. The erosion of disposable income as workers get poorer is shrinking demand for products as disposable incomes wane and hence reduces business viability' (CZI, 2007: 58). The survey highlights the loss of skills as a result of failure to pay economic living wages. It strongly recommended that the sector should

> seriously review remuneration practices in a manner that rewards the labour factor adequately. This entails paying living wages at the bottom end of the market while working out serious performance-related packages at the top end of the market. While this may result in short-term depleted profits, in the long run it will preserve and retain key skills in the country needed to take the shrinking economy through a recovery. We believe that a strategy that seeks to protect the bottom line at the expense of paying living wages is ultimately detrimental to both the company and the country at large. This strategy is not sustainable [ibid.: 58].

The 2008 *Manufacturing Sector Survey* observed that the situation had deteriorated further such that, in 2007, salaries at the lower end were below requirements for transport, resulting in workers absconding from work. A major development associated with the hyperinflationary environment was the disappearance of the middle class: the 'missing middle'. Holding down a formal-sector job became a disincentive as the returns from speculative informal activities were much more attractive.

In the worst-affected sectors such as agriculture and the civil service, the collapse in real earnings resulted in workers failing to turn up for work, representing a pool of dormant labour, ready to be re-engaged provided their conditions of service improved. In the agricultural and agro-industries, labour shortages emerged as workers withheld their services. While such a collapse in earnings elsewhere would have sparked protests, the use of repressive measures by the state created a semblance of stability. However, as shown below, a significant number of employees simply left the country or entered the informal economy.

### 7.4.2 Functional distribution of income and income differentials

The share of wages and salaries in Gross Domestic Income progressively declined between 1985 and 2007, from 49.4 per cent to 35.3 per cent, while that of profit increased (Table 7.2; Fig. 7.2). The percentage attributable to profit, on the other hand, increased from an annual average of 50.7 per cent to 65.3 per cent during the same period. Owing to the unstable macroeconomic environment, the increased share of profit was not accompanied by investment, which was, in fact, insignificant in gross terms and negative in net terms.

Income differentials for the unskilled, skilled and managerial grades during the period 1995–2000 show that the least-paid workers were the ones who bore the brunt of the economic crisis, violating the need for equity and consistency in the earnings structure, and thereby distorting the grading system (Zimbabwe Institute, 2007: 33).

**Table 7.2: Percentage share in the distribution of Gross Domestic Income by factor income**

|  | 1985–1990 | 1991–1996 | 1997–2007 | 2000–2007 |
|---|---|---|---|---|
| Wages and salaries | 49.4 | 41.5 | 37.2 | 35.3 |
| Rent | 2.3 | 2.2 | 1.5 | 1.3 |
| Profit | 50.7 | 58.4 | 63.8 | 65.3 |
| Financial interest services | −2.4 | −2.1 | −2.5 | −1.8 |
|  | 100.0 | 100.0 | 100.0 | 100.0 |

*Source:* Calculated from CSO, *National Accounts*, 1985-2003, and unpublished CSO data.

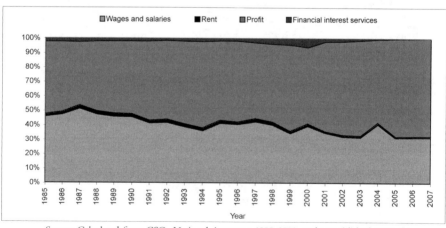

*Source:* Calculated from CSO, *National Accounts*, 1985-2003, and unpublished CSO data.

**Fig. 7.2: Percentage share in the distribution of Gross Domestic Income by factor income**

### 7.4.3 Growth and employment

It was argued above that employment is the link between growth and poverty reduction, and therefore that the extent to which growth reduces poverty depends on the elasticity factor and the integrability factor.

Real GDP growth averaged 4.6 per cent during 1986-90 but declined to -2.9 per cent during the crisis period, and employment growth declined from an annual average of 2.5 per cent to -1.6 per cent during the same period (Table 7.3). The rates of growth of employment for the period under review are well below the labour force growth rate of 3 per cent in the 1980s and 1990s and 1 per cent in the new millennium. Formal-sector employment declined from the peak of 1.4 million in 1998 to an estimated 700,000 by 2007. The percentage of the population employed in the formal sector declined from 14 per cent in 1980 to around 6 per cent by 2007.

Even before the onset of the crisis in 1997, growth was already erratic and sustained high levels of growth were not achieved – a critical aspect of employment creation and poverty reduction. Given the correlation between GDP and employment growth, the period of negative economic growth, 1997-2004, is, as would be expected, associated with negative employment growth. Employment appears to grow more slowly when the economy is expanding, and to decline more slowly when the economy is shrinking, owing to the lagged response

**Table 7.3: Real GDP and employment growth, 1986–2004**

| Sector/Year | GDP | | | Employment | | |
|---|---|---|---|---|---|---|
| | 1986–1990 | 1991–1996 | 1997–2004 | 1986–1990 | 1991–1996 | 1997–2005 |
| Agriculture | 1.3 | 4.1 | -1.7 | 1.0 | 3.1 | -6.2* |
| Mining | 0.8 | 2.0 | -2.5 | -1.0 | 2.7 | -0.4 |
| Manufacturing | 4.4 | 2.2 | -6.8 | 3.1 | -1.1 | -0.8 |
| Electricity and water | 11.1 | -2.2 | 3.0 | 2.5 | 6.8 | 5.1 |
| Construction | 10.7 | -1.5 | -8.4 | 11.2 | 0.8 | -7.0 |
| Financial services and real estate | 7.4 | 4.8 | 2.9 | 2.9 | 4.0 | 3.6 |
| Distribution | 6.3 | 3.3 | -6.3 | 4.2 | 1.0 | 0.8 |
| Transport and communication | 3.2 | 9.9 | -5.4 | 1.3 | -0.8 | -3.5 |
| Public administration | 0.8 | -4.4 | -1.2 | 0.6 | -4.3 | 0.5 |
| Education | 4.0 | 2.8 | 2.4 | 3.9 | 2.8 | 0.8 |
| Health | 3.4 | 5.1 | -0.9 | 4.7 | 1.1 | 7.6 |
| Private domestic services | 0.1 | 0.1 | -0.6 | 0.7 | 0.0 | -0.5 |
| Other | 5.1 | 4.1 | 1.7 | 5.1 | 4.1 | 1.5 |
| Total | 4.6 | 2.8 | -2.9 | 2.5 | 1.2 | -1.6* |

*Source:* Calculated from unpublished CSO data.
*Note:* While GDP data go up to 2008, employment data are available only up to the first quarter of 2004 for agriculture and up to the first quarter for all other sectors. Asterisks (*) denote data for 1997–2004.

resulting from the cost of hiring and firing workers. As noted in the CZI's 2007 *Manufacturing Sector Survey*, the trend was towards employment of casuals, who can be hired and fired more easily.

The extent to which GDP and employment growth are related, the employment intensity of growth, is measured by the employment elasticity of output. Overall, the employment elasticities of growth declined between 1991 and 2003, implying that the relationship between GDP and employment growth weakened over time. The employment elasticities for Zimbabwe differ from the world average and those for Sub-Saharan Africa in that the latter's elasticities increased before declining, while Zimbabwe's declined persistently (Table 7.4). Worse still, because Zimbabwe had the highest job-intensity of growth during 1991–95, its

**Table 7.4: Employment elasticities and GDP growth (%), 1991–2003**

|  | 1991–1995 | 1995–1999 | 1999–2003 |
|---|---|---|---|
| **Elasticities** | | | |
| Zimbabwe | 1.84 | 0.26 | −0.21 |
| World | 0.34 | 0.38 | 0.30 |
| Sub-Saharan Africa | 0.73 | 0.82 | 0.53 |
| **GDP growth** | | | |
| Zimbabwe | 0.1 | 3.7 | −6.3 |
| World | 2.1 | 3.6 | 3.5 |
| Sub-Saharan Africa | 1.1 | 3.2 | 3.2 |

*Source:* Compiled from Kapsos (2005), various tables. The ILO compiled employment elasticities for individual countries and regions worldwide.

decline thereafter was precipitous. Heintz (2006: 9) found that the employment elasticities for Zimbabwe's manufacturing sector declined from 0.65 between 1963 and 1979 to 0.06 between 1980 and 1996.[33]

With the labour regime having been deregulated since the early 1990s, rigidities in the labour market may not be responsible for this decline in Zimbabwe's elasticities. This is in line with the results of the 2007 and 2008 CZI *Manufacturing Sector Surveys*, which found that the main constraint to job creation was low levels of production, with labour-market constraints hardly featuring at all. The studies identified the major cause of the declining employment levels as constrained demand. Labour-market rigidity was not an issue, with no firm citing NEC compliance (labour standards) as an issue in 2006 and 2007. The onerous employment-security regulations that undermined employment creation in the 1980s were deregulated at the beginning of the ESAP period. Indeed, a World Bank study concluded:

---

[33] The 1995/96 ILO *Employment Report* suggests that the output elasticity of employment in the manufacturing sector in fact declined from 0.42 per cent during 1975–80 to 0.26 per cent during the late 1990s.

Often, African labour markets are blamed for competitiveness problems, but our analysis found that labour markets in Africa are flexible, and wages and employment are responsive to market forces. The most important issues for formal sector job creation are currently outside the narrow area of labour regulation, and are in the broader category of the investment climate [Fox and Sekkel, 2008: 12].

### 7.4.4 Growing informalization of the economy

In the absence of unemployment-benefit schemes, those who cannot find work or are retrenched cannot survive without working. It is for this reason that in 2004 levels of unemployment were as low as 9.3 per cent using the broad definition and 4.4 per cent using the strict definition.[34] This therefore implies that those who cannot find employment in the formal sector have to make do with work in the informal economy, which is 'unprotected', 'excluded', 'unregistered' or 'unrepresented' – in other words, decent-work deficits abound. At independence, the informal economy was relatively small, accounting for less than ten per cent of the labour force, which was attributed to the various laws and by-laws that prohibited the free movement of people, especially from the rural to urban areas. At independence, the new government permitted the free movement of people but was ambivalent about how to deal with informal activities in urban areas.

With the collapse of the formal sector as the crisis deepened, the informal economy blossomed. Based on data from the 2004 *Labour Force Survey*, Luebker (2008a) computed employment levels for the formal sector and informal economy using enterprise-based and job-based concepts. Using the enterprise-based concept, the formal sector employed 1.2 million people, compared to just over 710,000 in the informal economy. However, on the basis of the job-based concept, 975,000 people had formal jobs, while 4.1 million had informal jobs. This therefore implies that four out of every five jobs in Zimbabwe were informalized in 2004. The majority of these jobs (90.2 per cent) were unskilled, compared to the more than half of all formal-sector jobs that were professional or skilled. According to the 2004 *Labour Force Survey*, females accounted for 53 per cent of informal economy employment. According to the 2003 *Poverty Assessment Study Survey (PASS II)* of the Ministry of Public Service, Labour and Social Welfare (Zimbabwe, 2006b), nearly two-thirds (63 per cent) of informal economy employees were in urban areas; 31 per cent of the informal enterprises

---

[34] According to the broad (passive) definition, unemployment 'refers to the population age 15 years and above who, during the seven-day reference period, did not work and had no job or business to go back to, but who were available for work' (CSO, 2006: 27). The strict (active) definition requires that those who are without a job and are available for work look actively for work. Unemployment using the strict definition stood at 10.8 per cent in 1982, 7.2 per cent in 1986/87, 7.9 per cent in 1993, and 6 per cent in 1999 (CSO, 2006).

operated from a permanent building, 30 per cent from home, 20 per cent had no fixed location, and 11 per cent operated on footpaths. Eighty per cent of the enterprises had no employees, 18 per cent had 1–4 employees and 2 per cent had 5–9 employees.[35]

The *PASS II* report found lack of credit, capital and inputs to be the most common constraints facing household enterprises (31 per cent of the enterprises), followed by the lack of a market to sell produce (15 per cent), irregular supply of inputs and lack of access to market facilities (7 per cent each), transport (6 per cent), regulation (5 per cent), bad debts (5 per cent), and technology (3 per cent). Instead of addressing these challenges, the government unleashed a highly controversial military-style Operation Murambatsvina/Restore Order in 2005 which destroyed much of the 'sector' (UN, 2005). Be that as it may, the informalization of the economy is of concern because 'Informality is an undesirable form of employment since informal workers generally lack productive employment opportunities, cannot exercise their rights at work, are not covered by adequate social protection, and have no strong collective representation to voice their concerns' (Luebker, 2008b: 54).

At best, government policy towards the informal economy has been ambivalent, vacillating between tacit support and open revulsion. In a move that surprised many, Operation Murambatsvina was launched in May 2005, targeting the informal economy in urban areas. As the investigating UN envoy, Anna Tibaijuka, found out, the operation 'was carried out in an indiscriminate and unjustified manner, with indifference to human suffering, and, in repeated cases, with disregard to several provisions of national and international legal frameworks' (UN, 2005: 7). This resulted in what Tibaijuka referred to as a 'humanitarian crisis of immense proportions' (ibid.: 9). The UN report estimated that 700,000 people across the cities in Zimbabwe lost either their homes or source of livelihood, or both, with a further 2.4 million people affected indirectly. Operation Garikai/ Hlalani Kuhle, which was implemented shortly thereafter ostensibly to provide housing and workshops to those affected by Operation Murambatsvina made very little difference. In a study of one of the hubs of the informal economy in Harare, Glen View, Luebker (2008a) found that, of those affected by Operation Murambatsvina in the area (two-thirds of the respondents), only 2.5 per cent had benefited from the programme well over a year after its launch.

### 7.4.5 The impact of HIV and AIDS
It is now widely accepted, if only belatedly, that HIV and AIDS is a workplace challenge. It poses serious threats to workers' rights, since people living with

---

[35] One of the major challenges in measuring activities in the informal economy relates to the different definitions applied – see, for instance, *PASS II* (Zimbabwe, 2006b), Zimbabwe (2006a) and Luebker (2008b).

HIV and AIDS are subject to stigmatization, discrimination and hostility in their communities and at work. HIV and AIDS have a significant impact on the composition of the labour force in terms of age, skills and experience, with the productive age group, 15–49 years, the most affected. Losses of human capital due to HIV and AIDS are disproportionately higher among skilled, professional and managerial workers. The pandemic has profound adverse impacts on the economy, workforce and businesses, as well as on the infected and affected individuals and their families.

Estimates from UNAIDS and the IMF in Southern Africa suggest that GDP growth rates may decrease by 1–2 percentage points annually as a result of the pandemic (Lisk, 2002). It has been estimated that, over a twenty-year period in high-prevalence countries, economic growth could be 25 per cent lower than it might have been without the pandemic, their populations 20 per cent lower by 2015, and their labour forces 10–22 per cent smaller (ILO, 2000). Data from the 2002 population census suggest that the intercensal population growth rate declined from 3.9 per cent during the period 1982–92 to 1.2 per cent during the period 1992–2002, mainly due to the HIV and AIDS pandemic.

HIV and AIDS has manifested itself in the world of work through discrimination in employment, social exclusion, distortions in terms of gender inequality, an increased number of orphans, often resulting in increased child labour, and disrupted performance in small enterprises and the informal economy. It has also manifested itself in low productivity, depleted human capital, challenged social-security systems, and undermined occupational safety and health. The impact of HIV and AIDS at the enterprise level can be broken down into three categories: direct, indirect and systemic costs. Direct costs, which are easiest to quantify, arise from medical care and insurance costs, pension and retirement costs, recruitment and retraining costs, and costs of HIV and AIDS programmes. Indirect costs include reduced productivity, morbidity and absenteeism due to illness and bereavements. The systemic costs relate to loss of skills, loss of tacit knowledge, reduced morale, and breakdown of workplace discipline. HIV and AIDS is exacerbated by poverty, and vice versa, making it a challenge to fundamental principles and rights at work, and more importantly, to the Decent Work Agenda (SAfAIDS and HIVOS, 2007).

Even though government promulgated Statutory Instrument 202 of 1998, Zimbabwe Labour Relations (HIV and AIDS) Regulations, the response at the workplace was slow, especially since it was seen in the early years almost exclusively as a medical problem. For instance, the public-sector policy on HIV and AIDS was launched only in 2005 in response to the severity of the pandemic on the provision of public services. It had emerged that, between 1995 and 2002, the largest number of public employees who took sick leave of up to 90 days was in the 30–49 age group, including professional and technical grades, and that more female than male staff members had left the service on medical grounds. Terminations of service on medical grounds increased from 0.05 per cent in 1995 and peaked at 3.23 per cent in 2001 (Zimbabwe, 2007). As the report concedes, before 2005 the priority given to HIV and AIDS in government ministries was low, as most managers did not consider HIV and AIDS programmes as their core business, while others felt that they were not equipped to take a leading role in HIV and AIDS issues.

### 7.4.6 Overall poverty levels

A study by the Central Statistical Office (Zimbabwe, 1998) suggested that the incidence of poverty in Zimbabwe had increased from 40.4 per cent in 1990/91 to 63.3 per cent by 1995/96. The incidence of extreme poverty increased from 16.7 per cent to 35.7 per cent over the same period.[36]

*PASS II* suggested that poverty in Zimbabwe had increased markedly such that the proportion of the population below the Food Poverty Line increased from 29 per cent in 1995 to 58 per cent in 2003, a 102 per cent increase. The proportion of the population below the Total Consumption Poverty Line (TCPL) increased from 55 per cent in 1995 to 72 per cent in 2003, a 30 per cent increase. Per capita GDP declined from US$720 during 1997–2002 to US$265 by 2008. A higher percentage (71 per cent) of the people were below the TCPL in rural areas than in urban areas (61 per cent) in 2003, a situation which has worsened. Female-headed households experienced a higher incidence of poverty, with 68 per cent below the TCPL compared to 60 per cent for male-headed households. Thus, poverty has 'a rural face and a woman's face'. Furthermore, inequality increased from a Gini coefficient of 0.53 in 1995 to 0.61 in 2003.[37]

Persistent economic decline suggests that the Millennium Development Goals of halving poverty by 2015, and reducing malnutrition in the under-fives by two-thirds to 7 per cent by 2015, will not be achieved, considering that they are predicated on an annual real GDP growth rate of 6.6 per cent beginning in 2002, a far cry from what Zimbabwe has achieved. The *2004 Progress Report* (Zimbabwe, 2004: 20) observes that halving poverty by 2015 is unrealistic, extrapolating that, at real GDP growth rates of 5 per cent, 4 per cent and 3 per cent, poverty would be halved by 2020, 2026 and 2038, respectively. Far from abating, poverty levels are on the increase.

---

[36] Here, the incidence of poverty is measured in terms of the number of households (not people) whose incomes cannot meet the basic requirements for living, and extreme poverty as the number of those that cannot meet basic food requirements.

[37] A Gini coefficient of 0 implies total equality, while that of 1 denotes total inequality.

## 7.5 The Transitional Period, 2009–2010

The virtual collapse in real incomes and the redundancy of collective bargaining left many workers with no options other than joining the informal economy, absconding from work and engaging in survival activities, or emigrating. The public sector was the worst affected as most health centres closed down, while very little teaching and learning occurred in 2008.[38] As most public-sector employees stayed at home, the Ministry of Health and Child Welfare (through the Health Service Board) in conjunction with international partners, developed a human-resources retention scheme, which was applicable to health workers with critical skills in short supply.[39] This entailed payment of a US-dollar-based minimum allowance to enable eligible health workers to come to work. Thanks to this incentive, at least 95 per cent of those previously in post in late 2008 were confirmed back in January 2009 and were eligible for the allowance. In January 2009, this scheme was extended to cover all eligible health workers (see below). To cater for this extension, the funding envelope was enlarged from US$15 million to US$20 million in 2009.

From 1 March 2009, the retention allowance was considered to be a donation in addition to what the government was paying, to be treated as a bonus and not as an entitlement, and applying to Grades C5 and above.[40] The partners agreed to pay a once-off US$60 to all health workers in Grade C4 and below, including cadets in C5, in recognition of their continued importance to the public health sector. The eligible health workers would continue to receive retention allowances subject to confirmation of their being at work and with no record of unauthorized leave of absence in the month prior to their receipt of the allowance. The retention allowance is not taxable: if that happens, the funders will suspend their support. Should any health worker who has been on unauthorized leave of absence accept the allowance, it will be treated as fraud. The allowance will be reviewed in tandem with the availability of funds and changes in government allowances and pay, with input from the Human Resources for Health (HRH) Task Force.

With the adoption of the multiple-currency system in the national budget of 29 January 2009, the government announced that, while civil servants would continue to be paid their salaries in local currency, they would also receive a monthly allowance foreign currency to facilitate their access to a basket of goods and services now being charged in foreign currencies. This was to be done

[38] See Chapter 8.

[39] The participating international partners included the European Commission, the Expanded Support Programme (funded by CIDA, Irish Aid, Norway, SIDA, and DfID), DfID, UNICEF, UNFPA and Australian Aid.

[40] Grades in the public health sector start at A/B, rising to C1–C5, D1–D5, E1–E5, and F and F+.

initially through a voucher system pegged to a basket of goods for a family of six, which the Monetary Policy Statement of 2 February 2009 set at US$100. To circumvent the challenges associated with the voucher system, given the lack of adequate foreign-currency reserves to back it up, the new Minister of Finance announced that all civil servants would be given an allowance of US$100 in hard currency with effect from the end of February 2009.

Following this announcement, 'dormant' civil servants started returning to work. As a result, hospitals that had closed or scaled down their operations re-opened, with the bed occupancy at Harare Hospital rising from 180 patients in March to 576 patients by May 2009. Vacancy rates in the education sector declined from 60 per cent to 35 per cent by mid-June 2009 (Zimbabwe, 2009). In a bid to improve working conditions, the Mid-Term Fiscal Review of July 2009 introduced a modest pay structure for civil servants which recognized grades, albeit initially across only limited differentiated bands, with effect from the end of July 2009. The adjustment amounted to 50 per cent of the US$100 allowance, resulting in an average baseline salary of US$150, which is a far cry from the Poverty Datum Line of around US$500 per month. In the same budget review, the Minister of Finance observed that, at 35 per cent of total expenditures or 13 per cent of GDP,[41] the wage bill is far above international best practices of 30 per cent and 8–10 per cent, respectively. To address this paradox of low salaries leading to an unacceptably high wage bill because of a bloated public sector, the mid-term review argued that 'Government's capacity to accommodate higher remuneration packages would also be enhanced by payroll audits intended to remove ghost workers' (Zimbabwe, 2009: para. 301).[42] The payroll audit is expected to verify the payroll establishment, assess personnel capacities and competencies, and produce the following outputs/outcomes:

- A payroll aligned to the establishment.
- Rectification of all irregularities on the civil-service payroll.
- Strengthening of the systems and mechanisms of enhancing the validity of the payroll.
- A detailed profile of the civil service.
- Recommendations on attraction and retention measures [ibid.: para. 303].

While the decision to undertake the Public Service Payroll and Skills Audit was taken by Cabinet on 21 April 2009, the process started only on 16 November and was expected to be finalized by 18 December 2009; the issue was still not

---

[41] The Mid-Term Fiscal Review of 2010 indicated that the wage bill was 60 per cent of the budget and 15 per cent of GDP (Zimbabwe, 2010).

[42] In her 2009 report, the Comptroller and Auditor-General revealed that 10,277 youths were irregularly employed by the Ministry of Youth, Indigenization and Empowerment.

finalized a year later. Meanwhile, a tripartite study team – involving the Public Service Commission, two representatives of the public-sector unions, the Health Service Board and the ILO – visited South Africa from 16 to 19 November 2009 to study that country's public-sector negotiating framework with a view to strengthening the Joint Negotiating Forum in Zimbabwe. The public-sector negotiating framework in Zimbabwe has experienced serious challenges in that it is advisory, the final word resting with Treasury. Quite often in the past, Treasury would reverse agreed salary increments on the basis that there were no resources, creating bad blood amongst the negotiating parties. In one such instance, the Minister of Public Service, Labour and Social Welfare, Nicholas Goche, argued that

> The uniqueness of public service arrangements worldwide makes it difficult to apply the outcomes of consultative processes wholesomely. It is acknowledged that the fiscal determination of what should constitute the public service remuneration packages in any given year as a percentage of the Gross Domestic Product (GDP) militates against consultations on conditions of service in the public sector.[43]

Collective bargaining in the private sector is hampered by low levels of production, which limit the capacity of companies to pay realistic wages. In addition, the absence of a monetary base undermines recovery efforts that are intricately associated with the rebuilding of labour markets. In this context, deadlocks have become commonplace and resulted in arbitration, but arbitral awards have tended to be unrealistic (either too low or too high), with little regard to the reality on the ground, which creates serious distortions in the labour market.[44]

The process of developing a National Employment Policy Framework, which started during the latter half of 2007, gained momentum when the draft document was validated by key stakeholders in January 2009. Thereafter, it was formally adopted by the Tripartite Negotiating Forum in June 2009 before it was approved by Cabinet in 2010. The framework seeks to mainstream employment creation as a cross-cutting issues in all policies (macro and sectoral), and its implementation will be monitored by the Tripartite Negotiating Forum.

---

[43] The *Business Herald*, 17 October 2005, 4. The Minister of Finance, Dr Herbert Murerwa, reiterated the government's position regarding the sacrosanctity of macroeconomic targets, arguing that 'The current civil service wage bill, at 50 per cent of revenues and 40 per cent of expenditure or 19 per cent of gross domestic product, remains very high and unsustainable. The government finds itself in a paradox to the extent that the wage bill is very high yet civil servants' salaries are very low. Efforts are currently under way to rationalize the civil service, so that civil servants are better remunerated' (*The Herald*, 10 November 2005).

[44] For a detailed analysis of the arbitration system, see Madhuku (2010). While awards from voluntary arbitration (where an arbitrator is agreed on by the parties to the dispute) are, in general, final, those from compulsory arbitration (the arbitrator is appointed by the Minister of Labour) can be appealed against at the Labour Court.

## 7.6 Regulated Flexibility and the Global Decent Work Agenda

While structural adjustment programmes insisted on the pursuit of labour-market flexibility to aid adjustment, it became clear with time that it was associated with greater risks for workers, which had a destabilizing impact. As the Commission on Growth and Development[45] observed in *The Growth Report*, 'While creative destruction [the process through which new industries emerge and older ones disappear] is economically natural, it doesn't feel natural to those displaced in the process. If these casualties of growth are simply disregarded, they will seek to slow the economy's progress' (World Bank, 2008: 44). The Commission further noted (ibid.: 48) that

> Getting the labour market right is vital to both the economics and politics of growth. In too many developing countries, a portion of the population has not enjoyed the benefits of economic advance, and does not anticipate enjoying them in the future. If they are forever blocked from employment, the economy will miss out on their labour and any growth strategy will lose their support.

The International Financial Institutions replaced their SAP policies in September 1999 with Poverty Reduction Strategy Papers, which emphasized the importance of integrating social and economic objectives. This was in line with the resolutions of the World Summit on Social Development held in Copenhagen in 1995 which made the promotion of full employment a priority of economic and social policies.

Thus, contrary to the philosophy underlying the World Bank's 'Doing Business Index' – which ranks countries on the basis of the extent to which the economy is deregulated, including the labour market – evidence suggests that the need to cope with the increased risks in labour markets associated with globalization necessitates social insurance against them (Auer *et al.*, 2008). To reflect and promote this change, the ILO adopted the Decent Work Agenda at its 87th session in June 1999. Decent work is about productive work where rights are protected, generating adequate income, with adequate social protection. It is based on six dimensions: opportunity to work; productive work; freedom at work; equality at work; security at work; and dignity at work.

In line with this new thinking, Millennium Development Goal 8 on global partnerships speaks to the need to 'develop and implement strategies that give young people everywhere a real chance to find decent and productive work'. To implement this initiative, the Youth Employment Network, a global alliance between the UN, World Bank and ILO, was established in 2001 to support countries to develop national action plans on youth employment.

---

[45] This commission was set up by the World Bank to understand and unravel, over a period of two years, the phenomenon of growth. It was made up of nineteen eminent politicians, business leaders and economists; see Chapter 2.

Meanwhile, the Decent Work Agenda was further consolidated by the adoption of the Declaration on Social Justice for a Fair Globalization at the ILO's 97th session in June 2008, which places full and productive employment and decent work at the centre of economic and social policies. It also emphasizes the implementation of the Decent Work Agenda as a cross-cutting issue to be domesticated through Decent Work Country Programmes. The promotion of full and productive decent work was fully embraced by African heads of state and government at their meeting in Ouagadougou in September 2004, where concern was raised at the rising levels of youth unemployment, the failure to treat employment creation as a major objective of economic and social policies, and the inadequacy of current efforts to deal with the challenges of youth unemployment, underemployment and poverty. The Ouagadougou Declaration committed African governments to making employment creation and poverty reduction an explicit and central objective of economic and social policies; regional economic communities were requested to assist countries develop national employment policy frameworks. To concretize its implementation, the social partners (government, labour and business) adopted the Decent Work Agenda in Africa, 2007–2015, at a meeting in Addis Ababa, Ethiopia, in 2007.

Notwithstanding the enhanced recognition of the role of active labour-market policies (ALMPs),[46] there is an awareness that labour-market rigidity is to be avoided, implying a need to balance regulation and flexibility (negotiated flexibility or regulated flexibility or protected flexibility). As pointed out by Auer *et al.*, 'ALMPs are a potentially important weapon in the fight against unemployment and poverty, but produce mixed results' (2008: 2). They are considered to be second-best solutions when compared to regular jobs, but their importance arises in that they create or enhance access to such regular jobs. However, in the absence of adequate regular jobs, or where the match between available jobs and those seeking work is poor, problems arise. Abandoning them altogether is not an option in most developing countries, and hence the issue should be about making them work more effectively to insure against the risks of globalization to employment (ibid.). Instead of existing for their own sake, ALMPs are the microeconomic planks of an employment-oriented macro-economic policy.

---

[46] ALMPs are measures that enhance labour demand and the quality of labour supply. They support employment creation in two basic ways: directly, by job-creation measures (e.g. public works and enterprise creation and hiring subsidies), and indirectly, by improving employability through training and efficient labour exchanges that provide better labour-market information and enhanced job matching. They seek to 'activate' the (re)integration of the unemployed and underemployed into the labour market. They respond to the criticism that pure income replacement (passive measures) might entail disincentives to work once unemployment is of longer duration. Passive labour-market policies involve replacement income (transfer payments) such as unemployment benefits during periods of joblessness or job search. Both labour-market policies intermediate between supply and demand on the labour market, matching labour demand and supply. See Auer *et al.* (2008) for a detailed discussion.

Such employment-oriented macroeconomic policies have to be expansionary, at least in the spending items that concern employment such as public works (broadly incorporating employment-intensive infrastructure creation) and enterprise-creation schemes, as well as labour-market-related education and training measures. Spending on such programmes should be anti-cyclical, high during downturns and low when the economy is in a boom with low unemployment.[47] Essentially therefore, such a policy thrust obviates the restrictiveness of traditional macroeconomic policies that target price stability at the expense of the real economy (Islam, 2003).[48] In this regard, low unemployment is seen not as a labour-market problem but as a development challenge (Heintz, 2008). This is the approach that informs the Decent Work Agenda of the ILO and the Ouaga-dougou declaration referred to above.

Clearly therefore, the current discourse on the labour market is seized with achieving a balance between flexibility and job security (World Bank, 2008). The related concept of 'flexicurity' that was coined in the late 1990s seeks to achieve this balance in the context of the intense competition faced by firms in both domestic and export markets. The term captures the flexibility required by employers to adjust their labour forces as well as the security of the workers (Auer, 2007; de Gobbi, 2007). Flexicurity is often associated with labour-market security, where key elements of security are 'socialized' through policies and programmes administered by the state, such as retraining or unemployment insurance; protection is located outside firms (Auer, 2007; de Gobbi, 2007; Auer *et al.*, 2008). Where security is provided by the employer and policies focus on employment protection rather than transitions, such a system is one of 'job or employment security' and not of 'labour-market security'. In essence, labour-market security is the sum of employment protection in firms and social protection outside the firm. In a globalized economy, the latter is expected to provide a larger share of worker protection than in the closed and regulated economy of the past. Credible and affordable security networks are needed that provide security of both income and employability, and help people get into decent jobs.

An example of an attempt at socializing security are the Social Plan Guidelines gazetted in 1999 by the National Economic Development and Labour Council of South Africa (NEDLAC) as an effective solution for the management of large-scale retrenchments. Their primary objective is to avoid job losses and employment decline whenever possible, and seek to actively manage retrenchments

---

[47] For a detailed discussion of how an employment-friendly macroeconomic policy can be applied at the macro and sectoral levels, see Ehrenpreis (2008). An example in McKinley (2008) cites the instruments that can be used, including fiscal and monetary policies that focus on public investments in economic and social infrastructure where employment-intensive sectors are located, financial policies that facilitate banks to direct credit to SMEs, or trade policies that maintain tariffs to protect domestic food security.

[48] In the traditional macroeconomic framework, real economic performance is subordinated to monetary and inflation targets, being treated as a residual (see Ehrenpreis, 2008).

and to ameliorate their effects on individuals and local economies when large job losses are unavoidable. The plan accepts that the burden of employment decline should not be borne by the affected individuals and regions alone. Instead, it seeks to help reintegrate retrenched people into the economy, and revitalize affected local economies. The Guidelines require that, in the event that a retrenchment in excess of 500 people or 10 per cent of the labour force of a company (whichever is the greater) is proposed within a one-year period, the employer must notify the minister of labour. Where the procedures and codes of the Labour Relations Act have been followed, and large-scale retrenchments are anticipated, assistance may be requested from the Department of Labour, which offers the following services:[49]

a. Delivering information and services to retrenched workers and employers to promote re-absorption of retrenched workers into the labour market. To maximise the potential benefit of the services the parties are encouraged to jointly approach the Department of Labour.

b. The services which will be provided by the Department of Labour are divided into two separate categories, namely:

• Standard generic services offered across the board to employers, groups and individuals without charge.

• When requested by an enterprise facing retrenchments of 500 workers or 10 per cent of the workforce, whichever is greater, the Department of Labour will:

• set up a Retrenchment Response Team (RRT) competent in employment services, human resource development and unemployment insurance fund (UIF). Where necessary services linked to Labour Relations and Occupational Health and Safety will also be included. The RRT will liaise with the enterprise on the request of the workers and employers. The Department of Labour, with both workers' representatives and employers, will form a committee to determine:

i   The type of standard and additional services to be provided to the retrenchees.

ii   The financial resources needed to cover additional services where agreed upon and the extent of resource allocation from each partner.

iii   The time and people needed to offer these services.

iv   The technical resources needed to deliver an effective service.

v   Mechanisms on how to inform retrenchees on the purpose of the Job Advice Centre.

---

[49] <http://www.nedlac.org.za/reports/agreements–reports/archived/1998/social-plan.aspx>.

- A Job Advice Centre (JAC) will be opened on or close to the premises of the enterprise. It is the responsibility of the employers of the enterprise and/or worker representative to find a suitable venue for the JAC as well as for any group meetings which may be agreed, if the enterprise's own premises are not available. Depending on the number of retrenchees and any negotiated agreement between workers, employers and the Department of Labour, the JAC will offer the selected choice of services preferably 5–10 working, days before retrenchees leave the service of the enterprise. Standard as well as additional services will be offered during this time period provided it is practical.

Where there is a large-scale retrenchment which affects fewer than 500 workers, either party may approach the Department of Labour's provincial office or Labour Centre for standard services.

A major criticism of flexicurity is that it might encourage labour-market flexibility, resulting in more volatile employment – failing on security. For a developing country, the challenge is one of finding a source of funding for labour-market security. However, the positive impact of ALMPs makes them worthwhile, as shown in the *OECD Employment Outlook* of 2006, which places the Anglo-Saxon countries, low spenders on labour-market policies, at par with Nordic countries (high spenders) in terms of economic and labour-market performance, but the latter do much better on equity, achieving low levels of poverty and relatively equal income distribution (Auer *et al.*, 2008: 70).

## 7.7 Strategic Objectives and Recovery Policies

### 7.7.1 Strategic objectives and thrusts

The pro-poor growth approach requires that the link between growth and poverty reduction be enhanced through employment creation. The employment intensity of growth is therefore important for growth to be associated with the sustainable reduction of poverty and its eventual eradication. In the context of the dual and enclave structure that informs the Zimbabwean economy, when growth did happen, it left behind the majority of the population, an unsustainable situation that eventually resulted in the crisis that started in 1997. As shown above, the crisis period has further entrenched this dualism, making it even more difficult for growth to be inclusive and poverty-reducing. Against this backdrop, the key strategic objectives for recovery and growth include the following:

- Creating a basis for inclusive (shared) growth by consciously (re)integrating marginalized sectors (informal and communal) and groups (youths, women, people living with disabilities) into the mainstream economy.

- Enhancing the employment intensity of growth.
- Promoting decent employment, including the restoration of rights at work.
- Improving the match between labour demand and supply.

### 7.7.2 Recovery policies and policy measures

*Rebuilding labour markets*

The close relationship between product and labour markets is a stylized one. By implication, the rebuilding of the labour markets is closely related to the recovery of the economy. This therefore implies that, even though the ideals of achieving decent work are understandable, they need to be pursued in tandem with the recovery of the economy. In this regard, while external (push or positive) factors such as achieving the Poverty Datum Line, controlling inflation, comparative bargaining, and others, should continue to inform the collective-bargaining process, it is the internal factors (the permissive factors – ability-to-pay variables) that define the final outcome of collective-bargaining processes. This will help achieve sustainable outcomes that do not exacerbate unemployment or result in inflationary pressures. Whereas the process of destruction can happen quickly, rebuilding is a painstaking process.

In areas such as agriculture, where the structures for negotiating have been politicized, there is need to restructure the National Employment Council so that it reflects the interests of both workers and employers. In the public sector, efforts to create proper structures for genuine collective bargaining are most welcome. A study visit to South Africa during the week 16–19 November 2009 by the stakeholders in the Joint Negotiating Forum was a positive collective-learning process that should culminate in the establishment of collective-bargaining rights in the public sector in Zimbabwe. The involvement and facilitation of the ILO should promote the adoption of best practices in the area of public-sector collective bargaining. Attempts by the ZCTU and EMCOZ to create a common understanding of the challenges during the transitional period will help reduce the conflicts around collective bargaining, which have seen many deadlocks going for arbitration.

Ultimately, the pace of economic recovery will determine the transitional period. Hence it is important for the parties in the Inclusive Government to implement the Global Political Agreement and hasten the recovery process in order to catalyse the rebuilding of labour markets.

*Implementing the Decent Work Country Programme*

In line with the international Decent Work Agenda, Zimbabwe adopted its Country Programme in December 2005 for the period 2006–2007. The social

partners highlighted the following main country priorities for Zimbabwe:
- poverty reduction through employment creation;
- social and labour protection and reduced impact of HIV/AIDS at the workplace;
- enabling environment created through upholding and strengthening social dialogue;
- working out of poverty through promoting gender equality and empowerment.

This agenda is based on Zimbabwe's prioritization of MDG Goal 1 (Poverty), Goal 3 (Empowerment of Women) and Goal 6 (HIV and AIDS); Goal 8 (Developing Global Partnerships for Development) is taken to be cross-cutting. The 2005 Country Programme was later revised, with the implementation extended to 2011 (2007–2011). In this revised version, the themes agreed in 2005 were rephrased as follows:
- employment and poverty;
- social protection and HIV and AIDS at the workplace;
- tripartism, social dialogue and industrial relations;
- gender equality and women empowerment.

### Implementing the National Employment Policy Framework

In fulfilment of its obligations as agreed in Ouagadougou in 2004, and in line with its country Decent Work Agenda, Zimbabwe drafted its National Employment Policy Framework, which was validated by the social partners at a stakeholders' workshop held on 9–10 January 2009 and at a workshop organized by the Tripartite Negotiating Forum held on 27 July 2009. The draft framework is now awaiting the approval of Cabinet.

Essentially, the National Employment Policy Framework seeks to promote employment-intensive growth, facilitate the integration of the hitherto marginalized sectors (informal and communal) and groups (youths, women, and people living with disabilities) into the mainstream of the economy. It also seeks to mainstream employment creation across all policies, macro and sectoral.

Such an integrative and transformative agenda focuses on strengthening the backward and forward linkages through the exploitation of value chains and value systems among firms and sectors along the lines developed by Porter (1980). The value chain disaggregates a firm or sector into its strategically relevant activities, and a firm or sector's value chain is embedded in a larger stream of activities, the value system. Suppliers have value chains (upstream value) that create and deliver purchased inputs used in a firm or industry's chain. Thus, the extent of integration into activities plays a key role in broadening the scope of a firm or industry's influence. Thus, establishing firms and sectors with co-ordinated value chains can lead to a broad-based, more inclusive and employment-intensive growth path. Various business-linkage, mentorship and internship programmes aim to achieve more inclusive outcomes than is the case with individual firm or sector approaches. Such coalitions, involving co-ordinating or sharing value chains with partners, broaden the effective scope of the firm's or sector's chain, which is ultimately more integrative and employment-intensive.

To facilitate the matching of labour demand and supply, the employment framework proposes use of an active labour-market approach, with some of the following interventions (ILO, 2005: 24–5):

*Employability*
- Innovative, gender-sensitive training and skills-development programmes, such as apprenticeship programmes, mentorship, business incubators, promoting a culture of entrepreneurship, etc.
- Vocational training programmes designed and implemented in partnership with the private sector.
- Basic education programmes for school dropouts.

*Employment creation*
- SME and co-operatives promotion and development.
- Labour-based public works.
- Business linkages.
- Self-employment programmes.
- Service provision in fields such as HIV/AIDS, waste management and environmental protection, through public–private partnerships.
- Community-based service provision, such as access to micro-credit.

*Equal opportunity*
- Promoting the employment of young women.
- Programmes targeting people with disabilities and other vulnerable groups.

The National Employment Policy Framework also addresses the need for a labour-market information system, leveraging pro-poor employment-intensive infrastructure, promotion of SMEs, the restructuring and rationalization of the social dialogue structures to enhance efficiency and effectiveness,[50] the resuscitation of the National Productivity Institute,[51] and the creation of an integrated, co-ordinated and inclusive approach to labour administration, among others.

It is imperative that government, in conjunction with its social partners, fully implements the Decent Work Programme and the National Employment Policy Framework. These instruments should be disseminated widely for greater impact and inclusiveness.

---

[50] The Tripartite Negotiating Forum, the National Economic Consultative Forum, and the National Economic Council proposed in the GPA.

[51] See Chapter 10.

*Legislative reforms*

A plethora of draconian pieces of legislation have been enacted that undermine social and industrial relations and violate the rights of working people. These include the Public Order and Security Act, the Access to Information and Protection of Privacy Act, the Criminal Law (Codification and Reform) Act, and aspects of the amended Labour Act. These should, where applicable, be repealed or amended so that they are in line with international practice.[52] In addition, basic human and trade-union rights, including socio-economic rights, should also be included in the new constitution under the Bill of Rights.

Furthermore, the alternative dispute-resolution system should be reformed to enhance transparency and accountability by, among other things, creating an independent commission for conciliation and arbitration, as is the case in South Africa, Lesotho, Swaziland and Botswana (Madhuku, 2010).

# References

Amanor-Wilks, D. (ed.) 2001. *Zimbabwe's Farm Workers: Policy Dimension* (Lusaka: Panos).

Arrighi, G. and J. Saul 1973. *Essays on the Political Economy of Africa* (New York: Monthly Review Press).

Ashenfelter, O. and D. Card (eds.) 1999. *Handbook of Labor Economics, Volume 3B* (Amsterdam: Elsevier).

Auer, P. 2007. 'In Search of Optimal Labour Market Institutions' (Geneva: ILO, Employment Analysis and Research Unit, Economic and Labour Market Papers No. 3).

Auer, P., Ü. Efendioğlu and J. Leschke 2008. *Active Labour Market Policies around the World: Coping with the Consequences of Globalization* (Geneva: ILO).

Collier, P. 1995. 'Resource allocation and credibility', in *Regional Trade and Trade Liberalization in Sub-Saharan Africa* (Nairobi: AERC).

CZI 2007. *Manufacturing Sector Survey, 2007* (Harare: Confederation of Zimbabwe Industries).

CZI 2008. *Manufacturing Sector Survey, 2008* (Harare: Confederation of Zimbabwe Industries).

De Gobbi, M. S. 2007. 'Flexibility and Security in Labour Markets of Developing Countries: In Search of Decent Work for All' (Geneva: ILO, Employment Policy Department, Employment Policy Papers No. 6).

Ehrenpreis, Dag 2008. *Poverty in Focus*, 16: 'Jobs, Jobs, Jobs: The Policy Challenge'.

---

[52] While the Ministry of Labour and Social Services had indicated that these would be prioritized under the Inclusive Government's 100-day plan, which ended in August 2009, this had not been done by the end of 2010.

Ehrenpreis, Dag 2007. *Poverty in Focus*, 10: 'Analysing and Achieving Pro-Poor Growth'.

Fallon, P. R. and R. E. B. Lucas 1993. 'Job security regulations and the dynamic demand for industrial labour in India and Zimbabwe', *Journal of Development Economics*, 40.

Fox, L. and M. Sekkel 2008. 'Working out of poverty: Job creation in Africa', in Dag Ehrenpreis, *Poverty in Focus*, 16: 'Jobs, Jobs, Jobs: The Policy Challenge'.

Gann, L. H. 1965. *A History of Southern Rhodesia* (London: Chatto & Windus).

Ghose, A. K., N. Majid and C. Ernst 2008. *The Global Employment Challenge* (Geneva: ILO).

Harris, P. S. 1977. 'The wage and occupational structure of the Zimbabwean economy', *South African Labour Bulletin*, 3(5).

Heintz, J. 2006. 'Globalisation, Economic Policy and Employment: Poverty and Gender Implications' (Geneva: ILO, Employment Policy Unit, Employment Strategy Department, Employment Strategy Papers No. 3).

Heintz, J. 2008. 'Reintroducing Employment into Macroeconomic Policy', *Poverty in Focus* (December), 16: Jobs, Jobs, Jobs: The Policy Challenge, 18–19.

Horton S, R. Kanbur and D. Mazumdar 1991. 'Labour Markets in An Era of Adjustment: An Overview' (Washington, DC: The World Bank, PRE Working Paper Series, WPS 694).

ILO 1999. Decent Work, Report of the Director-General, International Labour Conference, 87th Session, Geneva.

ILO 2005. *Report of the Southern Africa Sub-Regional Conference on Youth Employment: The Youth Employment Challenge in Southern Africa: Policy Responses and Programmes Targeting Young Women and Men at National and Sub-Regional Level, 17-19 October, ILO-SRO.* <http://www.ilo.org/wcmsp5/groups/public/–ed_emp/–emp_policy/–invest/documents/meetingdocument/wcms_asist_8055.pdf>.

Islam, I. 2003. 'Avoiding the Stabilization Trap: Towards a Macroeconomic Policy Framework for Growth, Employment and Poverty Reduction (Geneva: ILO, Employment Sector, Employment Paper No. 53).

Kakwani, N. S., S. Khandker and H. H. Son 2004. 'Pro-Poor Growth: Concepts and Measurement, with Country Case Studies' (Washington, DC: International Poverty Centre, Working Paper Number 1).

Kanyenze, G. 2009. 'Labour Markets and the Rebuilding of Human Capital' (Harare: UNDP, Comprehensive Economic Recovery in Zimbabwe, Working Paper 3).

Kapsos, S. 2005. 'The Employment Intensity of Growth: Trends and Macroeconomic Determinants' (Geneva: ILO, Employment Strategy Department, Employment Trends Unit, Employment Strategy Papers No. 12).

Lewis, W. A. 1954. 'Economic development with unlimited supplies of labour' *The Manchester School*, 22, 139–91.

Lisk, F. 2002. 'The Labour Market and Employment Implications of HIV/ AIDS' (Geneva: ILO, ILO/AIDS Working Paper Number 1).

Loewenson, R. 1992. *Modern Plantation Agriculture: Corporate Wealth and Labour Squalor* (London: Zed Books).

Lucas, S., and P. Timmer 2005. *Connecting the Poor to Economic Growth: Eight Key Questions* (Washington, DC: Centre for Global Development, CGD Brief).

Luebker, M. 2008a. 'Decent Work and Informal Employment: A Survey of Workers in Glen View (Harare: ILO Sub-Regional Office for Southern Africa, Issues Paper No. 33).

Luebker, M. 2008b. 'Employment, Unemployment and Informality in Zimbabwe: Concepts and Data for Coherent Policy-making' (Harare: ILO Sub-Regional Office for Southern Africa, Issues Paper No. 32).

Madhuku, L. 2010. 'Audit of the Alternative Dispute Resolution System in Zimbabwe', paper commissioned by the ILO, Harare.

McKinley, T. 2008. 'Structural policies for poverty-reducing employment', in Dag Ehrenpreis, *Poverty in Focus*, 16: 'Jobs, Jobs, Jobs: The Policy Challenge'.

Mhone, G. 1999. 'Towards a National Employment Policy for Zimbabwe: A Proposed Policy Framework', discussion paper prepared for ILO/SAMAT.

Osmani, S. R. 2004. 'The Employment Nexus Between Growth and Poverty: An Asian Perspective', a report prepared for the Swedish International Development Agency (SIDA) Stockholm and the United Nations Development Programme (UNDP), New York <http://www.ipc-undp.org/emprego/paper/asia.pdf>.

Palmer, R. 1977. *Land and Racial Domination in Rhodesia* (London: Heinemann).

Phimister, I. R. 1976. 'The reconstruction of the Southern Rhodesian gold mining industry', 1903–10', *Economic History Review*, 29(3), 465–81.

Riddell, Roger C. 1979. 'Alternative development strategies for Zimbabwe', *Zimbabwe Journal of Economics* 1(3).

Rutherford, B. 1996. 'Another side to rural Zimbabwe: Social constructs and administration of farm workers in Urungwe District, 1940s', *Journal of Southern African Studies*, 23(1).

SAfAIDS and HIVOS 2007. *Managing HIV and AIDS in the World of Work: Experiences from Southern Africa* (Harare: Southern Africa HIV and AIDS Information Dissemination Service and HIVOS).

Schiller, C. 1990. 'Government pay policies and structural adjustment', *African Development Review*, 2(1).

Sibanda, A. E. 1992. 'The Political Economy of Zimbabwe: Focus on the Creation of a Proletariat: Implications for the Labour Movement' (Harare: ZIDS, A Discussion Paper Number 15).

Stoneman, C. and L. Cliffe 1989. *Zimbabwe: Politics, Economics and Society* (London: Pinter).

UN 2005. *Report of the Fact-Finding Mission to Zimbabwe to assess the Scope and Impact of Operation Murambatsvina by the UN Special Envoy on Human Settlements Issues in Zimbabwe, Mrs. Anna Kajumulo Tibaijuka* (New York: United Nations).

World Bank 1987. *Zimbabwe: A Strategy for Sustained Growth* (Washington, DC: World Bank).

World Bank 1989. *Sub-Saharan Africa: From Crisis to Sustainable Growth* (Washington, DC: World Bank).

World Bank 1997. *Country Assistance Strategy for Zimbabwe* (Washington, DC: World Bank, Africa Region, Southern Africa Department).

World Bank 2005a. *World Development Report, 2006: Equity and Development* (New York: Oxford University Press).

World Bank 2005b. *Economic Growth in the 1990s: Learning from a Decade of Reform* (Washington, DC: World Bank).

World Bank 2008. *The Growth Report: Strategies for Sustained Growth and Inclusive Development* (Washington, DC: World Bank, Commission on Growth and Development).

Zimbabwe 2004. *Zimbabwe Millennium Development Goals: 2004 Progress Report* (Harare: UNDP).

Zimbabwe 1981a. *National Manpower Survey: Vol. 1* (Harare: Ministry of Manpower Planning and Development).

Zimbabwe 1981b. *Report of the Commission of Inquiry into Incomes, Prices and Conditions of Service* [Chairman R. Riddell] (Harare: Government Printer).

Zimbabwe 1986. *First Five-Year National Development Plan, 1986–1990* (Ministry of Finance, Economic Planning and Development, 2 vols.)

Zimbabwe 1989. *The Promotion of Investment: Policy and Regulations* (Harare: Government Printer).

Zimbabwe 1998. *Poverty in Zimbabwe* (Harare: Central Statistical Office).

Zimbabwe 2006a. *2004 Labour Force Survey* (Harare: Central Statistical Office).

Zimbabwe 2006b. *Poverty Assessment Study Report* (Harare: Ministry of Public Service, Labour and Social Welfare).

Zimbabwe 2007. 'Public Service HIV and AIDS Workshop Programme' (Harare: Public Service Commission).

Zimbabwe 2009. *Mid-Term Fiscal Review* (Harare: Ministry of Finance).

Zimbabwe Institute 2007. *The Labour Market and Sustainable Growth and Transformation in Zimbabwe* (Cape Town: Zimbabwe Institute).

## Chapter 8

# Education and Training

## 8.1 Introduction

This chapter looks at education and training provision in Zimbabwe in historical perspective. It makes a distinction between education and training, even though in practice these are a continuum. At the level of education, the chapter explores the extent to which it meets the international norms and standards of availability, accessibility, acceptability and adaptability. However, to meet the skill needs of economies, societies and individuals, national training systems must be:

- Effective: offer meaningful, quality skills development, that avoids time-serving and irrelevant training.
- Efficient: avoid high-cost, inefficient provision.
- Competitive: to counter supply-driven training tendencies and facilitate the development of training effectiveness and efficiency.[1]
- Flexible: technically able in the short term to change the scope and direction of outputs (training provision), if necessary.
- Responsive: designed to be responsive to the changing demands of the market and the economy [Ziderman, 2003: 24].

The chapter examines education and training provision in terms of the four development phases in Zimbabwe – the first decade of independence (1980–1990), the ESAP period (1991–1996), the crisis period (1997–2008), and the transitional period (since 2009) – and provides some recommendations on the way forward.

## 8.2 The Concepts and Roles of Education and Training

Education and training are generally distinguished by the competencies taught – how general or specific these are. Programmes that aim to enhance competencies (such as literacy) that are useful in all occupations or are not focused on occupational effects are considered academic or general. Those that convey competencies useful only within a single firm or within a narrowly defined occupation are denoted as training. Another criterion that distinguishes education from training is the intention of the programme: general education does not prepare individuals for particular occupations, while vocational education and

[1] Supply-driven systems are dominated and controlled by line ministries in terms of both provision and funding, with limited participation of other key stakeholders (e.g. employers, employees, students and parents).

training clearly do. In practice, however, education and training exist along a continuum, with training more specific and more vocationally focused than education.

More generally, education tends to last much longer than training, it is generally open to all rather than restricted to specific groups, it provides a relatively standardized form of classroom-based teaching, and it takes place in well-developed institutions (e.g. schools). In most countries, education is administered by ministries of education. Training programmes are more likely supervised by labour or employment ministries, and are more concerned with labour markets.[2] In practice, therefore, education and training are often sharply divided by the public institutions that support them (Grubb & Ryan, 1999).

It is increasingly acknowledged that people's skills and capabilities, and investment in education and training (human capital), are critical for growth and development (World Bank, 2006; 2009). Human capital, the stock of productive skills and technical knowledge embodied in labour, refers to the acquired and useful abilities of all people to prepare them for the world of work. The concept of human capital goes beyond knowledge and skills to encompass attitudinal and behavioural traits (motivation, persistence, self-discipline and self-confidence), as well as morals and ethics which define good citizenship. This also includes social skills such as teamwork, the ability to negotiate conflict and resist peer pressure, which should be nurtured at an early age (World Bank, 2006: 72).

Skills and training stimulate economic competitiveness, raise productivity and incomes, and hence play an important role in poverty reduction (Grubb & Ryan, 1999; Ziderman, 2003). Yet concerns about the quality and relevance of education and training coincide with increased demand for advanced skills (e.g. problem-solving abilities). The framework connecting growth to poverty reduction emphasizes the importance of education and training, and of skills formation (Fig. 1). This is so because the poor need skills and assets in order to participate in and benefit from economic growth (World Bank, 2005; 2006; 2009).

In this regard, public investment in the productive capacity of the poor is critical to poverty reduction. This is so because personal and household livelihoods, and the potential to improve them, are defined by less-tangible assets that allow the poor to participate in and benefit from economic growth – their levels of education and health. For instance, education plays a key role, if not the most important role, in allowing farmers to increase their productivity and workers to transition from agriculture to other rural economic activities or from the informal to formal sector (Jonasson, 2008).

---

[2] In the case of Zimbabwe, the Ministry of Higher and Tertiary Education has been responsible for training since 1988.

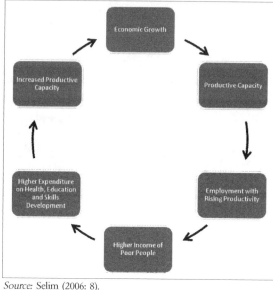

*Source:* Selim (2006: 8).

**Fig. 8.1: Virtuous cycle of links between growth, employment and poverty reduction**

It has been found that, in many poor countries, people with just one additional year of schooling earn ten per cent higher wages. Evidence also suggests that no country has ever achieved continuous and rapid growth without reaching an adult literacy rate of at least 40 per cent. With education, people are also far better able to prevent disease and to use health services effectively. For example, young people between the ages of 15 and 24 years who have completed primary education are less than half as likely to contract HIV as those who have little or no schooling (Lucas and Timmer, 2005).

It has been shown that education is an important empowering tool for gender equity (Zimbabwe, 2007). Improved female education and earnings levels are associated with falling fertility levels, lower infant-mortality rates, and increased investment in the education of future generations, all of which have positive impacts on economic growth. Since the majority of farmers in the developing world are women, greater female education leads to more productive farming and has particularly high returns in other areas, leading to lower fertility rates, lower infant-mortality levels, and higher education rates for the next generation. Female literacy also accounted for over 40 per cent of the global decline in malnutrition between 1970 and 1995 (Lucas and Timmer, 2005; World Bank, 2006).

Furthermore, new technological developments are meaningless if skills are in short supply, implying that there are significant synergies between new knowledge and human capital. As the 2007 *World Development Report* acknowledges, increased availability of skilled and educated workers induces faster skill-intensive technological change. Investment-climate surveys suggest that more than a fifth of firms in diverse developing countries cite inadequate skills as a major obstacle to their operations (World Bank, 2006). In a historical context, education and training have accompanied major advances in technological developments. In fact, all countries that have achieved significant economic growth over sustained periods – such as Japan, the Asian Tigers and, recently, China and India – overcame a lack of natural resources by investing in human capital. An important attribute of these countries is not only the high levels of education and training attained but the strong ethical and behavioural attitudes that resulted in a workforce that is hardworking and committed to work. In Africa, the education deficit still looms large.

Given its nature as a merit good, education is often seen as an empowerment or socio-economic right.[3] Thus, the right to education is enshrined in various international instruments:

- Universal Declaration of Human Rights, Article 26.
- International Covenant on Economic, Social and Cultural Rights.
- Committee on Economic, Social and Cultural Rights: General Comment 13: The Right to Education.
- International Convention on the Elimination of All Forms of Racial Discrimination.
- International Convention on the Right of the Child and Against Discrimination in Education.
- African Charter on Human and Peoples' Rights, Article 17.

Education also plays a critical transformational role as it raises the consciousness of a people and mobilizes them for the national agenda. The consumption aspect of education was long recognized as an asset for any society. Having an education is a good thing in itself. Better-educated citizens are better placed to participate in the affairs of their countries than their less-educated counterparts (Becker, 1964). Critically, therefore, education is not only acquired formally, as traditional norms and practices provide a useful foundation for primary socialization. These provide the intangible traits that define acceptable behaviour, norms and practices in any society (*ubuntu*). Other forms of non-formal education also provide second chances to those that might have missed opportunities or were left out for some reason. For instance, economic-literacy programmes create a capacity for enhanced citizen participation in economic-policy formulation, which is now a requirement for the national ownership of development programmes.

---

[3] A merit good is a good that, if left to the private-sector market mechanism, would be under-produced.

## 8.3 Education and Training Provision in Zimbabwe, 1980–2009

### 8.3.1 The state of education and training at independence

In line with the policy of separate development that had characterized the colonial period, a dual education system existed at Zimbabwe's independence, one for blacks and one for whites.[4] This was meant to ensure that there was no competition between blacks and whites in any sphere of life and to create and maintain an impoverished reservoir of cheap labour. The poor education for blacks was meant to block mobility that would threaten the doctrine of white supremacy. Thus, right from colonization, the education of blacks was left to missionaries. It was not until the 1940s that government participation in black education emerged, so missionaries bore the greater responsibility for black education throughout the colonial period, though Native Commissioners were empowered to withdraw the leases of schools that were suspected of promoting 'feelings of ill will or hostility against the State' (Zvobgo, 1987: 321).

From the early stages of colonization, the thinking was that African education should not be purely academic but should contain a fair degree of elements of vocational education to guarantee the existence of a large pool of cheap, un-skilled, uneducated and semi-skilled black labour.[5] African education was geared towards promoting manual work, and hence a culture of servitude (functionaries, and not competitors). Education for blacks was seen by the government to be closely related to broader issues of so-called 'community development', hence the focus on 'practical' subjects. The policy was meant to ensure 'the development of the native in such a way that he will come as little as possible into conflict or competition with the white man, socially, economically or politically' (Riddell, 1980, quoted in Raftopoulos, 1987: 276). The argument was that formal academic education was not relevant to the needs of African development in the rural areas, and that financial resources were insufficient to provide adequate facilities for a large African population. In addition, there was immense pressure on the administration from the white population for protection against competition from blacks. In this constraining framework, Africans were held to benefit more from industrial than academic education.

As the Chief Native Commissioner advised in 1918, 'the native should be trained not so much as a competitor with the white man in the business of life but as a useful auxiliary to help in the progress of the country' (quoted in Zvobgo, 1987: 322). To advance this practical focus, two notable institutions, Domboshawa and Tjolotjo (now Tsholotsho), were established in 1921 and

---

[4] An extensive discussion of the colonial education system appears in Zvobgo (1987), from which much of the information in this section is drawn.

[5] As was the norm during the colonial period, the terms African and black were used interchangeably, as were European and white.

1922, respectively, to promote industrial education for blacks to operate and survive in the confines of the Tribal Trust Lands (now Communal Lands). The plan was to 'stimulate effort amongst the people, to put purpose into their lives and to develop such skills in industries that [did] not offer direct competition to Europeans' (Keigwin, 1921, quoted in Zvobgo, 1987: 323). Hence, the courses offered were outside the European occupational structure.

On the pretext of limited resources, African education was not compulsory, and most blacks had to walk long distances to school. Meanwhile, in 1930, under the Compulsory Education Act, education became compulsory for all white children between the ages of seven and fifteen, and scholarships were provided at primary and secondary levels, while blacks had to pay for their education. As the first Premier of the Federation of Rhodesia and Nyasaland, Godfrey Huggins, noted in 1953, the only partnership he could envisage between blacks and whites was that of horse and rider. Things worsened during the era of the Rhodesian Front (RF) government, 1965–79, as central government took control of all aspects of European administration and development, leaving African district councils, with limited powers and resources, responsible for all African affairs, a principle that was also applied in the sphere of education.

Soon after coming to power, the RF government introduced a system of Community Development, under which the government proposed complete transfer of the development and administration of primary education from missionary churches to African local councils. The idea was to make Africans responsible for their own education and development in line with the RF's policy of separate development. After 1967, no mission church was allowed to establish a new primary school in rural areas; only local authorities could do so. The New Education Plan of 1966 introduced radical policy changes in the selection process into secondary education. Only 12.5 per cent of all Africans completing primary education each year would be allowed to proceed to academic secondary education (F1), and 37.5 per cent were to be admitted to the F2 vocational secondary education, a system of bottleneck screening.[6] The remaining 50 per cent were left without any provision of secondary education within the formal school system. In the past those that failed in a given year could apply the next year.

F2 secondary education had a stigma as it was deemed suitable for those considered unable to cope with academic work. This type of education was offered only to blacks and was perceived to be inferior to both the F1 stream and the technical and vocational system being run at the Salisbury Polytechnic

---

[6] The F2 secondary education stream was introduced following the Report of the Education Commission of 1962, chaired by Prof. A.V. Judges, starting with Msengezi Secondary School in 1966, introducing a purely practical curriculum in secondary education which ran parallel to the academic and more prestigious F1 stream.

and Bulawayo Technical College for Europeans, Asians and Coloureds. It was also a dead-end system in that its products could not proceed with education after their four-year secondary education. Graduates from the F2 stream were meant to return to the 'reserves', where they would use the skills acquired to develop their communities. As a result, teachers, parents and pupils resented it. Consequently, between 1966 and 1971, out of the projected 300 F2 schools, only 21 were operative and only 3,807 students had enrolled. Furthermore, government expenditure on African education was reduced from 8.6 per cent in 1965 to 2 per cent in 1967. Thus, the state of African education under the RF was depressing as the government curtailed its expansion. In a bid to protect the privileges of whites, an Education Act was passed in 1979 that adopted a zoning selection system whereby African children were barred from enrolling in Group A schools in areas where they did not reside. The Secretary for Education was given wide-ranging powers to restrict the majority of blacks to schools within their townships.

Thus, at the advent of independence, it was noted that 25 per cent of black children did not start school, while over 60 per cent of those that started school did not complete full primary education, and only 4 per cent completed four years of secondary education (Riddell, 1979). Per capita expenditure on education was as low as Z$40 for blacks compared to Z$450 for whites (Pakkiri, 1989). Expenditure at primary-school level was such that, on average, white students received twenty times more resources than blacks (World Bank, 1995).

The area of skills formation did not fare any better, as the economy relied on white immigrants for formally skilled labour, which seriously limited the development of vocational/technical training in the country.[7] The Salisbury and Bulawayo technical colleges were characterized by low (mainly white) enrolment and were not intended to provide the institutional technical training to service the economy in any comprehensive manner. Luveve Technical College in Bulawayo, which had been established to produce black skilled workers, was closed and its equipment was given to Salisbury Polytechnic because it was regarded as competing with white colleges, creating distortions in occupational roles in industry. The apprenticeship scheme, which was a central aspect of the skills-development process, was reserved for whites, with intakes highly controlled to ensure the continuity of a skilled 'labour aristocracy'. King (1990) observes that restrictions on intakes resulted from the pressure applied by the white, skilled unions, which kept intakes at an average level of only 1,000 per year in the period before independence.

As a result, at independence, blacks accounted for only 36 per cent of all

---

[7] Issues of human-resources development during the colonial period are discussed extensively in Raftopoulos (1987) and Ministry of Higher and Tertiary Education (2006), from which this discussion draws.

professional, technical and related staff, and only 24 per cent of managerial and administrative personnel (Zimbabwe, 1981). The limited stock of human capital was exacerbated by the skills drain that occurred towards independence, with the economy losing 15 per cent of white professionals and technical workers over the two-year period 1978-1979 (Riddell, 1979). Blacks had not received the necessary training and experience to adequately fill the yawning skill gaps so created.

Thus, the pattern of labour utilization and development during the colonial period includes:

- Reliance on imported white skills and limited training of blacks to ensure there was no competition to white skills.
- Skilled unions limiting the numbers of formally skilled labour on the market to create artificial shortages and maintain high salary premiums.
- Under-categorization of black skills, job reservation, and underutilization of black skills to protect white skills and engender an impression of a shortage of skills (and with this the indispensability of white skills).
- Serious wage/salary differentials.
- Reliance on imported skills undermined the comprehensive development of apprenticeship training and technical colleges, even though the Apprenticeship Training System had been introduced in 1934.
- Low enrolment at tertiary level, with low intakes in the technical areas.

Thus, at independence in 1980, Zimbabwe had a racially divided technical and vocational education and training system, and an inferior one for blacks that co-existed with that for whites, whose standard was benchmarked against the internationally acclaimed City and Guilds system of the UK, entrenching a dual and enclave outlook. The shortage of skills was used to forestall any radical policy agenda at independence on the strength that such an approach would trigger an exodus of white, skilled personnel. Precisely because of this, the far-reaching reforms undertaken at the advent of independence were designed to transform the inherited education and training system so that it served the interests of the majority.

## 8.3.2 Primary and secondary education provision, 1980–2009

### The first decade of independence, 1980–1990

The new government committed itself to democratizing the education system such that education was treated as a basic human right. The racially based F2 schools were phased out and converted into conventional schools in 1981. While the underlying idea of redressing the racial overtones associated with the F2 system is understandable, however, an opportunity to develop technical and vocational education using the framework already in place was lost.

The F2 system was replaced by the concept of Education with Production that had been experimented with in the camps during the liberation struggle. As a result, Zimbabwe Foundation for Education with Production (ZIMFEP) schools were established, whose curricula combined theory with practice. However, with time, ZIMFEP schools moved towards the conventional (academic) system, ostensibly to enable students in this stream to compete with others for A-level and university education. In addition, government adopted a policy of universal primary education, making basic education a right for all. Primary education was made free in September 1980.

Meanwhile, management of the education system was decentralized to the district council level, with community participation provided through School Development Committees. Even though government managed to remove the explicit forms of elitism, subtle aspects have remained to this day, such as the Group A, B and C ('Upper Tops' in rural areas) systems, reinforced by zoning, which implies that the best educational opportunities remain the preserve of the elites.[8] Hence, the colonial class structure persists as Group A schools continue to be elite institutions for the privileged, while Group B schools continue to cater for urban blacks and Group C for rural communities. Private schools and colleges also emerged after independence, charging high fees, and became a new haven for the elites. Financial discrimination has therefore replaced the racial discrimination of the colonial era, achieving the same result of creating enclaves in education provision. Group A schools are better resourced, with educational facilities such as textbooks, writing materials, and superior library and sporting facilities inherited from the past, better-trained and -qualified teachers and much lower pupil–teacher ratios. It is the Group B and C schools that have taken the greatest burden of overcrowding and inadequate resources as they struggle to cope with high enrolments.

Following the democratization and expansion of education provision, the number of primary schools in Zimbabwe increased by 88.7 per cent from 2,401 in 1979 to 4,530 in 1990. During the same period, enrolments in primary schools increased by 242.1 per cent, from 619,586 to 2,119,881.[9] An important development during the period of interventionist policies was the improvement in the gender-parity ratio in enrolments, from 90.8 in 1980 to 97.5 by 1990.[10] The number of teachers at primary-school level increased with enrolments, rising

---

[8] Primary schools in rural areas are now referred to as P3 schools, those in high-density urban areas as P2, while those in low-density urban areas as P1. Likewise, S3 secondary schools are located in rural areas, S2 in high-density urban areas and S1 in low-density urban areas (Zimbabwe, 2007).

[9] Unpublished data from the Ministry of Education, Sport, Arts and Culture.

[10] The gender-parity ratio is obtained by dividing female enrolment by male enrolment, and multiplying the result by 100.

by 114 per cent from 28,455 in 1980 to 60,886 by 1990.[11] The gender-parity ratio in teaching staff at primary-school level improved (with annual variations) from 60.9 in 1981 to 64.8 in 1990, averaging 68.6 over that period.

The number of secondary schools increased by 754.2 per cent, from 177 in 1979 to 1,512 in 1990, with the enrolments rising by 915.9 per cent from 66,215 to 672,656 during the same period. The gender-parity ratio of enrolments increased marginally, from 76.4 in 1980 to 76.5 in 1990, averaging 71.1 for the period; this was influenced by the deterioration in the ratio between 1981 and 1986.[12] Teaching staff at secondary-school level increased by 632.8 per cent, from 3,730 in 1980 to 27,332 in 1990, while the gender-parity ratio declined from 57.6 to 40.9 over the same time.

Secondary education witnessed greater expansion in the first five years of independence than during the whole period of colonial rule (Zvobgo, 1987). Such expansion strained resources – financial, human, infrastructural, teaching and learning – and could no longer be sustained under conditions of anaemic growth. The average teacher–pupil ratio of 1:40 during the period 1980–1990 was well above the recommended level of 1:28, and hence government resorted to using untrained teachers.

## The ESAP period, 1991–1996

In the absence of a strategy to deal with school-leaver unemployment, expanding education provision without addressing the labour absorptive capacity of the economy proved inadequate. Thus, there emerged a conflict between the political imperatives to democratize education provision and the strictures created by lacklustre economic performance, implying a need for education planning to go hand in hand with economic expansion. Faced with this stark reality, government adopted an economic structural adjustment programme (ESAP) in 1991, on the recommendation of the IMF and World Bank, in a bid to kick-start the economy and create jobs.

Substantial cuts in social expenditure, especially on education and health, were implemented during the ESAP period. As part of the strategy to reduce the budget deficit, ESAP sought to cut the budget for education from 9.2 per cent of GDP in 1990 to 8.7 per cent by 1995. Furthermore, cost-recovery and cost-sharing was introduced in a bid to diversify the sources of funding for social services, and to reflect the reduced role of the state that informed the ESAP strategy. In line with this thinking, school fees, which had been abolished at primary-school level at independence, were reintroduced in urban areas and for

---

[11] To deal with the shortage of teachers, government introduced an in-service teacher training programme, the Zimbabwe Integrated National Teacher Education Course (ZINTEC) with support from UNICEF in January 1981.

[12] Unpublished data from the Ministry of Education, Sport, Arts and Culture.

all secondary schools in 1992, with exemptions for children from households earning less than Z$400 per month, at a time when the Poverty Datum Line for a family of six was Z$593. This was done during the severe drought of 1992 when most families needed support.

The idea was to shift from a system of blanket subsidization towards targeted assistance for the poor through the Social Dimensions of Adjustment programme. As things turned out, the measures to mitigate the social impact of ESAP failed, as the programme was implemented belatedly in 1993, was highly centralized in Harare with weak structures, poor targeting that did not reach the intended beneficiaries, and limited resources (ZCTU, 1996). A marked decline in education expenditure as share of GDP and total government expenditure is evident during the ESAP period (Table 8.1). Furthermore, the bulk of the allocations (90 per cent for primary education) went to wages and salaries alone.

**Table 8.1: Education expenditure as a share of GDP and total expenditure**

|  | Education expenditure as a percentage of GDP | Education expenditure as a percentage of total government expenditure |
|---|---|---|
| 1980 | 1.8 | 10.3 |
| 1985 | 3.1 | 15.8 |
| 1990 | 1.9 | 16.9 |
| 1995 | 0.7 | 16.3 |
| 1996 | 0.5 | 15.8 |

*Source:* Dhliwayo (2001: 18).

The annual average growth rate of enrolments at primary-school level improved from -0.1 per cent for the total, -0.4 per cent for boys and 0.3 per cent for girls during the period 1985-90 to 2.8 per cent, 2.9 per cent and 2.7 per cent, respectively, during 1991-96. On the other hand, the annual average growth rates in enrolments at secondary-school level decelerated from 8.4 per cent for the total, 7.6 per cent for boys and 9.7 per cent for girls during 1985-90 to 2 per cent, 1.1 per cent and 3.1 per cent, respectively, during 1991-96. Studies have suggested a higher rate of drop-outs among girls, particularly at Grade 1 level (Dhliwayo, 2001).

However, the gender-parity ratios in enrolment at primary-school level improved from an average of 94.4 during 1980-90 to 96.5 during the ESAP period (97 by 1996) and from 71.1 to 81.5 (85.5), respectively, at secondary-education level. Even though the average pass rates at O level and A level improved from 18.7 per cent to 21 per cent, and 55.7 per cent to 63 per cent, respectively, during the two periods, the levels remained below 25 per cent at O level throughout the post-independence period, implying that the system was wasteful, forcing pupils to follow the academic route where their aptitudes and abilities were not located.

## The crisis period, 1997–2008

As a result of these challenges, a Presidential Commission of Inquiry into Education and Training was appointed in 1999 to restructure the education system as the new millennium beckoned.[13]

The commission highlighted the inability of the education and training system to produce graduates whose skills were marketable and relevant to the various fields of work. It noted that Zimbabwe's secondary education was too academic and examination-driven. Its report also observed that the secondary-school curriculum largely accommodated academic-orientated students, lacking a 'pathways approach'. The commission recommended restructuring the education and training system such that at the base of the system was an early childhood education and care programme that effectively prepared children for primary education. It recommended the introduction of a 'pathways system' that would cater for the diverse aptitudes, interests and abilities of students. This 'pathways approach' would divide pupils, after two years of junior-secondary education, into three streams based on performance and aptitude – two years of middle technical/vocational, middle academic, and middle commercial/business education – before proceeding to A level or joining a technical/vocational institution.

However, the challenges presented by the economic crisis that started in 1997 were unprecedented, as it brought economic decline, hyperinflation, shortages of foreign currency, shortages of basic commodities and food, and increased poverty. The situation was worsened by the withdrawal of international partners after 1999, recurrent droughts, floods, the fast-track land-reform programme, and ad hoc economic policies. These had a debilitating effect on education provision. Worse still, the HIV pandemic resulted in a dramatic increase in orphans and vulnerable children who needed assistance, which resulted in increased school absenteeism as some children were ill while others had to become care-givers (Zimbabwe, 2007).

## Gains reversed

The exponential expansion of education provision within a relatively short period of time had an adverse impact on quality, as reflected in the deterioration in the measures of internal efficiency of the education system.[14] The decline and reversal in the gains that had been made in the education sector were accentuated

---

[13] Zimbabwe, *Report of the Presidential Commission of Inquiry into Education and Training* [Chairman; C. T. Nziramasanga], 1999.

[14] Despite the improvement in the provision of primary education, its quality had been falling owing to a high teacher–pupil ratio – which averaged 1:37 (and was as high as 1:50) between 1990 and 2006 against a desired ratio of 1:28, high book–pupil ratios, high attrition levels, economic hardship and human-resource depletion due to HIV/AIDS, and the need to provide for newly resettled families under the land-reform programme (Zimbabwe, 2004; 2007).

by the crisis.[15] Enrolments at primary-school level, which had reached 2,480,094 by 2002, declined to 2,445,520 by 2006. While there was near gender parity at primary-school level, with an average ratio of 99.5 between 2000 and 2006, there was still gender inequality in enrolments at secondary-school level, where the gender-parity ratio averaged 90.7 during the same period. It is important to bear in mind that several United Nations declarations on education advocate for quality universal primary education by 2015, and gender equality in both primary and secondary education by 2005.[16]

This gender inequality is exacerbated by the inequality in terms of subject areas, with a higher proportion of boys doing science subjects, a gateway to the better-remunerating technical occupations; a higher proportion of girls pursue arts subjects. While the net enrolment ratio at primary schools peaked at 98.5 per cent in 2002, it had declined to 96.7 per cent by 2006.[17] Having reached 827,820 by 2001, enrolments at Form I to IV declined to 774,921 by 2006, the net enrolment ratio falling from 50.2 per cent to 46.3 per cent (Zimbabwe, 2007). This implies that a significant proportion of children who should be attending secondary school (13–16 years of age) are not doing so.

Presumably as a result of the economic hardships, the enrolment of pupils with disabilities declined from 18,932 in 2000 to 14,296 in 2002, rising to 21,296 in 2005 before declining by 21 per cent to 16,734 (0.7 per cent of primary school enrolments) in 2006. Of the 16,734 pupils with disabilities in primary schools in 2006, 43 per cent were girls, which may be a reflection of the stereotyping against the girl-child with disabilities (Zimbabwe, 2007).[18] Provision of special education in Zimbabwe is inhibited by a lack of trained staff, stereotyping, household poverty, limited stakeholder involvement, budgetary constraints, lack of facilities, and lack of co-ordination.

Transition rates from Grade 7 to Form I fell from 76.9 per cent in 2001 to 70 per cent in 2006, while those from Form IV to Form V rose from 8.8 per cent in 2000 to 17 per cent in 2006.[19] Drop-outs at primary-school level increased from 6.3 per cent in 2000 to 8.7 per cent in 2005, while at secondary-school level they increased from 7.5 per cent in 2000 to 8.5 per cent in 2005, mainly owing to financial constraints. Of the 30,359 pupils who dropped out

---

[15] At the turn of the new millennium, the education system in Zimbabwe was ranked second in Africa in terms of literacy and numeracy levels (UNESCO, 2003).

[16] These include Education for All (1990); Education for All (2000) Assessment; the World Education Conference, Dakar, 2000; and the Millennium Development Goals (2000), of which Zimbabwe is a signatory.

[17] The net enrolment ratio is the number of pupils enrolled who are of the official age group for a given level of education divided by the population for the same age group expressed as a percentage.

[18] It should be noted, however, that there was no national policy on special education in Zimbabwe until 1980, as the education of children with special needs was left to charitable organizations and churches.

[19] Primary-school education covers Grades 1 to 7, while secondary-school education goes from Form I to Forms IV (O level) and VI (A level).

of school in 2006, 48 per cent were girls. Drop-outs indicate the failure of the Basic Education Assistance Module (BEAM), which was introduced in 2001 to reduce the number of children failing to attend school because of hardships. The BEAM programme experienced problems related to limited financial resources and the management unit's weak capacity to administer the payment system.

According to an internal report of the Ministry of Labour and Social Services (May 2008), the BEAM programme has faced high staff turnover such that, of the thirteen posts (nine data capturers, one programmer, one programme officer, one programme manager and one systems analyst), only two were filled. Poor remuneration was cited as the reason for this. As a result, the programme was running behind schedule, failing to pay fees on time. Obsolete computer systems were also identified as requiring replacement, with the server that runs the programme having crashed in 2007, causing delays in the payment of fees. After April 2007, a programme of support for the National Action Plan for Orphans and Vulnerable Children was implemented to complement BEAM,[20] one aspect of which assists them with school-related support (including school fees). However, the scale of the assistance required was beyond these two interventions, hence the drop-outs.

Whereas the proportion of trained teachers improved from 89.3 per cent in 2000 to 96.7 per cent in 2006 at the primary-school level, at the secondary-school level it deteriorated from 97.8 per cent in 2001 to 91.9 per cent in 2006. By 2000, teacher morale was already low as a result of poor salaries, poor staff accommodation, especially in rural areas, and increased workloads, all of which culminated in an unprecedented brain drain of qualified teachers. Teacher absenteeism and deaths were reportedly on the increase as a result of the HIV and AIDS pandemic (Zimbabwe, 2004: 24; Zimbabwe, 2007).

### Differentiated impact: Worsening inequality

While the teacher–pupil ratio at primary level was almost constant during the period 2000–2006, averaging 38.2, a level well above the MDG-recommended target ratio of 1:28, it improved from 27 in 2000 to 24 by 2006 at the secondary level. Low-density areas had the lowest teacher–pupil ratio at primary-school level of 1:32 in 2006, while high-density areas had the highest at 1:39. Low-density secondary schools had the lowest teacher–pupil ratio in 2006 at 1:19, while high-density areas had the highest at 1:26. Government recommends a teacher–pupil ratio of 1:33 for Forms I–II, 1:30 for Forms III–IV, and 1:20 for Forms V–VI (Zimbabwe, 2007).

---

[20] This programme is funded by multi-donors under a basket fund managed by UNICEF. These funds are distributed to child care and protection NGOs and not to government, although the co-ordination role is left to government through the Ministry of Labour and Social Services.

The inadequacy of the infrastructure is reflected in the shortfall of classrooms at primary and secondary schools, both averaging 20 per cent between 2000 and 2006. The average shortfall in laboratories at secondary level worsened from 56 per cent in 2000 to 61 per cent in 2006. The shortfall in specialist classrooms at primary-school level increased from 86 per cent in 2000 to 96 per cent in 2006, very high levels indeed. In 2006, primary schools in high-density areas had the highest shortages (29 per cent) of ordinary classrooms, followed by commercial farming areas and resettlement areas (24 per cent), mining settlements (20 per cent), communal areas (17 per cent) and, lastly, low-density suburbs (11 per cent). For secondary schools, government schools had the highest shortfall of ordinary classrooms at 29 per cent, followed by city council and town board schools (28 per cent), church or mission schools (27 per cent), mining schools (24 per cent), farm schools (23 per cent), other private schools (22 per cent), town board schools (22 per cent) and, lastly, district schools (14 per cent).

Communal area primary schools had the highest shortfall of specialist classrooms (92 per cent), with low-density suburbs having the lowest (61 per cent). Furthermore, other relevant infrastructure – such as teacher accommodation, libraries and ablution facilities – were already inadequate by the turn of the new millennium (Zimbabwe, 2004: 24). The pupil–textbook ratio within primary schools deteriorated from two for English and two for Mathematics in 2000 to three and six, respectively, by 2006. During the period 2000–2006, nine out of the thirteen sporting disciplines experienced acute shortages of facilities in primary schools.

**Declining pass rates and lack of a pathways approach**

Pass rates at Grade 7 declined from 53.3 per cent in 1999 to 33.1 per cent in 2005, before improving to 56.1 per cent in 2006. Since 1999, girls have outperformed boys, presumably owing to their early maturity (Zimbabwe, 2007: 107), but the worsening pass rates applied to both boys and girls. Largely as expected, the Grade 7 pass rates were lowest in resettlement areas at 21.7 per cent in 2005, followed by communal areas at 24.9 per cent, commercial farms at 33.7 per cent, mining areas at 48.4 per cent, high-density areas at 51.7 per cent and low-density areas at 67.1 per cent.

At O level, the pass rates (Grade C or better in five subjects) collapsed from 25.4 per cent in 2000 to 14 per cent in 2006. The deteriorating pass rates were due to factors such as lack of teaching materials and other resources, unmotivated teaching staff, absenteeism due to the HIV and AIDS pandemic, and economic hardships. Unlike the pattern at primary-school level, boys outperformed girls at secondary-school level. For the period 2000–2005, for which disaggregated data by gender are available, boys consistently outperformed girls in science-oriented subjects, while girls did better than boys in Shona, Ndebele, English

Language, Fashion and Fabrics, and Food and Nutrition. This trend reflects the stereotyping of subjects by gender, where girls are socialized to believe that science and vocational subjects are difficult and therefore for boys, while the perceived 'soft' subjects (mainly the arts) are considered suitable for girls.[21]

Such low pass rates indicate that the education system is wasteful, apart from its having an academic focus. Having peaked at 83 per cent in 2003, the pass rates at A level (Grade E or better in two subjects) declined to 73.7 per cent in 2005 and 74.9 per cent in 2006. Although the transition rate from Form IV to Form V improved from 8.8 per cent in 2000 to 17 per cent in 2006, the majority of school-leavers had to join the ranks of the unemployed in the absence of new job opportunities. In addition, the relevance of the curriculum has been questioned in many reports.[22]

As has been pointed out, the current secondary-education curriculum does not effectively develop children according to their unique needs and inclinations, implying that it does not lay a solid foundation for the employability and integrability of its products into the economy; it lacks a functional dimension. The secondary-school curriculum is therefore not all-inclusive as it lacks a 'pathways approach' to take into account the diverse talents, aptitudes and preferences of students.

Faced with this challenge, the Ministry of Education, Sport, Arts and Culture made it compulsory for pupils to take at least one of the technical and vocational subjects at O level.[23] This made technical and vocational subjects compulsory at middle-secondary levels, as recommended by the 1999 Commission of Inquiry into Education and Training. Laudable as this move may have been, it was undermined by the lack of resources. The policies left the initiative to individual school heads, who depended on the availability of facilities and staff, as well as learner preferences. In the absence of adequate resources, most school heads allocated minimal funds to technical and vocational subjects.

The Ministry of Education, Sport, Arts and Culture required all secondary schools to implement a 'two-pathway education structure' with effect from 2006,[24] also in line with the recommendations of the Commission of Inquiry. These pathways involved the general/academic education pathway and the skills pathway, i.e. business/commercial/technology/technical–vocational education. The implementation of this two-pathway education structure begins after Form II in order to cater for the learners' varying aptitudes, interests and abilities.

---

[21] For a detailed discussion of the socialization and cultural norms that underpin these perceptions, see Chapter 6.

[22] The Report of the 1999 Commission of Inquiry, the Ministry of Higher and Tertiary Education's Report of 2006, and the Ministry of Education, Sport, Arts and Culture's Report of 2007 (Zimbabwe, 2007).

[23] Secretary's Circular No. 2 of 2001, reinforced by the Secretary's Circular No. 14 of 2004.

[24] By way of Policy Circular P77 of 2006.

Since its implementation is earmarked for the post-junior-secondary level, the ministry reintroduced the Zimbabwe Junior Certificate in 2007 for the 2006 cohort in order to facilitate the assessment and channelling of pupils into the two pathways. Within this new structure, the student is expected, at Form III level, to pursue one of the following options:

- Option 1: general/academic core subjects; business/commercial as major (at least two subjects); and one subject (elective) from technical–vocational.
- Option 2: general/academic core subjects; technical–vocational as a major (at least two subjects); and one subject (elective) from business/ commercial.

Most unfortunately, the success of this philosophy hinges on the availability of resources, lack of which has slowed down its implementation.

## The years of paralysis: 2007–2008

The impressive gains in expanding access to primary and secondary education were severely undermined by the socio-economic hardships that intensified after 2007, adversely affecting the teaching, learning and assessment (examination) processes. As the examination processes were badly affected, the overall rating of the education system was compromised, especially given the frequency and regularity of leaked examination papers and other misdemeanours. The hyper-inflationary environment made education provision expensive, and it became difficult for parents to afford such basic requirements as uniforms, food, fees and books, resulting in pupils dropping out of school, as reported above.

While the Education Act stipulates that no school authority shall increase fees by more than ten per cent per annum unless the Secretary for Education has approved such fees, the responsible authorities, faced with hyperinflation, did not observe this regulation. Internecine wrangles ensued between responsible authorities and the Ministry of Education, Sport, Arts and Culture as some of the fees were not approved on the grounds that they were unreasonably high. The Education Amendment Act of 2006 sought to regulate the national school fees system. Following the setting up of a National Incomes and Pricing Commission (NIPC) in July 2007, all fees had to be approved by this body, but the bullish approach it adopted created unwarranted tension among the stakeholders in education. Although Ministry of Education staff understood the impact of inflation, they feared that education could be rendered too expensive by arbitrary increases in fees and levies. However, with harmonized national elections coming up in March 2008, they tended to lean towards keeping fee levels down.

Consequently, schools had to review fees every term in order to sustain their operations, resulting in some charging fees in foreign currency or fuel coupons.[25] Since many people could not access foreign currency and fuel, a number of children could have dropped out of school as a result. Even when the new fees were approved, most schools still found it difficult to live within their budgets, which were soon eroded by hyperinflation and they had to ask for top-ups, which would also have had an adverse impact on school attendance in 2008. However, while private schools had the clout and resources to challenge the Ministry of Education and NIPC in order to raise fees, and obviated the controls by charging fees in foreign currency by way of 'units' and fuel coupons, public schools had to follow the letter of government directives. Furthermore, private schools reintroduced University of Cambridge examinations at Grade 7, and at Ordinary and Advanced levels, thereby avoiding the credibility crisis associated with local examinations.[26] As a result, rural and urban public schools were disproportionately affected by the economic paralysis (Box 8.1).

The disproportionate impact of the deteriorating quality in rural schools can be inferred from the fact that in 2006, the rural primary-school-going-age population accounted for 73 per cent of the national figure (Zimbabwe, 2007: 9). Sixty-eight per cent of all primary schools were in communal areas. The majority of primary schools (77 per cent) were run by district councils (which accounted for 68 per cent of primary-school enrolments); furthermore, 87 per cent of primary schools were P3 (primary schools in rural areas). Thus, the class structure in education provision was further entrenched, to the detriment of the poorer households, especially in the rural areas.

In 2006, 52 per cent of enrolments in Forms I–VI were in schools run by district councils; 98 per cent of pupils in primary schools were day scholars; 85 per cent of the students at secondary schools were in day schools; 64 per cent of the secondary-school enrolments (Forms I–VI) were in rural areas (S3), and 24 per cent in high-density areas (S2).

Media reports indicated that teachers were absent from schools for a considerable time in the year 2008. The first term was affected by the national elections, which went on until the end of June following the presidential run-off election necessitated by the failure of the 29 March elections to produce an outright winner. Furthermore, the academic calendar was disrupted by continuous industrial action by teachers, who protested against poor working and living conditions. This was not helped by the cash shortages at banks, which resulted in daily queues, as withdrawal limits did not allow people to meet basic daily expenses such as transport. Some teachers left the country for neighbouring countries in search of greener pastures.

---

[25] Fuel was available almost only through the use of coupons that had to be purchased with external funds. The coupons therefore had a value that made them tradable on the parallel market.

[26] Local examinations are administered by a division in the Ministry of Education, Sport, Arts and Culture, the Zimbabwe School Examinations Council (ZIMSEC).

**Box 8.1: UNICEF-SNV primary schools assessment report**

UNICEF-SNV (2009) found that school enrolments were adversely affected such that, during the third term of 2008, they were 16.3 per cent below those for the first term for Grades 3 and 6. Drop-outs were higher for girls (17.2 per cent) than for boys (15.4 per cent). The drop-outs were higher at Grade 6 (19.1 per cent) compared to Grade 3 (13.6 per cent). While attendance during the first term was affected mainly by elections, in the third term it was by industrial action by teachers.

School heads rated the general attendance of teachers and pupils in 2008. While 59.4 per cent of boarding-school heads rated teachers' attendance as high, only 41.1 per cent of urban day schools and 15.1 per cent of rural day schools rated it high.* Generally, boarding schools remained operational as a result of teachers' incentives provided after the regular review of school fees. A higher percentage of boarding-school heads (40.6 per cent) indicated that teacher attendance was in the medium range, as did 20.5 per cent of urban day-school heads and 26.3 per cent of rural day-school heads. A large number (58.6 per cent) of rural day-school heads rated teacher attendance as low, with 38.4 per cent of urban day-school heads and none at boarding schools rating teacher attendance in this category.

The ratings for high pupil attendance in 2008 were 56.5 per cent for boarding schools, 42.5 per cent for urban day schools, and only 8.6 per cent for rural day schools. Attendance was regarded as medium by 43.5 per cent of boarding-school heads, by 23.9 per cent of urban day-school heads, and by 41.1 per cent of rural day-school heads. None of the boarding school heads suggested pupil attendance in 2008 was low, yet 33.6 per cent at urban day schools and 50.3 per cent at rural day schools felt it was.

On whether or not there was any meaningful learning in 2008, 88.6 per cent of the teachers interviewed in boarding schools believed there was, but only 8.3 per cent in urban schools and none in rural schools agreed. Thus, all the teachers in rural schools and 91.7 per cent of those in urban schools felt that no meaningful learning took place in 2008. However, at all the private schools, the teachers indicated that the teaching and learning process was normal. Generally, therefore, 'no meaningful learning' took place in rural and most urban areas in 2008 as a result of the industrial action by staff, political disturbances, hunger, and lack of teaching and learning materials.

The results of the Basic Standardized Achievement Test (BSAT) in Mathematics, English and General Paper taken by Grade 4 and 7 pupils who were in Grade 3 and 6, respectively, in 2008 reflects the pupils' academic achievement in that year. The results are dismal, as reflected in mean pass rates of 33 per cent for Mathematics, 27.6 per cent for General Paper and 38.3 per cent for English at Grade 4. At Grade 7, the mean pass rates were 18.5 per cent for Mathematics, 24.1 per cent for General Paper and 45.6 per cent for English. The means for the three papers at Grade 7 are lower than those for the period 2004–2006, suggesting that pupils did not learn much in 2008. Given their disadvantaged position, rural pupils performed worse than their counterparts at urban and boarding schools. Girls outperformed boys in all the three subjects at both Grades 4 and 7.

The 2008 Grade 7 examinations were conducted in a haphazard manner, with serious problems experienced in the confirmation of candidates, the delivery of question papers, and the writing and invigilation of the examination. As well as the teacher and pupil absenteeism, it is not surprising that 2008 was a lost academic year. The study suggested a number of measures to remedy the situation, including weekend classes, holiday lessons, extended lessons for the key grades during the week, and reduced holidays. In fact, 76.4 per cent of the teachers interviewed indicated that they were prepared to make up for the lost teaching and learning time, provided their remuneration was reviewed.

*Source:* UNICEF-SNV (2009).

* High is when pupils and teachers attended school throughout the academic year; medium is when they attended for at least half the academic year; low is when they attended for less than half the academic year.

ZIMSEC was also affected by the economic hardships that reached a crescendo in 2008. By the time of the examinations, the teaching staff were on strike, resulting in Reserve Bank of Zimbabwe officials and the army coming in to invigilate. Such was the situation that, even after the examinations were written, markers refused to assess the examination scripts, citing the poor allowances being offered. The full extent of the crisis in the education sector occasioned by the economic paralysis of 2008 is captured in Box 8.1, which summarizes the major findings of a study by UNICEF-SNV (2009). The study was a rapid assessment of the impact of the socio-economic environment in 2008 on the teaching, learning and assessment processes, covering 190 of the 200 primary schools in Zimbabwe, and rural day, urban day and boarding schools. Its findings vindicate UNICEF's assessment of 2008 as a 'wasted academic year'.

## The transitional period, 2009–2010

Given the chaotic state of the education sector, the re-opening of schools was delayed until the end of January 2009. The absence of examination results de-layed enrolments at A level. It was only in April that government directed that students be enrolled on the basis of their mid-term (2008) examination results. The 2008 A-level examination results were eventually released during the last week of May, O-level results came out first week of June, while Grade 7 results appeared during the first week of July 2009. In an intriguing policy directive that was later reversed, the Minister of Education, Sport, Arts and Culture indicated that those who had been enrolled for Form V but failed their O-level examinations would be withdrawn from school. June O-level and A-level examin-ations scheduled to begin in the third week of May were postponed to July.

Meanwhile, in an attempt to lure teachers back to work, the national budget announced on 29 January indicated that civil servants would continue to be paid their salaries in Zimbabwe dollars but with a top-up allowance in foreign currency, underpinned by a voucher system pegged to a basket of goods for a family of six set at US$100 per month.[27] The budget statement liberalized the pricing regime and returned the responsibility of regulating school fees to the Ministry of Education, Sport, Arts and Culture; the NIPC was required simply to monitor the implementation of set fees. After the new Minister of Finance abandoned the Zimbabwe dollar and decided that, from end of February, all public employees would be paid an allowance of US$100, the teachers' strike was called off on 2 March 2009.

Teachers that had stayed at home because their salaries could not cover trans-port costs, and those that had gone to neighbouring countries or had taken odd jobs, started coming back when the Minister of Education, Sport, Arts and

---

[27] Monetary Policy Statement of 2 February 2009.

Culture indicated that waivers would be provided to facilitate their re-engagement. However, the euphoria that initially followed the announcement died down as the reality sank in that the same allowance would continue indefinitely. On 22 May 2009, public-sector employees in Harare demonstrated against the continued payment of the US$100 allowance. Some of the placards they carried read, 'US$100 is not enough' and 'Bills are more than our allowances'.[28] Nevertheless, the payment of the US$100 did reveal the existence of a significant number of 'ghost' employees.[29] Box 8.2 summarizes the results of a survey undertaken by the National Education Advisory Board to determine the state of education in the first term of 2009.[30]

In June 2009, the Minister of Education announced that tuition fees for the second term at state schools had been waived and that pupils had to pay only US$5 for primary schools and US$10 for secondary schools, in addition to whatever levy each school agreed to charge. This was a reduction from the fees for the first term that had been set at US$20 for primary schools and US$50 for secondary schools. Private schools were charging around US$1,000 per term for day schools. The implication of this development is that the resource gap between public and private schools will increase further, with serious implications for the overall quality of education.

The problems affecting the education sector spilled into the third term, when ZIMSEC workers went on strike demanding a review of their salaries, which resulted in the delay of the examinations that were scheduled to begin in October. Thus, even as the schools closed for the holiday at the end of the third term, classes taking examinations at O and A level continued, with their examinations scheduled to finish on 18 December.

Against this background, it is not surprising that the results of the 2009 examinations were unsatisfactory (Table 8.2). The Grade 7 results, with a 39.3 per cent pass rate, were the worst in a decade, rural schools being the worst affected, where in several cases zero pass rates were recorded. For instance, while the urban provinces of Harare and Bulawayo registered pass rates of 72 per cent, the predominantly rural province of Matabeleland North had the lowest pass rate (23 per cent), and those of other rural provinces were also very low. The overall pass rates at O and A level were slightly better than they had been in recent years. The poor pass rates were compounded by a decline in the number of candidates who registered to sit for the 2009 examinations. The number of

---

[28] *The Herald*, 23 May 2009.

[29] See Chapter 7.

[30] This board was set up in terms of the Education Act by the new minister in March 2009 to advise him on educational policy matters. It comprises eminent educationists, and includes the former Minister of Education, Fay King Chung, former Permanent Secretary, Isaiah Sibanda, and a representative of each of the two major teachers' unions, ZIMTA and PTUZ.

**Box 8.2: The state of primary and secondary education, first term 2009**

In July 2009, the National Education Advisory Board released the results of its survey, 'The Rapid Assessment of Primary and Secondary Education', covering 120 schools in all ten provinces of the country, 20 districts (two per province). Ninety of the schools were primary, 30 were secondary.

The survey found that enrolments in the 90 primary schools had remained fairly stable during the period 2003 to 2009. However, it found that the number of teachers had increased, thereby reducing the teacher–pupil ratio from 1:39 in 2003 to 1:35.9 in 2009. Enrolments in the secondary schools in the sample were less stable, experiencing close to a 10 per cent decline between 2006 and 2009. The teacher–pupil ratio had dropped from 1:25.6 in 2003 to 1:23.6 in 2009.

Despite the relatively stable enrolments at primary-school level, national data indicated a large number of drop-outs. The example given relates to the 1993 Grade 1 cohort which experienced a drop-out of 196,000 eight years later in 2000. The survey found that the majority of the teachers in both primary and secondary schools in the sample were qualified teachers. However, shortages of qualified teachers were experienced in A-level classes in Mathematics, Science and commercial subjects. In all the schools visited, teacher morale was very low owing to low salaries, lack of security in rural areas, where teachers were victims of political violence in 2008, lack of accommodation, and shortages of teaching and learning resources. As a result, the image of the teacher was at its lowest level since independence.

In spite of the demoralizing conditions, nearly all teachers were present at the schools during the field visits. The survey reports evidence of desertion by teachers, citing the rapid feminization of the teaching staff at both primary and secondary schools, implying that, as qualified male teachers left, they were replaced by qualified female teachers. A severe shortage of furniture in schools, particularly rural schools, was observed. Half the seats in rural primary schools and 18 per cent in urban schools were damaged and unusable, with the situation worse in secondary schools. Textbooks were in short supply, with over 20 per cent of the primary schools having no textbooks at all for English, Mathematics and African Languages, all compulsory subjects. A third of rural secondary schools had no textbooks for English language, and 22 per cent had no textbooks for Mathematics and Ndebele/Shona, compulsory subjects.

Furthermore, owing to a lack of resources, the ministry was failing to do quality checks. A large number of the schools sampled did not have substantive heads. In addition, no meaningful fees had been collected by the time of the study, resulting in schools operating on minimal budgets. Most parents were simply not able to pay the high fees, and the Advisory Board team noted that this would have an impact on the country's ability to meet the MDG target of basic education for all by 2015. The absence of regulations on teacher incentives was found to have exacerbated the conflict between teachers and parents. At the three special schools that were part of the sample, the survey found that government assistance for children requiring special education had declined considerably over the past decade.

The Rapid Assessment survey recommended that major inputs to improve the conditions and morale of teachers be provided, the poor relationship between parents and teachers being due to the fact that parents, including very poor ones, had to take over responsibility for teachers' remuneration when the state was unable to fulfil its obligations. The shortage of resources for the education sector should be addressed by the state, assisted by donors and parents. It also recommended that school fees and levies be unified. With respect to addressing the needs of the estimated 25 per cent of school children who are OVC, the study called for better co-ordination between Social Welfare, Education and donors.

*Source:* National Education Advisory Board.

**Table 8.2: ZIMSEC examination analysis, 2005–2009**

| Province | Grade 7: Candidates obtaining 4 to 24 units | | | | |
|---|---|---|---|---|---|
| | 2005 | 2006 | 2007 | 2008 | 2009 |
| Bulawayo | 82.82 | 85.03 | 87.82 | 79.00 | 72.00 |
| Harare | 83.34 | 81.70 | 84.57 | 74.56 | 72.00 |
| Manicaland | 52.67 | 54.78 | 69.33 | 44.88 | 34.77 |
| Mashonaland Central | 59.67 | 44.16 | 67.85 | 65.00 | 24.80 |
| Mashonaland East | 59.05 | 53.39 | 61.34 | 47.67 | 31.10 |
| Mashonaland West | 60.82 | 61.15 | 57.02 | 38.80 | 28.00 |
| Masvingo | 67.45 | 67.70 | 47.81 | 47.65 | 37.97 |
| Matabeleland North | 49.93 | 32.16 | 53.16 | 34.84 | 23.05 |
| Matabeleland South | 66.55 | 49.54 | 61.61 | 32.73 | 29.92 |
| Midlands | 69.99 | 64.71 | 74.98 | 50.70 | 39.40 |
| National | 62.42 | 68.03 | 70.45 | 51.50 | 39.30 |

| Year | Gender | O level | | | A level | | |
|---|---|---|---|---|---|---|---|
| | | No. of candidates entered | No. of candidates passing 5 or more subjects | National pass rate (%) | No. of candidates entered | No. of candidates passing 5 or more subjects | National pass rate (%) |
| 2006 | Female | 74,363 | 12,902 | 17.35 | | | |
| | Male | 79,866 | 18,345 | 22.95 | | | |
| | Total | 154,229 | 31,247 | 20.16 | | | |
| 2007 | Female | 85,291 | 10,354 | 12.14 | 13,014 | 10,151 | 78.00 |
| | Male | 93,983 | 15,319 | 16.30 | 21,112 | 15,686 | 74.30 |
| | Total | 179,274 | 25,673 | 14.32 | 34,126 | 25,837 | 75.71 |
| 2008 | Female | 71,450 | 8,910 | 12.47 | 13,079 | 9,012 | 68.90 |
| | Male | 71,390 | 11,722 | 16.42 | 19,526 | 12,973 | 66.44 |
| | Total | 142,840 | 20,632 | 14.44 | 32,605 | 21,985 | 67.43 |
| 2009 | Female | 44,209 | 7,472 | 16.90 | 9,694 | 7,567 | 78.06 |
| | Male | 42,992 | 9,381 | 21.82 | 13,908 | 10,574 | 76.06 |
| | Total | 87,201 | 16,853 | 19.33 | 23,596 | 18,141 | 76.88 |

Source: *The Herald*, 29 April 2010.

candidates that registered for the 2009 O-level examinations (87,201) represented 61 per cent of those registered in 2008 and 49 per cent of those in 2007, yet 2007 and 2008 were very difficult years. This decline emanated from the failure of most parents to afford the US$10 and US$20 per O-level and A-level subject, respectively, owing to poverty.

It was in this context that the Minister of Education, Sport, Arts and Culture observed that the education sector was 'in a critical state', arguing further that

there is a grave danger that the nation will suffer from a lost generation if this crisis is not taken seriously. Urgent steps need to be taken to rectify some of the obvious problems such as the scarcity of teaching and learning material, inadequacy of physical infrastructure and the no longer attractive working conditions for teachers.[31]

## 8.4 Higher and Tertiary Education (Vocational and University)[32]

A first task faced by the new government in 1980 was the assessment of the human-resource base and skills-shortage areas, and to formulate short- to medium-term training policies, given the fear that the economy would be haemorrhaged by an exodus of white skills as had happened in Mozambique. This was done through the *National Manpower Survey* (Zimbabwe, 1981), which highlighted the shortages of skills in technical areas arising from the neglect of technical training infrastructure and reliance on immigration. It identified the semi-skilled as an important reservoir of under-categorized skilled workers.

To correct the racial imbalances in the provision of technical and vocational education and training (TVET), the government established five more technical colleges between 1980 and 1990.[33] These were later upgraded into polytechnics in 2001. In order to deal with the under-categorization of skilled workers, a trade-testing and upgrading system was introduced in 1981 which classified workers into skilled-worker classes ranging from Class 4 to Class 1, the latter being the highest artisan grade within the industrial training and trade-testing system. To facilitate this process of upgrading semi-skilled workers through trade-testing, two vocational training centres were created at independence, Msasa in Harare (funded by the French government) and Westgate in Bulawayo (funded by the West German government).

Trade-testing provided an avenue for the recognition of skills obtained through on-the-job training, non-formal programmes such as adult and continuing education, and through the youth skills training centres and vocational training centres (VTCs) run by the Ministry of Youth Development and private organizations. Through this process, some 2,500 workers were re-categorized each year. However, this upgrading system waned over time as employers resisted it, since reclassification placed workers into higher-paying grades, effectively raising labour costs.

While the apprenticeship training system was retained, the recruitment process was centralized such that prospective apprentices had to apply to the Registrar of Apprenticeships at the Ministry of Labour.[34] After the initial selection, at least

---

[31] Quoted in *The Herald*, 29 April 2009.

[32] Tertiary education in Zimbabwe in 2010 consists of 13 universities (9 public and 4 private), 8 polytechnic colleges, and 14 teacher training colleges.

[33] The Manpower Planning and Development Act (No. 36 of 1984) sought to rectify the racial imbalances in skills formation.

[34] This function was later transferred to the newly formed Ministry of Higher Education in 1988.

twice as many candidates as there were places were sent to interested employers. To retain the trained cadres, apprentices were bonded for four years after the four-year training period. The apprenticeship system was complemented by a direct-entry programme into colleges.[35] However, notwithstanding the good intentions of centralized recruitment and government intervention in general, it created an adversarial relationship with employers which saw the numbers recruited into this scheme declining from 2,044 in 1981 to 1,164 in 1986, a level only slightly above average annual levels of the pre-independence era.

The development of TVET has been guided by the 'Rationalization of Technical and Vocational Education in Zimbabwe' policy document (Zimbabwe, 1990). This policy framework structured TVET into five levels: Pre-Vocational Certificate (PVC), National Foundation Certificate (NFC), National Certificate (NC), National Diploma (ND) and Higher National Diploma (HND). This affected all courses offered in government institutions and all providers of education and training under the aegis of the Higher Education Examinations Council (HEXCO), the successor examination body to the Further Education Examination Board (FEEB), which in turn had succeeded the City and Guilds in 1984. Through the 1990 policy reform, learners were for the first time afforded an opportunity to move from operative (PVC) to skilled operative grade (NFC), artisan grade (NC and Skilled Worker Class 1), technician (ND), and to technologist grade (HND), the equivalent of a degree. From 2004, polytechnics could upgrade TVET qualifications to graduate and post-graduate levels.

For the first time, the 1990 policy allowed mobility between TVET qualifications and the academic stream, providing a blueprint for the Zimbabwe Qualifications Framework. The Zimbabwe Qualifications Authority (ZIMQA) Bill that was drafted in 2005 is expected to come before Parliament during the period of the Inclusive Government, in line with provisions of the SADC protocol on Education and Training ratified in 1997 which envisages the establishment of a Regional Qualifications Framework. The current practice in Zimbabwe is such that, while students can move from one technical and vocational institution to another without losing credits, they are disadvantaged when they wish to join the academic stream since there is no policy to guide such movements. The discretion regarding the level at which the transfers are placed within universities is left with the individual departments; this is the distortion that the ZIMQA Bill seeks to correct.

University education has undergone similar radical transformation. In 1990, the University of Zimbabwe was the only university in the country; there are now nine state universities and four private ones.

---

[35] Apprentices recruited by private companies need at least four years to finish the programme, one of which is spent at the college/polytechnic. Direct-entry students do the programme in three years, two of which are spent at the college/polytechnic and one on industrial attachment.

### 8.4.1 Student enrolments

By 2009, higher and tertiary education institutions in Zimbabwe had a combined enrolment of 74,446 students, 45 per cent of whom were females (Table 8.3). The total enrolments work out at 555 students per 100,000 inhabitants, which is higher than the average of 538 for Sub-Saharan Africa but lower than the 967 for the whole of Africa. Female students are still under-represented at universities and polytechnics but are predominant at teachers' colleges, a reflection of the feminization of the teaching profession. Men appear to be disinterested in teaching because of the 'poverty and ridicule' associated with it. However, the overall percentage of female enrolments is below that of the SADC region.

**Table 8.3: Enrolments at higher and tertiary education institutions, 2009**

| Institution | Enrolment | Percentage female | Percentage change in enrolment 2007–2009 |
|---|---|---|---|
| Universities | 49,645 | 39.5 | –7.7 |
| Polytechnics | 13,217 | 44.3 | –7.0 |
| Teachers' colleges (primary) | 8,390 | 71.8 | –25.1 |
| Teachers' colleges (secondary) | 3,184 | 63.1 | –10.2 |
| Total | 74,436 | 45.0 | –10.0 |

*Source:* Adapted from Zimabwe (2009: Tables 6 and 7).

The largest decline in enrolments between 2007 and 2009 was experienced in teachers' colleges, caused by, among other factors, rising fees and the loss of qualified human capital. Of concern are the low enrolments in medicine, mathematics, science and technical studies due to a shortage of suitable candidates. Most secondary schools do not offer specialized science subjects such as physics, chemistry, biology and mathematics – they offer 'core science' instead because the country has lost qualified teachers in these areas (Zimbabwe, 2009).

### 8.4.2 Staffing

While the staffing situation at tertiary level varies widely, there is overstaffing in teachers' colleges and in non-teaching areas, and severe understaffing at polytechnics and universities (Zimbabwe, 2009). The brain drain has resulted in an acute depletion of skills, with medicine, applied sciences and engineering the worst affected. For instance, the loss of highly qualified staff is reflected by the low percentage (7.9 per cent) of lecturing staff with doctoral degrees at universities. Furthermore, women constituted only 32.6 per cent of lecturing staff, with the gender gap highest at universities and lowest in teachers' colleges.[36]

---

[36] Females constituted 27.3 per cent of lecturing staff at universities, 35.8 per cent at polytechnics and 40 per cent at teachers' colleges.

Comparing 2009 and 2007 levels, the number of staff at polytechnics declined by 20.1 per cent, at universities by 1.3 per cent, while those at teachers' colleges increased by 23.3 per cent, the overall staffing situation registering a decline of 2 per cent. However, while the average decline in staff at universities was generally low, the University of Zimbabwe recorded a decline of 22 per cent. Likewise, while the decrease in staff at polytechnics averaged 20 per cent, Harare Polytechnic experienced a decline of 43 per cent.

During the period 2007–2009, abscondings constituted 52.9 per cent at universities and 40.5 per cent at polytechnics, while resignations accounted for 41.1 per cent and 46.3 per cent, respectively; the remainder of the losses came from dismissal, retirement or death. Staff losses were highest in technical fields, accounting for 45.6 per cent and 73.7 per cent of all abscondings and resignations at universities and polytechnics, respectively. As a result, some universities suspended some courses owing to a shortage of staff. Replacements had lower qualifications and lacked experience, thereby affecting the quality of delivery. Consequently, vacancy rates ranged from zero to 74 per cent.

The reasons for the brain drain were varied: poor remuneration, limited opportunities to participate in collaborative research with intellectual peers in other universities or institutions around the world, and in staff exchange programmes, failure to honour professional incentives such as contact and sabbatical leave, staff development and other aspects of professional exposure, shortage of office space and computers, limited Internet access, shortage of teaching and laboratory equipment, and transport (Zimbabwe, 2009).

### 8.4.3 Infrastructure and equipment

Much of the infrastructure in tertiary education institutions is in a state of disrepair and dilapidated. Buildings and other structures are either inadequate or unsuitable for the institutions' needs or incomplete. The requisite equipment for teaching, learning, administration and sport is in short supply, and, where it is available, the bulk of it is obsolete. The number of students per computer was 28.8 for universities, 30.3 for polytechnics, and 87.7 for teachers' colleges, giving an average of 32.5, in 2009. The lecturer–computer ratio of 2.1 for universities, 6.3 for polytechnics, and 17.1 for teachers' colleges (with an average of 1.9) is similarly inadequate. The poor ICT connectivity in most institutions has adversely affected teaching, learning and operations. The existing capacity for student accommodation in universities and polytechnics can cater for only 7 per cent of the enrolment, resulting in some students living under sub-human conditions. Furthermore, electricity cuts, shortage of water and lack of proper sanitation have impacted on the operations of virtually all the institutions (Zimbabwe, 2009).

As with the TVET system, the universities were not spared the impact of a rapidly growing student body and the economic crisis, especially hyperinflation. Since the late 1980s, student riots had become a part of the University of Zimbabwe, the institution being closed on several occasions. However, the die was cast in 2008 when the university faced a myriad of challenges, ranging from an acute shortage of resources, deteriorating conditions of service for staff, infrastructural decay, and a failure to supply water and basic sanitation which resulted in the halls of residence being closed. While other universities trudged on, the University of Zimbabwe failed to open its doors in August 2008, only doing so, albeit for a very brief period, in November, when student protests against high fees charged in foreign currency and non-attendance of classes by lecturers forced the authorities to close it. It reopened during the first week of August 2009, but no new students were enrolled since the 2008 cohort had not received any meaningful teaching and learning and the halls of residence remain closed.

### 8.4.4 Funding

The provision of resources for TVET has been shared between government, the private sector and students. The 1984 Manpower Planning and Development Act provided for a fund, the Zimbabwe Manpower Development Fund (ZIMDEF), supported by a levy of 1 per cent of the salary bill on employers and administered by the Ministry of Higher and Tertiary Education. It is meant to meet the expenses for apprenticeship and direct-entry students, including the payment of grants to employees, the allowances and wages of trainees, and tuition fees for apprentices when they are at college. However, the 1994 Manpower Planning and Development Act, amended in 1996, is so flexible that ZIMDEF easily departs from its core business of financing training, delving into infrastructure and other non-core activities. Furthermore, the Minister of Higher and Tertiary Education, who is the sole trustee of ZIMDEF, has wide discretionary powers; he/she appoints the chief executive and fixes the terms and conditions of appointment, directs his/her activities, and approves the capital, revenue and recurrent expenditure budgets. For these reasons, the fund is seen as 'a striking case of governance shortcomings' (Ziderman, 2003: 70). Furthermore, the narrow definition of reimbursable training has resulted in low levels of company reimbursements, a development that riles business and other stakeholders (Zimbabwe, 2006a). In addition, ZIMDEF does not support training for the informal economy.

As expected, TVET provision is dominated by government, which in 2006 accounted for 55 per cent of enrolments, followed by the private sector with 28 per cent, parastatals accounting for the other 17 per cent (Fig. 8.2). Private training institutions finance themselves by charging fees to students, which has made entry into them the preserve of the elites. However, the role of the sector in training remains relatively small, as government tends to dominate.

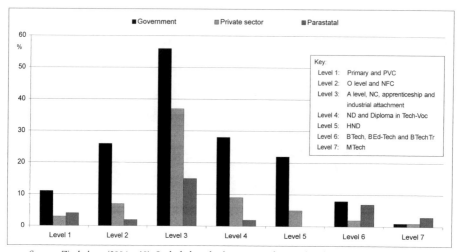

Source: Zimbabwe (2006a: 10). Included under 'government' are polytechnics, industrial training centres, government ministries, schools, VTCs, youth training centres and local authorities; 'private sector' comprises companies, churches, NGOs, the private sector and private colleges; 'parastatals' includes universities and parastatals.

**Fig. 8.2: Percentage of enrolments in TVET, by provider and level, 2006**

If parastatals and universities, which are publicly funded, are included under 'government' provision, its share rises to 72 per cent.

Donor financing in TVET is evident: USAID built and equipped Belvedere Technical Teachers' College and Mutare Polytechnic; GTZ equipped Harare Institute of Technology, Msasa VTC and Masvingo Polytechnic; the Chinese built Chinhoyi Technical Teachers' College (now Chinhoyi University of Technology); the French equipped Chinhoyi Technical Teachers' College and Westgate VTC. However, lack of refurbishment and replacement has resulted in the infrastructure and equipment deteriorating and the facilities being underused. Most institutions lack up-to-date equipment that matches developments in technologies in use in industry, with older institutions like Harare and Bulawayo polytechnics the worst affected. Specialized equipment for use by students with disabilities is also missing, and library facilities in TVET institutions are inadequate and out of date. The situation was worsened by the withdrawal of donors after 1999, the hyperinflationary environment, and budget constraints. Over-reliance on government is not in line with the 2002 UNESCO and ILO recommendations on TVET for the 21st century that regarded the funding of TVET as a shared responsibility between government, the private sector and students.[37]

Clearly, therefore, all publicly funded tertiary institutions have experienced serious financial problems. It is reported that treasury allocations represented less than 1 per cent of state universities' bids, and that, by July 2009, only 1 per cent,

[37] See <http://www.unevoc.unesco.org/pubsdir.php?akt=id&st=adv&id=2002_001&lg=ch>.

5.9 per cent and 7.8 per cent of the allocations for recurrent expenditure had been disbursed to universities, polytechnics and teachers' colleges, respectively. Corresponding allocations for capital expenditure were 0.8 per cent, 3.2 per cent and 2.4 per cent. While government contributed 82.4 per cent of the total funding for higher and tertiary education before the crisis, which was the highest for SADC countries, this share had dropped to 16.4 per cent by mid-2009, a level lower than the SADC average of 65.3 per cent. Student fees in public institutions were not only lower than those in private institutions, most students defaulted and the institutions could not turn them away as this would violate government policy (Zimbabwe, 2009).

An irony is that, while local tertiary institutions – and the education and training system in general – are faced with debilitating financial constraints, the government is financing over 3,000 Zimbabwean students in South Africa under the Presidential Scholarship Programme.[38]

### 8.4.5 Policy and institutional constraints

In spite of the recommendations of the Rationalization Policy (Zimbabwe, 1990), the Nziramasanga Commission (Zimbabwe, 1999), the joint GTZ/Ministry of Higher and Tertiary Education end-of-project evaluation of 2000, and the Ministry of Higher and Tertiary Education's policy review of 2006 to establish a national training authority to run vocational education and training, this has not been done. Even though the management of TVET was decentralized to institutions, the underlying problems associated with limited funding have remained. VTCs were transferred to the Ministry of Youth Development in 2000 to focus on skills training for youth, creating institutional fragmentation, overlap and mission creep.

Worse still, the vertical and lateral expansion of TVET tends to be driven by the desire for status in both the private and public sectors (Zimbabwe, 2006a). For instance, youth training centres and VTCs offer NDs and at times HNDs, yet they do not have the capacity in terms of lecturing staff, equipment and infrastructure. Even though UNESCO and the ILO strongly recommended that stakeholders be consulted,[39] the policy review found that 36.6 per cent of the 158 respondents indicated that they were not involved in policy formulation (Zimbabwe, 2006a).[40]

---

[38] *The Herald*, 20 November 2009. At a cost of around US$10,000 per student per year, the total cost of the programme is US$30 million, which could make a difference in meeting the funding needs of local tertiary institutions.

[39] UNESCO and ILO *Recommendations on Technical and Vocational Education and Training for the Twenty-first Century*, 2002; see fn. 37.

[40] A questionnaire was administered to all provinces of Zimbabwe covering a sample of 170 participants drawn from all sectors.

Most of those who indicated that they were involved (66.5 per cent) were civil servants, with 68 per cent of those who indicated no involvement in TVET policy formulation coming from the private sector and parastatals, hardly a solid building block for the evolution of a demand-driven system.[41] The study found that the curricula in use in institutions are continually drifting away from the needs of industry, despite the establishment of the Zimbabwe Occupational Standards Services in 1999 to produce occupational standards on which to base the TVET curricula. The National Manpower Advisory Council, which is supposed to bridge the gap between the government and industry, is not closely linked to the latter, creating a void between the expectations of industry and what the TVET system does (Ziderman, 2003: 70). Its mandate is restricted to an advisory role.

Sadly, there is no effective regulatory mechanism to monitor, evaluate and enforce regulations in order to assure quality in TVET institutions (Zimbabwe, 2006a). The inspectorate under HEXCO is ineffectual. The absence of a comprehensive policy in TVET implies that the guidance of operations of TVET, including the monitoring of standards and planning as well as the regulation of participation in TVET by NGOs and the private sector, is weak.

The failure to amend the enabling legislation (the Manpower Planning and Development Act, as amended in 1996) to accommodate the recommendations of the Rationalization Policy document (Zimbabwe, 1990) and the Nziramasanga Commission (Zimbabwe, 1999) has resulted in only marginal and haphazard reforms, which have been worsened by weakened capacity on account of the brain drain and acute shortage of resources. In addition, evidence of gender stereotyping in TVET abounds, with girls taking up courses socially perceived to be feminine (e.g. secretarial and other commercial courses), while the engineering field remains the preserve of boys (Zimbabwe, 2006a).

Regrettably, no TVET policy exists that targets the informal economy, where women and youths are predominant. Consequently, the integrability of such marginalized sectors and groups into the mainstream economy is undermined, reinforcing its inherited dual and enclave nature. This therefore implies a need for a comprehensive TVET policy in Zimbabwe that takes cognizance of the specificities of both the formal and informal economies, and of the needs of vulnerable and marginalized groups, requiring greater flexibility and diversity in TVET delivery, including the use of non-formal modes of education and training.

The report of the Ministry of Higher and Tertiary Education of 2006 ranked the constraints in TVET as follows: lack of funding; irrelevant curriculum;

[41] Ziderman (2003: 70) argues that, when TVET was transferred from the labour ministry to that of Higher Education and Technology in 1988, a change in orientation occurred, with the 'tripartite culture' (a readiness to work with industry) and a concern with labour-market issues being replaced with an education focus.

weak research and planning; inadequate monitoring and evaluation; inadequate qualifications framework; management shortcomings; inappropriate legislation; and political orientation.

In summing up the challenges facing education and training in Zimbabwe, a report by the Ministry of Education, Sport, Arts and Culture (Zimbabwe, 2007: 3) had this to say:

> The education sector is currently facing a number of challenges emerging from a highly competitive and integrated global economy and rapid technological and social changes which have brought about a diversity and complexity of the labour market. There is a mismatch between the demands of the labour market and the output of the education system resulting in high school leaver employment problems. A large amount of resources are required to bring about the qualitative reforms in education and training while sustaining the quantitative achievements. Shortages of textbooks, deterioration of infrastructure, availability of teaching materials and essential facilities such as laboratories and libraries especially in marginalized rural areas remain major challenges. The situation in the rural areas remains unattractive to trained teachers. High proportions of children without ECD [Early Childhood Development], low completion rates of girls especially at higher levels and low pass rates are a cause for concern in general.

## 8.5 The Brain Drain

Since the advent of independence in 1980, Zimbabwe has experienced three major waves of emigration. The first, in the early 1980s, was associated with the out-migration of disgruntled whites following majority rule. The UNDP (2008) observes that as many as 19,300 skilled and professional personnel emigrated, mainly to South Africa, Australia and the UK. This wave was, however, mitigated by the return of many Zimbabweans who had been working or studying abroad. The second wave was linked to the violence that followed the referendum of February 2000, when Zimbabweans rejected the government-sponsored new constitution, the fast-track land-reform programme that came immediately afterwards, the violent and disputed parliamentary elections of August 2000 and presidential elections of March 2002. This wave continued after the 2005 parliamentary and senatorial elections. The third wave is linked to the wrenching changes that took place after 2007 as the economy receded into paralysis in the context of hyperinflation.

Although estimates of the size of the Zimbabwean diaspora differ from study to study,[42] it probably ranges between three and four million, with South

---

[42] The word 'diaspora' was originally used to refer to the Jews who were displaced from their homeland. It is now widely used to define a homogeneous group of people with a common sense of displacement, both voluntary and involuntary, with a hope to return home once the factors that led to their leaving have been addressed (Makina, 2007).

Africa accounting for the largest group (over one million), followed by the UK, Botswana, the USA, Canada, Australia and New Zealand; Zimbabwe is now one of the top ten emigration countries in Sub-Saharan Africa.[43] Migration from the country is so widespread that there is almost one emigrant in every immediate family, and more from the extended family (Tevera and Crush, 2003: 29–30; Maphosa, 2004: 9).

The national human resources survey (Zimbabwe, 2006b) reported the extent of the brain drain in terms of the vacancy rates (the mean ratio of vacant posts to established posts) across all sectors of the economy. The study found emigration pressures to be severe, with 70 per cent of those interviewed intending to leave the country. The three most common reasons given for wanting to leave were economic (80 per cent), to work abroad (39 per cent) and self-advancement (46 per cent). People with higher qualifications were in the majority: 86 per cent for those with a Ph.D., 76 per cent for holders of Masters degrees or post-graduate diplomas, and 76 per cent first-degree graduates. These findings are in line with those of other studies, such as that of the Scientific and Industrial Research and Development Centre (Table 8.4).

While no sector has been spared by migration, its impact has been most pronounced in the social sectors, and in particular in health care, where it is estimated that more than 80 per cent of the doctors, nurses, pharmacists, radiographers and therapists who were trained after 1980 had left the country (UNDP, 2008). The national budget, delivered on 17 March 2009, observed that there was a 68 per cent vacancy rate for doctors, with the overall staff presence at most health institutions at between 15 and 50 per cent. The critical shortage of staff at major hospitals (Table 8.5) was compounded by staff shortages at the university medical training hospital in Harare. By March 2007, the overall vacancy rate was 60 per cent,[44] which resulted in a reduction in the yearly intake of medical students from 120 to 70.

In the mining sector, for instance, the Chamber of Mines of Zimbabwe estimates that more than half the industry's skilled personnel emigrated from the country in 2007 and that, in early 2008, 1,116 vacancies existed for professional and technical staff. Indeed, the picture is one of a severe and rapidly worsening skills shortage, exacerbated by the precipitous decline in the country's capacity to regenerate skills. Between 480 and 550 university graduates are required in mining disciplines, yet the maximum capacity of mining-related departments at the University of Zimbabwe is 124 students per year, implying that it will take four to five years to supply existing needs (Hawkins, 2009).

[43] Together with Mali, Burkina Faso, Ghana, Eritrea, Nigeria, Mozambique, South Africa, Sudan and the Democratic Republic of Congo.

[44] The vacancy rates were as high as 100 per cent in haematology, 96 per cent in anatomy, 95 per cent in physiology, and 88 per cent each in histopathology and anaesthesia and critical-care medicine.

**Table 8.4: Education and qualifications of Zimbabweans living abroad**

| Field of study | % | Qualification | % | Age group | % |
|---|---|---|---|---|---|
| Teachers | 26 | First degree | 34 | 20–29 | 25 |
| Doctors, nurses and pharmacists | 25 | Polytechnic education | 28 | 30–39 | 40.8 |
| | | Masters degree | 20 | 40–49 | 23.7 |
| Engineers and other scientists | 23 | Vocational training | 9 | 50+ | 10.5 |
| Accountants | 17 | Diploma | 2 | | |
| Farmers | 5 | None | 2 | | |
| Bankers | 2 | | | | |
| Clergy and others | 1 | | | | |

*Source:* Scientific and Industrial Research and Development Centre (2003).

**Table 8.5: Staff situation at the major referral hospitals (Harare, Parirenyatwa, Chitungwiza, Mpilo and United Bulawayo) as at 31 January 2006, selected posts**

| Designation | Establishment | In post | Vacancies | Vacancy rate (%) |
|---|---|---|---|---|
| Doctors/Specialist Heads of Department | 22 | 1 | 21 | 95 |
| Government Medical Officer | 106 | 27 | 79 | 75 |
| Chief Government Pathologist | 3 | 1 | 2 | 67 |
| Junior Registrar | 62 | 0 | 62 | 100 |
| Chief Medical Laboratory Scientist | 6 | 2 | 4 | 67 |
| Senior/Principal Medical Laboratory Scientist | 4 | 2 | 2 | 50 |
| State Certified Medical Laboratory Technician | 171 | 99 | 72 | 42 |
| State Certified Medical Laboratory Technician | 50 | 3 | 47 | 94 |
| Registered General Nurse/Sister | 2,852 | 1,936 | 916 | 32 |
| State Certified Nurse | 392 | 284 | 122 | 88 |

*Source:* 'A Review of National Strategies to Manage Mobility and Migration of Zimbabwean Skilled Professionals: The Health Sector Experiences', a presentation by Dr O. L. Mbengeranwa, Chairman of the Health Service Board at the 'Strengthening National Capacities for Addressing Migration and Development in Zimbabwe' Workshop, Troutbeck Inn, Nyanga, 18–19 September, 2006, cited in UNDP (2008: 110).

One consequence of the brain drain is 'grade inflation', a tendency for firms and organizations to promote inexperienced staff with low qualifications into positions that required better-qualified and experienced personnel. As the UNDP (2008) observed, the loss of skills and the deterioration in the country's training and education infrastructure is the most important single problem that industry will face in the post-crisis situation. Their study found that firms resorted to poaching skills from one another. Worse still, personnel previously categorized as technicians were graded as engineers, reflecting a downgrading of industrial capability across the board. This therefore suggests that the brain drain will be a major constraint to economic recovery, especially given the diminished capacity of the vocational education and training system to regenerate skills.

Measures to reverse the brain drain have been ad hoc,[45] and included the establishment in 2006 of a task force on skills' identification, deployment and retention, chaired by the Permanent Secretary in the Ministry of Higher and Tertiary Education. In spite of this, out-migration continued, especially in the context of the 2010 World Cup in South Africa, which created huge demand for technical expertise, particularly in infrastructure development and maintenance.

The brain drain is, however, mitigated by remittances from the diaspora, which provide a nexus between migration and development. Over time, remittances have assumed greater importance in Zimbabwe. World Bank estimates suggest that migrant remittance flows to Zimbabwe through official channels amounted to US$17 million in 1980, rising to US$33 million in 1982 before decreasing in subsequent years until 1994, when they were estimated to be US$44 million. The International Fund for Agricultural Development (IFAD) estimated remittance inflows at US$361 million in 2007, representing 7.2 per cent of GDP.[46] However, a more recent study of remittance strategies of Zimbabweans living in northern England estimated that US$0.94 billion was sent from the UK to Zimbabwe in 2007 (Magunha *et al.*, 2009). The contradictory figures reflect the challenges involved in estimating remittance flows as they depend on the concepts used and channels through which remittances are sent. According to the Zimbabwe Monetary Policy Statement of 31 January 2008, officially recorded foreign-currency receipts through the Homelink system were estimated at US$5.7 million in 2006 and US$47.5 million in 2007, a mere 13.2 per cent of the remittances estimated by IFAD for 2007.[47] This suggests that the bulk of remittances were transmitted through informal channels as a result of the huge exchange-rate differentials between the official and parallel exchange rates. A study by Makina and Kanyenze (2010: 19) estimated remittance flows to have risen from US$200,000 in 2001 to US$1.4 billion by the end of 2009.

As the social protection system in Zimbabwe collapsed with hyperinflation, remittances from abroad helped keep the Zimbabwean economy afloat. Bracking and Sachikonye (2006: 4) indicate that half of the 300 urban households surveyed in Harare and Bulawayo were dependent on migrant remittances for everyday consumption. Magunha *et al.* (2009) found the use of remittances to be as follows: cash for food (mentioned by 44.8 per cent of the sample), cash for household support (40.5 per cent), cash for school fees (31.7 per cent), cash for household bills (29.1 per cent), and cash for medicines (22.9 per cent). The

---

[45] Ad hoc in the sense that the underlying push factors such as the political and economic climate were not addressed.

[46] IFAD, *Sending Money Home: Worldwide Remittance Flows to Developing Countries, 2007*, <http://www.ifad.org/events/remittances/maps/index.htm>.

[47] Homelink is a private limited money-transfer and investment company of the Reserve Bank of Zimbabwe.

study concludes that a great deal of remitting appears to have been for everyday use for basic survival, with only one in five remitting consumer durables or for longer-term projects.

Studies suggest that a significant number (two-thirds) of diasporans are prepared to return home should political and economic stability be achieved so that they can participate in the recovery and development of their country (SIRDC, 2003; Bloch, 2005; Makina, 2007). This should be encouraging. However, whether it happens or not will depend on the success of the Inclusive Government in implementing the Global Political Agreement and embarking on a new era of peace, hope and freedom. In short, there must be a strong signal that the template and narrative are changing and are irreversible. The disharmony and bickering in the Inclusive Government is hardly a solid foundation for return migration and sustained recovery. Realistically, it is those who are doing menial jobs and those engaged in jobs outside their skill areas that may return.

With increased recognition of the development link between the diaspora and development, government, with support from the International Organization for Migration (IOM), established a Migration and Development Unit in the Ministry of Economic Development in April 2008 to co-ordinate efforts currently being undertaken by various government departments and ministries in the area of migration. However, the unit lacks sufficient capacity to carry out its work effectively and sits at too low a level to have sufficient clout to co-ordinate across ministries. Given the growing recognition of the importance of maximizing the developmental aspects of the diaspora, especially through remittances, government and the IOM have since 2007 organized a series of workshops on migration and development, which have culminated in the development of a migration policy framework that is now awaiting Cabinet approval. Joint efforts have been undertaken in the following areas (Makina and Kanyenze, 2010: 38–9):

- Engagement of diaspora organizations.
- Sequenced short-term return programme in respect of medical professionals.
- The Beitbridge Labour Migration Centre, which facilitates the registration and recruitment of farm-workers in South Africa.
- Development of the Zimbabwe migration profile with the Central Statistical Office.
- The human capital website in liaison with the Ministry of Higher Education.[48]
- The skills gap study.
- The health workers survey.
- The remittance regulatory framework study.

---

[48] See <http://www.zimbabwehumancapital.org.zw>.

## 8.6 International Experiences and Trends in Education and Training

The provision of education is guided by international principles and standards that have been developed and adopted at the global (UN) level. These include Education for All 1990, Education for All 2000 Assessment, the World Education Conference, Dakar 2000, the MDGs 2000, World Fit for Children (WFFC) 2002, with declarations to which Zimbabwe is a signatory. All these advocate the attainment of quality universal primary education by 2015 and gender equality in both primary and secondary education by 2005. The MDG process is considered to be one of the highest levels of development planning in Zimbabwe. MDG 2 relates to the need to 'Achieve universal primary education', while MDG 3 seeks to 'Promote gender equality and empower women'. WFFC target II is to 'Promote quality education', with an emphasis on promoting quality universal primary education and gender equality in education. It requires governments to expand and improve comprehensive early childhood care and education for girls and boys, especially the most vulnerable and disadvantaged children.

As well as education provision, countries throughout the world are increasingly concerned about skills development, with a new focus on training for employment. In the context of globalization, training has assumed greater importance to enhance national competitiveness or to improve the employability of job-seekers. In this regard, training systems are being reformed so that they can respond better to rapidly changing demands and opportunities. The need to deliver a 'workforce for the 21st century, highly skilled, productive and capable of restoring competitiveness, growth and equity' is now a common cliché in national development agendas. As Ziderman (2003) points out, at the heart of this consensus is the policy objective of developing an effective, efficient, flexible, competitive and responsive training system which is demand-driven.[49]

This shift away from supply-driven and centrally controlled training arises from the realization that wholly supply-driven programmes generally suffer from bureaucratic inertia, inefficiency and irrelevance with regard to the needs of the economy, are costly, often under-funded, ineffective and ultimately unsustainable (Atchoarena and Delluc, 2002; Middleton *et al.*, 1993; World Bank, 1991; Grubb & Ryan, 1999). Political decisions about TVET programmes undermine their effectiveness since such decisions are short-term, aimed at gaining political advantage. The long-run perspectives necessary for effective TVET programmes – the need to develop skills that can enable individuals to find and keep employment, to advance over time, to continue to improve productivity as technologies and work organization change – are easily undermined by short-term political goals, such as enrolling large numbers of individuals quickly.

---

[49] Demand-driven training provision aims at meeting the skill needs of the economy, of society, and of individuals (Ziderman, 2003; Grubb and Ryan, 1999; Middleton *et al.*, 1993).

System-building is also a problem in purely political decisions, where the temptation exists to add new programmes rather than consolidate and rationalize old ones. As such, TVET programmes have proliferated, creating a quagmire of overlapping interventions. TVET programmes in many countries became an agglomeration of unrelated programmes rather than constituting a coherent system. There is therefore a case for greater co-ordination to create more rational 'systems'. With decisions on trade-offs often scattered in independent ministries and agencies in the absence of a central political arena where such decisions are handled, a piecemeal approach leaves practitioners in TVET in a quandary as to whether unemployment will be reduced through training programmes or through macroeconomic policy. Consequently, the effective development of TVET policies requires some independence from political processes.

In addition, narrow, job-specific forms of TVET are increasingly inappropriate in an economic world where jobs and technology change quickly. Thus, failure to factor in the demand side has undermined the utility of education and training, resulting in a mismatch between skills demand and supply (De Moura Castro & de Andrade, 1990). Furthermore, efforts towards the integration of academic and vocational education to develop broader forms of vocational education suggest a growing aversion to narrow programmes. In the words of the World Bank (1991: 23), 'to respond to the needs of the economy demands a degree of freedom from short-term bureaucratic control that is difficult to achieve in line ministries. National training authorities have been found to be effective in this respect in several countries.'

Owing to the success of the German dual system, and to the weaknesses of school-based TVET, which has been criticized for being outdated and inconsistent with the demands of real work, many countries are trying to strengthen work-based approaches within their TVET systems. Work-based learning has taken the form of apprenticeship programmes, co-operative education, school-based enterprises and work experiences in developed countries, with parallel efforts in developing countries to promote traditional apprenticeships, 'education with production' or 'learning by doing'. However, an emerging concern is the need to attend to the learning/teaching process in work-based learning.[50] If a work-based programme is narrowly devised, then a trainee may have inadequate skills as work changes, and long-run employment experiences may be poor. It has proved difficult to implement work-based programmes in countries without supportive institutions (including stable tripartite discussions and agreements). Quite often, there is little integration with the school-based component.

Indeed, some forms of vocational education have moved closer to academic or general education, and education and training may have started to converge

---

[50] A key question is how much education and training is taking place alongside production.

(Caillods, 1994). Broader forms of vocational education integrate more academic competencies, yet broader and more-integrated TVET programmes lead to benefits only in the longer run, and their consequences in production – flexibility, the ability to anticipate and solve problems, the ability to perform as jobs become more complex or as individuals advance – are not immediately visible, and may not be supported by employers concerned with their current labour force. A present-oriented policy, or one responsive to present-oriented employers, will be likely to ignore the possibilities for broader programmes.

Although the general rule is that governments should not intervene where markets are working adequately, 'demand-driven training is a good idea but needs to be taken with a grain of salt' (De Moura Castro, 1995: 1). In view of their merit-good status, markets fail in education and training, especially in the context of the 'poaching' externality, where employers who pay for training fear to lose their skilled workers to other employers and hence cut back on training. Furthermore, the consumers of TVET – potential trainees and employers – may be uninformed, and providers of training may not respond to price-related incentives.

Therefore, intervention is necessary, as long as the associated bureaucratic inertia and political interference do not cause more inefficiency than the market failure itself. Intervention is particularly strong in two areas (Grubb & Ryan, 1999):

- At the educational end of the TVET spectrum, where the youthfulness, inexperience and lack of assets among potential participants make their decisions less attractive from an efficiency and equity standpoint.
- At the more transferable end of in-service training, where employers are least willing to provide and finance desirable amounts of training.

The continued role of the state is associated with the persistent concern for the poor and underemployed, the worst-off members of society. Thus, TVET is considered an attractive alternative to social welfare payments as it promises to create wealth and not merely to redistribute it.

Although the structures of successful organizations differ, the crucial aspect is a structure of governance that involves the various stakeholders (employers, unions, etc.) and creates adequate and stable funding, the freedom to use resources flexibly, and a high level of professional capacity (World Bank, 1991; Middleton *et al.*, 1993; Atchoarena & Delluc, 2002; Ziderman, 2003; Zimbabwe, 2006a). A stakeholder, co-operative and complementary approach is therefore expedient. As Middleton *et al.* (1993: 129) contend, 'co-operation between the government and the private sector is the cornerstone of the process through which the government's role changes as development proceeds'. Thus

> the challenge is to move from policies dominated by social and supply objectives
> and programs financed and provided by governments to policies and programs

that respond to market forces and promote employer and private training, and that establish appropriate complementary and supportive roles for the state [ibid.: 253].

One of the most contentious issues is as to whether pre-employment education should be academic or vocational or some mixture of the two (integrated education and training). This issue remains unresolved, as even the acclaimed German dual system is threatened by more students wanting to continue along academic rather than vocational tracks. The balance between academic and vocational content is one that every schooling system concerned with occupational preparation must confront. Nonetheless, English-speaking countries are making efforts to develop broader and more-integrated vocational education (Grubb & Ryan, 1999).

Even though education and training systems in developing and developed countries may seem worlds apart, many of the issues are remarkably similar, although a few (particularly the informal economy) are quite distinct. The world-wide trend in the restructuring of TVET systems has the following characteristics (Grubb & Ryan, 1999; Atchoarena & Delluc, 2002; Ziderman, 2003; UNESCO-UNEVOC, 2004):

- Declining role of the state – even in developed European countries with strong state traditions such that government-controlled TVET systems are opening up to form linkages with private institutions and other skills-development providers, sometimes co-financed from national budgets.
- Decentralization to sub-national governments – many countries have decentralized policy-making, and often funding of programmes, to sub-national governments. Regional variations provide 'natural experiments' where differences in TVET programmes can provide information on effective practices. However, decentralization itself raises the question of whether a country trying to establish a national TVET policy in order to compete more effectively in a global economy can accomplish this through local decisions.
- High-performance work, key skills, and broader conceptions of TVET – one of the common dreams of TVET is to create the highly skilled, flexible labour force necessary for work in high-performance firms and has led many countries to articulate 'key' or 'core' skills necessary for high-performance work, such as problem-solving or trouble-shooting, the ability to communicate effectively with others and to work in teams, the capacity to perform independently, etc.
- Move towards creating diversified schools combining vocational and academic skills training – the current manifestation of a much older debate about how general or specific preparation for employment

should be. There is a need for a broad and integrated programme. One challenge is the balance between academic and vocational skills, another is the breadth of skills. Whether the teaching is effectively integrated is important.

- Entrepreneurship in TVET and skills development is encouraged.
- Greater autonomy is being granted to public TVET institutions.
- The involvement of all partners is encouraged.
- New financing and certification mechanisms are being introduced.
- The curricula for the training of trainers and apprenticeship are being revised.
- Dual forms of training, where institutions and enterprises work closely, are being developed.

Special issues in developing and transitional countries include (Grubb & Ryan, 1999; Ziderman, 2003):

- Implementation problems – especially where economic conditions, political and cultural factors are not supportive, creating systemic problems. A system-building approach is therefore critical, with emphasis on what can be done to improve the conditions.
- Encouraging private-sector training – market failures lead firms to under-provide training.
- Promoting work-based learning, education with production (learning by doing), and traditional apprenticeships.
- Providing training for the informal economy – training has been proposed especially in the areas of basic business practices, literacy, health and safety, and technical skills. Whether training alone is sufficient, or whether it should be provided as part of a package of services (e.g. small loans, marketing advice, creation of co-operatives, etc.) is an issue to be addressed. Training for the informal economy must have characteristics of 'education with production' since production cannot stop engagement in training. Thus all the basic problems of work-based learning – the difficulty of disentangling training from production, the problem of identifying whether any learning is taking place – apply to the informal economy. This needs to be done in informal ways, as differently from schooling as possible for individuals who are distrustful of authority and formal organizations. Part of the training could include record-keeping and diaries.
- Growing social awareness of the needs of special groups, such as the poor, ethnic minorities, youths, people living with disabilities, and women.
- Developing systems and policies – national institutions and national policies about TVET. It is easier to create TVET programmes than to develop coherent systems.

In spite of the country-by-country declarations regarding the importance of improving education and training to enhance a country's growth, productivity, competitiveness, standard of living, and progress out of poverty, TVET policies that may help to achieve such goals are, as usual, undermined by the persistence of politics.

## 8.7 Sustainable Recovery Policies and Policy Measures

### 8.7.1 Strategic objectives and thrusts

In the context of the challenges posed by globalization and the high levels of unemployment and endemic poverty, it is imperative that education and training provide pathways to resolve these issues. This is particularly important in a country such as Zimbabwe where, historically, education and training were geared towards promoting the integrability of a particular group at the expense of others, thus promoting an enclave and dual system. Even though the racial discrimination that characterized the pre-independence period was abolished, a class-based one emerged and has been entrenched, especially after the onset of crisis, its deepening and the ensuing paralysis. The education and training system in Zimbabwe continued to focus exclusively on the formal sector, neglecting the non-formal (communal and informal) which is now the mainstay of the economy.

Given, then, the critical role of education and training in promoting employ-ability, enhancing productivity and external competitiveness, and in poverty reduction, the strategic objectives and thrust in this sector should be to:

- foster a 'pathways approach' that caters for the various aptitudes and interests of students;
- improve the quality of education and training by promoting a partnership, shared approach;
- improve the match between skills demand and supply by encouraging stakeholder participation in the design and provision of education and training;
- establish a national training authority, as recommended by the Nziramasanga Commission (Zimbabwe, 1999), to create a more demand-driven and flexible system at tertiary level;
- develop a comprehensive national skills-development policy framework for Zimbabwe;
- develop a manpower recovery plan for the public sector, and undertake sector-based human-resources audits;
- adopt and implement the migration and development policy framework;
- promote return migration and the use of diaspora skills;

- adopt immigration policies that make it easier to attract skills;
- engage in co-development programmes with countries with a high concentration of Zimbabweans.

## 8.7.2 Recovery policies and policy measures

*Harnessing the dormant human capital*

The collapse in real incomes increased the opportunity cost of being employed such that many professional and skilled persons ended up in the informal economy, particularly as money-changers, or were doing menial jobs in neighbouring countries. During 2008, the erosion of incomes was such that salaries could no longer cover even transport costs, resulting in workers, especially those in the public sector, staying at home. With the advent of the multiple-currency regime, the previously lucrative money-changing business was immediately shut out, and with the availability of goods on the local market, middlemen who were buying goods from neighbouring countries for resale found their sources of income drying up. They had to find alternative sources of livelihood quickly.

Following the inauguration of the Inclusive Government mid-February 2009 and the announcement that civil servants would be paid an allowance of US$100 from the end of February, a flurry of dormant teachers came back to be re-engaged. This experience suggests that, once a signal is out that government is working seriously towards substantially improving working conditions in the public sector, such dormant labour, which represents 'the low-hanging fruit', will return. In addition, some parastatals, such as the Zimbabwe Electricity Supply Authority (ZESA), have advertised for the return of skilled personnel who left the country in an attempt to take advantage of the global recession. Harnessing such dormant skills is attractive in that it may not be as costly as a comprehensive returnee programme.

A critical aspect in promoting the return of skilled workers from neighbouring countries will depend on the ability of the Inclusive Government to show that it is serious about delivering the much anticipated change and recovery. As things stand, the discord that characterizes the Inclusive Government will promote a wait-and-see attitude on the part of this dormant pool of human resources.

*Improving the quality and relevance of primary and secondary education*

One way of enhancing the quality of the education system is to broaden the scope of early childhood education (ECD) and care to cover every child, as recommended by the 1999 Presidential Commission of Inquiry into Education and Training.[51] The commission further recommended that ECD classes should

---

[51] The Nziramasanga Commission recommended this two-year programme as foundational.

be attached to existing primary schools. A World Fit for Children emphasizes the best possible start in life: having access to education and the opportunity to develop individual capacity in a safe and supportive environment. Target 5 of the WFFC binds countries to develop and implement national ECD policies and programmes to enhance children's physical, social, emotional, spiritual and cognitive development.

On the basis of the Education for All, MDGs and WFFC goals, Zimbabwe aims for all pupils enrolled in Grade 1 to have pre-school background by 2010. This therefore implies the need to strengthen the implementation of the early childhood education and care policy which seeks to establish a pre-school and two years of ECD at every primary school from 2005. To facilitate this, some teacher training institutions have introduced the training of ECD teachers.

While the percentage of Grade 1 pupils with a pre-school background increased from 49 per cent in 2002 to 64 per cent in 2006, 151,695 pupils did not have such an experience in 2006. At this rate, the WFFC target of 100 per cent by 2010 is unlikely to be achieved. The proportion of girls with pre-school education in 2006 at 64 per cent (77,645) was only slightly higher than the 63 per cent for boys (74,050). Urban areas had a higher percentage of Grade 1 pupils with a pre-school background (67 per cent) than rural areas (63 per cent). ECD attendance in rural areas was affected by higher incidences of poverty, long distances to school, and diseases (Zimbabwe, 2007). Low-density urban areas had the highest proportion of Grade 1 pupils with a pre-school background (77 per cent), followed by communal areas (66 per cent), high-density areas (65 per cent), and lastly commercial farms (51 per cent), reinforcing the inherited inequalities in education provision.

In addition, education is seen increasingly to be a shared responsibility, implying a need for all stakeholders to play their roles in the provision of this basic right. In this regard, the practice whereby government is responsible for the salaries of teaching staff in all schools, public or private, should be reviewed. This will allow government to give more attention to the development of the satellite schools established in resettlement areas into fully-fledged schools. In 2006, satellite schools accounted for 12.3 per cent of primary schools and 23 per cent of secondary schools (Zimbabwe, 2007). Furthermore, the reversals in achieving universal primary education and broadening the scope of secondary education are challenges that should be faced head-on by reprioritizing education in line with the MDG and other international agreements that Zimbabwe has acceded to.

The Nziramasanga commission of 1999 criticized the education system for being too academic, lacking an all-inclusive 'pathways approach' that catered for the divergent aptitudes, interests and abilities of pupils. While the Ministry of Education, Sport, Arts and Culture belatedly adopted this approach in 2006, it has been hampered by lack of resources, especially for the practical/skills pathway. The implementation of this two-pathway education structure begins after Form II, encompassing the general/academic education pathway and the skills pathway, i.e. the business/commercial/technology/technical–vocational. The practical/skills pathway requires resources that can be adequately provided only through the active participation of all stakeholders – parents, communities, the private and NGO sectors and government. Prince Edward secondary school in Harare is a good example of how this can be achieved through smart partnerships among stakeholders. The fact that Prince Edward is a government school provides ample evidence that this is feasible, with the school community building the requisite infrastructure.

*Reorganizing TVET*

As was pointed out above, technical vocational education and training worldwide is being reorganized to promote stakeholder participation, to make it more flexible and adaptable to the rapid changes in technologies associated with globalization, and to enhance the fit between the demand and supply of labour.[52] In the case of Zimbabwe, this issue was raised in various policy reviews which called specifically for the establishment of a National Training Authority.[53] The Nziramasanga commission recommended that the National Manpower Advisory Council be transformed into a national training council (Zimbabwe, 1999).

Also as mentioned above, the key ingredients of successful organizations include a governance structure that allows stakeholder participation, creates adequate and stable funding, the freedom to use resources flexibly, and a high level of professionalism. As is the case elsewhere where such reforms have been undertaken, funding is based on a shared approach. In most cases, the skills funds underpinned by the training (payroll) levy are used as the basis for the funding. This therefore suggests a need to amend the Manpower Development Act such that ZIMDEF finances the proposed National Training Authority.

One way that has been found to be effective in dealing with the misfit between labour supply and demand is the use of public–private partnerships in training. Typical examples of this are the school of mining and the hotel and hospitality departments at the Bulawayo Polytechnic, which have become fully-fledged public–private-partnership organizations. Some new partnerships are also emerging, such as the woodwork technology department at Mutare Technical College, where the private sector in the area is playing an active role as a beneficiary of the training, and hence as a strategic partner. Dairibord Zimbabwe

---

[52] An excellent detailed outline of such reforms can be found in Ziderman (2003: Tables 1.1, 11.1 and 12.1).

[53] See the Nziramasanga commission report (Zimbabwe, 1999), the *TVET Concept Paper for the 21st Century* (CPPZ, 2003), Zimbabwe (2006a), and UNDP (2008), among others.

Holdings Limited and the Harare Institute of Technology recently entered into a partnership whereby the latter provides training to Dairibord personnel in areas of food-processing, especially of milk and dairy products. Eleven employees of Dairibord recently graduated in food science technology programmes.[54] The Motor Trade Association has also mooted a similar arrangement with technical colleges, which suggests that this approach is viable and creates the win–win smart partnerships that are so vital for economic regeneration.[55]

National Employment Councils (NECs), which are bilateral structures of sectoral employer and worker representatives, could play an active role in training, as used to happen before independence, a departure from their current preoccupation with collective bargaining and industrial-relations management. Given the externalities associated with training, NECs offer the best avenue for collective effort and partnerships in training provision in order to build human-capital stock according to the specific requirements of each sector. By so doing, the NECs will emulate the experiences of South Africa, where the Sectoral Education and Training Authorities (SETAs) provide training on the basis of a one per cent payroll levy. SETAs also run internships for youths, where theoretical training at the colleges is complemented by attachments within companies in the respective sectors. The SETAs retain 80 per cent of the training levy collected in their sector, while the remaining 20 per cent goes to government for training not covered by the private sector.

To promote inclusiveness, curricula should be redefined so as to meet the specific demands of the non-formal (including informal) and small-scale sectors. Skill requirements of small-scale enterprises and the informal economy might be addressed using non-formal approaches such as the Informal Sector Training and Resource Network (INSTARN), which was launched in 1995 as a joint project of the Ministry of Higher and Tertiary Education and GTZ, providing a traditional apprenticeship programme. It started as a pilot project based at Masvingo Technical College, but was extended to become a national programme in 2000.

The apprentices were recruited from the ranks of the unemployed and were attached to a host informal business. They would undergo several weeks of formal training at a training college in their area. After training they would be placed with the host informal business, which would automatically become a client of the programme, receiving business training, regular support and monitoring from an INSTARN small business adviser. Supporting the host business was meant to create a conducive environment for training. The apprentices could opt for

---

[54] *The Herald*, 5 August 2009.

[55] This was mentioned at the organization's annual conference at Troutbeck Hotel, Nyanga, in September 2007.

trade-testing after twelve months to become certified. Upon qualification, those trainees who were keen on going into business were given business training, and would qualify for the tool hire-to-buy scheme operated by their local informal sector association. Thus, the project constituted an integrated approach to resolving the problems of the informal economy by providing technical training, business training and access to funding. However, the programme could not be sustained once the co-operating partner withdrew in 2000.

Yet another targeted initiative is the Integrated Skills Outreach Programme (ISOP), which was established by Cabinet in 2006 to alleviate poverty through employment creation. The programme administers training to equip unemployed youths with technical and entrepreneurial skills. It recognizes that not every student is academically orientated, so it is meant to provide an alternative source of livelihood for non-academically-orientated school-leavers. The programme runs short-term technical and entrepreneurial courses for five days to three months with a focus on employment creation. This initiative is chaired by the Ministry of Higher and Tertiary Education, in partnership with the Ministry of Youth Development, Indigenization and Empowerment, the Ministry of Small and Medium Enterprises and Co-operative Development, and the Ministry of Labour and Social Services.

### Human resource audits

Following the payment of the US$100 allowance to all civil servants, the existence of 'ghost employees' in the public sector was confirmed. In response, the mid-term budget review statement of 23 July 2009 indicated that government, through line ministries, was carrying out a payroll audit to verify the payroll establishment and assess the capacities and competencies of personnel. Such audits are critical in removing ghost workers from the public service, and they will also help to align the payroll to the establishment, rectify irregularities in the civil service payroll, and provide a detailed profile of the civil service. On the basis of such audits, a manpower recovery plan for the public sector can be developed.

Such audits are also necessary in the private sector in order to determine the impact of the brain drain, determine the skills gap, and assist in the formulation of appropriate sectoral responses. The NECs and relevant professional bodies should undertake such audits in their sectors or areas to assist in manpower planning for recovery, competitiveness and growth.

While there may be a case for carrying out a comprehensive national manpower survey along the lines of the one undertaken in 1981, this may be cumbersome as it requires a lot of resources and time. As a result, sector-based audits by the relevant stakeholders will be preferable. This approach is in line with the shift from centralized manpower planning to the more flexible labour-market analysis approach (Richards and Amjad, 1994). Such manpower audits can be the basis for the development of a comprehensive national skills-development policy framework. The government is in the process of developing such a policy framework in conjunction with the ILO.

*Diaspora development measures, voting rights and dual citizenship*[56]
As already pointed out, the IOM, ILO and relevant stakeholders are undertaking initiatives to harness the potential contribution of the diaspora in local development, including:

- the engagement of diaspora organizations;
- a sequenced short-term return programme in respect of medical professionals;
- the establishment of the Beitbridge Labour Centre;
- development of the Zimbabwe migration profile with the Central Statistical Office;
- the setting up of the human capital website;
- the skills gap study;
- the health workers survey;
- the remittance regulatory framework study.

A migration and development policy framework has been developed, and is awaiting Cabinet approval, which will help address the hitherto piecemeal and fragmented nature of interventions that are scattered across government ministries and departments. A more holistic and integrated approach, co-ordinated from one place (preferably the Migration and Development Unit in the Ministry of Economic Planning and Investment Promotion), is recommended. Countries such as the Philippines have gone to the extent of creating a specialized ministry to deal with issues of migration and development.

Such efforts to secure the maximum co-operation of people in the diaspora, as well as to harness remittances through formal channels, are commendable and should therefore be strengthened. Countries such as the Philippines, Bangladesh, Mexico, India, Moldova and Morocco have developed partnerships with home associations formed by their emigrants, through which the latter participate in the development of their home countries. Such recognition of those in the diaspora helps cement a close attachment to their home countries, an area Zimbabwe stands to reap benefits from, as most people in the diaspora feel a sense of being detached from their home country (SIRDC, 2003). Return migration should also be encouraged where applicable, especially with respect to dormant under-employed labour.

Such a strategy can work only if government addresses the push factors

---

[56] For a detailed outline, see Kanyenze (2009) and Makina and Kanyenze (2010).

behind the migration, namely governance and economic recovery. Returnees typically bring back with them human and financial resources, as well as social capital. Such measures should also include allowing those in the diaspora voting rights in local elections, as is the case in countries such as the Philippines, which promotes a sense of belonging and attachment to the home country. Furthermore, countries are increasing allowing dual citizenship so that migrants do not lose their home citizenship if they become citizens of destiny countries. This will therefore facilitate their return on short-term assignments and also maintain a close attachment with their home countries.

Government should also enter into co-development activities with countries that are major recipients of migrants from Zimbabwe. A good example is the partnership with South Africa that started in 2008, culminating in the establishment of the Beitbridge Labour Centre to facilitate the employment of Zimbabweans in the Limpopo Province of South Africa. Other initiatives could include the sharing of costs in skilled areas where the country has ploughed substantial resources into training (e.g. medical doctors).

*Immigration policies*

The world over, countries are relaxing immigration laws to facilitate the in-migration of skilled workers, especially in areas of critical skills shortage. For instance, developed countries such as the USA, the UK, Canada, Austria, New Zealand and Germany have actively sought and encouraged the immigration of ICT specialists into their countries. Closer to home, Mauritius also has such a policy. It is therefore necessary for Zimbabwe to review its immigration policies with a view to encouraging in-coming migration in areas of skills shortage.

## References

Atchoarena, D. and A. Delluc 2002. *Revisiting Technical and Vocational Education in Sub-Saharan Africa: An Update on Trends, Innovations and Challenges* (Paris: International Institute for Educational Planning/UNESCO).

Becker, G. S. 1964. *Human Capital* (Chicago, IL: University of Chicago Press).

Bloch, A. 2005. 'The Development Potential of Zimbabweans in the Diaspora. A Survey of Zimbabweans Living in the UK and South Africa' (Geneva: IOM, Migration Research Series No. 17).

Bracking, S. and L. Sachikonye 2006. 'Remittances, Poverty Reduction and the Informalisation of Household Wellbeing in Zimbabwe', GPRG-WPS-45.

Caillods, F. 1994. 'Converging trends amidst diversity in vocational training systems', *International Labour Review*, 133(2): Special Issue: Competitiveness, Equity and Skills.

CPPZ 2003. *TVET Concept Paper for the 21st Century* (Harare: Committee of Principals of Polytechnics of Zimbabwe).

De Moura Castro, C. 1995. 'The Elusive Fit Between Training and Its Demand', mimeo.

De Moura Castro, C. and A.C. de Andrade 1990. 'Supply and demand mismatches in training: Can anything be done?', *International Labour Review*, 129(3).

Dhliwayo, R. 2001. *The Impact of Public Expenditure Management under ESAP on Basic Social Services: Health and Education*, SAPRI/Zimbabwe, <http://www.saprin.org/zimbabwe/research/zim_public_exp.pdf>.

Grubb, N. W and P. Ryan 1999. *The Roles of Evaluation for Vocational Education and Training: Plain Talk on the Field of Dreams* (Geneva: ILO).

Hawkins, A. M. 2009. 'The Mining Sector in Zimbabwe and its Potential Contribution to Recovery' (Harare: UNDP, Comprehensive Economic Recovery in Zimbabwe, Working Paper 1).

Jonasson, E. 2008. 'Rural non-farm jobs: A pathway out of poverty?' *Poverty in Focus*, 16: 'Jobs, Jobs, Jobs: The Policy Challenge', 24–5.

Kanyenze, G. 2009. 'Labour Markets and the Rebuilding of Human Capital' (Harare: UNDP, Comprehensive Economic Recovery in Zimbabwe, Working Paper 3).

King, K. 1990. 'In-Service Training in Zimbabwe: An Analysis of Relationships Among Education and Training, Industry, and the State' (Washington, DC: World Bank, Education and Employment Division, Population and Human Resources Department).

Lucas, S. and P. Timmer 2005. *Connecting the Poor to Economic Growth: Eight Key Questions* (Washington, DC: Centre for Global Development, CGD Brief).

Magunha, F., A. Bailey and L. Cliffe 2009. 'Remittance Strategies of Zimbabweans in Northern England' (Leeds: University of Leeds, School of Geography), <http://www.zimbabweinstitute.org/File_Uploads/file/Remittances%20Paper.pdf>.

Makina, D. 2007. 'Survey of the Migrant Zimbabweans in South Africa', <http://www.idasa.org.za/gbOutputFiles.asp?WriteContent=Y&RID=2220>.

Makina, D. and G. Kanyenze 2010. 'The Potential Contribution of the Zimbabwe Diaspora to Economic Recovery' (Harare: UNDP, Comprehensive Economic Recovery in Zimbabwe, Working Paper 11), <http://www.kubatana.net/docs/econ/undp_contribution_diaspora_eco_recovery_100511.pdf>.

Maphosa, F. 2004. 'The Impact of Remittances from Zimbabweans Working in South Africa on Rural Livelihoods in the Southern Districts of Zimbabwe'.

Middleton, J., A. Ziderman and A. V. Adams 1993. *Skills for Productivity: Vocational Education and Training in Developing Countries* (Washington, DC: Oxford University Press for the World Bank).

Pakkiri, L. 1989. 'Education policies and economic development in Zimbabwe,' *Zimbabwe Journal of Educational Research*, 1(3).

Raftopoulos, B. 1987. 'Human resources development and the problem of labour utilisation', in I. Mandaza (ed.), *The Political Economy of Transition, 1980–1986* (Dakar: CODESRIA), 275–317.

Richards, P. and R. Amjad (eds.) 1994. *New Approaches to Manpower Planning and Analysis* (Geneva: ILO).

Riddell, Roger C. 1979. 'Alternative development strategies for Zimbabwe', *Zimbabwe Journal of Economics*, 1(3).

Scientific and Industrial Research and Development Centre 2003. *An Analysis of the Cause and Effect of the Brain Drain in Zimbabwe* (Harare: National Economic Consultative Forum and UNDP), <http://www.queensu.ca/samp/migrationresources/braindrain/documents/chetsanga.pdf>.

Selim, R. 2006. 'Employment–Poverty Linkages and Pro-poor Growth: A Synthesis Paper Based on Country Studies of Bangladesh, Bolivia and Ethiopia' (Geneva: ILO, Economics and Labour Market Analysis Department, Issues in Employment and Poverty Discussion Paper 23).

Tevera, D. and J. Crush 2003. 'The New Brain Drain from Zimbabwe' (Cape Town: SAMP, Migration Policy Series 29).

UNDP 2008. *Comprehensive Economic Recovery in Zimbabwe: A Discussion Document* (Harare: United Nations Development Programme).

UNESCO 2003. *Universal Primary Education, Goal for All: A Statistical Document* (Paris: UNESCO).

UNESCO-UNEVOC 2004. *Agencies for International Cooperation in Technical and Vocational Education and Training: A Guide to Sources of Information* (Bonn: International Centre for Technical and Vocational Training).

UNICEF-SNV 2009. *Final Research Report* (Harare: UNICEF-SNV).

World Bank 1991. *Vocational and Technical Education and Training* (Washington, DC: World Bank).

World Bank 1995. 'Zimbabwe: Achieving Shared Growth' (Washington, DC: World Bank, Country Economic Memorandum Volume 1).

World Bank 2005. *World Development Report 2006: Equity and Development* (Washington, DC: World Bank; New York: Oxford University Press).

World Bank 2006. *World Development Report 2007: Development and the Next Generation* (Washington, DC: World Bank).

World Bank 2009. *Africa Development Indicators: Youth and Employment in Africa: The Potential, the Problem, the Promise* (Washington, DC: World Bank).

ZCTU 1996. *Beyond ESAP: Framework for a Long-Term Development Strategy for Zimbabwe* (Harare: Zimbabwe Congress of Trade Unions).

Ziderman, A. 2003. *Financing Vocational Training in Sub-Saharan Africa* (Washington, DC: World Bank).

Zimbabwe 1981. *National Manpower Survey: Vol. 1* (Harare: Ministry of Manpower Planning and Development).

Zimbabwe 1990. *Rationalization of Vocational and Technical Education in Zimbabwe* (Harare: Ministry of Higher and Tertiary Education).

Zimbabwe 1999, *Report of the Presidential Commission of Inquiry into Education and Training* [Chairman: C. T. Nziramasanga] (Harare: Government Printer).

Zimbabwe 2004. *Zimbabwe Millennium Development Goals: 2004 Progress Report* (Harare: UNDP).

Zimbabwe 2006a. *Report on the Technical and Vocational Education and Training Policy Review Framework* (Harare: Ministry of Higher and Tertiary Education).

Zimbabwe 2006b. *Research on the Human Skills, Identification and Retention* (Harare: Ministry of Higher and Tertiary Education).

Zimbabwe 2007. *Primary and Secondary Education Statistics Report, 2000–2006* (Harare: Harare: Ministry of Education, Sport, Arts and Culture).

Zimbabwe 2009. *Baseline Study on the Status of Human Capital Development and Training Institutions in Zimbabwe* (Harare: Ministry of Higher and Tertiary Education).

Zvobgo, R. J. 1987. 'Education and the challenge of independence', in I. Mandaza (ed.), *The Political Economy of Transition, 1980–1986* (Dakar: CODESRIA), 319–54.

## Chapter 9

# Social Services:
# Housing, Health and Social Protection

This chapter looks at three aspects of social services: housing, health, and social protection. In each case, it follows through the policy and other pertinent developments since independence, and then proposes a way forward for each. The overriding issue is that the three are so closely interwoven that without any one of them it will be difficult to offer comprehensive social services to the population.

## 9.1 Housing

### 9.1.1 Introduction

Housing, also 'shelter', is one of the basic and fundamental human needs, offering protection from harsh weather conditions and providing security from societal threats. The UN Covenant on Economic, Social and Cultural Rights considers housing (shelter) as a basic socio-economic right.[1] Ideally, the provision of housing should be accompanied by the supply of other basic living needs such as safe drinking water, good sanitation, and accessible roads, schools and hospitals.

The provision of housing has been on Zimbabwe's national agenda since independence, not just because housing is an important social service but also because housing development contributes to national development through the creation of employment, investment, and the provision of markets for manufacturing industries. As stated in the 2010 National Budget Statement, housing not only uplifts the standard of living of people but also has multiplier effects on overall economic activity via the backward and forward linkages with the rest of the economy. The construction sector benefits from increased demand for building materials, and local authorities receive increased revenue. Housing is a physical expression of the socio-economic, cultural, political and ideological dynamics of a people, and also tells their history, as physical structures outlive their inhabitants.

The development of a housing policy in Zimbabwe stretches back to the

---

[1] This right is also enshrined in the UN's Universal Declaration of Human Rights, the Convention on the Elimination of All Forms of Discrimination against Women, the International Convention on the Elimination of All Forms of Racial Discrimination, and the Convention on the Rights of the Child, among others.

colonial period, when it catered separately for blacks and whites. Housing for Africans (blacks) was based on the premise that they were aliens in the urban areas, temporary dwellers whose permanent homes were in the rural areas, so were initially deprived of the opportunity to own houses. The colonial housing policy had the following elements:

- Rental housing schemes for Africans in urban areas.
- Segregated housing, with Africans staying in high-density areas.
- Financial institutions that catered for the needs of the whites only.
- No housing policy for rural areas.

As a result, twenty-eight years after independence, housing still reflects the dual and enclave nature of the economy, the following characteristics being very distinct:

- Race: There are locations where one race predominates, e.g. Arcadia suburb in Harare is occupied mainly by Coloureds, Belvedere is mainly an Indian community, and blacks live mainly in high-density suburbs.
- Location: The provision of houses has been concentrated in urban areas, with minimal development in rural areas.
- Gender: Rules and processes have tended to favour men in the acquisition of houses.
- Class: High-density areas are for the poor, medium-density areas for middle-income earners, and low-density areas for the rich.

## 9.1.2 The first decade of independence, 1980–1990

*Policy framework and ideological changes in Zimbabwe*
The two ministries responsible for the key aspects of housing during the early years of independence were the Ministry of Public Construction and National Housing and the Ministry of Local Government, Rural and Urban Development. Local authorities report to the latter, whose role is one of accountability for development finance as well as to ascertain tenure of occupancy. The Surveyor-General's Department is responsible for surveys and the registration of title deeds. The Ministry of Public Construction and National Housing was empowered by the Housing and Building Act, 1979 [*Chapter 22:05*] and the Housing Standards Control Act [*Chapter 29:08*] to formulate and administer the national housing policy, and its operations were broadly guided by two policy statements – one for urban housing and the other for rural housing.

At independence, the government sought to redress a myriad of social inequalities and injustices, and 'growth with equity' became the fundamental thrust in the reconstruction phase. The provision of better housing to low-income people became one of the government's measures for redressing inequalities in pursuance of its socialist goals.

During this transitional period, urban and rural settlement patterns changed drastically, posing a great challenge to the new government that viewed the provision of shelter both as a socialist right as well as a prerogative of the government. Before independence, 18.5 per cent of Zimbabwe's population lived in the urban areas; by 1982, the urban population had risen to 26.9 per cent owing to the return of refugees, exiles and 'ex-combatants', as well as movement from the rural areas (Zimbabwe, 2002). The urban areas had to cope with a population that was two to three times greater than they had been designed for. Squatter camps like Chirambahuyo in Chitungwiza, throngs of people sleeping on the streets and in storm drains, and a high number of tenants per household pointed to a looming housing crisis.

In order to correct the housing injustices and address rapid urbanization, the government formulated new policies and strategies that formed part of the *Transitional National Development Plan* (Zimbabwe, 1982). The main and long-term objective with respect to housing was to ensure that there was adequate housing and related services at affordable prices for all, irrespective of geographical location or socio-economic grouping. In an effort to achieve this, the following housing policies were adopted:

- Home-ownership would be the major form of tenure, with only a small percentage being developed for rental purposes.
- Cost-effective and labour-intensive modes of house construction were to be used in schemes funded by the public sector.
- There would be minimum housing standards.
- The public and private sectors would mobilize their resources to meet the housing needs of the country.

### Home-ownership policy

Before independence, about 90 per cent of the housing stock in high-density areas was rented accommodation and the remaining 10 per cent was allocated to middle-income blacks on freehold title. Under the home-ownership policy, local authorities converted the rental accommodation to home-ownership on rent-to-buy agreements. The process of allocating houses was based on a policy that gave sitting tenants the first option to purchase. The home-ownership scheme was designed to ensure that blacks could obtain title to houses as well as access the expanded credit facilities put in place through the public-sector funding. It encouraged individuals to invest in housing, which meant not only security of tenure for property-owners but also reduced maintenance costs for local authorities. The policy thrust shows an overwhelming commitment to home-ownership as the answer to the housing shortage and insecurity of tenure.

The perception that the problem was mainly the result of racial discrimination and insecurity of tenure was overstated, and gender inequalities and equity issues for marginalized groups such as orphans, the aged and people with disabilities did not receive the attention they deserved in the allocation of housing. The policy did not cater for the ultra-poor who could not pass the income criteria. The lack of policy for the marginalized resulted in the mushrooming of an informal private-sector housing market that offered accommodation that was affordable but had social and health hazards. The informal private-sector housing sector manifested itself in various forms such as shacks (*tangwenas*), several households lodging in one housing unit, several households renting a single apartment, and cottages or renovated servants' quarters located in medium- and low-density areas being rented out.

## Modes of house construction

For low-income housing programmes funded from public funds, government encouraged the use of labour-intensive and cost-effective modes of house construction: aided self-help, building brigades and co-operatives. Studies done by the Ministry of Public Construction and National Housing indicated that aided self-help was the most popular mode of construction during the period as it was cost-effective.

Through aided self-help schemes, notable housing projects were established. More than 7,000 serviced plots of 200 square metres, with ablution facilities, were allocated in Harare's Glen View high-density suburb between 1979 and 1981. In other suburbs – such as Warren Park, Dzivaresekwa, Hatcliffe and Kuwadzana in Harare – ablutions and 'core houses' were provided, which were supposed to benefit those in the low-income bracket. This scheme was also launched in other cities and towns, such as Bulawayo and Kwekwe.

Building brigades were not as cost-effective as intended for the following reasons:
- A lack of supervisory management, leading to increased costs.
- Inadequate and irregular flows of funds.
- Lack of transport, plant and equipment for implementing projects.
- Shortage of building materials which led to prolonged periods of completion time and hence an increase in labour costs.

## Minimum housing standards

In an effort to ensure the provision of decent housing to all, the following minimum housing standards were laid down:
- An expandable and detached four-roomed core house.
- Minimum stand area of 50 square metres.
- Minimum plot size of 300 square metres.
- Walls constructed of either burnt bricks, cement blocks or stabilized earth bricks.

- Floors made of cement and with a smooth finish.
- All housing estates in urban areas to be serviced with running water, sewage reticulation, electricity, and access to roads and storm-water drains.

These standards drastically improved the quality of high-density housing, but the government was immediately faced with increased construction costs. The beneficiaries of these stipulated housing standards were owners of new homes, but the policy failed to upgrade existing buildings that did not meet these standards.[2] A typical example is the now-dilapidated Mbare hostels, popularly known as 'Matapi flats', where each 'bachelor' had been entitled to one room, with communal cooking and ablution facilities. These buildings, now accommodating families, could not cope with the demands of the rapidly increasing urban population in terms of facilities and services, and although they had been condemned as unfit for human habitation, with plans on the national and council's agenda for years to demolish or upgrade them, nothing was done.

### Private-sector participation

Private-sector participation in low-cost housing development took several forms: mortgage loans advanced from building societies, employer-assisted housing schemes, private individuals and real-estate developers, as well as the activities of NGOs in various fields related to shelter provision.

Donors have played a crucial role in housing development. Kuwadzana suburb in Harare is a typical site-and-service scheme, and was funded by USAID. The scheme witnessed the provision of more than 7,000 plots to low-income earners, whose beneficiaries were given a loan to construct and finish a house within an 18-month period. The beneficiaries could either use private builders, building brigades (a cost-reduction measure), or their co-operatives. The World Bank also sponsored site-and-service schemes in Glen Norah, Budiriro and Sunningdale in Harare.

The most significant impact on private-sector participation was achieved in 1986 when government enabled building societies to be more competitive in attracting funds by allowing them to issuing tax-free paid-up permanent shares.[3] Twenty-five per cent of the funds generated were to be channelled towards low-cost housing. The government also succeeded in mobilizing the banking sector, which played a leading role in the provision of housing. The Zimbabwe Building Society, for example, built houses for all classes in society, financing the construction of low-income housing in Kuwadzana, medium-density houses

---

[2] It should be borne in mind that urban accommodation initially provided to blacks in the colonial period was for male labourers only. Women and children were expected to stay in the communal areas.

[3] Tax-free fixed-deposit investment that pays out capital plus interest at the end of a prescribed investment period.

in Waterfalls, and high-income houses in Borrowdale. Other building societies have also played a significant role for private buyers through the provision of mortgage facilities.

It should, however, be noted that it has never been easy getting a mortgage loan from a financial institution. Building societies cater mainly for people in formal-sector employment, as proof of employment is a prerequisite. In addition, life-insurance cover was required as collateral, but in order to get cover an HIV/AIDS test was (and remains) a prerequisite. These conditions had to be met to be eligible for a loan, and if they could not be met, it was necessary to resort to cash purchases, which was out of the question for the many low-income Zimbabweans.

Volume II of the *Transitional National Development Plan* (Zimbabwe, 1982) set out to deal with weaknesses observed in the implementation of the housing policies, where the objectives were to:

- reduce and eventually eliminate the housing backlog in municipal and rural council areas;
- improve the quality and number of houses in communal, resettlement, mining and commercial farming areas;
- reduce building materials and construction costs so as to bring adequate housing within the reach of ordinary urban and rural people.

In an effort to achieve these objectives, the government adopted the following strategies:

- The provision of serviced stands on an aided self-help basis.
- Provision at an appropriate level and form of financial and technical assistance to house-owners in both urban and rural areas;
- Setting up building brigades to undertake the construction of houses;
- Mobilizing people to solve the housing problem;
- Setting up and strictly enforcing housing standards in both urban and growth points (Zimbabwe, 1982; Mafico, 1991).

The city councils throughout the country play a central role in the provision of housing by providing stands, but demand for them has never been matched by supply (Table 9.1).

In principle, Harare City Council has a 'one person, one stand' policy, but in practice it is alleged that the rich and connected have benefited

**Table 9.1: Low-income housing waiting list in Harare, 1981–1989**

| Year | Number listed |
|------|---------------|
| 1981 | 17,384 |
| 1984 | 34,931 |
| 1985 | 36,457 |
| 1986 | 25,311 |
| 1989 | 50,053 |

*Source:* City of Harare, Department of Housing.

with more than one residential stand. This leaves the low-income earner with no choice but to compete with the rich on the open market, and since acquiring a house is a major investment, it means that the rich will get richer while the poor become poorer.

In a stable economy, the provision of stands is a noble idea, but in a depressed and highly inflationary economy, without any form of assistance to construct houses, it has proved to be a nightmare for low-income earners. As a result, in most instances low-income earners fail to develop their stands. Stand-owners resorted to building shacks on their properties without any health amenities like water and toilets, and a considerable number of stands allocated during this period remain undeveloped.

The United Nations Commission for Human Settlement endorsed a new Global Shelter strategy in 1989, which called for adequate housing for all by the year 2000. Its theme was 'the enabling approach', whose focus was to reduce the government's role as a direct provider of housing but urging it to concentrate on resource mobilization. Despite the various strategies and policies introduced during this period, the housing needs of the people of Zimbabwe were not realized.

### 9.1.3 The ESAP period, 1991–1996

The period of ESAP was characterized by a significant reduction in the economic role of the state, with the government cutting back on expenditure as well as introducing cost-recovery measures. In the area of housing, subsidies for government houses were removed; thousands of government workers were retrenched. With very little disposable income, the poor segment of society could not afford the high urban rentals.

The housing policy environment under ESAP was characterized by:

- Increased complementary participation of the private sector in housing delivery and opportunities for civil society to participate.
- Deregulation as a way of removing delivery bottlenecks, but this increased the vulnerability of home-seekers in the absence of measures to safeguard their interests against exploitation by developers.
- Demand still outstripped supply, and therefore consumers' choices were still limited, which continued to expose the marginalized to developers operating within limited restrictions.
- Inconsistency in the reform process. Local authorities relaxed the requirement for proof of formal income in the allocation of stands and houses, while the banks had different criteria for allocating mortgage finance, which stressed proof of a consistent and reliable source of income.

The tightening of resources through structural adjustment took a heavy toll on the ability of public budgets to finance much-needed infrastructure investment. For cities like Harare and Bulawayo, public investment as a share of GDP continued to decline. The housing shortages in Harare continued to escalate (Table 9.2). During the ESAP period, Harare quickly became an 'entrepreneurial city', where most retrenchees survived through self-employment conducted from their homes. More importantly, women were faced with lack of space to grow fresh vegetables, maize and sweet potatoes, which made up a family's dietary needs.

**Table 9.2: City of Harare's housing waiting list, 1991–1996**

| Year end | Active waiting list | Inactive waiting list | Total waiting list | No. of stands allocated | Allocation as a percentage of total waiting list |
|----------|---------------------|----------------------|--------------------|-------------------------|--------------------------------------------------|
| 1991 | 74,910 | 18,402 | 93,312 | 801 | 0.86 |
| 1992 | 82,934 | 18,797 | 101,731 | 563 | 0.56 |
| 1993 | 88,748 | 19,076 | 107,824 | 81 | 0.75 |
| 1994 | 94,527 | 20,000 | 114,527 | 6,453 | 5.63 |
| 1995 | 96,640 | 20,000 | 116,640 | 2,409 | 2.07 |
| 1996 | 78,504 | 24,564 | 103,168 | 4,327 | 4.19 |

*Note:* 'Active' waiting list refers to those who renew their membership annually, 'inactive' to those who register and do not renew. Mean annual allocation of total waiting list = 2.3 per cent.
*Source:* City of Harare, Department of Housing, June 1998.

In 1992 the Ministry of Public Construction and National Housing took steps that were contrary to the policy dictates of the World Bank by directly intervening in the construction of houses. This move was meant to increase the available housing stock through the following strategies:

- Mass production of houses through the 'turn the key' approach, i.e. completed houses available for occupancy.
- The use of affordable housing designs and economical land-use planning to achieve affordability.

Driven by its vision of 'Housing for all by the year 2000', the government launched the 'pay for your house' scheme in 1992, which was meant to speed up the construction of flats and houses. Initially it was confined to civil servants but was later opened up to the rest of the population. The scheme encouraged investment by individuals into a fund which was not specific to a particular housing scheme; members contributed to it monthly in advance. When their advance payments reached half the construction cost, a block of flats was built. The ministry was responsible for acquiring the land, preparing the plans, and the eventual construction of the units. The major drawback of the scheme was that individuals started contributing without knowing the value of the property, but its major strength was that it did not rely on budget allocations or any subsidies. The scheme saw the building of flats and houses in Willowvale, Budiriro, Mufakose, Tafara, Eastlea, Marimba Park and Mabelreign in Harare. The scheme was also extended with great successes to smaller urban centres.

Most Zimbabweans' dream of ever owning a house was shattered when the Ministry of Public Construction and National Housing abandoned the scheme, allegedly because of such sharp increases in the cost of building materials that it could not be sustained by the contributions. There were also allegations of corruption in the allocation of houses, with reported cases of multiple owner-ships, and allegations of misappropriating funds were levelled against ministry officials. Although its main focus was the low-income group, it also provided for high-income earners through such schemes as that at Donnybrook suburb in Mandara, Harare. The scheme was very noble as it went a long way towards addressing the plight of thousands of Zimbabweans.

This period was also characterized by low-income housing problems, marked by a sharp increase in the demand for shelter that far outstripped supply. This resulted in high prices for new houses. The income to house-price ratio in 1992 was 1:98 in Harare and 1:47 in Bulawayo.[4] This means that, on average, a house cost 98 times a Harare family's income. Furthermore, the cost of construction also rose significantly owing to shortages of building materials such as cement. In 1992, 44 per cent of household annual income went to rent payment, which compares with an internationally accepted expenditure of 10 per cent (Rakodi, 1989).

Faced with high construction costs, the minimum size of stands was reduced from 300 to 150 square metres; this was common in Kuwadzana Extension, Harare. The revision of the minimum standard size meant reverting to the pre-independence 150 square metres, with only a one-metre building line reserved between two houses on adjacent sides, which directly infringed on the privacy of each household. As the joke went, one merely needed to stretch one's arm through an open window to shake hands with a next-door neighbour.

A failure to meet the housing needs of society at large means that marginalized groups are further disadvantaged, as competition for limited resources stiffens. Given the limited ability to deliver adequate housing within the context of a deteriorating economy, questions arise as to the actual magnitude of the impact on already marginalized and vulnerable groups and the new poor. A new poverty category emerged as retrenchments from both the public and private sectors were effected. It had been observed that, under structural adjustment programmes, the already disadvantaged groups became more vulnerable, so attempts were made to cushion the effects of ESAP, and safety nets were put in place to deal with food, education, health, post-retrenchment training, and poverty alleviation. But neither strategy nor policy was put in place to deal with housing, particularly for the vulnerable groups, within the adjusting economy. The IMF and World Bank-sponsored ESAP had an adverse impact on housing

---

[4] The ratio of average income/earnings to the average price of a house.

development because it emphasized the need to curtail expenditure, resulting in soft options such as social services being affected. The thrust of policy was towards increased participation by the private sector in housing delivery. However, this should not negate the role of government in providing housing for vulnerable groups, and in ensuring gender equality when doing so.

To sum up, the effect of ESAP on housing was the increased proliferation of backyard shanties, high occupancy rates of up to ten people per room, and the rise of informal settlements characterized by poor sanitation and related sub-human conditions. Clearly, even before the onset of the crisis in 1997, the housing situation in Zimbabwe's urban areas was untenable.

### 9.1.4 The crisis period, 1997–2008

This period was characterized by persistent housing problems. The fast-track land-reform programme triggered the deterioration of relations between Zimbabwe and the international donor community and the country's isolation from the wider international community. In the past, housing had largely been co-funded by the Zimbabwean government and donors, the bulk of donor funding coming from USAID and the World Bank. Housing production was drastically reduced after the withdrawal of their funding.

Tenure status refers to the arrangement under which a household occupies its living quarters and the nature of its right to be there. In all provinces in the country, owners/purchasers constituted the largest portion, except in Harare and Bulawayo, where lodgers and tenants accounted for 64 and 48 per cent, respectively (Table 9.3). The high rate of lodgers in Zimbabwe's two major cities is an indication of severe housing shortages.

**Table 9.3: Percentage distribution of households by tenure status and province, 2002**

| Province | No. of households | Owner/ purchaser | Tenant[a] | Lodger[b] | Tied | Other | Not known |
|---|---|---|---|---|---|---|---|
| Bulawayo | 165,123 | 39.65 | 6.59 | 40.67 | 6.06 | 7.03 | 0.00 |
| Manicaland | 360,569 | 71.29 | 1.62 | 10.47 | 15.09 | 1.52 | 0.01 |
| Mashonaland Central | 217,431 | 66.09 | 1.08 | 5.66 | 24.66 | 2.51 | 0.00 |
| Mashonaland East | 265,045 | 69.86 | 0.89 | 7.69 | 18.68 | 2.87 | 0.00 |
| Mashonaland West | 275,736 | 52.29 | 2.37 | 13.66 | 28.91 | 2.76 | 0.01 |
| Matabeleland North | 144,803 | 75.21 | 1.72 | 5.50 | 14.66 | 2.90 | 0.01 |
| Matabeleland South | 134,496 | 77.21 | 1.07 | 6.28 | 13.20 | 2.24 | 0.00 |
| Midlands | 309,197 | 71.98 | 2.14 | 13.51 | 9.91 | 2.45 | 0.00 |
| Masvingo | 286,518 | 75.82 | 0.69 | 6.51 | 14.65 | 2.33 | 0.00 |
| Harare | 491,002 | 28.58 | 6.05 | 54.50 | 8.64 | 2.23 | 0.01 |
| Total | 2,649,920 | 59.94 | 2.65 | 19.61 | 15.14 | 2.65 | 0.01 |

[a] Using land or building for a fee. [b] Paying for a place or room to sleep in or to stay in someone else's house.
*Source:* Central Statistical Office; Zimbabwe (2002).

Although the government's objective at independence was to provide both rural and urban housing, in practice its main thrust has been on urban development, regardless of the fact that 80 per cent of the Zimbabwean population lived in rural areas. The housing structures in rural areas are built using sub-standard and non-durable building materials, and often do not guarantee adequate lighting and/or ventilation. The rural folk experience poor housing conditions, lacking adequate water supplies and basic sanitation. The 2002 census figures indicated that 53 per cent of Zimbabwe's population occupied dwelling units that were either 'traditional' or 'mixed', with only 43 per cent occupying modern types of dwelling (Zimbabwe, 2002a). The neglect of the development of the rural areas is partly the result of the absence of concrete policies for human settlement development in those areas before independence.

Although the government acquired land for resettlement after independence, the implementation of a rural shelter policy occurred only in those resettlement areas. It focused on planned settlements rather than on the already established settlements in communal areas. As a result, other basic requirements, such as safe drinking water and sanitation, were neglected and communal areas continue to lag behind. The 2002 Census found that 28 per cent of the population does not use any type of toilet facility, which in practice means using the bush.

One of the reasons for the poor performance of the housing sector in Zimbabwe has been inadequate finance. The housing finance system has not been sustainable as it relied heavily on loosely defined and inadequate government budget allocations. In 2004, the government came up with the *National Housing Delivery Programme* (Zimbabwe, 2003), which was a plan of action aimed at:

- clearing the urban housing backlog by year 2008, which was expected to have increased to 1,250,000 housing units;
- acquiring 310,406.6 hectares of peri-urban land to achieve the planned target;
- enhancing the housing-delivery system in order to increase the number of players involved and, consequently, the output;
- streamlining and enhancing the capacity of the Department of Public Works and National Housing within the Ministry of Local Government, Public Works and National Housing so that it directly participates, facilitates and monitors the housing-delivery process;
- creating an integrated institutional framework for housing delivery that will improve co-ordination and efficiency in the housing-delivery process.

One of the underlying principles of the programme was recognition of the need to expand the actors participating in housing and service delivery to ensure the participation of all stakeholders and to encourage both local and foreign investment in housing delivery. Learning from its past failures, the government recognized the need to establish appropriate institutional arrangements for financing the delivery of housing, and setting up the National Housing Delivery Programme and the Infrastructure Development Bank of Zimbabwe (IDBZ) were part of the government's strategies for mobilizing funds for infrastructure development. The bank was not only responsible for the co-ordination and administration of housing credit but was also an instrument through which government would intervene financially to support and sustain the housing-delivery programme.

Private-sector finance, dominated by the building societies, prefers the lucrative financial market rather than housing development, where quick returns are not realized. There are indications that the number of mortgage bonds issued by building societies was drastically reduced during this period and that they tended to benefit high-income earners only.

The lack of competition in the housing finance system has largely been blamed for the lack of growth in the housing industry. Land developers, including housing co-operatives, have been denied entry into the industry because of a lack of financial support from financial institutions, and when it has been available, the lending rates have been prohibitive.

The National Social Security Authority (NSSA) is one pension fund among many that have contributed to housing delivery in Zimbabwe, and it has launched many low-income housing projects throughout the country, notable examples being BHP-Chegutu and Marondera Rusike Housing Phase 2.

Food shortages, a negative balance of payments, budget deficits and chronic shortages of foreign exchange led to a contraction of the economy and rising urban and rural poverty. Urbanization accelerated rapidly, leading to increases in the urban population of between 6 per cent and 8 per cent per year, the explosive growth of the urban informal economy, and the proliferation of alternative housing solutions, many of them informal and unauthorized. The combination of economic decline, rapid urbanization and poverty growth, as depicted in Table 9.4, adversely affected the housing sector. There was also a shortage of building materials and a phenomenal increase in their prices, making it expensive to construct houses.

**Table 9.4: Urbanization trends in Zimbabwe, 1985–2005**

|                         | 1985  | 1990   | 1995   | 2000   | 2005   |
|-------------------------|-------|--------|--------|--------|--------|
| Total population ('000) | 8,392 | 10,241 | 11,190 | 12,627 | 13,805 |
| Urban population ('000) | 2,116 | 2,797  | 3,556  | 4,387  | 5,370  |
| Urbanization Level (%)  | 25.2  | 28.4   | 31.8   | 35.3   | 38.9   |
| Household ('000)        | –     | 2,031  | 2,331  | 2,664  | 3,088  |
| Average household size  | –     | 4.88   | 4.83   | 4.70   | 4.48   |

*Source:* UN estimates and projections, various years.

As the national housing policy acknowledged, there was a cumulative backlog of over one million housing units. A subsequent policy document, the *National Housing Delivery Programme*, further acknowledged the government's inability to provide decent and affordable housing (Zimbabwe, 2003). Government plans for housing fell short of the annual target of 162,000 units between 1985 and 2000, with actual production ranging between 15,000 and 20,000 units per annum. It further noted that the formal-sector housing production rate was decreasing and that, by 2002, only 5,500 plots were serviced in eight major urban areas compared to an estimated annual demand of 250,000 units.

By 2004, backyard tenancy had become the dominant source of housing for low-income households living in urban areas. In Mutare, for example, the United Nations Observer Mission of 2003 was informed that there were 34,000 backyard extensions and only 27,000 legally recognized and approved dwellings. In Victoria Falls, they comprised 64 per cent of the housing stock.

In an attempt to increase inflows of foreign currency, the government and Reserve Bank of Zimbabwe launched the Homelink housing scheme in May 2004 to encourage Zimbabweans abroad to invest in property at home. The Homelink Housing Development Scheme offers mortgage loans to non-resident Zimbabweans payable in foreign currency over five years. It therefore enables Zimbabweans in the diaspora to purchase or construct houses, purchase stands or improve residential properties. Eligible non-resident Zimbabweans were advanced a loan in Zimbabwean dollars equal to the value of the required funds, with the amount converted into foreign currency using the currency where the person was located, at the ruling auction rate on the day the funds were disbursed. Interest was charged at a rate of not more than 10 per cent on the foreign currency amount of the loan.

The third-quarter Monetary Policy Statement of 2004 set aside Z$750 billion to finance the purchase of residential stands, houses and the construction of homes. Homelink was transformed into a commercial subsidiary of the Reserve Bank in February 2005. However, the effectiveness of the initiative was undermined by the existence of a parallel market for foreign exchange, which offered a far more attractive exchange rate. Zimbabweans in the diaspora therefore chose to use the informal channels for remitting foreign currency and then buy the houses or stands with the proceeds. Another criticism of the programme was that it neglected the glaring housing needs of Zimbabweans at home.

As stated in the Monetary Policy Statement of 31 January 2008, officially recorded foreign-currency receipts through the Homelink system were estimated at US$5.7 million in 2006 (0.3 per cent of total foreign-currency receipts) and US$47.5 million in 2007 (2.2 per cent of foreign-currency receipts). If the estimates of the International Fund for Agricultural Development that US$361 million was remitted to Zimbabwe in 2007 are correct, the transfers through

Homelink constituted a mere trickle (0.1 per cent) of the inflows, implying that most of the transfers were through the informal system (Makina and Kanyenze, 2010).

On 19 May 2005, the government embarked on a crash operation, Operation Murambatsvina/Restore Order to 'clean up' the cities of illegal structures and 'illicit' activities. It lasted until 9 July 2005 and was carried out without consulting key stakeholders. Furthermore, in the vast majority of cases, it was conducted in contravention of many of the statutory procedures laid out by government's own Regional, Town and Country Planning Act [*Chapter 29:12*] regarding prior notice to households concerned.

The operation unleashed a humanitarian crisis by destroying homes, assets and means of livelihood for hundreds of thousands of women, men and children at a time when the economy was already struggling. According to the report of the UN special envoy, Anna Tibaijuka, an estimated 700,000 people in the cities across the country lost either their homes, their sources of livelihood, or both; a further 2.4 million people were indirectly affected (UN, 2005). Hundreds of thousands of people were made homeless, without access to food, water and sanitation, or health care, and the education of thousands of school-age children was disrupted. In a nutshell, the operation was conducted indiscriminately, with indifference to human suffering such that its impact will require substantial investment and assistance over many years to reverse (ibid.).

The net effect of the operation was that the economically disadvantaged and vulnerable populations were pushed deeper into poverty. The basic rights of the majority poor were infringed and their dignity was violated. Paradoxically, the operation used colonial-era laws and policies that had been designed as tools for segregation and social exclusion. The priority needs emanating from Operation Murambatsvina included shelter, non-food items, food, and health-support services. The emerging challenges include dealing with lack of security of tenure for the poor, conflicting and outdated housing and urban-development policies, as well as overlapping jurisdictions, especially between central and local governments with respect to the housing mandate. Operation Muramba-tsvina therefore needs also to be understood from the broader context of the urbanization crisis in Africa. Not surprisingly, therefore, Tibaijuka recommended that the outdated Regional, Town and Country Planning Act and other relevant acts be amended (UN, 2005).

With pressure mounting both internally and externally to relieve the effects of the operation, the government officially launched Operation Garikai/Hlalani Kuhle (Rebuilding and Reconstruction) on 30 June 2005.[5] Under this operation,

---

[5] In fact, on the day that the UN Special Envoy arrived in Harare, 26 June 2005, there was a presidential announcement that Operation Murambatsvina would be wound up and Operation Garikai/Hlalani Kuhle begin (UN, 2005: 91).

the local authorities were to provide access roads, trunk infrastructure and basic services to enable displaced people to build new homes in compliance with the government's Regional, Town and Country Planning Act.

Since the construction and occupation of the houses could not be done overnight, interim solutions to house the affected were required. Such solutions entailed finding temporary shelter/housing. The government identified and set up transit camps, such as the one at Caledonia Farm on the outskirts of Harare. However, they failed to provide the required basic needs at the camps, and those affected relied mostly on humanitarian assistance. According to Tibaijuka, the conditions at Caledonia Farm were well below international standards and what is normally found in refugee camps (UN, 2005). Because Operation Garikai was put together hastily, the UN report found that it failed to account for the immediate needs of those rendered homeless by Operation Murambatsvina at the onset of winter. An erroneous assumption underlying the operation was that the evictees would return to their rural homes.

The UN report questioned the strategy and methods used in Operation Garikai. To begin with, the operation was based on the assumption that government would provide stands for the homeless to build new homes, which raised a number of questions about:

- the capacity of the local authorities to provide the access roads, trunk infrastructure and basic services to allow the displaced to build new homes in compliance with the Regional, Town and Country Planning Act;
- the need for interim solutions (temporary shelter/housing);
- the sourcing of readily available and affordable building materials previously supplied in part by the informal sector;
- the availability of credit facilities for construction of houses (UN, 2005: 48).

The UN report also queried the capital-intensive methods of construction, estimating that this would require a foreign-exchange component of 35 per cent to 40 per cent of the total cost, which would translate to US$35–40 million in the first phase. While the use of the military and youth building brigades would speed up site preparation and construction, it was observed that this would undermine ownership by local authorities and communities, with far-reaching implications for downstream issues of sustainability and maintenance. Further-more, government's track record of supplying serviced sites in recent years, at less than 5,000 stands per year, made the stated national objective of delivering 4,900 stands under Operation Garikai within a few months unrealistic. As the UNDP (2008) found, the 3,325 houses constructed in the first year of Operation Garikai were a far cry from the 93,000 houses that were demolished under Operation Murambatsvina. In addition, given that the expenditure announced of US$300 million had not been envisaged in the 2005 budget, it was clear that, even with the best intentions, government would not be in a position on its own to deal with the emerging crisis.

With the beginning of hyperinflation in June 2007, the housing market went into frenzy, with those with access to foreign currency being the only players on the market. Dealing in the housing market in Zimbabwe dollars presented high risks: by the time a transaction was finalized and the proceeds accrued to the seller, the value of the sale had been eroded by hyperinflation. In the meantime, with a reduced stock of houses on the market, rentals became prohibitive. Many disputes around rentals emerged during this period as property-owners resorted to raising their rentals frequently to hedge themselves against hyperinflation. As the shortage of basic commodities escalated in 2007 and 2008, and as poverty deepened with hyperinflation, the construction of homes became a luxury the majority of the people could not afford.

### 9.1.5 The transitional period, 2009–2010

Following the introduction of the multiple-currency trading regime in February 2009, the housing market was dominated by those with access to foreign currency. In the context of limited fiscal space, government pronouncements on housing were reduced to statements of intent. For instance, in the Short-Term Emergency Recovery Programme (STERP) it was stated that government would prioritize national housing, with the state providing between 500 and a million hectares of fresh urban land for housing.[6] Local authorities, pension funds, building societies and public utilities were exhorted to mobilize resources for national housing, and priority was to be given to co-operatives and associations to acquire land for their members.

The 2010 national budget allocated US$26 million for housing, of which US$25 million was to be channelled through the IDBZ, and the remaining US$1 million used to resuscitate the Housing Guarantee Fund. As a percentage of the budget, the allocation represented 0.16 per cent (0.06 per cent of GDP), a slight decline from the 0.24 per cent for 2009 (0.06 per cent of GDP).

The Three Year Macro-Economic Policy and Budget Framework: 2010–2012 (STERP II) launched by the Minister of Finance on 23 December 2009 identified and prioritized the restoration of basic services, including health, water and sanitation, as part of the unfinished agenda of STERP. However, the limited fiscal space remains the most serious constraint, hence the renewed mortgage financing by building societies in 2010 is targeting the high-income group, further reinforcing the enclave nature of the housing market.

---

[6] See <http://www.zimtreasury.org/downloads/31.pdf>.

## 9.1.6 The way forward

Since independence, emphasis has been placed on the provision of detached shelter units; semi-detached units were shunned because of their lack of privacy. However, with escalating construction costs, coupled with worsening inflation and the multitude of people who cannot access affordable shelter, there is need to reconsider semi-detached housing as it facilitates intensive land use and lowers land-servicing costs.

Generally, the poor performance of the housing sector in Zimbabwe has been attributed to inadequate finance and the application of outdated colonial laws and policies that require standards levels that raise costs, thereby limiting supply. The current housing finance system has not been sustainable as it has relied heavily on loosely defined and inadequate government budget allocations. There is need for a joint effort between local authorities, other public-sector institutions and private-sector organizations to resolve the housing crisis in the country. Zimbabwe needs to mobilize pension funds, often referred to as institutional investors because of their role as investors in capital markets, for infrastructure finance. There are potentially good sources of investment in corporate bonds, government stock and equity. These institutions acquire funds from the public at periodic intervals on a contractual basis, transform these contributions into assets, and use the earnings to pay out benefits and claims. The savings mobilized are long term, stable, regular and, to some extent, accurately determinable, depending on the precision of the actuarial base.

Local authorities should carry out forward planning to ensure that off-site infrastructure services are adequate, e.g. sewage treatment, bulk water supplies, etc. Government and local authorities must make land available at affordable prices if housing is to benefit the low-income population.

The government gave rural repatriation as an alternative when Operation Murambatsvina destroyed the 'illegal' dwellings considered as homes. Ironically, the displaced were expected to head 'home' and live in much worse structures and conditions. There is need for government and other players to reformulate rural-development policies and strategies so as to ensure the provision of decent accommodation and amenities. The best way to promote rural shelter provision is to encourage the production and use of locally available building materials so as to minimize monetary inputs. Public efforts ought to be focused on the provision of clean water and sanitation. Public-sector contributions should be geared towards demonstration projects, training of manpower, and research into other applicable solutions. There is a need to come up with a rural policy that incorporates not only a homestead, but includes concepts of income generation and other activities that are central to a rural household economy.

Housing and urbanization need to be interrogated in processes of policy analysis and in assessments of policy implications. The process of policy analysis begins with the re-conceptualization of existing concepts. Several concepts used to define policies in the colonial state have been carried over to the post-colonial state. There is need to revisit each of these policies and analyse their significance and relevance in the post-colonial era, in line with the recommendations of the Tibaijuka report of 2005. A housing policy that captures gender issues should be adopted, as current policies remain laden with traits of pre-colonial policies, which were strikingly biased against women. The government should also consider renewing previously successful housing schemes such as the pay-for-your house scheme.

A United Nations study in 2000 supported the estimate by the Ministry of Local Government, Public Works and National Housing, and concluded that most of the world's population would be living in cities by 2007. It estimated that 48 per cent of the world's population was living in urban areas in 2003 and that more than 50 per cent would be doing so by 2007. This calls for co-ordinated efforts between developers, local authorities and government in housing the increasing urban population. There ought to be applicable standards within the reach of the poorest segments of society in order to avoid unplanned and illegal settlement development (revisiting the restrictively high colonial standards).

Given the political climate in the country, foreign players are not likely to assist in the immediate future: home-grown solutions are therefore required. This funding gap needs to be filled through the use of local resources. However, in future, with the re-engagement of international partners, these sources should complement local initiatives.

## 9.2 Health

### 9.2.1 Introduction

Health is an important component of an adequate standard of living. It is a human right enshrined in the UN's Universal Declaration of Human Rights, the African Charter on Human and Peoples' Rights, and the International Covenant on Economic, Social and Cultural Rights, among others. Every person (woman, man, youth and child) has the right to the highest attainable standard of physical and mental health, without discrimination, which includes access to adequate health care (medical, preventive and mental), nutrition, sanitation, clean water and air, and occupational health. The right to health is critical to a person's life and well-being, and is needed for the enjoyment of other rights.

Investment in health directly or indirectly impacts on economic growth and poverty reduction in a positive way. As Lucas and Timmer (2005) noted, workers who are healthy tend to be more productive over the course of longer lives. It has been established that improving basic maternal health and lowering fertility rates often result in higher household investment in the education and health of children. The history of society tells a sad story about the economic consequences of hunger, malnutrition and disease. For instance, when children are undernourished in the womb or in infancy, their cognitive development is retarded, and this can have permanent consequences, reducing their productivity and ability to benefit from education (World Bank, 2008).

However, the world over, there is concern about the performance of public health systems. Patients and the public are dissatisfied by the quality and cost of health care, while governments are grappling with the question of how to fund it in a sustainable way. Initial concerns about equity in health care in Zimbabwe during the first decade of independence were replaced by concerns about sustainable funding during the ESAP period, and issues of access and quality during the crisis period.

### 9.2.2 The first decade of independence, 1980–1990
The dominant health problems inherited by the new government in 1980 included nutritional deficiencies, communicable diseases, and inadequate access to reproductive health services. These problems were tilted against communal areas, where less than 10 per cent of the population was covered, yet in the urban areas there was 100 per cent coverage of safe drinking water and immunization and waste disposal. It is important to note that all resources prior to independence, including those for health, were distributed according to the needs of the settler economy, hence the great disparities in health status between rural inhabitants and urban workers (Table 9.5). This meant that the emerging health sector was redirected away from a curative bias to one where curative, preventive and promotive services were integrated.

**Table 9.5: Basic data on public hospitals at independence in 1980**

| Hospital category | Number | Beds | Doctors | Nursing cadres | Public hospital expenditure (%) |
|---|---|---|---|---|---|
| Central | 4 | 3,000 | 223 | 1,568 | 60 |
| General | 11 | 2,038 | 39 | 789 | 21 |
| District | 28 | 2,400 | 16 | 422 | 10 |
| Rural | 46 | 2,029 | 0 | 235 | 3 |

*Source:* Zimbabwe (1986).

At independence, Zimbabwe had a well-articulated vision called 'equity in health', which emphasized need rather than ability to pay as the basis for providing care. The policies contained in the document 'Planning for Equity in Health' were translated into the *Zimbabwe Health for All Action Plan* (Zimbabwe, 1986). This plan detailed all the programmes and services necessary to address the prevailing health problems for the period 1985–1990 and beyond. In fact, a long-haul policy of 'Health for All by the Year 2000' was espoused.

In 1982, the Ministry of Health adopted primary health care as the strategy to redress health inequities, achieve integration, and improve access to health services. The reallocation of resources from central and general hospitals to district hospitals, clinics and community outreach services became a major goal for the health sector. Tremendous progress was realized in the extension of health-care programmes and facilities to all segments of the population. As a result of government investment in primary health and preventive health, the infant mortality rate dropped from 90 per thousand in 1980 to 53 per thousand by 1988, and child immunization coverage rose from 25 per cent to 80 per cent for the same period (Fig. 9.1). The prevalence of malnutrition dropped over the same period from 22 per cent to 12 per cent.

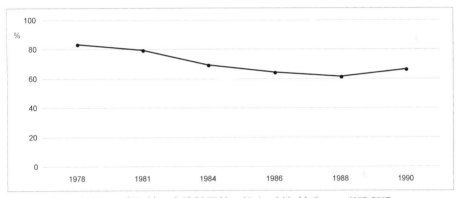

*Source:* Ministry of Health and Child Welfare, *National Health Strategy 1997–2007.*

**Fig. 9.1: Trends in infant mortality rates, 1978–1990**

The health sector's focus was on the previously underserved rural areas, to which it extended health infrastructure, training, deployment of greater numbers of health workers, and the development of health-management systems. The magnitude of the inequities government sought to redress at independence can also be reflected by the incidence of the preventable conditions that were dramatically lower among the white population of Zimbabwe (Table 9.6). Following the sustained efforts to improve the health status of the majority of its citizens, Zimbabwe experienced some of the most rapid improvements in health, nutrition and demographic indicators in all of Sub-Saharan Africa.

At independence, a service-delivery model was introduced that focused on a range of health services that the government could offer – in particular, public goods such as public-health infrastructure, extended programmes of immunization, accelerated training of health professionals, malaria control, and private health market regulation. In compliance with this service-delivery model, the share of health expenditure during the 1980s was maintained at over 5 per cent of total government expenditure, except during the 1983–85 drought years when

**Table 9.6: Selected notifiable infectious diseases at independence**

| | Africans | | Europeans | |
|---|---|---|---|---|
| | Cases | Deaths | Cases | Deaths |
| Pulmonary TB | 3,497 | 270 | 4 | 0 |
| Poliomyelitis | 28 | 1 | 0 | 0 |
| Tetanus | 114 | 58 | 0 | 0 |
| Diphtheria | 736 | 18 | 0 | 0 |
| Measles | – | – | 1 | – |
| Whooping cough | – | – | – | 1 |
| Nutritional deficiencies | – | – | – | 0 |

*Source:* Report of the Secretary for Health, 1981.

it plummeted. From 1980 to 1988, health expenditure rose by 94 per cent in real terms and 48 per cent in real per capita terms. As a percentage of GDP, health expenditure had increased from 2.2 per cent to 3.0 per cent by 1989.

The sweeping changes that took place within the health sector in support of resource redistribution towards health needs – including a shift in the budget allocation towards preventive care, the expansion of rural infrastructure, increased coverage of primary health care, the introduction of free health services for those earning below Z$150 (US$187.50) a month in 1980, increased manpower deployment in the public health sector, and the reorientation of medical training towards the health needs of the majority – placed huge constraints on the budget.

The government initiated a number of strategies to increase the health-sector workforce as part of the post-independence expansion. This involved increasing the intake at existing training schools and building multi-disciplinary training schools. Various programmes were also initiated to upgrade the skills of nursing and environmental-health technicians, and the curricula of doctors and nurses were changed in line with the new focus on primary health care. As a result, the number of health professionals increased (Table 9.7).

The critical area of state failure in public health delivery during the first decade of independence was the absence of adequate institutional and political capacity to push the policy agenda of 'equity in health'. Consequently, the implementation of equity policies in health have been challenged by several trends and features of the health-care system, which became more pronounced in the economic stagnation period after 1983. These include reductions in allocations to local authorities, increasing the pressure for fees, the static nominal level of the free-health-care limit despite inflation, the continued concentration of financial, higher-cost manpower and other resources within urban, central and private-sector health care, and the lack of effective functioning of the referral system, with high-cost central quaternary facilities being used as primary- or secondary-level care by nearby urban residents.

**Table 9.7: Number of health professionals registered by category, 1985 and 1990**

|  | 1985 | 1990 |
|---|---|---|
| Medical practitioners | 1,058 | 1,320 |
| Dentists | 94 | 131 |
| Pharmacists | 285 | 347 |
| Psychologists | 30 | 46 |
| Radiographers | 98 | 166 |
| Medical researchers | 7 | 11 |
| Nurses (all grades) | 9,533 | 12,518 |
| Midwives | 3,039 | 2,651 |
| Environmental-health technicians | 360 | 796 |
| Dental technicians | 14 | 22 |
| Medical-laboratory technologists | 150 | 168 |
| Environmental-health officers | 77 | 145 |
| Pharmaceutical technicians | 91 | 159 |

*Source:* Health Professions Council of Zimbabwe.

### 9.2.3 The ESAP period, 1991–1996

One of the prominent policies of ESAP was cost-recovery in social sectors like health and education, and during this period health expenditure declined from its highest level of total expenditure (6.2 per cent in 1990/91), to its lowest level (4.2 per cent in 1995/96), a sign that fewer resources, in relative terms, were being channelled to the sector (Figs. 9.2 and 9.3).

Given the continued decline in public resources to finance health, the government directed that all public hospitals charging user fees were to retain those fees. It was anticipated that this would improve the morale of health professionals, who would then raise revenue to procure medical supplies and other inputs that were increasingly in short supply. It was also meant to make local health facilities responsive to local community health needs. Despite the introduction of the health services fund between 1990

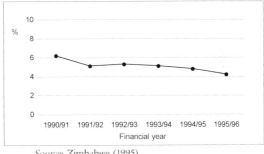

*Source:* Zimbabwe (1995).

**Fig. 9.2: Real health spending as a percentage of GDP**

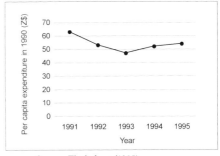

*Source:* Zimbabwe (1995).

**Fig. 9.3: Trends in real government expenditure on health and child welfare**

and 1996/97, Zimbabwe witnessed an acceleration in the decline of the public health sector, compounded by a combination of financial austerity, inflation, an expanding population, and an increased burden of disease attributed to the devastating effects of HIV and AIDS. Without sustainable strategies to enhance the health-financing role of the state, sustained progress in public health service delivery was dealt a major blow, as evidenced by the decline in health indicators (Table 9.8).

**Table 9.8: Hospital-based stillbirths, early neonatal and prenatal mortality, 1991–1996**

| Year[a] | Stillbirths | Stillbirths rate | Early neonatal deaths | Early neonatal mortality rate | Prenatal mortality | Prenatal mortality rate |
|---|---|---|---|---|---|---|
| 1991 | 5,033 | 19.3 | 3,741 | 14.4 | 8,774 | 33.6 |
| 1992 | 4,932 | 19.9 | 4,050 | 16.4 | 8,982 | 36.3 |
| 1993 | 4,797 | 18.9 | 3,561 | 14.1 | 8,358 | 32.9 |
| 1994 | 5,724 | 23.1 | 4,433 | 18.3 | 10,157 | 41.0 |
| 1995 | 5,855 | 23.4 | 4,425 | 17.8 | 10,280 | 41.1 |
| 1996 | 6,235 | 24.2 | 5,039 | 19.6 | 11,274 | 42.9 |

[a] Live births in 1991, 1992 and 1993 include live births in institutions and at home.
*Source:* T5 forms, all rates calculated per 1,000 live births.

While the public health system faced crippling service-delivery challenges, the private, for-profit health sector remained viable and enjoyed steady growth, serving less than 10 per cent of the mainly urban-based, formally employed population. Similarly, the private, not-for-profit mission hospitals and clinics became a more viable option. Mission hospitals are the single biggest private, not-for-profit health providers in the country because of their large consumer coverage. They are located mainly in the rural areas where, in most cases, they are the only health-service providers available to the local population. Their geographical location makes them very accessible to the predominantly socially and economically deprived groups of the population. Between 1990 and 2000, missions administered 62 hospitals and clinics, approximately 25 per cent of the 1,080 national health facilities, contributed about 38 per cent of the 18,200 national hospital beds, and also accounted for 68 per cent of national rural hospital beds (Zimbabwe, 1995).

ESAP's restriction of the service-delivery role of the state gave mission hospitals a lifeline, as most donors redirected their health resources through these not-for-profit hospitals. Not-for-profit private health providers, it was argued, have a reputation for reaching the poor and promoting local participation because of their small size and political independence, and were considered to be low-cost and innovative. It was common for salaries of a significant number of health professionals in mission hospitals to be paid, either in full or in part, by non-state actors, a measure to arrest the brain drain and retain qualified personnel.

Studies confirmed a disturbing reverse pattern in which patients from urban areas flocked to rural-based mission hospitals for treatment. This temporary migration has been sustained to date, and has been fuelled by the perceived availability of drugs and health professionals, as well as by the empathy and compassion historically associated with faith-based health institutions. This is reported to have stretched missions' health facilities to almost breaking-point.

Although ESAP lasted formally until 1996, government proceeded with the implementation of the health-sector reforms that had been designed in the last five years of the 1980s as a response to the dire situation bedevilling the health sector. Another outcome of ESAP was that it derailed the government's policy commitment to primary health care, as a disproportionate amount of public spending continued to go to tertiary and higher levels of care, instead of to the primary health care services that would have benefited the rural folk. This benefited, disproportionately, a minority of the population (the urban and better-off) and provided less cost-effective treatment in terms of health gain per dollar spent (Table 9.9).

**Table 9.9: Approximate ministry of health spending by level of service, 1995/96**

|  | Approximate 1994/95 share (%) | Approximate spending (US$ per head) | Approximate spending (US$m) |
|---|---|---|---|
| Parirenyatwa group of hospitals | 9.4 | 1.53 | 18.0 |
| Central hospitals | 24.2 | 3.94 | 46.9 |
| Provincial hospitals | 11.2 | 1.83 | 21.7 |
| District/General hospitals | 20.0 | 3.25 | 38.7 |
| Rural hospitals and clinics | 9.5 | 1.54 | 18.3 |
| Councils and voluntary organizations | 7.2 | 1.17 | 14.0 |
| Preventive services | 11.2 | 1.83 | 21.7 |
| Other | 7.3 | 1.19 | 14.2 |
| TOTAL | 100.0 | 16.31 | 193.5 |

*Note:* An exchange rate of US$1:Z$7 that prevailed during the mid-1990s has been used to present the US-dollar-equivalent amounts. *Source:* World Bank, *Public Expenditure Review*, 1995.

### 9.2.4 The crisis period, 1997–2008

From 1997 to 2008, Zimbabwe deteriorated progressively into macroeconomic, political and social crises. The economy went through unprecedented hyper-inflation and shortages of foreign currency. Hyperinflation eroded salaries of health workers (as it did those of all other workers) and drugs became unafford-able for the generality of the population. Shortages of foreign currency made it difficult to import drugs and hospital equipment, and other problems in-cluded increasing poverty and the high prevalence of HIV and AIDS, with an estimated 80 per cent of admissions to public hospitals attributed to HIV-related illnesses.[7]

In addition to hiving off the Ministry of Health and Child Welfare from the Public Service Commission to the recently formed Health Service Commission, results-based management was introduced in 2005 to improve individual and institutional performances. The concept proved highly unpopular among both health staff and management, as it was deemed time-consuming, tedious, elaborate, and incompatible with the demanding health professionals' work settings.

The period 1997–2008 also presented a major viability challenge for the private health sector. The National Incomes and Pricing Commission, which was given a broad-based mandate to approve and set prices for all manufacturers of goods and services, including the private health sector, was widely criticized for being insensitive and bureaucratic. It was also overwhelmed by submissions for price reviews, which precipitated a viability crisis in the private health sector. Any unauthorized price increase resulted in a breach of the law, and inevitably led to the arrest and even imprisonment of hospital executives.

Government introduced a wide range of measures to respond to these challenges. The Ministry of Health and Child Welfare was de-commissioned from the Public Service Commission (which administers all civil servants), and the Health Services Board was formed in 2006 to run the affairs of its employees.[8] However, this historic reform has done little to reverse or stop the departure of staff. A report from the Parliamentary Portfolio Committee on Health and Child Welfare confirmed that only 20 per cent of all health professionals trained in the country between 1990 and 2000 remained in the public health sector; 80 per cent had left.

This accelerated the crippling crisis gripping the public health sector. The Health Services Board reported that more than half of the key posts within the public health system were vacant in December 2005. Since then, additional numbers of skilled professionals (e.g. nurses, midwives and doctors) are widely reported to have moved abroad, although few reliable figures exist. The impact of these challenges in the health sector has hit rural areas the hardest, which have been historically marginalized. The introduction of the basic primary nursing course at all the mission hospitals, which had previously provided State Certified Nurse training, has also done little to reverse the brain drain in the public health sector. Reports of efforts to abolish the training of this new cadre further dampened the national capacity to respond to the deepening human resources crisis in the health sector.

---

[7] The HIV seroprevalence rate peaked at 24.6 per cent in 2004, but had declined to 15.6 per cent by December 2007. At one stage Zimbabwe was ranked the third worst affected in the world.

[8] Unfortunately, the Health Services Board lacks autonomy as it can only make recommendations.

The loss of trained and experienced health professionals has adversely impacted on the delivery of health services. According to the Ministry of Health and Child Welfare, as of September 2004, 56 per cent, 32 per cent and 92 per cent of the established posts for doctors, nurses and pharmacists, respectively, were vacant. The University of Zimbabwe's College of Health Sciences, which is the major institution teaching medicine in Zimbabwe, has not been spared. As of March 2007, it had an overall vacancy rate of 60 per cent, the worst affected departments being Haematology, Anatomy and Physiology, with vacancy rates of 100 per cent, 96 per cent and 95 per cent, respectively.[9]

Further losses of lecturers without replacement could lead to further reduction in the number of courses offered. More ominous, though, is the threat to the core courses, which ensure the university's ability to continue offering entry-level courses, as well as staff-development courses. In the same vein, new programmes that some departments have been contemplating offering have been put on hold. For a long time, Zimbabwe has been the main regional trainer of doctors in the East, Central and Southern Africa region, a position that is threatened under the current scenario.

Probably the most debilitating development was the emergence of cholera in August 2008 as a result of the failure by the Zimbabwe National Water Authority and local authorities to provide water in urban areas and the deteriorating sanitation situation in the country. All ten provinces were affected in what became a serious humanitarian crisis. The epidemic was considered Africa's worst in fifteen years, killing 4,300 people and infecting 98,309 by 26 May 2009, with an unacceptably high death rate of 4.4 per cent. In terms of international norms, a 'controlled cholera outbreak' leads to a fatality rate of one per cent or less. The severity of the outbreak in Zimbabwe is attributed to the collapse in water, sanitation and health infrastructure, with the deadly efficiency of the epidemic enhanced by food shortages following a poor harvest in 2008.[10]

In their joint *Epidemiological Bulletin*, the World Health Organization and the Ministry of Health and Child Welfare reported that, from September 2009, 10 out of the 62 districts were affected by the ongoing cholera epidemic, compared to 51 districts in 2008, and by 3 January 2010, the crude death rate was 3.4 per cent, having reached 5 per cent at its peak.[11]

What made the situation critical was that the epidemic coincided with a period when health workers were not coming to work because their salaries could not meet their transport costs, and also at a time when some hospitals

[9] For a detailed analysis of the impact of emigration on health service delivery, see UNDP (2008).

[10] See the report by IRIN Africa, 'Zimbabwe: Cholera is not going away anytime soon', <http://www.irinnews.org/Report.aspx?ReportId=84562>.

[11] World Health Organization and Ministry of Health and Child Welfare, *Epidemiological Bulletin* No. 40 (2010), <http://ochaonline.un.org/cholerasituation/tabid/5147/language/en-us/default.aspx>.

had closed and others had reduced the number of wards owing to a lack of staff and resources. International partners therefore provided a salary top-up in US dollars in order to get staff back to work and deal with the epidemic.

### 9.2.5 The transitional period, February 2009–2010

The Inclusive Government that was inaugurated in February 2009 was fully aware of the extent of regression in the health sector. In his budget statement of 17 March 2009, the Minister of Finance observed that 'the economic decline has contributed to the deterioration of health delivery, including the shortage of health professionals, inadequate supply of essential drugs, equipment and other medical supplies, inadequate provision and maintenance of equipment, infrastructure, ambulances and service vehicles'.[12] In STERP, health (including dealing with the outbreak of cholera) was identified as a priority area.

STERP recognized the sharp decrease in health funding, in real terms, and the resultant deterioration in the delivery of health services to the populace. Some of the problems it identified were human resources flight, shortages of essential drugs, obsolete medical equipment, and the inability of the public health system to detect and prevent communicable diseases. Therefore, STERP focused on interventions in line with the objectives of the Millennium Development Goals towards reducing infant, child and maternal mortality, improving access to reproductive health services, as well as halting and reversing the spread of HIV and AIDS. The immediate thrust in the sector would be to mobilize resources to capacitate Natpharm, the government pharmaceutical agency, to supply all government health institutions with drugs and pharmaceutical products.

The Mid-term Fiscal Policy Review of July 2009 emphasized that the government would continue with its targeted approach in resuscitating and rehabilitating the health-delivery system through public–private partnerships. Harare Hospital was the first to undergo extensive refurbishment, followed by Mpilo Hospital in Bulawayo.

In the same vein, the Inclusive Government proposed to develop and implement a health-sector recovery plan intended to contribute to the restoration of basic health services to a functional state. Pursuant to this, a document entitled 'Health Action Plan for the First 100 Days' was prepared at a health summit held in 2009. At the centre of the plan is the need to protect vulnerable groups through the development and implementation of social safety nets that will ensure the sustainability of the policy on universal access to primary health care by vulnerable groups.

The plan focuses on the following areas: health financing, human resources, drugs, medical sundries and other supplies, medical equipment, health infra-

---

[12] Paragraph 13.3.1, <http://www.zimtreasury.org/downloads/198.pdf>.

structure, communication and transport, and broader policy issues. It laments the continual decline, in real terms, of health financing in Zimbabwe from the various sources of financing, which has led to the deterioration in health indicators, especially in rural areas.

Human resources in the health sector suffer from three problems: the inability to train sufficient health professionals to fill vacant posts, a deterioration in the quality of training owing to the scarcity of qualified trainers, and the flight of trained health personnel. The number of health workers per head of population has therefore declined. The health sector has also experienced widespread stock-outs of essential drugs, vaccines and medical supplies, which has compromised access to basic health services, mainly by the poor and most vulnerable sections of society who cannot afford to purchase drugs from the private sector. Medical equipment has also become obsolete owing to extended periods of neglect, as has the physical health infrastructure, which is in a serious state of disrepair.

Some of the recommendations that came out of the summit were that:

- Rural Health Centres should offer health services for free.
- The government should increase budget allocations to the health sector to attain the Abuja Declaration target of 15 per cent.
- A human-resources policy that encourages staff retention should be developed and adopted.
- Health-delivery synergy should be formed between the Ministry of Health and Child Welfare and NGOs and mission hospitals, for the last two to offer an agreed health package on behalf of the ministry.
- The government should adopt a sector-wide approach to health development.

With respect to the Abuja Declaration target of 15 per cent, budget allocations to the health sector for 2009 and 2010 amounted to 8.7 per cent and 7 per cent, respectively. However, a positive development arising from the emergence of the Inclusive Government is that hospitals that had closed or scaled down operations reopened: for instance, the bed occupancy at Harare Hospital rose from 180 patients in March to 576 in May 2009.

Meanwhile, Zimbabwe is one of the countries in Southern Africa worst affected by HIV and AIDS, a region at the epicentre of the pandemic. At the national level, life expectancy fell dramatically from just over 57 years in 1982 to about 50 years in 1995 and an estimated 39 years in 2003; it was estimated to be 37 years in 2007. The dramatic decline in life expectancy is a result of the HIV and AIDS pandemic, which saw the HIV adult prevalence rate reach a level of 24.6 per cent in 2003. A total of 1.6 million Zimbabweans under 50 years of age are living with HIV and AIDS. However, recent data from the Ministry of Health and Child Welfare suggest that adult HIV prevalence had declined to 14.3 per cent in 2009, when an estimated 1,187,822 adults and children were living with

HIV and AIDS, and an estimated 389,895 adults and children were in urgent need of antiretroviral therapy. The decline in HIV prevalence in Zimbabwe is attributed to prevention programmes, behavioural change, prevention of mother-to-child transmission, and the impact of mortality.[13]

### 9.2.6 The way forward

Without strategies to enhance the health-financing role of the state, programmes to institute a sustained recovery programme for the public health sector will suffer. To address these acute health challenges, the state should develop a three-tier response (immediate-term, mid-term and long-term responses) to assist it to disaggregate and unlock the problematic and complex state failure in health-service delivery. The following should be put into motion as immediate steps to resuscitate the failing public health service delivery system:

- Equip and capitalize health institutions.
- Put in place strategies to train more health workers, and policies to retain them.
- Strengthen the primary health care system as a way of combating communicable diseases such as cholera and other diarrhoeal diseases.
- Resuscitate and strengthen the disease-surveillance system in order to contain outbreaks of communicable diseases.
- Reactivate the country's emergency preparedness and response system on disease outbreaks.
- Facilitate health workforce strengthening and retention in districts with low staff levels.
- Support the strengthening of the District Health Management Systems initiative of the Ministry of Health and Child Welfare.
- Facilitate the sequenced short-term return of medical professionals.

The consensus view is the one that endorses health reforms that deal immediately with the crippled supply side of the health-delivery system. Health-sector reforms that inject drugs into the public health sector immediately, decentralization as means of achieving greater openness and accountability, and the pursuit of policies that increase access to and coverage of health programmes are rightly supported by most health professionals, politicians and stakeholders because of the immediate relief they bring to the population.

In view of the foregoing, both the medium-term and long-term responses should be informed and inspired by overall state strategies to trigger and sustain economic growth and to re-engage international partners.

---

[13] Zimbabwe [2010], 'Zimbabwe Country Report', UN General Assembly Special Session Report on HIV and AIDS: Follow-up to the Declaration of Commitment on HIV and AIDS, Reporting period: January 2008 to December 2009, <http.//data.unaids.org/pub/Report/2010/Zimbabwe_2010_country_progress_report_en.pdf>.

## 9.3 Social Protection

### 9.3.1 Introduction

Various definitions of social protection, also known as social security, have been proposed. Cichon *et al.* (2004: 619) define social expenditure as

> cash and in-kind transfers paid by state or public organizations or agreed upon through collective bargaining on 'social' grounds. Transfers include cash benefits such as pensions, employment injury benefits, short-term cash benefits (sickness and maternity benefits, unemployment benefits) as well as benefits in kind such as health services ...

According to Holzmann and Jorgensen (2001), social protection centres on the concept of risk management, as they define it as consisting of 'public interventions to (i) assist individuals, households, and communities better manage risk, and (ii) provide support to the critically poor'.

Social protection is recognized as a human right in Articles 22 and 26 of the Universal Declaration of Human Rights. The Ministry of Public Service, Labour and Social Welfare (2002: 6) define it as 'a set of public and private, formal and informal measures that assist people to manage risks and minimize the incidence and impact of welfare losses that might lead to unacceptable living standards'.

This section looks at social security protection policy development in Zimbabwe within the framework of social risk management as part of the analysis of the broader social services sector. This is important because the primary objective of the activities of the social services sector is to afford the population some degree of social protection, whether in kind, e.g. housing and health, or in cash.

### 9.3.2 Social security systems and their design

How social security can best be delivered to the population is a subject of debate. However, two approaches are common: the ILO's approach that puts emphasis on publicly mandated schemes, and the World Bank's model that emerged in the 1980s, which has three pillars but whose focus is on market-oriented, privately managed schemes.[14]

The ILO's approach emphasizes publicly mandated schemes that are administered by a public entity where, as far as possible, risks are pooled within a generation or across generations. The World Bank argues that privately managed systems would create savings, thereby raising investment capital. It also argues

---

[14] The World Bank model 'ideally' consists of three pillars: i) a mandated, unfunded, defined benefit system, which is publicly managed and in charge of the poverty alleviation objective; ii) a mandated, funded, defined contribution system which is privately managed and in charge of the income replacement objective; and iii) voluntary and funded retirement provisions to compensate any perceived retirement income gap for individuals, in particular at the higher income end.

that such an arrangement ring-fences funds from direct government borrowing and the purported resultant inefficient deployment of such funds. One major criticism against privately managed, defined contribution schemes is that they have only a very limited component of intra- and inter-generational solidarity, putting squarely on the shoulders of the individual the financial risks that periods of sickness, disability, unemployment and old age pose. Unlike publicly managed schemes, privately managed schemes do not have the financial back-up of government during periods of insolvency.

While the ILO's definition of social protection entails that the state plays a paternalistic role in the organization of the provision of social protection, the World Bank's approach, which is more market-oriented, diminishes the role of the state. This seemingly polarized approach has its roots in theories of social justice and the state. The World Bank seems to draw its approach to social protection from the libertarian theory of social justice. Libertarians glorify the operations of private markets and promote individual freedoms as a way of creating economic benefits. They argue that the role of the state in the distribution process should be extremely circumscribed (Nozick, 1974). The ILO recognizes the redistributive role that the state should play in the provision of social protection. This follows a utilitarian approach that seeks to narrow the income gap between individuals and between groups of individuals in society – the primary role of social security (Barr, 2004).

In Zimbabwe, the statutorily mandated social protection systems follow the ILO model, so the schemes discussed in this section generally follow this model, in which the state plays a prominent distributional role in the provision of social protection. The World Bank model has found application mainly in Latin America, with Chile providing the most cited example. However, an eclectic approach is feasible.

### 9.3.3 Social protection within the framework of social risk management
As defined by Holzmann and Jorgensen (2001), social protection is a means to better manage risks and to provide support to the critically poor. Basically, three institutions are used to take care of risks: the market, the family and the state. For risk management to work within the first two institutions, a counter party is required. For example, if individuals resort to the family for risk management, a family member who is willing to offer assistance should exist. In the case of the market, another person should be willing to enter into a transaction. The problem with family and market solutions to risk management is the absence of counter parties, resulting in market and family failure. As a result, individuals cannot rely solely on the family and the market for satisfying needs and taking care of risks. The state and other agencies are therefore required as they can deal with market and family failures.

There are two forms of risk: idiosyncratic and covariant risks. Idiosyncratic risks affect isolated individuals or households; covariant risks are caused by outside factors that affect a large number of individuals or households. While informal or market-based risk-management instruments can often handle idiosyncratic risks, they tend to break down when facing high covariant, macro-type risks. Covariant risks require agencies outside the family and the market. Table 9.10 presents the main sources of risk and the degree of covariance, which can range from pure idiosyncratic (micro), to regional covariant (meso), and to national covariant (macro) events.

This section analyses social protection systems and their development in Zimbabwe within the framework of social risk management as explained above. In Zimbabwe, there are specific social protection programmes that target idiosyncratic risks while others are designed to deal with covariant risks (Table 9.11). It is important to see how social protection policies designed to deal with the social risks have evolved over time.

**Table 9.10: Main sources of covariant risk**

| | Micro (Idiosyncratic) | Meso | Macro (Covariant) |
|---|---|---|---|
| **Natural** | | Rainfall Landslides Volcanic eruption | Earthquakes Floods Drought Strong winds |
| **Health** | Illness Injury Disability | Epidemic | |
| **Life cycle** | Birth Old age Death | | |
| **Social** | Crime Domestic Violence | Terrorism Gangs | Civil strife War Social upheaval |
| **Economic** | Unemployment Harvest failure Business failure | Resettlement | Balance of payments Financial/currency crisis Trade shocks |
| **Political** | Ethnic discrimination | Riots | Political default on social programmes Coup d'état |
| **Environmental** | | Pollution Deforestation Nuclear disaster | |

*Source:* Adapted from: Holzmann and Jorgensen (1999); Sinha and Lipton (1999); World Bank (2000) [in Holzmann and Jorgensen (2001)].

**Table 9.11: Current social protection programmes in Zimbabwe within a social risk management framework**

|  | Idiosyncratic | Covariant |
|---|---|---|
| **Prevention or mitigation** | National health insurance (government) | BEAM (government) |
|  | Food price controls (government) | Education block grants (DfID/NGOs) |
|  | Savings and loans (SIDA/NGO) | Agricultural support interventions (DfID/NGOs) |
|  | Migration |  |
|  | Private health insurance |  |
| **Coping** | *Zunde raMambo/Insimu yeNkosi* | Drought-relief public works programme (government) |
|  | Remittances | Medical treatment orders (government) |
|  | Old age | Feeding programmes (WFP/DfID/NGOs) |
|  | Workers compensation | • school |
|  | Occupational schemes | • vulnerable groups |
|  | War victims | • urban supplementary |
|  | National health insurance | • nutrition support |
|  | Free health for the poorest | Home-based care for AIDS (WFP/NGOs) |
|  |  | Emergency relief (DfID/NGOs) |
|  |  | Food vouchers (DfID/NGOs) |
|  |  | Cash transfers (UNICEF – under discussion) |

*Source:* Adapted from Singleton (2006).

### 9.3.4 Social protection in Zimbabwe

In Zimbabwe, traditional African society relied on informal social security within the family. The family unit, with its extended relationships, offered social protection in the form of support to its orphaned, aged, sick and destitute members. In this set-up, the right to social protection depended on the strength of relations among kinsmen. The only problem with this form of social protection is that it fails when covariant risks visit a family, and the criteria used to include individuals for social protection are highly subjective.

When the country urbanized, new forms of social protection were required as the risk profile changed and the family support system was weakened. This saw the government introducing various forms of social security schemes, as explained below. Social security provision under the colonial governments was, however, fragmented along racial lines (Kaseke, 1988). At independence, the new government continued with most of the social security arrangements but in an expanded format that included all races.

The Department of Social Welfare, under the Ministry of Public Service, Labour and Social Welfare, runs a public-assistance programme that provides financial assistance to destitute members of society – those who do not have an adequate and reliable income to meet their basic needs. Their destitution may arise from such factors as old age, unemployment, sickness, disability, or death or desertion of a breadwinner. Prior to independence, assistance was granted to the aged, blind and sick only after it had been determined that applicants had severed links with their rural folk. After independence, public assistance was made accessible to all destitute citizens. The public assistance is a non-contributory scheme financed from general taxes. It is also means-tested in that assistance is granted only to persons who are unable to obtain assistance from their families and to those who can prove that they lack the income necessary to meet their basic needs.

### 9.3.5 Public assistance during the ESAP period
ESAP introduced variations in the form of public assistance, but its funding mechanism and delivery channels remained largely unchanged. Assistance was no longer restricted to the traditionally deserving, i.e. the aged, disabled and the sick, but extended to cover economic and social casualties of structural adjustment.

One of the objectives of ESAP was to improve living conditions, especially for the poorest groups, through rising incomes and lowering unemployment via the generation of sustained economic growth. Government acknowledged, however, that ESAP would have a wide range of detrimental effects as well. The vulnerability faced by the poor would arise from price effects – the removal of subsidies from maize meal and other basic food items, and the introduction of cost-recovery in education and health. As a result, there existed a need to cushion the impact of ESAP on adversely affected vulnerable groups through its Social Dimensions of Adjustment (SDA) component.

The SDA centred around a Social Development Fund (SDF) with two parts: a social safety net, which provided support for food expenses and school-examination and health fees; and an employment and training programme for those affected by the down-sizing. These measures failed to completely protect the population from the adverse impacts of ESAP as they were confined mainly to the urban areas.

The food-money programme supplemented the food budgets of urban poor households through a direct cash transfer of Z$4 (less than US$1) per capita per month. Its target was urban households with less than Z$150 (US$20) per month. The education assistance programme targeted the unemployed, the retrenched and those earning less than Z$400 (US$55) per month. The health programme targeted those earning below Z$400, the aged with no pension, the unemployed, and the retrenched (with proof of retrenchment).

One important lesson learned from the SDA was that it was abused by undeserving people, and it was also difficult for the deserving ones to access (Kaseke *et al.*, 1997). The SDF budgets were underfunded and, because of delays in disbursing the funds, they lost value from inflation and devaluation by the time they were received. Furthermore, the offices were centralized in Harare. Given these weaknesses, a process to review the social protection programme gained momentum at the end of the 1990s, and involved the World Bank, civil society and government.

### 9.3.6 Public assistance in the new millennium

*The Basic Education Assistance Module*
In January 2001, the government introduced the Enhanced Social Protection Project, which had a five-component package comprising the Basic Education Assistance Module (BEAM), the Public Works component, the Children in Especially Difficult Circumstances Module, the Essential Drugs and Medical Supplies component, and the development of a longer-term Social Protection Strategy. The BEAM programme replaced the Department of Social Welfare's school fees assistance programme.

The primary objective of BEAM is to reduce the number of children dropping out of school, and to bring in children who have never been to school owing to economic hardships. Its main development objective is to prevent parents from withdrawing children from school (an extreme coping mechanism) in response to increasing poverty. It targets children of school-going age (6–19 years), and the Ministry of Public Service, Labour and Social Welfare, in conjunction with the Ministry of Education, Sport and Culture, implemented the programme.

BEAM assists primary- and secondary-school children to pay school fees – those who have dropped out of school and those of school-going age who have never been to school as a result of economic hardships. Some of the problems faced by BEAM included enrolling undeserving children, favouritism, and lack of proper records on the programme at various schools. The scheme also suffered from poor targeting and sometimes the loss of continuity of support before a student sat for examinations.

*War victims' compensation*
The Ministry of Public Service, Labour and Social Welfare administered the War Victims Compensation Act [*Chapter 11:16*] that came into effect in 1980 and provides for compensation for injuries caused by the liberation war. Compensation also extends to dependants of people who died as a result of the war, but only war-related injuries or deaths that occurred before 1 March 1980 are considered. The scheme is non-contributory and financed by the state, and was based upon the understanding that war injuries impaired claimants' capacity to earn incomes and that dependants had had their source of support cut off.

## Old-age pensions

Old-age pensions were provided under the Old Age Pension Act of 1936 prior to independence and catered only for non-Africans over the age of 60 years (Clarke, 1977). Africans were excluded on the assumption that, upon reaching old age, they would fall back on their extended families for support. Africans in urban areas were regarded as temporary residents and thus expected to return to their rural homes on reaching old age or ceasing employment. The old-age pensions were scrapped when Zimbabwe attained its independence, although those who were receiving pensions before 18 April 1980 continued to receive them, and non-Africans, like anyone else who becomes destitute on account of old age, can be considered for assistance under the public assistance programme.

## Occupational pension schemes

Table 9.12 highlights the active contributors and pension payouts for the period 2000–2006. Before independence, the extension of social protection under this scheme was dependent on the goodwill of employers. As noted above, this was due to the erroneous assumption that, on retirement, Africans would fall back on the peasant economy. Occupational pensions were thus a preserve

**Table 9.12: Active contributors and pension payments: Occupational schemes, 2000–2006**

| Year | Number of active contributors | Pension payments (US$)[a] |
|------|------|------|
| 2000 | 626,896 | 85,073.00 |
| 2001 | 881,456 | 143,745.50 |
| 2002 | 910,229 | 258,872.70 |
| 2003 | 898,932 | 27,349.90 |
| 2004 | 846,669 | 42,973.50 |
| 2005 | 853,869 | 9,359.40 |
| 2006 | 843,492 | 157,490.00 |

[a] Irregular fluctuations in the pension payments is caused by the use of the official exchange rate which was fixed artificially by the government. *Source:* Insurance and Pensions Commission.

of non-Africans, though the Public Service and a few companies did provide occupational pensions to Africans. Employees contribute towards occupational pensions, usually matching the employer's contribution. At the end of 1984, 617,824 people were covered by occupational pensions, as compared to 338,775 in 1979.[15]

## The National Social Security Authority

The National Social Security Authority (NSSA) is a statutory corporate body, constituted and established in terms of the National Social Security Authority

[15] Report of the Registrar of Pensions, 1984.

Act of 1989 [*Chapter 17:04*], and is tasked by the government to administer social security schemes in Zimbabwe on behalf of workers, employers and the government. NSSA currently runs two compulsory schemes: the Pension and Other Benefits Scheme, also known as the National Pension Scheme, and the Accident Prevention and Workers' Compensation Insurance Fund.

The NSSA scheme was introduced after government realized that the generality of Zimbabwe's workforce did not have adequate and comprehensive social insurance. Workers could access social protection only under occupational schemes, which were not compulsory and whose coverage was limited. This meant that only a small fraction of the labour force had social security cover, which lacked portability and transferability.[16] The fragmented occupational schemes could not adequately pool risks and lacked intergenerational risk-sharing and government financial backing in times of insolvency and economic turbulence. Occupational pension schemes catered for only one risk – loss of income due to retirement. It should be noted, however, that the introduction of the NSSA scheme was not a response to ESAP but to the generally inadequate social protection cover among the working population; in fact, the law that gave birth to NSSA was passed in 1989 – two years before the start of ESAP.

### Pension and Other Benefits scheme

The Pension and Other Benefits scheme is a long-term, public, mandatory social security scheme that is fully contributory and started collecting contributions on 1 October 1994. The scheme pays old-age pensions, disability pensions, survivor's benefits, and funeral assistance. All employed persons between the ages of 16 and 65 who are citizens or residents of Zimbabwe are covered by the scheme – except domestic workers. In 2006, the scheme covered 1,240,423 workers. The employer and the employee each contribute 3 per cent of the earnings covered (i.e. a total contribution rate of 6 per cent) up to a ceiling that is adjusted from time to time.

The normal retirement age to qualify for an old-age pension is 60 years. However, workers in arduous employment can elect to retire at 55 years with at least ten years of contributions. There is also allowance for late retirement at 65 years. A retirement grant can also be paid if the insured does not meet the qualifying conditions for the pension. Disability pension is paid to workers who are younger than 60 years of age and have been assessed by a medical doctor as disabled and permanently incapable of work. They should have contributed for at least one year and the disability must not be work-related.

Survivor benefit is paid if the deceased was receiving or had met the qualifying

---

[16] If a worker resigns from employment he/she receives all contributions plus interest earned, and if the worker finds another job, he/she starts contributing afresh.

conditions for the old-age or disability pension at the time of death. Eligible survivors (in order of priority) are the widow/widower, children younger than age 8 (age 25 if a student; no limit if permanently disabled), parents, and other dependants. If there is no widow/widower, dependent children are paid through the legal guardian. The scheme also pays a funeral grant to the contributor if he or she had contributed for at least one year. Table 9.13 captures the pension and other benefits scheme's membership, expenditure and revenue since 2000.

**Table 9.13: Pension and Other Benefits scheme's membership, expenditure and revenue**

| Year | Active members | | | Benefit outlays | Contribution revenue | Old-age demographic protection ratio | | |
|---|---|---|---|---|---|---|---|---|
| | Male | Female | Total | US$ millions[a] | | Male | Female | Total |
| 2000 | 590,767 | 167,567 | 758,334 | 3.22 | 27.93 | 38.9 | 9.7 | 24.0 |
| 2001 | 635,905 | 180,370 | 816,275 | 5.16 | 36.96 | 42.1 | 10.5 | 26.0 |
| 2002 | 906,629 | 257,158 | 1,163,787 | 8.12 | 69.26 | 59.1 | 13.9 | 35.4 |
| 2003 | 958,624 | 271,906 | 1,230,530 | 1.37 | 16.78 | 63.4 | 14.9 | 38.0 |
| 2004 | 1,006,577 | 285,508 | 1,292,085 | 6.85 | 30.04 | 43.3 | 10.4 | 26.1 |
| 2005 | 1,044,444 | 296,249 | 1,340,693 | 1.67 | 5.93 | 45.1 | 11.1 | 27.4 |
| 2006 | 966,331 | 274,092 | 1,240,423 | N/A | N/A | 45.2 | 11.3 | 27.5 |

[a] Irregular fluctuations in the pension amounts is caused by the use of the official exchange rate which was fixed artificially by the government. *Source:* NSSA annual reports – various years.

The old-age demographic protection ratio for contributors affiliated to the scheme reflects the extent to which the current working-age population is protected in old age (Fig. 9.4). It is calculated as the number of current affiliates to

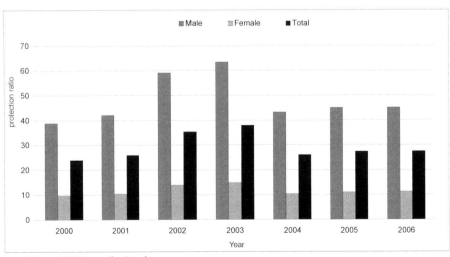

*Source:* NSSA contribution data.

**Fig. 9.4: Old-age demographic protection ratio of affiliated members**

a social security institution providing benefits in old age as a proportion of the working-age population. Indications are that, while this ratio improved between 2000 and 2003, it deteriorated in subsequent years. Generally, protection is higher among males than among females.

### 9.3.7 Accident prevention and workers' compensation insurance fund

The workers' compensation insurance fund (WCIF) was introduced in 1920 as the Workmen's Compensation Scheme, and is a scheme in which the employer insures his or her workers against work-related injuries. The rates of contribution are based on an industry assessment of accident records, so each industry pays premiums according to its accident profile. All workers except those in government and private domestic employment are covered by the scheme. Contribution premiums are based on industry-risk-assessed rates levied on the total wage bill up to a ceiling on earnings.

The main objective of the scheme is to remove from the employer the burden of looking after an injured worker, both in terms of medical expenses and of wages during periods of temporary lay-off. The WCIF scheme pays out both short-term and long-term benefits, the short-term benefits including periodic payments that provide income where it had stopped owing to work-related accidents or injuries. The scheme also pays for all medical fees that include transport, drugs, hospitalization and prostheses, and there is no ceiling on medical expenses. The scheme pays long-term benefits in the form of employees' pensions, dependants' pensions, and rehabilitation services.

*Medical treatment orders and the social health insurance*

Medical treatment orders (MTOs) have been in existence since 1980. An MTO is a fee waiver/voucher issued to indigent persons to facilitate access to intermediate and tertiary health services, such as a provincial or national hospital or other specialist facility. The Ministry of Public Service, Labour and Social Welfare provided block grants to clinics until the year 2000 to facilitate access to health services by the very poor. The MTOs covered the following categories of people:
- Those over sixty years of age.
- Those who are handicapped.
- Those who suffer continuous ill health.
- Dependants of people who are destitute or incapable of looking after themselves.
- Orphans and vulnerable children (OVC). Community members alert the authorities to the situation of OVC requiring medical attention, and extended family members apply for an MTO on behalf of the OVC.

Zimbabwe does not have a national health insurance scheme, although plans are currently under way to introduce one. There are private medical-aid societies, primarily for urban formal-sector workers on a voluntary basis. It is estimated that private medical-aid societies cover less than ten per cent of the population;[17] in 2001, it was found that eleven per cent of households had some form of private health insurance.[18]

Leaving health-care funding to private, voluntary health insurance might not be desirable for various reasons. There is an element of adverse selection, which arises if a customer conceals that he or she is a bad risk. For example, it is possible for individuals to hide their medical condition from the insurer (hidden knowledge). What most private insurers would do to lessen the impact of adverse selection is to try to insure good risks only; this is called 'cream-skimming' or the avoidance of 'bad lemons'. Other problems are those of market failure, stemming from provider monopoly power,[19] and ignorance and uncertainty among consumers about when or whether to use health services (Normand and Weber, 1994). Besides this ignorance and uncertainty, there is also asymmetry of knowledge about illness and health care between patients and health-care professionals, which also leads to market failure because health-care professionals act both as advisers on appropriate services and at the same time provide those services.

It is because of these problems with health-care financing in Zimbabwe that the government seeks to introduce a national health insurance scheme and has asked NSSA to introduce a scheme that would increase the extent of coverage of the population. The proposed scheme would be compulsory and cover all workers in formal employment and their dependants.[20] According to the principles of the scheme, no worker will be excluded on the basis of his or her health condition – in other words, the risks would be shared among the population covered, with low rates of contribution. To start with, the scheme will cover basic primary health services, and members wishing to access private hospital services can 'top up' with their private medical-aid schemes; the scheme will therefore not be in competition with existing medical-aid schemes but will complement them.

The scheme seeks to redress inequities in coverage, improve the quality of health care, introduce transparency in the financing of health care, and separate the roles of purchasers and providers of health-care services. It will also lessen

---

[17] Association of Health Funders of Zimbabwe database.

[18] 2001 National Health Accounts Study.

[19] Medicine is generally a closed field, with a few doctors who have a degree of monopoly. In Zimbabwe the monopoly power of doctors is expressed through their perennial disagreements with health funders and the hiking of medical fees to an extent that accessing medical care is practically on a cash basis instead of on an insurance basis.

[20] It is estimated that the scheme will cover nearly half the population of Zimbabwe.

the financial burden on government of offering free health services. The scheme also seeks to bridge existing geographical inequalities in access to health care (which are pronounced between urban and rural areas), which points to the need for further investment in the provision of rural health centres if the target of a 'clinic within 8 km for all' is to be met.

There are inequalities in accessibility between the 'rich' who enjoy sophisticated levels of services, largely financed through medical-aid societies, and the 'poor', who receive only basic services. The national health insurance scheme will share the risks among all its members and redress imbalances and inequalities in the provision of health care. Finally, there is need to bring in new sources of financing and to reconsider how the limited funds that are available can be rationed effectively to meet the government's overall health and equity objectives.

It is anticipated that the health insurance scheme will be implemented in three phases. Phase I will cover all employed people, Phase II will include indigent groups (the very poor), whose contributions will be paid by government in advance, while Phase III will include other groups such as farm communities. NSSA will manage and administer the scheme along the same lines as the WCIF's medical aid fund and the NSSA pension fund; the Ministry of Health and Child Welfare will lead in the provision of health services.

### 9.3.8 Other social protection programmes

Numerous other programmes intended to prevent or cope with the effects of covariant risks are being implemented in Zimbabwe, some by government and some by NGOs. The Regional Hunger and Vulnerability Programme made an inventory of national social protection policies, institutions and frameworks in 2007. Among those it identified are the Drought Relief Public Works Programme, the national policy on drought management, and the orphan-care policy.

#### Drought Relief Public Works Programme

The Drought Relief Public Works Programme provides free cash assistance to the elderly, chronically ill and disabled. The able-bodied can benefit on condition that they participate in community projects for a 15-day working month. The programme's target beneficiaries are the poorest households, particularly in the rural areas, though the programme has since been extended to urban areas. It offers temporary employment on labour-intensive public works programmes in return for cash income that enables participants to buy inputs or food or to pay school fees. There is also an element of skills development. In the current economic climate, the impact of cash transfers may not be felt immediately, as this is just a short-term social safety net which focuses on drought response and relief.

## National policy on drought management

The objective of the policy on national drought management is to build the capacity of individuals and communities at the household level to plan and undertake activities that utilize household resources efficiently. The key policy recommendations include:

- Formulation of a drought-management plan.
- Mobilization of funds for drought management.
- Provision of food security and grain reserves.
- Capacity-building for drought management.
- The need for a rural industrialization policy.
- Provision of a policy framework for integrating women into the mainstream of national economic activities.
- Extended extension services and research. This sees drought as part of long-term development programming and stresses the importance of an integrated approach to drought response.

## Orphan-care policy document

A national orphan-care policy document was produced in 1998, whose objective was to promulgate a package of basic care and protection for orphans in the light of HIV and AIDS and the consequential high incidence of orphanhood. The policy seeks to ensure that orphans are accorded all their rights, as prescribed by the UN Convention on the Rights of the Child and the African Charter on the Rights and Welfare of the Child. It recommends the establishment of a six-tier safety-net system of orphan care, focusing on biological families, nuclear families, extended families, community care, formal foster care, adoption, and institutional care. One of its strengths is that it uses established legislation and also adopts a multi-sectoral approach to the problem. However, it has been criticized for not allowing participation and direct links between orphans and decision-makers.

## Rural livelihoods programmes

Between January 2002 and June 2006, Action Aid International implemented a rural livelihoods support programme for vulnerable households affected by HIV and AIDS in seven districts: Bulilima, Mangwe, Shurugwi, Kadoma, Sanyati, Makondi and Nyanga.

## Education block grants

The USAID and DfID block-grant programmes, implemented by NGOs, provide annual payments negotiated with individual schools in exchange for fee waivers for orphans and vulnerable children. The schools use the funds to purchase books and other materials, or furniture, or to invest in improved classrooms or vital infrastructure needs. In this way, block grants support entire schools as well as individual OVC who receive fee waivers.

### Zunde raMambo/Insimu yeNkosi

There is a traditional method of caring for orphans in Zimbabwe, which is one of the responsibilities of traditional leaders: the chief's *Zunde raMambo* or *Insimu yeNkosi*. This is a collective field that is worked by the community under the leadership of the chief and the village head for the benefit of indigent persons, specifically orphans. Zimbabwe's legislative and policy framework for OVC – the orphan-care policy and the National Plan of Action for Orphans and Vulnerable Children – builds on this social protection mechanism. However, owing to institutional and resource constraints, they are not being fully mobilized at the local level.

### 9.3.9 Social protection in the transitional period, February 2009–2010

On social protection, STERP seeks to cushion the vulnerable groups, the elderly, orphans and child-headed families, as well as the physically handicapped, from its possible adverse effects. As a result, STERP will enhance support for publicly funded social safety nets, with specific allocations made for vulnerable groups and those institutions catering for such people. Humanitarian assistance will be in the form of food and non-food relief: food relief will target acquisition of 80 per cent of the cereal requirements of the country, and input support; non-food relief will be in the form of water and sanitation assistance, with the aim of curbing water-borne diseases. This will call for the revamping of the water-reticulation system and provision of adequate water-treatment chemicals.

One of the results of the stand-off between government and international partners has been that two systems of social protection emerged – one under the Ministry of Labour and Social Services, the other co-ordinated by UNICEF. Since April 2007, development partners have been implementing the Programme of Support for the National Action Plan for Orphans and Vulnerable Children, which will end in December 2010.[21] In view of the imminent closure of this programme, efforts are under way to come up with a comprehensive social protection programme integrating both aspects.

### Shortcomings of the social protection delivery mechanisms in Zimbabwe

Social protection mechanisms that are related to employment are designed along the enclave nature of the economy, where they cater only for people who are in the formal sector. For example, the NSSA scheme covers only 1.2 million people

---

[21] This programme is funded by multi-donors under a basket fund managed by UNICEF. The funds are distributed to child-care and -protection NGOs, not to government, although the co-ordination role is left to government through the Ministry of Public Service, Labour and Social Welfare.

(17 per cent)[22] in a labour force of 6.9 million. As noted above, occupational pension schemes cover only 840,000 members of the working population. Besides, during the hyperinflationary period, all pension arrangements were tottering on the brink of irrelevance, their benefits having become meaningless with pensioners not collecting their pensions. The introduction multiple currencies has breathed some life into some of them, notably NSSA, which started disbursing pensions in US dollars in April 2009.

In the wider context, which includes social protection mechanisms that are not employment-based, social protection in Zimbabwe is not based on long-term risk management but is dominated by short-term emergency responses. These short-term responses do not build the capacity of vulnerable communities and households to deal with the various shocks they are exposed to. In addition, small-scale, donor-funded, NGO-implemented social protection programmes operate at a low scale and are not institutionalized as national government-run programmes. There is also a general lack of political will to scale-up support for social protection in Zimbabwe. The current approach, which is preoccupied with social transfers, does not address structural vulnerabilities such as market failure, for which more sustainable interventions are required.

Studies carried out by the Ministry of Public Service, Labour and Social Welfare in 2002 provided the following underlying reasons for the failure of the three components of social protection (social security, income security and social safety nets):

- Failure of macroeconomic policies to deliver on social imperatives.
- The unco-ordinated, incoherent and sectoralization of social protection (even in the Ministry of Public Service, Labour and Social Welfare, two parallel management structures exist – the Department of Welfare and the Social Dimensions Fund, creating a bureaucratically complex situation).
- Lack of mutually supportive and clear policy objectives has led to disjointed approaches.
- Inaccurate targeting of needy communities and individuals owing to the absence of clearly defined selection criteria.
- Inadequate per capita benefits/rewards, especially in the context of no or irregular reviews of benefits.
- Minimum community participation in decision-making, resulting in most of the poor being unaware of the existence of social protection programmes and of their benefits.
- Limited political will and commitment, as verbal policy statements and

---

[22] Zimbabwe (2002a).

policy objectives were not followed by effective and tangible support, especially in the annual budgets.
- Inadequate monitoring and evaluation to facilitate prompt remedial actions.
- Weak management and organizational structures, exacerbated by cumbersome, tedious and costly procedures and manual programme operations.
- Limited programme coverage.
- Inadequate human resources as a result of poor working conditions in the public social protection schemes.
- Non-demand-driven programmes and poor customer services.
- Lack of public confidence in social protection programmes owing to a lack of transparency and accountability and the perceived prevalence of corruption, politicization of the programme, non-adherence to agreed selection criteria, and undue pressure from persons of influence.
- High public dependency, especially as a result of increased unemployment, poverty, the breakdown of traditional social and family relationships, HIV and AIDS, etc.
- A non-supportive and unconducive economic environment [Zimbabwe, 2002b: 16–18].

### 9.3.10 The way forward

With the high prevalence of poverty in Zimbabwe, there is a need to design policies and take action that reduce these poverty levels. Social protection, if well designed, can play a crucial role in reducing poverty. Therefore, any future approach to social protection mechanisms should focus on preventing, mitigating and coping with risks that plunge the population into poverty, through the provision of income or in-kind security.

### Safety nets

The government should put in place new safety nets and expand existing ones to prevent people who have not yet slid into poverty from doing so. Transfers in cash or in kind can do this by creating a minimum income that is paid to those who have no other source of income.

### Comprehensive coverage of the population

The National Social Security Authority currently covers people in formal employment, yet the formal sector is shrinking while the informal economy is expanding. To increase social security cover, NSSA should consider extending coverage to the informal economy. If workers in the informal economy are not covered, they will become a burden on the fiscus when their income streams are cut off.

## National Health Insurance Scheme

There is need to expedite the implementation of the National Health Insurance Scheme. Less than ten per cent of the population is covered by the existing private medical-aid schemes, leaving the rest of the population to access medical services on a cash basis. NSSA data show that by enlisting only formal-sector employees into the scheme, health cover will increase to 50 per cent of the population. The scheme should also consider providing cover to rural communities. When the proposal was put to stakeholders and parliament, they all agreed that it was a good idea to implement it, but the timing was not right because of the economic hardships. It is hoped that once the economy stabilizes, the scheme will be implemented since all the preparatory work has been done.

## Include more contingencies

The currently NSSA scheme covers only long-term contingencies, such as retirement, invalidity and survivors' pensions. The list of contingencies covered should be expanded to include short-term benefits for circumstances like maternity, unemployment and sickness.

## Create an integrated national social protection strategy for Zimbabwe

Current efforts to create an integrated national social protection strategy for the country are worthwhile. Integrating the lessons learned so far will help create a better co-ordinated and inclusive approach to social protection. Ideas around the establishment of an income grant are a step in the right direction. The involvement of all stakeholders is particularly critical for ownership and sustainability.

## Resource mobilization

The government may not, in the initial stages, be able to afford to finance the whole spectrum of social protection arrangements; as a result, it may have to seek external support to finance them. However, the government should introduce schemes that it would be able to sustain in the event of the donor community pulling out.

## References

Barr, N. 2004. *Economics of the Welfare State* (New York: Oxford University Press).

Cichon, M. *et al.* 2004. *Financing Social Protection* (Geneva: ILO).

Clarke, D. 1977. *The Economics of Old Age in Subsistence Rhodesia* (Gwelo: Mambo Press).

Holzmann, R. and S. Jorgensen 1999. 'Social protection as social risk management: Conceptual underpinnings for the social protection sector strategy paper', *Journal of International Development* 11, 1005–27.

Holzmann, R. and S. Jorgensen 2001. 'Social risk management: A new conceptual framework for social protection, and beyond', *International Tax and Public Finance* 8(4), 529–56.

Kaseke, E. 1988. 'Social security in Zimbabwe', *Journal of Social Development in Africa*, 3(1), 5–9.

Kaseke, E., J. Dhemba and P. Gumbo 1997. 'Transforming Resources to Poor Households: The Case of Social Safety Nets in Zimbabwe', a consultancy report produced for the Ministry of Public Service, Labour and Social Welfare and UNICEF Zimbabwe by the School of Social Work, Harare.

Lucas, S. and P. Timmer 2005. *Connecting the Poor to Economic Growth: Eight Key Questions* (Washington, DC: Centre for Global Development).

Mafico, J. C. 1991. *Urban Low-income Housing in Zimbabwe* (Avebury: Brookfield).

Makina, D. and G. Kanyenze 2010. 'The Potential Contribution of the Zimbabwe Diaspora to Economic Recovery' (Harare: UNDP, Comprehensive Economic Recovery in Zimbabwe, Working Paper 11), <http://www.kubatana.net/docs/econ/undp_contribution_diaspora_eco_recovery_100511.pdf>.

Normand, C. and Weber, A. 1994. *Social Health Insurance: A Guidebook for Planning* (Geneva: WHO).

Nozick, R. 1974. *Anarchy, State, and Utopia* (Oxford: Blackwell).

Rakodi, C. 1989. 'The production of housing in Harare, Zimbabwe: Components constraints and policy issues', *Trialogue*, 20, 7–13.

Singleton, G. 2006. 'Social Service Delivery Analysis in Zimbabwe' (unpublished, draft 2: 17 February).

Sinha, S. and M. Lipton 1999. 'Undesirable Fluctuations, Risk and Poverty: A Review' (Washington, DC: World Bank (draft, mimeo)).

UN 2005, *Report of the Fact-Finding Mission to Zimbabwe to assess the Scope and Impact of Operation Murambatsvina by the UN Special Envoy on Human Settlements Issues in Zimbabwe, Mrs. Anna Kajumulo Tibaijuka* (New York: United Nations).

UNDP 2008. *Comprehensive Economic Recovery in Zimbabwe: A Discussion Document* (Harare: United Nations Development Programme).

World Bank 2000. *World Development Report, 2000/1: Attacking Poverty* (Washington, DC: World Bank).

World Bank 2008. *The Growth Report: Strategies for Sustained Growth and Inclusive Development* (Washington, DC: World Bank, Commission on Growth and Development).

Zimbabwe 1982. *Transitional National Development Plan, 1982/83 – 1984/85* (Harare: Ministry of Economic Planning and Development, 2 vols.).

Zimbabwe 1986. *Zimbabwe Health for All Action Plan* (Harare: Ministry of Health and Child Welfare).

Zimbabwe 1995. *The National Health Profile, 1995* (Harare: Ministry of Health and Child Welfare).

Zimbabwe 2002a. *Census 2002 National Report* (Harare: Central Statistical Office).

Zimbabwe 2002b. *National Social Protection Strategy for Zimbabwe: Social Development Fund* (Harare: Ministry of Public Service, Labour and Social Welfare).

Zimbabwe 2003. *National Housing Delivery Programme* (Harare: Ministry of Local Government Public Works and National Housing).

*Chapter 10*

# Science and Technology Development

## 10.1 Introduction

Although African governments recognize the importance of science and technology (S&T) in development and in uplifting standards of living, they have not made much progress in harnessing it for the benefit of their people. Investments in S&T have a long gestation period and therefore require foresight, serious commitment, and leadership with vision. There is a need to strike a balance between current consumption and the long-term productivity and welfare improvements that such investments can bring about. African governments have focused on immediate problems of macroeconomic stability – attempts at addressing inflation and budget deficits to remain credit-worthy in the eyes of the Bretton Woods institutions and the international community – at the expense of S&T.

Notwithstanding this, African countries do have the capacity to formulate appropriate and effective S&T policies. Unfortunately, that capacity is scattered among individuals in various organizations who tend to view S&T from the narrow confines of their own organizations rather than with a national perspective. This calls for a need to co-ordinate, harmonize and harness that capacity and apply it to formulating S&T policies, action plans and programmes. Furthermore, the national innovation systems and S&T policy-making structures of most African countries are fragmented and disarticulated, and there is greater interaction in the international sphere than there is among the various internal actors.[1] Regrettably, S&T policy is developed with a formal-sector bias and ignores the non-formal sectors that account for the majority of the population and labour force, thereby reinforcing the inherited dual and enclave structures of the African economy.

The hardware components of the national innovation system are the major players in S&T, namely basic scientific research institutes, public research and development (R&D) institutions, the private sector, policy-makers (in government) and policy researchers. The disarticulation is manifested in the fact that the priorities of basic scientific research are not guided by the desire to address national problems. Rather, they are based on scientists' desire to publish in

---

[1] The following are the major actors in the national innovation system and stakeholders in the S&T policy-making arena: research and development institutions in various sectors of the economy, institutions of higher learning, policy researchers, policy-makers, and the private sector, including small and medium-sized enterprises.

international journals, whose research interests do not necessarily coincide with the problems and priorities of African countries. Research outputs are not taken up by R&D institutions or industry for transformation into useful products, and, as a result, the existing stock of knowledge is grossly underutilized (if it is ever utilized) in improving the lives of the population.

Policy-makers in Africa rarely consult local policy researchers for advice and rely on foreign 'experts', normally provided by international finance institutions and the donor community, whose interests do not always coincide with national long-term strategic interests. The private sector does not engage in much research and development, and those firms that do have the resources to undertake this type of activity are mainly foreign-owned. However, they undertake R&D at their foreign headquarters and the results, normally in the form of products but in some cases processes, are then passed on to local subsidiaries and remain internalized in the firm.

This disarticulation of the national system of innovation brings about a disjuncture in the process of technological change and impedes the desired reinforcing interaction between scientific enquiry (basic research), technological innovation (R&D), and production and consumption patterns (Fig. 10.1). This hinders the development of national technological capabilities that address the needs of the domestic populace. This point is discussed in more detail below as a critique of the regional integration of S&T initiatives.

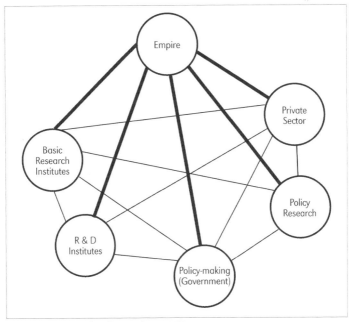

Source: Zwizwai and Halimana (2006: 361).

**Fig. 10.1: Disarticulation of the science and technology system in Africa**

A regional study on science and technology came up with a broad framework that is appropriate for S&T development in the Southern African Development Community (SADC) region and applicable to Africa as a whole. That framework was constructed after taking into consideration the experience of the South-East Asian countries that have done well in the area of S&T development, and is premised on the self-discovery approach (Hausmann and Rodrik, 2003).

This approach argues that most significant productive diversification is the result of concerted government action and of public- and private-sector collaboration. Discovery entails that entrepreneurs experiment with new product lines in order to identify (discover) new activities that can be produced at a cost low enough to be profitable. The discovery approach justifies government intervention in economic and industrialization processes and technological development on the basis of market failure arising from information and co-ordination externalities.

### Objectives

This chapter seeks to develop an alternative science and technology strategy to promote inclusive growth and development. More importantly, its main objective is to explore how an inclusive S&T strategy can be formulated to facilitate the integration of the non-formal sectors of the economy, thereby dissolving the inherited dual and enclave structure of the economy.

In that respect, the chapter traces the development of S&T in Zimbabwe in terms of policy, management and performance, and the extent to which an inclusive S&T policy has been adopted and implemented. It examines and critically analyses the major initiatives undertaken during three post-independence periods – the first decade (1980–1990), the ESAP period (1991–1996), and the crisis period (1997–2008) – with the objective of identifying good and bad practices, and taking into consideration prevailing constraints. The same is done with regard to the national S&T policy thrust. The role of both the public and private sectors is considered in the process.

Since there is a powerful movement towards regionalism, and Zimbabwe – or, indeed, any other African country – is not strong enough on its own to withstand the pressures from a globalizing world, the study examines the role played by SADC in contributing to the development of S&T through their protocols, memorandums of understanding and agreements.

The role of science and technology in development is then discussed, and literature on S&T in that regard reviewed. This is followed by a section that traces the development of S&T in Zimbabwe and then discusses the role of regional blocs. Finally, a way forward is proposed in the form of a set of policy guidelines and implementation modalities for an S&T strategy.

## 10.2 Science, Technology and Development

African countries have tried different industrial development strategies but have had little success in achieving higher levels of industrialization, largely because of their lack of appreciation of the role of S&T in economic and industrial development. In recent years, they have begun to appreciate it, but have not succeeded in designing development strategies that integrate technology policies systematically into national economic development plans and programmes.

Mainstream economics, which has had a major influence on economic and industrial development, takes technical and institutional change as largely exogenous to economic and industrial development. This is why there has been no serious effort to formulate and implement technology policies as an integral part of the development strategies pursued.

In the 1960s and early 1970s, discussions on the role of S&T in development evolved around the concept of 'technology transfer'. Within this context, technology was viewed mainly as hardware, i.e. machinery and equipment that could be imported by (transferred to) developing countries. The general perception was that developing countries did not need to invest much in S&T since there was a wide range of technologies available that they could simply import from the 'shelf' of techniques in developed countries. The bulk of the technological effort of developing countries was therefore put into choosing the most appropriate technologies from the 'world shop', and in that respect they were seen as passive recipients of technology.

Africa's disappointing experience in the use of imported machinery and equipment (technology) led to questions and doubts about the technology-transfer paradigm and its appropriateness. The positive change in the quality of life and technological dynamism of the newly industrialized countries shifted the focus of enquiry to how and why technology had been mastered in those countries. This brought about the concept of 'technology acquisition' that was developed in the late 1970s, and in the 1980s evolved into the concept of building of 'technological capabilities' (Lall, 1992).

The term 'technology acquisition' recognizes that developing countries should play an active rather than passive role and go beyond choosing, assimilating and deploying imported technologies. They need to seek new information about the technologies and develop appropriate skills, not only for operating but also for maintenance and repair. Further, the buyer should make investments in the learning process to master the technology and adapt it to local/national environmental conditions,[2] the point being that the buyer can never successfully obtain all the required information from blueprints, manuals and even training. Most plants have characteristics that are peculiar to themselves, and solutions that

[2] This point was dwelt on extensively by Bell (1984) and Dahlman and Westphal (1981), among others.

may have worked in one plant may not work in a similar one under different environmental conditions.

Building 'technological capabilities' is a further development, beyond that of technology acquisition, and applies to both the macro and micro levels of technological activity. At the macro level, the focus is on building 'national technological capabilities', which recognizes the fact that many complementarities are required among different components of the economic system to achieve successes in S&T development and its application for sustainable enterprise and national development. What this means is that there are intra-sectoral and cross-sectoral interactions among enterprises that have the effect of influencing technological developments among each other because of the nature of their production and marketing relations. Developments in one enterprise have demands and effects on both downstream and upstream industries.

At the micro level, there has been a mix-up in the understanding of production capacity and technological capability, and this has been a source of policy confusion and misdirection in the past (Bell and Pavitt, 1993). Production capacity refers to equipment, machinery and other resources necessary to produce goods and services at certain levels of efficiency from given input combinations; technological capability concerns the skills to initiate, manage and generate technical change, and includes human resources, knowledge, experience and institutions. Production capacity is mainly capital-embodied, while technological capability is a dynamic resource that induces change in creative industrial and economic development.

The distinction between production capacity and technological capability is important for at least three reasons. Firstly, conventional investment analysis places a lot of emphasis on capital-embodied resources as the major vehicle for technological development. Next, any given technology (embodied in machinery and equipment) was assumed to be fixed and with unalterable properties, implying that, once a machine had been designed, it could not be subjected to further alterations in its lifetime. In fact, the machine, equipment or plant was seen as the technology. Such mistaken assumptions had conceptual and policy implications that rendered technological capability irrelevant or, at best, a commodity that would emerge in time through 'learning by doing'; post-investment learning was not given further consideration. The confusion of production capacity and technological capability led policy-makers to conceptualize international technology transfer as no more than a transplant of a given plant from one country to another. The important long-term aspect of technology creation, using the imported technology as the base, was hardly ever considered.

According to Marleba (1992), technological learning, which is an important factor in building technological capability as opposed to production capacity, can set a firm or industry on any of three types of technical-change trajectories.

The first is that it can lead to an increase in production through dynamic efficiency and yield improvements. This may come about as a result of actual plant modification, incremental innovation or by organization of production. The second is that the characteristics and physical properties of a product may be altered to improve its reliability and performance. This may come about through dynamic learning and through improved performance in terms of horizontal and vertical differentiation. Finally, processes and products may be scaled up, and this can happen in situations of indivisibilities and high capital intensity and when there are difficulties in modifying a production process. Under such circumstances, engineers may resort to capacity-stretching through incremental investments in technology up to a certain vintage.

'National systems of innovation' is a relatively new approach to analysing and understanding the relationships between S&T and development. It is a deviation from the 'pipeline' model, which assumes a linear process from basic research, to applied research, design, development and production. The national system of innovation is more systemic and lays emphasis on the process by which enterprises – in interaction with each other and supported by institutions (a set of rules, policies and laws that define behaviour) and organizations (industry associations, R&D institutes, innovation and productivity centres, regulators) – play a key role in the generation and utilization of new knowledge and technologies. Its pillars are networking, learning and collaborations (Oyelaran-Oyeyinka, 2006).

The more recent concept of 'systems of innovation', which is basically a systems approach to innovation and the application of technology to development, builds upon, and is closely related to, that of technological capability. It is a way of systematically examining the various components of the economic and social system and mapping out their role in the application of technology to development. It is useful at this point to state clearly what innovation is, and what constitutes the system of innovation. Innovation is not research (though it is often confused with this), nor is it science and technology. It is the *application* of knowledge in production. This knowledge might be acquired through learning, research or experience. However, until it is applied in the production of goods or services, it cannot be considered to be innovation.

A system of innovation consists of a network of economic agents and the institutions and policies that influence their innovative behaviour and performance. It is conceptualized as the interactive process by which enterprises – in interaction with each other and supported by institutions and organizations such as industry associations, R&D institutions, innovation and productivity centres, standards-setting bodies, universities and vocational training institutions – bring new products and processes and new forms of organization into economic use. The advantages and strengths of the system of innovation approach are that it takes a holistic approach that places innovation and learning at the centre while taking a historical evolutionary perspective. Innovation is viewed not only from the perspective of products and processes but also, and very importantly, from the institutional perspective. The role of institutions is recognized rather than being assumed away.

Institutions play an important role in stimulating innovation, and innovations need to be supported by the introduction of new institutions. Institutions can be conceptualized in a narrow and in a broad sense. In a narrow sense, they refer to S&T organizations such as R&D institutions and productivity centres; in a broader sense, they include the political context, including the constitution and the rules and regulations (laws and statutes, patents and quality standards) pertaining to innovation activities. The major functions of institutions with regard to innovation are the management of uncertainty, provision of information, and management of conflict and promotion of trust among groups. Seven systems functions have been identified in the literature (Oyelaran-Oyeyinka, 2006: 2–3):

- Knowledge generation, including R&D: R&D is an important source of learning for innovation. It is not only an avenue for economic and social diversification (new products and processes) but also contributes to the building of scientific and technological competencies.
- Competence building, i.e. formal and non-formal training in educational institutions and training of technical personnel in firms and organizations.
- Supply of inputs, particularly finance, for production and innovation and for the development of scientific, technical and managerial human resources, venture capital and loans.
- Provision of regulatory frameworks and measures, standards and quality functions (such as product-quality tests), and provision of incentives to the development of new products and services.
- Facilitation of the exchange and dissemination of knowledge and information.
- Stimulation of demand and creation of markets.
- Reduction of uncertainties and resolution of conflicts through appropriate institutions such as industrial arbitration.

The above framework forms a good basis for reviewing Zimbabwe's performance in the development of the national system of innovation, and how S&T capabilities have been harnessed (or not) for national development purposes and improvements in the well-being of the masses. Given the uneven development that characterized the inherited economy at independence in 1980 (the dual and enclave typology), it is critical to examine the extent to which science and technology have been used to facilitate the integration of the disadvantaged, non-formal sectors into the mainstream economy in order to achieve an integrated, inclusive, pro-poor growth path.

## 10.3 Development of Science and Technology in Zimbabwe

Generally speaking, a policy is an official statement with a specific purpose, a set of objectives, clearly defined goals and outcomes, and a set of criteria for choosing among competing alternatives. For a policy to go beyond mere rhetoric, a policy statement should be backed up by a policy instrument, and this consists of three elements (Mudenda, 1995: 84):

- The legal device that gives the policy its normative force (act, decree or statute).
- An organizational framework in the form of a state structure or a ministry that ensures implementation of the policy after its adoption.
- An operation mechanism, normally in the form of a government department or directorate that oversees the day-to-day implementation of the policy.

Policies can be explicit or implicit. Explicit policies aim at inducing a direct effect to achieve a specific goal. Mudenda (1995) identified three primary objectives of explicit technology policies: the management of international technology transfer, the execution and management of technical change, and the acquisition of technological and managerial capability.

He defines implicit technology policies as all those aimed at inducing general economic, cultural, ecological and demographic activity in society, with residual effects on the technology-transfer process, the management of technical change, and the nurturing of local technological capacity. Such policies include educational policies, control of the movement of skilled personnel, and advocacy of trade liberalization or trade barriers, depending on the relative power in the marketplace.

The three major elements of explicit technology policies are elaborated upon as follows:

*Management of international technology transfer:* Policies that deal with issues connected with the search for, and the selection of, the most appropriate technical systems, as well as the negotiation of the best terms for the relocation of imported technical systems.

*Management of technical change:* Policies aimed at ensuring that, once the technical systems are relocated, the host country, industry or firm is able to assimilate and adopt the technical system. They are also aimed at ensuring that imported technical systems are easily replicated (diffused) in the national economy and that, in the long run, it is easy to make innovations based on such technology.

*Development of local technological capacity:* These policies are intended to develop S&T human resources, S&T infrastructure, the national innovation system, and a dynamic industrial infrastructure.

It is important to note that these types of policies are interrelated and cannot be tackled sequentially or piecemeal. The state has an important role in the formulation and implementation of these policies.

### 10.3.1 The pre-independence period

From the time that the country was colonized in 1890, and after an abortive mineral prospecting effort, agriculture became topmost on the colonial agenda. As a result, white commercial agriculture provided the take-off base for industrial and technological development in mid-colonial-era Rhodesia. The first generation industries were established to meet agricultural input needs such as fertilizers, agro-chemicals and implements, as well as basic consumer goods – mealie-meal, soap, bread, flour, edible oil and beer. Heavy industries started to emerge in the 1950s, and these included iron and steel, structural engineering, agricultural machinery and sugar refining. These were followed by light-engineering industries that produced components and spares.

When the Rhodesian Front declared UDI, it counted on a vibrant agro-industrial and manufacturing economy to withstand the economic sanctions imposed by the United Nations. The Rhodesian government responded to the sanctions by adopting and implementing state controls and interventionist policies in the major sectors of agriculture, industry and mining. It viewed industry as the engine of economic growth, with the ability to absorb a larger proportion of the labour force than the extractive sectors of agriculture and mining. It adopted an import-substitution industrialization strategy that entailed the use of quantitative restrictions on imports, an administered foreign-exchange-allocation system, and investment controls. It used the Industrial Development Corporation to spearhead industrial development by venturing into 'green pasture' investment projects that were too risky for the private sector to take on, and eventually offloaded them to the private sector after proving their viability. It also put in place infrastructure to support the economy, such as transport (road and rail), electricity, dams, telephones, and serviced industrial land.

The black majority were excluded from mainstream economic activities through land policies that condemned them to areas with the most infertile soils and unreliable rainfall, and that were generally unsuitable for productive agricultural activity, thereby transforming them into a pool of cheap labour for industry, commercial agriculture and mining.

To provide guidance in the area of science and technology policy and research, the government established the Scientific Council of Rhodesia, an advisory body in the Prime Minister's department, with the following terms of reference:

- to undertake a review of the areas of research carried out in Rhodesia;
- to indicate other areas of research which, in the national interest, could be usefully investigated, and to suggest suitable lines of research within such areas, together with responsibility for this research;

- to recommend ways and means whereby the above review could be carried out on a continuing basis;
- to keep under review those areas of science for which responsibility was not clear-cut and to make recommendations thereon;
- to provide, when required, advice on scientific priorities to the Treasury and the Ministry of Commerce and Industry;
- to advise Government on matters affecting overall national scientific policy.

The sector that experienced a lot of progress in the harnessing of science and technology for economic growth was the agricultural sector. The foundation of the national agricultural research infrastructure that was inherited at independence was laid in 1948 with the establishment of the Department of Research and Specialist Services to develop technologies that increased crop yields and intensified production. This was necessary because, with the rapid increase in the white settler population after the Second World War, increased production could no longer be achieved through the physical extension of productive land. Its impact on national crop production was described as impressive. Between 1950 and 1965, there was a five-fold increase in the use of fertilizer, compared to a fifty per cent increase in cropped area, and there was a significant increase in crop yields between 1948 and the mid-1960s: tobacco, 300 per cent; wheat, 185 per cent; maize, 155 per cent; cotton, 100 per cent. Between 1950 and the mid-1960s, beef take-off increased by 150 per cent per head, and calving rates increased from 49 per cent to 60 per cent.

The Agricultural Research Council was established in 1970, initially as an advisory body, and was restructured in 1976 to assume direct responsibility for agricultural research programmes, complementing other government departments. The Council was made up of members of the Rhodesian Farmers' Union, the directors of Research and Specialist Services, the Department of Conservation and Extension, the Tobacco Research Board, and representatives from the University of Rhodesia and agro-industry; it received research grants from several producer associations in addition to government funding. The representation of such stakeholders ensured their participation in the formulation of research priorities and strategies, and this made the research and the technologies developed more appropriate and relevant.

On the whole, a well-developed agricultural research system was established that generated the type of technologies that facilitated the diversification and intensification of the large-scale commercial farming sector. As has been pointed out before, there was deliberate neglect of the technological needs of the African smallholder farmers confined to poor agricultural regions. Therefore, the technology-driven agricultural revolution experienced prior to independence was confined to the large-scale white commercial farming community, with the

Africans eating crumbs from the table, as it were, in the form of spill-over research, particularly relating to drought-tolerant maize and cotton-seed varieties, thereby contributing to the dual economy inherited at independence (Rukuni *et al.*, 2006).

A very important characteristic of policy-making in general in pre-independence Zimbabwe, that influenced the development of technology in agriculture, is that it proceeded on a consultative basis between the government and the various stakeholders. Farmers, intellectuals, industrialists and organized foundations had a lot of influence in policy-formulation during this period (Zwizwai *et al.*, 2004).

Farmer organizations provided enormous political and financial support to the government, and strongly determined pricing, marketing, labour and wage policies in the agricultural sector. The Confederation of Rhodesia Industries played a leading advisory role, and also provided a critique to the government on industrial-development strategies. Academics and researchers at the University of Rhodesia provided additional policy backup. In the 1960s and after, the university formed the core of the thinking of the Rhodesian Front government on science and technology development.

## 10.3.2 The first decade of independence, 1980–1990

### 10.3.2.1 *Science and technology policy thrust*
The new government of Zimbabwe inherited a fairly well-developed and diversified economy, with an industrial base stronger than that of most Sub-Saharan African countries. In 1980, Zimbabwe's share of manufacturing value-added in GDP was 25 per cent, compared to 14 per cent for Sub-Saharan Africa and 23 per cent for South Africa (World Bank, 1998).

In pursuing its development objectives during the first decade of independence, government adopted a number of policy blueprints, including *Growth with Equity* in 1981, the *Transitional National Development Plan (TNDP)* (1982–85) and the *First Five-Year National Development Plan* (1986–90). It is mainly on the basis of these documents that the national S&T policy thrust and the contextual development strategy during this period is analysed.

The main development objectives, as stated in *Growth with Equity*, were to 'achieve a sustainable high rate of economic growth and speedy development in order to raise incomes and standards of living of the people' (Zimbabwe, 1981: 2). The national policy thrust was inspired by the need to correct the economic imbalances inherited from the colonial regime, particularly with regard to the distribution of incomes and resources. The S&T policy thrust was logically expected to be shaped and inspired by these national aspirations, and dovetailed into contributing towards the same.

*Growth with Equity* pointed to the need for the country to have a unified and co-ordinated national policy on science and technology that was lacking at that time. It made proposals 'to review as a matter of urgency, the provisions of the Research Act and, if necessary, promulgate a new Science and Technology Act with the view to establishing necessary and appropriate institutions in this field' (Zimbabwe, 1981: 14). One such institution proposed was a Science and Technology Council, whose functions would include establishing policy guidelines and priorities in science and technology research in the country and monitoring developments outside the country so as to assess the possibility of their application in Zimbabwe. In addition, a Science and Technology Foundation was proposed whose function would be to mobilize resources internally and externally to fund science and technology research.

The *TNDP* (Zimbabwe, 1982) did not explicitly discuss the need for a clear technology policy, nor did it follow up on the proposals for technology-related institutions mentioned in *Growth with Equity*. However, it did refer to elements of technology policy in the course of discussing investment policies and human-resources development.

Science and technology policy re-emerged in the *First Five-Year National Development Plan* (1986–1990), where it was noted that 'the medium-term objective of science and technology is to develop and strengthen endogenous scientific and technological capability in terms of human resources, institutions, information collection and dissemination' (Zimbabwe, 1986: 22). The long-term objectives of science and technology as instruments of socio-economic development, according to that plan, were to generate employment, raise the living standards of the majority of the people by raising labour productivity, and solving the balance-of-payments problems. During 1986/87, government made its first attempt to draw up a national science and technology policy through the Ministry of Industry and Technology, but unfortunately the draft document was never finalized and did not get beyond the offices of the ministry into the national policy-formulation process.

The importance of S&T in development continued to be recognized in the *Second Five-Year National Development Plan* covering 1991–1995, which was drawn up before ESAP but was never implemented, having been replaced by the latter. This plan had given considerable attention to the issue of science, technology and development, and lamented the lack of progress in the formulation of a national S&T policy, despite the fact that government had made commitments in this direction much earlier in *Growth with Equity*. In that plan, government had recommitted itself to the policy objective of developing national scientific and technological capacity, but it was abandoned at a very early stage in favour of ESAP.

What is important to note here is that government had paid only lip service to the development of a comprehensive science and technology policy and to serious programmes of developing national technological capabilities to uplift the living standards of the majority. It is fair to say that the concept of S&T capability was not clearly conceptualized for its proper integration into national development and industrialization plans and programmes. In the *TNDP*, science and technology was referred to only indirectly within the context of investment policies and human-resources development. Policies were being designed based on existing implementation mechanisms: human-resources development fell briefly under the Ministry of Manpower Development and, after 1988, under the Ministry of Higher and Tertiary Education, while investment policies came under the Ministry of Economic Planning and Development. This implies that the strategy was fragmented.

The discussion of S&T within the framework of investment policies in the *TNDP* reflects the common mix-up of productive capacity and technological capability. This confusion is further reflected in the objectives for S&T in the *First Five-Year National Development Plan*, particularly the long-term objectives, which were to be achieved 'by raising labour productivity, and solving the balance of payments problems'. What was clearly lacking in the long-term objectives was the transformation of the economy to one with an inclusive, pro-poor, more robust, competitive and dynamic industrial base. Within the context of an S&T-motivated development strategy, improvement in labour productivity is an ongoing phenomenon that occurs through learning by doing, continuous innovation, and minor incremental or major technological change, plant modifications, changes in processes, the reorganization of production, and capacity-stretching through incremental investment.

The long-term productivity improvements expected in the plan are associated more with increases in production capacity than with the improvement of technological capability. Furthermore, employment generation and solutions to balance-of-payments problems can be resolved through the attainment of an inclusive, pro-poor, robust, competitive and dynamic economic and industrial base – which should be the major focus of a national S&T policy. This is what leads to the long-term, sustainable uplifting of living standards in a nation. The preoccupation with short-term macroeconomic concerns and considerations is significant.

The conclusions that emerge from the S&T thrust during this first decade of independence are that:
- Government was aware that S&T could play as important a role in development as it had during the colonial era, even though it then had benefited only a few, and that S&T resources should be mobilized for those purposes.
- Despite that recognition, government was not able to put policy

guidelines in place to harness S&T for development that were integrated with national development policies.

- Government was preoccupied with short-term macroeconomic problems, and these concerns blurred it from taking bold steps to build the necessary S&T foundation that is the prerequisite for national economic and industrial transformation.
- There was some 'confusion' and a failure to distinguish between production capacity and technological capability.

In short, Zimbabwe did not have an explicit and coherent policy to guide the activities and performance of scientific and technological efforts, institutions and systems in contributing to the building of national S&T capabilities within the various economic sectors of the country – a prerequisite for building a solid, resilient and dynamic national economic and industrial base.

### 10.3.2.2 *Management of science and technology*

During the first decade of independence (and beyond), S&T policy evolved through the interactions of rules and regulations set up by various departments whose functions affected, or were affected by, science and technology. Such departments and institutions did not, therefore, establish an overall S&T policy since they were sector-specific. When it comes to co-ordinating scientific research and policy-making, at least in terms of statutory mandate, the Research Council of Zimbabwe (RCZ), established long before independence, was more central.

After independence, the government took a number of steps to strengthen science and technology-related institutions both at the policy-making and co-ordination level and at the level of human-resources development. In 1984, the government restructured and strengthened the RCZ and expanded its role to include:

- to promote, direct, supervise and co-ordinate scientific and technological research in Zimbabwe;
- to provide for the establishment of research councils and institutes to conduct research;
- to advise government on matters affecting overall national scientific policy and to vet foreign researchers.

The RCZ became the central institution in respect of science and technology policy advice and the co-ordination of S&T and R&D activities in the country. The Council worked closely with the Scientific Liaison Office, which fell under the office of the President and Cabinet, and provided it with secretarial and support services. It maintained contact with scientific and technical developments inside and outside Zimbabwe, and provided scientific and industrial organizations in the country with direct access to sources of information in other countries.

In undertaking its functions as outlined above, the RCZ had, and still has, eight Standing Committees, which are effectively its operational arms:

*Agricultural sciences*
- Promoting research and development to boost the country's agricultural base, including crop and animal production.

*Natural and environmental sciences*
- Promoting research and development in natural sciences, environmental planning and conservation of the environment.

*Industrial development*
- Industrial-support research in areas such as meteorology and standardization, biotechnology, microelectronics and material sciences, especially in relation to natural resources.
- Energy resources, including conventional and renewable technologies.

*Mineral resources and earth sciences*
- Mineral-resources exploration and mapping, extraction and utilization of water and mineral resources.
- Promoting research in metals and minerals and their beneficiation.

*Health sciences*
- Promoting research in preventive health services, nutrition and sanitation.
- Encouraging research in vaccines, pharmaceutical drugs development and epidemiology information systems.

*Remote sensing*
- Early-warning systems in crop monitoring, assessment of yields and monitoring of droughts.
- Location of underground water and targeting of mineralized zones and cartography.

*Social sciences*
- Base-line data in socioeconomic, cultural and demographic indicators for appropriate planning.

*Informatics*
- Planning and facilitating the establishment of a science and technology information system, specializing in the information area.
- Encouraging the development of a science and technology information centre through liaison and co-operation with national institutions which are users or potential users of science and technology information in support of national research and development activity.
- Defining, recommending and encouraging the application of common standards for data communications.
- Advising on policies and procedures for the selection and procurement of hardware and software.

The RCZ has been involved in organizing biannual symposia in an attempt to co-ordinate and popularize scientific research. This has provided a debating forum on matters related to the type and direction of research in Zimbabwe by bringing together a wide range of individuals involved in research, industry and other institutions.

The Council's added responsibility of vetting foreign researchers gave it increased contact, recognition and acceptance by research institutions wishing to involve foreign experts. However, it lacks instruments for influencing the thrust of research in the country at a practical level because it does not command the financial resources to do so.

The Scientific Liaison Office produced the following publications for the scientific community in Zimbabwe:

- *Current Literature* available from the Scientific Liaison Office.
- *Zimbabwe Research Index*.
- *Directory of Organizations* concerned with research and technical services, which was supposed to be produced on a triennial basis.

During the early 1980s, government established a technology portfolio in the Ministry of Industry and transformed it into the Ministry of Industry and Technology. Unfortunately, there was no clear demarcation of responsibilities between this ministry and RCZ. The RCZ fell under the President's office and did not feel obliged in any way to report to the ministry. The national administrative and management structures for S&T-related activities were not streamlined clearly and this was a recipe for territorial wars. The ministry took bold initiatives to lay foundations for harnessing S&T for development and went on to draw up a draft national science and technology policy but, unfortunately, this document never found its way to Cabinet. The lack of clear demarcation of responsibilities between the two partly contributed to this outcome. The technology portfolio was dissolved in 1987/88 and no other line ministry was assigned that portfolio until 1998, when the responsibility of the Ministry of Higher Education was expanded to include technology.

### 10.3.2.3 National performance in science and technology: Scientific support systems

At independence, Zimbabwe inherited a national innovation system characterized by a strong R&D network in the agricultural sector, a fairly strong R&D network in the health sector, and a weak R&D infrastructure in the industrial sector. On the whole, the government recognized the importance of the prevailing national innovation system and, before ESAP, did not invoke any policies that undermined these institutions. In fact, it went on to strengthen some and restructured others, particularly in agriculture and health, with a view to expanding extension and outreach programmes. This was consistent with the government's desire to improve service delivery to communal areas that had previously been neglected.

Below is a summary of some of the important R&D institutions and their roles.

**Agriculture**

The apex organization in agricultural research was the Agricultural Research Council that was established by the Agricultural Research Act of 1970 [*Chapter 18:05*] and became operational in 1971. At independence, the Ministry of Agriculture had 31 institutes or units that provided S&T-based services to the agricultural industry and were distributed across the whole country, although they focused on providing services to the large-scale commercial farmers. These institutions covered the whole range of R&D requirements for the agricultural sector, such as the following:

- *Agricultural engineering:* Developing tillage systems that minimize erosion and maximize crop production with minimal inputs, developing technologies that reduce crop losses during processing and storage, and those that are suitable to the farmer, including water pumping for small-scale irrigation.
- *Veterinary services:* Animal disease control, veterinary public health, including meat inspection, and the registration of stock remedies and vaccines.
- *Other:* Agronomy, crop breeding and seed services, plant protection, horticulture, experimental research, chemistry and soil research, research focused on specific crops.

The Department of Agricultural, Technical and Extension Services (Agritex), now known as the Department of Agricultural Research and Extension (AREX), has over the years played an important role in the dissemination of research results to farmers and hands-on education of the same. Through its extensive outreach programme, i.e. extension officers resident in the country's 52 districts, it afforded farmers skills and production methods that were the products of R&D.

After independence, the new government sought to maintain the gains made in the large-scale commercial sector while improving research and extension services to the previously neglected small-scale communal farmers. It therefore invested heavily in social, economic and productive infrastructure in the rural areas, and provided support in the form of subsidies, favourable pricing policies and investment in marketing infrastructure. There was a tremendous increase in production among small-scale farmers, particularly in maize and cotton. The achievements of the first decade of independence in terms of increased agricultural productivity have been described as a 'second agricultural revolution' in Zimbabwe, spearheaded by the small-scale farmers (Rukuni *et al.*, 2006).

**Health**

In the health sector, the scientific support and national innovation system was well developed at independence, and continued to be so throughout the period prior to ESAP. The public sector dominated in R&D and supported the majority of the key health institutions in the country (Chandiwana and Shiff, 1998):

- The Ministry of Health's *Blair Research Institute*, which incorporates eleven research thrusts in vector-borne diseases, communicable and infectious diseases, and health systems and public health technologies.
- The *Medical Research Council of Zimbabwe*, a statutory body which co-ordinates all health research in the country and promotes Essential National Health Research (ENHR) and Institutional Ethical Review Committees (IERCs) as strategies for sound research for health development.
- The *University of Zimbabwe Medical School*, which has the major concentration of health professionals in the country and is involved in clinical work, research and education of medical personnel.
- *Technical Units of the Ministry of Health*, which include Epidemiology and Disease Control, Government Analyst Laboratory, Zimbabwe Regional Drugs Control Laboratory, Public Health Laboratories, the National Blood Transfusion Services, and the Zimbabwe National Family Planning Council.
- The Harare-based *Biomedical Research and Training Institute* for the Southern Africa Development Community, which is a centre of excellence for biomedical sciences and training.

**Manufacturing**

During the first decade of independence, there was a virtual absence of public-sector R&D institutions for the manufacturing sector in Zimbabwe. The only public institutions that could do research for industry were the technical departments of the University of Zimbabwe and the technical colleges. But very few firms collaborated with the university – and that collaboration was limited to advising the university on training programmes and internships for students and, in some cases, metallurgical and chemical testing rather than technological upgrading or research. There was and still is very little in-house research in Zimbabwean industry, and the experience of other countries is that there should be some research capabilities within firms for them to be able to make good use of R&D institutions.

- *Scientific and Industrial Research and Development Centre (SIRDC):* Government recognized the need for an R&D institute to undertake science and technology research aimed at supporting the development of industry in the country. It therefore initiated efforts aimed at establishing such an institution, culminating in the formation of SIRDC in 1993. Although SIRDC was eventually established during the ESAP period, the idea was mooted before then and a lot of the ground work was done at that time.

- *Standards Association of Zimbabwe (SAZ):* The SAZ is a non-government and non-profit-making body that was set up in 1957 to promote standardization and quality improvement, provide an information service on national and international standards and technical regulations, and provide technical services for testing manufactured goods and raw materials. It also operates certification mark schemes, and registration schemes for international standards such as ISO 9000 and 1400.

  An institution like the SAZ can play a very important role in promoting export competitiveness by encouraging the adoption of internationally recognized quality-management standards. Importers in most countries, particularly in the developed counties, now require ISO 9000 series certification as verification of a supplier's control of material procurement, in-process testing, and continuous monitoring of product quality. The 1400 series of ISO standards, related to the environment, has also become very important for the ability to export to developed countries. SAZ product certification acts as an effective marketing tool. The certification mark promotes the name of the manufacturer and also enhances production efficiency, minimizes wastage, and hence promotes competitiveness.

Although the government continued to support research institutes and strengthened extension services, towards the end of the 1980s, faced with an economy that was heating up because of budgetary constraints, some of the institutions began to experience cuts in their budget allocations. However, these cuts did not reflect a change in policy but, rather, a shrinking of the national financial resource base.

### 10.3.2.4 National performance in S&T: Human-resource development

As discussed in the previous chapter, Zimbabwe made considerable strides in promoting the development of education and science and technology-related training institutions during the first decade of independence. The World Bank (1995) noted that Zimbabwe's educational base was relatively advanced by regional standards, and that its expansion in the 1980s was truly impressive. In that report, the World Bank went on to remark (para. 3.20) that 'Zimbabwe's achievements in education are among the country's most impressive gains since independence, putting Zimbabwe near the top of the list in Africa in terms of absolute achievements and the pace at which these results have been attained.'

Notable to S&T were government's efforts to develop technical manpower by creating new technical colleges and expanding intakes, as well as the establishment of the National University of Science and Technology (NUST), which was the second government-funded university in the country.

Another step that government took to encourage the development of local human resources and skills acquisition on the part of Zimbabweans was to establish a Foreign Recruitment Committee within the Ministry of Labour, Manpower Planning and Social Welfare. Its purpose was to minimize the recruitment of expatriate labour and, where this occurred, a framework was set up to ensure that no expatriates were recruited when Zimbabweans were available. Any company or organization recruiting expatriate staff had to ensure that expatriates would transfer their skills to Zimbabweans so that, by the time of contract fulfilment, an expatriate could be replaced by a qualified Zimbabwean, thus removing reliance on expatriate labour in that particular field.

The Foreign Recruitment Committee realized that, in a developing country like Zimbabwe, whose economy was dominated by transnational corporations, there was a danger that some companies might promise to provide training simply as a means of obtaining permission to recruit personnel from abroad. Because expatriates enjoyed excessively high salaries and other fringe benefits compared to their Zimbabwean counterparts with similar qualifications, they generally wanted to extend their contracts and were reluctant to train local Zimbabweans to replace them. To prevent this, the committee required companies applying for foreign recruitment to submit a training schedule which spelt out the nature, duration and goals of the proposed training in addition to particulars of the trainees. A monitoring committee was established to make follow-up operations on a monthly basis to ensure that the training obligations were fulfilled.

### 10.3.2.5 *National performance in S&T: Ideology, macroeconomic policies*

In the 1980s, government pursued an import-substitution industrialization strategy, characterized by a highly regulated economic environment, similar to that implemented by the colonial regime but declaring that the controls would be used to bring about a more equitable form of growth in the economy. New measures were introduced in respect of minimum-wage legislation and hire-and-fire regulations intended to protect workers, in addition to the foreign-exchange, investment, price and agricultural-marketing controls that existed.

But it would be fair to say that, during that first decade of independence, government simply implemented measures aimed towards industry but did not have in place clear industrial development policies and strategies: they are not evident in the successive policy and development plans. While the *First Five-Year National Development Plan* (1986–90) did recognize the important role of industrialization in economic development and employment creation, it failed to put in place the necessary measures to ensure that industrialization would take place and progress.

The government articulated a socialist ideology. It was suspicious of white business-owners and feared economic sabotage through the creation of artificial shortages. Consequently, its priorities in industry targeted ownership and not enterprise creation. National economic security was a major preoccupation, particularly in the early years of independence. In pursuit of its socialist policies, government focused on penetrating and controlling the 'commanding heights of the economy' instead of developing industry. Parastatals were the main instrument for effecting this, and, naturally, take-over bids did not go well with most private entrepreneurs. The *First Five-Year National Development Plan* stressed the need for government control of strategic enterprises, relegating foreign investment to areas of shortfalls in skills and capital (Zimbabwe, 1986: 29–30).

The commitment to socialism, without a socialist-owned and -controlled economic base, had a disruptive impact. Industry, commerce, banking, insurance and agriculture remained firmly within the capitalist ethic, albeit with very little expansion in some sectors during the years of independence. Business remained jittery and dubious about the future ideological thrust of the government.

The absence of the rapport with the private sector that had existed under the UDI regime led to a situation in which the bureaucracy became a major obstacle to doing business in the economy. Business was frustrated by the bureaucracy that was involved in dealing with price controls, labour regulations, particularly those relating to security of employment, the sourcing of foreign exchange, and investment approvals. The manufacturing sector maintained much of its form and structure, but with very limited deepening of industrialization. Although there was some diversification after the introduction of export incentive schemes, particularly the export retention scheme, this outcome was more the result of importers having an opportunity to earn foreign currency in order to purchase inputs to produce for the highly lucrative local market rather than any serious commitment to developing international markets.

### 10.3.3 Science and technology policy thrust during ESAP

#### 10.3.3.1 *Overall national policy thrust/framework*

In 1990, the government abandoned its import-substitution industrialization strategy and socialist ideology in favour of an open-market economy, by adopting the World Bank-sponsored ESAP. The decision to make this dramatic policy change came about because of the economic problems that the country was facing in the second half of the 1980s – low rates of economic growth, low levels of investment and export growth, high budget deficits and inflation, growing unemployment, and the deterioration of infrastructure.

The root causes of these problems lay in, among other things, the egalitarian policies pursued by the post-independence government, particularly high social expenditure that was not matched by increases in productive capacity. This imposed a heavy burden on the government budget at a time when the economy was not expanding and the prices of primary commodities were declining on the international market.

### 10.3.3.2 Science and technology policies under ESAP

A major requirement of ESAP was that government should let the private sector be the driving force in the economy, while its role was to create an environment conducive for private-sector investment. In this regard, the government had to reduce its expenditure, and hence its budget deficit, so as not to compete for resources with the private sector. Government investment in S&T, particularly R&D support programmes, suffered as a result of this philosophy. Unfortunately, R&D investment has a long gestation period and is unattractive for private-sector investment. Furthermore, most large private-sector firms in Zimbabwe were subsidiaries of multinational companies that preferred to undertake R&D at their headquarters in the developed world.

The ESAP policy document sidelined government on matters related to S&T and R&D, the point being that, if government confined itself to creating a conducive national economic and policy environment, the private sector would take care of the rest. There is nothing worthwhile to talk of about S&T policies during ESAP, and this was time lost in relation to S&T policy development.

### 10.3.3.3 Administration of science and technology

The technology portfolio was unpackaged from the Ministry of Industry and Technology some two years before the adoption of ESAP, and the technology management and administration functions 'reverted' to the Research Council of Zimbabwe, with the Scientific Liaison Office serving as its secretariat. For all practical purposes, the role of this office was confined to registering and over-seeing foreign researchers and monitoring and compiling a database of local scientific research. The office did not have significant resources to allocate for scientific and technological research.

### 10.3.3.4 National performance in science and technology

Technological capabilities that had evolved and accumulated within industry were lost with the evident de-industrialization that occurred during this period. Domestic industry was exposed to international competition without any measures being put in place to strengthen its technological competencies and competitiveness. Furthermore, the national innovation system was experiencing pressure owing to the tight fiscal policies that reduced allocations to state-funded

S&T and R&D institutions. ESAP was not just a drawback but was nearer to a disaster with regard to the development of national scientific and technological capabilities.

Rukuni *et al.* (2006) illustrate how the S&T infrastructure with respect to agriculture was decimated during the ESAP period. As a result, a country that had experienced two S&T-driven agricultural revolutions – in the 1950s and 1960s, led by large-scale white farmers, and in the 1980s, driven by small-scale black farmers – lost its ability to provide food security to its populace.

### 10.3.4 Science and technology policy thrust, 1997–2008

#### 10.3.4.1 Overall national political–economic context
As shown in Chapter 2, the years after 1996 can be characterized as a crisis period in that the economy experienced persistent and accelerating decline. Within this context, the government found it more compelling to harness S&T to support the local drive for economic survival, and a lot of progress was made in the area of science and technology by their putting in place a much more coherent national management and administrative structure for S&T development and in S&T policy formulation.

At the same time, it is important to note that the implementation of certain sectoral regulatory frameworks, against the background of a perceived political threat from opposition parties, resulted in certain decisions being made that held back progress in some areas of technological development. On the one hand, the government needed creative indigenous business entrepreneurs to invest in and lead the revival of the industrial sector, but, on the other, it was no longer confident of the political views of some indigenous entrepreneurs in view of the increasing popularity of the opposition, particularly in the urban areas.

#### 10.3.4.2 National management and administration of science and technology
Science and technology re-emerged as an important component of the national development strategy with the establishment of the technology portfolio in the Ministry of Higher Education in the face of the country's increasing isolation by the international community. The functions of the ministry in the area of S&T were not spelt out, nor was its relationship with the Scientific Liaison Office and the Research Council of Zimbabwe that had the statutory mandate to oversee and advise government on science and technology-related issues and policies, and promoting, directing, supervising and co-ordinating scientific and technological research. No budget allocation was made for the technology department, and no staff complement was established except for the single 'scientific liaison officer' who reported to a director in a different department. There was clear confusion over roles and responsibilities among these organizations, and this

was reflected particularly in the duplication of effort in drawing up a national science and technology policy, with two government institutions coming up with documents for consideration by Cabinet.[3] Further, the relationship between Ministry of Higher Education and Technology and other line ministries, such as those of agriculture, industry and health, which oversee S&T programmes within their sectoral responsibilities, was again not defined.

With the failure of the economic-reform programme, lack of support from the international financial institutions, and deteriorating economic performance, the government finally woke up from its slumber with regard to S&T and decided to take appropriate steps in that direction. However, as demonstrated by the situation described above, it was initially unclear how to go about it.

The situation was finally resolved by the establishment of the Department of Science and Technology Development in the Office of the President and Cabinet in 2002. This department was elevated to a fully-fledged Ministry of Science and Technology Development in April 2005, and its functions were then clearly spelt out. As pointed out in the ministry's annual report,

> This elevation was not just a mere transformation of the Department to a Ministry, but was clear testimony of Government's realization of the critical role that science and technology should play in the struggle towards the achievement of national economic development objectives particularly the attainment of the Millennium Development Goals.

The Ministry of Science and Technology Development is responsible for co-ordinating and promoting the development and application of scientific and technological resources for national development and improvements in the living standards of the population. Its main functions are to co-ordinate, facilitate, monitor and evaluate, undertake advocacy, and popularize the development and utilization of S&T. It is also responsible for mainstreaming and harmonizing S&T policies, providing seed financing for S&T programmes and projects, and creating a regulatory framework for S&T institutions. The ministry has two departments: Policy Development and Management, and Programmes and Projects Development (Table 10.1).

The ministry supervises and works closely with the following organizations established in terms of the Research Act: Research Council of Zimbabwe, Scientific and Industrial Research and Development Centre, the National Bio-technology Authority (formerly Bio-safety Board) and Zimbabwe Academic and Research Network (ZARNet). These organizations have contributed to designing and implementing programmes of the ministry. The ministry also works closely with the Zimbabwe Association of Inventors, researchers, Young Scientists Exhibition, and women's and youth groups.

---

[3] This issue is discussed below.

**Table 10.1: Strategic objectives of the Ministry of Science and Technology Development**

| Policy development and management | Programmes and projects development |
|---|---|
| • Develop science and technologies that promote the attainment and sustenance of a technology-driven economy.<br>• Develop and manage regulatory frameworks that facilitate science and technology development.<br>• Develop an institutional framework that facilitates effective science and technology policy implementation.<br>• Establish and operationalize effective monitoring and evaluation systems of S&T policies. | • Promote the development of a science culture.<br>• Co-ordinate and promote ICT development and application nationwide.<br>• Promote and advocate commercialization of R&D and innovations/outcomes.<br>• Identify and co-ordinate the implementation of S&T programmes and activities.<br>• Create and foster synergies with national, regional and global S&T institutions.<br>• Mobilize resources for the effective implementation of S&T projects and programmes. |

*Source:* Ministry of Science and Technology Development, <http://www.mstd.gov.zw>.

Science and technology is a cross-cutting issue, and most S&T programmes fall under the authority of other sectoral line ministries. It is important therefore to develop a national S&T management and administration system that ensures that initiatives taken by the Ministry of Science and Technology Development are taken on board and implemented by the responsible line ministry. The then Department of Science and Technology Development constituted an inter-ministerial committee at director level from relevant line ministries to guide and direct the implementation of S&T activities. The committee had the following terms of reference:

• Ensure the mainstreaming of S&T into line ministries' programmes and activities.
• Provide guidance and direction for the development and formulation of internal and sectoral science and technology policies.
• Provide technical expertise and feedback on the implementation of the sectoral science and technology policies and programmes.
• Oversee the development and reviews of relevant science and technology regulatory frameworks that facilitate science and technology development.
• Provide guidance and direction for the establishment of an appropriate institutional framework that facilitates the effective implementation of the science and technology policy.
• Recommend ways and means by which the impact of science and technology policies can be monitored and evaluated.
• Recommend appropriate science and technology policies for adoption by government.

- Advise on the mobilization of funding and incentives that facilitate the effective implementation of science and technology policies.

The Ministry of Science and Technology Development established eight provincial Science and Technology Development committees to forge partnerships between government, industry, R&D institutions and communities. Provincial Scientific Officers were appointed in an effort to decentralize the ministry's activities to grassroots level. However, the effectiveness of these decentralization efforts has been hampered by budget constraints.

### 10.3.4.3 *Progress in the formulation of national science and technology policies*

**National science and technology policy**

When the Ministry of Higher Education was assigned the technology portfolio, the incumbent minister used existing national institutions to backstop the ministry in drawing up and implementing programmes for the new department. In particular, the ministry took advantage of the Science and Technology Dialogue Forum housed at the Institute of Development Studies of the University of Zimbabwe to assist it in coming up with a national science and technology policy. The Forum was the outcome of an S&T policy advocacy project undertaken at the Institute within the framework of the Africa Technology Policy Studies Network funded by the Carnegie Corporation of New York. The activities of the Forum included S&T policy seminars with members of parliament, senior policy-makers, provincial development committees, S&T policy researchers, R&D institutions, the private sector and other stakeholders. These seminars were conducted at national and at provincial level and were aimed at lobbying government to come up with a national S&T policy and at creating a framework for stakeholders to contribute towards the S&T policy-making process. In this regard, the Forum established chapters in all nine provinces, based in the Provincial Administrator's office under the Provincial Governor.

The Institute of Development Studies, through the Forum, drew up a draft Science and Technology Policy for the country and submitted it to the ministry in June 1999 at the request of the minister. That document had been drafted after nationwide consultations and had been subjected to a national review seminar involving all S&T stakeholders, both inside and outside government, and with external resource persons.[4]

The efforts by the ministry to come up with a national S&T policy document encouraged the RCZ to revive and accelerate its efforts to come up with a national science and technology policy, in apparent competition with the

---

[4] From the United Nations Institute for Economic and Development Planning, Africa Technology Policy Studies Network, and the Carnegie Corporation of New York.

ministry. The document it produced, with input from the ministry's document, was submitted to Cabinet by the Minister of Higher Education and Technology and adopted as Zimbabwe's official national S&T policy and launched on 5 June 2002. After its launch, and the establishment of the Department of Science and Technology that was transformed into the ministry, a lot of progress has been made in laying the framework for harnessing S&T for development and in implementing S&T-related programmes.

### Science and technology action plan

In 2004, the ministry developed a ten-year action/work plan, with the following focus:

- Promotion of and advocacy for science and technology activities.
- Support for research and development through the practical integration of inventions and innovations on the one hand and enterprise development on the other.
- Development and application of information and communication technologies (ICT) in order to bridge the digital divide and create a knowledge-based economy.
- Transfer of technology for import substitution and export promotion.
- Harmonization of science and technology activities in partner institutions.

### Innovation and Commercialization Fund

The ministry went on to establish an Innovation and Commercialization Fund in terms of the Audit and Exchequer Act [*Chapter 22:03*] as venture capital to support the implementation of the 2004 action plan. It is open to the general public (individuals and corporate organizations), and through it the ministry provides seed funds and encourages beneficiaries to court other partners. Some of the projects that have benefited from this fund have become national projects – the biodiesel jatropha project and the coal-to-fuel conversion project.

### Biotechnology policy

The Department of Science and Technology Development, through the Biosafety Board, facilitated the formulation and adoption by Cabinet of the Biotechnology Policy. The National Biotechnology Authority Act (No. 3 of 2006) provides for the establishment of the Authority, which will be responsible for spearheading the development of biotechnology in Zimbabwe and ensuring that such development does not pose any danger to human health, environment, the national economy and the country's norms and values.[5]

---

[5] The act had not been brought into force at the time of writing.

## National ICT policy

The Ministry of Science and Technology Development also developed a national Information and Communication Technology (ICT) policy framework in three stages. The first stage was to conduct a national e-Readiness survey, which assessed the nation's preparedness for the utilization of ICTs.[6] Five attributes are critical to e-Readiness across the economy and society:

- *Network Access:* Availability, cost and quality of ICT networks, services and equipment.
- *Networked Learning:* How well the education system integrates ICTs into its processes to improve learning, and whether or not it has training programmes in ICT.
- *Networked Society:* Whether or not there are employment opportunities in the sector, and to what extent individuals are using ICTs at work and at home.
- *Networked Economy:* The degree to which business, organizations and government are using ICTs to interact with the public and with each other.
- *Network Policy:* The degree to which the policy environment promotes or hinders the growth of ICT adoption and use.

The e-Readiness survey covered ICTs, government, governance, education and training, agriculture, commerce and SMEs, health, mining and manufacturing, transport, tourism and environment and cross-cutting issues of gender, youths, disabled and the aged/elderly. The survey found out that networked access, network policy and networked society were at Stage 1 (low state of readiness) while networked learning and networked economy were at Stage 2, giving an overall rating of 1.4.

The second stage in the formulation of the national ICT policy framework was termed the e-Period phase, and this involved information dissemination and a publicity campaign. Stakeholders discussed the findings of the e-Readiness survey and had an opportunity to propose policies and strategies that would guide the development and use of ICTs in their respective sectors. The third stage was the drafting phase, which involved collecting, synthesizing and incorporating the inputs of all the stakeholders into a draft document, which was finalized and launched in December 2005. The ICT policy framework addresses e-Governance, education and training, commerce and SMEs, agriculture, tourism and environment, health, manufacturing and mining, transport, gender, youth, disabled and the elderly, and roles of government, parliament and research institutions.

---

[6] The survey was conducted with support from the UNDP and in collaboration with the project steering committee, the National Economic Consultative Forum, and the National University of Science and Technology. It was measured using the Harvard University Guide, a model that uses a four-stage scale, 1 being a low state of readiness, and 4 being an ideal state of readiness.

Among other things, the policy seeks to develop and improve national ICT infrastructure (communications, electricity and transport), increase bandwidth on the national backbone and international gateway systems to enhance speed and efficiency, promote local production of ICT products to ensure relevant content and use of appropriate technologies, promote local research and development in software and hardware and rationalizing the ICT tariff structure to make ICTs more affordable and accessible.

**The ICT bill**

The ministry began working on an ICT bill, an important implementation aspect of the national ICT policy.[7] The ICT policy points to the need for a National Information and Communication Technology Authority (NICTA) to rationalize the governance and regulation of the ICT sector in Zimbabwe. A number of actors are involved in the regulation of the ICT sub-sectors of telecommunications, broadcasting, information technology and e-commerce, including government ministries, the Broadcasting Authority of Zimbabwe, the Postal and Telecommunications Regulatory Authority of Zimbabwe, and even the Zimbabwe Electricity Supply Authority. These authorities do not have a framework for co-ordinating their policies in relation to ICT to ensure that they are harmonized in order to achieve a common desired goal. Because ICTs converge at the technology front, there is a need for the rationalization of the governance and regulatory framework of the ICT sector.

**The Science, Innovation and Technology bill**

The Ministry of Science and Technology Development also began work on developing a Science, Technology and Innovation bill. This was aimed at defining the roles of the various players in S&T and at establishing a national research fund that can be accessed by various bodies. The target was to allocate 1 per cent of GDP for R&D purposes.

*10.3.4.4 Science and technology initiatives*

A number of initiatives were undertaken in promoting the development and use of S&T during the crisis period, driven from different fronts: the Ministry of Science and Technology Development, the Office of the President, the Ministry of Agricultural Mechanization, and the Reserve Bank of Zimbabwe.

During his election campaign, the President embarked on a countrywide programme of donating computers, printers and accessories to schools and tertiary institutions with the stated aim of promoting general computer literacy

---

[7] This was continued by the new Ministry of Information and Communication Technology that was formed under the Inclusive Government; see below.

and the use of ICTs in education and educational administration. As noble as this effort was, the teachers at most schools were not computer literate, and many of the schools that received the computers did not have electricity and could not use them. In most cases, the computers were not used as effectively as they could have been.

The Ministry of Science and Technology Development initiated and/or supported several programmes in different sectors of the economy, which are presented below.

## Mining

The ministry financed, facilitated and co-ordinated the technology refinement/optimization of the Oliken submerged arc furnace project which produces ferrochrome from locally available resources mainly for export. The second phase of the project is aimed at producing stainless steel.

It assisted Mining Enterprises with technical and financial support in the development of a bankable project proposal for a project aimed at producing aluminium sulphate in Rutenga, which is used in water-purification processes. The country imports all its water-treatment requirements, and this development provides a substitute for the imports that save on foreign currency.

## Housing

The ministry undertook a comparative study of alternative and affordable building technologies with various partners: SIRDC, for rammed earth technology; PG–Zimtile, for prefabricated concrete blocks; the Forestry Commission, for wooden shell technology; and the Ministry of Public Construction, for conventional brick walls. It also hired a consultant to develop a design for a model barrier-free, user-friendly homestead that addresses challenges experienced by people with physical disabilities.

## Energy

The ministry is responsible for spearheading the National Biodiesel Project, which has the potential to bring considerable benefits to the country (Box 10.1).

## Agricultural engineering

The multipurpose plough: The Ministry of Science and Technology Development supported an invention initiative by the Zimbabwe Association of Inventors and the Industrial Development Corporation for a multipurpose plough. The plough tills the soil, plants seeds, applies fertilizer and covers the furrows, all in one operation. The four-in-one operation provided by this plough reduces the strain on draught power, bearing in mind the recurrent droughts in the region and the depletion of the national herd, and plans to commercialize and develop a motorized version were in hand. This is a development that has the potential to address real problems faced by farmers and can go a long way in increasing agricultural productivity. If the plough is commercialized, this will create opportunities for import substitution and reduce foreign-currency requirements for the importation of agricultural equipment for these purposes.

---

**Box 10.1: The National Biodiesel Project**

The National Biodiesel Project was initiated by government to produce biodiesel from *Jatropha curcas* seed with the objective of reducing oil imports and the related foreign-currency requirements. Finealt Engineering (Private) Limited, a wholly government-owned company, was designated as a 'Special Purpose Vehicle' to implement it.

Through this project, Zimbabwe is one of the first African countries to implement a renewable biodiesel energy initiative. Interest in biofuels is growing all over the whole world due to increasing oil prices. There are also concerns over environmental issues such as global warming and the fast depletion of non-renewable energy resources.

If successfully implemented, the project has potentially tremendous benefits to the country in terms of technological capacity building, employment creation, development of rural areas, reduction in rural–urban migration, and reduction of dependency on oil imports. Biodiesel production contributes to sustainable development by addressing national energy needs and has positive ripple effects on the economy. The cake produced in the oil-extraction process can be used as organic fertilizer or stock feed after detoxification. Glycerine is a by-product of the biodiesel production process and can be used in downstream industries such as the manufacture of cosmetics and pharmaceuticals.

*Developments*
- The project was allocated land for setting up the biodiesel plant and offices in Mutoko.
- The project environmental impact assessment was carried out and approved.
- Work on the design and construction of the biodiesel production plant had progressed well by 2006 and civil works commenced in 2007.
- Individual farmers, teachers and Agricultural Research and Extension (AREX) officers received training in jatropha propagation and management.
- Planting materials, in the form of cuttings, seeds and seedlings, were provided to farmers and institutions, including schools, the army, police, prison services and women's organizations.
- A research and demonstration plot was established at the biodiesel plant site.
- In preparation for the commissioning of the biodiesel production plant, the project has been purchasing jatropha seed from villagers in the province.
- Research and development work on the detoxification of *Jatropha curcas* cake, activated carbon manufacture, soap production and glycerine purification is in progress.
- The Standards Association of Zimbabwe is involved in developing Zimbabwean Biodiesel Standards.

*Source:* Finealt Engineering (Pvt.) Ltd., *Annual Report, 2006*.

---

## Farm mechanization programme

Despite there being a Ministry of Agricultural Mechanization, this programme was spearheaded by the Reserve Bank of Zimbabwe. According to the Governor of the RBZ, the mechanization programme was conceived as part of the land-reform programme and aimed at revitalizing and capitalizing the agricultural sector. Its objective was to transform the equipment and productive landscape of the sector by mechanizing both communal and commercial farmers. Combine harvesters, tractors and animal-drawn equipment were distributed to thousands of farmers across the country. The mechanization programme involved a considerable amount of agricultural equipment, most of which was imported, and the RBZ planned to continue with phase four of the same programme across all clusters of farmers, covering A2, A1, communal and resettlement categories.

However, a number of concerns were raised relating to the manner in which the programme was implemented. Most of the beneficiary farmers did not have the necessary skills to operate and maintain the equipment. Some basic introductory lessons were given on how to operate sophisticated equipment such as combine harvesters, but the adequacy of the training was questionable. There were reports that some of the equipment soon began to suffer stress; the tractors, especially, turned out not to be sufficiently robust to operate under local conditions, and incidents of front-suspension arms breaking were reported. This was the case mostly with tractors from China.

While some local companies could provide backup services such as basic repair and maintenance, spare parts turned out to be a problem, with the more serious farmers having to travel to South Africa to purchase the requisite spares. Adequate foreign-currency provision was not made for the companies supplying the backup services, which might indicate a need that had not been anticipated because the imported equipment and machinery were new.

In addition, some of the farmers did not have adequate knowledge about the appropriate loads that the machinery and equipment could take. Some combine harvesters lay idle when wheat was due to be harvested because the farmers could not operate them properly. Others lost valuable planting time, as the situation was compounded by delays in the provision of inputs such as seed and fertilizer, and all these affect the level of harvests. This factor alone undermined the noble objective of increasing yields that was behind the mechanization programme.

Finally, in view of the hyperinflationary conditions that prevailed at the time, because of the grace period before the 'loan' had to be repaid and the designation of the loans in local currency, this equipment was basically provided for free. What did this mean to the farmers in terms of the value that they attached to these very important productive assets? Some farmers were reported to have used the tractors for commercial transport businesses, using heavily subsidized fuel.

## SIRDC

As mentioned above, the Scientific and Industrial Research and Development Centre was established in 1993 during ESAP, although its conception was mooted prior to that period. Its building and operationalization were delayed by ESAP policies that restricted government expenditure on research and development. During its first phase, SIRDC consisted of seven research institutes, eventually expanded to eleven in addition to the Business Operations Unit.[8]

During the crisis period, government put more resources into SIRDC and assigned it greater responsibility in addressing the problems that the country was facing. The Department/Ministry of Science and Technology Development recognized the importance of SIRDC in fulfilling its mandate of co-ordinating and promoting the development and application of scientific and technological resources for national development, and created space for SIRDC to contribute to addressing the problems that the country was facing as a result of isolation by Western countries.

Despite its limited resources, both financial and human, SIRDC made significant progress in implementing its mandate during the crisis period. It established a subsidiary company, SIRTECH (Private) Limited, through which SIRDC provides technology-based incubator facilities that combine affordable rent, shared facilities and services, business-consulting services, and on-the-job entrepreneurial development for young enterprises. Its primary purpose is to help start-up firms to overcome the technical problems associated with their first few years of operation.

In 2004/05, SIRDC, through SIRTECH, went into partnership with the RBZ's business entity, FINTRUST, that supported the commercialization of four research products: roofing tiles known as SIRTILE; animal antibiotics – brand name SIRDAMECTIN; a foundry branded SIRMET, and science laboratory and teaching equipment known as SLATE.[9] The commercialization of the four projects was expected to result in downstream employment and save foreign currency through import substitution (especially of science laboratory equipment and foundry projects). The production of antibiotics for veterinary use to control both external and internal parasites would greatly benefit the beef industry.

### National Productivity Institute

In 2003, government launched the National Productivity Institute, housed at SIRDC, in line with SADC's commitment to establishing National Productivity Organizations (see below). Unfortunately, it is dormant owing to lack of funding.

---

[8] Biotechnology Research, Building Technology, Electronics and Communication, Energy Technology, Environmental Sciences, Geo-information and Remote Sensing, National Metrology, Production Engineering, Food and Biotechnology, Metallurgy Research and Informatics.

[9] See <http://www.sirdc.ac.zw/sirtech>.

Nevertheless, this was an important development in view of the strategic role that such institutes can play in contributing to the competitiveness of industry by promoting higher industrial productivity. Productivity is the efficiency with which inputs of capital and labour are used, and relates to the conversion of inputs (resources) into outputs (goods and services) efficiently and effectively with the optimum use of human capital and physical resources. It involves the enhancement of human-resources development and technological capabilities at the enterprise, sectoral and national levels.

### 10.3.4.5 Impact of the crisis on scientific and technological development

The objective of developing national scientific and technological capacity and capability is to facilitate the dynamic development of different sectors of the economy for the benefit of the general populace. The benefits of S&T are realized through efficient and competitive production and service provision by both the private and public sectors, and these need to operate within a conducive national socio-economic and political environment. The socio-political environment prevailing during the crisis period undermined the full realization of the positive impact that S&T developments during this period could have achieved. The point is that S&T does not exist for its own sake: it is an input which works with other inputs to achieve desired outcomes and, in the absence of other inputs, the desired outcomes may not be achieved.

As an example, the multipurpose plough, which has the potential to save foreign currency and increase agricultural productivity and food security, may not achieve those outcomes if agricultural policies are in bad shape or if enterprises involved in the commercialization of that plough fail to operate efficiently because of a stifling macro-policy and business environment. The same can be said about SIRDC's efforts to commercialize research results that have been referred to above. The conclusion that emerges is that, given the decline in manufacturing, agriculture, the private sector, the formal economy and skills that has characterized the crisis period, the objectives of developing S&T were not realized. On the contrary, there was a decline in overall national technological capabilities as these are embodied in the various sectors of the economy, particularly industry, and in human capital.

The socio-political environment during the crisis period brought about certain decisions that were inimical to certain aspects of S&T development, particularly through the regulatory process. A case in point has been the telecommunications sector, a very important sector for the development of ICTs, which government itself believes to be of strategic importance to national development. Under the Postal and Telecommunications Act [*Chapter 12:05*], the government established the Postal and Telecommunications Regulatory Authority of Zimbabwe (POTRAZ), whose main objectives are to promote competition, efficiency, innovation and investment in the telecommunications sector, achieve universal access, and ensure that customers get quality services at fair price. In executing its mandate, and with the desire to achieve these objectives, POTRAZ awarded international gateway facilities to mobile telephone companies Telecel and Econet on 26 June 2002 and 17 September 2002, respectively.

The issuing of these licences was expected to bring about greater efficiency in telecommunications in the country, but government had a different focus and believed that, in the interests of national security, the international gateway facility should be confined to the government-owned Tel•One. The POTRAZ board was dissolved for its decision, and government legislated the withdrawal of the other licences. Government's worries on the political front superseded 'rational' economic decisions. In particular, government felt a need to control the media, which became more pronounced after the initiation of the land-reform programme.

### 10.3.4.6 Education and human-resources development

The impact of the crisis on human capital was discussed in Chapter 8, where the brain drain and its implications on recovery were highlighted. For any country to establish and maintain a vibrant national innovation system and build upon its scientific and technological capabilities, it must have a critical mass of science and technology personnel, and continue producing them to meet new demands as well as replace those that exit the market through natural attrition. The adverse impact of emigration on S&T takes on a more long-term perspective when it involves personnel from educational and technical training institutions. An example is the case of the University of Zimbabwe, where the shortage of lecturers resulted in some courses having to be suspended, the most affected departments being in the faculties of medicine, engineering, science, mathematics and law.

### 10.3.5 Science and Technology in the Transitional Period, 2009–2010

When the Inclusive Government was formed, science and technology fell under two ministries: the Ministry of Science and Technology and the Ministry of Information and Communication Technology. This move was based on political expediency rather than measures to streamline the national management and administration of science and technology policies and programmes. In fact, the establishment of a ministry of ICT brought about territorial squabbles between that ministry and the Ministry of Media, Information and Publicity.

The government drew up a Short-Term Emergency Recovery Programme (STERP)[10] in March 2009 and a 100-day plan a month later. STERP recognizes

---

[10] See <http://www.zimtreasury.org/downloads/31.pdf>.

technology as 'the critical engine for the transformation of Zimbabwe from a developing country to a modern industrial state' (para. 268), and the government committed itself to speeding up the implementation of the science and technology policy through the allocation of adequate resources, and to strengthening the strategy of promoting information and communication technology to cover all the public sectors, including educational institutions.

In the 100-day plan, the Ministry of Science and Technology targeted, among other things, the following:

- Linkages with diaspora experts.
- Identification of R&D projects for commercialization.
- Commercialization of Research and Development and Science and Technology Integration.
- Popularization of Science and Technology.
- Identification of individual needs through sector requirements.

The Ministry of ICT committed itself to developing the county's national Website, increasing bandwidth to the Internet gateway by 40 per cent, improving service delivery, particularly in telephone and mobile communication services, reviewing the national ICT policy framework, and completing the drafting of the ICT bill.

What was important was that the Inclusive Government recognized the importance of S&T in development. S&T development programmes, particularly those being addressed by the Ministry of Science and Technology, are of a medium- to long-term nature and cannot be addressed within the context of a 100-day plan. A case in point is the commercialization of R&D; this fact was not explicitly acknowledged. Furthermore, the government lacked financial resources even for salaries of civil servants, let alone for the S&T commitments.

## 10.4 Regional Blocs and Science and Technology Development

### 10.4.1 The SADC science and technology initiative

Regional co-operation offers scope for S&T development by pooling financial and scientific human resources. Even though Zimbabwe belongs to both SADC and COMESA, it is SADC that has given attention to science and technology development in the region: S&T has an important role to play in making the region competitive and SADC is very aware of this. In the *Regional Indicative Strategic Development Plan (RISDP)*, S&T and ICT are identified separately as cross-cutting issues that are among the priority areas of intervention (SADC, 2003: Chapter 4). Matters relating to S&T are also raised within the context of sectoral policies and initiatives in areas such as agriculture and natural resources, in education and training, and in some thematic areas such as human and social development.

According to the *RISDP*,

> The overall aim of the intervention in Science and Technology in the region is to develop and strengthen national systems of innovation in order to drive sustained socio-economic development and the rapid achievement of the goals of the SADC Common Agenda including poverty reduction with the ultimate aim of its eradication (SADC, 2003: 59).

It identifies the following areas of focus in the area of science and technology:

- Strengthening of regional co-operation on S&T.
- Development and harmonization of S&T policies.
- Intra- and inter-regional co-operation in S&T.
- Research capacity in key areas of S&T.
- Technology development, transfer and diffusion.
- Public understanding of S&T.

ICT is covered under SADC's Protocol on Transport, Communications and Meteorology,[11] which represents member states' commitment to the creation of reliable transport and communication infrastructure and the need to take maximum advantage of ICTs for the development of the region. The overall goal of the ICT intervention is to go beyond 'backbone infrastructure development' and move towards addressing structural bottlenecks such as:

i) Reinforcement of citizens' connectivity and ability to effectively use ICT, and be involved in ICT planning and national development.

ii) Development of skills at individual and institutional levels to increase ICT use and capitalize on innovative ICT applications.

iii) Strengthening of governments' capacity to develop effective policy and regulatory frameworks to create conducive environments to ensure market development and public participation in the information and knowledge-based society.

iv) Building a self-sustaining process with the positioning of the community as an effective participant in the information and knowledge-based society – i.e. transition from e-readiness to e-participation [SADC, 2003: 60].

The *RISDP* gives special attention to agricultural research and training. The overall goal of agricultural research and training is 'to contribute to poverty alleviation and sustainable growth', while specific objectives, among others, are to promote partnerships and improve the information communication system (ibid.: 35). SADC desires to move towards initiating research on indigenous technical knowledge and emerging issues, such as biotechnology and intellectual property rights, to which it had previously not given much attention.

---

[11] See <http://www.sadc.int/index/browse/page/162>.

The Protocol on Education and Training, that was signed in September 1997 and came into force in July 2000,[12] provides for co-operation in areas such as educational and training policy, basic, intermediate and higher education and training, and research and development. Article 8 places emphasis on regional co-operation in higher education. S&T is to be achieved through first-rate programmes in postgraduate education and training and both basic and applied research for the development of the region. The protocol also emphasizes the need to share facilities at regional level and to set up 'centres of excellence' in order to maximize scarce resources.

At national level, the protocol encourages member states to strengthen research capacities by allocating adequate resources to universities and research institutes to enable them to undertake socio-economic and technological research. It also recognizes the need for universities to forge links with non-university institutes, the private sector and SADC sectors to access research facilities for joint use. The networking of professionals within the region is also encouraged.

An important SADC initiative that is relevant for the development of techno-logical capabilities at the enterprise, national and regional levels is the concept of National Productivity Organizations (NPOs). In August 1999, SADC heads of state and government signed a Declaration on Productivity,[13] committing them to establishing NPOs with the involvement of key stakeholders, particularly labour and business, who could contribute to their creation, sustenance and effective operation. At the macro level, they committed themselves to formulating trade, industrial and labour policies to ensure adequate access to economic assets and income-generating activities for the majority of the labour force, and to enhance human-resource development and technological capabilities at the enterprise, sectoral, national and regional levels. They also committed themselves to pro-moting and strengthening horizontal and vertical linkages among micro, small-, medium- and large-scale enterprises at national, regional and international levels.

South Africa and Botswana have National Productivity Institutes that are already playing an important role in improving productivity in their countries. In particular, the National Productivity Institute of South Africa has been very vibrant, and has been implementing its 2004–2009 programme of action that involves:

- Provision of productivity competencies and improvement solutions.
- Research to monitor the nation's productivity performance.
- Supporting job retention/creation and poverty reduction.
- Skill development.
- Workplace collaboration.

[12] See <http://www.sadc.int/index/browse/page/146>.
[13] See <http://www.sadc.int/index/browse/page/177>.

The focal areas of the programme include SMEs and community development, support to national strategic initiatives, productivity-improvement advisory services, productive behaviour and competencies, productivity promotion and research, and knowledge management.

### 10.4.2 A critique of the SADC science and technology initiatives

Although SADC's initiatives are on the right track in addressing some of the basic problems relating to S&T within the region, two important issues arise. The first is how and to what extent the regional member countries dovetail their national science and technology development programmes into regional initiatives and into their national development plans and policy frameworks. The second, and more important, is whether these initiatives are sufficient to come up with S&T programmes that address the needs of the people of the region rather than those in the developed countries.

On the first issue of streamlining the SADC strategy with national development policies, Zimbabwe has made some strides. As noted above, this has mainly been in the areas of streamlining the national administration of S&T and of policy formulation. Whether this progress has been the result of the SADC initiative or not is debatable,[14] but this is not of much consequence. What might be more telling are the measures that have been taken that go against the general SADC thrust, as reflected in the *RISDP* in the area of telecommunications regulatory practices.[15]

On the second point, it should be emphasized that S&T is not a neutral phenomenon that, when harnessed, will ensure national prosperity and the fulfilment of the needs of the majority. It is very possible, and indeed very likely, that there can be significant scientific and technological progress that does not benefit the majority. The challenge really is to ensure that harnessing national S&T capabilities is directed at addressing the prevailing dualism that has seen progress in certain sectors of the community to the neglect of the majority. Unless measures are put in place to address this, the SADC regional S&T development efforts are likely to reproduce the unequal development that has characterized the region, but at a higher level. This is where the aspect of dovetailing regional S&T initiatives into national development policies comes in. In other words, there has to be a paradigm shift at the national policy level – a movement away from neo-liberalism to define the role of S&T within the context of the need to satisfy the requirements of equitable development.

It is useful at this stage to restate the difficulties that Zimbabwe and other countries in the region face in harnessing S&T for development and industrial-

---

[14] Zimbabwe's science and technology policy documents do not make reference to SADC.
[15] See above on the decision of POTRAZ versus that of government.

ization in a way that benefits the majority of the population, and this is best achieved by making a comparison between the developed and the developing countries. As Mhone (1992) pointed out,

> in the developed countries, the process of technological change and industrialization is manifested in a mutually beneficial and reinforcing interaction between the development of science, technological innovation, production processes and consumption patterns. The mutual interaction and feed-back among the foregoing not only propels technological change but also evolves an industrial fabric of upstream, downstream and lateral complimentary activities ... that reinforce the virtuous circle of efficiency, growth, and development through increasing spread effects and positive externalities.

The point is basically that there is a virtuous articulation between science, technology, production and consumption that is autonomous and endogenously driven. This characterization of the developed countries was equally applicable to both market- and socialist-oriented economies.

Zimbabwe and other developing countries on the periphery face a disarticulation of the national innovation system, particularly the process referred to above of scientific investigation, technological innovation, production and consumption. Science is not only underdeveloped but it is not shaped by the production and consumption needs of the domestic economy and therefore proceeds independently of these needs. This is the situation described previously, where components of the national system of innovation are more closely connected to the centre and are disarticulated among themselves. The dependency of the production sector on imported capital goods and production processes further undermines the need for technological innovation to a considerable extent.

The SADC initiative on S&T, as pointed out, addresses a number of problems that member countries are facing in this area. However, success requires the creation of a virtuous circle similar to that prevailing in the developed countries as described above. As long as the SADC strategy does not address these issues, S&T development will not be geared to addressing the needs of the majority. The question that arises is – what is the entry point to break the vicious circle that Zimbabwe and other countries in the region are facing? This issue is addressed now.

## 10.5 The Way Forward

### 10.5.1 Summary of the key issues

The experience of Zimbabwe in S&T development brings out a number of issues that need to be taken into consideration in mapping the way forward.

The pre-independence government managed to establish a strong industrial base that had developed significant technological capabilities within the context of import-substitution industrialization. One important factor that accounted for the survival and success of the economy despite the sanctions was the internal cohesion among the minority white community, and a collective/ inclusive approach (though only to the whites) in policy-making and strategic programmes design. That government managed to establish a strong agricultural research infrastructure that brought about the first agricultural revolution in the country which was rooted in the large-scale commercial farming sector. It was predicated on R&D programmes that were developed and implemented in close consultation and collaboration with the commercial farmers.

The post-independence government managed to achieve a second agricultural revolution by 'democratizing' the agricultural research infrastructure during the first decade of independence and making R&D services accessible to the previously neglected communal areas while continuing to provide support to the national agricultural R&D network, thereby maintaining the gains made in the large-scale commercial sector. This was accompanied by pricing and marketing policies and an infrastructure that promoted agricultural development and output growth in these areas. On the educational and human-resources development front, the government made appropriate investments that addressed this constraint to industrial and technological development to a considerable extent.

However, during that period, the government failed to put in place a national science and technology policy, despite expressing a desire to do so, partly because of its preoccupation with short-term macro-economic stabilization and the fact that investment in S&T has a long gestation period that does not provide immediate results. The national administration of S&T was not streamlined and was rectified only during the crisis period. The post-independence import-substitution industrialization had limited success, particularly towards the end of the decade, partly because the rapport with the private sector that had existed under the UDI regime no longer did so, and there was some level of distrust of government because of the latter's pronounced socialist ideology. In addition, the bureaucracy had become a major obstacle to the running of business in the economy.

The period of ESAP, with its policies of rolling back the state in areas such as science and technology, witnessed the erosion of the scientific and technological capabilities that the country had accumulated. In industry, this occurred with the de-industrialization that resulted from poorly designed liberalization policies, and in agriculture from declining government support for R&D and extension services. A key lesson of this period is that market forces on their own cannot lead to S&T development and industrial transformation that benefits the majority of the population. There is need for government intervention and support for the development of a national system of innovation. This support should be strategic and purposeful and guided by the needs and aspirations of the general populace. These same beneficiaries of S&T and industrial development should be involved in defining their needs, priorities and aspirations that, when all put together, will constitute a national vision.

The crisis period saw significant progress in the national administration, formulation and implementation of S&T policies and programmes. However, realization of the potential benefits of these developments was thwarted by the socio-economic and political environment prevailing in the country. What became clear was that developments in science and technology in the absence of a conducive business environment and developmental policies could not lead to an improvement in society's well-being.

The national system of innovation has basically remained disarticulated, with limited interaction among its various components. Until the middle of the crisis period, the system had much stronger linkages with the developed countries than among themselves, and this led to a situation where the development of science was not conditioned by the production and consumption requirements of the country, and science itself was underdeveloped. This led to the perpetuation of the phenomenon of dependency and a dualistic economy.

Unlike during the UDI era, policy-making in the post-independence period has largely been the preserve of government, with limited input from other actors. This did not help in bridging the gap between government and the business community or in creating a common agenda and vision.

### 10.5.2 The extended discovery approach

The alternative approach being proposed takes the S&T policy-making process as the foundation upon which strategies can be developed to harness science and technology for the benefit of the majority. This process should be inclusive and involve all stakeholders, such as the policy-makers themselves, the private sector, scientists (basic research institutions), technologists (R&D institutions), academia (policy researchers), the labour movement, civil society, women support groups, the youth and, very importantly, the communities whose problems are to be addressed by these policies and initiatives. Women support groups are singled out to ensure gender mainstreaming within the policies and programmes. Within this inclusive process, the starting point is not what S&T can do for society but, rather, the collective identification of the needs and aspirations of society.

> The next step is to identify the various activities that need to be undertaken to fulfil those needs and aspirations. Such activities may include investments in several projects, training/capacity-building in various areas, infrastructure development, etc. In most cases several activities will need to be undertaken simultaneously and with one feeding into the other. This creates a virtuous circle as opposed to vicious one. It facilitates regional development by creating linkages between agriculture and small and medium enterprises (SMEs) through agro-

processing and metal-working industries. There is also need to link SMEs with large industries [Zwizwai, 2007].

When the activities that need to be undertaken to fulfil the needs and aspirations of the relevant communities have been identified, the next step is to assign roles, as it were – to identify who does what. The roles of government, the private sector (local, national and international), financial intermediaries, R&D institutions, extension services, labour, training institutions and scientific enquiry should all be defined.

Zimbabwe has already formulated a national science and technology policy, a national ICT policy, and is developing a National Science Technology and Innovation bill. Of particular interest is the manner in which the national ICT policy was formulated, in that it involved extensive consultations, which is consistent with the approach being recommended here. Also of interest is the initiative undertaken by the Ministry of Science and Technology to establish provincial S&T organs, though they are not yet fully functional owing to budget constraints. These are structures that can be utilized in implementing the extended discovery approach (EDA) being advocated here, but existing functional Provincial Development Committees could be used for the same purposes in lieu of the provincial S&T committees that are not yet functioning.

The important point here is that, with a lot of ground work having been covered at the S&T policy-formulation level, the time is almost ripe for moving in to consider developing programmes along the lines suggested. At the risk of labouring the point, the programmes referred to here are not S&T programmes but development programmes aimed at fulfilling the needs and aspirations of communities, and S&T programmes will therefore be based on the role-assignment exercise, and will dovetail into and contribute towards sustainable implementation of the development programmes.

But for the EDA to be implemented successfully, there are fundamental requirements for a sound national S&T and industrial infrastructure. The point here is that S&T influences the trajectory of economic and industrial development, but at the same time the type of economic and industrial infrastructure will determine the extent to which S&T can be harnessed for national development. These will then reinforce each other, creating a virtuous circle.

The prolonged economic crisis that Zimbabwe has been going through has greatly eroded the production and technological capabilities that it had acquired over time. The solution to this crisis lies at both the political and macroeconomic-management level, but this is not what we seek to address here; at some point in the future, the political dimensions that have resulted in Zimbabwe's isolation and the withdrawal of support by the international community will be resolved.

There are three critical areas that require government's involvement and that need to be nurtured to facilitate the development and utilization of national technological capabilities for the benefit of the masses: human resources, the national system of innovation, and a robust industrial infrastructure.

## 10.5.3 Critical areas of intervention

### Human resources

The development of human resources is one of the most important requirements for economic, technological and industrial development. In this regard, a good educational system is imperative, as is industrial and management training. Zimbabwe had managed to establish a well-respected, modern education and human-resources-development system consisting of primary, secondary and tertiary education, and technical, vocational and professional training. It had also developed formal industrial training through apprenticeship and on-the-job training, certified through trade-testing. Industrial training equips the employee with skills needed for the job, or provides the employee with an opportunity to acquire skills for a given industry. This training is important in that it increases local capacity to assimilate, adapt and diffuse imported technology. It also develops the potential for innovativeness.

As pointed out before, the educational system is under severe stress because of a shortage of qualified teachers and lecturers. As part of the process of recovery, the education sector and technical training institutions will need to be revitalized, complemented by the promotion of return migration. Addressing the problem of human resources will need to be given priority, and human-resources development should be revitalized as a strategic requirement for industrial development.[16] One of the major challenges of the education system is its academic focus, without offering a pathways approach: the vocational aspect at the secondary level was weak, hence attempts to vocationalize the system. Vocational education has traditionally been held in low esteem in Zimbabwe, leading to low-quality applicants and poor staffing and equipment. The low pass rate in science subjects at O level does not provide a meaningful basis for S&T development, and this needs to be addressed seriously.

### National system of innovation infrastructure

Zimbabwe needs to strengthen its national system of innovation. Along the lines of the SADC initiative, government should allocate more resources to institutions involved in basic scientific research and collaborate with regional and international partners. Research priorities should be set in ways that take into account the aspirations and needs of the people of Zimbabwe, as determined

---

[16] See Chapter 8.

through a consultative process. Government should invest in infrastructure for basic research that advances scientific knowledge that has the potential for wide application.

Another important aspect of the national system of innovation is the R&D institutions. These engage in applied research that is aimed at translating the results into fairly immediate productive use. Zimbabwe has good R&D infrastructure in agriculture and health, although it has been declining because of the hardships the country has been facing. These need to be re-equipped and strengthened to bridge the gap effectively between scientific enquiry and the production and delivery of services. In the area of industry, SIRDC is of national strategic importance, since it has the greatest potential to undertake industrial research and development that is missing in the private sector. It is important to develop and strengthen the linkages between these R&D institutions and the private sector in order to facilitate the translation of the outcomes of R&D into productive use.

A National Productivity Institute is an important component of the national innovation system as it contributes to enterprise, sectoral and national efficiency and competitiveness, as well as complementing and contributing to technological development, particularly incremental technical and organizational change. Since one had already been established at SIRDC which is currently dormant, it is important that it is resuscitated.

### Industrial infrastructure

Zimbabwe had developed a fairly strong industrial infrastructure comprising a number of strategic industries including basic metals, metal-working, and engineering and chemicals. However, many of these have closed shop, and the share of industry in gross national product has been declining. These industries should be resuscitated because of their strategic nature in the process of economic and technological development outlined below.

The basic-metal industry is often divided into two: ferrous (iron and steel) and non-ferrous, such as copper, lead, zinc, tin and nickel. On the whole, the basic-metal industry involves mining, metallurgy, rolling and extrusion, and produces inputs for the metal-working industry. The metal-working industry involves metal forming (forging and foundry), cutting (milling and machining) and sheet-metal working (fabrication). This industry is strategic in the production of capital goods and spare parts for industrial equipment.

The engineering industry can be categorized broadly into machine-building and technical services. It consists of a number of elements, including engineering design and development, tool engineering and production, production engineering, materials engineering and maintenance engineering. The important point to note is that all these together translate S&T innovations and developments into new, more efficient and more economical machines, plant and equipment. This industry has the capacity to design, adapt and manufacture the components of new technical systems, as well as to repair, modify, and rehabilitate existing industrial plant and equipment.

Zimbabwe needs to put in place policies, strategies and incentives not only to revive this industry but to ensure that it takes off at a higher technological level given the advances that have been occurring: in particular, computer-aided design and computer numerical controlled technology should be assimilated. The chemical industry is strategic in that it produces and supplies intermediate products to other industries, and almost all industries use products from the chemical industry.

### 10.5.4 Science and technology research priorities

It has already been pointed out that the setting of priorities in S&T should be determined by the requirements of programmes aimed at satisfying the needs and aspirations of the national population. However, there are two major areas of technological development – biotechnology and ICT – which emerge as priority areas because both are forefront technologies that have wide application across the major areas of development such as agriculture, health and industry. The benefits from these technologies are huge. Any country that ignores them will certainly lag behind in development, continue to suffer from technological dependence, and will find it increasingly impossible to catch up with the advanced and the advancing countries.

*Biotechnology*

Biotechnology has applications in addressing problems in all areas of agricultural production and processing. These applications include improving crop yields, increasing resistance to pests and diseases, increasing tolerance to drought, salinity and low soil fertility, and increasing the nutritional content of foods. Industrial biotechnological processes are being applied widely in the chemical industry, pulp and paper production, textiles and leather, food processing, metals and minerals.

In health, biotechnology can be used in various ways, including diagnosis of genetic diseases, preventive health care and gene therapy. Medical biotechnology has also assisted in the development of new drugs. Animal biotechnology involves, among other things, developing animal vaccines and medicines, cloning, and the genetic modification of animals and insects. Other applications include improving animal health and performance, increasing livestock and poultry productivity, and using animals for the production of pharmaceuticals. The bottom line is that biotechnology is frontline technology that has so many applications and potential benefits that Zimbabwe cannot afford to ignore it.

SIRDC is already involved in biotechnology research, but the financial and human-resources constraints it faces obviously limit the progress that can be achieved. National scientific capabilities should be developed in this and other areas that have the potential to benefit the majority.

*Information and communication technology*
Another strategic area is information systems, which are important in the dissemination of innovations. Advances in ICTs have led to the opening up of new markets, reduced the cost of search for investment opportunities across the globe, increased the speed of trading, and expanded the boundaries of the tradability of services. ICTs are at the forefront of development in this globalizing world. Knowledge and information are key factors in competitiveness and productivity as well as in social and political development. Basically, knowledge empowers people and provides them with the opportunity to make their own informed choices as to what works best for them in their particular environment (Zwizwai, 2007). Zimbabwe has already developed an ICT policy. ICT development programmes should therefore be prioritized on the basis of their potential to improve the quality of life.

## References

Bell R. M. 1984. 'Learning and the accumulation of industrial technological capacity in developing countries', in M. Fransman and K. King (eds.), *Technological Capacity in the Third World* (London: Macmillan).

Bell, R. M. and K. Pavitt 1993. 'Technological accumulation and industrial growth: Contrast between developed and developing countries', *Industrial and Corporate Change*, 2(2).

Chandiwana, S. and S. Shiff 1998. 'Science Based Economic Development: Eureka Factor', paper presented at the New York Academy of Sciences Conference on Science and Technology for Africa Development, Harare.

Dahlman. C. J. and L. E. Westphal 1981. 'Technological Effort in Industrial Development: An Interpretive Survey of Recent Research' (Washington, DC: World Bank).

Hausmann, Ricardo and D. Rodrik 2003. 'Economic development as self-discovery,' *Journal of Development Economics*, 72 (December).

Lall, S. 1992. 'Technological capabilities and industrialization', *World Development*, 20(2), 165–86.

Marleba, F. 1992. 'Learning by firms and incremental technical change', *Economic Journal*, 102, 845–59.

Mhone, G. 1992. 'A Macro-economic Strategy for Industrialisation and Indigenisation of Technology', in Proceedings of the Third Symposium on Science and Technology, Vol. IIIB (Harare: Research Council of Zimbabwe).

Mudenda, G. 1995. 'Formulating technology policy in Africa: New directions', in O. Ogbou *et al.* (eds.), *Technology Policy and Practice in Africa* (Ottawa: IDRC).

Oyelaran-Oyeyinka, B. O. 2006. 'Systems of Innovation and Development: Institutions for Competence Building', paper presented at the ATPS Conference on 'Science, innovation, technology and the African society: Implications for achieving the MDGs', 27–29 November, Maputo.

Rukuni M., P. Tawonezvi and C. Eicher (eds.) 2006. *Zimbabwe's Agricultural Revolution Revisited* (Harare: University of Zimbabwe Publications).

SADC 2003. *Regional Indicative Strategic Development Plan* (Gaborone: SADC).

World Bank 1995. 'Zimbabwe: Achieving Shared Growth' (Washington, DC: World Bank, Country Economic Memorandum Volume 1).

World Bank 1998. *World Development Indicators, 1998* (Washington, DC: World Bank).

Zimbabwe 1981. *Growth with Equity: An Economic Policy Statement* (Harare: Ministry of Economic Planning and Development).

Zimbabwe 1982. *Transitional National Development Plan, 1982/83–1984/85: Volume 1* (Harare: Ministry of Economic Planning and Development, 2 vols.).

Zimbabwe 1986. *First Five-Year National Development Plan, 1986–1990: Volume 1* (Ministry of Finance, Economic Planning and Development, 2 vols.)

Zwizwai, B. M. 2007. 'Information and Communication Technology, Gender and Human Development', thematic paper for the *Zimbabwe Human Development Report, 2007* (Harare: UNDP (forthcoming)).

Zwizwai, B. M. and M. C. Halimana 2006. 'An alternative science and technology framework for southern Africa', in G. Kanyenze, T. Kondo and J. Martens (eds.), *The Search for Sustainable Human Development in Southern Africa* (Harare: ANSA).

Zwizwai, B., A. Kambudzi and B. Mauwa 2004. 'Zimbabwe: Economic policy-making and implementation: A study of strategic trade and selective industrial policies', in C. Soludo *et al.* (eds.), *The Politics of Trade and Industrial Policy in Africa* (Ottawa: IDRC).

## Chapter 11

# Trade and Trade Policy

This chapter explores trade and trade policy in Zimbabwe since independence in 1980 and is structured into six parts. The first provides an introduction and brief review of literature on trade policy and development. The second focuses on the first decade of independence (1980–1990) while the third assesses trade measures and performance during the ESAP period (1991–1996). A review of trade policy and performance during the crisis period (1997–2008) is undertaken in the fourth section, and the fifth looks briefly at the transition period after 2009. A conclusion and recommendations on the way forward appear in the final section.

## 11.1 Introduction: The Conceptual Framework

The question as to whether or not free trade is associated with superior growth and employment performance has attracted much debate and intrigue. Developed countries and multilateral organizations (the IMF, World Bank, WTO, OECD, etc.) typically espouse the doctrine of free trade, arguing that it is good for growth and is welfare-enhancing. In fact, such policies were central to the structural adjustment programmes implemented in developing countries at the behest of the multilateral institutions, where it was argued that economic openness produces predictably positive growth and employment outcomes.

In an address to the ILO's International Labour Conference in June 1999, US President Bill Clinton argued that 'Competition and integration lead to stronger growth, more and better jobs, more widely shared gains ... Moreover, a failure to expand trade further could choke off innovation and diminish the very possibilities of the information economy. No, we need more trade, not less.'[1] The EU also contended that[2]

> The multilateral trading system has for fifty years contributed to stable and continued economic growth, with all the benefits that this implies. Eight rounds of trade liberalization and strengthening of rules has made a major contribution to global prosperity, development, and rising living standards. Since 1951, global trade has grown seventeen-fold, world production has more than quadrupled, and world per capita income has doubled. The multilateral system has helped many developing countries to be integrated into the international economy, experience

[1] See <http://www.ilo.org/public/english/standards/relm/ilc/ilc87/a-clinto.htm>.

[2] 'The EU Approach to the WTO Millennium Round', 8 July 1999, <http://aei.pitt.edu/4942/01/003151_1.pdf>.

showing that countries with more open markets achieve higher levels of economic growth and development. The record of the WTO since the conclusion of the Uruguay Round has been particularly positive, bringing major improvements in market access and more predictable rules. Growth has become increasingly trade-driven, and trade accounts for an increasing proportion of economic growth.[3]

The theoretical premise for this position goes back to David Ricardo's trade theory of 1817 which stated that, when countries specialize according to their comparative advantage, compared to autarky, free-trading countries would benefit more. A body of literature also emerged supporting the virtues of free trade. A study by the OECD (1999) contended that more open and outward-orientated economies consistently outperform restrictive trade and [foreign] investment countries. In the same vein, the IMF (1997) extolled openness as a primary factor behind economic growth and convergence among developing countries.[4] This prediction has also been supported by some growth regressions which found some indicators of outward-orientation (e.g. trade ratios or indices of price distortions or average tariff level) to be strongly associated with per capita income growth (Stiglitz, 1998). At the heart of this positive prognosis is that trade liberalization, the opening up of the economy to international trade, realigns domestic prices of tradable goods with world prices. It is argued that, where governments relied on import controls, tariffs or export taxes and subsidies, domestic prices deviated from world prices, thereby distorting resource allocation (World Bank, 1990). In this regard, it is argued that 'trade liberalization results in the contraction of inefficient sectors and the expansion of new, efficient ones. Over time, a new and more efficient production structure develops that will be better suited to the international environment (Michalopoulos, 1987: 24).

However, critics have questioned the presumed automatic link between free trade and economic and employment growth. For instance, Rodríguez and Rodrik (2000) contend that, once the methodological approaches employed in the studies that provide a positive relationship between openness and economic growth are questioned, the results are open to diverse interpretations.[5] They argue that, in many cases, the indicators of 'openness' used in the regressions are poor measures of trade barriers, or are for that matter highly correlated with other sources of poor economic performance. Their study found little evidence that open trade policies (lower tariff and non-tariff barriers to trade) were significantly associated with economic growth.

---

[3] A similar text appears in the opening paragraph to the Doha and other WTO ministerial declarations. The EU is pushing for the conclusion of Economic Partnership Agreements (EPAs) with the African, Caribbean and Pacific (ACP) countries that seek to introduce reciprocal liberalization of trade between the EU and regional groupings of the ACP countries.

[4] See also Krueger (1998).

[5] See also Helleiner (1990), Taylor (1988) and Krugman (1987).

The existence of market imperfections as a hindrance to the expected positive outcomes from liberalizing trade have long been acknowledged (Helleiner, 1990; Taylor, 1988; Krugman, 1987, among others). The movement towards managed trade, the contentious and often self-serving trade negotiations under the WTO, especially around agriculture, and frequent trade wars illustrate the reality of market imperfections in international trade.[6] Rodrik (2006) cites empirical evidence on developments that defy the notion of trade liberalization as a basis for economic prosperity. He cites China and India, which were able to sustain high economic-growth momentum without employing conventional approaches.[7] These countries registered robust growth despite maintaining high levels of trade protection, extensive industrial polices, and lax fiscal and financial policies, without resorting to privatization, throughout the 1990s. 'On the basis of the evidence available, however, to suggest that there is already a universal optimal *trade* policy prescription that will generate improved economic performance for all who embrace it is to ignore too much recent experience' (Helleiner, 1995: 47).

Other critics have also raised the technical challenges associated with trade reforms, arguing that the rapid and significant reduction of tariffs recommended (World Bank, 1990) disregards the political sensitivities involved and the fact that most African governments derive a significant proportion of their revenues from trade taxes (Rodrik, 1990). Both proponents and critics agree that the sequencing of such reforms is problematic, as economic theory offers little guidance on the optimal sequence for removing market distortions (Michalopoulos, 1987). It has also been argued that, given supply constraints, the output response in developing countries may not happen in the short term. As Kapoor (1995: 3) noted, 'Given the weak implementation capacity in African economies ... structural adjustment programs, in general, have unrealistic expectations about how fast adjustment can occur; consequently, the political costs of speedier implementation are also often underestimated'.[8] In essence, therefore, trade policy is rarely a first–best instrument (Neary, 2001). For Taylor (1988: 33), 'it is fair to say that in the mid-1980s the trade liberalization strategy is intellectually moribund, kept alive by life support from the World Bank and International Monetary Fund.'

Krugman (1987: 132) asks whether free trade is passé. He argues that, while this is not true, 'it is an idea that has irretrievably lost its innocence. Its status has shifted from optimum to reasonable rule of the thumb'. Hausmann *et al.* (2004) advocate a strategy that confines reformers to focusing on the areas

---

[6] See, for instance, Keet (1999).

[7] See Chapter 1.

[8] Kapil Kapoor was the chief economist of the World Bank in Harare during the ESAP period.

that have the greatest pay-off instead of casting widely on all distortions. The distortions that have the greatest pay-off – or, rather, pose a major binding constraint to trade growth – are identified through an empirical approach which should guide the intervention strategy.

More-recent work from the World Bank (2005 and 2008) acknowledges that, while trade reforms can play a part in accelerating integration into the global economy and anchor an effective growth strategy, the redistributive effects of trade liberalization remain diverse and may not always be poverty-alleviating or, rather, pro-poor.[9] The World Bank notes that the conventional package of reforms that focused on liberal trade measures had an obsession with dead-weight loss triangles, motivated by the desire to reap efficiency gains from their elimination without paying attention to the dynamic forces that drive economic growth. The World Bank study also observes that the world trade system is still biased against the poor, with global markets still hostile to the products the world's poor produce – agricultural products, textiles and labour-intensive manufactures – and problems of escalating tariffs, tariff peaks and quota arrangements deny the poor access to markets and skew incentives against value-addition in poor countries.[10]

## 11.2 The First Decade of Independence, 1980–1990

### 11.2.1 Trade and trade policy overview
At independence, the new government took over a fairly well-diversified economy with an industrial base stronger than that of most Southern African countries. The post-independence period's policy environment saw the restoration of peace, the lifting of economic sanctions, and the re-admission of the country into the international community. Zimbabwe's re-entry into the international community paved the way for access to new markets, and the country immediately became a member of the Southern African Development Co-ordination Conference, now the Southern African Development Community (SADC), which provided a region-wide market.[11] In addition, it acceded to the Lomé Convention, thereby obtaining preferential entry for agro-exports into the European Economic Community markets.[12] It also joined the Preferential Trade Area, now the Common Market for Eastern and Southern Africa (COMESA), thus accessing

---

[9] See also WTO and ILO (2007).

[10] The assessment of trade and trade policy here is not exhaustive, highlighting only the main arguments.

[11] SADC members are: Angola, Botswana, Democratic Republic of Congo (DRC), Lesotho, Madagascar, Malawi, Mauritius, Mozambique, Namibia, Seychelles, South Africa, Swaziland, Tanzania, Zambia and Zimbabwe. This market currently has an estimated population of 210 million people.

[12] The Lomé Convention is now known as the ACP–EU Cotonou Agreement that seeks to promote trade between 77 African, Caribbean and Pacific countries and the European Union.

an extra-regional market in Southern and East Africa.[13] The government also negotiated bilateral agreements with neighbouring countries and barter-type trade agreements with a number of socialist countries, including North Korea, Hungary, Cuba and China, among others.

However, the new Zimbabwe continued the pre-independence trade policy aimed at protecting local industrial development and the diversification of domestic markets through import restrictions and foreign-exchange controls. It is worth noting that the regulation of foreign trade in Zimbabwe dates back to the UDI era of 1965–1980, the motivation being one of economic survival under conditions of international isolation on the back of international sanctions. Strategic domestic and industrial policies had to be devised to combat the sanctions and sustain production, and hence survival. These circumstances induced import-substitution industrialization, which was maintained after independence (Rattso & Torvik, 1998).

A stable currency and favourable exchange rate during the early years of independence played a crucial role in promoting Zimbabwe's trade then. Between 1982 and 1990, the Zimbabwe dollar was pegged to a trade-weighted basket of fourteen currencies,[14] which took into account the inflation differentials with the major trading partners. All the foreign exchange earned by exporters was surrendered to the state and there were no foreign-currency accounts. In turn, importers received foreign-exchange allocations from the Reserve Bank of Zimbabwe (RBZ) after being granted import permits by the Ministry of Industry and Commerce. This policy regime, coupled with the lifting of international sanctions, accounted for the post-independence economic boom, which recorded GDP growth rates of 10.6 per cent (1980) and 12.5 per cent (1981), before a severe drought reversed this positive trend in 1982.[15]

Even without accounting for the devastating economy-wide effects of the 1982 drought, Rattso and Torvik (1998) observed that the post-independence economic boom was unsustainable on foreign-exchange grounds, compelling the new government to restore administered foreign-exchange allocations to put a check on the current-account deficit. The policy adjustments of the mid-1980s made an attempt to strike a balance between the pursuit of a managed industrial protectionist policy (inward-looking industrial strategy) while at the same time promoting exports. The focus was on responding to the economic-growth-limiting nature of the administered foreign-exchange system that was choking

---

[13] COMESA members are: Angola, Burundi, Comoros, Democratic Republic of Congo (DRC), Djibouti, Egypt, Eritrea, Ethiopia, Kenya, Madagascar, Malawi, Mauritius, Rwanda, Seychelles, Sudan, Swaziland, Uganda, Zambia and Zimbabwe. This market currently has an estimated population of 389 million.

[14] Including the South African rand, British pound, US dollar, West German deutschmark, Japanese yen and Botswana pula.

[15] See Chapter 2.

industrial capacity by constraining import capacity. In any case, 'by the end of 1982, government became concerned about the long-term debt implications of the [early economic] boom and began to pay more attention to macroeconomic balance' (Bhalla *et al.*, 1999: 10). Coupled with the drought, the weakening global economic conditions and, in particular, declining commodity prices and worsening terms of trade impacted adversely on the balance of payments.[16] The terms of trade at 1975 levels, for instance, continued to deteriorate from 94.5 in 1981 to 87.2 in 1982 and 86.0 in 1983.

To address the emerging challenges, government adopted a stabilization programme, beginning with a twenty per cent devaluation of the Zimbabwe dollar in December 1982. The RBZ then adopted an exchange-rate policy focused on ensuring that the local unit would not appreciate, marking a break from the import-substitution industrialization that had characterized the early years of independence. Other measures implemented included export incentives designed to address the anti-export bias. Of note is that import controls and the rationing of foreign exchange was motivated primarily by the need to control the current account as an instrument of macroeconomic policy rather than of industrial policy. The policy adjustment included export subsidies, export retention schemes, and an incremental export bonus scheme to influence decisions in the private-sector towards exports. The export retention scheme allowed exporters to retain export earnings initially to finance imports of strategic inputs for exports, though this was eventually adjusted to allow the import of inputs to address domestic production bottlenecks.

On balance, these incentives marked a departure from the largely regulated foreign-exchange rationing system that had been predominant in the early 1980s, broadening the magnitude of resources (foreign exchange) that were then allocated outside the administered allocation system. To buttress this policy shift, by the end of the first decade a substantial proportion of foreign exchange transacted in the economy was no longer going through the official, regulated system, giving rise to some form of market system.

In 1986, the Minerals Marketing Corporation of Zimbabwe (MMCZ) and the Zimbabwe State Trading Corporation (ZSTC) were established, the former assigned to market mineral resources while the later was responsible for managing domestic commercial procurement services. The MMCZ is still operational, but the ZSTC gave way to the Zimbabwe Export Promotion Programme (ZEPP) in 1987. A criticism of the ZSTC was that, instead of being a service organization to exporters and importers, it acted more like a rival (ZCTU, 1996: 60). The ZEPP initially enjoyed seed capital in the form of a grant of US$5.5 million from the European Union under the Lomé III Convention. Within three years,

---

[16] See Chapter 2.

it had achieved its export target of US$100 million and generated about US$185 million in income.

These export incentives had a positive impact on economic growth towards the end of the decade, with GDP growth at 7.7 per cent, 5.2 per cent, and 7.0 per cent, respectively, for the years 1988, 1989 and 1990. As a percentage of GDP, exports remained static during the last half of the decade, at levels that were below the peak of 30.3 per cent achieved in 1980 (Table 11.1).

**Table 11.1: Exports and imports of goods and services as a percentage of GDP, 1980–1990**

|         | 1980 | 1981 | 1982 | 1983 | 1984 | 1985 | 1986 | 1987 | 1988 | 1989 | 1990 |
|---------|------|------|------|------|------|------|------|------|------|------|------|
| Exports | 30.3 | 25.2 | 21.9 | 22.5 | 26.7 | 22.0 | 24.0 | 23.9 | 23.9 | 23.6 | 23.0 |
| Imports | 33.3 | 32.5 | 27.8 | 25.7 | 26.1 | 21.8 | 21.5 | 21.2 | 20.5 | 22.0 | 22.0 |

*Source:* IMF, *International Financial Statistics.*

In spite of the measures to stimulate exports, the government's own assessment was not upbeat. Overall export growth was disappointing, rising by only 3.4 per cent per annum in real terms over the period 1980 to 1989. Coupled with debt-service payments that rose to a peak of 34 per cent of export earnings in 1987, this severely constrained the growth of imports, which declined by 0.4 per cent per annum in real terms over the period 1980 to 1988. This severely constrained utilization of existing capacity as well as investment in new production capability (Zimbabwe, 1991).[17] Other studies have noted how the developments in the decade could not guarantee sustainable economic transformation for Zimbabwe in the medium to long term. The six years from 1982 to 1987 witnessed very low and volatile economic growth, stagnant employment, foreign-exchange shortages, inadequate investment, and large, rising structural deficits (Mumvuma *et al.*, 2006).

## 11.2.2 Policy results

As if to magnify the impact of the largely restrictive trade policies of the 1980s, the foreign-exchange shortages put a damper on the expansion in productive capacity, with the Confederation of Zimbabwe Industries estimating that, for the year 1987 alone, import allocations committed to production for the domestic market were below 40 per cent of their value in 1980 (Rushinga, 1987). The major reason for the foreign-exchange bottleneck was the fact that allocations were, by and large, done at unrealistic and non-market prices. This scenario no doubt curtailed the exploitation of business opportunities, narrowing the scope for the recreation of capital. The only visible uplift in export growth was

---

[17] It has been observed that exports grew at an average rate of 9 per cent per annum in US dollar terms at the end of the 1980s following the stagnation caused by droughts and the world depression during the early and middle parts of the decade (ZCTU, 1996).

recorded at the dawn of independence, that is, 1980 and 1981, as the new nation enjoyed its access to a global market space after having endured fifteen years of political and economic isolation.

Notwithstanding these constraints, it would appear that, after recovering from the distortions of sanctions, 'Zimbabwe had developed the best balanced trade structure in Sub-Saharan Africa with manufactured exports accounting for about 20% of the total, or nearly 40% if cotton lint, ferrochrome and steel are included' (ZCTU, 1996: 59). Manufactured goods accounted for much of the growth in exports, rising from 29 per cent to 36 per cent of the total by the end of the decade (World Bank, 1995). The success was surprising considering that it occurred during a period of destabilization by South Africa under apartheid, in the absence of any coherent industrialization strategy, and also in a context where trade policy was ad hoc and often incoherent (ZCTU, 1996). Interestingly,

> in terms of trade policy, Zimbabwe was at best a semi-NIC, having stumbled on some policies that gave it a much better (though still inadequate) record than that of most African countries. Trade, especially in non-traditional manufactured goods, did expand. Yet there were many distortions and frustrations, and it is easy not to show that many exporters suffered from an anti-export bias that was only partially cancelled by other incentives' (ZCTU, 1996: 60).

The trade ratio (imports and exports as a percentage of GDP) is a measure of the degree of opening up of the economy: from a level of 71 per cent in 1980 it closed the decade much lower (Table 11.2). This trend can be blamed largely on the fairly rigid trade-promotion policies during the first decade, a trend also apparent in Table 11.1.

**Table 11.2: Trade ratios: Imports and exports as a percentage of GDP, 1980–1989**

|           | 1980 | 1981 | 1982 | 1983 | 1984 | 1985 | 1986 | 1987 | 1988 | 1989 |
|-----------|------|------|------|------|------|------|------|------|------|------|
| Ratio (%) | 71.1 | 71.2 | 62.3 | 56.8 | 69.8 | 48.1 | 47.4 | 46.7 | 45   | 48.4 |

*Source:* Bhalla *et al.* (1999: 19).

The picture painted here is one of trade expansion that did not reach optimal levels during the first decade, and the export support policies adopted managed only to sustain a mediocre trend, particularly since the support was also available for domestic production. In an attempt to explain this mixed export performance, the UNDP/UNCTAD Zimbabwe Country Assessment Report underscored the insignificance of the export retention scheme in promoting exports from the mid-1980s onwards, arguing that 'one of the problems with the export retention scheme ... was that the profitability of the domestic market induced firms to export below cost, knowing that they would be able to make up the loss by the profits they would make domestically' (Bhalla *et al.*, 1999: 12). The trade performance scenario can thus be explained largely by corporate-specific microeconomic decisions that limited initiatives to expand aggressively into exports, given the traditionally insulated and profitable domestic market they had been used to since 1965 and also in the absence of any radical policy changes during the first decade of independence.

Also of note is the fact that government had apparently continued to use an import-substitution strategy in order to promote local industrial development when opening up the country to global markets, and international sympathy would have lent credence to its adoption of a more outward-looking industrial strategy from the outset. It is thus no coincidence that the development of industry during this period was much slower than in the pre-independence period.[18] This was partly because the shallow phase of import substitution, which involved consumer products, had been exhausted, and opportunities lay in the 'deeper' phase that required huge capital outlays, greater technological capabilities, and detailed economic, financial and technical feasibility studies (Green and Kadhani, 1986). The growth-limiting effect of the earlier policy regime was used to advocate a radical shift in economic policies that had had far-reaching effects.

## 11.3 The Period of ESAP, 1991–1995

### 11.3.1 Policy overview

By the end of the 1980s, the limitations of the import-substitution strategy had been fully acknowledged and the need for change was accepted, although there was no agreement on its nature and content. Even before the adoption of ESAP in 1991, the government's trade policies were already being altered, with the Open General Import Licence (OGIL) being expanded to accommodate more products. With effect from July 1990, government introduced the export retention scheme that allowed exporters to retain 5 per cent or 7.5 per cent of their export earnings, based on the type of export, and use the retained proceeds to finance strategic imports such as capital goods or raw materials. There was a 12 per cent real depreciation in the Zimbabwe dollar during 1990, following the 8 per cent during 1989. Government began to remove a substantial number of commodities from the price-control list with effect from October 1990, with the exception of foodstuffs. In the budget statement announced in July 1990 and accompanied by a policy statement, government provided a strong signal of its changing policy position.

The launch of ESAP in January 1991 marked the full embrace of market reforms in Zimbabwe. In fact, opening up foreign trade – trade liberalization – was the *raison d'être* of ESAP. At the heart of structural adjustment programmes

[18] See Chapter 4.

was a desire to change the composition of national output in favour of tradable goods (both exportables and importables) via exchange-rate depreciation. Thus, with the adoption of ESAP, rapid export growth was to become the means for launching the economy on to a faster growth path.

## 11.3.2 Specific trade reforms

The main thrust of ESAP on trade reforms was the elimination of quantitative controls and the reduction and harmonization of tariffs and duties, with specific components of this policy direction taking the form of the removal of export incentives and phasing out import licensing. The programme set a target of 9 per cent growth in exports on an annual basis over the five-year period to 1995. The reforms were phased in as follows:

*Phase 1: 1991–1993*
Additional inputs were put on OGIL and, by the end of 1992, 15 per cent of imports were placed under unrestricted OGIL, while 10 per cent remained restricted; by 1993, 20 per cent were unrestricted. Foreign-exchange allocation was phased out, with tariffs remaining the only source of protection to local industry. The exchange rate was devalued in August 1991, allowing the Zimbabwe dollar to depreciate in real terms to encourage export competitiveness. The export retention scheme allowed productive sectors to retain a proportion of their export earnings for the purchase of machinery and raw materials to expand their productive capacity. At first, mining and agriculture were allowed to retain only 5 per cent of their export proceeds, while manufacturing, tourism, construction and road hauliers could retain 7.5 per cent.

In November 1993, the Investment Centre, a division in the Ministry of Finance, was upgraded into a stand-alone, 'one-stop shop', the Zimbabwe Investment Centre. It was responsible for the appraisal and approval of investment projects that produced either for the domestic market or for export, with an upper export threshold of below 80 per cent. All projects with an export threshold in excess of 80 per cent were appraised and approved by the Export Processing Zones Authority, which was set up in 1996.

*Phase 2: 1993–1995*
The OGIL list was expanded to include intermediate inputs and then other imports, and by 1994 most goods were on OGIL, with the exception of a small negative list that included textiles and strategic imports such as fuel. OGIL was eventually replaced by an open import system. The progressive expansion of an unrestricted OGIL was meant to facilitate the nurturing of an export-oriented industrial regime, and hence engender a competitive environment for local firms. Industrial protection shifted away from quantitative restrictions to

tariffs, and tariff rates were reduced such that an average nominal tariff of 16 per cent was reported in the WTO's *Trade Policy Review* for Zimbabwe in 1994 (Bhalla *et al.*, 1999).

Adjustments to the proportions retained in the export retention scheme were effected over time, with companies allowed 100 per cent by 1994. Foreign-exchange reforms were deepened, with exporters eventually being empowered to trade their retentions, thereby establishing a foreign-exchange market and an element of a market-determined exchange rate. With a widening in the magnitude of export earnings, transactions on the foreign-exchange market increased, providing an incentive for the government to unify the dual exchange-rate regime in 1994. Foreign-currency accounts which allowed 60 per cent retention were introduced in January 1994, and this was increased to 100 per cent in July 1994.

*Phase 3: 1995*

This signalled the end of ESAP, with the government capping the period by implementing commitments under the WTO framework, accounting for significant reductions in tariffs, and converting non-tariff barriers into tariffs, thereby giving prominence to tariffs as the only source of industrial protection. During the trade-liberalization phase, tariffs were, on balance, reduced, as reflected in the declining percentage of duty collected to import values (Table 11.3).

**Table 11.3: Ratio of duty collected to value of imports, 1990–1996**

|           | 1990 | 1991 | 1992 | 1993 | 1994 | 1995 | 1996 |
|-----------|------|------|------|------|------|------|------|
| Ratio (%) | 24.3 | 24.1 | 22.5 | 19.9 | 15.7 | 13.0 | 13.5 |

*Source:* Bhalla *et al.* (1999: 19).

Further liberalization of the foreign-exchange regime was effected, leading to currency convertibility and culminating in Zimbabwe acceding to the obligations of the IMF's Article VIII (Sections 2, 3 and 4), which committed the country to maintaining liberalization of all payments for current transactions (Zimbabwe, 1998: 5). The Export Processing Zones programme was introduced in 1995 at the end of ESAP. Investors were to access incentives that included: a tax holiday for five years, after which a tax level of only 15 per cent would apply; duty-free importation of raw materials and capital equipment and machinery associated with operations; exemption from fringe-benefits tax for employees; and the non-application of labour laws.[19]

Meanwhile, ZimTrade succeeded the Zimbabwe Export Promotion Programme in 1992 with a mandate to provide incentives, grants and other trade-promotion

---

[19] Following protestations from the ZCTU, labour regulations were promulgated in 1998 to cater only for EPZs. The Labour Act was allowed to operate in Export Processing Zones only after the 2002 amendments.

support from a 0.1 per cent surcharge on imports and exports, which government agreed to match. ZimTrade's board had equal representation from government and the private sector, and its divisions included export development, export information, and a unit providing a complete package for new exporters.

### 11.3.3 Policy results

Though trade liberalization had been envisaged to be gradual, actual implementation was accelerated, generating mixed effects across the various sectors of the economy. Rattso and Torvik (1998) note that, to the surprise of most observers, the government chose to go for full trade liberalization – a more radical approach than that implemented in most developing countries. They argue that this must be understood against a background of increased political pressure to join the international trend of implementing liberal economic reforms, and assurances from the Bretton Woods institutions that liberalization would unlock funding.

To demonstrate this, by 1994 the foreign-exchange allocation system had stopped operating, the financial sector had been liberalized, price controls had been lifted, labour laws and investment laws had been relaxed. All current transactions were being done liberally, the only restrictions being those on the capital account and, more specifically, on returns to investments made before independence and on holding foreign assets abroad. The economy's response to the 'shock therapy' type of reforms was not good, triggering bouts of macroeconomic instability in the short run. The immediate experience was the contraction of output and employment, a consumption boom, the inflow of imports, and a rising trade deficit (Rattso and Torvik, 1998). Exports as a percentage of GDP increased from 23.9 per cent in 1991 to 36.1 per cent in 1996, while the share of imports in GDP increased from 27.2 per cent in 1991 to 38.1 per cent in 1995 (Table 11.4). Events were complicated by a severe drought in 1991/92.

**Table 11.4: Exports and imports of goods and services as a percentage of GDP, 1991–2000**

|         | 1991 | 1992 | 1993 | 1994 | 1995 | 1996 | 1997 | 1998 | 1999 | 2000 |
|---------|------|------|------|------|------|------|------|------|------|------|
| Exports | 23.9 | 27.3 | 30.7 | 34.7 | 35.6 | 36.1 | 35.4 | 42.5 | 47.8 | 37.9 |
| Imports | 27.2 | 36.6 | 32.4 | 36.6 | 38.1 | 35.9 | 42.0 | 44.2 | 46.1 | 38.2 |

Source: IMF, *International Financial Statistics*, and Central Statistical Office, *National Accounts Tables*.

### The manufacturing sector

The manufacturing sector was the hardest hit by the trade-liberalization programme, particularly since it had previously been protected and had to face up to new business conditions. Trade liberalization was implemented hurriedly without full attention being paid to the structural problems of the manufacturing sector, which then had serious supply-side constraints that included obsolete capital that had not been replenished owing to acute shortages and rationing of foreign currency. The combined effect of exchange-rate depreciation and high financing costs made exposure to external competition unbearable. These conditions resulted in company closures, particularly of small-scale and medium-sized companies. De-industrialization occurred, with the sector's contribution to GDP declining to less than 16 per cent during the reform period for the first time since 1960, yet in the 1970s and 1980s it had averaged 25 per cent. Manufacturing output fell by more than 20 per cent as competition from foreign imports intensified. The downturn in industrial output was a major structural challenge, signifying a wave of de-industrialization as protection barriers were removed. The major sectors to be affected were textiles, clothing, footwear, wood and furniture, paper, printing and publishing, and transport and equipment. On the textiles side, liberalization accounted for a major influx of Asian garments that were relatively cheaper, and local players were squeezed. According to the ZCTU, the textiles sector lost at least 15,000 employees between 1992 and 1997.

The accelerated movement of goods on to OGIL in the absence of adequate balance-of-payments support placed pressure on the scarce foreign currency, thus compounding the deterioration of the balance-of-payments position as imports were rising faster than exports. The liberalization of imports allowed import-dependent industries to expand, thus enabling the protected, domestically focused producers to prosper. This did not involve any structural change at all, and companies that had suffered from restricted access to imports prior to the reforms benefited immensely when liberalization was effected. As the reforms progressed and the influx of imports heightened, import-competing industries could not withstand the foreign competition and were rendered unprofitable. There is also no doubt that the 1991/92 drought and its aftermath compromised agricultural income and aggregate demand, further dampening the manufacturing sector (Tekere, 2001).

### Trade performance

During the reform period, merchandise imports rose by more than 20 per cent on an annual basis while real exports fell. The value of exports shrank on average at an annual rate of 4.6 per cent between 1991 and 1995, and that of imports by about 3.8 per cent. This was in sharp contrast to the pre-ESAP period, when exports had grown at an average rate of 9 per cent per annum between 1985 and 1990 (ZCTU, 1996). The bulk of imports were final consumer goods, rather than intermediate inputs and capital goods, which put a damper on domestic industrial capacity in the short to medium term in the absence of the value-adding potential of capital goods and other strategic inputs. This points to reduced investment potential both in terms of replacement capacity and future production capacity.

The response of trade to the liberalization measures was also observed to have been quite noticeable. The trade ratio increased significantly from 48.4 per cent in 1989 to peak at 92.6 per cent in 1995 (Table 11.5). This observation serves to confirm that, despite the shortcomings of the programme, some degree of trade openness was registered through the reforms embarked on under ESAP, yet export performance was dismal; in fact, it worsened in comparison with the first decade of the 1980s.

**Table 11.5: Trade ratios: Imports and exports as a percentage of GDP, 1989–1996**

|  | 1989 | 1990 | 1991 | 1992 | 1993 | 1994 | 1995 | 1996 |
|---|---|---|---|---|---|---|---|---|
| Ratio (%) | 48.4 | 50.6 | 61.2 | 80.1 | 71.0 | 81.1 | 92.6 | 81.8 |

*Source:* Bhalla *et al.* (1999: 19).

## Structure of exports

During the trade-reform era, the composition of exports also changed: although primary exports remained more prominent, their significance declined after 1990 (Table 11.6). However, despite these positive structural movements, absolute expansion in export earnings was not realized, owing mainly to a persistent weakening in macroeconomic fundamentals that accounted for high budget deficits and interest rates. This had a direct bearing on the cost of production, and hence curtailed industrial production. The trade-liberalization framework had no supporting export incentives apart from the exchange rate, whose adjustment always lagged behind in making exports competitive.

**Table 11.6: Composition of exports (percentage of total exports, US$), 1985, 1990–1996**

|  | 1985 | 1990 | 1991 | 1992 | 1993 | 1994 | 1995 | 1996 |
|---|---|---|---|---|---|---|---|---|
| Primary | 84.2 | 81.3 | 76.5 | 75.6 | 69.8 | 76.4 | 72.6 | 77.1 |
| Agricultural | 51.3 | 50.4 | 48.9 | 46.2 | 45.9 | 59.0 | 47.7 | 56.8 |
| Mineral | 32.9 | 30.9 | 27.6 | 29.4 | 24.0 | 17.4 | 25.0 | 20.2 |
| Non-primary | 15.8 | 18.7 | 23.5 | 24.4 | 30.2 | 23.6 | 27.4 | 22.9 |
| Agriculture-based | 3.1 | 3.6 | 5.6 | 4.9 | 5.4 | 4.9 | 5.6 | 4.7 |
| Food manufactures | 0.8 | 1.1 | 4.2 | 1.2 | 2.7 | 1.6 | 2.2 | 1.7 |
| Mineral-based | 1.7 | 2.2 | 2.2 | 1.9 | 2.4 | 1.6 | 2.4 | 1.7 |
| General | 10.2 | 11.8 | 11.5 | 16.3 | 19.8 | 15.5 | 17.1 | 14.8 |

*Source:* Chipika and Davies (2002).

The implementation of the trade reforms was totally divorced from complementary environmental policies and the management of fiscal policy, which had over the years accounted for an inflationary episode. The official development assistance to finance ESAP had the effect of raising the relative prices of non-tradable goods and thus of taxing exports (Collier and Gunning, 1992). Manufactured exports' performance was confined to agro-processing, which, according to Tekere (2001), emerged as a high-growth sub-sector, particularly in dairy products, meat products, grain foodstuffs, other foodstuffs and beverages (Table 11.7). This demonstrates the agriculture sector's capacity to expand into exports under more open trading conditions and in the absence of any major externalities.[20] Machinery, electrical machinery and transport equipment, all part of high-technology production, registered weak growth, demonstrating the limited export capacity in these products. Metal products, leather, hides, wood and furniture – the country's resource-based manufactured exports – responded positively to trade reforms. High-technology industries emerged as low-growth sub-sectors, particularly in iron and steel, ferro-alloys, textiles and clothing exports. During this reform period the manufacturing sector, which for years had enjoyed protection from foreign competition and thus always exhibited the attributes of an infant industry, was exposed to immense competition with trade liberalization.

## 11.4 The Crisis Period, 1997–2008

Zimbabwe's economic management during the period between 1997 and 2008 was dominated by stop-gap policies and the incoherent implementation of trade policy. When ESAP was phased out in 1995, the government was not eager to continue pursuing economic reforms following resistance from civil society, resulting in a two-year gap between the expiry of ESAP and the implementation of the Zimbabwe Programme for Economic and Social Transformation (ZIMPREST). The major characteristic of the ZIMPREST era was the attempt to deepen market reforms in the absence of a supporting multilateral framework from the IMF. 'ZIMPREST sought to further deepen trade liberalization measures adopted under ESAP. During the ESAP period, Zimbabwe fully implemented the trade policy liberalization component of the economic programme. Since 1998, however, there has been a divergence between official policy and practice' (SAPRIN, 2004: 45). However, the programme, which covered the period 1998–2000, was marred by poor economic performance and the weak implementation of trade policies, most policies being implemented half-heartedly.

The post-ESAP experience with respect to trade policy is well articulated in *The SAPRI Report*:

> Within ZIMPREST (1998–2000), and even the Millennium Economic Recovery Programme (MERP), the official position on trade has been further liberalization, yet in practice the government has taken several measures that indicated trade policy reversals. These included the tariff rationalization of 1998, Zimbabwe's mid-loading of tariffs within the SADC trade protocol, the removal of several

---

[20] The externalities referred to here are related to weather, land reform, etc., or uncontrollable factors that might compromise the smoothness of production.

**Table 11.7: Exports of manufactures, US$ millions, 1990–1995**

| | 1990 | 1991 | 1992 | 1993 | 1994 | 1995 | 1990–95 growth rate |
|---|---|---|---|---|---|---|---|
| | US$ millions | | | | | | (% p.a.) |
| Cotton lint | 87 | 63 | 27 | 24 | 60 | 51 | –10.2 |
| Refined sugar and honey | 12 | 6 | 5 | 1 | 8 | 14 | 4.3 |
| Ferro-alloys | 155 | 123 | 113 | 114 | 99 | 214 | 6.7 |
| Iron and steel | 56 | 51 | 51 | 61 | 24 | 16 | –21.8 |
| Meat products | 5 | 8 | 10 | 13 | 12 | 12 | 21 |
| Dairy products | 5 | 3 | 4 | 9 | 10 | 12 | 18.5 |
| Grain products | 7 | 7 | 8 | 29 | 26 | 40 | 40.2 |
| Other foodstuffs | 13 | 11 | 14 | 17 | 23 | 23 | 11 |
| Beverages | 0.2 | 2 | 2 | 13 | 3 | 3 | 86.2 |
| Tobacco (processed) | 6 | 6 | 6 | 9 | 17 | 11 | 12.4 |
| Textiles | 44 | 48 | 60 | 61 | 76 | 63 | 7.3 |
| Clothing | 38 | 41 | 51 | 50 | 67 | 65 | 11.2 |
| Footwear | 5 | 8 | 10 | 13 | 12 | 14 | 21.7 |
| Leather, hides, etc. | 13 | 14 | 18 | 14 | 19 | 27 | 16.5 |
| Wood products | 9 | 8 | 13 | 21 | 31 | 38 | 34.3 |
| Furniture and fixtures | 6 | 6 | 8 | 14 | 31 | 21 | 31.3 |
| Paper, printing and stationery | 7 | 6 | 8 | 25 | 26 | 18 | 19.0 |
| Rubber products | 3 | 3 | 4 | 5 | 3 | 5 | 8.7 |
| Chemicals and plastics | 26 | 28 | 39 | 41 | 60 | 51 | 14.8 |
| Petroleum and coal products | 9 | 5 | 4 | 7 | 12 | 22 | 18.2 |
| Non-metallic mineral products | 15 | 12 | 11 | 14 | 15 | 17 | 2.5 |
| Metal products | 24 | 25 | 23 | 39 | 39 | 53 | 17.1 |
| Machinery | 10 | 8 | 7 | 5 | 11 | 14 | 7.2 |
| Transport equipment | 28 | 10 | 17 | 15 | 26 | 23 | –3.2 |
| Electrical machinery | 16 | 10 | 14 | 11 | 13 | 27 | 6.5 |
| Art works | 6 | 5 | 7 | 9 | 12 | 15 | 20.3 |
| Jewellery | 0.4 | 0.6 | 1.7 | 13 | 16 | 28 | 130.1 |
| Other manufacturing | 18 | 14 | 13 | 3 | 6 | 7 | –18.1 |
| Total manufacturing | 623 | 533 | 546 | 634 | 751 | 898 | 7.6 |
| Pure manufactures[a] | 313 | 289 | 349 | 450 | 544 | 602 | 13.9 |

[a] Pure manufactures excludes the first four products.    *Source:* Tekere (2001: 12).

tariff exemptions, and the proposed reintroduction of price controls [SAPRIN, 2004: 45–6].

As a result of the inconsistent policy regime during the ZIMPREST era, manufacturing output and exports declined. Developments after this largely reflect a deepening crisis, with land reform triggering the inevitable collapse of the productive sector.

Government's decision to nationalize nearly all the country's commercial farms led to a sharp decline in export earnings as well as in food production.[21] Agriculture's share of exports fell substantially, as continued land redistribution contributed to large declines in production (Kramarenko *et al.*, 2010: 32). It is thus worth noting that the land reform brought a new dimension into Zimbabwe's political economy, and shaped the relationship between capital and labour thereafter. It is a stark reality that one of the major costs of the programme was the immediate erosion of both productive and trade capacity, with the slump in export capacity compounding exchange-rate instability and balance-of-payments pressures. As Munoz (2006: 3) observed,

> Before the start of the fast-track land reform in 2000, the official and the black market value of the Zimbabwe dollar were close (about Z$40:US$1). In 2000, when the land reform program started, the black market rate began to deviate from the official rate. As the years went by, the black market premium widened to 600% at the end of 2003. As a result a heavily managed auction system was in place during January 2004 – October 2005.

After ZIMPREST, economic policy blueprints were seized with short-term goals, effectively marginalizing trade policy.

The period 2003–2008 coincided with the tenure of a new Governor of the Reserve Bank of Zimbabwe, who took on a central role in economic policy, often using unorthodox methods. During this period, multiple exchange-rate regimes were employed, ranging from a fixed exchange rate, managed two-tier exchange rates, and a foreign-exchange auction, all of which faltered. In the event, exports declined at an annual average rate of 1.7 per cent during the whole period of crisis (1997–2008).

Kramarenko *et al.* (2010: 30) summed up the external trade record during the crisis period as follows: 'During its decade-long economic down-turn, Zimbabwe's external position deteriorated sharply, with the country unable to meet many of its external obligations and accumulating arrears.' They noted also (ibid.: 31) that

> The initial conditions in terms of competitiveness are unfavourable for exports and foreign and domestic investments, making it difficult to achieve a rapid increase in exports and FDI, including in mining. Indeed, Zimbabwe performs poorly in terms of competitiveness whether it is measured by governance (including rule of law, property rights, and corruption), investment climate (including enforcement of property rights and infrastructure), or price indicators.

Investment in key export sectors was adversely affected by the disruptive economic environment, inadequate infrastructure, high operational costs and the poor business climate.

---

[21] See Chapter 3.

## 11.5 The Transitional Period, 2009–2010

A key development in trade relations was the signing of interim Economic Partnership Agreements (EPAs) by some ACP countries in 2009, a time when civil-society organizations were lobbying governments not to do so in view of the potential dangers inherent in Free Trade Areas between developed and developing countries. EPA negotiations began in earnest in September 2002, when they were formally launched in Brussels by the ACP countries and the European Union. The intention was to finalize the negotiations by the WTO deadline of 31 December 2007 designed to bring trade relations into conformity with the institution's norms; a new trade arrangement had to be signed and become operational by 1 January 2008. However, none of the African negotiating groups was able to reach a final agreement by the deadline and instead most of the non-Least Developed Countries (LDCs) initialled interim EPAs with the EU to avoid trade disruption. Exports from non-LDC countries faced the threat of higher tariffs in the EU if no agreement was reached to replace the preferences established by the Lomé conventions. LDCs were covered by the EU's 'Everything But Arms' initiative that allows their exports to enter the EU duty-free and quota-free.

Zimbabwe was one of the few COMESA countries that signed an interim EPA agreement with the EU in August 2009.[22] The problem with EPAs is that they disregard the experiences with trade liberalization under structural adjustment programmes, insisting on a reciprocal liberalization of trade by ACP countries. Soon after signing, the Ministry of Trade and Industry in Zimbabwe issued a statement contradicting what it had just done:

> Is Zimbabwe prepared for a Free Trade Area with developed countries? The definitive answer is an emphatic no. In a Free Trade Area, countries trade on a duty free and quota free basis. EC countries will only pay VAT for 80% of the products by the year 2023. All duties and charges of equivalent effect will be gone. Why will Zimbabwean industries not be able to compete? A lot of things are not in place.[23]

This goes to illustrate the absence of a strategic approach to trade issues. In this regard, the African Union and its Regional Economic Communities highlighted the need for EPAs to help achieve sustainable development, eradicate poverty, reinforce regional integration, improve market access and the gradual integration of Africa into the global economy (African Union, 2010a and 2010b).[24] This conference observed that Africa is in fact more integrated into

---

[22] Zimbabwe chose to negotiate EPAs under COMESA, thereby weakening the SADC grouping, which remained with only seven countries.

[23] Extract from the report on the ESA–EC interim economic partnership agreement signing ceremony held on 29 August 2009 in Grand Baie, Mauritius. Zimbabwe, Ministry of Trade and Industry.

[24] These concerns were also raised and elaborated by trade unions and civil-society groups in Southern Africa (ANSA, 2006 and 2007).

the global economy, the share of trade in Sub-Saharan Africa's GDP being 34.5 per cent, compared to only 13.5 per cent for the USA and Japan and 14.3 per cent for Europe. Contrary to expectations, this greater integration has not been accompanied by any significant investment inflows into manufacturing to enhance competitiveness and enable the continent to join the international value chains. The statement concedes that, in the EPA negotiations and outcomes, 'the critical issues that will allow Africa to move forward on the path to industrialization and sustainable economic growth and development have still not yet been addressed' (AU, 2010a: 4).

The AU Commission and Regional Economic Communities identify the key areas of contention in the EPA negotiations with the EU to include the following:

1. *Development dimension*

   The outstanding issues include the mobilization of additional resources (especially for specific development assistance and support for EPA adjustment costs and implementation); financing mechanisms (the EU prefers use of its European Development Fund and general budget, while the African countries insist on using their own internal mechanisms); development benchmarks (the African countries want to link trade liberalization to the achievement of some development benchmarks, while the EU is against that, even though the Cotonou Partnership Agreement states that one of the objectives of EPAs is development); and development matrix (the African EPA regions have worked out a costed and prioritized development matrix to support the implementation of EPAs, while the EU is questioning this).

2. *Definition of 'substantially all trade' coverage and transitional period*

   The EU insists on a 'one size fits all' approach whereby all African countries (whether LDC or not), should liberalize at least 80 per cent of their value of trade within fifteen years for EPAs to be WTO-compatible. This implies that the sensitive products of African countries cannot cover more than 20 per cent of their trade with the EU. African countries are offering to liberalize 60 per cent of their trade over a period of twenty years and the EU has rejected such offers on the basis that they are not WTO-compatible. This has resulted in most African countries refusing to initial or sign EPAs on the basis that tariff-liberalization schedules and implementation periods vary widely among the various bilateral agreements notified at the WTO, and these have not been contested by any member, including the EU. Such agreements take cognizance of the difference in the levels of development between the parties (the principle of special and differential treatment). Even though the WTO provides rules for a transitional period of ten years, it recognizes the need for deviations in exceptional circumstances. Moreover, there is no specific threshold under WTO rules on what constitutes 'substantially all trade'. Furthermore, the AU has argued that all African non-LDCs are part of customs unions with LDCs. In this regard, there is need for longer transitional periods and flexibility on the scope of 'substantially all trade' to enable all African states to submit market-access offers that accommodate both LDCs and non-LDCs, and at the same time enable all LDCs to participate in regional EPAs that support regional integration processes instead of promoting regional fragmentation as the EPA negotiating configurations have already done.

3. *Most-favoured nation clause*

The EU would like to include the 'most-favoured nation' (MFN) clause, arguing that, since it provides all ACP countries with duty-free, quota-free market access, its exclusion would discriminate against it in relation to other developed and large developing countries. The AU insists that this clause should be excluded as it violates GATT/WTO rules that recognize South–South co-operation among developing countries. In this respect, if Africa were to sign a preferential agreement with China, India or Brazil, it would have to extend it to the EU as well. Brazil intimated that it will challenge an agreement that includes the MFN clause. The AU fears that an MFN provision will also undermine its ability to diversify export markets. It has also raised the issue that a number of EU Free Trade Agreements have no MFN clause (e.g. the EU–Mexico FTA in which Mexico is required to liberalize 54.1 per cent).

4. *Non-execution clause*

The non-execution clause would allow the EU to unilaterally suspend co-operation in the event of democratic troubles in the beneficiary country; hence African countries reject its inclusion on the basis that EPAs should be purely about trade and that the issue was adequately dealt with in the Cotonou Partnership Agreement.

5. *Treatment of community levy*

The EU would like to have community levies, where they exist, phased out of EPAs. The AU argues that a community levy is an important mechanism in financing regional integration and is therefore non-negotiable unless the EU provides guaranteed alternative sources of finance that will last for the duration of the EPAs.

6. *Export taxes*

The EU insists on prohibiting export taxes in EPAs, a requirement the AU sees as a WTO-plus condition.[25] The AU is opposed to the removal of export taxes on the grounds that African countries cannot continue exporting raw

---

[25] WTO-plus refers to issues that were rejected in the WTO negotiations (the 'Singapore issues') such as investment policy, competition policy, government procurement, and trade facilitation.

materials and hence, since they are at a nascent stage of their development, reserve the right to use export taxes to protect infant industries, enhance value addition, economic diversification, food security, revenue generation and environmental protection. The EU's position is informed by its desire to access raw materials (AU, 2010a: 11).

7. *Quantitative restrictions*

Similarly, the interim EPA foresees, at best, very limited scope for quantitative restrictions (quotas, import/export prohibition). The AU's position is that, as with export taxes, the policy space afforded by such a tool is useful for promoting infant industries, value addition, diversification, and food security and environmental concerns.

8. *Standstill clause (modification of tariffs)*

The EU is reluctant to allow future tariff modifications and, if they are allowed, they should not undermine WTO compatibility. The AU recalls that WTO/GATT Article XXVIII allows members to modify their schedule of concessions, subject to renegotiation and compensation to any interested party. African governments would like to modify tariff commitments when the need arises in line with the evolution of their regional integration programmes.

9. *Special agricultural safeguards*

The EU has reservations on both the principle and mechanism proposed by the African countries. However, the AU insists on the need to take provisional measures to limit or redress the harm that agricultural imports from the EU can cause in their markets. The African states are in favour of the elimination of agricultural export subsidies provided by the EU on entry of EPAs into force, in line with promises made by the EU at the WTO Hong Kong Ministerial to remove these by 2013. As such, the African countries would want to be able to raise duties to the level they consider appropriate for those products for which the EU provides subsidies, even if those products are not part of the sensitive list.

10. *Rendezvous clause*

African countries are reluctant to include the 'Singapore issues', except trade facilitation, as there is no WTO obligation to cover more than trade in goods. The EU introduced these issues and is insisting on binding legal commitments.

11. *Rules of origin*

Two issues remain contentious on the rules of origin: asymmetry in rules applying to imports from the EU into African countries and vice versa, and cumulation. Taking into account the difference in the levels of development, the African states have proposed the principle of asymmetry in the rules of origin such that there are two sets of rules – one for goods coming from EU countries and the other for goods from African countries.

The AU has also identified risks associated with EPAs as currently conceived. It is argued that the elimination of tariffs for 80 per cent of trade, as advocated by the EU, restrictions on the use of export taxes and quantitative restrictions, and the standstill clause, among others, will undermine Africa's industrialization prospects and its ability to move up the industrial value chain. This would imply that Africa will remain a supplier of raw materials in the international division of labour. The AU observes that no country, except for Hong Kong, has industrialized without protecting its infant industry. The unfair competition arising from the EU's agricultural subsidies will have adverse implications for food security and rural livelihoods in Africa. Unfortunately, these subsidies and domestic support are not being removed at the WTO or in EPA negotiations.

The possible flooding of African regional markets by EU products following the liberalization of 80 per cent of trade is considered a real risk for African countries, a development which will undermine their ability to increase intra-African trade, diversify and industrialize. Furthermore, it is also contended that EPAs are breaking down existing African customs unions, with the EU demanding the rapid implementation of bilateral interim EPAs where states have initialled or signed, even as sub-regions are still negotiating. In the wisdom of the AU (2010a: 15), 'EPAs have potentially created tension and could seriously rupture existing regional integration programmes'. In addition, it is feared that, since most tariffs will eventually be reduced to zero under EPAs, most African governments will lose revenue, especially given that tariff revenues constitute a significant source of government revenue in these countries. This, it is reasoned, will worsen an already difficult financial situation on the African continent, where many governments are already heavily indebted.

Another source of risk relates to the likely impact of including services, investment, competition, and government procurement in EPAs, which will undermine local enterprises and industries since foreign companies from the EU will have to be treated as local firms should the Singapore issues be included. The inclusion of WTO-plus intellectual-property rules, as the EU advocates, would make it difficult for African countries to access the knowledge and technology necessary for industrialization and enhanced agricultural production. It would also make it hard for African countries to import affordable generic medicines or to manufacture them locally.

The above contentious issues have led the AU (2010a: 17) to conclude that the 'divergencies between the EU and Africa seem to be intractable, and not resolvable, despite ten years of negotiations'. The AU is nudging the EU to consider alternatives to EPAs, as stipulated in Article 37.6 of the Cotonou Agreement. According to the AU, in the event of the failure to conclude a development-oriented EPA, or the expansion of Everything But Arms coverage to all of Africa and Generalized System of Preferences regulation, African countries should discontinue EPA negotiations and focus on deepening African regional integration and the development of South–South co-operation.[26]

At the regional level, Zimbabwe is a member of the SADC Free Trade Area and the COMESA Customs Union. The SADC FTA was officially launched on 17 August 2008 and allows for duty-free trade in goods within the SADC region. The COMESA Customs Union was launched on 7 June 2009 in Victoria Falls. A customs union is a trade agreement that involves the free movement of goods between member states and the application of a common external tariff on imports from non-member states. A customs union invariably entails the adoption and application of a uniform trade policy, hence, it builds on a Free Trade Area by, in addition to removing internal barriers to trade, requiring participating nations to harmonize their external trade policy.

A major challenge that has hampered the smooth movement of goods within both SADC and COMESA has been the proliferation of non-tariff barriers that hamper trade amongst member states. Non-tariff barriers are trade barriers that restrict imports but are not in the usual form of a tariff. These include import licensing, rules and regulations for the valuation of goods at customs, pre-shipment inspection, and complex rules of origin, among others. The proliferation of these non-tariff barriers has the effect of slowing down regional integration.

The SADC FTA and COMESA Customs Union should not be viewed as ends, but rather as a means to an end. The end here is development, and therefore regional integration should be viewed as a vehicle to achieve development and eradicate poverty. More importantly, regional integration efforts should be underpinned by measures to address the inherent structural rigidities and distortions in the regional economies, and infrastructure deficits, and adopt institutional reforms that enhance confidence in the regional economies.

However, in light of the current global trend towards regionalism (the proliferation of regional trading blocs) rather than multilateralism, the formation of the SADC FTA and COMESA Customs Union may not have been a matter of choice but of necessity. However, an issue that needs addressing is overlapping membership, which has undermined regional integration. Zimbabwe belongs to both SADC and COMESA, but has chosen to negotiate EPAs under the Eastern and Southern Africa grouping. Since WTO provisions do not allow a country to belong to more than one customs union, Zimbabwe will have to make a choice. However, this may be superseded by a political decision to create one customs union for SADC, COMESA and the East African Community countries.

---

[26] The AU (2010b) expresses concern at 'the current loss of dynamism in the EPA negotiations that has been due to the lack of progress in resolving the differences between the parties on a number of contentious issues.'

Given the intrinsic* link between trade and production, Zimbabwe must enhance its productive capacity. While the Inclusive Government has improved confidence and resulted in capacity utilization levels rising to 40–50 per cent, this has flattened out in 2010 as a result of the Global Political Agreement not being implemented in full. As Kramarenko *et al.* (2010: 30) put it, 'After many years of falling output and hyperinflation, Zimbabwe has been experiencing a fragile recovery since 2009.' The country is still to benefit fully from the policies implemented under STERP.

## 11.6 Conclusion and the Way Forward

### 11.6.1 Conclusion
It has been argued that conventional trade theory begins with an economy which is competitive and small, such that individual consumers and firms do not influence domestic prices and the economy cannot affect world prices. In this context, free trade maximizes real national income by removing the constraint that domestic production must match consumption patterns. With specialization in production for which there is comparative advantage, the value of aggregate output at world prices is enhanced, while consumers benefit by buying from the cheapest supplier worldwide. Thus, trade theorists emphasize efficiency gains and opting to use programmes of adjustment assistance to help those adversely affected.

However, it has also been shown that, even when the case for free trade is clear, the best way to achieve it may not be politically feasible. Two rules for piecemeal trade liberalization are available: the uniform reduction rule, whereby all tariffs are reduced by an equi-proportionate amount, leaving relative tariff rates unchanged; and the concertina rule, where the focus is on reducing the highest tariff rate. In this regard, it can be concluded that trade policy is rarely a first–best instrument.[27] A different scenario emerges in the case of oligopolies, with barriers to entry and a relatively small number of firms. In such a situation, firms see themselves as interdependent, and hence behave 'strategically' by taking into account the expected reactions of rivals. Within such a scenario, there may be scope for government intervention favouring home firms – an idea referred to as the theory of strategic trade policy.

Recent literature attempts to provide endogenous explanations for economic growth, stressing the importance of resources targeting research and development (R&D) in promoting technological innovations and the introduction of new and higher-quality products. In such a situation, externalities become important since the benefits of R&D cannot be fully appropriated, which has implications

---

[27] See Krugman (1987) and Neary (2001), among others.

for trade policy. For instance, where a sector is disproportionately engaged in R&D, protection for that sector will raise long-run growth, arguments associated with an older infant-industry argument justifying transitional protection to allow new firms to benefit from 'learning by doing' and scale economies. However, such arguments justify production or R&D subsidies and are therefore a case for strategic industrial, rather than trade, policy (Neary, 2001).

The most visible result of the trade regime over the last thirty years is that trade liberalization does not always lead to sustained export growth, economic growth, and hence an increase in societal welfare. The net benefits are a function of initial conditions, and the capacity of the country to work round binding constraints to contain the costs of adjustment and devaluation may not necessarily translate into expansion in exports, as other dynamics – such as elasticity of demand in target markets, non-tariff barriers in the same markets, as well as supply elasticity parameters in exporting countries – may have a bearing on trade outcomes. The Zimbabwean situation also brings out the fact that structural reforms are an important prerequisite for export promotion, especially to achieve pro-poor, equitable growth and development.

The developments over the last thirty years have entrenched the inherited dualistic structure of production in Zimbabwe. Furthermore, growth does not always translate into poverty reduction, unless the growth model is inclusive and prioritizes expanding opportunities for the poor to participate meaningfully in development. What also emerges is that, for trade reforms to be effective, a more inclusive and holistic alternative to neo-liberal economics is required. This model recognizes from the outset that the state has a more strategic role to play in discharging a development mandate.

### 11.6.2 Recommendations on the way forward

Zimbabwe needs to maximize its trade potential by addressing binding constraints, with the state taking a lead in discharging a development-state mandate, and to reassert itself in the regional markets (SADC, COMESA, AU) in order to garner sufficient muscle to penetrate the global economy. In view of the dual and enclave nature of the Zimbabwean economy, it would be imperative for the country to adopt a proactive and strategic trade policy aimed at stimulating both the formal and non-formal sector that should focus not only on export-oriented trade (regional and global) but also on reforming the domestic industrial structure.

Furthermore, it will be important to deepen regional trade-integration initiatives. In this regard, the country should actively engage its regional partners and support both regional and international forces seeking to make a strong regional trading bloc a reality (ZCTU, 1996). A strategic trade policy should extend protection to strategic and labour-intensive sectors, at the same time promoting export diversification and value addition (beneficiation). Adequate funding and subsidies should be made available for research and development activities.

To lower trade costs, Zimbabwe should invest in upgrading infrastructure,[28] and in addition it will be important to plan infrastructure investment as part of regional initiatives. As UNCTAD (2010: 7) has observed:

> The development of transport corridors provides an example where public and private investment and joint efforts are focused on improving commonly identified trade facilitation and transportation bottlenecks across national borders. Developing cross-border infrastructure would strengthen regional integration initiatives. Building transnational structures such as roads, railways, waterways, air transport links, telecoms and energy supply lines (development corridors) has an even stronger impact on the development of productive capacities of neighbouring countries if it is accompanied by local development projects in different sectors (e.g. agriculture and industry).

To underpin the alternative trade policy advocated, there is need for a supportive institutional framework that is geared towards restoring the country's competitiveness. In conjunction with key stakeholders, there is need to identify activities and those sectors with strong export value chains. The institutional framework governing trade policy should therefore be realigned to ensure owner-ship of the process by all stakeholders, and thus a broad-based and integrated trade agenda is a sound basis for policy credibility in the medium to long term. Given the strong linkages between trade, industry, and science and technology, the policies recommended in these areas facilitate trade promotion. Studies have suggested that the role of trade policy in economic growth is largely auxiliary. Better results arise from focusing on dealing with the binding constraints on economic growth, such as investment in human resources and infrastructure and enhancing the credibility of institutions for macroeconomic management (Rodrik, 1997).

The *Africa Competitiveness Report* of the World Economic Forum (2009) indicates that African businesses can become far more competitive – but African governments need to improve access to finance, resist pressure to erect trade barriers, upgrade infrastructure, improve healthcare and educational systems, and strengthen institutions. Limited access to financial services is identified as a major obstacle for African enterprises. In addition, underdeveloped infrastructure, limited healthcare and educational services, and poor institutional frameworks also make African countries less competitive globally.

---

[28] See Chapter 2.

# References

African Union 2010a. 'African Union Commission/Regional Economic Communities Common Position Paper on EPAs', AU Conference of Ministers of Trade, 6th Ordinary Session, 29 October – 2 November, Kigali, Rwanda.

African Union 2010b. 'Kigali Declaration on the Economic Partnership Agreement Negotiations', AU Conference of Ministers of Trade, 6th Ordinary Session, 29 October – 2 November, Kigali, Rwanda.

ANSA 2006. 'EPAs Declaration', Southern African Trade Union Coordination Council (SATUCC) Regional Workshop on EPAs, Big Five Hotel, Gaborone, Botswana, 16–17 February.

ANSA 2007. 'EPAs Communiqué', Civil Society, Global Unions, Regional Trade-related NGOs, Business Community, Farmer and Church Organizations Regional Workshop on EPAs, Randburg Towers Hotel, Johannesburg, South Africa, 26–27 July.

Bhalla, A. *et al.* 1999. 'Globalisation and Sustainable Human Development: Progress and Challenges for Zimbabwe', UNCTAD/UNDP Occasional Paper, Presented at a National Workshop, 13–19 December.

Chipika, J. and R. Davies 2002. 'Economic reforms and non-traditional exports in Zimbabwe: Is anything taking shape?', in G. K. Helleiner (ed.) *Non-traditional Export Promotion in Africa* (Basingstoke: Palgrave Macmillan).

Collier, P. and J. W. Gunning 1992. 'Aid and exchange rate adjustment in African trade liberalisation', *Economic Journal*, 102, 925–39.

Green, R. H. and X. Kadhani 1996. 'Zimbabwe transition to economic crisis, 1981–1983: Retrospect and prospect', *World Development*, 14(8).

Hausmann, R., L. Pritchett and D. Rodrik 2004. 'Growth accelerations', *Journal of Economic Growth*, 10(4), 303–29.

Helleiner, G. 1990. *The New Global Economy and the Developing Countries: Essays in International Economics and Development* (Aldershot: Elgar).

Helleiner, G. K. 1995. *Trade, Trade Policy and Industrialisation Reconsidered* (New York: UN University, World Institute for Development Economics Research, World Development Studies 6).

IMF 1997. *World Economic Outlook* (Washington, DC: International Monetary Fund).

Kapoor, K. 1995. 'Overview of the Seminar', in Kapil Kapoor (ed.), *Africa's Experience with Structural Adjustment: Proceedings of the Harare Seminar, May 23–24, 1994* (Washington, DC: World Bank, World Bank Discussion Papers, 288).

Keet, D. 1999. *Globalisation and Regionalisation: Contradictory Tendencies, or Strategic Possibilities?* (Braamfontein: Foundation for Global Dialogue, Occasional Paper No. 18).

Kramarenko, V. L. *et al.* 2010. *Zimbabwe: Challenges and Policy Options after*

*Hyperinflation* (Washington, DC: International Monetary Fund).

Krueger, A. O. 1998. 'Why trade liberalization is good for growth', *Economic Journal*, 108 (September), 1513–22.

Krugman, P. R. 1987. 'Is free trade passé?', *Journal of Economic Perspectives*, 1(2).

Michalopoulos, C. 1987. 'World Bank Programmes for Adjustment and Growth', in V. Corbo *et al.* (eds.), *Growth-oriented Adjustment Programmes* (Washington, DC: World Bank and IMF).

Mumvuma, T., C. Mujajati and B. Mufute 2006. 'Understanding reform: The case of Zimbabwe', in J. Mensah (ed.), *Understanding Economic Reforms in Africa: A Tale of Seven Nations* (Basingstoke: Palgrave Macmillan).

Munoz, S. 2006. 'Zimbabwe's Export Performance: The Impact of the Parallel Market and Governance Factors' (Washington, DC: International Monetary Fund, Working Paper Number WP/06/28).

Neary, J. P. 2001. 'International Trade: Commercial Policy' (Dublin: University College Dublin and Centre for Economic Research, WP01/23), <http://www.ucd.ie/economics/research/papers/2001/WP01.23.pdf>.

OECD 1999. 'Open Markets Matter: The Benefits of Trade and Investment Liberalization', *OECD Observer* (October), <http://www.oecd.org/dataoecd/18/51/1948792.pdf>.

Rattso, J. and R. Torvik 1998. 'Zimbabwe trade liberalization: Ex post evaluation', *Cambridge Journal of Economics*, 22, 325–46.

Rodriguez, F. and D. Rodrik 2000. *Trade Policy and Economic Growth: A Skeptic's Guide to Cross-National Evidence* (Cambridge, MA: National Bureau of Economic Research, NBER Working Papers 7081).

Rodrik, D. 1990. 'How should structural adjustment programmes be designed?', *World Development*, 18(7).

Rodrik, D. 1997. 'Trade Policy and Economic Performance in Sub-Saharan Africa', paper prepared for the Swedish Ministry for Foreign Affairs, November.

Rodrik, D. 2006. 'Goodbye Washington consensus, hello Washington confusion? A review of the World Bank's *Economic Growth in the 1990s: Learning from a Decade of Reform*', *Journal of Economic Literature*, XLIV (December), 973–87.

Rushinga, A. 1987. 'New loans may ease forex shortages', *African Business* (May).

SAPRIN 2004. *Structural Adjustment: The SAPRI Report: The Policy Roots of Economic Crisis, Poverty and Inequality* (London: Zed).

Stiglitz, J. E. 1998. 'Towards a New Paradigm for Development: Strategies, Policies and Processes', Prebisch Lecture at UNCTAD, Geneva, 19 October 1998.

Taylor, L. 1988. 'Economic Openness: Problems to the Century's End' (New York: UN University, World Institute for Development Economics Research, Working Papers No. 41).

Tekere, M. 2001. 'Trade Liberalisation under Structural Economic Adjustment: Impact on Social Welfare in Zimbabwe', paper for the Poverty Reduction Forum, SAPRNI Initiative.

UNCTAD 2010. 'Developing Productive Capacities in Least Developed Countries: Issues for Discussion', pre-conference event to UNLDC-IV: Building Productive Capacities in LDCs for Inclusive and Sustainable Development, 15 October 2010.

World Bank 1990. *Making Adjustment Work for the Poor: A Framework for Policy Reform in Africa* (Washington, DC: World Bank).

World Bank 1995. 'Zimbabwe: Achieving Shared Growth' (Washington, DC: World Bank, Country Economic Memorandum Volume 1).

World Bank 2005. *Economic Growth in the 1990s: Learning from a Decade of Reform* (Washington, DC: World Bank).

World Bank 2008. *The Growth Report: Strategies for Sustained Growth and Inclusive Development* (Washington, DC: World Bank, Commission on Growth and Development).

World Economic Forum 2009. *The Africa Competitiveness Report, 2009* (Geneva: World Economic Forum).

WTO and ILO 2007. *Trade and Employment: Challenges for Policy Research* (Geneva: ILO), <http://www.ilo.org/global/publications/books/WCMS_081742/lang–en/index.htm>.

ZCTU 1996. *Beyond ESAP: Framework for a Long-Term Development Strategy for Zimbabwe* (Harare: Zimbabwe Congress of Trade Unions).

Zimbabwe 1991. *Zimbabwe: A Framework for Economic Reform (1991–1995)* (Harare: Government Printer).

Zimbabwe 1998. *Zimbabwe Programme for Social and Economic Transformation (ZIMPREST): 1996–2000* (Harare: Government Printer).

*Chapter 12*

# Finance for Inclusive Growth

## 12.1 Introduction

A lot of empirical and theoretical literature on the finance–growth nexus shows that a well-developed financial sector plays a causal and central role in promoting socio-economic development. As long ago as 1873, Walter Bagehot argued that the financial system played a critical role in igniting industrialization in England by facilitating the mobilization of capital for growth. Schumpeter (1934) noted that banks actively spur innovation and future growth by identifying and funding productive investments. Economies require advanced and sophisticated financial markets that can mobilize and make available for investment financial resources from such diverse sources as the banking sector, the stock market, venture capital and pension funds. An efficient financial sector facilitates the trading, diversification and management of risk. A large body of empirical and theoretical evidence also shows that financial development reduces income inequality and absolute poverty.

A country's development is therefore dependent on the level of sophistication of its financial sector (McKinnon, 1973; Shaw, 1973; World Bank, 1989) and the level of inclusiveness of the financial sector. The recent financial crisis has highlighted the potentially disastrous consequences of weak financial sector policies and the need for transparency and robust regulation of the financial sector to protect investors and depositors. In developing countries, where access to financial services is limited, it is important to broaden access to the underserved, especially those in the non-formal economic sectors (communal areas and the informal economy). Governments do have a strategic role to play in promoting well-functioning and inclusive financial systems.

By the 1970s, Zimbabwe's financial sector had become one of the most developed in Sub-Saharan Africa outside South Africa (Harvey, 1998). It comprised four commercial banks, two discount houses, three merchant banks, three building societies, three finance companies, the Post Office Savings Bank (POSB), the Zimbabwe Stock Exchange (ZSE), a large number of pension and provident funds, three development finance institutions, including the Agricultural Finance Corporation established in 1924 to fund agricultural projects, and two stockbroking firms (ZCTU, 1996).

This chapter analyses the evolution of the financial sector in Zimbabwe from 1980. It looks at the government policy framework that shaped the financial sector and assesses whether it facilitated the widespread availability of financial products and services to the majority of the community. The main objective is to ascertain the extent to which the financial sector development process contributed to the attainment of pro-poor and inclusive growth. The analysis will be undertaken in four periods; the first decade of independence, 1980–1990, the ESAP period, 1991–1996, the crisis period, 1997–2008, and the transitional period, from February 2009. The chapter concludes with a discussion of possible strategies that can be employed in order to achieve financial inclusiveness that can foster inclusive growth through the financial deepening of the sector.[1]

## 12.2 The First Decade of Independence, 1980–1990

At independence, the new government did not make any fundamental changes to the financial sector (Harvey, 1998), whose institutions remained highly segmented by function (ZCTU, 1996). Throughout the 1980s, the financial sector remained tightly controlled and oligopolistic. Market entry was restricted, while competition among institutions within the sector was non-existent. Pricing of the products and services on offer bore little or no resemblance to the cost of supplying them.

The financial system remained exclusive of the majority of the country's population, as financial services were available only to the urbanites that constituted less than thirty per cent of the population. Lack of access to finance is a critical factor in generating persistent income inequality as well as slower economic growth. Small and medium-sized enterprises (SMEs) could not seize the opportunities that appeared through the reconstruction programme owing to their failure to access credit to fund their inputs and working-capital requirements. Households, the majority of whom were indigenous Zimbabweans who lived in the rural areas, did not have access to finance because of their long distance from the formal financial system, their lack of knowledge about the availability of financial services, low level of literacy, and the unwillingness of banking institutions to provide services to the low-income group of the population.

Furthermore, money and bond markets were generally underdeveloped, and sophisticated banking products were therefore naturally absent, so consumers had a limited range of banking products from which to choose. In fact, banks supplied services on a 'take it or leave it' basis. The number of financial institutions in the banking sector remained relatively small in view of the strict entry requirements. Both local and foreign investment in the financial sector were

---

[1] Financial deepening is the increased provision of financial services through a wider choice of financial intermediaries that are geared to the development of all levels of society. It is the transmission mechanism through which the financial sector facilitates access to financial services to all sections of the community. Nzotta and Okereke (2009) contend that the contribution to the economy of a financial system depends on the quality and quantity of its services and the efficiency with which it performs them.

restricted, and the marketing of services was rare as banks sold similar products across the board. In view of the controls on the operation of the financial sector, it was rare for financial institutions to venture into 'risk management', often requiring 100 per cent collateral security from borrowers. There was a lack of active asset and liability management, and incentives to increase efficiency were non-existent.

This invariably meant that banks avoided lending to SMEs and other 'risky' projects, as most did not have acceptable security to offer to the lending institutions. Those with small savings in rural areas could only deposit them with the widely spread branch network of the POSB. Banks often referred to the high transaction costs as a major impediment to lending to small but numerous borrowers. As a result, bank lending focused on the needs of 'big business' at the expense of small, but sometimes financially more viable, projects. In fact, it was primarily because of their failure to expand lending to small firms and low-income groups that the government set up the Small Enterprises Development Corporation (SEDCO). In addition, the government and the commercial banks set up the Credit Guarantee Company to boost lending to marginalized groups to fund small-scale projects. It was for this reason that, in 1987, the Reserve Bank of Zimbabwe (RBZ) decreed that five per cent of banks' assets comprise loans to the black indigenous sector, which, to all intents and purposes, implied the SMEs and the poor (Muzulu, 1995).

Although the determination of interest rates was left to each individual institution, in a typical case of financial repression, the RBZ determined the minimum lending and deposit rates. As a result, banks often took deposits at rates very close to the minimum, but lent at rates well above the minimum lending rate. Consequently, margins were high and most financial institutions were making huge profits, even after adjusting for administrative and other costs.

Furthermore, although sanctions were removed at independence in 1980 and financial pledges of US$2.2 billion were made at the Zimbabwe Conference on Reconstruction and Development (ZIMCORD) in March 1981, not much attention was paid to the terms of the offers. Consequently, part of this total amount turned out to be commercial loans (Green and Kadhani, 1986), while much of the other part remained undisbursed five years after the conference (Robinson, 1987; Stoneman, 1989).[2] Export performance was poor, thanks to an over-valued Zimbabwe dollar and domestic firms' lack of marketing skills in international markets owing to the long period of international isolation. Moreover, the relatively low quality of Zimbabwe's manufactured goods, arising from under-investment because of foreign-exchange shortages, rendered them internationally uncompetitive (Muzulu, 1994).

---

[2] The IMF described Zimbabwe as being under-borrowed at independence.

The resultant foreign-exchange constraint forced the government to adopt the previous government's foreign-exchange allocation system *in toto*. Thus, the financial sector continued to be heavily involved in applications for import licences on behalf of their clients from the Ministry of Industry and Commerce and the RBZ. By 1987, however, low foreign-currency inflows and high demand rendered the system terribly unworkable (Muzulu, 1993).

In view of the high import intensity of investment in Zimbabwe, only those companies accessing foreign exchange could borrow from the domestic money market for investment purposes. In fact, access to foreign exchange determined who got credit from the formal financial institutions (Harvey, 1998) and this perpetuated the dualism in access to financial resources. By 1989, there was a growing consensus on the need to implement reforms, although there was no agreement on the content and sequencing of them. In 1991, therefore, government adopted reforms under the omnibus title of an Economic Structural Adjustment Programme (ESAP).

## 12.3 The ESAP Period, 1991–1996

In January 1991, the government launched ESAP, whose main objective was to improve the living conditions of the poorest groups in the nation by generating sustained higher economic growth as a result of increased competition and productivity (Zimbabwe, 1991: 3). An integral part of these reforms was the mobilization of savings by liberalizing the interest-rate regime and transforming it into a market-based framework. This followed government's recognition that excessive regulations and controls had interfered with competition and made banks less efficient, more fragile, and reduced industry's access to finance. The understanding then was that administered interest rates had led to negative real interest rates for the greater part of the first decade of independence and that it was necessary to create conditions that would allow interest rates to follow inflation trends in order to allow savers to receive positive real interest margins. This was in line with the theoretical underpinnings of financial sector reforms, which emphasized the link between interest rates and savings, as postulated by McKinnon (1973) and Shaw (1973).

According to the model, interest-rate liberalization is expected to increase financial savings and improve both the quantity and quality of investment. The theory predicts that positive real interest rates will generate enough domestic and foreign savings to finance development. A number of channels were identified through which this would occur. Firstly, theory predicts that interest-rate liberalization would, other things being constant, generate incentives for savers to increase their savings with formal financial institutions, thereby increasing the pool of internally generated loanable funds. Secondly, theory also predicts an increase in foreign-capital inflows with a rise in domestic interest rates. According to theory, domestic savings, deposit rates and expected changes in the exchange rate would influence portfolio allocation between foreign and domestic assets. An increase in domestic interest rates relative to foreign rates is, therefore, expected to encourage capital inflows which, in turn, will augment domestic savings, resulting in a large pool of loanable funds. In this instance, investment was expected to increase since, in developing countries, investment is constrained by the availability rather than the cost of funds (ZCTU, 1996).

Theory also predicts that, even if investment does not increase, it is expected that positive real interest rates would raise the average efficiency of investment. Thus, investment improves through a quality rather than a quantity effect. Furthermore, interest-rate liberalization is expected to influence production techniques away from capital-intensive ones to labour-intensive ones, as real positive rates raise the price of capital relative to the more abundant factor, labour. To the extent that labour is the more abundant resource in developing countries, the choice of more labour-intensive techniques would therefore be beneficial (Muzulu, 1994).

Regulations pertaining to the entry of new financial institutions were relaxed following the implementation of reforms. With this liberalization, it was expected that the range and quality of financial products and services adaptable to changing consumer needs would improve (dynamic efficiency) as a direct result of competition. Following the adoption of ESAP, the government committed itself to maintaining export competitiveness through an exchange-rate policy that allowed the Zimbabwe dollar to depreciate over time by the inflation differential between Zimbabwe and its major trading countries. In addition, the exchange-rate adjustment was designed to prevent leakages of domestic savings in the form of capital flight. As Chandavarkar (1990: 30) put it, 'the most operative causes of capital flight are the conjunctual ones such as persistent overvaluation of the real exchange rate'.

In addition, Zimbabwean residents and companies were allowed to open foreign-currency denominated accounts with authorized dealers within Zimbabwe. Foreigners were allowed to purchase shares on the Zimbabwe Stock Exchange subject to a 25 per cent limit on a counter, while a single foreign investor was limited to 5 per cent. Remittance of dividends was progressively raised to as high as 100 per cent of net after-tax profits for all investors as from January 1995. Restriction on access to domestic borrowing by foreigners was abolished. In fact, Zimbabwe agreed to commit itself to Article 8 (full current-account convertibility) of the IMF in February 1995.

An extensive review of Zimbabwe's financial performance under ESAP appears in Finhold (1995) and ZCTU (1996). Financial liberalization not only deregulated interest rates but also facilitated the onset of the first stage of financial deepening – the emergence of new financial intermediaries and banks.

A number of banking institutions, most of them owned by indigenous Zimbabweans, had entered the market by the end of the 1990s (Table 12.1). The number of banking institutions increased more than threefold – from ten before ESAP in 1991 to thirty by the end of 1999, constituting fourteen commercial banks, four merchant banks, three finance houses, six discount houses and five building societies. The banking sector was one of the sectors where economic empowerment of the indigenous people was achieved smoothly without any adverse impact on either investment flow into the country or output.

The influx of new entrants into the financial sector resulted in intense competition for customers between the new indigenous Zimbabwean banks and the old, 'orthodox' banks, mainly foreign-owned. However, the community did not benefit much from this competition, as the pricing of banking products did not improve. Average lending rates increased from 12 per cent in 1990 to 34.7 per cent in 1997, while interest on three-month deposits rose from 10.3 per cent to 32.5 per cent over the same period (Makina, 2009). In addition, when measured in terms of depth of products and services offered, the new banking institutions did not offer any innovative services, choosing to fight for space in the market for generic banking products, mainly deposit mobilization and lending to well-established companies and individuals with high net worth. A lack of risk-management skills and weak corporate-governance structures limited the capacity of the new institutions to develop new products. As a result the banking sector continued to serve prime clients, leaving SMEs and other marginalized sections of the community without access to financial services.

The problem worsened with the increases in inflation and nominal interest rates to which the expansionary fiscal and monetary policies gave rise. High nominal lending rates accompanied by high rates of inflation increase the risk of borrowing because the higher the rate of inflation, the greater its variability, which sharply increases the cost of borrowing at high nominal interest rates (Harvey and Jenkins, 1992). As Makina (2009) notes, it is hardly surprising that both existing and new banks did not expand lending to the small-scale sector and low-income groups. Indeed, evidence elsewhere shows that financial liberalization is more successful in countries that maintain moderate inflation (Cho and Khatkhate, 1989). As the ZCTU (1996) argued, the little improvement in lending to the indigenous sector (mainly SMEs) during ESAP came largely through political pressure for the indigenization of the economy rather than from liberalization per se.

With respect to the responsiveness of savings deposits to interest-rate liberalization, evidence shows a positive but weak relationship (Muzulu, 1995). Studies show that other important non-price factors influence savings, such as the appropriateness of financial instruments compared to available alternatives, cultural values, proximity of bank branches, and so on, which may be more

**Table 12.1: Banking sector architecture by the end of 1999[a]**

| | Banking institution | Date licensed |
|---|---|---|
| **Commercial banks** | | |
| 1 | Agribank | 4 June 1999 |
| 2 | Barclays Bank | 1 May 1965 |
| 3 | Commercial Bank of Zimbabwe (Jewel Bank) | 11 November 1991 |
| 4 | First Banking Corporation | 7 February 1997 |
| 5 | Kingdom Bank | 22 December 1997 |
| 6 | Metropolitan Bank | 14 April 1998 |
| 7 | NMB Bank | 8 June 1993 |
| 8 | Stanbic Bank | 14 April 1993 |
| 9 | Standard Chartered Bank | 1 October 1983 |
| 10 | Time Bank | 13 February 1997 |
| 11 | Trust Bank | 2 January 1996 |
| 12 | Zimbabwe Banking Corporation (Zimbank) | 16 July 1979 |
| **Merchant banks** | | |
| 1 | ABC Zimbabwe (formerly First Merchant Bank) | 1 May 1965 |
| 2 | Genesis Merchant Bank | 20 July 1995 |
| 3 | Interfin Merchant Bank | September 1999 |
| 4 | Merchant Bank of Central Africa (MBCA) | 1 May 1965 |
| **Finance houses** | | |
| 1 | ABC Asset Finance (formerly UDC Ltd.) | 1 April 1968 |
| 2 | Leasing Company of Zimbabwe | 20 May 1996 |
| 3 | ZDB Financial Services | 20 October 1997 |
| **Discount houses** | | |
| 1 | ABC Securities (formerly Bard Discount) | 1 May 1965 |
| 2 | Discount Company of Zimbabwe | 1 August 1959 |
| 3 | Intermarket Discount House | 30 October 1990 |
| 4 | National Discount House | 12 December 1997 |
| 5 | Rapid Discount House | 26 August 1997 |
| 6 | Tetrad Securities Limited | 1 November 1996 |
| **Building societies** | | |
| 1 | Beverley Building Society | 4 April 1950 |
| 2 | Central Africa Building Society (CABS) | 8 September 1954 |
| 3 | First National Discount House | 10 June 1996 |
| 4 | Intermarket Building Society (formerly Founders Building Society) | 1 July 1961 |
| 5 | Zimbabwe Building Society | 27 November 1991 |

[a]This list includes banks that were licensed but had not yet commenced operations, and excludes banks that were licensed but had their licences cancelled within the same period, e.g. United Merchant Bank. *Source:* Reserve Bank of Zimbabwe.

important than financial savings (Kariuki, 1993).[3] According to the ZCTU (1996), non-interest factors are important in determining portfolio allocations of savings among the various alternative forms, ranging from holding cattle, seed, etc., to holding financial savings. Therefore, the expected portfolio changes arising from high real interest rates may not always be desirable to savers. The introduction of a thirty per cent withholding tax on interest income from savings held with some financial institutions may also have discouraged savings. Indeed, even in periods of high deposit interest rates, tax on interest income effectively lowers the returns on savings held with formal financial institutions, which discourages them. Further analysis by Muzulu and Moyo (2002), which looked at both aggregate and micro-level data from individual financial institutions, showed that only twenty per cent of the banks sampled listed interest rates as being significant in mobilizing savings, with sixty per cent emphasizing the effect of deposit promotions.

An analysis of the financial deepening index, as measured by the conventional ratio of money supply to GDP, during the post 1996 period shows some interesting patterns. From 1997, the ratio of broad money (M3) to GDP fell consistently – from 45.8 per cent in 1997 to 32.2 per cent in 1999 – reflecting, in the main, the banking crisis that culminated in the closure of United Merchant Bank. There was public mistrust of the banking system, and it is possible that most people kept their money rather than depositing it with formal financial institutions.[4]

From 2000, however, the financial deepening index rises consistently, reaching a high of 72.5 per cent in 2003. As the UNDP (2008) notes, this period saw the entry of many new banks into the financial sector, resulting in a rise in the degree of monetization within the economy. In 2004, the ratio fell somewhat to 67.2 per cent,[5] largely reflecting the financial shake-up of the 2003/04 period, which resulted in many indigenous institutions facing liquidity challenges that forced them into either curatorships or judicial management. After 2006, however, the index increased sharply to 81.9 per cent. The quasi-fiscal activities of the RBZ, financed by printing money, increased during this period, resulting in an acceleration in the rate of money-supply growth.

An analysis by the UNDP (2008) shows how government expenditure closely traces the degree of financial deepening in the economy, further confirming that the rise in the money supply to GDP ratio during the post-ESAP period did not reflect a healthy financial sector. Such a development can largely be

---

[3] Chigumira and Masiyandima (2001) also found the same relationship.

[4] This is consistent with the findings of the UNDP (2008).

[5] The UNDP puts the ratio at just 40 per cent. While the differences may reflect data inadequacies, the fact that no institution closed down during this period suggests that the 40 per cent may be an exaggeration.

attributed to the lack of independence of the RBZ. Although it announced a series of contractionary monetary policies between 2003 and 2007, the RBZ continued to accommodate government demands to finance the ballooning deficit through extensive political interference by the executive. In addition, the central bank governor appeared to be keen to please politicians by doling out financial presents to them in a classic case of patronage. Yet central bank independence is crucial in fighting inflation. As an IMF research report argued, 'central bank independence is seen as essential to counter the natural preference of politicians for expansionary policies that promise short-term electoral gains at the risk of worsening inflation in the long run' (Quintyn and Tailor, 2004: 4).

Although the opening up of the banking sector resulted in an increase in commercial banks, their intermediation role did not improve. The proportion of commercial banks' lending to GDP remained largely the same over the reform period, the ratio showing a negligible improvement from 11.8 per cent in 1989 to 12.2 per cent in 1996 (Fig. 12.1). There was no change in the general credit philosophy of bankers as the new entrants chose to follow the conservative ap-proach of their seniors. The magnitude of lending to the private sector doubled from 12.4 per cent in 1989 to 24.3 per cent in 1996, as represented by the claims on the private sector to GDP curve in Figure 12.1. This was mainly because the removal of trade restrictions and price controls provided industry and commerce with an opportunity to boost production and increase sales. As a result, they turned to the banking sector for financial support to acquire inputs and replace machinery. The new banking institutions identified an opportunity to lend to firms that were not only perceived to be viable but had also abundant collateral to support their credit applications.

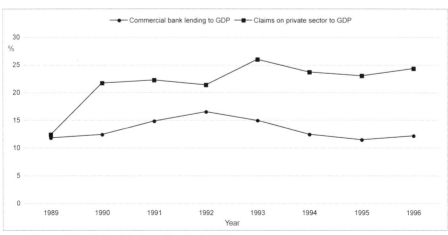

*Source:* CSO, *National Statistics Year Book, 1998.*

**Fig. 12.1: Commercial banks' lending and claims on the private sector to GDP, 1989–1996**

It was not surprising that the majority of new banks were licensed as merchant banks and discount houses rather than as commercial banks, or that they competed for established corporate clients and government business (Makina, 2009). Consequently, the increase in the value of loans extended to the private sector did not benefit SMEs, most of whom operated in the rural areas and as home industries and did not have the title deeds that banks demanded as collateral. The reforms failed to deal with the embedded structural impediments to financial inclusiveness, and the country therefore missed the opportunity to embark on the path of inclusive economic growth.

By their nature, merchant banks and discount houses operate in the wholesale arena of banking, which makes them more inclined to do business with large organizations and corporate clients. They have no appetite for small enterprises, let alone those in the marginalized sections of the community. In a country where seventy per cent of the population is rural-based, and seventy per cent of the economically active population has no access to financial services, these institutions are not strategically placed to address the challenge of financial exclusion decisively.

The success of financial sector reforms in fostering financial inclusion and promoting inclusive growth also depends on other, complementary policies.[6] Zimbabwe's financial sector reforms were overshadowed by macroeconomic instability owing to high government deficits during ESAP. As the ZCTU (1996) argues, fiscal policy influences the level of domestic savings both directly, through the government's own expenditure relative to revenue, and indirectly, through its influence on savings incentives and the decisions of private savers.

During the ESAP period, the government consistently ran a primary budget deficit that increased over time, implying that its recurrent expenditure exceeded current revenue and resulted in dissaving. It should be noted that dissaving per se is not necessarily bad, particularly if real economic growth exceeds the level of real interest rates and government finances its deficit out of voluntary private savings. Unfortunately, during the period under review, Zimbabwe's real economic growth was below the level of real interest rates, which meant that total savings could increase only with a fall in the budget deficit, as happened in South-East Asia. Most of the South-East Asian countries that exhibited high levels of savings (of over 30 per cent of GDP) maintained near-balanced budgets with surpluses on their primary accounts, a strategy that enabled their governments to contribute positively to total domestic savings. Results from a more rigorous test of the link between investment and interest rates showed a positive,

---

[6] A good definition of financial inclusion was given in the 2008 Report of the Committee on Financial Inclusion in India: that it represents a 'process of ensuring access to financial services and timely and adequate credit where needed by vulnerable groups such as weaker sections of the community and low income groups at an affordable cost'.

but statistically insignificant, relationship, implying that interest rates were not a significant deterrent to investment in the manufacturing sector during the ESAP period (Muzulu, 1993). In fact, the results showed that it was the quantity and not cost of capital that was more important in influencing investment decisions.

Although Zimbabwe's interest rates were, by and large, higher than those of a selection of OECD economies between 1993 and 1995 and the country should have witnessed an increase in capital inflows, such interest-rate differentials become important only if exchange-rate movements do not erode the ensuing beneficial effects. From the evidence, only in the case of savings in short-term maturities (90-day negotiable certificates of deposit, for example) in 1993 and 1994, were increases in real deposit rates large enough to make it profitable to save in Zimbabwe if account is taken of exchange-rate movements. This, together with the liberalization of the current-account transactions as well as the introduction of foreign-currency accounts (FCAs) in 1994, appears to have resulted in a large inflow of foreign exchange. FCA deposits, which accounted for 3.5 per cent of the money stock in January 1994, accounted for 8.8 per cent by December 1994, although 77.7 per cent of these deposits were in the form of short-term deposits. Foreign-currency reserves were very high during this period, at around six months of import cover.

## 12.4 The Crisis Period, 1997–2008

The economic problems afflicting Zimbabwe arguably began in the last quarter of 1997 and reached a crescendo in 2008.[7]

### 12.4.1 Financial inclusion

The financial reforms that were initiated during ESAP continued into the next decade. New banking institutions continued to enter the market as the minimum capital requirement became more affordable – by 2002 the number had increased dramatically to forty-three (Fig. 12.2). Particular growth was noted in the commercial-banking sector, where the number of institutions more than trebled from five in 1990 to seventeen in 2002, and in the discount-house sub-sector, from only two in 1990 to eight by 2002. In addition, by end of 2003 more than twenty applications for banking licences were pending, two-thirds of which were for merchant-banking licences. This avalanche of applications was driven mainly by the relatively low minimum capital requirements for banking licences, which ranged from Z$200 million for a discount house to Z$500 million for a commercial bank.[8]

---

[7] See Chapter 2.

[8] The official exchange rate was pegged at Z$824:US$1 while the black-market rate averaged Z$6,000:US$1. Using the official rate, Z$200 million and Z$500 million translate to US$242,718 and US$606,796, respectively, while using the black-market rate, they translate US$33,333 and US$83,333.

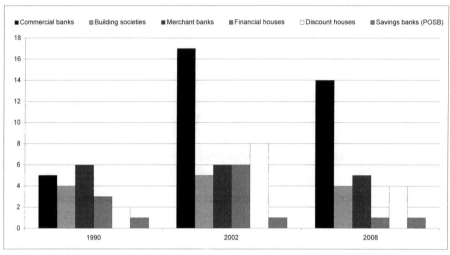

Source: IMF and Reserve Bank of Zimbabwe.

**Fig. 12.2: Number of banking institutions, 1990, 2002, 2008**

Financial inclusion can be measured by, among other indicators, the number of bank branches or ATMs at the disposal of the community. The growth in the banking sector intensified competition, as the old guard fought to defend their market stronghold while the new entrants enticed clients with new products and efficient methods of service delivery. There was a proliferation of branches and ATMs, as banks stretched their outreach programmes to far-away Growth Points in the rural areas. The newly licensed banks, the majority of which were indigenous-owned, sought to meet niche markets that had endured long periods of poor banking services: these included the SMEs, the middle-income earners and communal farmers. Most of the branches were opened by commercial banks and building societies. Some new banks entered into arrangements with retail chain stores, leading to the introduction of in-store banking facilities. The arrangements between Kingdom Bank and the Meikles group and between Century Bank and OK stores became popular with clients, who could combine their shopping and banking under one roof.

In addition to branch intensity, access to financial services can also be measured by the number of bank accounts opened as a percentage of the population, particularly savings accounts, which are regarded as a better indicator of banking penetration than other deposit accounts (Mohan, 2006). Although the proportion of the country's population that had a bank account showed a steady increase, to a peak of 49.5 per cent in 2006, the majority did not have one (Fig. 12.3). The banking crisis that was triggered by the closure of ENG Asset Management early in 2004 resulted in a number of commercial banks being placed under curatorship or closing, quarantining all the accounts that were held

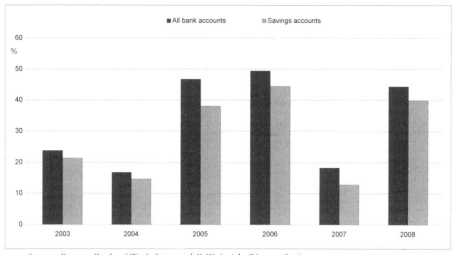

*Source:* Reserve Bank of Zimbabwe, and IMF Article IV consultative reports.

**Fig. 12.3: Percentage of population with banking accounts, 2003–2008**

with them.[9] As a result, the number of people operating bank accounts decreased. However, the Bank Use Promotion and Suppression of Money Laundering Act 2004 [*Chapter 24:24*], and the subsequent establishment within the RBZ of a division to administer this legislation, forced people to open bank accounts: by 2006, nearly half the population had a bank account, with 44.5 per cent operating a savings account. In addition, the Sunrise Project 1 initiated by the RBZ in August 2006 also forced many people to open bank accounts as they searched for ways to legitimize their cash holdings to be able to convert them into the new currency.[10]

As the fast-track land reform programme continued to cause havoc in the farming community by displacing the commercial farmers, most banking institutions that had established strategic rural branches to serve them were affected. All of a sudden business at these branches dwindled, and their operations were rendered unviable, leaving the banks with no alternative but to close them. By end of 2006, over ten branches had been closed in the rural towns of Zvishavane, Mhangura, Mberengwa, Shamva, Maphisa Growth Point, Hwange and Shurugwi, to mention only a few, most of them belonging to commercial banks. A combination of branch closures and the persistent rigid monetary policy that set unrealistic maximum daily withdrawal limits encouraged people to transact

[9] See 'Zimbabwean central bank to take measures to solve banking crisis', *Xinhua*, 4 January 2004, available at <http://www.zimbabwesituation.com/jan5_2004.html#link7>.

[10] Sunrise Project 1 was a programme of monetary reforms conducted by the RBZ in which three zeros were removed from the local currency. This was meant to reign in inflation, which had shot above the 1,000 per cent mark in August 2006.

outside the banking system, thereby furthering financial exclusion. As a result, by 2007, only 18.3 per cent of the population had access to a bank account.

In addition, the excessive money supply that emanated from the RBZ's unrestricted printing of money saw the country experiencing twenty-two months of continuous hyperinflation between March 2007 and December 2008 – the longest episode of hyperinflation ever recorded in history. By July 2008, inflation had officially reached an overwhelming 231 million per cent, leading to high transaction demand for money. The increasing cost of printing notes forced the authorities to issue higher denominations of 'bearer cheques', which were cheaper to print, and to impose further daily cash withdrawal limits on both individuals and corporates. However, as political governance increasingly became an international concern, the German company, Giesecke and Devrient, that supplied the RBZ with banknote paper halted deliveries in 2008. The RBZ responded by printing even more inferior notes on locally manufactured paper. Not only were the security features compromised further, but the durability of the notes also suffered at a time when the RBZ was also not able to get spare parts to service the printing press.

During this period, the black-market premium widened,[11] to the extent that it became almost impossible to conduct illegal foreign-currency dealings on the street as large bags were required to carry local currency cash, which, of course, was a security risk. As a result, foreign-currency speculators perfected their art and introduced what came to be known as 'burning'.[12] This unorthodox strategy forced many people to return to the banking system and open accounts to facilitate illegal foreign-currency trading, hence the growth in accounts in 2008 shown in Figure 12.3. There was a marked increase in Internet banking and cell-phone banking. Banking institutions were overwhelmed to the extent that RTGS transfers which, under normal circumstances, would be processed within twenty-four hours needed at least two days, and internal transfers, which were normally effected the same day, needed at least twenty-four hours. The national payments system was choked and experienced frequent system grid-locks as a result of the volume of transactions that had to be processed. This exposed the banking system to high operational risk and also delayed the processing of genuine transactions, thereby adversely affecting trade.

These developments resulted in a redenomination of the almost worthless local currency three times between August 2006 and February 2009 by the removal a total of twenty-five zeros. The exercise proved useless as long as the RBZ continued to engage in quasi-fiscal activities that resulted in a higher rate

---

[11] The difference between the official exchange rate and the black-market exchange rate.

[12] Burning was the illegal dealing in foreign currency when payment of the equivalent local-currency amount was effected through transfers (RTGS or internal) from the buyer's to the seller's local-currency account.

of growth in money supply. As it became increasingly difficult to print more notes, the RBZ reintroduced, at face value, coins that had fallen out of the system in 2002, when inflation was 135 per cent, as legal tender. This made the whole process of controlling money-supply growth and inflation all the more difficult because the RBZ lost track of the monetary base. The hyperinflationary environment worsened, with an astronomical monthly inflation rate estimated at 79.6 billion per cent in mid-November 2008 (Hanke and Kwok, 2009).[13] At that point, people simply refused to transact in Zimbabwe dollars, making them worthless.[14]

In order to normalize the situation, on 2 October 2008 the RBZ suspended the use of bank transfers. This accelerated the voluntary (but unlawful) rejection of the local currency as legal tender for the majority of transactions, as people generally preferred the other currencies, particularly the South African rand and the US dollar, despite the existence of an official ban on the use of foreign currency as a medium of exchange. In fact, it was estimated that half of all transactions in Zimbabwe were conducted in foreign exchange.[15] Prices in foreign currency were more stable and more favourable than those in local currency.

The whole national payments system became confused. There were various legal tenders, various foreign-exchange rates; some progressive employers introduced foreign-currency-based allowances, while the government and the central bank continued to pay their employees in the local currency, which was no longer accepted as a medium of exchange by the majority of traders. The majority of the population was pushed into financial exclusion, and the worst hit were the rural poor. In most areas, people resorted to barter trade. A bucket of maize was being exchanged for a goat, while a grinding miller would accept a gallon of fuel to grind one bucket of maize. A commuter would, for example, pay an agreed number of chickens to board a bus from Mukumbura to Harare.[16] The major reason for this was that the majority of the rural folk did not have any foreign currency, since the Grain Marketing Board and cotton merchants were paying local currency for grain and cotton delivered to them.

A number of factors led to the voluntary substitution of foreign currency for local currency during this period. Firstly, there was a general loss of confidence in the Zimbabwe dollar as it rapidly lost value in the hyperinflationary environment. Secondly, there was loss of confidence in the banking sector as the RBZ imposed

---

[13] Although no official data on inflation are available between August and December 2008 inclusive, Hanke and Kwok (2009) used the Purchasing Power Parity concept to generate figures for this period in line with Frenkel (1976).

[14] See also Chapter 2.

[15] This was said by the financial director of one of the major exhaust-manufacturing companies in Zimbabwe in an interview on dollarization at the time.

[16] This writer experienced this situation first-hand in September 2008.

cash-withdrawal limits that became meaningless with hyperinflation. Thirdly, as most inputs were now imported, holding foreign exchange was preferable to holding local currency with respect to stock replacement: using foreign currency helped both firms and consumers to preserve the value of their savings. Clearly, therefore, the RBZ's introduction of Foreign Exchange Licensed Warehouses and Shops (FOLIWARS), Foreign Exchange Licensed Oil Companies (FELOCS) and Foreign Exchange Licensed Outlets for Petrol and Diesel (FELOPADS) towards the end of 2008, as well as the dollarization of the economy at the beginning of 2009, was the formalization of a process that was already entrenched.

The parallel market also received a boost from the RBZ's policy inconsistencies with respect to the conduct of FCAs that had been in operation since the mid-1990s. Although the foreign-exchange market was partially liberalized on 5 May 2008 for private transactions, while the government continued to access foreign currency for next to nothing, the RBZ's continued interference with the operations of the inter-bank market continued to sustain the existence of the parallel market for foreign exchange.

### 12.4.2 Financial sector performance

The unstable macroeconomic environment adversely affected the performance of Zimbabwe's financial sector during the crisis period. More fundamentally, the banking crisis of the 1990s exposed the inefficiencies associated with bureaucratic banking supervision and monitoring whereby the RBZ, as the regulatory authority, could not take appropriate supervisory action against a non-compliant bank without the concurrence and approval of the Registrar of Banks at the Ministry of Finance. As the IMF (2005: 53) notes, 'even when serious problems were identified in the banking sector, there was more likely to be forbearance than decisive supervisory action'. Partly for this reason, and partly because of the strong linkages within the financial services sector, other institutions also suffered from the public's general loss of confidence in the banks.

Notwithstanding these problems, the financial sector in Zimbabwe remained generally sound during the 1990s, with an average capital-adequacy ratio of over 13 per cent, well above the standard 8 per cent recommended by the Basel Accord of 1988 (Mushayakarara, 1998). Moreover, more financial institutions continued to enter the sector, implying that there was scope for increased growth in the banking sector. However, the continued deterioration of the macroeconomic environment revealed underlying weaknesses in the sector during 2003–2004. These weaknesses included:

> poor standards of corporate governance, inadequate risk-management, and use of depositors' funds for speculative investments. In addition, there was abusive self-dealing, including unreported insider transactions, use of subsidiaries and affiliates to evade prudential limits, and use of RBZ liquidity advances to support group

companies and deliberate misreporting to RBZ to conceal losses and overstate capital [IMF, 2005: 53].

Naturally, these problems were more pronounced in the newer banks registered in the 1990s. Thus, by December 2003, pressure was already evident in the banking sector, as reflected by the level of RBZ liquidity support, which rose from about 4 per cent of total bank deposits around June 2003 to 15 per cent by the end of December 2003. The liquidity problems for non-compliant commercial banks worsened following the increase in statutory-reserve requirements from 20 per cent to 30 per cent, effective January 2004.

The RBZ therefore set out to address both the underlying weaknesses that had led to the emergence of problem banks and to strengthen them through a package of measures designed to enhance supervision and prudential standards. One of the most important changes designed to enhance the soundness of the banking system related to the transfer of the powers of the Registrar of Banking Institutions from the Ministry of Finance to the RBZ through the Financial Laws Amendment Act in August 2004.[17] The RBZ now ensures that potential entrants meet stringent standards, thereby avoiding the problems of licensing weak banks, and it now has the ability to take corrective action. The placement of a number of banks – Trust Bank, Royal Bank, Barbican Bank, Time Bank and Century Bank – under curatorship or liquidation in 2004 signified a break from the previous practices of forbearance. The move reduced the competition within the financial sector that had ushered in innovative products in a classic reversal of the liberalization of the early 1990s. In addition, financial deepening and financial inclusion suffered, as many more people shunned the banking system as they were unsure which banking institution might be next in the firing line. People started to keep cash outside the banking system, as reflected by the general fall in the proportion of deposits to GDP (Fig. 12.4).

It can be seen from Figure 12.4 that the proportion of total deposits to GDP has followed a generally declining trend, from above 52 per cent in 1997 to as little as 0.01 per cent in 2007. The 1997 figure represents the result of the liberalization of the financial sector during the ESAP era. The determination of interest rates through the demand-and-supply mechanism resulted in favourable interest rates, as discussed above, which encouraged clients to keep their cash within the banking system. In addition, the new banking and financial institutions also boosted the amount of money that passed through the banking sector.

During early 2000, unit trust management companies emerged that were registered by the Registrar of Collective Investment Schemes. These encouraged even low-income earners to save by pooling their small savings into one big fund,

---

[17] The Banking Act Amendment Number 1 of 2005, which requires the RBZ to consult with the Minister of Finance prior to granting or revoking a licence, appears to have been a regressive move as it undermined the ability of the RBZ to take corrective action on time.

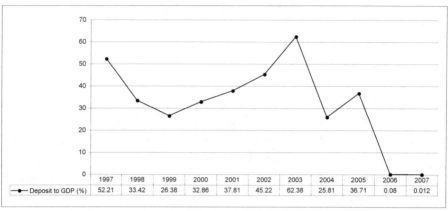

Source: IMF and Reserve Bank of Zimbabwe.

**Fig. 12.4: Deposits as a percentage of GDP, 1997–2007**

which was either invested in the money market or as security investments on the Zimbabwe Stock Exchange. In 2002, as well as the new banking institutions, other financial institutions such as asset-management companies, which were not dealing in collective-investment schemes, emerged. Since these were not regulated, they offered attractive interest rates on clients' deposits, thereby attracting more clients to the detriment of the formal banking institutions. However, they would negotiate favourable interest rates with banking institutions, where they placed clients' funds at rates higher than those they offered their clients, ensuring that they benefited on the margin. As a result, there was marked increase in the proportion of deposits to GDP, which reached 62.4 per cent by the end of 2003.

However, as more and more asset-management companies emerged and operated without any regulatory authority as there was no legal framework to govern their operations, some began to abuse clients' funds, engaging in foreign-currency dealings and fuelling parallel-market activities as well as causing inflationary pressure in the whole economy. Since only companies that engaged in collective-investment schemes (unit trusts) were required to be registered in terms of the Collective Investment Schemes Act [*Chapter 24:19*], asset-management companies started to operate like banking institutions, accepting deposits at high interest rates and offering loans to both individuals and companies. While these entities virtually conducted banking activities in violation of the Banking Act [*Chapter 24:20*], which requires every institution to be licensed by the Registrar of Banks, they managed to attract many people back into the banking system by offering higher deposit rates than banks offered. Nevertheless, the lack of a regulatory framework to supervise these operations made them high-risk activities and, if one failed, it had the potential to destabilize the whole financial sector, as their operations were intertwined with the banking sector.

Indeed, the country had to pay dearly when, in early 2004, one such entity, ENG Asset Management, failed to pay clients' maturing deposits. This marked the beginning of the banking crisis that shook the country in the third decade of Zimbabwe's independence: deposit levels as a proportion of GDP plummeted to 25.8 per cent as clients withdrew their funds from the banking system in response to the crisis, which had a contagion effect. From that time on, the financial sector was hit by severe systemic risk, which resulted in more banking institutions and asset-management companies being placed under curatorship and liquidation, respectively, and driving the majority of the country's already impoverished citizens further into financial exclusion.

### 12.4.3 Access to financial services

Both supply-side and demand-side factors affect access to financial services in Zimbabwe (Table 12.2). Supply-side factors are the challenges that prevent banks from making financial services available to the rural and marginalized communities, while demand-side factors are those that induce people to shun the banking system. Furthermore, during the period of hyperinflation, communities preferred to hold cash as they had lost confidence in the banking system owing to the inconsistent and unreliable monetary policy which introduced unrealistic cash-withdrawal limits and made it difficult for them to access their money.

The National Microfinance Survey undertaken between December 2005 and March 2006 (Ernst & Young, 2006) revealed that an alarming 70 per cent of the economically active population did not have access to formal financial services and relied on informal financial service providers. In his 2010 national budget statement, the Minister of Finance said that 85 per cent of the population were 'submerged and drowning' in poverty, 13 per cent were 'floating or dog-

**Table 12.2: Factors affecting access to financial services**

| Supply-side factors | Demand-side factors |
| --- | --- |
| Unavailability of appropriate infrastructure in terms of reliable electricity, telecommunications connectivity which facilitate the provision of information-technology-driven products and services | Banking facilities are between 50 km and 100 km away |
| Poor road networks, which retard accessibility | Unreliable and unaffordable transport |
| High information, transaction and monitoring costs | Low income levels – low-income people generally have the attitude that banks are only for the rich |
| Seasonality in deposits | High bank charges and low interest rates erode savings and discourage deposits |
| Lack of fiscal benefits | Lack of information on banking services available |
| | Stringent account-opening requirements |
| | Inflexible products |

paddling', and only 2 per cent were the wealthy few. This confirms empirical evidence that countries with high levels of financial exclusion have high levels of poverty and income inequality (Mohan, 2006).

It is imperative that governments strive to ensure that the majority of their people have access to financial services. When a large proportion of the population uses the formal financial system, a country experiences high savings mobilization and pooling, which enables financial institutions to provide efficient payment systems that facilitate trade and a rapid growth in the incomes of the poor, who are presented with an opportunity to catch up with the rest of the economy as it grows (Demirgüc-Kunt, 2008). In addition, facilitating equal access to financial services for citizens will provide a platform for individuals and small enterprises to obtain credit, which results in increased demand, while improved delivery of raw materials and the availability of working capital leads to a rise in production volumes and, ultimately, in an improved supply of consumer goods. Furthermore, as access to financial services improves, financial deepening will widen as financial intermediaries develop new products and delivery channels in order to gain comparative advantage over competitors.

### 12.4.4 Lending

Studies have shown disappointingly low numbers of micro-enterprises and SMEs borrowing from formal financial institutions (Muzulu, 1995; Muzulu and Moyo, 2002). Muzulu and Moyo found that SMEs showed little appetite for borrowing from formal financial institutions primarily because of a lack of interest on their part: high interest rates, lack of knowledge about bank requirements, and the onerous conditions attached to such borrowings all served to reinforce the sector's lack of interest in borrowing from them. This suggests that financial institutions need to develop and market products that are appropriate to the micro and small-scale sectors along the lines of the Grameen Bank of Bangladesh (Box 12.1).

While in nominal terms there appears to have been growth in bank lending between 2000 and 2006, in real terms there was hardly any growth at all. Statistics show that the share of loans and advances in total assets held by commercial banks fell from 21.2 per cent in 2004 to 12.2 per cent in 2005 before rising to 16.8 per cent in 2006. Liquidity management took up much of the energy of banks as they operated on a knife-edge, where any liquidity surplus or deficit at the end of each day incurred huge penalties (Robinson, 2006).

What there was was subsidized lending, directed by the RBZ through the Agricultural Sector Productivity Enhancement Facility (ASPEF), the Productive Sector Facility (PSF) and the Basic Commodity Supply Side Intervention (BACOSSI). The effect of such lending on output is, however, not apparent. One major problem with concessionary facilities when money-market rates

## Box 12.1: The Bangladesh Grameen Bank model: Financial inclusion

The Grameen Bank (Grameen means 'rural' or 'village' in Bangla/Bengali language) was established in 1976 as a way of fighting poverty by extending banking facilities to poor men and women in Bangladesh. By providing small loans to very poor people, mostly women, Grameen empowers people to start small businesses that will lift them out of poverty. Muhammad Yunus, the founder, and Grameen Bank were jointly awarded the Nobel Peace Prize in 2006 for advancing economic development in Bangladesh. The success of the Grameen model has inspired similar efforts in a number of countries throughout the world.

Grameen Bank has reversed conventional banking wisdom by focusing mainly on women borrowers, dispensing with the requirement of collateral, and extending loans only to the very poorest; 97 per cent of its members are women. Women suffer disproportionately from poverty and are more likely than men to devote their earnings to their families. The bank does not require any credit history or business experience for providing loans. The poor do not come to the bank, the bank goes to the poor. By September 2008, Grameen had 140,016 centres, 198,038 groups, and about 7.6 million members.

By November 2009, Grameen had provided US$8.6 billion in small loans to almost 8 million people, with a nearly 97 per cent repayment rate. Ninety-four per cent of the bank's shares are owned by borrowers, and 65 per cent of borrowers have risen above the poverty line. The entire Grameen system is built on peer support, with the framework of a five-member group and the broader framework of a centre.

Grameen has both loan and savings products. The period for a basic loan can vary from three months to three years; the period for a housing loan is ten years. Micro-enterprise loans are also given for a period up to three years, and education loans for the period of education. Grameen also has a scholarship programme for the children of its members. The basic loan, which includes all income-generating loan activities, constitutes about 98 per cent of the total loan portfolio.

According to Muhammad Yunus, poverty-focused micro-credit programmes should charge a lower rate of interest, which may be equal to the cost of funds at the market rate plus up to 10 per cent. He calls it the Green Zone. It may be in the Yellow Zone as well, which equals the cost of funds plus 10 to 15 per cent. If any programme charges an interest rate higher than the Yellow Zone, they operate in the Red Zone, which, according to Muhammad Yunus, is the territory of the moneylenders. This is for maximizing profit and not for maximizing social benefit.

Grameen Bank has developed a decentralized system. It always delegates decision-making power and authorities to the lower level – zonal offices, area offices, branches, centres and groups. It operates a transparent system so that everything remains visible, and follows a participatory process. Grameen monitors all its activities continuously and thoroughly. It reaches out even to the remote and dark corners of the system to keep them clean. It has developed a strong management information system, and all its branches are computerized. Grameen has a well-organized internal audit system which conducts both financial and management audits of its offices at all levels.

*Source:* H. I. Latifee, 'Financial Inclusion: The Experience of Grameen Bank', paper presented at the Conference on 'Deepening Financial Sector Reforms and Regional Cooperation in South Asia' held at the Gulmohar Hall, India Habitat Centre, Lodi Road, New Delhi-110003, India, 6–7 November 2008, <http://www.grameentrust.org/The%20Experience%20of%20Grameen%20Bank.pdf>.

are higher than interest rates offered to participants is that opportunities for arbitrage abound. It is always more lucrative to redeploy the funds in order to get more certain returns from money-market investments than to undertake the uncertain and more demanding pursuits for which the money was intended.

Moreover, it is difficult to measure the technical efficiency of banks when they have to lend at absurdly negative real interest rates for political reasons. Banks had to lend at 25 per cent while the official year-on-year rate of inflation was 231.2 million per cent. Real commercial lending rates were positive in only five out of the eleven years between 1997 and 2007. If one takes into account the fact that interest cost is tax-deductible, then the real cost of borrowing was hugely negative. In addition to compromising the profitability of banks, the subsidized credit came with onerous conditions imposed on the borrower. As a result, most firms were not keen to borrow through this window. Clearly, it becomes inherently difficult to have any real idea of the technical efficiency of the banks, as the profitability indicators do not indicate this properly.[18]

Another negative effect of subsidized credit on commercial lending was the very high statutory reserve requirements (over 50 per cent for demand deposits) needed to fund the programme. Although the RBZ (2006: 48) argued that low commercial lending was a result of banks exercising caution 'in view of the perceived high credit risk in the high interest rate environment', the high reserve requirements left banks with limited surpluses to lend to the private sector on commercial lines.

Furthermore, bank lending on commercial lines declined owing to their preference for holding government securities in the form of one-year treasury bills to fund the government deficit, at a nominal coupon rate of 340 per cent. In addition, the RBZ also issued its own bills, designed to sterilize monetary expansion arising from financing losses from its quasi-fiscal activities. Statistics show that commercial bank holdings of both government and RBZ bills, which accounted for 26 per cent of total bank assets in 2004, rose to just over 26 per cent in 2005 and to 29.1 per cent in 2006 before falling to just 12 per cent by 2007, thanks to the hyperinflation that reduced government's recourse to the market for funds.

### 12.4.5 The microfinance sector
The microfinance sector in Zimbabwe emerged in the 1990s following financial liberalization, with a variety of organizations providing services to hitherto marginalized members of the community as well as to SMEs. The sector

---

[18] The RBZ concluded that the financial sector was profitable, as reflected in their results, although the indicators shown are in nominal terms. However, it admitted that the bulk of the profits came from interest income on securities and investments, which accounted for 70 per cent of total income for banks in 2006 (RBZ, 2006).

experienced phenomenal growth, with organizations such as commercial banks, NGOs, credit and savings co-operatives, development banks and high-net-worth individuals joining in their formation. The providers of microfinance services can be categorized as banks, non-bank microfinance institutions, moneylenders, savings and credit co-operative societies, as well as government-managed microfinance programmes such as SEDCO.

Before 1 January 2004, the licensing of microfinance service providers was handled by the Ministry of Finance in conjunction with the Ministry of Public Service, Labour and Social Welfare in relation to those providers who were financially backed by NGOs. In December 2003, there were over 1,600 registered moneylenders.[19] However, when the RBZ took over the licensing and supervision of the microfinance sector, with effect from 1 January 2004, a total of 245 applications were received (from 47 non-bank microfinance institutions and 198 moneylenders) while the rest shied away from the prospect of operating under a rigorous regulatory and supervisory regime. This figure had further deteriorated to 73 (32 non-bank microfinance institutions and 41 moneylenders) by 15 July 2010. As at 28 February 2006, 208 savings and credit co-operative societies had been registered by the Ministry of Youth Development, Employment Creation and Co-operatives.

The most common financial products provided by microfinance institutions worldwide are credit for enterprise development, savings accounts, consumer loans, housing loans, and services such as insurance and payment systems like money transfers, cash cards, etc. In Zimbabwe, however, development finance is provided mainly by banks, some non-bank microfinance institutions, government-managed institutions and some savings and credit co-operative societies. Moneylenders provide mainly consumer loans, especially to civil servants and other sections of the community that are shunned by the formal banking sector, and they play a significant role in the financial system by meeting human needs – the payment of school fees, food and shelter-related payments, medical expenses, etc. – that lead to poverty alleviation, which is a development goal.

Their low levels of capitalization hinder the capability of moneylenders to provide business-development loans, as these ordinarily require a substantial loan amount with a longer loan period, which the institutions cannot afford. Furthermore, moneylenders lack project-evaluation expertise and are therefore unable to assess the viability of such applications, leaving them to prefer consumer loans, which are normally salary-based and repayable through direct debit or deduction. Consumer-loan facilities are offered over a short term, usually for maximum periods of thirty days at exorbitant interest rates. Credit and

---

[19] In terms of the Moneylending and Rates of Interest Act [*Chapter 14:14*], as revised in 1996, this definition included non-bank microfinance institutions and moneylending institutions.

savings co-operatives mobilize deposits from members in addition to providing consumption and business-development loans and operate under the umbrella of the National Association of Savings and Co-operative Unions of Zimbabwe.

Studies show that, despite the proliferation of microfinance institutions in the 1990s, they remained concentrated in the urban centres, depriving the majority of the population from access to financial services, with only about 10 per cent of the informal sector accessing credit from them by early 2000 (Muzulu and Moyo, 2002). In addition, these constraints have also limited the product and service diversity of the microfinance sector, the majority of the institutions confining themselves to generic products of loans and savings for member-based institutions like credit and savings co-operatives.

The new dispensation that was ushered in with the formation of the Inclusive Government and the subsequent dollarization of the economy requires micro-finance institutions to move away from the standard branch-and-loan-officer model of delivering credit and to consider introducing non-traditional or altern-ative channels. Alternative channels for service delivery include kiosks, mobile banking, business units, the Internet, call centres, banking agents, ATMs, leveraging on the nationwide presence of the POSB, and participating in national payments and remittance facilities.

### 12.4.5 Remittances from the diaspora

Following the drying up of foreign financial inflows in 1999 and the rising demand for foreign currency, the RBZ authorized the formation of Money Transfer Agencies (MTAs) in 2004. This move came out of the belief that remit-tances from the diaspora formed a significant source of foreign exchange that fuelled the movement of the Zimbabwe dollar on the parallel market. Most of the MTAs were separate entities of commercial banks, but the RBZ also formed its own, Homelink (Private) Limited, in direct competition with commercial banks, solely to channel the perceived foreign currency from the diaspora to government. The high minimum capital requirement of US$100,000 imposed on these MTAs acted as a huge barrier to entry, as did the restrictions on what they could do – they could not engage in the bureau de change functions of buying foreign exchange from any person or entity whatsoever. Moreover, they could not levy any commissions, fees or charges on customers, but instead received agency fees from the RBZ in Zimbabwe dollars.

Statistics on total remittances to Zimbabwe through both MTAs and in-formal channels have been a subject of intense debate.[20] The predominant use of informal channels, and the fact that some of the remittances are in kind, creates immense problems of measurement. Makina (2007), for example, found

---

[20] See Chapter 8.

that only two per cent of Zimbabwean migrants in South Africa used formal channels to send money home, while the majority used a variety of informal channels. What is required, therefore, are policies that improve remittance flows into formal channels in order to strengthen their developmental impact.

One of the major reasons for the poor capital inflows into the formal financial institutions was the policy shift displayed by the RBZ on the receipt of remittances. When MTAs were established in 2004, remittances could be received in foreign currency, but from 2005, recipients had to get their money in Zimbabwe dollars at an exchange rate that was usually unfavourable relative to that on the parallel market. This naturally encouraged people to use informal channels, resulting in a decline in foreign-currency inflows through MTAs. When the policy changed again in 2007, and recipients were allowed to receive money in foreign currency, inflows through official channels improved somewhat, although the fear of another sudden policy reversal kept a significant portion of remittances outside formal channels. The RBZ's failure to maintain a competitive exchange rate drove remittances from official to informal channels, where demand-and-supply factors determined a more competitive rate. As the UNDP (2008) notes, the difference between the official and parallel exchange rates forced Zimbabweans in the diaspora to look for alternative ways of sending money to relatives at home.

## 12.5 The Transitional Period, 2009–2010

When the RBZ introduced FOLIWARS in late 2008, marking the beginning of official dollarization, banks were not allowed to levy charges in foreign currency, even though their costs were denominated in foreign currency, which naturally worsened their losses in real terms. Even when they could officially levy charges in foreign exchange, the public had very little confidence in the financial sector, and total deposits held by banks started from a very low base of around US$200 million in February 2009. Although they rose to US$800 million by end of September 2009 as confidence grew, this was low relative to the demand for loans after a decade of capital consumption. It is also noteworthy that 70.9 per cent of the deposits comprised demand and short-term deposits, reflecting a combination of low incomes, low confidence in banks, and an inclination towards cash (RBZ, 2009b). Moreover, because the RBZ could no longer act as 'lender of last resort' owing to a tight liquidity constraint worsened by its inability to issue its own liabilities, banks lent out only a tiny fraction of their liabilities in order to reduce the risk of not being able to meet the demand for cash. As a result, most financial institutions rationalized their operations by closing branches in rural and peri-urban areas, which naturally worsened the dualistic nature of financial resource allocation as it left 65 per cent of the population unbanked (Zimbabwe, 2009b).

However, a nascent recovery in both deposit levels and loans and advances has been noticed since then, reflecting a gradual normalization of operations in the banking sector. The biggest challenge, though, continues to be liquidity, which has impacted on the capacity of banks to offer credit facilities (Fig. 12.5). Although the volume of deposits increased by 113.8 per cent following dollarization to US$1,016.40 million in October 2009, the intermediation ratio increased by only 16 percentage points from 33.2 per cent in April 2009 to 49.2 per cent in October 2009. The short-term nature of deposits has restrained banks from offering long-term credit facilities suitable for the recapitalization of industrial operations, so the government will need to consistently pursue strategies that offer opportunities for inclusive industrial development that is anchored in universal access to financial services.

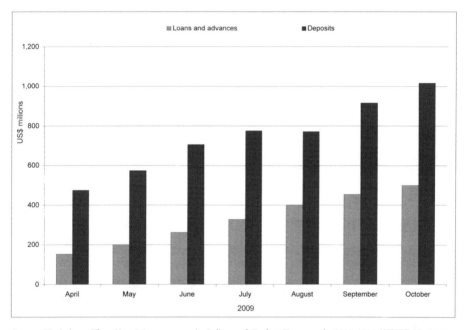

*Source:* Zimbabwe, *Three-Year Macroeconomic Policy and Budget Framework, 2010–2012* (STERP II), 2009.

**Fig. 12.5: Loans and deposits and advances, April–October 2009**

In spite of these developments, the macroeconomic policies contained in the Short-Term Economic Recovery Programme (STERP) (Zimbabwe, 2009a), the 2009 budget statement,[21] and the July 2009 monetary policy statement (RBZ, 2009a) have all conspired to improve the economic environment. As a result, there has been a nascent recovery in most sectors of the economy (IMF, 2009).

[21] See <http://www.zimtreasury.org/downloads/196.pdf>.

## 12.6 Strategies for Financial Sector Recovery and Inclusive Growth

In his 2010 national budget statement, the Minister of Finance, Hon. Tendai Biti, bemoaned the fact that 85 per cent of Zimbabweans languished in poverty while, in 2006, 70 per cent of the population was unbanked. To address this anomaly, there is need to 'ensure that a broad-based macro-economic recovery and growth is achieved' (Zimbabwe, 2009b: 24). This means that the government must adopt strategies that are conducive to inclusive growth and are anchored in inclusive financial intermediation by ensuring ease of access, availability, and use of the formal financial system by all members of the economy.

Since the financial sector is the lifeblood of the national economy, there cannot be any economic development and growth to talk about if it is not adequately diversified and developed. The challenge for governments of developing countries, particularly of Zimbabwe, is to design macroeconomic policies and strategies that encourage the full participation of all citizens in the process of economic development by, among other things, enabling their access to financial services. The following are some of the strategies that the government can implement to facilitate inclusive, pro-poor growth.

### 12.6.1 Building an inclusive financial framework

As reported above, a survey conducted December 2005 and March 2006 found that 70 per cent of the economically active population were excluded from access to formal financial services (Ernst & Young, 2006). To expand the access of poor people to financial services, inclusive financial systems are therefore needed that provide appropriate services for all types of clients. Microfinance has been accepted as one vehicle to achieve financial inclusiveness. An inclusive financial system recognizes that the massive number of people who are excluded will gain access only if financial services for the poor are integrated into all three levels of the financial system: micro, meso and macro (Helms, 2006).

*Micro-level interventions* involve defining microfinance clients and the service providers. Poor people need a variety of services that include insurance, remittances and transfers, pensions, loans for emergency needs, micro-enterprise loans, and safe places to save. Microfinance clients are often self-employed and typically home-based entrepreneurs in rural areas – they are small farmers and others engaged in small income-generating activities; in urban areas, they are more diverse and include street vendors, shopkeepers, service providers, artisans, etc.

*Meso-level interventions* are about building financial infrastructure and associated systems. Financial infrastructure refers to the payments and clearing systems that allow the transfer of money among participating financial institutions. Usually, microfinance institutions that serve the poor lack direct access to the payments system, so they must work through public and private banks by forging alliances. Transparency and information infrastructure are critical elements in building inclusive financial systems: accurate, standardized and comparable information on financial performance is fundamental to integrating microfinance into the financial system. Credit bureaux are critical building blocks of transparency.

*Macro-level interventions* have to do with the role of government in building inclusive financial systems. Helms (2006: 76) identifies three ways in which governments become involved in the financial system:

- First and foremost, the government sets policies that affect the financial system. These policies include ensuring macroeconomic stability, liberalizing interest rates, and establishing banking regulation and supervision which make viable microfinance possible. A major component includes the development of an efficient infrastructure with widespread access to information technology, passable road networks, and a readily available power supply.

- Secondly, the government can proactively promote inclusion by offering fiscal incentives to encourage financial institutions to make financial services available in those regions of the country where poor or low-income people are in the majority. Such incentives may include tax holidays for every brick-and-mortar bank branch opened in the rural areas, exemption from reserve requirements of deposits mobilized from such branches, streamlining of local government bureaucracy to speed up business registration and licensing, and provision of discounted land for business premises. These incentives should be applied to all stakeholders interested in developing an inclusive approach to financial and economic development, such as SMEs, microfinance institutions, and commercial banks and building societies.

- Thirdly, the government delivers financial services directly and indirectly, usually by disbursing credit to preferred groups or channelling resources to financial institutions through wholesale arrangements. Although history has shown that this system has often been politicized (as with SEDCO and the Social Development Fund) and used to serve the few who are perceived to be 'politically correct', government-owned banks such as the POSB and Agribank have had a good track record in mobilizing savings or transferring money through their wide network of branches that cover some of the most remote areas of the country.

### 12.6.2 Maintenance of political and macroeconomic stability

One of the most important contributions government can make to the attainment of inclusive growth is to maintain macroeconomic stability through appropriate monetary and fiscal policies. The experience of the past decade has shown beyond reasonable doubt that business does not thrive on coercion and instability. Policy inconsistencies are major impediments to making investment decisions and attracting capital. Research has shown that political uncertainty and macroeconomic instability may lead to a deterioration in business conditions (Demirgüc-Kunt, 2008). Since both monetary and fiscal policies affect the taxation of financial intermediaries, and thus the provision of financial services, it follows that a well-functioning financial system requires fiscal discipline and stable macroeconomic policies.

Furthermore, other studies have shown that countries with low and stable inflation rates experience higher levels of banking and stock-market development, and high inflation and real interest rates are associated with a higher probability of systemic banking crises. At the height of the meltdown from 2007, Zimbabwe witnessed a wave of sustained bank-branch closures, especially in regions where political uncertainty was widespread owing to violence. The revival and recovery of the financial sector requires that the government implement policies that en-sure political stability and sustained macroeconomic stability, which will promote the restoration of the real value of savings and allow longer-term planning by both business and households.

### 12.6.3 Infrastructure rehabilitation and development

During the RBZ's Sunrise Project conducted in August 2006, communities indicated that a major reason that they kept large sums of cash at home instead of in a bank was that had to travel between 50 and 100 kilometres to get to the nearest banking facility; banking institutions indicated that they shunned rural areas because they were inaccessible because of the poor infrastructure.[22] It became clear that inclusive development requires infrastructure that will facilitate the participation of all citizens of the country – that is, both households and business alike. When, in November 2005, the Reserve Bank of India requested banks to make basic, 'no-frills' accounts available, the initiative was unsuccessful, as residents did not use them owing to long distances and other factors unrelated to the cost of operating an account. Thus, distance is a major obstacle in access to financial services and markets for communal farmers.

The absence of adequate and cost-effective infrastructure is a major impedi-ment to branch expansion. Reliable power supply, roads that are passable all year round, affordable transport, and good communication networks are neces-sary for viable branch networks and the provision of innovative channels that facilitate access to financial services. To enhance private-sector participation in the provision of financial services to low-income members of the community and the development of small enterprises in remote areas, government should

---

[22] RBZ, *Rural Banking, Financial Inclusion and Empowerment of Small to Medium Enterprises*, Supple-ment to the January 2007 Monetary Policy Review Statement, 31 January 2007.

implement policies that facilitate the provision of cost-effective electricity, clean water, a comprehensive road network, and an efficient telecommunications system.

### 12.6.4 Development of legal and information-sharing frameworks

The protection of property rights and the enforcement of contracts are critical elements in the development of financial systems: outside investors are reluctant to invest if their rights are not protected. The Zimbabwe government needs to come up with a competitive and conducive investment environment that is underpinned by security of investment, property rights, ease in starting a business, favourable tax legislation, flexible and adaptable conflict resolution, and judicial enforcement. The timely availability of good-quality information is equally important since it reduces information asymmetries between borrowers and lenders, which improves financing opportunities for SMEs and the poor. The availability of asymmetric or imperfect information is considered socially inefficient as it leads to the denial of credit to creditworthy borrowers by lenders who cannot distinguish between good and bad borrowers.

One way of reducing information asymmetry is by establishing a credit reference bureau that would become a base for information-sharing among all stakeholders in the financial sector. A credit reference bureau collects information from a variety of sources and provides, for example, records on the repayment behaviour of individuals and firms, which allows lenders to screen borrowers at low cost, thereby reducing risks and fostering increased access to credit by SMEs and individuals. For a credit reference bureau to have access to various sources of information, there is a need for partnership between the public and private sectors and the design of a regulatory framework to facilitate information-sharing between regulated and unregulated institutions and corporates, moneylenders and credit stores.

### 12.6.5 Encourage expansion of branch networks

The period from 2000 witnessed a sustained reduction in the size of the branch networks of banks following the supervisory action by the RBZ and because of political and macroeconomic instability. While a single branch of a bank served an average of 12,000 people in urban centres, in the rural areas one branch served 170,000 people in mid-2006. There is no doubt that more has to be done to expand banking institutions' outreach, especially in the rural and remote areas of the country; they should be given incentives to build more branches to counter the effects of long distances and expensive transport. Government needs to improve rural development and enhance the profit potential for rural branches in order to induce banks and other financial service providers to venture into these areas.

### 12.6.6 Promote affordable bank accounts

In modern life, ownership of a bank account is a ticket to a land of opportunities, yet over 70 per cent of the population have no bank account, which limits their participation in economic activities. One of the major impediments to owner-ship of bank accounts is the universal application of rigid account-opening requirements which have stringent 'know your customer' assessments whose conditions cannot be easily fulfilled by rural folk and the poor. In addition, exorbitant bank charges that are not commensurate with service delivery, as well as low interest on deposits, have encouraged citizens to shy away from banking institutions.

Governments have implemented a variety of country-specific measures to increase the rate of bank-account ownership among their citizens (Box 12.2). These experiences show that it requires unity of purpose between government, the banking sector and other stakeholders to design appropriate home-grown banking products aimed at boosting confidence in the banking sector and at enticing the majority of the community into the formal financial sector. The groundwork was laid by RBZ's National Microfinance Policy, whose full implementation should be the next logical step.[23]

### 12.6.7 Promotion of access to credit

One of the major tools used to ensure the participation of SMEs and poor communities in the process of inclusive economic development is provision of credit. Unfortunately, access to low-risk and low-cost financing has remained out of reach for many of the rural poor, making it nearly impossible for them to invest or to diversify into other types of income-generating activities.

### 12.6.8 Promotion of alternative delivery channels

The quest for a financial inclusion system that fosters a participatory economic development process has intensified worldwide, and studies were commissioned in search for solutions to this predicament (ACCION, 2009; ADBI, 2009). These studies concluded that there was a need for governments to create environments that facilitate the diversification of financial services delivery systems through alternative channels. Alternative channels are non-traditional ways of distributing credit and other financial services to the poor. The emphasis is on branchless banking, since most of these service-delivery methods do not depend on the presence of branches, and channels that have been implemented include agent banking, mobile banking, cell-phone banking, and e-banking.

---

[23] The policy was issued as a supplement to the 'First Quarter Monetary Policy Statement: A Focus on Food, Foreign Exchange Generation, Producer Viability and Increased Supply of Basic Commodities', Reserve Bank of Zimbabwe, 30 April 2008.

Agent banking is when a licensed financial institution enters into collaboration with another enterprise, financial or non-financial, to provide distribution outlets for financial services and products. Such entities may include post offices, retail chain stores, supermarkets, pharmacies, and local or district councils, and are a cheaper alternative for the banking poor and communities in remote rural areas. To promote such schemes, government, through the central bank, should come up with a regulatory framework and guidelines to address matters of permissible agent activities, security, liquidity management, liability to the customer (agent or bank), and general consumer protection, including pricing transparency and disclosure.

---

**Box 12.2: Country experiences in the promotion of basic bank accounts***

France and Belgium have undertaken initiatives committing banks to open an affordable account with bare minimum facilities. Termed 'call deposit account' in Belgium, it offers three basic types of transactions: money transfers, deposits and withdrawals, and bank statements. However, individual banks may opt to offer other services if they wish.

In Germany, a voluntary code was introduced by the German Bankers' Association in 1996. This makes provision for an 'everyman' current account, offering basic banking transactions, without an overdraft facility.

In France, the law on exclusion of July 1998 reiterated the right to an account first set out in the 1984 law and has since then simplified the process of exercising the right to an account.

In Canada appropriate legislation, which was enacted in June 2001, requires all banks to provide accounts without minimum opening balances to all Canadians, regardless of employment or credit history, with minimum identification requirements. A Financial Consumer Agency of Canada was set up to monitor financial institutions' adherence to their public commitments.

In November 2005, the Reserve Bank of India advised banks to make available a basic banking 'no-frills' account with low or no minimum stipulated balances as well as charges to expand the outreach of such accounts to vast sections of the population. Several banks took up the challenge and introduced the no-frills accounts with and without value-added features.

In South Africa, all financial institutions together with other stakeholders like the government, labour and community adopted a voluntary agreement, the Financial Sector Charter, whose main objective is making the sector more racially inclusive and representative. In October 2004, a 'Mzansi account' which is a basic, standardized, debit-card-based transactional and savings account was launched at the initiative of South Africa's four largest commercial banks together with the state-owned Postbank. By April 2009, over six million Mzansi accounts had been opened, the majority of them (around 90 per cent) by people who had not previously banked at the same bank at which the account was opened. These accounts do not have monthly administration fees and have 'know your customer'-driven ceilings on transaction value.

*Adapted from Mohan (2006); and Bankable Frontier Associates, *The Mzansi Bank Account Initiative in South Africa*, Final Report, 2009, <http://www.finmark.org.za/documents/R_Mzansi_BFA.pdf>.

---

Mobile banking is the use of vans or other customized vehicles that circulate among communities and provide the services of a standard bank branch; Zimbank and the POSB were famous for such services among the rural and farming communities. In the rural areas, banking institutions can make use of local leadership structures as venues for such services. The major concern with this scheme is the need to ensure adequate security in transit and at the venues.

Cell-phone and Internet banking involve the use of ICTs to provide access to financial services for the unbanked and communities in remote rural areas. The uptake of these services has remained weak. Cell-phone banking accounted for under US$500,000 between April and October 2009, though the value of Internet-banking transactions was better, with a total of US$25.9 million over the same period.[24] While there is no aggregated data on the geographical location of the users, it is generally believed that the majority were from the urban centres. Cell-phone and Internet technologies can facilitate access to financial services, such as cash deposits and withdrawals, third-party deposits into a user account, retail purchases and bill payments, transfer of cash or airtime credits between user accounts. The smooth operation of this delivery channel requires mutual co-operation between the various regulatory authorities involved to ensure that risk-management measures are taken to prevent money-laundering activities.

### 12.6.9 Consumer protection

Consumer protection seeks to level the playing field between providers and consumers of financial services. Bank customers have less information about their financial transactions than the financial institutions providing the services, which can result in excessively high interest rates paid, lack of understanding about financial options, and insufficient avenues for redress. Thus, without adequate consumer protection, the benefits of financial inclusion can be lost. Consumer-protection policies are necessary to address technical and delivery security, reduce predatory lending and increase disclosure of information, facilitate efficient dispute settlement, enhance data protection and improve comparability of offers. A good consumer-protection policy should therefore provide for transparency, fairness, responsibility and fair recovery practices.

The government should encourage competition to reduce credit prices, and civil-society organizations should campaign vigorously for transparency and disclosure of cost of credit across providers to enable borrowers to compare. Since financial literacy is low, financial education must be pursued alongside the promotion of plain language to help the less literate and less financially experienced.

---

[24] Zimbabwe, *Three-Year Macroeconomic Policy and Budget Framework, 2010–2012* (STERP II), 2009.

## 12.7 Conclusion

International experience has shown that to achieve inclusive growth governments should strive to broaden SMEs' access to economic opportunities and to build the resilience of the most vulnerable against economic shocks. However, inclusive growth cannot be achieved in a country with high levels of financial exclusion. Policies to encourage the provision of financial services to the vast majority of the population in the rural areas should be implemented. As the country moves out of a decade of depressed economic activity, with the consequent slump in economic growth and development that forced most formal economic activities into the informal economy, promotion of and support for the development of SMEs and microfinance will be a key driver.

The need for the government to perform its facilitatory role efficiently and effectively cannot be overemphasized. The rehabilitation and development of run-down infrastructure should be undertaken, and public–private partnerships should be encouraged. The provision of finance for infrastructure development will depend on the availability of credit, which also relies on savings. One way of harnessing savings is to make banking services accessible to a majority of the population. In this regard, the financial-inclusion initiatives initiated by the RBZ in 2007 should be pursued vigorously. Respective stakeholders identified in the National Microfinance Policy should do their part to bring the poor and the rural communities into the formal banking system. Members of the Bankers' Association of Zimbabwe should consider reopening branches that were closed at the height of the financial crisis and adopt new, alternative delivery channels to widen access to financial services.

In the end, a combination of government initiatives and other stakeholders' participation in promoting financial inclusion will lead to an overall financial and economic development programme that facilitates inclusive, pro-poor growth.

## References

ACCION 2009. 'Accelerating financial inclusion through innovative channels', *InSight*, 27 (December) <http://resources.centerforfinancialinclusion.org/insight/IS27en.pdf>.

ADBI 2009. 'Promoting Financial Inclusion through Innovative Policies', proceedings of the workshop on Promoting Financial Inclusion through Innovative Policies, Asian Development Bank Institute, Tokyo, Japan, 31 March – 3 April.

Chandavarkar, A. 1990. *Macroeconomic Aspects, Foreign Flows and Domestic Savings Performance in Developing Countries: A 'State of the Art' Report*, (Paris: OECD Development Centre, Technical Paper, 11).

Chigumira, G. and N. Masiyandima 2001. 'Did Financial Sector Reforms Result in Increased Financial Savings for Lending to all Sectors of the Economy including the SMEs and the Poor?' (Harare: Unpublished paper for ILO Project on Financial Sector Reforms).

Cho, Y. J. and D. Khatkhate 1989. 'The Effects of Financial Liberalization on the Development of the Financial Market and the Allocation of Credit to Corporate Sectors: The Korean Case' (Washington, DC: World Bank, Development Research Department, Discussion Paper 166).

Demirgüç-Kunt A. 2008. *Finance and Economic Development: The Role of Government* (Washington, DC: World Bank).

Ernst & Young 2006. 'RBZ National Microfinance Survey and Proposed Legal and Regulatory Framework' (Harare: Ernst & Young).

Finhold 1995. *Zimbabwe Economic Review* (Harare: Zimbabwe Financial Holdings).

Frenkel, J. 1976. 'A monetary approach to the exchange rate: Doctrinal aspects and empirical evidence', *Scandinavian Journal of Economics*, 78, 200–24.

Green R. H. and X. Kadhani 1986. 'Zimbabwe: Transition to economic crisis: Retrospect and prospect', *World Development*, 14(8).

Hanke, S. H. and A. K. F. Kwok 2009. 'On the measurement of Zimbabwe's hyperinflation', *Cato Journal*, 29(2).

Harvey, C. 1998. 'The Limited Impact of Financial Sector Reforms in Zimbabwe' (mimeo).

Harvey, C. and C. Jenkins 1992. 'The Unorthodox Response of the South African Economy to changes in Macroeconomic Policy' (IDS Discussion Paper 300).

Helms, B. 2006. *Access for All: Building Inclusive Financial Systems* (Washington, DC: Consultative Group to Assist the Poor).

IMF 2005. *Zimbabwe: Selected Issues and Statistical Appendix* (Washington, DC: International Monetary Fund), <http://www.imf.org/external/pubs/ft/scr/2005/cr05359.pdf>.

IMF 2009. 'Statement at the Conclusion of an IMF Staff Mission to Zimbabwe', Press Release 09/249, <http://www.imf.org/external/np/sec/pr/2009/pr09249.htm>.

Kariuki, P. W. 1993. 'Interest Rate Liberalization and the Allocative Efficiency of Credit: Some Evidence from the Small and Medium-scale industry in Kenya' (Brighton: Sussex University, IDS, D.Phil. thesis).

McKinnon, R. I. 1973. *Money and Capital in Economic Development* (Washington, DC: The Brookings Institution).

Makina, D. 2007. 'Profiling Zimbabwean migrants in South Africa', *Africa News*, <http://www.africanews.com/site/Profiling_Zimbabwe_migrants_in_South_Africa/list_messages/11806>.

Makina, D. 2009. 'Recovery of the Financial Sector and Building Financial Inclusiveness' (Harare: UNDP, Comprehensive Economic Recovery in Zimbabwe, Working Paper 5).

Mohan, R. 2006. 'Economic Growth, Financial Deepening and Financial Inclusion', address given at the Annual Bankers' Conference 2006, Hyderabad, 3 November.

Mushayakarara, E. N. 1998. 'The "Banking Crisis" and the Current State of the Financial Services Industry', paper presented to Deloitte and Touché Senior Management, Nyanga, Zimbabwe.

Muzulu, J. 1993. 'Real Exchange Rate Depreciation and Structural Adjustment: The Case of the Manufacturing Sector in Zimbabwe (1980–1991)' (Brighton: University of Sussex, D.Phil. thesis).

Muzulu, J. 1994. 'The impact of currency depreciation on Zimbabwe's manufacturing sector', *Development Policy Review*, 12(2).

Muzulu, J. 1995. 'Financial Sector Policies for Sustainable Development', background paper to ZCTU 'Beyond ESAP' study.

Muzulu J. and T. Moyo 2002. 'Financial Sector Development in Zimbabwe', mimeo.

Nzotta, S. M. and E. J. Okereke 2009. 'Financial deepening and economic development of Nigeria: An empirical investigation', *African Journal of Accounting, Economics, Finance and Banking Research*, 5(5).

Quintyn, M. and M. W. Taylor 2004. *Should Financial Sector Regulators Be Independent?* (IMF: Washington, DC).

RBZ 2006. *Annual Report 2006* (Harare: Reserve Bank of Zimbabwe).

RBZ 2008. *National Microfinance Policy* (Harare: Reserve Bank of Zimbabwe).

RBZ 2009a. *January 2009 Monetary Policy Statement* (Harare: Reserve Bank of Zimbabwe).

RBZ 2009b. *The 2009 Mid-year Monetary Policy Statement* (Harare: Reserve Bank of Zimbabwe).

Robinson, P. 1987. *Trade and Financing Strategies for the New NICs: The Zimbabwean Case* (London: Overseas Development Institute).

Robinson P. 2006. 'Zimbabwe's Hyperinflation: The House is on Fire – But Does the Government Know it is Dousing the Flames with Petrol?' *Hintergrundinformationen aus der internationalen Entwicklungszusammenarbeit Afrika* (Bonn: Friedrich Ebert Stiftung), <http://library.fes.de/pdf-files/iez/03894.pdf>.

Shaw, E. S. 1973. *Financial Deepening in Economic Development* (New York: Oxford University Press).

Schumpeter, J. A. 1934. *The Theory of Economic Development* (Cambridge, MA: Harvard University Press).

Stoneman, C. 1989. 'The World Bank and the IMF in Zimbabwe', in, B. K. Campbell and J. Loxely (eds.), *Structural Adjustment in Africa* (Basingstoke: Macmillan).

UNDP 2008. *Comprehensive Economic Recovery in Zimbabwe: A Discussion Document* (Harare: United Nations Development Programme).

World Bank 1989. *World Development Report* (Washington, DC: World Bank).

ZCTU 1996. *Beyond ESAP: Framework for a Long-Term Development Strategy for Zimbabwe* (Harare: Zimbabwe Congress of Trade Unions).

Zimbabwe 1991. *Zimbabwe: A Framework for Economic Reform (1991–1995)* (Harare: Government Printer).

Zimbabwe 2009a. 'Short-Term Emergency Recovery Programme (STERP): Getting Zimbabwe Moving Again' (Harare: Ministry of Finance).

Zimbabwe 2009b. 'The 2010 National Budget Statement: Reconstruction with Equitable Growth and Stability' (Harare: Ministry of Finance).

## Chapter 13

# Synthesis: Beyond the Enclave

## 13.1 Summary of Zimbabwe's Economic Experience

### 13.1.1 The conceptual framework

Because Zimbabwe achieved its independence relatively later than other African countries, it was hoped that the country would draw lessons from others' experiences, build on the strengths and avoid the same mistakes; that it would break from its past colonial experiences, take advantage of good practices from elsewhere, and build a country that would become a beacon of Africa. As the analysis in this book has shown, Zimbabwe not only failed to learn from the past but eventually slipped into an unprecedented crisis, resulting in almost complete paralysis.

The main argument in this book is that the perennial problem of under-utilization of resources, especially labour, can be traced to the legacy of dualism and enclavity associated with the grafted type of capitalism that was carved out under colonialism.[1] Evolving social formations suggest the co-existence of the dominant capitalist and pre-capitalist modes of production that have been fused together in a rather uneasy and tenuous manner (grafted capitalism). From the capitalist perspective, pre-capitalist forms of work constitute non-productive labour in that the labour is not profit-oriented. From a market, and therefore capitalist, point of view, under-employment manifests itself as non-productive labour in that it is not harnessed by capital for accumulation. The capitalist part of the economy is the formal sector, while the pre-capitalist part is the non-formal (informal and subsistence) sector. The non-formal sector therefore accommodates the remnant of pre-capitalist forms of production (non-productive labour).

An important requirement for development under capitalism is the need to capture non-productive labour into its realm of operation; in this way, a dynamic impulse is imparted to social relations based on the imperative to accumulate. Thus, the disruption of pre-capitalist relations imparts to a country the potential of internally driven growth. The issue is that, while both developed and developing countries have elements of both productive and non-productive labour, it is the predominance of non-productive labour that constitutes the

---

[1] See Chapter 1. This analysis draws heavily from ZCTU (1996) and ANSA (2006). The ideas were borrowed from the work of the late Prof. Guy Mhone, who contributed extensively to these studies (Mhone, 2000).

major problem in developing countries. In other words, the tragedy in most African economies is that the majority of its labour force, mainly women, are trapped in pre-capitalist forms of production that are not driven by the need to employ labour to generate profit and the further expansion of capital. Thus, the low resource absorptive capacity of African economies is related to the enclave growth emanating from the structural legacy of economic dualism, which explains the vicious cycle of perpetual underemployment that afflicts the majority of the labour force, and especially women.

Apart from the underutilization of resources, and especially labour, another legacy of colonialism is the absence of an internal (endogenous) dynamism for growth and transformation, since the economies are dependent on, and constrained by, external factors. This lack of an internal dynamism is reflected in the following:

- *Demand deficiency:* An enclave economy is limited by its very nature: the existence of a large segment of the labour force engaged in low productivity implies that effective demand is low.
- *Limited internal savings:* The fact that a majority of the labour force lives close to subsistence level implies that they cannot save, and when they do, their savings are not captured through financial intermediation, hence the reliance on foreign investment and foreign aid which pre-empts the need for self-generated savings.
- *Asymmetry between national, regional and international growth and development needs:* As a consequence of the above problems, African countries find themselves in a dilemma whereby disarticulations at national level, coupled with external dependency, militate against effective regional co-operation and national development as well.
  In the absence of an internally motivated and conscious process of transformation, the growth process would not only marginalize the majority of the labour force but would also marginalize the developing country itself in the international arena.

A consequence of this structural deformity is that trickle-down effects from the formal sector are too weak to transform and absorb non-formal sectors into formal activities. The market forces on their own would simply perpetuate this dualism, even in the presence of some growth, implying the need for a proactive role on the part of the state in order to integrate the non-formal economy and endogenize the growth process in a manner that allows the majority of the labour force to engage in productive activities.

Using this conceptual framework of dualism and enclavity, this book has demonstrated how this structural distortion was entrenched, eventually becoming an albatross around the government's neck, and culminating in a loss of confidence in and support for the political parties that had spearheaded the struggle for independence and who had ruled until the Inclusive Government was formed in 2009. Tellingly, no less than ten economic blueprints were launched after independence, yet the policies implemented bore little resemblance to those promulgated. For much of the post-independence period, government was more concerned with crisis management than with following a well-mapped-out development strategy. As the ZCTU (1996: 89) pointed out, 'an analysis of the policies adopted in the 1980s does not give one a single teleological goal for the country's development'. Indeed, this can be said of all the three decades since independence.

### 13.1.2 The first decade of independence, 1980–1990

While the first decade of independence started promisingly, with government adopting the aptly titled policy of *Growth with Equity* in 1981, failure to achieve robust growth during that decade meant that the commendable social programmes pursued (especially in education and health) could not be sustained into the 1990s. During this period, investment levels remained depressed, result-ing in stunted growth, increased unemployment and other social deficits. As a result, government latched on to the diametrically opposite programme of ESAP, with its formulaic reliance on market forces, on the recommendation of the World Bank and IMF.

### 13.1.3 The ESAP period, 1991–1996

Predictably, the ESAP programme failed to revive the economy and address the social deficits that emanated largely from the structural deformity inherent in a dual and enclave economy. As the chief economist at the World Bank in Harare at the time, Kapil Kapoor, admitted towards the end of the programme, relying on exchange-rate depreciation to achieve a structural shift towards exports was misplaced, as successful exporting requires 'the upgrading of export infrastructure, the provision of export finance, and the development of market intelligence' (Kapoor, 1995: 4). In this regard, we may conclude with Kapoor that, 'given the weak implementation capacity in African economies ... structural adjustment programs, in general, have unrealistic expectations about how fast adjustment can occur; consequently, the political costs of speedier implementation are also often underestimated' (1995: 3).

In addition, ESAP maintained the bias in favour of the formal sector, mean-ing that the majority of the people remained locked in the non-formal sector (communal and informal), where economic activities are of the survival type. Not surprisingly therefore, the number of households living in poverty increased from 40.4 per cent in 1990/91 to 63.3 per cent in 1995/96 (Zimbabwe, 1998). As the World Bank (1995: 10) observed, ESAP 'entailed considerable pain but little visible gain'. The same World Bank document goes on to suggest that, 'unless the programme is seen to be generating benefits for everybody in Zimbabwe, it might not be possible to follow through with and maintain the momentum of many of the recent policy changes. This will require dealing more effectively with poverty and with the social dimensions of adjustment' (1995: 18). A critical learning point from ESAP was that 'the Zimbabwe case demonstrates the importance of popular ownership and participation throughout the process of adjustment. An open, transparent dialogue can help generate realistic expectations, reduce uncertainty, and contribute to a unified sense of national ownership for reforms' (ibid.).

### 13.1.4 The crisis period, 1997–2008

The painful experiences with ESAP, the resultant discord within government, and in particular the rise of civil society as a countervailing force in the mid-1990s threw the government's plans to extend ESAP into a quandary. What emerged after the crisis began in 1997 can hardly be described as a coherent and credible set of policies as government resorted to populism, implementing knee-jerk policies on the spur of the moment. A penchant for unbudgeted expenditures emerged, beginning with the award of a gratuity and pension to each of the 50,000-strong war veterans at the end of 1997, and followed by the entry into the DRC war in August 1998, among others. As a result, the budget deficit, which had been targeted to decline to 3.8 per cent of GDP by the end of 2000, shot up from about 6 per cent in 1998 to about 18 per cent by the end of 2000.[2]

Instructively, from the new millennium, all government policies were short-term, of one year's duration, as crisis management took effect. Worse still, policy inconsistencies and reversals, institutional overlap and decay, degradation and collapse of infrastructure, severe human-resources deficits emanating from out-migration, and serious governance deficits conspired to achieve an unprecedented eleven years of persistent economic decline between 1997 and 2008. During the period of negative economic growth (1999–2008), the economy declined by a cumulative 51 per cent.

The unchecked extensive role of the state during this period, reflected in unsustainable budget deficits and an unmanageable public-sector debt (foreign and domestic), resulted in off-budget, quasi-fiscal activities by the Reserve Bank of Zimbabwe. The lack of transparency and accountability in the conduct of state affairs promoted clientelism, patronage and populism, with corruption emerging as a serious vice. Unsurprisingly, these policies resulted in the destruction of the economic base, with government resorting to printing money to sustain itself, which in turn generated hyperinflation and the paralysis of 2007 and 2008.

[2] See Chapter 2.

The exchange-rate system was volatile and unpredictable, characterized by multiple exchange rates and rapid dollarization as the local currency collapsed. The productive sector faced a litany of problems, including lack of secure and predictable property rights, a rapidly worsening shortage of skills arising from out-migration, a hostile investment climate, acute shortages of essential inputs – especially fuel, raw materials and intermediate inputs – uncertain agricultural land rights, land-tenure insecurity, inadequate and dilapidated productive infra-structure, inefficient and subsidy-dependent public enterprises, diminished inter-national competitiveness, and gross capacity underutilization (UNDP, 2008).

The paralysis that followed was demonstrated in the collapse of the formal sector and the resurgence of the informal economy, which became the dominant segment of the economy such that four out of five jobs in Zimbabwe had been informalized by 2004 (Luebker, 2008). This process of destruction also saw the obliteration of the middle class, as poverty became pervasive, implying that this spectre of the 'missing middle' will also need to be addressed (Simpson and Ndlela, 2010). The inter-linkages between the sectors, especially between agriculture and manufacturing, were decimated through the fast-track land-reform programme, which began a worsening disarticulation of the economy and wrenching structural changes that will have far-reaching consequences for recovery.

The height of this destruction was the wanton implementation of the 'clean up' Operation Murambatsvina in May 2005 that targeted the informal economy and resulted in 700,000 people losing their homes, sources of livelihood, or both, with a further 2.4 million people indirectly affected (UN, 2005). The follow-up Operation Garikai/Hlalani Kuhle, which sought to construct housing and workshop facilities for those affected, could not rectify the impact of this man-made tsunami. Luebker (2008) found that in one of the hubs of the informal economy targeted by Operation Murambatsvina, Glen View in Harare, a meagre 2.5 per cent of the two-thirds that were affected were assisted.

At this stage, the state could no longer provide basic services, matching the description of a failed or fragile state with a huge dose of cronyism. The sorry state of sanitation resulted in a nationwide outbreak of cholera in 2008, at a time when hospitals, clinics and the education system had ground to a halt as a result of a lack of material and human resources. Thus, the re-emergence of hitherto controlled diseases (malaria, cholera and TB) while the HIV and AIDS pandemic was taking a huge toll on the economy generated unprecedented levels of social distress, which were worsened by recurrent food shortages associated with the fast-track land-reform programme. Public-sector employees, in particular, could no longer go to work because their salaries did not cover their transport costs, leading to the collapse of service delivery when it was needed most.

The cost of the descent into lawlessness, with deteriorating governance indi-cators, was the estrangement of Zimbabwe from traditional development partners and processes, with dire consequences to the economy and populace. Zimbabwe's isolation from the 'mainstream' of international development effectively reduced it to pariah status. Not even the so-called friends of the country would help, hence the failure of the 'Look East' policy. Migrant remittances, which are counter-cyclical, provided much-needed social protection at a projected US$1.4 billion by the end of 2009 (Makina and Kanyenze, 2010).[3] In the short to medium term, the economy will rely increasingly on mineral exports, implying a need for greater transparency and accountability in the way such resources are managed and utilized.

### 13.1.5 The transitional period, 2009–2010

The hung parliament that emerged in the 2008 elections and the contested outcome of the presidential run-off in June 2008 saw the main political parties negotiating a Global Political Agreement (GPA) in September 2008, which resulted in the formation of the Inclusive Government in February 2009. The lack of credibility of the local currency resulted in the adoption of a multiple-currency regime towards the end of January 2009, which effectively stabilized the economy by killing hyperinflation. In the event, Zimbabwe experienced deflation during 2009, which averaged –7.7 per cent for the year.

However, the optimism that had followed the formation of the Inclusive Government and the adoption of the Short-Term Economic Recovery Programme (STERP) in March 2009 was compromised by a lack of progress in implementing the GPA. In the event, recovery remained fragile, especially in the context of limited fiscal space, policy inconsistencies, and the absence of sufficient progress to convince the sceptical international community on re-engagement. Systems to promote and support the aid business (e.g. a credible Tender Board and aid-management systems) had not been put in place. Furthermore, successful implementation of STERP required the mobilization of US$8.4 billion, a task that proved elusive as pledges amounted to only around US$500 million, targeting mainly humanitarian assistance.

Recovery efforts were also hampered by the emergence of the global recession triggered by the sub-prime-mortgage crisis in the USA in August 2007, the worst since the Great Depression of the 1930s. The slump in global demand led to a collapse in commodity prices. Sources of funding, including foreign direct investment, lines of credit and migrant remittances were projected to decline significantly, with the duration and depth of the recession dependent on the efficacy of the stimulus monetary and fiscal-support measures.

The global crisis came at a time when Zimbabwe was already experiencing a

---

[3] A study of the remittance strategies of Zimbabweans living in Northern England by Magunha *et al.* (2009) estimated that US$0.94 billion was sent from the UK alone in 2007.

worsening balance-of-payments deficit, from US$33 million in 2007 to US$410 million in 2008. Exports declined from US$762.02 million between 1 January and 1 July 2008 to US$475.52 million over same period in 2009, a decline of 37.6 per cent. Thus, the global crisis magnified the recovery challenge that Zimbabwe was facing, suggesting that much-needed external support might not be forthcoming at the levels required when re-engagement takes place (RBZ, 2009).

## 13.2 Lessons from Current International Development Thinking

Just as the Zimbabwean crisis was emerging in the late 1990s, there was a major rethink of the international development discourse, resulting in far-reaching changes to international aid architecture. This therefore implies that, if Zimbabwe is to be a credible, effective and strategic partner, it has to invest in understanding the latest developments in international development thinking. Mastery of these will help the country ride on their crest and leverage international development space to meet the strategic interests of the country in the international arena. If a country fails to take advantage of them, the development discourse will be based on others' interpretation of these processes, procedures and frameworks.

### 13.2.1 A balanced approach that integrates economic and social objectives

At the Social Summit on Social Development held in Copenhagen in 1995, world leaders noted with concern the rising social deficits, reaffirming the goal of attaining full employment and hence an integrated vision of development that incorporated economic and social objectives as equally important. The ILO took the issue further by adopting the Declaration on Fundamental Principles and Rights at Work at the International Labour Conference in June 1998. This was followed by the adoption of the Decent Work Agenda at the 87th Session of the ILO International Labour Conference in 1999. Likewise, at the September 1999 Board meetings, the IMF and World Bank introduced Poverty Reduction Strategy Papers (PRSPs) as their new lending programmes. As discussed in Chapter 1, PRSPs had to be government-led but prepared with the participation of key national stakeholders to engender broad-based ownership. However, the imposition of a macroeconomic framework that maintained the old mantra of 'stabilize, privatize and liberalize' led to criticism that the programme was not fundamentally different from preceding SAP policies.[4]

At the Millennium Summit of September 2000, 189 heads of state and government adopted the UN Millennium Declaration, which put employment creation and poverty reduction (and its eradication) at the heart of development policies, to be implemented through the eight MDGs. This marked a departure from the focus of the past on conventional approaches to development (such as

---

[4] See Chapter 1.

structural adjustment programmes) that were preoccupied with achieving macro-economic stability through fiscal and inflation targets at the expense of growth, employment and poverty reduction.[5]

In this new paradigm, the role of labour markets, and decent employment in particular, were acknowledged as the intermediary (nexus) between growth and poverty reduction. In this regard, a development strategy that fully employs a country's human resources and raises the returns to labour is considered a powerful tool for poverty reduction/eradication. Within this framework, growth is seen as a necessary but insufficient condition to generate significant improvements in employment and poverty reduction. For growth to be equitable (shared, inclusive) and contribute towards sustainable poverty reduction, it must be mediated through policies that strengthen individual capabilities and, in particular, create opportunities for poor people so that they, too, can contribute towards and benefit from the growth process.[6] In this regard, human development is both an 'output' of growth and one of its most important inputs.

Since the launch of the first global *Human Development Report* in 1990, the UNDP has popularized the concept of sustainable human development (SHD) which puts people at the centre of the development process, creating an enabling environment where people can enjoy long, healthy and creative lives.[7] In the context of SHD, growth is a means rather than an end in itself. What is critical for human well-being is the quality of growth, not just its quantity, hence the concept of pro-poor, broad-based and inclusive growth. SHD questions the presumed automatic link between expanding income and expanding human choices, arguing that such a link depends on the quality and distribution of economic growth. The link between growth and human well-being has to be created consciously through deliberate public policy such as public spending on social services and fiscal policy to redistribute income and assets. This link may not exist in the marketplace, which can further marginalize the poor. Thus, development is the sustained elevation of an entire society towards a better and more humane life.

Three core values capture the essence of development and represent the common goals sought by all individuals and societies: life sustenance (the ability to provide basic necessities – food, shelter, health, protection), self-esteem (a sense of worth and self-respect) and freedom (to be able to choose). This way of looking at development therefore implies a more holistic approach, emphasizing the building of people's human capabilities, translating the benefits of growth into people's lives, and ensuring that the people themselves actively participate

---

[5] The stabilization trap – see Chapter 7.

[6] See Chapter 7.

[7] See Chapter 1.

in processes that shape their destiny. It has implications for the state, which is expected to play a leading and strategic role in expanding capabilities and opportunities and ensuring that growth is broad-based and inclusive. It implies a human-rights approach as a critical aspect of it. Thus, governments must create an enabling environment to improve empowerment, co-operation, equity, sustainability and security.

As highlighted in Chapter 7, three factors are critical for sustainable poverty reduction – the growth factor, the elasticity factor and the integrability factor. This therefore suggests that for growth to be poverty-reducing it needs to be broad-based and inclusive, implying a need to address issues of marginalization, vulnerability and capability-deprivation up front as a prerequisite for shared growth outcomes. To achieve this requires the adoption of supply-side interventions (active labour-market policy programmes) and other social interventions that influence the quality of labour supply and demand.

This new approach was domesticated on the African continent at the Ouaga-dougou extraordinary meeting of heads of state and government in September 2004. At this summit, regional economic communities were tasked with assisting member states to develop national employment policy frameworks as a basis for poverty reduction. The Decent Work Agenda in Africa (2007–2015) was adopted by the social partners – government, business and labour – at the 11th African regional meeting of the ILO held in Addis Ababa in April 2007. At the 97th Session in June 2008, the ILO adopted the Declaration on Social Justice for a Fair Globalization, which institutionalizes the Decent Work Agenda as the key policy and operational concept of the ILO.

The Declaration is a commitment 'to place full and productive employment and decent work at the centre of economic and social policies'. It emphasizes the need for policy coherence for sustainable development between social, environmental and economic objectives: the need for a holistic, integrated and balanced approach in support of decent work. This effectively places employment at the heart of economic policies and calls for new partnerships with non-state actors.

### 13.2.2 Lessons from the past: New insights from the World Bank

Meanwhile, with the benefit of hindsight, and more than two decades after their introduction, the World Bank came up with a damning indictment of structural adjustment programmes, as highlighted in its 2005 report on *Economic Growth in the 1990s* and *The Growth Report* of 2008, both of which were quoted extensively in Chapter 1 (World Bank, 2005 and 2008). These two documents rightly observed that the successful East Asian economies employed diverse policies and advised against formulaic approaches, highlighting the importance of country-based experimentation and learning. In essence, the success stories had had to discover for themselves, through trial and error, a process of 'self-discovery' which was helped along by the government's hand.

These two documents acknowledge that common to all economic success stories is the fulfilment of four functions: rapid accumulation of capital, efficient resource allocation, technological progress, and sharing of the benefits of growth, implying the need for a balanced approach to development. The policy ingredients of growth strategies from the successful reformers were distilled in *The Growth Report* as falling into several loose categories: accumulation, innovation, allocation, stabilization and inclusion. Under 'accumulation' is the need for strong public investment, which helps to accumulate the infrastructure and skills needed for sustained growth. Innovation and imitation speak to the importance of learning to do new things, such as venturing into unfamiliar export industries, and to do things in new ways. The successful reformers also avoided 'big bang' approaches to economic and governance reforms, employing a more pragmatic approach, referred in the report as 'strategic incrementalism', which implies exploiting the willingness to reform, being grounded in political realities, and being consistent with the country's capacity constraints. In addition, credible, sustainable reforms depend on the checks and balances provided through political institutions.

Equity and equality of opportunity were flagged as essential ingredients of sustainable growth strategies, the former being outcomes or results, the latter referring to starting points. In the words of the report, 'The Commission strongly believes that growth strategies cannot succeed without a commitment to equality of opportunity, giving everyone a fair chance to enjoy the fruits of growth' (World Bank, 2008: 7).

The importance of political leadership and sound governance, credible commitment to growth, credible commitment to inclusion, and capable administration are also emphasized in *The Growth Report*. It notes that successful cases share this aspect: an increasingly capable, credible and committed government. Such leadership requires patience, a long planning horizon, and an unwavering focus on the goal of inclusive growth. As pointed out in Chapter 1, strong technocratic teams, focused on long-term growth, are another feature of successful cases. In the words of the Commission:

> In recent decades governments were advised to 'stabilize, privatize and liberalize'. There is merit in what lies behind this injunction – governments should not try to do too much, replacing markets or closing the economy off from the rest of the world. But we believe this prescription defines the role of government too narrowly. Just because governments are sometimes clumsy and sometimes errant does not mean they should be written out of the script. On the contrary, as the economy grows and develops, active, pragmatic governments have crucial roles to play' (World Bank, 2008: 5).

As they emphasize, a coherent growth strategy will therefore set priorities, deciding where to devote a government's energies and resources.

The role of the state will loom large in Zimbabwe's recovery and development, especially given the extent of state failure. The characteristics of fragile or failed states are evident in Zimbabwe,[8] and exhibit the following:

- State structures lack political will and or capacity to provide the basic functions needed for poverty reduction, development and to safeguard the security and human rights of their population.
- Susceptible to crisis in one or more of its sub-systems.
- Vulnerable to internal and external shocks and domestic and international conflicts.
- Internecine conflicts and conflagration.
- Institutional arrangements embody and preserve the conditions of crisis, such as inequality.
- Lack political cohesion.
- Lack credibility.
- Lack governance capacity.
- Centralization of decision-making.
- Weak state or political institutions.
- Lack will/capacity to create economic opportunities for citizens.
- Fail to provide basic services.
- Lack forward development momentum, hence generate a lot of human suffering.
- Have spill-over effects that impact on development prospects elsewhere.[9]

The real danger is that it is easy to recommend a minimalist role for the state to counteract state failure, yet market failures are real and should also be addressed. In this regard, a strategic role for the state needs to be mapped out along the lines discussed above.

In a nutshell, the main message of *The Growth Report* was succinctly summarized by the renowned economist Edmar Bacha as follows: 'The three "dos" for growth that I care most about in the report are economic openness, social inclusiveness, and effective governments. The message can be spelled out equally well in three "don'ts": inwardness, exclusion, and bloated governments – a recipe for stagnation' (World Bank, 2008: 24).

Notwithstanding these positive developments, the lending programmes of the international financial institutions are still steeped in the traditional mode. Even though a shift has been made from the Washington Consensus to the

---

[8] Fragile states are poor countries with weak state structures and/or whose legitimacy is challenged; see <http://www.bbc.co.uk/blogs/theeditors/2010/02/fragile_states_and_internation.html>.

[9] See Claire Mcloughlin, *Topic Guide on Fragile States* (Birmingham: Governance and Social Development Resource Centre, 2010), <http://www.gsdrc.org/go/topic-guides/fragile-states>.

Augmented Washington Consensus, the strategy entails adding institutional and governance reforms (institutional fundamentalism) on to the traditional requirements (stabilize, privatize and liberalize). As Rodrik (2006 and 2007) argues, this stretches the limited capacity of developing countries; furthermore, it retains the discredited 'one size fits all' formulaic approach to development.

### 13.2.3 International debt-relief framework

Since issues of debt relief will feature prominently in Zimbabwe's recovery efforts, it is important that there is an understanding of the international debt-relief framework so that the country is adequately prepared for debt negotiations. Of note is that all countries seeking assistance (debt relief) under the Highly Indebted Poor Country (HIPC) initiative are required to have a PRSP, or an interim one, in place by the decision point.[10] As discussed in Chapter 1, at the 2005 summit of the G8 countries, it was proposed that the IMF, World Bank and AfDB cancel 100 per cent of the debt of countries that had reached (or would reach) completion point under the HIPC initiative; debt accumulated prior to the end of 2004 was covered under this Multilateral Debt Relief Initiative. While the reduction in debt-servicing requirements increased poverty-reducing spending through enhanced fiscal space arising from debt relief, evidence suggests that countries have not made significant improvements in domestic resource mobilization and that export performance did not improve. In addition, given that international debt-relief efforts were meant to ensure a permanent exit from rescheduling, some slippage is evident. As reported in Chapter 1, of the thirteen post-completion countries for which data were available in 2005, external debt sustainability deteriorated in eleven cases, with eight above HIPC thresholds.

As assessment of international debt-relief efforts suggests that they are not in themselves sufficient to achieve export diversification, enhance national debt-management capacity or the ability to deal with shocks (Simpson and Doré, 2009). This therefore suggests that Zimbabwe needs to negotiate its debt in a more strategic manner. A resource audit may constitute a useful starting point, which includes a national debt audit as a basis for developing a national strategy that will form the basis for negotiations with creditors.

### 13.2.4 The international aid architecture

The latest developments in aid architecture suggest a shift in aid delivery from project-based approaches towards programme-based strategies through which support to the various sectors is channelled via Sector-Wide Approaches and the national budget of partner countries (see Chapter 1). Since 2005, donor-partner relations have been guided by the Paris Principles: ownership (partnering

---

[10] A detailed discussion of the processes involved can be found in Simpson and Doré (2009).

government leadership and country ownership of development programmes), alignment (donor support based on partner countries' national development strategies and priorities), harmonization (donors use common arrangements in the areas of planning, funding, disbursement, monitoring and reporting), managing for results, and mutual accountability.

Clearly, therefore, the partner country has to take responsibility and leadership, with donors playing a supportive role, which requires diligence, capacity, credible management systems, and good management skills on the part of the partner country, in this case Zimbabwe. In addition, it requires a culture of broad-based participation by key stakeholders, including parliamentary oversight to engender national ownership of development programmes. This is indeed a far cry from past experiences, where governments would act without the active participation of their legislators and non-state actors.

### 13.2.5 Evidence-based policies
A recurring observation throughout the analysis in this book is that, as the crisis deepened, government policies were driven more by expedience than evidence. As a result, not only did the quality of national data deteriorate at the turn of the millennium but it also became highly politicized. Even when inflation data were available, they would not be published: hence the latest inflation data before 2009 were for July 2008. The latest employment data are for 2003; a new labour force survey is overdue, and so is an update study on poverty. *The Growth Report* emphasized the importance of undertaking growth and poverty diagnostics as a basis for understanding the factors behind growth and development. Zimbabwe therefore needs a new data set covering key economic and social variables, on the basis of which policies can be formulated.

### 13.2.6 Financing sustainable human development: Fiscal space
An important issue in financing SHD is the creation of 'fiscal space' – 'concrete policy actions for enhancing domestic resource mobilization, and the reforms necessary to secure the enabling governance, institutional and economic environment for these policies to be effective' (Roy *et al.*, 2009c: 6). This definition goes beyond that of the international financial institutions, which sees fiscal space as the availability of budgetary room to provide resources for desired purposes without prejudicing government's financial position or solvency.

As noted in Chapter 1, the 'fiscal space' discussion is a recognition of a conflict between the desire to use the state to lift as many people as possible out of poverty and the need for prudent economic management to achieve inclusive development. Conventional approaches to fiscal restraint focus on the intertemporal budget constraint, insisting that an expansion of public expenditure should not compromise short-term macroeconomic stability, thus failing to address the link between fiscal policy and growth. This reflects the tension between securing fiduciary and developmental outcomes, with policy-makers resolving this conflict by making one payback (developmental) contingent upon satisfactory fulfilment of the other (fiduciary).

By focusing narrowly on solvency as measured by the ratio of debt to GDP, IMF programmes ignore the longer-term supply-side effects of higher public expenditure. They underestimate the long-term payback to fiscal sustainability from the implementation of a transformational development strategy. In this case, the short term continues to act as a binding constraint on the long term as it ignores the positive endogenous effects of additional public investment on solvency and stability. The observed decline in ratios of public investment, especially in infrastructure, to GDP is a result of the inappropriateness of the evaluation criteria used by international financial institutions which insist that borrowing countries meet strict fiscal targets that do not make the requisite distinction between recurrent and capital expenditure (Roy *et al.*, 2009b).

On political grounds, governments find it easier to protect current programmes than capital projects. Cuts in public investment were not compensated for by private investment as expected. Moreover, the relationship between public and private investment is complementary rather than conflictual since public investment can 'crowd in' private investment. Countries whose macroeconomic frameworks included strong public-investment strategies achieved substantial and stable economic growth with high poverty elasticities, while those that sought to achieve deficit targets without reference to growth and poverty objectives experienced economic stagnation. Not only are the levels of spending important, but also what the government is spending its resources on (Roy *et al.*, 2009a).

The fiscal diamond is a diagnostic tool used to widen government's policy options (Roy *et al.*, 2009a).[11] It also helps to identify the endogenous and exogenous, short-term and long-term nature of the available options. The fiscal instruments for creating fiscal space include: i) overseas development assistance through aid and debt relief; ii) domestic revenue mobilization through improved tax administration and tax-policy reforms; iii) deficit financing through domestic or external borrowing; and iv) reprioritization and raising the efficiency of expenditures. A fiscal rule that distinguishes between current and capital expenditures will ensure that fiscal restraint does not discourage growth in the aggregate public capital stock. In such a case, the current budget deficit/surplus is viewed as the logical indicator to use, with a zero current deficit an important long-term policy target for fiscal responsibility.

A diagnostic tool such as the fiscal diamond is indeed relevant to understanding the financing options for recovery and unleashing a transformative growth and

---

[11] See Chapter 2.

development agenda in Zimbabwe. Given the restricted options available in the absence of the re-engagement of the international community and the narrow tax base, Zimbabwe needs to focus carefully on how it can create the required fiscal space for short-term recovery and the medium- to long-term imperatives of identifying a pro-poor growth path.

## 13.3 Strategic Objectives and Thrusts, and Recovery and SHD policies

### 13.3.1 Strategic objectives and thrusts
On the basis of the foregoing analysis, and on the principle of logical derivation from such analyses, the key broad strategic objectives and thrusts would be as follows:[12]

- Consolidate macroeconomic stability by restoring the rule of law, bringing to closure the land issue, and enhance fiscal space by, among other things, re-engaging the international community, adopting a sustainable debt strategy, restructuring state-owned enterprises.
- Adopt a holistic approach to development, integrating economic and social objectives (pro-poor, inclusive growth and human-centred development).
- Create the basis for evidence-based policy-making by enhancing national data collection, analysis and collation.
- Rebuild and strengthen the role of the state as a basis for transforming it into a developmental state and promote good governance.
- Expand and strengthen the national institutional framework for broad-based stakeholder participation in decision-making, implementation, monitoring and evaluation.

### 13.3.2 Broad recovery and SHD policy measures

*Consolidate macroeconomic stability*
While the introduction of the multiple-currency regime stabilized the macro-economy by immediately killing off hyperinflation, further work remains to be done to strengthen the rule of law, bringing to closure the land issue by under-taking a land audit through an independent Land Commission.

An important outstanding challenge is the need to enhance fiscal space. In the short to medium term, this could be achieved by focusing on reprioritizing and enhancing the efficiency of expenditure and re-engaging the international community. As domestic revenues recover with growth, the country will

---

[12] The macro and sector-specific objectives, thrusts, and recovery and SHD policies appear in the relevant chapters; only the more generic ones are covered here.

hopefully be in a position to reduce its dependence on external assistance. It is therefore critical that an exit strategy be developed so that Zimbabwe is not dependent on external assistance in the long term (aid obsolescence strategy). A critical component of the strategy to enhance fiscal space will be the negotiation of the country's debt, based on the results of a national resource audit that includes an audit of the national debt, and the strengthening of debt contraction and management systems. As recommended by the UNDP (2008), it is also necessary to develop a national aid policy framework, with the participation of civil society and parliament.[13]

### Adopt a holistic SHD policy framework with a pro-poor, inclusive approach

In line with the latest trends in development thinking and aid architecture, it is important that Zimbabwe develops an SHD strategy that is pro-poor and inclusive. In such a strategy, economic and social objectives are integrated into a coherent, pro-poor approach. Such a human-centred approach to development is also informed by a human-rights framework, where decent work, food security, health care, education, housing, basic utilities (water, electricity and sanitation), infrastructure (including transport), and an adequate standard of living form the core of the strategy.[14]

Furthermore, this strategy is employment-intensive and explores the use of employment-enhancing strategies such as value chains and channels, clusters and other business-networking strategies in all sectors of the economy. The existing SME policy framework should be a central component of this employment-intensive strategy. This approach is contained in the National Employment Policy Framework adopted by the Tripartite Negotiating Forum (TNF) in July 2009, which, at the time of writing, is awaiting Cabinet approval.[15] As a basic requirement for operationalizing this approach, all key sectors should develop employment-intensive strategies based on this framework.

The rapid improvement of human development indicators through the adoption and implementation of human development strategies across all ministries, as well as the design and operationalization of social safety nets, is a useful starting point. More fundamentally, an SHD approach should consciously seek to transform the inherent enclave and dualistic structure of the economy by adopting an integrability (active labour-market policy) programme and enhancing an inclusive approach in all sectors of the economy.

The education and training system needs to be reformed such that it is

---

[13] These issues were developed in detail in Chapter 2.

[14] These rights are enshrined in such international law instruments as the UN Charter, the UN International Covenant on Economic, Social and Cultural Rights, and the African Charter on Human and Peoples' Rights. In countries such as Brazil and South Africa, they are included in a Bill of Rights in the Constitution.

[15] See Chapter 7.

more demand-driven to ensure better fit between skills demand and supply. At the level of tertiary education, this is done by establishing a stakeholder-driven national training authority funded by a restructured ZIMDEF, and, in the arena of human capital, it is also important to develop and implement a policy framework for return migration and a mechanism for harnessing the skills of those in the diaspora.[16] The provision and maintenance of social infrastructure is also an important component of a pro-poor strategy. The development of such a strategy through stakeholder participation should be the basis for re-engaging international partners, who now insist on the Paris Principles of national ownership of programmes, alignment with national programmes, harmonization of donor support, managing for results, and mutual accountability.

### Evidence-based policies

A break with the past, when policies were based more on expedience than evidence, should be hastened. This requires the production of timeous, quality data, so the process of creating an autonomous Central Statistical Office should be speeded up to wean it from political interference. In addition, key economic and social indicators should be developed: the labour-force and poverty surveys need to be updated as a basis for inclusive recovery. Given the focus on poverty reduction/eradication, it is imperative that the national poverty analysis capacity be strengthened.

### Transform the state's role into a developmental one, and promote good governance

As argued above, Zimbabwe exhibits the characteristics of a fragile or failed state. Fragile states can be strengthened through some of the following measures:
- Enhancing stability by jointly addressing sources of conflict and stress.[17]
- Improving security by providing an environment that enhances personal safety.
- Co-ordinated national stakeholder approach, with international stakeholders playing a supportive role.
- Promoting inclusive decision-making.
- Developing the capacity of institutions to respond effectively to citizens' needs.
- Identifying strategic priorities that can provide quick wins.
- Provision of basic services, especially targeted to the poorest and most vulnerable groups.
- Inculcation of a culture of tolerance of diverse opinions.

[16] See Chapter 8.

[17] For example, the Kadoma Declaration on the Country Risk Factor in Zimbabwe, adopted by the Tripartite Negotiating Forum and launched by the President in February 2010.

- Encouraging reform related to the conditions that are driving fragility that will increase the likelihood of long-term stability.
- Promoting learning from countries that have experienced similar challenges, and drawing from institutions that focus on rebuilding fragile states (sub-regional bodies, UN agencies, etc.).
- Engaging in peace-building activities for all key stakeholders.
- Promoting public–private partnerships to deliver basic services.[18]

Given the politicization and decay of national institutions in Zimbabwe, there is an urgent need to reform them so that they can be made efficient and effective. The process of reviewing these institutions should incorporate thorough investigations into areas of institutional overlap, and audits such as the ongoing human-resources audit. What should inform this process of reforming and strengthening public institutions is a strategic review of the role of the state. Employees of such institutions, including the public sector, should be properly trained, with key staff trained in results-based management and budgeting. Thus, efficient government would require a strategic-planning capacity based on sound scientific and technical knowledge.

In line with the World Bank (2008), Rodrik (2006 and 2007), ANSA (2006), and the ZCTU (1996), among others, the proposed role of the state is neither minimal nor extensive but, rather, a strategic one. While ensuring macroeconomic stability, as required in traditional approaches, the state is expected to intervene in the economy purposefully as follows:

- To resolve market failures and rigidities related to ownership of and access to productive assets such as land, finance and human capital.
- To augment the market where such markets fail to arise or fail to allocate resources in a manner that maximizes net social welfare, such as when market indicators channel investment into unproductive or speculative investment and consumption activities.
- Where the market has indicated prospects for growth but is unable to exploit opportunities owing to specific constraints, to intervene in a manner that is market-friendly in order to resolve these constraints.
- When the market is failing to realize specific opportunities in the domestic and foreign markets, to intervene to lead the market by providing supply-side incentives that will entice the private sector to undertake such activities. These incentives should be time-bound (ZCTU, 1996: 18–19).

In intervening in this way, the state should not attempt to substitute the market by engaging in activities that could be undertaken by the private sector.

---

[18] See Mcloughlin, *Topic Guide on Fragile States* (fn. 9).

Its interventions must be targeted, without unduly distorting the macroeconomic environment, in such a way that it supports 'learning by doing' (self-discovery); with such an approach, partnerships between the state, the private sector and civil society become a critical aspect.[19] The explicit aim of such interventions is to maximize net social benefits and not to promote partisan interests.

Furthermore, the policy formulation, implementation and monitoring process should be transparent and consultative, implying a need for government to treat stakeholders as partners in development (ZCTU, 1996: 19). The creation of a dynamic, participatory and radical democracy, which regards people's mobilization, demonstrations and open hearings as part of the struggle for an ethical and developmental state, is therefore emphasized (ANSA, 2006).

To achieve these requires a return to international norms and standards of good governance and reviewing laws that infringe on individual and collective rights of citizens (freedom of speech and association). These values, norms and standards should be entrenched in the Constitution, which should include socio-economic rights in a Bill of Rights.

### Expand and strengthen stakeholder participation in national decision-making processes

The issue of broad-based stakeholder participation in policy formulation, implementation, monitoring and evaluation is an important requirement for the national ownership of development programmes, which is now entrenched in international aid architecture. However, what is emerging is that such participation is more effective when it is institutionalized, as is the case with the National Economic Development and Labour Council of South Africa (NEDLAC).

Consultative processes and procedures are best developed within the framework of the ILO. Social dialogue refers to all types of joint and collaborative relationships, which include negotiations, consultations and exchanges of information between representatives of governments, employers and workers on issues of common interest relating to economic and social policy (Ishikawa, 2003).

The most developed forms of consultation are between representatives of government, employers or workers at tripartite or bipartite levels, at national, sectoral or workplace levels. The ILO is the only tripartite UN specialized agency. Tripartism in the ILO is guided by Convention 144 of 1976 on Tripartite Consultation (International Labour Standards) and Recommendation No. 113, which provide for effective consultation and co-operation at national level between public authorities and employers' and workers' organizations. Such consultation and co-operation should ensure that the competent authorities seek the views, advice and assistance of employers' and workers' organizations on matters such as the preparation and implementation of laws and regulations that affect their

---

[19] See Chapter 1.

interests and the elaboration and implementation of plans of economic and social development.

From the ILO's perspective, social dialogue has three major components: the first involves the exchange of information, which is followed by consultations and negotiations. Negotiations are meant to achieve mutual gains or win–win outcomes. The range of issues subject to social dialogue is vast, and include: macroeconomic policy framework and economic growth; structural change and transformation of the economy; wage increases, inflation, and monetary policy; education and vocational training; social welfare, security and protection; gender equality; taxation and fiscal policy; productivity and economic competitiveness; employment policy; and wider economic and social policy issues (Ishikawa, 2003).

In countries such as South Africa and Ireland, social dialogue has been extended to stakeholders outside the traditional tripartite arrangement ('tripartite-plus'), a development increasingly seen as 'best-practice'. In the case of Zimbabwe, tripartite consultations are institutionalized at the national, sectoral (National Employment Council) and workplace (works council) levels. Following recommendations from the ZCTU (1996), the National Economic Consultative Forum (NECF) was established in July 1997. However, it deviated from the original proposal in that members were appointed by the President in their individual capacity, and as a result the ZCTU withdrew its participation. Nonetheless, the NECF continued operating as a consultative forum. It has an independent secretariat.

Following increased tension between the ZCTU and government over economic and social policies, the TNF was established in September 1998 as a tripartite forum that brought together government, organized labour, and business. Its mandate went beyond that of the NECF to negotiate policy. However, it does not have a secretariat of its own, such functions falling to the Ministry of Labour and Social Services. While the TNF has developed and signed a number of protocols, they were not implemented owing to a lack of political will. A process of strengthening the TNF by, among other things, establishing an independent secretariat is under way, including exploring the possibilities of making it a statutory body.

Under the Global Political Agreement of September 2008, yet another consultative body, the National Economic Council was proposed. It will comprise representatives of the mining, agriculture, manufacturing, tourism, commerce, financial, labour, academia and other sectors. Its mandate is to advise government in formulating economic plans and programmes for approval by government.[20]

---

[20] This structure had not been established at the time of writing.

A key challenge is that there are now three structures vying to be the premier national consultative forum. This competition is not healthy, given the scarcity of resources and capacities and the need to harmonize such social dialogue processes. As stated above, the TNF is in the process of restructuring itself into a tripartite-plus structure, and is in the process of moving towards the creation of an independent secretariat. A tripartite delegation visited NEDLAC in August 2009 to study the South African experience and structures. It would appear that the TNF is the best placed to take on the role of housing social dialogue in Zimbabwe: it has over ten years' experience in negotiating policies and has enjoyed technical backstopping services from the ILO and UNDP.

As stated by the ZCTU (1996: 90),

> A truly national compromise can only be arrived at when all interest groups and stakeholders participate in policy formulation, decision-making and implementation. This entails that representatives from the informal and communal sectors as well as representatives from other civil society groups be invited to become members of the proposed [Zimbabwe Economic Development Council]. Moreover, participation and decision-making by all levels of society has to be guaranteed through a broad, participatory and decentralized approach.

In addition, the oversight role of parliamentary portfolio committees needs to be strengthened, as well as the decentralized structures of governance. A strong resource-watch mechanism should be put in place to safeguard the exploitation of resources and the management of mineral resources. The UNDP (2008) recommends the establishment of a Sovereign Wealth Fund through which such mineral resources can be used to fund investment rather than for consumption.

## References

ANSA 2006. *The Search for Sustainable Human Development in Southern Africa* (Harare: Alternatives to Neo-Liberalism in Southern Africa).

Ishikawa, J. 2003. *Key features of National Social Dialogue: A Social Dialogue Resource Book* (Geneva: ILO).

Kapoor, Kapil (ed.) 1995. *Africa's Experience with Structural Adjustment: Proceedings of the Harare Seminar, May 23–24, 1994* (Washington, DC: World Bank, World Bank Discussion Papers, 288).

Luebker, M. 2008. *Decent Work and Informal Employment: A Survey of Workers in Glen View* (Harare: ILO Sub-Regional Office for Southern Africa, Issues Paper No. 33).

Magunha, F., A. Bailey and L. Cliffe 2009. 'Remittance Strategies of Zimbabweans in Northern England' (Leeds: University of Leeds, School of Geography), <http://www.zimbabweinstitute.org/File_Uploads/file/Remittances%20Paper.pdf>.

Makina, D. and G. Kanyenze 2010. 'The Potential Contribution of the Zimbabwe Diaspora to Economic Recovery' (Harare: UNDP, Comprehensive Economic

Recovery in Zimbabwe, Working Paper 11), <http://www.kubatana.net/docs/econ/undp_contribution_diaspora_eco_recovery_100511.pdf>.

Mhone, G. C. Z. 2000. 'Enclavity and Constrained Labour Absorptive Capacity in Southern African Economies' (Harare: International Labour Office Southern Africa Multidisciplinary Advisory Team (SAMAT), Discussion Paper No. 12).

RBZ 2009. *Mid-term Monetary Policy Review* (Harare: Reserve Bank of Zimbabwe).

Rodrik, D. 2006. 'Goodbye Washington consensus, hello Washington confusion? A review of the World Bank's *Economic Growth in the 1990s: Learning from a Decade of Reform*', *Journal of Economic Literature*, XLIV (December), 973-87.

Rodrik, D. 2007. *One Economics, Many Recipes: Globalization, Institutions, and Economic Growth* (Princeton and Oxford: Princeton University Press).

Roy, R., A. Heuty and E. Letouzé 2009a. 'Fiscal space for what? Analytical issues from a human development perspective', in R. Roy and A. Heuty (eds.), *Fiscal Space: Policy Options for Financing Human Development* (London: Earthscan), 31-67.

Roy, R., A. Heuty and E. Letouzé 2009b. 'Fiscal space for public investment: Towards a human development approach', in R. Roy and A. Heuty (eds.), *Fiscal Space: Policy Options for Financing Human Development* (London: Earthscan), 67-92.

Roy, R., A. Heuty and F. Rodriguez 2009c. 'Introduction', in R. Roy and A. Heuty (eds.), *Fiscal Space: Policy Options for Financing Human Development* (London: Earthscan), 1-14.

Simpson, M. and D. Doré 2009. 'International Aid and its Management: Some Insights for Zimbabwe in the Context of Re-engagement' (Harare: UNDP, Comprehensive Economic Recovery in Zimbabwe, Working Paper No. 2).

Simpson, M. and D. Ndlela 2010. 'Informal economy, and the "Missing Middle" in Zimbabwe: Some Observations' (Harare: UNDP, Comprehensive Economic Recovery in Zimbabwe, Working Paper No. 9).

UN 2005, *Report of the Fact-Finding Mission to Zimbabwe to assess the Scope and Impact of Operation Murambatsvina by the UN Special Envoy on Human Settlements Issues in Zimbabwe, Mrs. Anna Kajumulo Tibaijuka* (New York: United Nations).

UNDP 2008. *Comprehensive Economic Recovery in Zimbabwe: A Discussion Document* (Harare: United Nations Development Programme).

World Bank 1995. *Performance Audit Report: Zimbabwe Structural Adjustment Program* (Washington, DC: World Bank, Operations Evaluation Department).

World Bank 2005. *Economic Growth in the 1990s: Learning from a Decade of Reform* (Washington, DC: World Bank).

World Bank 2008. *The Growth Report: Strategies for Sustained Growth and*

*Inclusive Development* (Washington, DC: World Bank, Commission on Growth and Development).

ZCTU 1996. *Beyond ESAP: Framework for a Long-Term Development Strategy for Zimbabwe* (Harare: Zimbabwe Congress of Trade Unions).

Zimbabwe 1998. *Poverty in Zimbabwe* (Harare: Central Statistical Office).